Ve-Eileh Divrei David

Culture and History of the Ancient Near East

VOLUME 88

The titles published in this series are listed at *brill.com/chan*

Ve-Eileh Divrei David

Essays in Semitics, Hebrew Bible and History of Biblical Scholarship

By

S. David Sperling

BRILL

LEIDEN | BOSTON

The Library of Congress Cataloging-in-Publication Data is available online at http://catalog.loc.gov
LC record available at http://lccn.loc.gov/2016057028

Typeface for the Latin, Greek, and Cyrillic scripts: "Brill". See and download: brill.com/brill-typeface.

ISSN 1566-2055
ISBN 978-90-04-34086-2 (hardback)
ISBN 978-90-04-34087-9 (e-book)

This book is printed on acid-free paper and produced in a sustainable manner.

Contents

Preface

I am delighted that Professors W. Randall Garr and Baruch Halpern encouraged me to submit my favorite articles for publication in Brill's CHAN series. *Ve-Eileh Divrei David* (2Samuel 23:21) comprises articles written over four decades in the areas of Comparative Semitics, Bible and the history of modern, especially Jewish, biblical scholarship. While I have not revised the substance of the articles, this publication has enabled me to make numerous minor revisions, correct old errors and clarify what I earlier obscured. In numerous instances I updated bibliographical references to primary sources and contemporary dictionaries. I hope that this collection will be of use to scholars and students.

I was privileged to study with outstanding scholars and teachers who inspired me to devote my life to teaching and research. At the age of seventeen, fresh out of an old school yeshivah, I walked into a Bible class taught by Moshe Held at what was then The Seminary College of Jewish Studies of the Jewish Theological Seminary of America (JTSA). Held's dynamism and his passionate commitment to deciphering ancient texts opened up a new world to me and led me eight years later to become his doctoral student at Columbia. In the Seminary College and later at the Seminary's Rabbinical school I studied Bible with H. L. Ginsberg, Nahum Sarna and Moshe Greenberg. I was introduced to the serious study of rabbinics by David Weiss Halivni and Saul Lieberman. Early in my teaching career I came under the influence of Theodor Gaster who was my senior colleague at Barnard. Scholars familiar with the work of these masters will, I hope, see the fruit of their teaching in the present collection. I must also thank Baruch Levine who over twenty years ago aroused my interest in the history of biblical scholarship.

Much of my work was inspired by questions directed to me by students, especially at the New York School of The Hebrew Union College-Jewish Institute of Religion where I have taught happily for almost four decades. I also have to thank the College for its support of my work by providing generous book allowances over the years. I am especially grateful to the College and its provost Dr. Michael Marmur for allotting funds for typing and editorial assistance for this book.

I dedicate this book to my beloved wife Jennifer Jaech who knows me better than I know myself. Jennifer has enabled me to fulfill the advice of Ecclesiastes 9:9, "Enjoy life with the woman you love."

Peekskill, New York, 2016

List of Abbreviations

Note: For additional abbreviations, consult *The* SBL *Handbook of Style, The Assyrian Dictionary of the Oriental Institute of the University of Chicago* (CAD), *Dictionary of Jewish Babylonian Aramaic* (DJBA), and *Dictionary of Jewish Palestinian Aramaic* (DJPA).

1QapGenar	*Genesis Apocryphon*
AbB	*Altbabylonische Briefe in Umschrift und Übersetzung*
ABD	*Anchor Bible Dictionary*
ABL	*Assyrian and Babylonian Letters*
AfO	*Archiv für Orientforschung*
AH	*Aramaic Handbook*
AHw	*Akkadisches Handwörterbuch*
AIT	*Aramaic Incantation Texts from Nippur*
AKA	*Annals of the Kings of Assyria*
ANEP	*Ancient Near East in Pictures*
ANET	*Ancient Near Eastern Texts Relating to the Old Testament*
ANRW	*Aufstieg und Niedergang der römischen Welt*
AOAT	*Alter Orient und Altes Testament*
AOB	Altorientalische Bibliothek
Ar	Aramaic
ARI	*Assyrian Royal Inscriptions*
ARMT	Archives royales de Mari (texts in transliteration and translation)
Aruch Supp	*Additamenta ad Librum Aruch Completum Alexandre Kohut.* Edited by S. Krauss
AS	*Assyriological Studies*
ATD	Das Alte Testament Deutsch
ATHE	B. Kienast. *Altassyrische Texte Heidelberg Erlenmeyer*
BA	*Biblical Archaeologist*
BAL	R. Borger. *Babylonisch-assyrische Lesestücke*
BASOR	*Bulletin of the American Schools of Oriental Research*
BBEA	Landsberger Brief
BDB	Brown, Driver, and Briggs. *A Hebrew and English Lexicon of the Old Testament*
Ber.	*Berakot*
BeO	*Bibbia e Oriente*
BH	Biblical Hebrew
BHS	*Biblia Hebraica Stuttgartensia*

Bib.	*Biblica*
BiOr	*Bibliotheca Orientalis*
BMS	*Babylonian Magic and Superstition*
BN	*Biblische Notizen*
BSOAS	*Bulletin of the School of Oriental and African Studies*
BT	Babylonian Talmud
BuA	B. Meissner. *Babylonien und Assyrien*
BWL	*See* Lambert BWL
BZAW	Beihefte zur Zeitschrift für die alttestmentliche Wissenschaft
CAD	*Assyrian Dictionary of the Oriental Institute of the University of Chicago*
CANE	*Civilizations of the Ancient Near East.* Edited by J. Sasson
CH	Code of Hammurabi
CHI	*Cambridge History of Iran*
CRAIBL	Comptes rendus de l'Academie des inscriptions et belles-lettres
CTA	Corpus des tablettes en cunéiformes alphabétiques découvertes à Ras Shamra-Ugarit de 1929 à 1939. Edited by Andrée Herdner. See also *KTU*
CTB	C. Kasowski. *Thesaurus Talmudis*
CTY	M. Kosovsky. *Concordance to the Talmud Yerushalmi*
DBI	*Dictionary of Biblical Interpretation.* Edited by John Hayes
DCH	*Dictionary of Classical Hebrew.* Edited by David Clines
DDD	*Dictionary of Deities and Demons.* Edited by Karel van der Toorn
DISO	*Dictionnaire des inscriptions sémitiques de l'ouest*
DJBA	M. Sokoloff. *Dictionary of Jewish Babylonian Aramaic*
DJPA	M. Sokoloff. *Dictionary of Jewish Palestinian Aramaic*
DLU	G. del Olmo Lete and J. Sanmartin, *Diccionario de la Lengua Ugaritica*
DN	divine name
DNWSI	*Dictionary of the North-West Semitic Inscriptions*
EA	*El Amarna* letters
Ebeling Handerhebung	E. Ebeling. Die *akkadische Gebetsserie "Handerhebung"*
EncJud	Encyclopaedia Judaica
Enc. Rel.	*Encyclopedia of Religion*
En. el.	*Enuma Elish*
ErIsr	*Eretz Israel*

ET	*Expository Times*
FSAC	W. F. Albright. *From the Stone Age to Christianity*
Gen. Rab.	*Genesis Rabbah*
Gilg.	Epic of Gilgamesh
GN	geographic name
HAE	*Handbuch der althebräischen Epigraphik*
HALAT	*Hebräisches und aramäisches Lexikon zum alten Testament*
HRCS	E. Hatch and H. Redpath. *Concordance to the Septuagint and Other Greek Versions of the Old Testament*
HSS	Harvard Semitic Studies
HTR	*Harvard Theological Review*
HZ	M. Boyce. *History of Zoroastrianism*
IDB	*Interpreter's Dictionary of the Bible*
IEJ	*Israel Exploration Journal*
IOS	*Israel Oriental Studies*
JA	Jewish Aramaic
JA	*Journal Asiatique*
JAAR	*Journal of the American Academy of Religion*
JANES	*Journal of the Ancient Near Eastern Society*
JAOS	*Journal of the American Oriental Society*
Jast	M. Jastrow. *Dictionary of the Targumim, the Talmud Babli and Yerushalmi and the Midrashic Literature*
JBA	Jewish Babylonian Aramaic
JBA	*Jewish Book Annual*
JBL	*Journal of Biblical Literature*
JCS	*Journal of Cuneiform Studies*
JEA	*Journal of Egyptian Archaeology*
JJS	*Journal of Jewish Studies*
JNES	*Journal of Near Eastern Studies*
JPA	Jewish Palestinian Aramaic
JPS	Jewish Publication Society
JQR	*Jewish Quarterly Review*
JRAS	*Journal of the Royal Asiatic Society*
JSS	*Journal of Semitic Studies*
KAI	H. Donner and W. Röllig. *Kanaanäische und aramäische Inschriften*
KAR	Keilschrifttexte aus Assur religiösen Inhalts
KJV	King James Version
KTU	*Die keilalphabetischen Texte aus Ugarit*

Kut	E. Y. Kutscher
Lambert BWL	W. Lambert. *Babylonian Wisdom Literature*
LE	Laws of Eshnunna
Leš.	*Lešonenu*
Lev. Rab.	*Leviticus Rabbah*
Levy, *TMW*	J. Levy. *Wörterbuch über die Talmudim und Midraschim.* Berlin, 1924
Levy, *TW*	J. Levy, *Wörterbuch über die Targumin.* Leipzig, 1881
LH	Late Hebrew
LSJ	H. Liddell, R. Scott, H. Jones, *A Greek-English Lexicon*
LSp	F. Schulthess. *Lexicon Syropalaestinum*
LXX	Septuagint
m.	*Mishnah*
MAARAV	*Journal for the Study of the Northwest Semitic Languages and Literatures*
MAD	Materials for the Assyrian Dictionary
MAOG	*Mitteilungen der Altorientalischen Gesellschaft*
Mek.	Mekilta
Melamed Millon	E. Z. Melamed. *Millon Arami-Ivri le-Talmud Bavli*
MT	Masoretic Text
MVAG	*Mitteilungen der Vorderasiatisch-ägyptischen Gesellschaft*
NEB	New English Bible
NESE	*Neue Ephemeris für semitische Epigraphik*
NIN	*Journal of Gender Studies in Antiquity*
NJPS	New Jewish Publication Society
Nr.	Number
NRSV	New Revised Standard Version
NT	New Testament
OB	Old Babylonian
OBS	E. A. Speiser. *Oriental and Biblical Studies*
OECT	Oxford Editions of Cuneiform Texts
OIP	Oriental Institute Publications
OLZ	*Orientalische Literaturzeitung*
Or	*Orientalia*
OT	Old Testament
P8WCJS	*Proceedings of the Eighth World Congress of Jewish Studies*
PAAJR	*Proceedings of the American Academy for Jewish Research*
PBS	University of Pennsylvania. Publications of the Babylonian Section
PN	Proper Name

PRU	*Le Palais royal d'Ugarit*
PSm	*Thesaurus Syriacus*. Edited by R. Payne Smith
PsmCom	Compendious Syriac Dictionary
PT	Palestinian Talmud
RA	*Revue d'Assyriologie et d'archéologie orientale*
RAcc.	F. Thureau-Dangin. *Rituels accadiens*
RANE	*Records of the Ancient Near East*
RB	*Revue biblique*
REB	Revised English Bible
RLA	*Reallexikon der Assyriologie*
RSV	*Revised Standard Version*
SAA	State Archives of Assyria
SAHG	*Sumerische und akkadische Hymnen und Gebete*
SGA	E. Y. Kutscher. *Studies in Galilean Aramaic*
SGL	A. Falkenstein. *Sumerische Götterlieder*
Sok Dict	See *DJBA* and *DJPA*
Sperling Studies	S. David Sperling, "Studies in Late Hebrew Lexicography in the Light of Akkadian."
TAD	*Textbook of Aramaic Documents from Ancient Egypt*
TCL	Textes cunéiforms du Louvre
TDOT	*Theological Dictionary of the Old Testament*
TDP	R. Labat. *Traité akkadien de diagnostics et prognostics médicaux*
Tg.	Targum
Tg.Neof.	Targum Neofiti
Tg. Onq.	Targum Onqelos
Tg. Ps-J.	Targum Pseudo-Jonathan
THAT	*Theologisches Handwörterbuch zum Alten Testament*
Tn.	Tukulti-Ninurta
TSSI	*Textbook of Syrian Semitic Inscriptions*
TuL	E. Ebeling.*Tod und Leben*
TWAT	*Theologisches Wörterbuch zum Alten Testament*
UF	*Ugarit Forschungen*
USQR	*Union Seminary Quarterly Review*
UT	*Ugaritic Textbook*
Vg.	Vulgate
VT	*Vetus Testamentum*
VTSup	Supplements to Vetus Testamentum
WO	*Die Welt des Orients*
WUS	J. Aistleitner, *Das Wörterbuch der ugaritischen Sprache*

YOS X	*Yale Oriental Series, vol. X*
ZA	*Zeitschrift für Assyriologie*
ZAH	*Zeitschrift für Althebraistik*
ZAW	*Zeitschrift für die alttestamentliche Wissenschaft*
ZDMG	*Zeitschrift der Deutschen Morgenländischen Gesellschaft*

Semitic Philology

CHAPTER 1

ḥgr I and *ḥgr* II

Lexicographers[1] disagree about the relationship between Biblical Hebrew (BH) *ḥgr*, "to gird (oneself) with,"[2] and Late Hebrew (LH) *ḥgr*. LH *ḥgr*, likewise means "to gird (oneself) with"[3] but attests the additional senses "to limp," "to be halt," "to be lame," "to stumble," and "to be impeded." The meaning "gird," is related to the substantives *ḥagōrāh/ḥagōr*,[4] "belt," "girdle," "sash," *ḥagīrāh*, "enclosure,"[5] and *maḥger*, "ox collar."[6] The additional meanings of the LH verb are related to the substantive *ḥigger*, "a lame person," "a cripple," and to its correspondents in Aramaic and Syriac *ḥigrā, ḥagirā, ḥagir*. The Akkadian verb *egēru*, "to twist," as well as the verb *ḥgr* attested in Jewish Aramaic (JA) and Syriac[7] must also be considered.[8] In this study we attempt to demonstrate that Hebrew *ḥgr* should

1 For rabbinic abbreviations not found in the standard manuals see *DJPA*, *DJBA*. The following are among those who separate *ḥgr* I and *ḥgr* II: Jast, 424; Dalman, Handwörterbuch, 137; M. Zuckermandl, *Tosephta*, lxvi. A contrary view is taken by Levy, TMW II, 14–15; and by the standard Hebrew lexicons. See BDB, 291; *GKC*, 214; KBL, 276; *HALAT* I, 279.

2 See H. L. Ginsberg, "Interpreting Ugaritic Texts," *JAOS* 70 (1950), 158.

3 LH *ḥgr* has a slightly wider semantic range than BH *ḥgr*. Thus the Mishnah (*m. Mid.* 3:1) in describing the temple-altar notes that: *wḥwṭ šl sqrʾ ḥwgrw bʾmṣʿ*, "And a red strand wound round its midsection." In some cases the verbal form *ḥagūrāh* may mean "adhering to," "cleaving to." See Saul Lieberman, *Tosefta Ki-fšhuṭāh* Order Zeraim, Part I, 23. Lieberman translates these instances by *dəbūqāh*.

4 LH prefers the form without final *-āh*. *ḥagōrāh* does not occur in the Mishnah or Tosefta and only once in the Babylonian Talmud (*b. Šabb.*, 9b).

5 For *ḥagīrāh šel ʾabānīm*, "stone partition," see Lieberman, *Tosefta*, I, 271:43–44; *idem, Tosefta Ki-fshuṭāh*, (Order Zeraʿim, Part II), 783. Lieberman *ibid.*, translates *ḥagirah* by *məḥiṣṣāh*. In *m. ʿErub.* 2:4, we follow Lieberman's reading (*ibid.*): *ʿōśin ḥagīrāh*, "They make an enclosure." The printed editions read: *ḥagōrāh*; See further, DS III, 82; Albeck-Yalon, Mishnah II, 88, accepts the reading *ḥagōrāh* and translates *heqep šel ḥabālīm*, "a rope encirclement."

6 *m. Kel.* 14:4; See Levy, TMW II, 14; Albeck-Yalon, *Mishnah*, VI, 66; D. Hoffman, *Mischnajot*, (Teil VI), 70, n. 55.

7 For JPA see below. For Syriac, see Payne Smith, col. 1192.

8 Some scholars compare Ugaritic *ḥgr* to the cognate forms in the other Semitic languages. See for example: C. H. Gordon, *UT*, 394, no. 837; KBL, 276; *idem*, *HALAT* I, 279; H. Sauren, G. Kestemont, "Keret, roi de Ḫubur," *UF* 3 (1971), 200; Unfortunately, the two sole attestations of Ugaritic *ḥgr* (IK:148=*KTU*³ 1.14:iii:44); SS:17= *KTU*³ 1.23:17) are in unclear contexts. It is likely that "gird" was expressed in Ugaritic by *šns*. (See VAB B:ll–13=*KTU*³ 1.3:ii:11–13; cf. 1Kgs18:46.); Arabic *ḥǧr* which is generally compared (GKC, 214; BDB, 291; KBL, 276; *HALAT* I, 279; *UT*, 394,

 | DOI 10.1163/9789004340879_002

be divided into two distinct words: 1) *ḥgr* I, "to gird," attested in BH and LH. 2) *ḥgr* II, associated with lameness and difficulty of movement, attested only in LH.[9] We relate LH *ḥgr* to *ḥgr* of the Aramaic dialects and to Akkadian *egēru*, but separate *ḥgr* I from all of these.

We turn first to an examination of the view that LH *ḥgr* is not to be separated from BH *ḥgr*. Those scholars who adhere to this view justify their position by alleging a semantic development from the concept "to tie," to that of "to be bound (in regard to the limbs)."[10] Following this line of reasoning, a *ḥigger* is one whose feet are bound. In and of itself, such a semantic development is reasonable and can, in fact, be demonstrated in Akkadian[11] and in Sumerian.[12] This semantic development is however unlikely in the case of *ḥgr* for the following reasons:

---

no. 837) corresponds neither to BH *ḥgr* nor to LH *ḥgr*. According to Lane, Book I, Part 2, 516, Arabic *ḥǧr* means "prevented," "hindered," "withheld," "restrained," "debarred," "inhibited," "forbade," "prohibited," and "interdicted." The Arabic correspondent of *ḥgr* I is *qallada, taqallada.*Thus, Saadia translates *ḥgr* by *qld* in Ps 65:13, 76:11, and 109:19. (J. Kafah/Kafih, *Tehillim ʿim Targum u-Feruš Haggaʾon Saadia ben Yosep Fayyumi* [Jerusalem. 1963], 157–158, 181, 240); Similarly, al-Fasi translates Hebrew *ḥgwr ʿrb* by *tqld syp* (S. Skoss, *Kitab jamiʿ al-Alfaẓ* I [New Haven: Yale, 1936], 520); In fact, the Arabic correspondent of LH *ḥgr* is *ʿrǧ*. cf. al-Fasi's statement (*ibid.*): *wpy ʾlmšnh ysmwn ʾl ʿrǧ ḥigger*, "In the Mishnah they call the lame, *ḥiggēr*."

9 Cf. however Rashi's comments on 2Sam 22:46 and Ps 76:11.

10 The fullest statement is found in Levy, TMW II, 14. Levy sees here a development from "umgürten, umspannen." Translating LH *ḥgr* as "anstossen, stolpern, lahmen," he explains: "Diese Bedeut. hängt mit nr. 1 (umgürten, umspannen) zus.; dah. *ḥāgar* anstossen, als ob die Hand u. dgl. gebunden sind, wodurch er am Gehen verhindert ist."; cf. F M. Cross, Jr. and D. N. Freedman, "A Royal Song of Thanksgiving: II Samuel 22= Psalm 18," *JBL* 72 (1953), 33, n. 104.

11 *kasû* regularly means "to bind," (*CAD K*, 250f,; AHw., 455) and is attested in contexts describing lameness and paralysis. Note the following example: *akkannu ša ana ritkubi tebû mannu unniḫka sisû ezzu sa tebûšu našpandi* [*m*]*annu mešrêtika ukassi mannu šerʾānika uramme*, "Wild ass erect for mating, who has tired you? Raging stallion whose ardor is devastation, who has paralyzed, your limbs? Who has slackened your muscles?" (Biggs Šaziga, 17:12–13); Similarly we read: *minâtiki ubbir mešrêtiki ukassi manāniki ukannin*, "I have magically bound your figure, paralyzed your limbs, contorted your nerves."(Maqlu, VII:71–72); According to von Soden (AHw., 414, 497), the common Akkadian word for "a cripple," *kubbulu/kumbulu* is to be related to the verb *kabālu*, allegedly meaning "to bind." If he is correct, we have a second example of the transition from "tie," "to cripple." However, von Soden's etymology is hardly convincing. The *CAD* rightly takes a different view. It renders *kabālu* by "to be paralyzed," "to be lame," and makes no reference to a meaning, "bind." (*CAD K*, 3) The problem merits a detailed study, taking into consideration Akkadian *k/qapālu*, "to roll up," and West Semitic *qpl, kbl, kpl*.

12 See W. W. Hallo, "The Lame and the Halt," *Eretz Israel* 9 (1969), 68.

1) *ḥgr* I does not have the general sense "to bind," "to tie," but only the specific sense "to gird." A partial interdialectal distribution for "to bind," "to tie," yields:

Hebrew (BH and LH)	Aramaic	Akkadian
qšr[13] *ḥbr*[14] *rks*[15] *ʾsr*[16] *ḥbš*[17] *ʿqd*[18] *kpt*[19]	*qṭr*[20] *zrz*[21] *ʿṣb*[22] *kpt*[23] *ṣmd*[24]	*kaṣāru*[25] *rakāsu*[26] *ṣamādu*[27] *kasû*[28] *kamû*[29] *eʾēlu*[30]

13 E.g.: Deut 6:8; Josh 2:18; Jer 51:63; Prv 7:3; *m. Kil.* 8:4; *m. Šabb.* 7:2; *m. Yoma* 4:2, 6:8; *m. Parah* 3:3.

14 E.g. Exod 26:3, 36:10; *m. Parah* 12:8; *m. Kelim* 17:13.

15 Exod 28:28, 39:21.

16 E.g. 1Sam 6:7; 2Sam 3:34; Jer 39:7; Ezek 3:25.

17 E.g. Gen 22:3; Exod 29:9; 1Kgs 13:13; Ezek 30:21; The standard Hebrew lexica associate BH *ḥbš* with LH and Aramaic *ḥbš* as well as with Arabic *ḥabasa*. (See BDB, 289–90; GKC, 212–13; KBL, 274–275; *HALAT* 277–78; cf. *ATHE*, 15.) It must be noted, however, that in LH and BH *ḥbš*, a different semantic range is in evidence. BH *ḥbš* functions essentially like Akkadian *ṣamādu*. (See Landsberger Date Palm, 25, n. 7; Contra Kienast, *ATHE*, 15, *ḫabāšu* does not mean "binden.") BH *ḥbš* is used for tying on apparel (Exod 29:9; Ezek 15:10, 24:17); preparing an ass for riding (Gen 22:3; Num 22:21); and for binding wounds (Isa 30:25, 51:1; Ezek 30:21, 34:4. For Job 23:11, 40:13, see Tur-Sinai, *Job*, 401, 555.); LH *ḥbš*, however, is used for the notions of "confinement," "detention," "restriction," and "imprisonment." It thus largely corresponds to Akkadian *esēru*. Note the following examples:
šhyh ḥbwš bbyt hʾswrym, "(one who) was confined in prison." (*m. Soṭah* 4:5)
hʾšh šnḥbšh bydy gwyym, "A married woman who was detained by gentiles." (*m. Ketub.* 2:9)
wky tʿlh ʿl dʿtk šzh mhlk bšwq wzh nhrg ʾlʾ mlmd šḥwbšyn ʾwtw wʾy mt qṭlynn lyh, "Would it occur to you that if the one were walking about in the street, that the other be executed? Rather (the verse) teaches that we imprison him and if (the victim) died, we execute him." (*b. Ketub.*, 33b; cf. *b. Sanh.*, 78b; H. S. Horovitz and I. Rabin, eds., *Mechilta d'Rabbi Ismael*, (Jerusalem, 1970), 270:12–13.
ʾyn hbwš mtyr ʿṣmw mbyt hʾswrym, "The prisoner cannot release himself from prison." (*b. Ber.*, 5b)
lʾ ʾhyh ḥwbš lʾ ʾhyh mḥwbšy ʿṣmn bbyt hmdrš wbbyty ʾyn lḥm wʾyn śmlh šʾyn bbyty lʾ mqrʾ wlʾ mšnh wlʾ gmrʾ, (Midrashic interpretation of Isa 3:7) "I am not a *ḥōbēš*—I am not one of those who confine themselves (*ḥōbšē ʿaṣmān*) to the academy. For in my house there is no bread and no garment—I possess neither Scripture nor Mishnah nor Gemara."
(*b. Šabb.*, 120a; cf. *b. Ḥag.*, 14a)

2) More telling is the fact that in BH "girding," as described by *ḥgr* is generally of the type that facilitates movement. Thus, it is well known that the expression *ḥgr mtnym*[31] and its synonyms[32] connote "activity," "industry," "zeal," "avidity," "bravery," and the like.
3) This sense of *ḥgr* survives in LH. We note the following passages: *kl 12 ḥdš šʿśw btybh hyw ḥwgryn mtnyhm wznyn hbhmh whḥyh*, "During the entire twelve

---

The association of BH *ḥbš* with Aramaic *ḥbš* is extremely tenuous. Significantly, the Aramaic versions of the Bible do not employ Aramaic *ḥbš* as the regular, correspondent of BH *ḥbš*. (The only extant examples are Peshitta to Jon 2:6 and to Job 40:13. In the Jonah passage Peshitta appears to have had a different reading than the Masoretic Text. The Job passage is problematic in its own right.) For example, in Exod 29:9 (apparel) Onqelos has *tqn, Tg.Ps-J. kbš* and Peshitta *sym*; At Ezek 34:4 (binding wounds) the Targum has *ṣmd* (=*ṣamādu*) and the Peshitta *ʿṣb*; In 1Kgs 13:13 (riding preparation) the Targum has *zrz* to Peshitta's *rmʾ ʿl*; In contrast, the association of LH *ḥbš* with Aramaic *ḥbš* appears certain. Thus we note JA *ʾtḥbš bpylky* (φυλακή) "He was confined in prison." (*Lev. Rabb.* 30:5); For Syriac attestations see PSmCom, 125. Similarly, Arabic *ḥabasa* goes with the LH and Aramaic uses of *ḥbš*. Note that Saadia translates Hebrew *klʾ* by Arabic *ḥbs* in Gen 8:2; Ps 88:9, 119:101. (See J. Derenbourg, *Version arabe du Pentateuque*, [Paris, 1893], 14; Kafah/Kafih, *Tehillim*, 203, 256.); See further Lane, 500–501.

18 Gen 22:9; *m. Tamid* 4:1.

19 *b. Giṭ*, 14b; *b. Sanh.*, 70b, 77a; *b. Mak.*, 23a; *b. Šebu.*, 28a.

20 E.g. *Tg. Onq., Tg. Ps.-J., Tg. Neof, Sam. Tg.* and Peshitta to Deut 6:8; *Tg. J. to* Josh 2:18; Jer 51:63; Targum to Prv 7:3; See also Ezek 46:22 with the Targum and Qimhi ad loc.

21 See below.

22 E.g. Peshitta to Isa 1:6, 30:26, 61:1; Job 5:18 (MT: *ḥbš*).

23 E.g. *b. Ber.*, 56b; *b. Šabb.*, 94a; *b. Moʿed Qaṭ.*, 16a; *b. Sanh.*, 95a; *Tg. Ps.-J.* to Gen. 22:9.

24 Targum to Ezek 34:16; Note *b. Ber.*, 22b: *ʾṣṭmyd ḥṣbyh drb nḥmn*, "Rabbi Nahman's (broken) pot (= Akkadian *ḫaṣbu*) has been put back together."

25 *CAD K*, 257 ff.; AHw., 456–457.

26 AHw., 945–947.

27 *CAD Ṣ*, 89ff.

28 *CAD K*, 250ff.; AHw., 455–456.

29 AHw., 433–434; cf. *CAD K*, 128–131.

30 *CAD E*, 40–41; AHw., 189.

31 2Kings 4:29, 9:1; Prv 31:17. cf. Gersonides a.l.; See further E. Dhorme, *L'emploi métaphorique*, 132.

32 E.g. *ʾzr mtnym* (Jer 1:17); *šns mtnym* (1Kgs 18:46); *ḥzq mtnym* (Nah 2:2); *ʾzr ḥlṣym* (Job 38:3, 40:7); In BH, weakness is expressed by terms for ungirding. Thus *wmtny mlkym ʾptḥ* (Isa 45:1) connotes that no kings will be able to oppose Cyrus. We may see this further in Job 12:21 where *mzyh* (=Akkadian *mēzeḫu*) *ʾpyqym rph* is translated: *tqwp tqypyʾ mḥlš* "He weakens the power of the mighty."

months that they spent in the ark, they zealously fed the cattle and the wild animals."[33]

wmšl lmlk škʿs ʿl ʾštw whwṣyʾh lʾḥrymym ntrṣh lh myd ḥgrh mtnyh qšrh ktypyh[34] *whyth mšmšt ʾwtw ywtr mdʾy*, "And this is like the case of the king who became angry with his wife and divorced her. After a while he became reconciled to her. She immediately began to work zealously and fastidiously and served him even more than necessary."[35]

wyhy ʾyš mṣlyḥ hyh ḥwgr mtnyw wʾdwnw ʾwmr lw mzwg ly kws ḥmyn whwʾ mwzg tn ly ṣwnn whwʾ nwtn lw mʾwtw kly, "He was a successful man.[36] He worked industriously. When his master would tell him, 'Mix me a hot cup,' he would mix it. When his master would say 'Give me a cold drink,' he would serve him from the same utensil."[37]

4) As we have seen, this idiomatic use of *ḥgr* I extends to its BH synonyms. Nor is this phenomenon confined to BH. A regular JA correspondent of BH *ḥgr* is *zrz*.[38] The verb *zrz* is well attested in JA and LH in contexts describing dexterity and facility of movement.[39] The abstract noun *zərizut* means "skill," "agility,"

---

33 Tanḥ I, 46.

34 Note *ptḥ ktp* in Ezek 25:9. The Targum a.l. reads: *hʾ ʾnʾ tbr yt tqwp Moab*, "Behold I am breaking Moab's power."

35 Sipra, 43d.

36 Gen 39:2.

37 Tanḥ I, 186; B. Landsberger has shown (Landsberger Brief, 73, n. 145) that Akkadian *qablī rakāsu* has a very similar meaning. He translates the idiom as,"im Amt, im Dienst sein," "seinem Geschäft nachgehen." This phrase has its idiomatic as well as literal antonym in *qablī patāru* which Landsberger renders, "der Ruhe pflegen." To Landsberger's examples for the former idiom we should probably add: *libbaka ṣabbit qablēka rukus*, "Be determined and be firm." (K. Deller, "Die Briefe des Adad-šumu-uṣur," *AOAT* 1 [1969], 58:18'–19').

38 See below for attestations; In LH *zerez* is a "belt," or "girdle." We read in *ʿErub.*, 18b that as part of Adam's penance, *hʿlh zrzy tʾynym ʿl bśrw* 130 *šnh*, "He put girdles of fig leaves on his body for 130 years." The word is also attested as a wide strap used in girding a riding animal. (See *m. Kelim* 23:2 and Bertinoro a.l.; cf. Sipra, 76c.) The LH vocable is presumably borrowed from Aramaic. Note that *zərāzēh* translates *ḥagōrō* in *Tg. J.* to 1Sam 18:4. Both the LH and Aramaic words may be related to NA *zurzu*, but this is uncertain. See *CAD Z*, 168.

39 Thus Ps 70:2, *yhwh lʿzrty ḥwšh* appears in the Targum as *yy lsʿdy zryz*; We note further: *ʾybʿy lhw lzrwzy npšyyhw*, "they are obligated to bestir themselves." (*b. Pesaḥ*, 65a; further, *b. Ned.*, 8a); *kywn dʿbdynn lyh ṣrh kl škn dmzdrz ṭpy*, "Since we make a rival for him he will certainly be more fastidious." (*b. Yoma*, 13a. Note that *ṣrh* is grammatically feminine, though it refers to a male rival. [cf. Ugaritic *ṣrt*]); For LH *zrz* note the following comment to Exod 14:13: *wyʾmr mšh ʾl hʿm ʾl tyrʾw htyṣbw wrʾw hry mšh mzrzn lhwdyʿ ḥkmtw šl mšh hyʾk hyh ʿwmd wmpyys lkl ʾwtm hʾlpym whrbbwt*, "Moses said to the people, 'Fear not. Stand firm and see.' Behold, Moses was actively urging them on. It goes to show how wise Moses was,

"alertness," "industry," "preparedness," "speed," "fastidiousness," and the like.[40] The LH substantive *zārīz*, when referring to a person, describes one who is zealous, industrious, or apt.[41] It seems, therefore, that the notion of "gird," in

---

how he was constantly placating all of those thousands and myriads." (Horovitz-Rabin, *Mechilta*, 93:19–94:1); *mzrzyn l'dm bš't tlmwd wmzrzyn 't h'dm bš't m'śh*, "They encourage a man in time of study and they encourage a man in time of action." (*ibid.*, 218:1–2); *b' aḥr w'mr lw 'l tšth ṣwnn … šl' tmwt kdrk šmt plwny wzh zrzw ywtr mkwlm*, "Another came and said to him 'Do not drink cold water so that you do not die as did So and So.' This one roused him more than all the rest had." (Sipra, 79d); *my š'lh zrzw šl' yr'h wmy šl' 'lh zrzw sl' y'lh*, "Whoever had ascended, he admonished not to look. Whoever had not ascended he admonished not to ascend." (J. N. Epstein and E. Z. Melamed eds., *Mekhilta de Rabbi Shim'on ben Yohai* (Jerusalem, 1955), 145:7).

40 We can see two nuances of *zərīzūt* in the following passage: *bzryzwt yṣ'w yśr'l mmṣrym šn'mr ky bḥzq yd hwṣy' yhwh 'tkm m'rṣ mṣrym* (Exod 13:3; misquoted. MT: *mizzeh*) *dbr ḥ'ḥr bzryzwt 'ṣmn yṣ'w yśr'l mi-Miṣraim šn'mr wkkh t'klw 'wtw mtnykm ḥgwrym wgw'* (Exod 12:11), "The Israelites left Egypt by means of (divine) agility as it is said, 'For Yahweh took you out of the land of Egypt with a strong arm.' Another interpretation: By bestirring themselves the Israelites left Egypt. As it is written, 'In this manner shall you eat it, with your loins girded, etc.' " (*Mechilta* [ed. Horovitz-Rabin] 62:13–15) Note that this passage depends for its point on the semantic connection between BH *ḥgr* and LH *zrz*.); A slightly different nuance is found in the following comment to Num 22:21: *wyqm bl'm bbwqr wyhbš 't 'twnw wky l' hyh lw 'bd 'w špḥh 'l' ššn't yśr'l qdmtw w'md bzryzwt hw' b'ṣmw*, "Balaam rose in the morning and saddled his donkey mare. Did he not have a male servant or a maid-servant? (He did) but hatred of Israel came upon him so that he himself rose with alacrity." (Tanḥ II, 137).

41 E.g.: *yš zryz wnśkr zryz wmpsyd špl wnśkr špl wmpsyd*, "There is an industrious person who benefits and an industrious person who suffers a loss. There is a sluggard who benefits and a sluggard who suffers a loss." (*t. Yebam.* 4:8); Similarly we read in *b. Ned.*, 36a, *m'śh hyh wqdmw bnwt lbnym wnmṣ'w bnwt zryzwt wbnym šplym*, "There was a case in which the daughters preceded the sons. Thus, the daughters turned out avid but the sons turned out to be sluggards.") cf. *b. Pesaḥ*, 89a; *b. Giṭ*, 25a); Ginsberg relates LH *šāpēl* to late BH *šiplūt yādayim* in Qoh 10:18. See H. L. Ginsberg, *Koheleth* (Jerusalem, 1961), 124; A further comparison may be made to Syriac *šaplūtā* which the Peshitta to Qoh 10:18 employs for both *šiplūt yādayim* and *'ṣltym*. For other examples: *r'h tynwq šnpl lym pwrs mṣwdh wm'lhw whzryz hry zh mšwbḥ w'yn ṣryk lyṭwl ršwt mbyt dyn*, "If one saw a child fall in the sea (on the Sabbath) he should spread a net and pull him up. He who acts quickly is to be commended, nor does he need to obtain permission from a court." (*b. Yoma*, 84b); *'m bnw zryz … wtlmwdw mtqyym bydw*, "If his son is apt … and retains his learning … (*b. Qidd.*, 29b); *dtny' wbywm hšmyny ymwl bśr 'rltw mlmd škl hywm kšr lmylh' l' šhzryzyn mqdymyn lmṣwwt*, "As it is taught, 'On the eighth day his foreskin shall be circumcised.' (Lev 12:3) This teaches that the entire eighth day is licit for circumcision. However, the punctilious discharge ritual obligations early."(*b.Yoma*, 28b).

LH has developed in the direction contrary to that postulated by those scholars who link *ḥgr* I and II.

We turn now to the relationship between BH *ḥgr* and its alleged Aramaic cognates. We can do this simply by examining the Aramaic translations of the Bible. The Peshitta employs a number of verbs to translate BH *ḥgr*. These are *kbn*,[42] *ʾsr*,[43] *lbš*,[44] *ḥzq*,[45] *rmʾ*,[46] *zwn*,[47] and *mḥʾ b*.[48] For example, the Peshitta translates 2Sam 3:31, *ḥgrw śqym* as *ʾtkbnw sqʾ*. The phrase *whwʾ ḥgwr* (2Sam 21:16) appears as *ʾsyr hwʾ*. For Dan 10:5, *wmtnyw ḥgwrym* the Syriac offers *wḥṣwhy ḥzyqyn*. We find a similar situation when we consult the Peshitta's renderings of the synonyms of BH *ḥgr*. For *ʾzr* the Peshitta has *ʾsr*,[49] *ʿšn*,[50] *ḥzq*,[51] and *kbn*.[52] Thus, Peshitta to Ps 93:1 translates *htʾzr* by *ʾṭʿšn*. For *wtʾzrny* (Ps 18:40), Peshitta has *tḥzqny*. The hapaxlegomenon *šns* (1Kgs 18:46) is translated by Syriac *ʾsr*. In no case[53] does the Peshitta employ Syriac *ḥgr* to translate BH *ḥgr* or its synonyms.

---

42 Isa 15:3, 22:12; Jer 4:8, 6:26, 49:3; Ezek 7:18, 27:31; Joel 1:8, 13; Lam 2:10; In LH *rəḥēlīn kəbūnōt* are lambs whose fleece is protected by a covering tied round their bodies. (See *m. Šabb.*, 5:2; Lieberman, *Tosefta Moʿed*, 16:2; *Šabb.*, 54a and Rashi ad loc.) Aramaic -LH *kbn* may be behind *kabnu* which is equated in the lexical texts with *kušāru*, "reed stalk," "reed shelter." (*CAD K*, 593; AHw., 516) For a possible connection between *kbn* and *kabnu*, see W. von Soden, "Aramäische Wörter in neuassyrischen und neu-und spätbabylonischen Texten. Ein Vorbericht. I (aga-*muš)," *Or* 35 (1966), 12; von Soden (*ibid.*) translates *kabnu* by "Umhüllung," "Reifen." See further, AHw., 417; *CAD K*, 22 renders *kabnu* as "(a tree?)."

43 1Sam 25:13; 1Kgs 20:11; 2Kgs 3:21, 4:29, 9:1; Prv 31:17.

44 1Sam 2:18; 2Sam 6:14.

45 Lev 16:4.

46 Ps 45:4.

47 Deut 1:41.

48 Isa 32:11.

49 Jer 1:17; 2Kgs 1:8.

50 Ps 65:7.

51 2Sam 22:40; Ps 18:33, 40; Job 30:18.

52 Ps 30:12.

53 2Sam 22:46 is no exception. The Peshitta has *bnyʾ nwkryʾ ntklwn wntḥgrwn mn šbylyhwn* for MT *bny nkr yblw wyḥgrw mmsgrwtm*. However, Peshitta offers exactly the same translation for Ps 18:46 where MT reads *wyḥrgw mmsgrwtyhm*. Whatever the meaning of the problematic Psalms verse, the Syriac translates as: "The foreigners are impeded, they are held back from their paths." Since *ntklwn* and *ntḥgrwn* are synonymous, we have here a good Syriac hendiadys, but unrelated to BH *ḥgr*. We further note that the Peshitta reads the other verb in this verse as a form of *klʾ* (cf. Peshitta to Gen 8:2), rather than as a form of *nbl*. cf. Peshitta to Exod 18:18; Isa 1:30.

The situation in JA is similar. When we turn to the Aramaic of the Targums, we find BH *ḥgr* translated by *zrz*,[54] *ʾsr*,[55] and *qmr*.[56] BH *ʾzr* appears variously as Aramaic *ʾsr*,[57] *zrz*,[58] *tqp*,[59] and *sʿd*.[60] The Targum translates *šns* by *zrz*.[61] Finally, whenever Hebrew *ʾsr* has the sense, "to gird," both Targum and Peshitta translate it by Aramaic *ʾsr*.[62] An interdialectal distribution for "to gird," would never include Aramaic-Syriac *ḥgr*,[63] but rather one of the verbs listed above. We may illustrate this by tabulating the following attested phrases:

---

54 Judg 18:11; 1Sam 25:13; 2Kgs 4:29, 9:1; Ps 45:4; JA *zrz* also renders *ḥlṣ*. See Targums to Num 32:17, 20, 21, 27, 29, 30, 32; Josh 6:7, 9, 13. (Peshitta translates *zwn*.); cf. also LH *ḥillūṣ ʿaṣāmōt* (*b. Ber.*, 16b) and JA *zrwzy grmy*. (*b. Yebam.*, 102b).

55 1Sam 12:18; 2Sam 3:31, 6:14, 21:16; 2Kgs 3:21; Isa 22:12; Jer 4:8, 6:26, 49:3; Ezek 7:18, 27:31; Joel 1:8, 13.

56 Lam 2:10.

57 2Kgs 1:8.

58 Ps 18:33, 30:12, 65:7, 93:1; Job 30:18.

59 Isa 8:9; 50:11; Jer 1:17.

60 Isa 45:5; *sʿd* was loaned into NB and LB as *sêdu*. See von Soden, "Aramäische Wörter ... II," 266.

61 2Kgs 18:46.

62 Job 12:18; See further Peshitta to Neh 4:12.

63 Jast, 424 cites a JA *ḥgr* with the meaning "tie," from *b. Ned.* 49b. It is true that the passage in question is partially transmitted in Aramaic, but the relevant phrase is Hebrew: *wḥwgrny* (var: *wḥwgr ʾny*) *ṣydʿy mn hpsḥ ʿd hʿṣrt*, "I gird my temples (i.e., tie a bandage to ease the throbbing caused by drinking wine) from Pesah to Shabuot"; Both Jast (*ibid.*) and Levy, TMW II, 14) list *p. Ned.*, 37d as an instance of JA *ḥgr*, "'to bind." The phrase in question reads: *ḥgr ʿlyh mwtnʾ*. Jastrow translates, "tied a rope around it," in agreement with Levy, TMW and the traditional commentators. It is difficult to determine what the phrase means in context because that involves higher critical problems that go beyond the scope of this study. We must, therefore, limit ourselves to the following remark: Levy, Jastrow and their predecessors identify *mwtnʾ* in our text with JA *mtnʾ*/*mytnʾ* attested several times in the Baylonian Talmud (*b. Šabb.*, 51b, 102a; *b. ʿErub.*, 34a, 35a; *b. B.Qam*, 113b; *b. Bat.*, 86a, 89a; *b. Menaḥ*, 35b) in the meaning "cord," "rope," "string," "strap." (It is certainly related to Akkadian *matnu*, "sinew," "bowstring." For the Akkadian see AHw., 633; *CAD M/I*, 412. For West Semitic cognates see M. Held, "Studies in Comparative Semitic Lexicography," *AS* 16 [1965], 402–405.) Thus *mtnʾ* is the cord holding the scale balances (*b. B. Bat.*, 89a); a rope by which to hoist an object through a window (*b. ʿErub.*, 34a); a small rope by which to control a cat (*b. Šabb*, 51b); a strap attached to phylacteries; a rope with which to drag objects (*b. B. Bat.*, 86a); a rope used together with a lock (*b. ʿErub.*, 35a; a flax strap tied round the waist (*B. B. Meṣ*, 113b). If *mwtnʾ* in our passage is indeed identical with TB *mtnʾ*/*mytnʾ* there is still no reason to assert the existence of JA *ḥgr* "to bind." Talmudic *mtn*(Rashi *mytnʾ*) is found in a pure Hebrew context in *b. B. Bat.*, 89a. There is no reason

a) "wearing a belt"

Hebrew	JA	Syriac	Äkkadian
ḥgwr ḥgwrh[64]	*ʾsyryn zrzyn*[65]	*ḥzyqyn mḥzqtʾ*[66]	*ša nēbeḫi raksu*[67]

b) "girded with weapons"

Hebrew	JA	Syriac	Akkadian
ḥgwr kly[68] *mlḥmh*	*mzrzyn bmny qrbʾʾ*[69]	*mzynyn bmʾny qrbʾ*[70]	*kakkē ētezīḫ*[71]

not to read *ḥgr ʿlyh mwtnʾ* as *hāgār ālēhā motna*. Note that Samuel, the author of our statement, when quoted in an unquestionably Aramaic context, speaks about *mʾn dʾsr mytnʾ dkytnʾ rṭybʾ ʾḥrṣyh*, "one who binds a wet strap of flax around his midsection." (*b. B. Meṣ*, 113b) Similarly, "tied by a rope," is JA *qṭyr bmtnʾ*. (*b.ʿErub.*, 35a).

64 2Kgs 3:21.

65 Targum Ezek 23:15; MT has *ḥagōrē*, noun; Note *ʾsr hmynʾ*. (*b. Ber.*, 60b).

66 Peshitta to Ezek 23:15.

67 Racc. 90:28, 119:28; cf. AHw., 773; Alternatively, in Akkadian one can say *nēbeha ezēhu*. Note: *ī*[*s*]*iḫūšu nēbaham*,"with a girdle they girt him." (O. R. Gurney, "The Poor Man of Nippur," *Anatolian Studies* 6 [1956], 154:82) The reading *īziḫūšu* seems preferable in light of Hebrew *mēzaḥ* (Ps 109:19) which is, incidentally, associated with *ḥgr; nēbeḫa labāšu* is also attested. See e.g. BRM IV 25:46. In Akkadian "girding" may also be expressed by *šitpuru*. Note: *apluḫta ezzata ina šitpurikī*, "when you gird yourself with the fierce harness." (MSL V, 198; cf. Lambert BWL, 227:29–30, 231); Less well attested terms for "girding" are *ebēḫu* and *ebēṭu*. (*CAD E*, 8, 13; AHw., 181, 182); the Akkadian nouns corresponding to *ḥagōrāh* are *ḫuṣannu* (e.g. OIP 2:46:14–15); *meserru* (TuL 141:13); *šibbu* (e.g. OIP 2:46:15–16, KB VI /1: 84:54–55 (Descent of Ishtar), and *aguḫḫu*. (e.g. Gilg. VI:4)

68 Judg 18:11.

69 Targum, *ibid.*

70 Peshitta, *ibid.*

71 *kakkē ētezih namurru la*[*biš*], "He girt himself with weapons, was clad in awesomeness." (LKA, No. 63 r. 3)

c) "girded the midsection"

Hebrew	JA	Syriac	Akkadian
ḥgrh . . . mtnyh[72]	*ʾsrt . . . ḥrṣh'*[73]	*ʾsrt . . . ḥṣyh*[74]	[*q*]*ablīša ītezih̯*[75]

BH *ḥgr* therefore, is not associated with Aramaic *ḥgr*. The BH semantic equivalent of Aramaic *ḥgr* is *psḥ*.[76] Thus, for example, *wypsḥ* in 2Sam 4:4 is translated *wʾytḥgr* by the Targum and *wʾtḥgr* by the Peshitta. It is hardly surprising then that the Aramaic-Syriac substantive *ḥgyrʾ* is used to translate BH *pissēaḥ*[77] in Lev 21:18 and 2Sam 19:27.[78]

There has never been any doubt about the relationship between Aramaic *ḥgr* and LH *ḥgr*. Like its Aramaic counterparts, LH *ḥgr* corresponds to BH *psḥ*. The LH substantive *ḥiggēr*[79] replaces BH *pissēaḥ* almost completely.[80] For example, the Midrash to Lev 21:18 comments: *pissēaḥ byn ḥiggēr bšty rglyw*

72 Prv 31:17.

73 Targum, *ibid.*

74 Peshitta, *ibid.*

75 [*q*]*ablīša ītezih̯ ikarrab*, "Having girded her midsection, she pronounces the blessing." (Lambert-Millard Atra-hasīs, 62:286); See further AHw., 887b; cf. above n. 37.

76 Another BH correspondent is *nkh rglym*. In 2Sam 4:4, 9:3 the Targum reads: *lqy btrtyn rglwhy*, while Peshitta has *msrḥn rglwhy*. However, both the Targum and Peshitta to 2Kgs 23:29 explain Pharaoh Necho's name as *prʿh ḥgyrʾ*, "Pharaoh the lame." Cf. Qimhi ad loc.; The same tradition recurs in *b. Moʿed Qaṭ*, 28b. The feminine substantive appears as *ḫagirtāʾ* in line 16 of the Aramaic incantation in cuneiform from Uruk.

77 Cf. Akkadian *pessû*. See Hallo, "Lame and Halt," 69; AHw., 856b- 857a; The attestations of feminine *pessatum* are problematic. See CH XXII r. 83; J. J. Finkelstein, "An Old Babylonian Herding Contract and Genesis 31:38f.," *JAOS* 88 (1968), 32; Cf. E. Szlechter, "Les tablettes juridiques datées du regne d'Abi-Ešuḫ conservées au Musée d'Art et d'Histoire de Genève," *JCS* 7 (1953), 91; *idem*, Szlechter TJAA, 86; *CAD Ḫ*, 208b.

78 See further Targum and Peshitta to Deut 15:21; Isa 33:23; Jer 31:7; Mal 1:8, 13; Prv 26:7; Job 29:15; cf. Peshitta to Isa 35:6.

79 *ḥiggēr* is constructed on the same nominal pattern as *pissēaḥ*. Both BH and LH use the *qittēl* pattern as a means of expressing physical defects: cf. M. H. Segal, *A Grammar of Mishnaic Hebrew* (Oxford: Clarendon Press, 1970), 108–109.

80 An exception is: *wkl psḥ ʾw ʿwr ʾw ḥgr* (Y. Yadin, *The Scroll of the War of the Sons of Light against the Sons of Darkness* (Jerusalem, 1957), 300:4 .

byn ḥigger brglw ʾḥt, "(the disqualification of a lame priest for temple service includes) a person lame in both of his legs or in one of his legs."[81]

Having thus shown that there is no connection between Aramaic *ḥgr* and BH *ḥgr*, we must likewise reject any connection between BH *ḥgr* and the LH substantive *ḥiggēr*. LH does not conceive of the *ḥiggēr* as a "bound man," but rather as a "crooked man." This may be seen by comparing the antonyms of the verbs in question. We cite the interdialectal equivalents of the pair "gird-ungird."

Hebrew	JA	Syriac	Akkadian
ḥgr—ptḥ[82] *ntr*[83]	*zrz -šrʾ*[84]	*ʾsr*[85]*-šrʾ*[86]	*rakāsu-paṭāru*[87]

By contrast, the antonym of *ḥgr* II is *pšṭ*. This may be seen clearly in the following passages: *ḥiggēr bywm rʾšwn wntpšṭ bywm šny*, "A cripple on the first day who became free-moving on the second."[88]

ḥiggēr šykwl lhtpšṭ, "A cripple who is able to become free-moving."[89]

šhyw ḥgryn ʿd hprq wkšhgyʿ hprq ntḥgrw … šhyw pwšṭyn ʿd hprq wkšhgyʿ hprq ntḥgrw, "They were lame until puberty and at puberty became free-moving … they were free-moving until puberty and at puberty became lame."[90]

We need scarcely demonstrate that the verb *pšṭ*, here translated "free-moving," literally means "straightened out." The word *pšṭ* is well attested as an antonym of words for "crooked," or "twisted." The Talmud refers to a straight ram's

81 Sipra, 95b.

82 1Kgs 20:11; cf. 2Sam 3:31 and Jer 6:26 with Ps 30:12; cf. further 2Kgs 4:29, 9:1 with Isa 45:1.

83 Note *mšytyr ḥgwrw*, "as soon as he opens his girdle.." (*b. Šabb.*, 9b and *mšytyr ḥgwrh* [*ibid.*]) In BH, *ntr* and *ptḥ* occur in synonymous parallelism. See Isa 58:6; Ps 105:20.

84 Targum to Isa 5:27.

85 Peshitta to 1Kgs 20:11.

86 *Ibid.*

87 See Gilg. X:IV:9; cf. n. 37 above.

88 *b. Ḥag.*, 2a; f. *ibid.*, 9a; *b. ʿArak.*, 2b.

89 *Ibid.*, 6a.

90 *t. ʿEd.* 1:14,

horn, as *šōpār pāšūṭ*, and its opposite a crooked ram's horn, as *šōpār kāpūp*.[91] Similarly, *pšṭ* is used for straightening wrinkles: *sdyn hmqwmṭ mpšṭyn 't qwmṭyw wr' wyn 't ngʿw*, "(To examine) a wrinkled sheet, we straighten its wrinkles and examine its 'affection.' "[92]

We see from the above texts that a *ḥiggēr* in LH is one who is crooked or twisted. His cure is described by LH as a process of straightening out. In contrast, a free-moving individual is a *pāšūṭ* or *pōšēṭ*.[93] This antithesis provides us with the link to Akkadian *ēgēru* as well as with an etymology for the Akkadian word.

Akkadian *egēru* is well attested in the meaning, "to twist," in both transitive and intransitive senses.[94] Thus, for example in the omen series Šumma Izbu some anomalies are described as *kīma pillurti itgurū* or *kīma pillurti itlupū*; both phrases meaning, "twisted like a cross."[95] Further, *egēru* is equated with *šapāṣu*, "to wrestle."[96] The adjective *egru*[97] means "twisted," "perverse,"[98] in both the physical and moral senses.

91 *'mr R.Levi mṣwh šl r'š hšnh wšl ym hkpwrym bkpwpyn wšl kl hšnh* (=Akkadian *ša kal šatti* [RAcc. 76:13]) *bpšwṭyn*, "Rabbi Levi said, 'The ritual obligation of Rosh Hashanah and Yom Kippur requires bent (rams' horns) but the ones used throughout the year (on fast days) must be straight.' " (*b. Roš. Haš.,*. 26b).

92 *t. Neg.* 1:8.

93 For the variant see Zuckermandl, *Tosephta*, 456.

94 See *CAD E*, 41–42; AHw., 190; note, for example, En. el. V:59: *ēgir zibbassa durmaḫ*[*iš*] *urakkis*. "He (Marduk) bent back her tail and bound (it) to the great band."

95 Cf. TCS IV:85–86:14, 15–18; *egēru* has a moral connotation as well. Note e.g. *ša kišpūpušūni ikpudūni nullâ*[*ti*] *itgur libbašunuma malû tuššat*[*i*], "Those who have worked witchcraft against me, who have plotted baseness against me, perverse is their heart, they are full of malice." (OECT 6, 49:20–21).

96 *CAD E*, 41b lexical section; Note that the I/3 of *egēru* describes the function of a *muštapṣum*, "wrestler" in ARMT I:5:4–9. On this passage see M. Held, "A Faithful Lover in an Old Babylonian Dialogue," *JCS* 15 (1961), 13; See further, W. Moran, "New Evidence from Mari on the History of Prophecy," *Biblica* 50 (1969), 47:16–17.

97 See *CAD E*, 47; AHw., 190; In En. el. VI: 154, Marduk is termed *mu'abbit egrūti za'iri* "destroyer of the perverse enemies." The term *egru* is somewhat synonymous with *ṣalpu*, "slanting," "crooked," "dishonest." (*CAD Ṣ*, 86) Both *ṣalpu* and *egru* are associated with *lā šēmû*, "disobedient," in a difficult passage. See W. G. Lambert, "Three Literary Prayers of the Babylonians," *AfO* 19 (1959), 65:53; *CAD I/J*, 175a 3 translates *egrātum* by "shady dealings." For lexical equivalents of *egēru*, see MSL 9:134: 508–516.

98 Lambert BWL, 310 note to 1.279, cites Latin *perversus* as a semantic parallel to *egēru*.

Akkadian *egēru*, like LH *ḥgr*, is attested in contexts describing immobility and difficulty of movement. We read in a well-known Mari passage: *ana dâk nakrim šibqī teštenê u tēteneggirāšu u nakrum qātamma ana kunūšim šibqī ištenê u īteneggirkunūti*, "You constantly seek strategems against the enemy and would trip him. But the enemy likewise constantly seeks strategems against you, and he would trip you."[99]

It is significant that Akkadian *egēru*, "to twist," and *ešēru*, "to go straight," are attested as antonyms in regard to mobility of the legs. This is in no way different from the antonymy of *ḥgr* and *pšṭ* discussed above. Note the following: *kaššāptī limqutma anāku lut*[*bi*] *šî linnēgirma anāku lū*[*šir*], "May my sorceress fall but may I rise, may she hobble, but I walk straight."[100]

Like its West Semitic counterparts,[101] *egēru* may be used of speech. An Old Babylonian text of Hammurabi speaks of foreign countries *ša šadûšunu nesû lišanšunu egru*, "Whose mountains are distant, whose languages are distorted."[102] The term *lišanu egru* is very similar to JA *ḥgr pwm' wḥgr mmll*,

99 ARMT 1:5:4–7; See M. Held, "Faithful Lover," 13; Cf. W. von Soden, "Zu den politischen Korrespondenzen des Archivs von Mari," *Or* 21 (1952), 76. Von Soden translates *egēru* here as "jemand uber Kreuz, in die Quere kommen, in den Weg treten."; *CAD E*, 42 translates "to maneuver for position."; In the same letter, lines 15–16, however, we read: *a*[*ssu*]*r*[*r*]*i nakrum ina šubatim l*[*ā īteni*]*ggirkunūti*. This substantiates Held's rendering, "trip" and should be translated, "Heaven forbid the enemy trip you from ambush."

100 Laessøe Bit Rimki, 40:44–45. Note that Laessøe (*ibid.*, 43–44) mistakenly derives *linnegir* from *nakāru*.

101 *ḥgr* II may be used of various parts of the body. Thus, if a person breaks a bone of the paschal lamb, he is only culpable if the break is *kdy šth' hyd mḥgrt*, "large enough for a hand to be impeded by it." (*p. Pesaḥ*, 35b) The verb *ḥgr* II may even be used of a fingernail. According to *b. Ber.*, 37b, a ritual slaughtering implement is rendered unfit for use if it has a fault, *kdy šṭḥgr bh ṣprn*, "large enough for a fingernail to be impeded." Rashi a.l. translates: *št'kb bh ṣprn*. In addition, *ḥgr* II is employed to describe furniture which does not stand firm. See *m. Zabim* 3:1, 3.

102 UET I, 146 IV:6–8; Cf. I. J. Gelb, *Hurrians and Subarians* (Chicago, 1944), 41; See further, W. von Soden, "Der hymnisch-episch Dialekt des Akkadischen (Schluss)," *ZA* 41 (1932), 170, n. 3; For the most part Akkadian *lišānum* is feminine. (AHw., 556) Hence the expected stative is *egret*. The antonym of *lišanu egru* is probably *lišān mithurti*, "harmonious speech." See W. von Soden, "Das akkadische t-Perfekt in Haupt-und Nebensätzen und sumerische Verbalformen mit den Präfixen ba-, imma- und u," *AS* 16 (1965), 110; AHw., 662; S. N. Kramer, "The 'Babel of Tongues': A Sumerian Version," 88 (1968), 109; Contrast *CAD E*, 361a; TCS 3, 83–84.

"lame of mouth and distorted in speech,"[103] and to Syriac *ḥgr lšn'*, "of stammering, halting tongue."[104]

The use of words meaning "twist," for "lameness," is obvious. As a result, it is no surprise that other Akkadian verbs with the meaning, "twist" are also attested in the senses of "lameness," "deformity" and "disability." Thus, Akkadian *pasālu*[105] means, "to twist, contort, distort." The II *quttulu* form *pussulu* refers to a crippling defect. Note the following equivalencies:[106]

A. ŠU. GÌR. KU_5 = *kuṣṣudu*[107]
[A].ŠU. GÌR. KU_5 = *ussulu*[108]
A. ŠU. GÌR. KU_5 = *pussulum*

Similarly, Akkadian *kanānu*, "to twist," is attested in contexts dealing with lameness and paralysis. Note the following: *šumma šēpāšu ittenenṣilā u ittanaknannā*, "If his feet become more and more paralyzed and contorted."[109] In like manner we read in Maqlu: *ša ... ukassû mešrêtīya ukanninu manānēya*, "(The sorceress) who has paralyzed my limbs, contorted my sinews."[110]

We make one qualification with regard to the conclusions reached in this study. Akkadian does not employ *egēru* as widely as LH and Aramaic-Syriac employ *ḥgr* II to express difficulties of bodily movement. This maybe accounted for by the existence of a wide variety of Akkadian terms that serve

103 *Tg. Ps.-J.* to to Exod 4:10; Cf. the fragment a.l. *ḥagir pum uqəaše mamlel*. The Peshitta a.l. reads: *lʿg mmlly wʿl lšn'*.

104 See PSmCom, 126. In Syriac, as in LH, *ḥgr* is the antonym of *pšṭ*. Thus *wtrwn lšwn 'lm* (Isa 35:6) is translated by the Peshitta as : *wntpšṭ lšnh dp'q'*.

105 See TCS 4: 157:70. The commentary (*ibid.*, 223) reads: *pasālum*:kub-bu-[lu]. See CAD K, 3, *ibid.*, 483; Contrast AHw., 838a; Note further the lexical equation AL.GÚ.GÚ=*pussul* "he is crooked." See MSL 4:72:168; For a discussion of the verb *pasālu* see W. von Soden, "Zum akkadischen Wörterbuch. 31–40," *Or* 18 (1949), 399–401.; cf. AHw., 882.

106 Lambert BWL, 306 (note to l. 76); cf. MSL 12:143:23'–24; 13:219:48–54.

107 Note Lambert BWL, 76:76 (Theodicy): *ilânni kuṣṣudu panânni lilli*, "The cripple is on top of me, the fool is my superior."

108 *ussulu* is a variant of *uṣṣulu* related to Hebrew *ʿṣl* and Aramaic *ʿṭl*. In one LH source (H. S. Horovitz, *Siphre D'be Rab* [Jerusalem, 1976], 97:6–8) *aṣēlim* are grouped with amputees (*qṭʿyn*) and lame individuals (*ḥygrym*) in a context which seems to suggest that LH *ʿāṣēl* is closely related in meaning to Akkadian *uṣṣulu*.

109 Labat TDP, 142:IV:13'.

110 Maqlu, VII:64–65; Cf. above, n. 11.

that purpose. Among the relevant terms are: *aḫāzu,*[111] *akû,*[112] *amāšu,*[113] *ḫamû,*[114] *ḫašḫāšu,*[115] *ḫummuru,*[116] *kasû,*[117] *kubbulu,*[118] *muqqu,*[119] *pessû,*[120] *rummû,*[121] *šābulu,*[122] *šamāmu,*[123] and *šapāku.*[124]

---

111 E.g. *šaddihā ahāya kilatta ittahzā,* "My once active arms have both become paralyzed." (Lambert BWL, 34:76 [Ludlul I]).

112 See *CAD A/I*, 283, 286; *E*, 73.

113 Landsberger rendered *šumma ... qātāšu u šēpāšu amsā* as, "wenn seine Hände und Füsse heiss sind." (B. Landsberger, "Jahreszeiten im Sumerisch-Akkadischen," *JNES* 8 [1949], 285, n. 120); Labat TDP, 81 translates, "si ses mains et ses pieds sont crispés(?)" *CAD A/II*, 28 has, "to be cataleptic." AHw., 42, "zusammenziehen." Cf. *ibid.*, 315, s.v. *ḫamāsu*, 318, s.v. *ḫam/nšu* II.

114 See Gilg. V:iii:l2.

115 E.g. *akú bēl emūqi ikattam hašḫāšu petân birki ibâ',* {The powerless overwhelms the strong one, the cripple overtakes the swift one." (Cagni Erra 104:10–11).

116 E g. *Ugaritica* 5:294:35; *aškāpu ḫummuru* (ABAW, 38:7) is problematic; Cf. *CAD Ḫ*, 235; *CAD A/II*, 443; See further *MSL* 8/1: 9:29, 12: 201: 9–11.

117 See above, n. 11.

118 See *CAD K*, 483.

119 E.g. *minšu kî šībi muqqi tūšib ina āli,* "Why did you remain in the city like a crippled old man?" (Cagni Erra 62:47).

120 See above, n. 77.

121 See *CAD A/I*, 206.

122 See TCS 4, 63:85, 86, 155:39, 40.

123 Labat 188:1, 238:67; Cf. E. K. Ritter, "Magical-Expert (=Āšipu) and Physician (=Asû) Notes on Two Complementary Professions in Babylonian Medicine," *AS* 16 (1965), 305; For the noun *šimmatu*, "paralysis," see *CAD A/II*, 375b.

124 E.g *aḫīya išpukū birkīya urammû,* "They have made my arms limp, they have slackened my knees." (KAR 32:44); For *našpaku* see *CAD B*, 255; Cf. AHw., 760b 3.

CHAPTER 2

Akkadian *egerrû* and Hebrew *bt qwl*

Rabbinic Judaism generally avoided recourse to the divinatory methods that were in vogue in the Hellenistic world.[1] A notable exception to this avoidance was the rabbinic reliance on the *bt qwl* (= *bat qôl*). The *bt qwl* was generally considered a licit form of divine revelation and hence specifically excluded from the biblical prohibition against *nḥš* or divination.[2] Lieberman made a major contribution to the understanding of *bt qwl* in an appendix to his *Hellenism in Jewish Palestine.*[3] Briefly, it had been clear all the while that the rabbis recognized the revelatory character of various pronouncements that were subsumed under the heading *bt qwl*. The Palestinian Talmud, followed by medieval Jewish commentators,[4] explained the term as a synonym of

1 Dream interpretation was sanctioned by the Bible's writers and consequently, never viewed as illicit. See S. Bar, *A Letter That Has Not Been Read: Dreams in the Hebrew Bible* (Cincinnati, 2001). The activities of the rabbis in interpreting dreams are well-documented in the Babylonian Talmud. For some interesting examples see J. Neusner, *A History of the Jews of Babylonia*, Vol. IV (Leiden, 1969), 341–347. An interest in such matters on the part of Babylonian Jewry is hardly surprising considering the well-known Babylonian predilection for the art. Rabbinic Judaism would naturally be compelled to modify or adapt those features which opposed its basic religious tenets. Thus, the Babylonian *ilu ša šunāte*, "the god of dreams," became *bʿl ḥḥlmwt* (*b. Ber.* 10b) or *bʿl ḥḥlwm* (*b. Sanh.* 30a) "the master of dream(s)" explained by Rashi a.l. as "the prince who reveals dreams at night." See further Oppenheim, *Dreams*, 236–237. Similarly, the interest of the Hellenistic world in dream-interpretation accords nicely with native Palestinian Jewish tendencies. Some of the Greek methods of dream-interpretation were appropriated by the early rabbis and employed as aids in their biblical exegesis. See Saul Lieberman, *Hellenism in Jewish Palestine* (New York, 1950), 60–78.

2 See Lieberman, *Hellenism.*, 197. The severe rabbinic strictures against *nḥš* recorded in *y. Šhabb.* 8d may indicate that the prohibition was widely ignored. In actual fact, the Bible specifically refers to one aspect of *bt qwl* as *nḥš*. See n. 28 below.

3 Lieberman, *ibid.*, 194–199. E. A. Urbach made an extensive collection of *bt qwl* references in an appendix to his article "Halacha and Prophecy," Tarbiz 18 (1947), 1–27. For an early study see S. Schechter, "On the Study of the Talmud," in Studies in Judaism (Philadelphia, 1908), 112–114. Schechter translated bt qwl by "daughter-voice."

4 See Lieberman, *ibid.*, 194, n. 3. Add the comment of Issachar Katz-Berman, the author of *Matnot Kehunah* to *Exod. Rab.* 29:9. Note the explanation of Tosafot in *b. Sanh.*, 11a: "There are those who say that they did not hear a voice (*qwl*) emanating from heaven. Rather, from that (heavenly) voice emanated another. It is like those instances in which a man strikes

 | DOI 10.1163/9789004340879_003

hbrh,[5] "echo," "reverberation," taking *bt qwl* as a derivative of an original *qwl*.[6] This "reverberation" might be human[7] or non-human[8] in origin. It might

something forcefully and hears the sound of that striking far off in the distance. It was this (secondary voice) which they heard. Therefore it is called *bt qwl*."

5 For the meaning "reverberation," "echo," see *m. Roš. Haš.* 3:7. J. J. Finkelstein tentatively connected this Late Hebrew (LH) word with Akkadian *ḫubūru* "din," in his paper "Hebrew חבר and Semitic **ḪBR*," *JBL* 75 (1956), 331. There can be little doubt that he was correct. His hesitation was apparently based on translation errors in Jast, 330. In fact, *hbrh* clearly attests the meaning, "din," "clamor," and "uproar," in addition to "echo," "reverberation." See e.g., *b. Yoma* 19b; *b. Giṭ.* 89a. Morphologically, *hbrh* is even closer to Akkadian *ḫabarratum*. Note the following OB passage from an inscription of Ipiq-Eshtar, king of Malgium: *inūmišu urdam mātum innapḫari kalûšu iškun ḫabarratam rabītam u maruštam ī[pu]uš* "At that time the entire people, all of them, came down here, raised a great clamor and committed an enormity." Cf. RIME 4, 678. With this passage compare the usage of *hbrh* in *y. Šheq.* 5:2 (48d): *myd nplh hbrh bʿyr* "A clamor immediately broke out in the city." For the pair *hubūru/rigmu* "clamor/din," see Finkelstein, "**ḪBR*," 329; W. Moran, "Atrahasis and the Biblical Story of the Flood," *Biblica* 52 (1971), 51–61. See further W. von Soden, "Der hymnisch-epische Dialekt des Akkadischen," ZA 41 (1932), 168. Other synonyms of *ḫubūru* are *ikkillu, šisītu* and *tanūqātu*.

6 See n. 4. This interpretation is borne out by *Exod. Rab.* 29:9: *kšʾdm qwrʾ lhbrw yš lqwlw bt qwl whqwl šhyh ywṣʾ mpy hgbwrh lʾ hyh lqwlw bt qwl*. "When a man calls his fellow his voice has a reverberation but the voice which was emanating from God had no reverberation." Similarly, *Cant. Rab.* 1:21: "Just as oil has no reverberation (*bt qwl*) when poured, so Israel has no reverberation in this world." Cf. Jast, 200. According to Payne-Smith, col. 596 *s.v. brt qlʾ*, Wis 17:18 has *brt qlʾ* for Greek ἠχώ. There is at least one instance, however, in which *qwl* and *bt qwl* are used interchangeably. In *b. Sanh.* 96b there is a midrashic elaboration of the destruction of the first temple in which Nabû-zēr-iddin is addressed first by a *qlʾ* and then by a *bt qlʾ* with no apparent difference in meaning. The Munich manuscript has *npqt* (*sic*) *qlʾ* which the editor emends to *npqt bt qlʾ*. See R. Rabbinovicz, *Variae Lectiones in Mischnam et in Talmud Babylonicum* Pars IX (Nürnberg, 1926), 282.

7 *m. Yeb.* 16:6; *t. Yeb.* 14:7. The human voice could be masculine or feminine: see *b. Meg.* 32a.

8 In *b. Ber.* 3a it is related that R. Yose heard *bt qwl šmnhmt kywnh* "an oracular voice moaning like a dove." The moaning of a dove is a familiar image. Aramaic *mnhmyn* renders *hmwt* in Ezek 7:16. Biblical Hebrew expresses the same concept by *qnn* (Jer 48:28) and by *hgh*. (Isa 38:14, 59:11; Nah 2:8) The same simile is well attested in Akkadian as *kīma summati damāmu*. (Ebeling Handerhebung, 132:64; Ludlul 1:107) By itself this comparison would merely take its place alongside the biblical and Akkadian similes for sorrow and mourning. However another rabbinic passage indicates that the *bt qwl* could actually be conceived of as sounding like a bird in a context which has nothing to do with sorrow and mourning. In Petiḥta 23 of *Lam. Rab.* we find the following interpretation of the enigmatic phrase in Qoh 12:4: *wyqwm lqwl hṣpr* "'And he will rise up at the sound of the bird.' This refers to Nebuchadnezzar the wicked … for eighteen years an oracular sound (*bt qwl*) reverberated in Nebuchadnezzar's palace saying: O wicked slave, go and destroy the temple of your master whose children do not obey him." That the *bt qwl* should sound like a bird is in keeping with

emanate from heaven,[9] from Mt. Horeb,[10] from the temple sanctuary,[11] or from an unspecified origin.[12] It would assume various forms.[13] The contents of the *bt qwl* were likewise diverse. These could consist of factual information,[14] evaluative statements,[15] legal decisions,[16] predictions of coming events[17] or counsels concerning individual courses of action.[18] In performing these functions, the *bt qwl* largely filled the vacuum created by the extinction of recognized prophecy in the Persian period of Jewish history.[19] Though most of the above had been noted by scholars,[20] Lieberman was the first to recognize the significance of the fact that the term *bt qwl* could be applied to such cases as the following:[21] *r. ywḥnn wrby šmʿwn bn lqyš hww mtḥmdyn myḥmy ʾpwwyy dšmwʾl ʾmryn nlk ʾḥr šmyʿt bt qwl ʿbrwn qwmy sydrʾ šmʿyn qlyh dṭlyyʾ wšmʾl mt wsyynmwn wkn hwt lyh* "Rabbi Yohanan and Rabbi Shimon b. Laqish wished to see Samuel in person. They said, 'let us act in accord with a *bt qwl* oracle.' They passed a synagogue and heard the voice of a child (reciting the biblical verse) 'Samuel died.'[22] They noted the time of the pronouncement and (later) established that this had in fact happened to him."[23] In the above passage the *bt qwl* was merely a biblical

what we know of the *egerrû*. (See below and contrast Blau, *Zauberwesen*, 65.) Note the following: [*šumma amēlu*] *egerrī esṣūri ina šamê īpul*[*šu*] "If the oracle of (an ominous) bird answers a man from heaven ..." (CT 39:42:33; cf. CT 43:32 and see *CAD I/J*, 212.) An *egerrû* could originate from various animals. See A. L. Oppenheim, "Sumerian: inim.gar, Akkadian: *egirrû* = Greek: *kledon*," *AfO* 17 (1954/6), 50, 55. On Qoh 12:4 see H. L. Ginsberg, "Koheleth 12:4 in the Light of Ugaritic," *Syria* 33 (1956), 99–101; cf. *idem*, *Koheleth*, 130.

9 *b. B. Qam.* 59b; *b. Sanh.*11a.

10 *m. Abot* 6:2; *b. Ber.* 17b.

11 Horovitz-Rabin *Mechilta*, 200:13–14.

12 *b. Ber.* 51b; *b. Šabb.* 56b; *b. ʿErub.* 13b; *b. Taʿan.* 24b; *b. Ḥul.* 86a.

13 See *b. ʿAbod. Zar.* 17a. I refer here not to the *bt qwl* designated as such, but rather to the prostitute's interpretation of her flatulence as oracular. This has well-attested Akkadian parallels. See *CAD Ṣ*, 107 s.v. *ṣarātu*.

14 *m. Yeb.* 16:6 and *b. Yeb.* 122a.

15 See below.

16 *b. ʿErub.* 13b; *b. B. Meṣ* 59b.

17 *b. Soṭah* 2a.

18 *b. B. Bat.* 3b.

19 *t. Soṭah* 13:2.

20 For bibliography see *EncJud*, vol. 4, 324 s.v. *bat kol*.

21 *y. Šabb.* 6:9 (38c).

22 1Sam 28:3.

23 That this is the meaning of *sym* is evident from *y. Soṭah*, 24b: *mʿśh šyṣʾw nʿrym lhlḥm bʾntwkyʾ wšmʿ ywḥnn khn gdl bt qwl ywṣʾ mbyt qdš hqdšm wʾmrt nṣhw ṭlyyʾ dʾgḥw qrbʾ bʾntwkyʾ wktbw ʾwth hʿt wntnw bw zmn wkwwnw šbʾwth šʿh hyth* "It happened that the young men went out

verse recited by a student in the course of his studies. For the two rabbis, however, it possessed oracular significance.[24] On the basis of this and similar examples, Lieberman concluded that the *bt qwl* was identical to the Greek φήμη or κληδών.[25] Both the Hebrew and Greek phenomena attribute oracular efficacy to "an omen contained in a chance uttering."[26] Lieberman noted similar phenomena in other parts of the classical and Hellenistic world.[27] A few years later A. L. Oppenheim demonstrated the existence of a close relationship between the Greek φήμη and κληδών phenomena and the Mesopotamian phenomenon known as Sumerian *inim.gar* and Akkadian *egerrû*. Though he adduced Biblical and Islamic parallels to the phenomenon,[28] Oppenheim overlooked Lieberman's study. Consequently, he did not refer to the rabbinic material in his discussion. The obvious conclusion resulting from these two studies is that the *egerrû* and the *bt qwl* are indeed related phenomena. It is the purpose of this study to draw attention to that relationship and to demonstrate that the *bt qwl* and the inim.gar/*egerrû* may mutually elucidate one another.[29]

---

to do battle with Antioch. Yohanan the high priest heard an oracle (*bt qwl*) emanating from the innermost sanctuary saying, 'The lads who battled Antioch were victorious.' So they wrote down the date and indicated the hour and (later) determined that the event had occurred at that very time." The parallel to the above in *t. Soṭah* 13:5 has *wkywnw ʾt ʾwth hšʿh wkywnwʿsnṣhw ʾwth šʿh.*

24 A similar story is related in *y. Šabb.* 6:9 (8c) about Bar Kappara who applied a recited verse to himself. It is important to note that though the children involved quote biblical verses, the rabbis do not consult these verses directly. Their method is not to be confused with stichomancy. In *b. Ḥul.* 95b the following distinction is made among methods favored by different rabbis: *rb bdyq bmbrʾ wšmwʾl bdyq bsprʾ wr. ywḥnn bdyq bynwqʾ* "Rab consults (the omen offered) by a ferry, (*mbrʾ* = *mʿbrʾ*; see Jast, 725, 813 [= Akkadian *nēberu*]), Samuel consults a Bible (stichomancy) and R. Yohanan consults a child." The consultation as narrated in the above talmudic passage was direct. R. Yohanan asked the child: *pswq ly pswkyk* "Recite your verse for me." Presumably, the verse would be the most recent one studied by the child. For other examples see *b. Ḥag.* 15a–b. R. Yohanan also taught, "If one rose in the morning and found himself uttering a biblical verse—this is minor prophecy." (*b. Ber.* 55b) Stichomancy survived in the medieval Jewish *šimmūša*. See M. Gaster "Divination (Jewish)" in *Encyclopedia of Religion and Ethics*, ed. J. Hastings (New York, 1955), Vol. 4, 813.

25 *Hellenism*, 194.

26 *Ibid.*, 195.

27 *Ibid..*, 196–198.

28 Oppenheim, "Sumerian: inim.gar," 52–53. His interpretation of 1Kgs 20:30 indicates that what the rabbis termed *bt qwl* was termed *nḥš* by the Bible.

29 The linguistic relationship between inim.gar and *egerrû* was elucidated by B. Landsberger in "Das gute Wort," *MAOG* IV (1929), 315.

The terms *bt qwl* and *egerrû* are semantically close. Akkadian *egerrû* is a loan from the Sumerian compound inim.gar, composed of the elements *inim* corresponding to Akkadian *amatu* "word," and *gar* corresponding to Akkadian *šakānu* "to put, place." Accordingly, it is best rendered as "utterance."[30] LH *bt qwl* may denote "echo," "reverberation,"[31] "voice,"[32] and possibly "word."[33] The respective etymologies of both terms indicate that the respective phenomena are acoustic. This borne out by the verbs employed in describing their operation. Turning first to *bt qwl* we note that the verbs associated with it are *yṣʾ* in Hebrew (=*npq* in Aramaic sources), *ʾmr, šmʿ* and *hšyb*. The following examples are characteristic: *yṣʾ: yṣth bt qwl wʾmrh lw ršʿ bn ršʿ bn ršʿ bn bnw šl ʿśw hršʿ* "A voice rang out and said to him: O wicked man (Titus)! Son of a wicked man (Vespasian)! Scion of Esau the wicked!"[34]

npq: npq bt qlʾ wʾmrh kl mn dhwh bʾškbtyh drby mzwmn hwʾ lḥyy hʿwlm hbʾ "A voice rang out and said: Whoever was present at the death of R. Judah the Prince is designated for life in the world to come."[35]
ʾmr: ywmʾ ḥd šmʿ hhwʾ gbrʾ bt qlʾ dʾmr kl ʿbdʾ dmryd hštʾ mṣlh "One day that man heard a voice saying: Any slave who rebels nowa(days) is successful."[36]
šmʿ: šmʿty bt qwl šmnhmt kywnh "I heard a voice moaning like a dove."[37]
hšyb: ʾmr r. ywḥnn b. zkʾy mh tšwbh hšybtw bt qwl lʾwtw ršʿ "R. Yohanan ben Zakkai said: What answer did the voice give to that wicked man ...?"[38]

---

30 See CAD E, 45.
31 See n. 6 above.
32 This meaning of *bt qwl* is the most common one; cf. e.g., *b. Ber.*12b, 17b, 51b; *b. Šabb.* 33b (bis), 56b; *b.Yoma* 22b; *b.* Ket. 103b; *b. Giṭ* 56b; *b. B. Meṣ* 59b; *b. B. Bat.* 3b; *b. Sanh.*, 96b. The Arabic *ṣaut* (=Hebrew *qwl*), "voice," "sound," corresponds to Syriac *brt qlʾ* in the Ahiqar story; see F. C. Conybeare, J. Rendel Harris, and Agnes Smith Lewis, *The Story of Aḥikar* (Cambridge, 1913), 38:4 (Syriac numeration) and page 1 of the Arabic version.
33 I could find no clear case of this usage in Rabbinic sources. Lieberman infers this meaning from R. Yohanan's homiletical interpretation of *dābār* in Isa 30:21. See *b. Meg.*, 32a; *Hellenism*, 195.
34 *b. Giṭ* 56b. For additional examples of *bt qwl* with *yṣʾ* see *m. Abot* 6:2; *b. Ber.* 61b; *b. Šabb.* 33b, 56b, 88a; *b. Roš. Haš.* 21b; *b. Meg.* 3a, 12a; *b. Ḥag.* 15a; *b. Soṭah* 2a; *b. B.Meṣ* 59b, 85a, 86a; *b. Sanh.* 104b; *b. Mak.* 23b; *b. ʿAbod. Zar.* 10b, 17a; *b. Ḥul.* 87a.
35 *b. Ket.* 103b; cf. further e.g., *b. Ber.* 51b; *b. ʿErub.* 54b; *b. Pesaḥ* 114a; *b.Ket.*77b, 103b; *b. B. Bat.*73b; *b. Sanh.* 96b.
36 *b. B. Bat.* 3b, Usually *ʾmr* is part of a sequence with *yṣʾ*; e.g., *b. Taʿan.* 29a; *b. Moʿed Qaṭ.* 18b; *b. Ḥag.* 15a.
37 *b. Ber.* 3a. See n. 8.
38 *b. Pesaḥ* 94a = *b. Ḥag.* 13a.

The verbs employed with *egerrû* indicate that it too is acoustic. It is particularly noteworthy that a number of these verbs correspond closely to those associated with *bt qwl*. Thus, Akkadian *šūṣû, dabābu/qabû, šemû* and *apālu* correspond to *yṣʾ, ʾmr, šmʿ, and hšyb* respectively attested in the above passages. Note the following references:

šūṣû: [*ina*] *qūlti mūši ina sūq erbetti*... *tazzazāma*... *egerrâ tušeṣṣi*[39] "You (figurines) will stand at a crossroad in the stillness of the night... and call forth an *egerrû*."

dabābu: šumma inūma uššī bīti nadû egerrû damqu idbub (var. *īpul*)[40] *bītu šû libbašu ṭāb šumma inūma uššī bīti nadû egerrû lemnu uttazam bītu šû niziqtum sadrassu*[41] "If a favorable *egerrû* spoke when the foundations of a house were laid, that house will experience happiness. If an unfavorable *egerrû* cried out when the foundations of a house were laid, constant vexation is in store for that house."

šemû: šuttušu deʾiqte amrat egerrâšu asseme[42] "His favorable dream has been seen. I heard the oracle concerning him."

apālu: šumma amēlu egerrû ina šumēlišu īpulšu kašād ṣibûti[43] "If an oracle answered a man on his left (this means): achievement of objective."

When *egerrû* and the *bt qwl* have the meaning "oracular response," that response may be a detailed one or a simple "yes" or "no" answer which might be repeated for emphasis. This may be seen when we compare the following two statements, the first from the Talmud, the second from an Akkadian source: *wʾmr r. špṭyh ʾmr r. ywḥnn mnyyn šmštmšyn bbt qwl šnʾmr*... *whwʾ dʾmr hn hn whw dmr lʾw lʾw* "R. Shephatiah said in R. Yohanan's name: Whence (the scriptural permission) to employ a *bt qwl*? It is written...[44] The *bt qwl* is reliable if it repeats 'Yes, yes' or if it repeats 'No, no.' "[45]

39 LKA 93 r. 5–7.

40 Though not indicated in *CAD A/II*, 155–165, *apālu* here merely means "speak up," in full agreement with its semantic equivalents Hebrew *ʿnh*, Aramaic *ʿny* and Ugaritic *ʿny*.

41 CT 38, pl. 10:20–21.

42 ABL 1347 r. 2–3.

43 CT 39, pl. 41:16; See further ABL 76 (=*AOAT* 5/1: 76) r. 4–5.

44 His source is Isa 30:21 "Your ears shall hear a message (perhaps understood as 'prophetic message') behind you." Does this indicate that the *bt qwl* was heard from behind? An *egerrû* could come from any direction. Note: *egerrī eṣṣūri ana panīšu īpulšu* "An oracle of a bird answered (a man) in front of him"(CT 39: 42:32) and *egerrû ana arkīšu ītanappalšu* "an oracle keeps answering (a man) in back of him." (*ibid.*, 41:23).

45 *b. Meg.* 32a.

šumma amēlu egerrû anni 2-sŭ īpulšu tazbiltum šumma amēlu egerrû ulla 2-šu īpulšu kašād ṣibûti[46] "If an oracle twice answered a man 'yes' (this means) deferment... If an oracle twice answered a man 'no' (this means) attainment of goal." The Akkadian material clearly emphasized that it is the repetition that is crucial rather than the affirmative or negative quality of the response.[47] We may surmise that the same holds true of the rabbinic material though as yet no final conclusion is possible.

Lieberman drew special attention to the *bt qwl* in its aspect as an unintentional oracular statement. This is likewise a feature of the *egerrû*, as noted by Oppenheim in the following Akkadian prayer: *šutlimamma egirrî dumqi ina suqi lū magir qabûa*[48] "Grant me a propitious oracle (to utter) so when I walk along in the street my utterances will be pleasing." The wish of the worshipper is to make statements that will promote well-being for other people. The fact that the statement is purely accidental in no way detracts from the effect it can have in the real world. This was seen above, in the example of the *egerrû* uttered when the foundations of a house were laid, and can be seen in greater detail in the following story related in the Palestinian Talmud.[49] *r. ywnh wrb ywsh slqyn mbqrh lrby ʾḥʾ dhwʾ tšyš ʾmryn nlk btr šmyʿt bt qwl šmʿyn qlyh dʾttʾ ʾmrh lḥbrth ʾṭpy bwṣynh ʾmrh lh lʾ yttpy wlʾ myṭpy bwṣynhwn*[50] *dyśrʾl*, "Rabbi Yonah and Rabbi Yosah were going to visit Rabbi Aha who was ill. They said, 'let us follow a *bat qôl* oracle.' They heard the voice of one woman saying to another, 'has the lamp gone out?' She answered her, 'It will not go out'; and the lamp of Israel is not (to this day) extinguished." (Rabbi Aha was still alive

46 CT 39, pl. 41:10.

47 Cf. Oppenheim, "Sumerian: inim.gar," 54–55.

48 *Ibid.*, 51, 53; For the text cf. Langdon, OECT 6, 84:21–22 and Schollmeyer, 75:23–24; Cf. Ebeling's translations in Ebeling Handerhebung, 49 and 51:119–120.

49 *y. Šabb.* 8c. Listening to two people in order to get a *bt qwl* has a close parallel in ARMT X:4 in which Queen Shibtu questions a man and woman in order to elicit an *egerrû*. See A. Finet, "Un cas de clédonomancie à Mari," in *Zikir Šumim: Assyriological Studies Presented to F. R. Kraus on the Occasion of his Seventieth Birthday*, eds. G. van Driel, Th. Krispin, and K. R. Veenhof (Leiden, 1982), 48–56; A. Malamat, "The Prophetic Experience in Mari and the Bible-A Re-examination," *Shnaton* 7–8 (1983–1984), 48–55, especially 173–174.

50 *bwṣynʾ* = Akkadian *buṣīnu* (*m*). See AHw., 143a. Both the Akkadian and the Aramaic term can refer to a plant. The respective plants, however, are quite dissimilar. See Landsberger, "Wortgleichungen," 194, n. 4. The metaphor of death as the extinguishing of a flame is widespread. See T. H. Gaster, *Thespis* (New York, 1950), 335, n. 2; Cf. further *napista bullû* in *CAD B*, 73f. For the phrase "to extinguish a flame," in the Semitic languages see M. Held, *JBL* 84 (1965), 276, n. 19: Add *mkbš ʾwr* (=Akkadian *išāta kabāsu*) attested in *y. Šabb.* 8d.

at the time that this story was transmitted.) Similarly, a negative accidental pronouncement could bring about a misfortune. Again, this is best illustrated by another passage from the Palestinian Talmud.[51] *r. ywḥnn hwʾ ʿbr bšwqʾ ḥmʾ ḥd mzbyn mn ʾylyn mlṭmhʾ*[52] *ʾmr lyh mn ʾylyn ʾt ḥyy ʾmr lyh ʾyn šbqyh wʾzl lyh btr šʿh ʿbr gbyh ʿmr lyh rby ṣly ʿlwyy dmn hhyʾ šʿth lʾ zbnyt klwm* "R. Yohanan was walking along the street when he saw a man selling honey cakes. He said to him, 'do you make a living from these?' He told him, 'yes.' R. Yohanan left him and went on his way. A while later the man came over to him and said, 'Rabbi pray for me, for since that time (we encountered one another) I've sold nothing.' "

The first story, specifically termed a *šmyʿt bt qwl*, is an illustration of an *egerrû dumqu*, which resulted in R. Aha's recovery. The second is an *egerrû lemnu*, resulting in economic hardship. Though the text is not without difficulty, it appears that the unfavorable street oracle is a major source of complaint on the part of the suffering protagonist in Ludlul: *dalḫā têrētūa*[53] *nuppuḫā uddakam itti bārî u šāʾili*[54] *alakti ul parsat*[55] *ippî sūqi lemun egerrûa attilma* (for *attâlma!*) *iššāt mūši šuttī pardat* "My omens are confused and inflamed daily; the diviner and the dream-priest cannot investigate (the circumstances of) my case; at the crossroad (?) oracles are of ill-portent for me; when I go to bed at night my dream is terrifying."[56]

---

51 *y. Šabb.* 8c–d.

52 See Krauss, *Lehnwörter* II, 340a.

53 Cf. *Ugaritica V*, 267:5′ *dalḫā têrētum šutābulum šīru.*

54 On these two priests see Lambert BWL, 284, n. 52; J. Renger, "Untersuchungen zum Priestertum der altbabylonischen Zeit," ZA 59 (1969), 203–218.

55 *CAD E*, 43b (cf. *CAD A/I*, p. 299a) has: "I can not stop going to the divination priest." Since CAD recognizes here the idiom *alakta parāsu,* the required translation would be: "I am not impeded from going to ..." though *itti* would still be problematic. Cf. the objections in Lambert BWL, 284. Lambert himself (*ibid.*, 33) translates, "the omen of the diviner and dream priest does not explain my condition." This too is problematic for the following reasons. First, it requires *parsat* to have an active rather than a stative connotation. Secondly, if *itti* is understood as the construct of *ittu* "omen," it can only be an omen about the priest. It is more likely to take *parāsu* here as an ellipsis of *arkata parāsu* (=Mishnaic *bdq ʾḥry* "investigate." See e.g. *m. Qidd.* 4:4–5). The sufferer is complaining about the inability of the priests to perform their functions. Compare his complaint in Ludlul II:6–7 (Lambert BWL, 38): *bārû ina bīri arkat ul iprus ina maššakki šaʾīlu ul ušāpi dinī* "The diviner through divination has not been able to investigate, through libanomancy has not elucidated my case." Similarly, a *barû* complains, *dīnu šupšuqma ... parās arkatu nesânni* "The case is very confounding ... investigation of it eludes me." See Landsberger Brief, 21, n. 28. Similar Akkadian idioms meaning "investigate, examine" are (*w*)*arkata šaʾālu* and (*w*)*arkata ḥâṭu.* See *CAD A/II*, 277b.

56 Lambert BWL, 32:51–54. The meaning of *pî sūqi* is unclear. It may mean "crossroad."

An important point of contact between the *egerrû* and the *bt qwl* is the evaluative function performed by both of them. In the polytheistic Mesopotamian cults, the worshipper depends on the lower gods to speak favorably of him before the high gods. Thus Hammurabi prays: *šēdum lamassum ilū ēribūt TN libitti TN egirrê ūmišam ina maḫar DN bēliya u DN2 bēltiya lidammiqū* "May the protecting spirits, the gods who have access to the Esagil temple and the very brickwork of the Esagil temple, cause my oracles to be propitious in the presence of Marduk my lord and Zarpanitu my lady."[57] At the same time, the worshipper could call upon the lower gods to malign his enemies.[58] The *bt qwl* was similarly conceived of as offering statements about the relative merits and demerits of individuals. Because of the monotheistic character of rabbinic Judaism, the divine speaker remained anonymous: *ʾmr r. yhwdh ʾmr rb bkl ywm wywm bt qwl yṣʾt mhr ḥwrb wʾmrt kl hʿwlm kwlw nyzwnyn bšbyl ḥnynʾ bny wḥnynʾ bny dy lw bqb ḥrwbyn mʿrb šbt lʿrb šbt* "R. Yehudah said in Rab's name: Every single day a voice emanates from Mt. Horeb and proclaims: The entire world is sustained for the sake of My son Hanina. Yet my son Hanina is content with but one qab of carobs weekly."[59] Or, to cite another example: *ḥlš dʿtyh ʾmr rbwnw šl ʿwlm lʾ plplty twrh kmwtw yṣth bt qwl ʾmrh lw twrh kmwtw plplt twrh kmwtw lʾ rybṣt* "He became distraught and said, 'Master of the world, have I not argued Torah on a par with him?'A voice spoke up and said to him, 'you've argued Torah on a par with him but you haven't disseminated as much Torah as he has.' "[60]

57 CH xxv: 48–58. Cf. Oppenheim, "Sumerian: inim.gar," 53.

58 *Ibid.*, xxvi:81–97: DN ... *mudammiqat egirrêya* ... *ašar šiptim u purussîm ina maḫar DN2 awassu lilemmin šulput mātišu halāq nišīšu tabāk napištišu kīma mê ina pî DN2 šarrim lišaškin* "May Ninlil ... the lady who produces propitious oracles for me, malign his case before Enlil at the place of judgment and decision. May she cause to be placed in the mouth of Enlil the king (a decree bringing about the) destruction of his land, extinction of his people, and the pouring out of his lifebreath like water." (Cf. Šurpu, VII:72; B. Hruška, "Das spätbabylonische Lehrgedicht Inannas Erhöhung," *ArOr* 37 [1969], 484:46.) Though Yahdun-Lim does not explicitly employ the term *egerrû* in his inscription, he expresses Hammurabi's sentiment in different words: DN *kallatum* ... *lū mulemminat awātišu ina maḫar DN2 ana dariātim* "May Aya the bride ... be the one who maligns his deeds before Shamash forever!" (RIME 608: 149–152).

59 *b. Ber.* 17b; *b. Taʿan.* 24b; *b. Ḥul.* 86a. The reference is to the first-century scholar Hanina b. Dosa whose piety was legendary. For the episode of the carobs see Held, *AS* 16 (1965), 397–398.

60 *b. B. Meṣ* 85b.

CHAPTER 3

Late Hebrew *ḥzr* and Akkadian *saḫāru*

The verb *ḥzr* is very common in Late Hebrew (LH) and in Western Aramaic.[1] Its semantic range includes the concepts, "turn, return, repeat, circle, surround, besiege, seek."[2] Our verb has correspondents in Eastern Aramaic as well. These are respectively *ḥdr*[3] and the weakened form *hdr*.[4] While these correspondences are well known, the relationship between *ḥzr* and Akkadian

---

* This article presents a revised version of a point which I examined in my dissertation, "Studies in Late Hebrew Lexicography in the Light of Akkadian," in the Department of Middle East Languages and Cultures of Columbia University. I sincerely thank Professors Isaac Barzilay, H. L. Ginsberg, David Weiss Halivni, and David Marcus who read the manuscript and made valuable suggestions. I particularly wish to thank my mentor Professor Moshe Held for his unflagging aid and encouragement.

It is a great privilege to present this article to Professor Theodor Gaster. He, more than any other individual, has enabled contemporary students to penetrate the veil of ideological and theological biases that the millennia have woven between the ancient near eastern world and our own. In so doing he has made us appreciate that lost world and taught us the necessity of understanding it in its own terms: Y'RK BᶜL ŠMM YMW WŠNTW.

Text citations from the Tosefta follow S. Lieberman, *The Tosefta* (New York, 1955–1988). Abbreviations of Assyriological sources follow *CAD*. Biblical and rabbinic sources are abbreviated according to *The SBL Handbook of Style*. For abbreviations of rabbinic sources not found in *The SBL Handbook*, this article follows M. Sokoloff, *A Dictionary of Jewish Babylonian Aramaic* (Baltimore, 2002). In addition note the following abbreviations: BH=Biblical Hebrew; LH=Late Hebrew; GN=geographic name; DN=divine name; PN=personal name; Levy, TW=J. Levy, *Chaldäisches Wörterbuch über die Targumim* (Leipzig, 1881); Levy, TMW= J. Levy, *Neuhebräisches und aramäisches Wörterbuch über die Talmudim und Midraschim* (Berlin, 1924); OBS = J. J. Finkelstein and M. Greenberg, *Oriental and Biblical Studies Collected Writings of E. A. Speiser* (Philadelphia, 1967); Sperling Studies = S. David Sperling, "Studies in Late Hebrew Lexicography in the Light of Akkadian," (Ph.D. dissertation, Columbia, 1973).

1 For attestations see Kasowski, *Thesaurus Talmudis* 13:288–324; Jastrow, 446–47; Levy, *TW*, 1:248; *idem, Wörterbuch*, 2:32.

2 See below.

3 E.g., *Or* 10 (1941), 129:9; for Syriac *ḥdr* see Payne Smith, col. 1203, and see below.

4 For Jewish Aramaic (JA) *hdr*, see Kasowski, *Thesaurus Talmudis* 10:175–202; *TW*, 1:194–95; for Mandaic *hdr*, see Drower and Macuch, *Mandaic Dictionary*, 131–32; for the shift of /ḥ/ to /h/ see E. Kutscher, VTSup 16 (1967), 172; J. N. Epstein, *A Grammar of Babylonian Aramaic* (Tel Aviv, 1960), 18. The verb *hdr* may be hidden in Dan 4:33. See the commentaries.

 | DOI 10.1163/9789004340879_004

saḫāru[5] has not been previously noted. It is the purpose of the present study to examine that relationship.

Jacob Levy first proposed the verb *sḥr* as an etymology for LH *ḥzr*.[6] Phonetically, the derivations present no problems[7] and may be accepted in principle.[8] It is our contention, however, that the etymon of LH *ḥzr* is to be sought in Akkadian *saḫāru* rather than in the Biblical Hebrew (BH) *sḥr*. In order

5 For attestations see AHw., 1005–8; *CAD S*, 37–54.

6 Levy, TMW, 2:32; cf. TW, 1:194. Levy attempted erroneously, to associate these words further with biliteral stems. Levy buttressed his argument semantically by demonstrating that the different Targums alternate between Aramaic *sḥr* and Aramaic *ḥzr* when translating Hebrew *sābīb*. Thus, in Gen 23:17 Onqelos reads *s^e^ḥōr s^e^ḥōr* while Pseudo-Jonathan has *ḥazōr ḥazōr and* Peshitta has *kd ḥdr*. Sefire Aramaic, which was unavailable to Levy, provides his view with additional support. In one of the Sefîre inscriptions we encounter the phrase, *wkl mlky' zy sḥrty* "All the kings of my surrounding region." See J. Fitzmyer, *The Aramaic Inscriptions of Sefîre* (Rome, 1995), 134:7–8. Cf. Fitzmyer's translation a.l.; cf. further *ANET*³, 660; *KAI*, 2:264, 268; R. Degen, *Altaramäische Grammatik* (Wiesbaden, 1969), 134; contrast A. Dupont-Sommer apud F. Rosenthal, *An Aramaic Handbook* (hereafter AH; Wiesbaden, 1967), 1/2:5. Aramaic *sḥrt* is most likely to be equated with Akkadian *siḫirtu* "Umgebung" (surroundings) a synonym of *limūtu*. See AHw., 1040; *CAD S*, 235. Cf. this phrase with the Targums to Deut 17:14 *kol haggôyîm ašẹr sebîbōtāy*). Onqelos translates:… *dī b^e^saḥarānây*. Pseudo-Jonathan renders:… *dib^e^ḥazrānūtây*. (Peshitta reads *dbḥdry*.) A further case in point is the expression *wayyassēb 'ẹt pānā(y)w* (*m. Ber.* 2:5; *m. Ma'aś.* 2:2). The BH, Aramaic and LH idioms are to be equated with Akkadian *panī suḫḫuru*, "to turn the face." The sense may be either the positive "zuwenden" (turn towards) or "abwenden"(turn away). See AHw., 819a, 1007a–b; Mullo Weir Lexicon, 292; *CAD S*, 49–50.

7 For similar combination of voicing and metathesis, cf., e.g., the respective words for "honey" in Akkadian, Hebrew, and Aramaic:

Akkadian	Hebrew	Aramaic
dišpu	*d^e^baš*	*dūbš'ā*.

Contrast GvG, 1:278, 1g.

8 The Aramaic forms with medial /d/ remain to be explained. I consider two possibilities: a) We have a case of false etymologizing. Aramaic knows other such examples. Thus *p^e^tōrā*, "table" is a well-known loan from Akkadian *paššuru*, which is in turn borrowed from Sumerian BANŠUR. Similarly, Mandaic *zql'* "date-palm" corresponds to *dql'* of the other Aramaic dialects and to LH *dẹqẹl*; b) Professor Ginsberg has suggested (privately) that the Aramaic forms with medial /d/ have resulted from blending or contamination with some word on the order of Arabic *dāra*, which, like the verbs *sḥr, saḫāru*, and *ḥzr*, is a synonym of Hebrew *sbb*. See Saadia's translations of Ps 3:7, 114: 3, 5; note that a verb *dar* in this sense may be attested in Old Akkadian. See W. von Soden, ZA 62 (1973), 273; I. Gelb, *Sargonic Texts in the Ashmolean Museum* (Chicago, 1970), 8:22. H. L. Ginsberg has illustrated the operation of the linguistic phenomenon of blending in BH in *Louis Ginzberg Jubilee Volume* (New York, 1945), 161, n. 8. For other illustrations in Semitic and elsewhere, see C. Brocklemann, ZS 5 (1927), 6–38.

to establish this correspondence, we will attempt to show that the respective semantic ranges of *ḥzr* and *saḫāru* largely go hand in hand.

Levy made no distinction between BH and LH *sḥr* nor between Hebrew and Aramaic *sḥr*. It will be recalled that the meaning of BH *sḥr* is a matter of controversy. Though the meaning of the noun *sōḥēr* "merchant,"[9] is an established fact, ancient and modern commentators alike dispute the meaning of the finite verb *sḥr* in Gen 34:10, 21, and 42:34.[10] Some explain the finite verb as "to trade, engage in commerce,"[11] while others prefer "to circle, travel"[12] seeking support in Akkadian *saḫāru*[13] and Aramaic *sḥr*.

---

9 Though Speiser, (OBS, 99) has remarked that *sōḥēr* lacks the "outwards credentials of a professional term," this should give us no pause. The same is true of *rōkēl*, which is close in meaning to *sōḥēr*.

10 Possibly related as well are Jer 14:18 and Ps 38:11. Speiser (OBS, 100) is justified in terming the Jeremiah verse as "much too obscure." As regards the Psalms passage, Speiser (along with Rashi, Qimhi, and Saadia) parses *seḥarḥar* as reduplicated form of *sḥr*, which he translates "to circle." Consequently, he translates the difficult *libbī seḥarḥar* as "my heart goes round and round, pit-a-pat." This is difficult to accept because no other biblical passage describes the troubled heart as going round in circles. (For the terms actually employed, see Sperling Studies, 28, n. 9.) Apparently, this is why Rashi translated *muqqāp yāgôn*. Cf. his comment on *b. Giṭṭ.* 70a, s.v. *sḥrḥr*. Qimhi for his part preferred *maḥšebôtā(y)w ḥōlekôt wesobebôt ʾānāh weʾānāh*. Though not without difficulty, Landsberger's comparison with Akkadian *libbašu šuḫarrur* "his heart is dead silent" is preferable from the viewpoint of style and idiom. See B. Landsberger, "Akkadisch-Hebräisches Wortgleichungen," VTSup 16 (1967), 176–204, especially 189, n. 1.

11 For the medievals see Sforno to Gen 34:10 and Qimhi *ad loc.*; Among the modern proponents of this interpretation are W. F. Albright (*BASOR* 163 [1961], 44f; *ibid.*, 164 [1961], 28); C. Gordon "Abraham of Ur," in *Hebrew and Semitic Studies presented to Godfrey Rolles Driver... in Celebration of His Seventieth Birthday 20 August, 1972*, eds. D. Thomas and W. McHardy (Oxford, 1963), 78; Landsberger, VTSup 16, 188–190.

12 Rashi is the medieval proponent of this view. We read in his comment on Gen 42:34: *tisḥārû tesōbebû wekol lešôn sōḥarîm ûseḥōrāh ʿal šęmeḥazzerîm wesōbebîm ʾaḥar happraqmaṭiyā*- "*tisḥārû* 'you shall go round.' The entire terminology of *sōḥarîm* and *seḥōrāh* derives from (the fact) that they (the merchants) move about constantly in search of trade." See Berliner, *Raschi*, 84–85. Rashi's use of *meḥazzerîm* indicates that he was not only mindful of LH *rōkelîm meḥazzerîn bāʿayyārôt* "peddlers traveling between towns" (*m. Maʿaś.* 2:3; *b. B. Qam.* 82a) but that he may have equated the roots *sḥr* and *ḥzr*. Speiser, being in almost complete agreement with Rashi, asserts that "the Heb. verb *sḥr* signified originally 'to circle, follow an irregular course'... The connotation to 'trade' is a late secondary development in Heb. and Jewish Aramaic based on the noun *sōḥēr* 'merchant,' i.e., 'peddler, one who makes the rounds.'" See E. A. Speiser, *Genesis. A New Translation with Introduction and Commentary* (AB; Garden City, 1964), 264–265; Cf. OBS, 97–105. Speiser's assertion, however, is unsupported. There is no evidence as to what "the Heb. verb *sḥr* signified

Though a final decision in this matter is still impossible, the present evidence weighs heavily in favor of translating the BH verb *sḥr* by "to trade, engage in commerce." We note that despite the alleged identity of BH *sḥr* and Aramaic *sḥr*, none of the Aramaic versions employs the verb *sḥr* in translating the verses in question.[14] Secondly, although Aramaic *sḥr* is attested as a *verbum movendi*, one may question whether it is ever attested in the sense "travel, journey." In the absence of conclusive evidence to that effect, Aramaic *sḥr* cannot serve to corroborate such a meaning for BH *sḥr*.[15] Thirdly, in LH, a dialect considerably influenced by Aramaic, *sḥr* means "to trade, engage in commerce," never "to circle, travel, make a circuit."[16] Finally, we think it possible to demonstrate

---

originally." In fact, though Akkadian knew a *sāḫiru* "merchant"(see Landsberger, VTSup 16 176–190; cf. AHw., 1009, s.v. *sāḫḫiru* and *sāḫiru*) and a *sāḫirtu/saḫartu* "merchandise" (Landsberger, VTSup 16, 176–190; cf. AHw., 1008b; K. Balkan, *Or* 36 [1967], 405, it never employed the common verb *saḫāru* to describe the movement of either, preferring *etēqu* for the merchant and *wabālum/šūbulum* for the goods. (See Landsberger, VTSup 16, 180–182, 188.) As such, we surely are not compelled to treat the ambiguous BH verb *sḥr* as the source of the unambiguous noun *sōḥēr*. Quite possibly (with Speiser) the verb "to trade" is a secondary development from the noun. But (contra Speiser) the attested Akkadian noun forms allow a loan into West Semitic and a consequent secondary verbal development well within the generally accepted limits of the patriarchal period.

13 Landsberger has shown that Speiser's appeal to Akkadian *saḫāru* does not alleviate the syntactic difficulties of the Genesis verses. See VTSup 16, 189.

14 For example, *Tg. Onq.* to Gen 34:21 has: *wyʿbdwn bh sḥwrtʾ*. *Tg. Ps.-J.* a.l. reads: *wyʿbdwn bh prqmṭyyʾ*. A manuscript fragment reads: *wytgrwn bh* (AH, I/1:57); Peshitta reads: *wnttgrwn bh*. Cf. further Saadia's *wʾtgrw pyh*.

15 The Targums usually express the notion "travel" by *nṭl* (e.g., Gen 11:2, 12:9; 33:17), while Peshitta prefers *šql* (e.g., Peshitta to above verses). Speiser has called attention to Aramaic *sḥr* allegedly construed with *ʾrʿʾ* as a direct object in IQapGen 21:15 and has adduced this verse in corroboration of his interpretation of BH *sḥr ʾrṣ* (OBS, 101–2). However, the following considerations must not be ignored. First, the phrase actually reads: *lmsḥr wlmḥzʾ ʾrʿʾ*, the noun *ʾrʿʾ* being the direct object of the verb *ḥzʾ*, not of *sḥr*. Second, the passages immediately following IQapGen 15–18 employ *sḥr* as a *verbum movendi* with the sense "to make a circuit around." However, this sense is not necessarily synonymous with "traverse, journey, travel." The preceding lines of the narrative provide a motive for Abraham's movements: he is to circle the land in order to symbolize his formal acquisition of that land in behalf of himself and his descendants in perpetuity. The BH passages in which the finite verb *sḥr* occurs do not intend to bestow any such land grant. Finally, it is worth noting that IQapGen itself expresses "travel, traverse" by terms other than *sḥr*. Note *wʾzl lʾrk mt* in 2:23 and *hlk wʾzl* in 21:13.

16 Thus we read in a midrash: *ʾāmar* PN *mah hallāšôn dᵉrôr kimᵉdayyēr bê dayyārā ûmᵉsaḥēr bᵉkol mᵉdînah* "PN said, 'What is the meaning of the term *dᵉrôr?* (The beneficiary) of the *dᵉrôr* is comparable to a person who lodges at an inn and can engage in commerce

that the actual etymological correspondent of Akkadian *saḫāru* in BH is *šḥr* rather than *sḥr*.[17] Accordingly, we separate BH *sḥr* from Aramaic *sḥr*[18] and from Akkadian *saḫāru*.[19]

In contrast, when we compare LH *ḥzr* with Akkadian *saḫāru*, we note close semantic parallels between them. First, note that both verbs mean "circle, revolve."[20] We see this for example in astronomical contexts: *ḥakmê yiśrāʾēl ʾōmrîn galgal qābūʿa ûmazzālôt ḥōzᵉrîn wᵉḥakmê ʾummôt hāʿôlām ʾōmrîn galgal ḥōzēr ûmazzālôt qᵉbûʿîn*[21] "The Jewish sages say, 'The vault of heaven is stationary but the heavenly bodies revolve.' But the gentile sages say, 'The vault of heaven revolves while the heavenly bodies are stationary.'"[22]

Akkadian employs *saḫāru* similarly to describe the motion of heavenly bodies. For example, we read in a neo-Assyrian (NA) letter: *Ṣalbatānu kīma ištu libbi zuqaqīpi ittuṣia issuḫra ina libbi zuqaqīpi ētarab* "Mars, having come forth from Scorpio, circled round and reentered Scorpio."[23]

In the intensive conjugation, LH *ḥzr* (*hizzēr*) means "to travel, make a circuit." We note the following LH paraphrase of a biblical verse: *šęhāyā PN haṣṣaddîq mᵉḥazzēr bᵉkol mᵉqômôt yiśrāʾēl wᵉdān ʾōtām bᵉʿārēhęm šęnęʾęmar wᵉhālak middē šānāh bᵉšānāh wᵉsābab GN wGN2 wGN3*. "For the righteous Samuel used to travel to all the Israelite cities and judge them (the people) in

---

in every province.'" (Sipra [ed. Weiss] 107a); for a variant of *kimᵉdayyēr bê dayyārā*, see Kohut, *Aruch Completum*, 3:134.) A parallel text of the last phrase reads: *ûmôbîl sᵉḥōrāh bᵉkol mᵉdînāh* "transports merchandise (=*saḫirtam wabālum/šūbulum*; see above, n. 12) in every province." (*Roš. Haš.* 9b. Contrast Rashi to Lev 25:10. See Berliner, *Raschi*, 268. Rashi does not comment on the second half of the parallel text in his commentary to *Roš. Haš.* 9b. We are therefore unaware of his reading of the crucial passage.

17 See below.

18 The most common BH equivalent of Aramaic *sḥr* is *sbb*. See e.g., *Tg. Onq.* to Gen 42:24; (*Tg. Ps.-J.* offers *ḥzr*); Exod 13:18 (*Tg. Ps.-J.* has *ḥzr*); Num 34:4, 5; *Tg. J.* to 1Sam 5:8, 9, 10; 2Sam 5:23, 14:24). Other BH correspondents of Aramaic *sḥr* are *swg* (see Targum to Isa 42:17, 59:14; Jer 38:22, 46:5; Zeph 1:6); and *zwr* (Targum to Isa.1:4). We note that in JA, alone among the Aramaic dialects, *sḥr* is attested both as a *verbum movendi* and as a verb denoting "to trade, do business." (For an attestation of this latter sense, see Theodor-Albeck, *Bereschit Rabba*, 2: 551:2–3.) In all likelihood, this second sense of *sḥr*, restricted to JPA, is a Hebraism.

19 Akkadian *saḫāru* never denotes "to do business, engage in commerce" or anything of that sort. For the relevant Akkadian terms, see Landsberger, VTSup 16, 186.

20 *ḥzr* occurs in hendiadys with *glgl* "revolve, spin" in *b. B. Bat.* 16b.

21 Akkadian employs *kânu* to describe the stationing of heavenly bodies. See *CAD K*, 160.

22 *b. Pesaḥ* 94b.; for a metaphorical use of this image see *b. Šabb.* 151b commenting on Deut 15:10.

23 ABL 519:21–23 =*AOAT* 5/1, 13:21–23.

their own cities. As it is stated: (1Sam 7:16) every year he went on circuit to GN, GN2 and GN3."[24]

Further, the Babylonian Talmud credits Ezra with the following mercantile reform: *šẹyehû rōklîn meḥazzerîn bāʿayyarôt miššûm*[25] *takšîṭê nāšîm* "That peddlers be allowed to travel between towns for the purpose of (selling) women's trinkets."[26]

Akkadian *suḫḫuru* has this very same meaning. We read in a letter from Mari: *inanna šumma libbi bēliya* ^{lú}*bēl arnim ina ne<pā>rim lidūkūm*[*a*] *qaqqassu likkisūma birīt*[27] *ālānê adi* GN *u* GN2 *lisaḫḫirū aššum ṣābum ipallaḫma* [*arḫ*]*iš ipaḫḫuram* "Now if my lord approves, let them execute a criminal (kept) in jail, and let them cut off his head, and go round (with it) between the settlements as far as GN and GN2 so that the troops will be afraid and will assemble here quickly."[28]

Both LH *ḥzr* and Akkadian *saḫāru* are attested in the meanings, "seek out, search for, attempt to find." We note first some LH passages which illustrate these senses of *ḥzr: ḥizzēr* DN *ʿal*[29] *kol middôt ṭôbôt littēn l*^{e}*yisrāʾēl w*^{e}*elōʾ māṣāʾ ʾẹllā ʿaniyyût* "DN searched through all the good qualities in order to bestow (them) upon Israel but found only poverty";[30] *darkô šẹlāʾ ʾîš laḥazōr ʿal ʾiššāh w*^{e}*ʾēn darkāh šẹlāʾiššāh laḥazōr ʿal ʾîš māšāl lāʾādām šẹʾābdāh lô ʾabēdāh mî ḥôzēr ʿal mî baʿal ʾabēdāh m*^{e}*ḥazzēr ʿal ʿabēdātô* "It is a man's custom to seek a wife actively, but it is not a woman's custom to seek a husband actively. The situation is analogous to a person who has lost an article. Who seeks what? The owner of the lost article keeps seeking his lost article."[31]

Akkadian *saḫāru* is attested in the meanings, "search, seek," as early as Old Babylonian (OB). In an OB letter, a prospective oil-buyer writes: *šamnam*

---

24 *b. Šabb.* 56a. This midrash makes a specific semantic connection between *ḥzr* and *sbb.*

25 The use of *miššum* in our passage is very similar to Elephantine *bšm* (e.g., *AP* 8:12[=TAD B2.3:9], *AP* 13:9 =*TAD* B2.7:9) and to Akkadian *aššum* followed by a substantive. See *CAD A/II*, 468–469.

26 *b. B. Qam.* 82a–b; cf. *b. B.Bat.* 22a.

27 Cf. LH *ḥizzēr bēn*, e.g., Lieberman, *Tosefta* (Order Zeraʿim), 49:36.

28 ARMT II, 48:14–20. Compare Oppenheim, *Letters from Mesopotamia* (Chicago, 1967), 98. *CAD N/II*, 341 offers "they shall put the criminal to death in the warehouse."

29 Usually *ḥzr* in this sense is followed by the preposition *ʿal*. Occasionally *b* is employed as in the following: *ʾillū hāyîtā meḥazzēr bekol ʾohālê* GN *ʾēn ʾat môṣēʾ*... "Even if you were to search through all the tents of GN, you would not find ..." (*Yalqut* Shimoni, 80b).

30 *b. Ḥag.* 9b.; for the similar Akkadian construction *lā* ... *ela*, see Sperling Studies, 40, n. 42; contrast Lieberman, *Hellenism in Jewish Palestine* (New York, 1950), 49, n. 19; see further, A. Bendavid, *Biblical Hebrew and Mishnaic Hebrew* (Tel Aviv, 1967), 148.

31 *b. Qidd.* 2b.

damqam ... šāmamma liqiā šamnum mād šumma šamnum ša PN lā damiq suḫurma šamnam damqam šāmamma liqiā. "Buy for me oil of good quality and get (it). Oil is plentiful. If PN's oil is not of good quality, look around, and buy for me only oil of good quality and get (it)."[32]

We call attention to a particularly poignant passage in the Gilgamesh epic: *Gilgameš êš tadâl balāṭam ša tasaḫḫuru lā tutta* "O Gilgamesh, to where are you roaming? The (lasting) life that you are looking for you shall not find."[33]

The connotation of *saḫāru* as "seek" is further corroborated by its association with *seʾû* and *buʾû*, the most common Akkadian words for "to seek." In Maqlû for example, we find the following sequence: *šēdū libaʾūki utukkū lišteʾûki eṭemmū lissaḫrūki* "May the genies look for you, the spirits always seek you out, the shades of the dead search you out."[34]

Finally we note that *saḫāru* and *šeʾû* are equated in a lexical list, to wit:

> Ú-KIN=*ri-tam šu-teʾ-ú* "to seek pasture."
> Ú-KIN=MIN *sa-ḫa-rum* "to look for pasture."[35]

---

32 AbB 2:144:17–25.

33 Gilg. X:i: 7–8 (OB). Cf. XI: 198 *balāṭa buʾû* and XI:7 *balāṭa šeʾû*; note that the sequence *saḫāru ... (w)atû(m)* is the semantic equivalent of *ḥzr ... mṣʾ* as cited above in our text and in the passage quoted in n. 29.

34 Maqlû II:210–12. Cf. 206–8.

35 MSL XIII, 193:272–73. The synonymous relationship of *saḫāru and šeʾû* may provide us with an etymological distinction between BH (and rare JPA) *sḥr* "to engage in commerce" on the one hand and Akkadian *saḫāru*, Aramaic *sḥr*, and Aramaic-LH *ḥzr* on the other. Professor Held has noted (oral communication) that the parallelism of *saḫāru/šeʾû* corresponds to the Hebrew parallelism of *drš/šḥr.* See Ps 78:34; cf. Prov 11:37. At the same time Held noted the equivalence of the Akkadian idiom *sāḫiru damqāti* (OIP 2, 23:6) and Hebrew *šōḥēr ṭōb* (Prov 11:27; cf. Esth 10:3) "seeker after good." Note further that the Aramaic versions at times translate Hebrew *šḥr* by *b*ʿy. (See Peshitta to Prov 8:17; Job 7:21, 8:5; Targum to Job 7:21.) The Hebrew-Aramaic correspondence has its parallel in the inner-Akkadian correspondence of *saḫāru* and *buʾû.* It is additionally noteworthy that in LH, where *šḥr* survives vestigially in literary contexts, it is associated with *šqd* and *ḥqr*. See Buber, *Midrash Tehillim*, 492; cf. Targum to Isa 8:20. We conclude therefore that the Hebrew etymon of Akkadian *saḫāru* is BH *šḥr* "to seek, search, look for" and possibly, "turn." See Job 8:5. If we are correct, it is likely that the BH orthography reflects an etymological **śḥr* which shifted to *sḥr* in the later dialects in keeping with a well-known phenomenon in Hebrew and Aramaic. (See e.g. M. Segal, *A Grammar of Mishnaic Hebrew* [Oxford, 1970], 32.) We would then be justified in distinguishing BH **šḥr* "to seek" and BH *sḥr* "to engage in commerce." Additional support for our hypothesis is furnished by Mari *IŠ-ḫu-ra-am-ma* (ARMT II, 129:21). Although von Soden reads the initial sign here as *ís* (AHw., 1005b, 3f, cf. 1006a, 6e; von Soden Syllabar no. 139), the evidence for his

An additional meaning shared by *ḥzr* and *saḫāru* is that of "besiege, surround." For *ḥzr* in this sense we note the following passage in Tosefta: *bāri'šônāh hāyû mannīḥin zēnān babbayit hassāmûk laḥomāh pa'am 'aḥat ḥāzᵉrû 'alēhẹm wᵉhāyû nidḥāqîn liṭṭōl 'ẹt zēnān wᵉhārᵉ gû zẹh 'ẹt zẹh hitqīnû šẹyᵉhē kol 'eḥād wᵉ'ẹḥād maḥazîr lᵉbêtô* "Originally they used to deposit their weapons in the house nearest the city wall. One time they were besieged; while pressing to reach their weapons, they killed one another (in the confusion). They decreed (therefore) that (henceforth) each person should take his weapon home."[36]

Akkadian *saḫāru*, with the connotation "besiege" is attested in a well-known inscription of Nabonidus: *palḫiš atamma ana enlil ilāni Marduk bīta šu'ātim ša taqbû epēšu ummān-manda saḫiršumma puggulū emūqāšu* "Reverently I spoke with Marduk, the Enlil of the gods (saying) 'That very temple which you have ordered me to rebuild, the Medes are besieging it and their armed force is very strong.'"[37]

It is well-known that LH *ḥzr* attests the sense "return," and thus is a synonym of *šwb* and often a substitute for *šwb*. This synonomy and substitution may best be illustrated by comparing pairs of BH and LH idioms, e.g., *šāb l'ētānô*[38] and *ḥāzar l'ētānô*,[39] "returned to full strength"; *šāb rēqām*[40] and *ḥāzar rēqām*,[41] "returned empty-handed"; *šāb 'ẹl 'āpār*[42] and *ḥāzar lᵉ'āpār*[43] "returned

preference is not compelling. (Bottéro, ARMT XV, 43:139, lists only one occurrence of this value which is itself not entirely convincing. For a critique of von Soden's procedure in assigning values to the sign *IŠ*, see Held, *JAOS* 79 [1959], 173, n. 87.) Finally, note that K. Riemschneider has recently listed *šaḫāru* as a MA variant of *saḫāru*. (K. Riemschneider, *Lehrbuch des Akkadischen* [Leipzig, 1969], 174, 269; see further, Sperling Studies 44, n. 58.) Taken together, the Akkadian occurrences and the Hebrew orthography may indicate the nature of the original initial sibilant.

36 Tosefta (Mo'ed), 99–100; 23–25; cf. further *Tg. Ps.-J.* to Gen 19:4; Targum to Ps 22:13, 17.

37 VAB 4, 218:23–25; see further ARMT X, 81:8–10. For *saḫāru* in hendiadys with *lawû*, the more common word for "besiege," see *Ugaritica* 5, 31:30–32.

38 Exod 14:27; *Tg. Onq.* and *Tg. Ps.-J* offer *twb*; *Tg. Neof.*, The fragment Targums *FTP* and *FTV* render by *ḥzr*; *Sam. Tg.* translates *'zr* (=*ḥzr*); Peshitta has *hpk*.

39 *b. B.Bat.* 75a.

40 Jer 50:9; Targum: *twb*.

41 *b. Roš. Haš.* 17b.

42 Gen 3:19; Qoh 3:20.

43 Theodor- Albeck, *Bereschit Rabba*, 213:8; *b. Sotah* 17a; *b. Sanh.* 92a.

to dust, died"; *hēšîb limᵉqômô*[44] and *hẹḥẹzîr limᵉqômô*[45] "returned (transitive), restored"; and similar pairs.[46]

Similarly, Akkadian *saḫāru,* like its LH counterpart, attests the meaning "return." We note the following passage: *lā emūqā balātuššunu rēš ḫurāṣi lā anašši kīma issuḫrūne ana* GN *allak … ina panīšunu rēš ḫurāṣi anašši* "Without their presence I have no authority to examine the gold. As soon as they have returned here, I shall go to Uruk … and examine the gold in their presence."[47]

In fact, the relationship between the Hebrew pair *ḥzr/šwb* has its parallel in the Akkadian pair *saḫāru/târu,* it being recalled that *târu* is the semantic equivalent of *šwb.*

Akkadian *saḫāru* and *târu* are employed in synonymous parallelism as in the following passage: *ilī šabsu litūra ištarī zenītum lissaḫra* "May my angry personal god return to me, my enraged personal goddess come back to me."[48]

The two verbs are likewise attested in hendiadys as in the following passage: *aṣû siḫru u târu simat tāhāzi lā kullumū* "They (the foals) had not been trained on how to advance, turn about and turn away as is befitting for battle."[49]

In various idioms *saḫāru* and *târu* are interchangeable. Thus the idiom *kišāda turru* is synonymous with *kišāda saḫāru,* both denoting "to turn the neck."[50] similarly, *ana lā bašî literrūšu* "May they make him (the demon) nonexistent" is in no way different from *kīma lā nabšî kalâša ussaḫḫir* "it made all (the land) like (something) that had never existed."[51]

---

44 1Sam 5:3.

45 *b. Makk.* 9b, based on *hēšîb* in Num 35:25; cf. *m. Yad.* 4:4 expounding on Jer 49:6 and R. Yohanan's comment on Lev 5:23 (*b. B. Qam.* 94b). In general, midrashic explanations of biblical verses are extremely valuable in determining BH-LH sequences.

46 For additional examples see Bendavid, *Biblical Hebrew and Mishnaic Hebrew*, 364.

47 *AOAT* 5/1, 277;3. 1–5; note that *alāku* occurs as an antonym of *saḫāru* in Lambert BWL 128:44. (Cf. EA 44:9–10.) This sequence has its parallel in *hlk … ḥzr* (*m. Sanh.*10:3). Cf. further Aramaic *ʾzl … mḥzr* (Targum Qoh 1:6).

48 Ebeling Handerhebung, 46:87; cf. *ZA* 32 (1918–19), 174: 56; See further Lambert BWL 343:8 (Ludlul).

49 TCL 3:28:173.

50 Oppenheim, *JAOS* 61 (1941), 256.

51 Cf. *ZA* 28 (1914), 77:60 and *JCS* 11 (1957), 86:iv:12; The synonymy of *saḫāru* and *târu* extends as well to the terminology of the Schlussklauseln, or closing legal clauses. We read in an Neo-Babylonian document: … *nadin maḫir apil rugummâ ul īši u aššu matīma lā saḫārimma ana muḫḫi amēlūtu šuʾātu lā ragāmu dayyānū tuppi išṭurū …* ["The money] has been given, received and paid. He is satisfied and has no (further) claim. The judges have inscribed a tablet so that a claim will never again be raised against these men …" (Nbn. 668:17–20) Generally *târu* is employed in clauses of this type. (For examples see

Furthermore, both *târu* and *saḫāru* may be employed as auxiliary verbs in sense of "again, a second time," in a manner very similar to Hebrew employment of *šwb* and *ḥzr*.[52]

In this last connection the manner in which both Akkadian *saḫāru* and LH *ḥzr* are employed is significant. Each of these, when employed as an auxiliary verb generally functions to repeat the action of the main verb, or to revert to a former condition referred to by the main verb. At times, each of these auxiliary verbs may introduce an action opposed to the main verb.

An illustration of the repetitive use of *ḥzr* is the following: *hikkāh zęh wᵉḥāzar wᵉhikkāh zęh qillēl zęh wᵉḥāzar wᵉqillēl zęh* "He struck one, then turned and struck the other. He cursed one, then turned and cursed the other."[53] For an example of *ḥzr* introducing an action opposed to the main verb see the folowing passage: *kēwān šęhiggîd šûb ʾēnô ḥôzēr ûmaggîd* "Once he has testified he may not change his testimony."[54]

For Akkadian *saḫāru* in similar functions, note the following examples: [*ša*] *matīma ina šarrāni kullat nākirī lā isḫuru lā išnû qabalšu mamman* "Against whom no one among all the hostile kings ever returned to wage his battle again."[55] Similarly, *ilu ušeṣṣâ u usaḫḫar ušerrab* "He will cause the god to go forth (in procession) and then to reenter (his sanctuary)."[56]

šar māt GN *ittišu* [*i*]*sl*[*i*]*m ittasḫarma šar māt* GN *itti šar māt* GN2 *ittaškan*, "The king of Aleppo made a pact with him. But then the king of Aleppo proceeded to compact with the king of Hanigalbat."[57]

ABAW NF 51 [Munich, 1960], passim.) Note further that *saḫāru ... ragāmu* corresponds to LH *ḥzr ... ṭʿn* (e.g., *b. B. Bat.* 31a).

52 For *šwb* in this sense, see, e.g., Mic 7:10; for *târu* see e.g., En. el. IV:26.

53 *b. Makk.*, 16a.

54 *Ibid.*, 3a.

55 Borger Esarh 103:27.

56 ABL 65 rs. 3; Cf. LH *ḥāzar wᵉhiknîs* in *m. Shab.* 10:1.

57 *JCS* 8 (1954), 61, n. 132.

CHAPTER 4

Genesis 41:40: A New Interpretation

The basic sense of Gen 41:40 has always been clear to readers. It is certain from the context that the writer of the passage wished to describe Pharaoh as conferring wide-ranging authority on Joseph. Unclear, however, is the precise intention of the text, particularly of the second clause. The ancient, medieval, and modern translations and commentaries have attempted—unsuccessfully in our opinion—to resolve the difficulty.[1] Our study examines earlier suggestions and proposes a fresh solution.

The Hebrew of the Masoretic text reads: *ʾth thyh ʿl byty wʿl pyk yšq kl ʿmy rq hksʾ ʾgdl mmk* "You shall be in charge of my palace[2]... Only the throne shall be greater than you."[3] For the moment we leave untranslated the highly

1 The Septuagint (hereafter LXX) translated: *kai epi tō stomati sou hypakousetai pas ho laos mou* "And all my people shall be subject to your mouth." Perhaps this reflects a reading *yqšb*. Note that Prov 17:4, *mrʿ mqšyb ʿl śpt ʾwn* is translated by LXX as *kakos hypakoúei glossēs paranómon* "A bad man hearkens to the tongue of transgressors." In addition, see LXX to Prov 29:12. Peshitta translated: *wʿl mlt pwmk nsb dynʾ klh ʿmy* "And by the word of your mouth shall all my people be judged." The Syriac is more likely a guess than a witness to the reading *yšpṭ* (contrast *BH*³). Saadia offers: *wʿly ʾmrk ynqʾd ǧmyʿ qwmy* "All of my people will be directed by your command." See J. Derenbourg, ed., *Version arabe du Pentateuque* (Paris, 1893), 65. Elsewhere Saadia employed *qāda* to translate the term for "lead" and "drive" Hebrew *nhg*. See Y. Kafah/Kafih, ed., *Tĕhillîm ʿim Targûm u- Fērûš ha-Gāʾôn Rabbēnû Saʿadyāh ben Yôsēf Fayyumî* (Jerusalem, 1965) for Saadia's translations of Ps 78:26, 52 (185, 188); Ps 80:2 (*ibid.*, 191) In his essentially correct translation of Gen 41:40 Saadia has been followed by a number of moderns. Thus *NJPS*: "By your command shall all my people be directed." Cf. *Gesenius*¹⁷, 527b (with reservations).

2 Cf. Gen 39:4, 5. According to 44:1 Joseph has his own *ʾšr ʿl bytw*, translated literally by LXX as *ho ĕpì tēs oĭkiàs autou*.

3 The verb *ʾgdl* appears to be a first person imperfect. Yet the grammatical subject of the clause is the throne. Scholars have therefore generally taken *rq hksʾ* as an accusative of extent. Ibn Ezra, for example, wrote "Its sense is, 'I shall not have more greatness than you, except in regard to the throne.'" (A. Weiser, ed., *Ibn Ezra* [Jerusalem, 1976], 1:116); cf. *Gesenius' Hebrew Grammar*, 118h. A slight modification of this is Redford's "Only on the throne shall I be greater than you." See D. Redford, *A Study of the Biblical Story of Joseph* (Leiden, 1970), 166. However, both the presence of the definite article (*hksʾ*) as well as the relative position of the accusative and that which it allegedly determines make this explanation unlikely. (See Ehrlich, *Randglossen* 1:210; contrast *idem, Mikrâ Ki-Pheschutô* 1:113.) There is manuscript support though, for *ygdl* (third person; see *Randglossen* 1:210). But there is no need for textual

 | DOI 10.1163/9789004340879_005

problematic second phrase. Joseph was thus to be major domo. Indeed, Egyptian sources know such an official who is designated as *mr pr*. His activity however was restricted to the royal household while Joseph's authority was not.[4] It is more likely that the Hebrew writer had in mind the Israelite *ʾšr ʿl hbyt*, an official of very high standing who was, by the ninth pre-Christian century, first minister of state.[5] A biblical account of the meeting of a Judahite royal delegation and its Assyrian counterpart during the reign of Hezekiah names the *ʾšr ʿl hbyt* first in the Judahite group.[6] Significantly, the first Assyrian official mentioned is the *trtn* (Akkadian *tartānu/turtānu*) who followed the king in *limmu*, or eponym succession.[7] Furthermore the title *ʾšr ʿl hbyt*[8] appears in an inscription from a burial cave in the Kidron Valley from about 700 BCE. Joseph would thus be pictured as a sort of grand vizier.[9] We would not err in expecting the next phrase to expand on this depiction.

If we derive *yšq* in the second phrase from the well-attested verb *nšq* I "kissed" with semantic etymons in Ugaritic, Aramaic, and Akkadian, then the Masoretic Text admits of only two translations a) "All my people shall kiss you on the mouth."; b) "At your command[10] all my people shall kiss." The first

---

emendation, for *ʾgdl* and *ygdl* may simply be alternative orthographies. In classical Hebrew the imperfect prefixes *alep* and *yod* were frequently interchanged and both pronounced *iqtol*. See Qimhi apud *Gesenius' Hebrew Grammar*, 47b; cf. H. L. Ginsberg in *Mordecai Kaplan Jubilee Volume* (New York, 1953), 257; M. Held, *ErIsr* 9 (1969), 77, n. 55. "Throne" is used here metonymically, representing the royal authority; cf. E. L. Greenstein and D. Marcus, *JANES* 8 (1976), 90, comment to l. 81.

4 R. de Vaux, *Ancient Israel* (New York, 1965), 1:130.

5 H. J. Katzenstein, *IEJ* 10 (1960), 150, n. 9; Ginsberg, in *Kaplan Volume*, 252–253.

6 2Kgs 18:17–18; cf. Isa 36:2.

7 See AHw., 1332.

8 See S. Aḥituv, Echoes from the Past. Hebrew and Cognate Inscriptions from the Biblical Period (Jerusalem: Carta, 2008), 44. The name of the office holder is broken. See *ibid.* for a suggestion.

9 Further light is shed on the narrator's conception of Joseph's office by the association of *ʾšr ʿl hbyt* and *skn* in the description of Shebna in Isa 22:15. The high standing of the *skn* is assured by the description of Shebna's duties, by the occurrence of the title in Phoenician and Aramaic sources, and especially by the mention of the *skn* immediately following the *mlk* "king" in the Ahiram sarcophagus inscription. (See *KAI* 1:2; vol. 2: 211–12; *DNWSI*, 785.) The Hebrew and Phoenician titles are reflected in Amarna *sūkinu* (*EA* 256:9; 362:69), which is functionally equivalent to Akkadian *rābiṣu* and Egyptian *wpwty* "commissioner, agent" and in Ugaritic *skn* (see Bohl, *Sprache*, 83: Albright, in *CAH*³, 11/2, 102; Gordon, *UT*, Glossary No. 1754; Aistleitner, WUS⁴, No. 1909; *DLU* II, 401.

10 For this idiomatic sense of *ʿl py*, see, e.g., Gen 45:21; Exod 17:1; Num 3:16, 9:20, 27:21. For post-biblical Hebrew, cf. *b. Sukkah* 2b.

translation makes grammatical sense but is unlikely in a context describing Joseph's authority.[11] The alternative translation takes *ʿl pyk* idiomatically but leaves the apparently transitive verb *yšq* without a direct object.

Because of these difficulties commentators and translators have sought other solutions. Targum Onqelos translated *yšq* by *ytzn*[12] "shall be fed, shall be provided for." Rashi followed Onqelos and in addition related *yšq* to *bn mšq byty* of Gen 15:2.[13] It must be objected, though, that the context of Gen 41:40 leads the reader to expect mention of Joseph's authority and privileges rather than of his duties.[14] More significant, there is no philological basis for

11 Cf. H. Gunkel, *Genesis* (Göttingen, 1910), 438; Ehrlich, *Randglossen*:1: 210; S. R. Driver, *The Book of Genesis* (New York, 1904), 343. Though a kiss may be an act of homage, biblical and near eastern sources do not indicate that oral or facial kissing was an appropriate gesture of submission, at least, in non-romantic contexts. Joab's deceitful kiss of Amasa (2 Sam 20:9) illustrates a practice of equals. Note Herodotus's remark that Persians kissed equals on the mouth and those somewhat superior on the cheeks (*The Histories*, 1:134; cf. further C. Sittl, *Die Gebärden der Griechen und Römer* [Leipzig, 1890], 78, n. 6). Akkadian sources speak of kissing the feet of a superior, especially a sovereign, as a gesture of submission or reverence (references in AHw., 759a). An inferior might also kiss a superior on the knees (*CAD B*, 256a), a practice which has parallels in the Babylonian Talmud and Greco-Roman custom (see *b. Sanhedrin* 27b; *b. Ketubot* 49b, 63a; Sittl, *Gebärden*, 169). According to the Babylonian Talmud a superior might show affection or appreciation for an inferior by kissing him/her on the head (*b. Ḥagigah* 14b; *b. Megillah* 14a; *b. Nazir* 29b). One modern commentator cites two midrashic statements to explain Gen 41:40. The first comments on it directly: "No one shall kiss me without your permission." (J. Theodor and Ch. Albeck, *Der Midrasch Bereschit Rabba* [Reprint: Jerusalem, 1965] 3:1100) The second (*ibid.*, 577, 709) explains the proper name Phicol (Gen 21:22; 26:26) as "The-Mouth-of-Everyone—All his minions kiss him on the mouth." See A. Kahana, *The Bible with Critical Commentary* (Zhitomer, 1904), 117–118 (in Hebrew). Though certainly of interest, these sources are irrelevant to Gen 41:40. First, they reflect Greco-Roman practice. Secondly, the earlier comment says simply that the Pharaoh might not be kissed without Joseph's permission, not that either he or Joseph might be kissed on the mouth. The second citation claims that Phicol or, more precisely, whomever the midrashist actually had in mind, did not receive the tribute due his office or was perhaps known for homosexual promiscuity. For related midrashic comments, see D. Hyman, D. Lerrer, and I. Shiloni, *Yalqut Shimʿony ʿal Hattora* (Jerusalem, 1973), 1:426, 2:533; S. Buber, *Lekach-Tob* (Vilna, 1880), 96. For the gesture of kissing in general in Greco-Roman sources, see Sittl, *Gebärden*, 166–173; H. J. Rose, in *Oxford Classical Dictionary* (Oxford, 1970), 466.

12 For the Onkelos text, see A. Sperber, *The Bible in Aramaic* (Leiden, 1970), 1:70; cf. A. Diez Macho, *Neophyti I* (Barcelona, 1968), 275.

13 Saadia apparently made the same connection. He translated *mšq* by *qyʾd*; see ad loc. (ed. Derenbourg, 22).

14 Cf. K. A. Kitchen, *ET* 69 (1957), 30.

the Targum's translation. Rashi notwithstanding, the term *bn mšq byty* is itself highly problematic[15] and cannot elucidate *yšq*. It is likely that Onkelos was influenced by the inner-Aramaic closeness of *zwn* "provide," "feed" and *zyyn* (*paʿel*) "to arm, equip with weaponry."[16] By analogy to Aramaic, Onkelos may have reasoned that Hebrew *nšq* II, which is associated with weaponry, could likewise by associated with food-provision.

Indeed, some medieval Jewish scholars explicitly related *yšq* to *nšq* II, a verbal root connected with the noun *nšq* (*nešeq*) "weapon," etymologically distinct from *nšq* I, as shown by Ugaritic.[17] Ibn Janah, for example, raised the possibility of translating Gen 41:40 "At your command my people shall bear weapons, i.e., they will battle their foes."[18] But this translation is likewise objectionable. Though the noun *nešeq* is well-attested, the verb *nšq* II appears only

---

15 The phrase occurs nowhere else. Furthermore, the Masoretic cantillation breaks the construct-genitive chain in an unexpected and ungrammatical manner. Onkelos translated, *br prnsʾ hdyn dbbyty* "this overseer who is in my house." (ed. Sperber, 1:20). The Peshitta either ignored *mšq* or did not have the vocable in its Hebrew source. Indeed *mšq* looks suspiciously like a partial dittography of *dmśq* (cf. vs. 2). See further *Gesenius*[17], 473; H. L. Ginsberg, *BASOR* 200 (1970), 31–32. For a provocative, if overly ingenious, solution see Ehrlich, *Mikrâ Ki-Pheschutô*, 1:39. For a derivation of the meaning "overseers" see A. Neubauer, ed., *The Book of Hebrew Roots by Abu ʾl Walid Marwan ibn Janah, called Rabbi Jonah* (Oxford, 1875), 396 = W. Bacher, ed., *Sepher Haschoraschim* (Berlin, 1896), 277; J. Biesenthal and F. Lebrecht, ed., *Rabbi Davidis Kimchi Radicum Liber* (Berlin, 1847), 203.

16 Targum Onkelos employs *zwn* to translate Hebrew *klkl* "sustain, support." (Gen 45:11; 47:12; 50:21) Similarly it translates *rʿh* "lead, pasture" by *zwn* (Gen 48:15) and also employs it for *nhl* "lead." (Gen 47:17) The noun *nšq* "weapon" appears in Targum as *mny zynʾ* (1Kgs 10:25; 2Kgs 10:2). In addition see the Targums to Isa 22:8 and Job 39:21; cf. Levy, *TW* 1:215, 219.

17 Ugaritic "kiss" is *nšq* with etymological *šin*. See *DLU* II, 336. The vocable is to be distinguished from *nṯq*. See *DLU* II, 338. In *PRU* II, 123:1–3 (=*KTU*[3] 4.169:3) *nṯq* appears as a specific weapon along with *ḥẓ* "arrow," *qšt* "bow," and and *qlʿ* "shield." Note the similar association in the parallelism *nšq*//*qšt* in Job 20:24. See M. Dahood, *AnOr* 49 (1972), 333, who translates *nṯq* as "dart." Analogously, in Akkadian the general term for "weapon," *kakku*, refers as well to a specific weapon whose exact translation thus far eludes us. See *CAD K*, 52. More problematic is the Ugaritic phrase *nṯq dmrm* (*CTA* 4, vii: 39= *KTU*[3] 1.4:vii:39). Even the reading is uncertain, for though Herdner's transcription has *dmrm*, the autograph has *dmrn*, which seems closer to the photograph (pl. 10). Caquot translated the phrase as "l'arme du Vaillant." (*Textes ougaritiques* [Paris, 1974] 1:217); De Moor preferred "armor-bearers of the place of perdition." (*AOAT* 16 [Neukirchen-Vluyn, 1971], 164, 166. Perhaps the wisest course was taken by H. L. Ginsberg (*ANET*, 135) who hesitated to offer any translation.

18 He translated *yšq* by *ytslḥwn* (*Roots*, 465 = *Haschoraschim*, 326) but suggested *yltzmwn* "will cleave to" as an alternative (ad loc.). Ibn Ezra likewise opted for *nšq* II; see ad loc. (ed. Weiser, 1:116).

three times in the Hebrew Bible, twice in the phrase *nšqy qšt*[19] and a third in the apparently conflate form *nwšqy rwmy qšt*.[20] Each of these seems to be an active participle with a direct object much like *tpś qšt*[21] "bow holder" and *drky qšt*[22] "bow stringers." In fact, biblical Hebrew generally favors similar active participles with direct objects in its descriptions of military personnel. Note for example *šlp ḥrb*[23] "sword drawer"; *nśʾy mgn wḥrb*[24] "bearers of shield and sword"; *tpśy ḥrbwt*[25] "sword holders"; and *nśʾy ṣnh wrmḥ*[26] "holders of buckler and lance." We should expect *nšqy qšt* to conform to this pattern and to have some active sense rather than a passive "armed with." If *rwmy* in the expression *nwšqy rwmy qšt* is an explanatory gloss or a conflate of two synonymous expressions, then we should translate *nwšqy qšt* as "bow shooters" and the verb *nšq* II as "shoot" or perhaps as "cast, fling." Note the phrase *rmh qšt* "archer."[27] Accordingly, were we to derive *yšq* in Gen 41:40 from *nšq* II we would be compelled to translate *ʿl pyk yšq kl ʿmy* as "At your command shall all my people shoot/cast/fling," which is unlikely.

The Egyptian setting of the Joseph story has led some scholars to suggest that an Egyptianism underlies *yšq*. Yahuda suggested that *yšq* reflects Egyptian *śn* "kiss," which is sometimes attested with food as a direct object and thus means both "kiss" and "eat."[28] In effect, the Targum's translation would be justified by this procedure. However, Gen 41:40 has no direct object following the verb *yšq*. Furthermore, other scholars have shown that *śn* does not mean "eat" even in Yahuda's alleged prooftexts.[29] Kitchen, who criticized Yahuda, himself

19 1Chr 12:2; 2Chr 17:17.

20 Ps 78:9; see *BH*³.

21 Amos 2:15.

22 1Chr 5:18; cf. 2Chr 14:7; note the apparently conflate form *tpśy drky qšt* "bow-holders/stringers." (Jer 46:9).

23 Judg 8:10, 20:2, 15, 17, 35, 46; 2Sam 24:9; 2Kgs 3:26; 1Chr 21:5. For the plural, see Judg 20:25.

24 1Chr 5:18; cf. 2Chr 14:7. Cf. also *tpśy mgn* "shield-holders." (Jer 46:9).

25 Ezek 38:4.

26 1Chr 12:25; cf. 1Chr 12:9.

27 Jer 4:29. Cf. the alternation of *rmh* and *yrh* in Exod 15:1,4. Akkadian shares with Hebrew the preference for constructing active participial phrases to describe military personnel. Note *nāš kabābi muttabbilat kakkī* "wielder of weapons." (Ebeling Handerhebung, 130:6).

28 A. S. Yahuda, *Die Sprache des Pentateuch in ihren Beziehungen zum Ägyptischen.* (Leipzig, 1929), 6–7 = *idem*, *The Language of the Pentateuch in its Relation to Egyptian* (Oxford, 1933), 7–8.

29 See E. König, *JBL* 48 (1929), 342; cf. T. E. Peet, *JEA* 16 (1930), 158; K. A. Kitchen, *ET* 69 (1957), 30; Redford, *Joseph*, 166 n. 4.

saw in *yšq* a reflex of Egyptian *śn t3* "kiss the earth."[30] Contextually, Kitchen's suggestion is superior to that of Yahuda. Nonetheless the text still lacks the required direct object, in this case a correspondent of Egyptian *t3*, such as *ʾrṣ* "earth, ground" or *ʿpr* "dust." Furthermore, one need not turn to Egyptian for "kiss the earth" as a figure connoting submission[31] but may adduce Akkadian examples as well.[32]

One of the more popular approaches to the problem has been to translate *yšq* as "arrange, order themselves" on the basis of Arabic *nasaqa*.[33] While it is true that Arabic *nasaqa* attests these meanings, even a casual reading of the standard Arabic lexica demonstrates that the verb is employed primarily for the stringing of pearls and the composition of discourses.[34] The meaning alleged here for *yšq* would most likely be expressed in Arabic by *iǧtamaʿa*, the eighth form of *ǧamaʿa* "gather, collect." A dialectal distribution[35] for the notion of people, troops, subjects, etc. ordering themselves follows:

---

30 *ET* 69 (1957), 30.

31 Thus P. Heinisch, *Das Buch Genesis* (Bonn, 1930), 374–375, explained *yšq* by reference to Ps 72:9 in which *ʿpr ylḥkw* "shall lick the dust" stands parallel to *ykrʿw* "will bend the knee."(Cf. Isa 49:23.) In addition, see *EA* 100:34–36 with Weber's note ad loc., 1195.

32 Akkadian *qaqqara našāqu/nuššuqu* "kiss the earth (repeatedly)" provides a more exact parallel to Egyptian *śn t3*. See e.g., Streck Asb., 34:19–20; *ibid.*, LXXXVII, n. 2; *ibid.*, 539; *RLA* 3, 668.

33 E.g., J. Skinner, *A Critical and Exegetical Commentary on Genesis* (New York, 1917), 469; S. R. Driver, *The Book of Genesis* (New York, 1904), 343; König, *JBL* 48, 342; *RSV*.

34 See G. W. Freytag, *Lexicon Arabico-Latinum* 3:275; J. Hava, *Arabic-English Dictionary* (Beirut, 1921), 766; H. Wehr, *A Dictionary of Modern Written Arabic* (Ithaca, 1961), 962.

35 The importance of the principle of dialectal distribution can scarcely be overstated. Of particular significance is Held's "stress on disclosing the meanings of words by the inductive method rather than the etymological one." (See *JAOS* 79 [1959], 169; cf. W. F. Albright, *From the Stone Age to Christianity* [Garden City, N.Y., 1957], 46–47; B. Landsberger, *JNES* 24 [1965], 295–296.) Over-reliance on the etymological method often leads scholars into allegedly clarifying an obscure term in language X by reference to a term in language Y when the contextual sense of the term in language Y is inappropriate to the obscure term of language X. By establishing the attested semantic range of a term with the aid of dialectal distribution we are able, within limits, to be precise about the probable synchronic associations which a speaker would have made, irrespective of ultimate etymological relationships. It is worthy of note that neither Saadia, nor Ibn Ezra, nor Ibn Janah, who were native speakers of Arabic as well as outstanding Hebraists, associated *yšq* of Gen 41:40 with Arabic *nasaqa*.

Hebrew	Aramaic	Akkadian	Arabic
nqbṣ[36]	*ʾtknš*[37]	*paḫāru*[38]	*ʾǧtmʿ*[39]
nʾsp[40]		*kutaṣṣuru*[41]	
nqhl[32]			

A. B. Ehrlich likewise turned to Arabic. He suggested revocalizing *yiššaq* to *yašaq* and translating *ʿl pyk yšq* as "soll sich deinem Befehle unterwerfen." In so doing he parsed *yšq* as a *qal* imperfect of *šuq*,[43] related it to *tšwqtk*[44] (Gen 3:16) which he understood as "your submission." He connected *tšwqh* and **yāšaq* to Arabic *sāqa* "seine Sache dem Belieben eines anderen überlassen, sie ihm anheim geben." His final tour de force was to assert that the sense "anheim geben"[45] underlies the noun *sūqatun* "Untertanenschaft (state of submission)."[46] Though it cannot be denied that the meaning "anheim geben" and "überlassen" are attested by Arabic *sāqa*, these are clearly secondary to its

36 E.g., Gen 49:2; Isa 49:18, 60:4; Ps 102:23.

37 E.g. *Tg. Onq.* to Gen 49:2; Lev 8:4; Num 16:3; Deut 33:5.

38 See ARMT II: 48:6–20; AHw., 210; *CAD P*, 23.

39 See Saadia to Gen 49:2 (ed. Derenbourg, 77); Isa 49:18; 60:4; (ed. Derenbourg, 76, 90); Ps 102:23 (ed. Kafih, 224). We have not included Ugaritic in this distribution. Though several nouns have the sense "assembled multitude," e.g., *qbṣ* and *pḫr* (*CTA* 14, iii:15=*KTU*³ 1.15:15), it is unclear which verbs have the required meaning. See *CTA* 14, ii:85–87 (=*KTU*³ 1.14:ii:32–34) with Caquot, *Textes ougaritiques* 1:516, with reference to previous literature.

40 Judg 9:6, 10:17, 16: 23.

41 References in *CAD K*, 262, sec. 7.

42 Lev 8:4; 1Kings 8:2; Jer 26:9.

43 See *Randglossen*, 1:14–15, *ibid.*, 210. Presumably his vocalization was based on forms such as *yāqām* (= *yāqom*; see *Gesenius' Hebrew Grammar*, §72f). Previously Ehrlich had followed LXX, though not without reservations; see *Mikrâ Ki-Pheschutô*, 1:113. The *Randglossen* proposal was accepted by E. A. Speiser, *Genesis* (Garden City, 1964), 313.

44 Saadia apparently related *yšq* of Gen 41:40 to *tšwqtk* of Gen 3:16 a millennium before Ehrlich, though he did not invoke *sāqa*. He simply translated *tšwqtk* by *qyʾdk* and *yšq* by *ynqʾdw*.

45 "leave to the discretion of."

46 Ehrlich discussed *tšwqtk* in *Randglossen*, 1:14–15. It must be noted, however, that the Masoretic Text differs from LXX *he apostrophe sou*; Old Latin *conversio tua* (*BH*³). Ehrlich differs from most and translates that passage, "und es ist meine Pflicht mich ihm hinzugeben." (*Randglossen*, 7:16) It seems simpler to derive *tšwqh* from *šūq* which occurs in the *polel* as a synonym of *rʿb* "hungry" (Ps 107:9) and *ʿyp* "thirsty." (Isa 29:8).

basic meaning "drive."[47] Arabic *sāqa* is a semantic equivalent of Hebrew *nhg*[48] and *nhl*.[49] Like those verbs, *sāqa* may be employed for the driving of cattle or beasts. The noun *sūqatun* refers to "mob, rabble, subjects" and the like, in the sense of those driven by another. If Ehrlich were correct in deriving *yšq* from *sāqa*, we would have to translate Gen 41:40 as "All my people shall drive," which is most unconvincing.

Our contention is that the Masoretic text be emended slightly to read *ʿl pyk yšb* (*yešeb*) *kl ʿmy*. The ancient signs for *bet* and *qof* were not graphically distant.[50] Indeed, the Masorah and versions vacillate between *tšwqtk* and *tšwbtk* in Gen 3:16, and a similar situation obtains in Cant 7:11.[51] The proposed emendation would enable us to translate *ʿl pyk yšb kl ʿmy* literally as "all my people shall sit at your command," an exact reflex of Akkadian *ana pī X ašābu* "to sit at the command of x," which attests the idiomatic sense "obey." As an example we may cite an omen text based on observations of anomalous births: *šumma izbū 2-ma pīšunu 1-ma mātum ana pī šarrim uššab*[52] "If anomalies are double, but have only one mouth, the land will be obedient to the king." Similarly an OB omen text reads: *šarrum massu ana pīšu uššab*[53] "As regards the king, his land shall obey him." In an Old Assyrian royal inscription King Irišum declares: *ālī ana pīya ūšib*[54] ... "My city obeyed me."

47 For references, see Lane, 1/4:147–71; Wehr, *Dictionary*, 442–443.

48 See S. Skoss, ed., *Kitab jamiʿ al-alfaẓ* (New Haven, 1945), 2:257; Saadia to Gen 31:18 (ed. Derenbourg, 48); Exod 10:3 (*ibid.*, 95).

49 See Saadia to Ps 23:2, 31:4 (ed. Kafih, 91, 101).

50 See conveniently the chart in *IDB*, 4:914 and the Aramaic script charts appended to F. Rosenthal, *Die aramaistische Forschung* (reprint: Leiden, 1964).

51 See n. 46.

52 Leichty lzbu (= TCS 4), 87:26. Cf. 132:20. The omen interpretation is transparent. The presence of one mouth eliminated the possibility of disagreement. We may compare idioms along the line of *pâ ištēn mitḫariš iššaknū* "(Rebellious countries) had united themselves under one command." (Weidner, Tn. 3:36–37; Grayson RAI, 1:103; cf. Josh 9:2 and see E. Dhorme, *L'emploi métaphorique des noms de parties du corps en Hébreu et en Akkadien* [Paris, 1923], 84.) Similarly, *pâ ištēn kullat nākirī* [*aškun*] "I made all the foes submit to (my) unified command." (Weidner, Tn. 5:36–37; Grayson, RAI, 1:104; further, AHw., 872–873, meaning D). Extremely close to *pâ ištēn šakānu* literally, "to place one mouth" is *pâ ēda šakānu* literally, "to place a single mouth." We read in the "Fable of the Fox and the Wolf": *pâ ēda iššaknūma ... ana kalbi reʾīšina išteneʾū marṣāti* "(The fox and wolf) having reached an agreement ... constantly seek the discomfiture of the dog their shepherd." (Lambert BWL, 207:14–15).

53 *YOS X*, 11:4:17–9. W. von Soden translates, "'Der Land des Königs wird für seinem Mund sitzen' d.h. seinem Geheiss folgen" (*Or* 21 [1952], 76).

54 AOB I, 12:7:18; cf. Grayson, RAI, 1:10.

Inasmuch as *pû* means "word" and "command" as well as "mouth"[55] the vocable is often a virtual synonym of *qibītu.* Now, the idiom *ana pī X ašābu* has a causative parallel in *ana qibīt X šūšubu,* literally "to cause to sit at the command of x." Note the following examples: *išdī ayyābī u lemnim in mātim lū assuḫ napḫar mātim ana qibītišu ušēšib*[56] "I extirpated enemy and foe from the country. I caused the entire country to be obedient to my command"; *napḫar māt Šumerîm u Akkadîm uštešmi kibrāt erbettim ana qibītišu ušēšib*[57] "He compelled obedience from the entire land of the Sumerians and Akkadians. He imposed his command on the Four Quarters."

The above references demonstrate the use of the Akkadian idioms "to sit at the command of/cause to sit at the command of X" in rulership contexts that are extremely similar to Gen 41:40. That text, as emended by us, is in keeping with the tendency of the Semitic languages to construct idioms making verbal use of the parts of the body.[58] Note this in the very continuation of the Joseph narrative in Gen 41:44: *ʾny prʿh wblʿdyk lʾ yrym ʾyš ʾt ydw wʾt rglw bkl ʾrṣ mṣrym* "I am Pharaoh; but without your consent no man shall lift his hand or his leg throughout the land of Egypt." Each of these idioms simply means that the movements of the subjects will be so much in their ruler's control that their very abilities to sit, move or walk will depend on him. An American speaker might say, "They won't make a move without his permission."

As to the prepositional equivalency of *ʿl* and Akkadian *ana* in the respective idioms we may compare *ʿl py htwrh* (Deut 17:11) "according to the instruction" with *ana pī kankim ša PN našû*[59] "according to the document which PN bears."

We translate Gen 41:40: "You shall be in charge of my palace, and all my people shall obey you. Only the throne shall be greater than you."

55 See AHw., sub D "Aussage, Befehl."

56 *RA* 39 (1942–44), 8:49–53 (Samsu-Iluna B).

57 *RA* 63 (1969), 36:123–28.

58 In general see Dhorme, *L'emploi métaphorique*; Holma, *Körperteile*; H. Vorwahl, *Die Gebärdensprache im Alten Testament* (Berlin, 1932); A. L. Oppenheim, *JAOS* 61 (1941), 251–67; S. D. Sperling, "Studies in Late Hebrew Lexicography in the Light of Akkadian," (unpublished Ph.D. dissertation: Columbia, 1973), chap. 5: A. D. Kilmer, *JAOS* 94 (1974), 177–183 and especially 182, n. 24; M. Gruber, *Nonverbal Communication.*

59 AbB 2:1:23–24. More frequently the Hebrew prepositions *ʿl* and *l* correspond to *ana.* Note, however, the alternation of *ʿl py* and *lpy* in Num 35:30 and Deut 17:6.

CHAPTER 5

A šu-íl-lá to Ištar (Ebeling Handerhebung 60)

One of the most important Akkadian prayer collections was the series[1] known as šu-íl-lá[2] "Lifting of the Hand." The name describes a gesture employed widely in the ancient Near East.[3] A long prayer to Ištar may be the earliest example of šu-íl-lá. Though that text dates from the mid-second milennium,[4] most of the members of the Akkadian series are attested in copies made after 800 BC.[5]

---

1 For bibliography on the šu-íl-lá prayer series see E. Dalglish, *Psalm Fifty-One in the Light of Ancient Near Eastern Patternism* (Leiden, 1962), 45–51. Add Mayer Gebetsbeschwörungen; M.-J. Seux, *Hymnes et prières aux dieux de Babylonie et d'Assyrie* (Paris, 1986) and the bibliographies in each. For a recent detailed study with bibliography see C. Frechette, *Mesopotamian Ritual-prayers of "Hand-lifting" (Akkadian Šuillas). An Investigation of Function in Light of the Idiomatic Meaning of the Rubric* (Münster, 2012).

2 The Sumerian prayers known as šu-íl-lá must be distinguished from the Akkadian prayer series "Lifting of the Hand" on linguistic, historical, religious and literary grounds. See Dalglish, *Psalm Fifty-One*, 35–36, 43–51; Mayer Gebetsbeschwörungen, 31. The Akkadian name of the series whose individual pieces bear the subscript šu-íl-lá is not completely certain. There are some indications that the Sumerian was translated literally into Akkadian as *nīš qāti*. (See Mayer Gebetsbeschwörungen 7, n. 14; AHw., 797, s.v. *nīšu* I 4.) An additional complication is that even when the reading *niš qāti* is certain it is difficult to decide whether the term refers to a šu-íl-lá prayer or to prayer in general. See for example BMS 12 (= Ebeling Handerhebung, 80): 79, 88; BMS 50 (= Ebeling Handerhebung, 148) :21. Outside of the prayer series proper, Akkadian sources usually give the Sumerian writing. (See AHw., 1262; Mayer Gebetsbeschwörungen, 25, n. 57.) The apparently plural *šu-íl-lá-ka-nu* which occurs three (sic!) times in LAS 334 (Obv. 2, 4, Rev. 6) implies a singular *šuʾillakku*.

3 See S. Langdon, *JRAS* 1919, 531–558; M. Gruber, *JANES* 7, (1975), 73–83. In Hebrew, *maśśat kappay* "my hand-lifting" is found in synonymous parallelism with *tᵉpillāti* "my prayer." (Ps141:2) See E. Dhorme, *L'emploi métaphorique des noms des parties du corps en Hébreu et un Akkadien* (Paris, 1923), 145. Cf. further Ugaritic *šʾa ydk šmm* "Lift your hands to heaven (i.e. pray)." See *CTA* 14:ii:75–76; cf. iv:167–168 (=*KTU*³ 1.14: ii:22–23; cf. iv:4–5); In addition, see Aramaic *wʾśʾ ydy ʾl bʿlšmyn wyʿnny bʿlšmyn* "I prayed to Baalshamayn and Baalshamayn answered me." (*KAI* 202:11).

4 A šu-íl-lá to Ištar first published by King as STC II, Pl. LXXV ff. and edited as Ebeling Handerhebung, 130 turned out to be a Neo-Babylonian version of a text found at Boğazköy dating from the middle of the second millennium. We cannot know whether the text served as a šu-íl-lá in its original form. See E. Reiner and H. Güterbock, *JCS* 21 (1967), 255–266; Cf. Mayer Gebetsbeschwörungen 28–29.

5 See Mayer Gebetsbeschwörungen, 28–31.

 | DOI 10.1163/9789004340879_006

Virtually all of the exempla of the genre bear the rubric ÉN (Akkadian *šiptu*[6]), usually translated "incantation," as well as a subscript inim.inim.ma.šu.íl.lá ᵈX-kam/kám[7] indicating their membership in the series and identifying the divinity to whom they are addressed. On internal grounds of terminology and style many of the šu-íl-lá texts might be described more accurately as prayers than as incantations.[8] Modern scholarship echoes what may have been

6 Mayer (*ibid.*, 22–23) is of the opinion that ÉN/*šiptu* was simply an aid to the officiant directing him to the point where the ritual recitation began. This begs the question of just what the officiant thought he was reciting. It is clear that the Akkadian language was capable of distinguishing conceptually between prayer and incantation and that *šiptu* is clearly at home in undisputed incantation contexts. Note that it occurs in parallelism and hendiadys with the Sumerian loanword *tû* "spell," "incantation" in En.el. iv:91 and passim in Maqlu. See the references in AHw., 1247. It is significant that the most common verbs employed with *šiptu* are *nadû* and *manû* (Renger, ZA 59 [1969)], 226–228), "hurl," "recite." The verb *nadû* points to the quasi-physical character of the incantation and *manû* to a special manner of recitation. (See Meissner BuA II, 208; Renger ZA 59, 227; Gaster Janes 7 [1975], 41.) The use of manû is an indication that the šu-íl-lá texts were considered at least to some extent as incantational. The threefold repetition instructed by the subscript to many of these texts, including the one under study, is a further indication. Actual usage rather than ultimate origin aids us in determining whether a particular piece should be treated as a prayer rather than as an incantation. Modern Jewish prayer books for example, are fond of repeating the priestly benediction (Num 6:24–27) followed by Ps 121:4, three times as part of the Shema liturgy recited before retiring. It is instructive that in the same liturgy Ps 121:4 is followed by a three-fold repetition of Gen 49:18, a three word verse, beginning each time with a different word viz. *lîšuᶜātᵉkā qiwwiti* YHWH *qiwwiti* YHWH *lîšuᶜātᵉkā* YHWH *lîšuᶜātᵉkā qiwwiti*. The entire section then proceeds with the tell-tale incantation formula "in the name of YHWH" and then names the guardian angels who surround the sleeper on all sides much in the manner of the *ilu ištaru šēdu* and *lamassu*. Cf. the Sumerian examples in Falkenstein Haupttypen, 30.

7 The reading of KA.KA.ma is not completely certain. See Mayer Gebetsbeschwörungen 23, n. 56; E. Ritter, *AS* 16 (1965), 309, n. 17; R. Labat, *Manuel d'épigraphie akkadiene* (Paris, 1976), Nr. 15.

8 Perhaps the essential difference between prayer and incantation is that prayer does not attempt to compel the deities or bypass them. The gods retain the option of non-compliance. Incantation attempts to realize the wish of the reciter automatically. Cf. F. Heiler, *Prayer, a Study in the History and Psychology of Religion* (New York, 1932), 72; C. Fossey, *La Magie assyrienne* (Paris, 1932), 139. Akkadian speakers differentiated terminologically between prayer and incantation. The common terms for "prayer" are *karābu* (n.) (*CAD K*, 192); *ikribu* (B. Landsberger, *MAOG* 4 [1929], 294–315; *CAD I/J*, 62–66; RLA III 160–161); *sup(p)û* (AHw., 1060b; *AfO* 23 (1970), 46–47; VAB 4: 122:51–54; 124:3–5 // *unnennu*; Lambert BWL 108:11; H. Hunger, *Babylonische und assyrische Kolophone* (Neukirchen-Vluyn: Neukirchener, (1968), 102 Nr. 328:9–11 //*taslītu*; OIP 2:81:29–30); *sul(l)û* (Ebeling Handerhebung, 134:99 with *supû*; Lambert BWL 134:130 with *supû* and *karābu*; further, AHw., 1056b); *teslītu/taṣlītu* (AHw., 1351); *niš qāti* (Šurpu II:78; Lambert BWL, 218:4; *idem*, "Dingir.šà.dib.ba Incantations." *JNES* 33

an ancient equivocation.[9] The pioneer Assyriologist Leonard W. King included many šu-íl-lá pieces in his *Babylonian Magic and Sorcery*[10] while Erich Ebeling, to whom we owe the standard edition of the šu-íl-lá texts referred to them as a prayer series as shown by the title he chose, *Die akkadische Gebetsserie "Handerhebung*."[11] The most popular modern designation is that of Benno

---

(1974), 276:36); *tespītu* (TCL 3:125 // *teslītu*; Mullo Weir Lexicon, 379). Furthermore, unlike incantations which are "hurled" (*nadû*) and "spelled" (*manû*), prayers are "prayed" (*ba'ālu*) and "offered in homage." (*karābu*) See references in *CAD B*, 2; AHw., 101 (s.v. *bâlu*.); Meissner BAW I, 11–12; *CAD K* 192; AHw., 445. Other important prayer verbs are *sullû*/ *ṣullû* (AHw., 1056, 1110); *suppû* (AHw., 1060); *šutēmuqu* (AHw., 214a); *utnennu* (Mullo Weir Lexicon, 382; *CAD E*, 163;AHw., 144); *maḫāru* (Ebeling Handerhebung, 146:20; Lambert BWL 134:134, 136, 138, 140, 142, 144); *nīš qāti našû* (Lambert BWL 218:4, Cf. Šurpu II; 76); *šasû* (Ebeling Handerhebung, 72:4; Lambert BWL 134:132; Cagni Erra 88:23. Akkadian *šasû* "call out" as a prayer term finds its semantic parallels in Hebrew *ṣʿq, zʿq, qrʾ, šwʿ*; *še'û* (Lambert BWL 74:70; 76:73; Mullo Weir Lexicon, 339); *saḫāru* (*ibid*., 291; With *še'û* and *saḫāru* cf. their semantic parallels Hebrew *drš* and *bqš* which are part of the lexicon of prayer. See M. Held, *AOAT* 25 (1976), 233, n. 34.) To this list we should also add verbs of praise such *dalālu, šitmuru, šurruḫu* and the like. (See Mayer Gebetsbeschwörungen, 319–321.) In addition to the terminological distinctions between prayer and incantation, prayers were usually in the precative while incantations were in the indicative to underline the assertion that the very pronouncement of the spell was efficacious. Cf. T. H. Gaster, *The New Golden Bough* (New York, 1959), 171. Furthermore, anyone might pray alone and should do so often. (Lambert BWL 104:135; 108:11–13; Landsberger *MAOG* 4, 303) In contrast, incantations were left to the *āšipu* or *masmaššu* priest who viewed his lore as secret (*niṣirtu* or *pirištu*). See KAR 44 Rs. 7–8. In his recitation the priest often addressed directly the evil he wished to combat without invoking the aid of a particular god or goddess (e.g. Maqlu iii: 104–117, 118–127, iv:76–87). At other times the invocation of the divinities was little more than name-dropping with the intent to activate automatically the gods mentioned (e.g. Šurpu IV: 87–8). Sometimes the priest took care to deny any originality and attributed his formulae to Ea, Marduk or another prominent divine exorcist. (See Falkenstein Haupttypen, 44–67; Ritter, *AS* 16, 1965, 309.) Indeed, in incantation the priest might go so far as to identify himself with the exorcist god. Note *šiptu šipat Marduk āšipu ṣalam Marduk* "The incantation is the incantation of Marduk, the exorcist the very image of Marduk." (*CAD A/II*, 431b, lexical section). Cf. C. Frank, *Studien zur babylonischen Religion* (Leipzig, 1911), 24. See further CT 16:2:70–79.

9 Ancient Mesopotamians doubtless regarded prayer and incantation as different attempts to control the multitude of phenomena which moderns call the universe. Prayer and incantation have generally existed side by side in all cultures. See G. van der Leeuw, *Religion in Essence and Manifestation* (N.Y., 1963), 422, n. 2.

10 London, 1896.

11 Berlin, 1953.

Landsberger,[12] followed by his students Walter G. Kunstmann[13] and Wolfram von Soden,[14] "Gebetsbeschwörung (prayer-incantation)."[15] In his form-critical study of the šu-íl-lá series Werner Mayer[16] raised objections to the term and retained it with reluctance.

The subject of the present study is a šu-íl-lá composition[17] to Ištar which was edited critically by F. W. Geers[18] accompanied by a German translation and brief commentary by von Soden[19] who translated it again in *Sumerische und akkadische Hymnen und Gebete* (SAHG).[20] Since then it has been translated by Ebeling in Ebeling Handerhebung[21] and subsequently by Seux.[22]

To our knowledge, though, ours is the first detailed study of this piece. We treat philological problems, structure, and literary devices, and provide comparisons to other Near Eastern literature including the Bible. We also provide a fresh translation of Geers's critical text. For the convenience of the reader we have normalized the Akkadian.

Vs. 1) *qarittum* ᵈ*Ištar kanūt ilāti*
Valiant Ištar, darling of the goddesses
2) *dipār šamê u erṣeti šarūr kibrāti*
Torch of heaven and earth, splendor of regions
3) ᵈ*Ininni bukrat* ᵈ*Sîn ilitti* ᵈ*Ningal*
Ininni, daughter of Sin, child of Ningal
4) *tu'amti d/ṭarri šupê qurādi* ᵈ*Šamši*
Twin of bearded shining Šamaš the hero
5) ᵈ*Ištar anātīma šamê tabellī*
Ištar, You are Anu for You rule the heavens

12 *OLZ* 1925, 480.

13 W. G. Kunstmann, *Die babylonische Gebetsbeschwörung* (Leipzig, 1932), 1.

14 RLA III, 169–70; AHw., 797a, sv. *nīšu* 4.

15 Landsberger was led to his decision by the equation of inim. inim.a = *šiptu*. Cf. now Labat, *Manuel*, Nr. 15; Note further lú-inim-inim-ma = (*w*)*āšipum* (*ZA* 59 [1969], 223). This equation is not undermined by ⁱ⁻ⁿⁱᵐKA=*a-ma-tum*, inim.inim.ma = *a-ma-a-tum* (*CAD A/II*, 29b) for *awatu/amatu* may mean "formula," "wondrous word."

16 Mayer Gebetsbeschwörungen, 7. Cf. Seux, *Hymnes*, 24.

17 The rubric ÉN is missing from the text, probably by accident. See SAHG, 402.

18 *ZA* 42 (1934), 220–222.

19 *Ibid.*, 222–225.

20 SAHG, 333–336.

21 60–62.

22 *Hymnes*, 321–323.

6) *itti* ^{d}*Enlil māliki taṭemmī dadmī*
With Enlil the counselor You direct the inhabited lands

7) *mummu bān parṣi u šuluḫḫī*
Primal (Ea) are you, creator of divine rites and lustrations

8) *taklimti* ^{d}*Ea ina apsî tukalli riksāti*
In the deep You hold the bonds, the instructions of Ea

9) *ēma bašmūma asurrû nadât libittu*
Wherever damp courses have been built, a foundation brick placed

10) *ša pâ šaknū tapaqqidī kīma* ^{d}*Šamši*
You care for all humanity (lit.: all endowed with speech) as does Šamăs

11) *šumma ina* ^{d}*Igigī ayyu māḫirki*
Who is Your rival among the gods of heaven?

12) *šumma ina* ^{d}*Anunnaki ali šāninki*
Who is Your equal among the underworld divinities?

13) *attīma ina libbi tarbaṣ nišī lupna … išdiḫa tukannī*
You alone end poverty and establish prosperity in the farmsteads of the people

14) *tuštepellī šīmatamma idammiq lemnu*
You bring about a change in fortune so that the wretched thrives

15) *eš'ēma in(a) ilāni supû šarkūki*
asḫurma in(a) ^{d}*ištarāti kâšīma ša bâli*
I searched among the gods: To You are prayers offered.
I sought among the goddesses: Only You are to be supplicated.

16) *pānukki* ^{d}*šēdu arkatuk* ^{d}*lamassu*
Before You stands a genie, behind you a guardian spirit.

17) *imnuk mīšari šumīlukki dumqu*
At Your right is Justice, at Your left Good Fortune.

18) *kunnū ina rēšiki tašmû magāru*
Serving You are Compliance and Favor.

19) *itātūki šutasḫurā balāṭa šulma*
Encircling You about are Life and Well-being.

Rs. 20) *ki ṭābu suppûki ki qerub nešmûki*
How sweet are prayers to You! How nigh Your attentiveness!

21) *napluski tašmû qibītki nūru*
Your glance is favorable hearing, Your word, light.

22) *rēminnīma* ^{d}*Ištar qibî naḫāši*
Pity me Ištar! Ordain my prosperity.

23) *kīniš naplisinnīma leqê unninīya*
Yea, regard me with favor. Accept my prayers.

24) *erdi ūski išdiḫu likūna*
Your path I followed. May my prosperity endure.
25) *serdâki āḫuz lubēl ṭūb libbi*
I grasped Your pole. May I have contentment.
26) *ūbil abšānaki pašāḫa šuknī*
I have borne Your yoke. Grant peace.
27) *uqeʾi rēški līšira salīmu*
I have anticipated Your wishes. May reconciliation come straight to me.
28) *aṣṣur šarūrūki lū tašmû u magāru*
I have heeded Your splendor. May there be compliance and acceptance.
29) *ešʾe namrirrīki limmirū zimūʾa*
I have looked for Your rays. May my face gleam.
30) *asḫur bēlūtki lū balāṭu u šulmu*
I have sought out Your dominion. May there be life and wellbeing.
31) *lurši* ᵈ*šēda damqa ša pānīki*
ša arkīki ālikat lamassa lurši
Would that I possessed the good genie who stands before You.
Would that I possessed the guardian-spirit who follows You.
32) *ša imnukki mešrâ luṣṣip*
dumqa lukšuda ša šumēlukki
Let me add the wealth at Your right
Let me gain the good fortune at Your left
33) *qibīma liššemi zikri*
Speak out so that my word may be heard
34) *amāt aqabbû kīma aqabbû lū magrat*
May the word I speak be pleasing just as I speak it
35) *ina ṭūb šēri u ḫūd libbi itarrinni ūmišam*
In joy and gladness guide me constantly, daily
36) *ūmīya urrikī balāṭa šurkī*
lubluṭ lušlimma luštammar ilūtki
Prolong my days. Grant life.
May I live in health to sing Your praises.
37) *ēma uṣammaru lukšud*
šamû liḫdûki apsû lirēški
May I attain whatever I wish
May the heavens rejoice in You, the deep exult over you
38) *ilāni ša kiššati likrubūki*
ilāni rabûti libbaki liṭibbū

May all the gods of the pantheon bless You
May the great gods satisfy Your desires

39) INIM-INIM-MA ŠU-ÍL-LÁ *dIštar-KÁM ana pan dIštar nignak burāši tašakkan*
Prayer-incantation to Ištar. You set up a censer with juniper.

40) *miḫḫa tanaqqīma* ŠU-ÍL-LÁ III-*šú tamannūma tuškên*
You pour out libation-beer, recite this šu-íl-lá prayer thrice and then you prostrate yourself.

Notes to the text:

1. *kanūt ilāti.* For *kanūtu* in general see Tallqvist Götterepitheta, 112: AHw., 441; CAD K 171–172. Of special importance are the studies of the verb *kunnû* and the substantive *kanūtu* by A. Schott (ZA 42 [1934], 125–129) and P.-R. Berger ZA 60 (1970), 131–133. Ištar is referred to as *kanūt bēlēti* in Ebeling Handerhebung, 142:25; See further Ebeling, ArOr 17 (1949), 187:25. Note as well the description of Ninsigga: *kanūt ištarāti bēlet dadmī šagapurti ilat pāṭ gimri* "Darling of the goddesses, mistress of the habitations, goddess of totality." (*JAOS* 88 [1968], 125:Ia:2, cf. 7) Though *kunnû* is a virtual synonym of *kubbutu* "to honor" and *šurruḫu* "to extol" it may be applied as well to the pampering of a child, *šerra kunnû.* See Šurpu iv: 28; B. Landsberger, ZA 42 (1934, 129), n. 1. Indeed, *kunnû* is even employed for the careful treatment of inanimate objects (Borger Esarh., 93:8–9); the modern distinction into categories of animate and inanimate was not always made by the ancients (Berger, ZA 60, 132). Some passages refer to the pampering or babying of divinities male and female. Gula says of her youth: *uldanni Antum kīniš ukannanni ušāḫizanni milka damqa uza'inanni kuzbi* "Antu bore me. She cared for me steadfastly. She taught me my good counsel and adorned me with my sexual charm." (*Or* 36 [1967], 124:139–40) An OB hymn refers to Nana as *ettum muštarḫat u kanât* "An only (child), haughty and pampered." (ZA 44 [1938], 32:19; See further SAHG 238; *CAD E*, 396.) The male god Nergal is referred to as *māru kunnû libbi dEnlil* "Pampered son, darling of Enlil's heart." (*AOAT* 11 [1971], 359) The nuance of babying carries over into Ugaritic where the wives of Baal are termed *klt knyt* "darling brides." (*KTU*3 1.4: i:15, 53)

1.2 Ištar is elsewhere referred to as *namirtum dipar šamê u erṣeti šarūr kal dadmē* "Shining torch of heaven and earth, splendor of all habitations." (Ebeling Handerhebung, 132:65) We may follow Tallqvist Götterepitheta, 133 and compare *phos tou kosmou* "light of the world" in John 8:12. Note as well the Syriac to that verse, *nureh dʿalmā,* medieval Hebrew *ziw haʿōlam* and Quranic *nuru as-samawati wàal'arḍi* (Sura 24:35).

1.3. *ilitti Ningal.* In Ugaritic myth Ningal appears as Nikkal, bride of Yariḫ, the Canaanite correspondent of Sin (*KTU*[3] 1.24). As Nkl, the goddess apears in Aramaic inscriptions along with the moon god Śhr (*KAI* 225:9; cf. 226:9).

1.4. *qurādi Šamši.* Cf. Hebrew Šemeš "Sun(god)" described as *gibbor* "hero" in Ps 19:6. See N. Sarna in *Proceedings of the Fourth World Congress of Jewish Studies* (Jerusalem, 1969), 172.

1.5. *Anātīma.* The ancient Mesopotamian who worshiped many deities often compared one to another. By saying "*Anātīma*" our poet has identified Ištar with Anu. In the previous line he spoke of Ištar as the twin of Šamaš (Cf. Ebeling Handerhebung, 128:3) while in 1.6 he described Ištar as sharing power *itti Enlil* "with Enlil." Another option of the worshiper may be seen in Ebeling Handerhebung, 14 in which the various high gods are described as attributes of Marduk. Thus his divinity (*ilūtu*) is Sîn, his princeliness (*malkūtu*) is Anu, his lordship (*bēlūtu*) is Dagan and his wisdom (*ḫasīsu*) is Ea. Yet another type of comparison is the language of KAR 102 (translated in SAHG 258–259) in which the many gods are described as physical features of Ninurta. Anu and Antu are his lips (1.6, 1.16) and Ea and Damkina, his ears (1.21). None of these rhetorical devices attempts to go beyond comparison to conceptual identification.[23] In contrast, Ištar's identification with Sumerian Ininni (1.3) was complete and included a merger of cult, prayer and myth. On the need to distinguish between comparison and conceptual identification see T. H. Gaster, *Journal of the History of Ideas* 16 (1955), 424.

1.6 *itti Enlil māliki.* For Enlil as *māliku* "counsellor" see Ebeling Handerhebung, 38:35, 142:27; Maqlu II:6; Lambert -Millard Atra-hasīs I:8, 43, 45, 57; III: viii:11.

taṭemmī. *CAD Ṭ*, 97, *s.v.* *ṭêmu v.* translates "you command the inhabited world." Despite the emphatic [ṭ], *CAD ad loc.* suggests a connection with *tu'umu* A, translated "to bid, command," in *CAD T*, 500. See further, AHw., 1387.

mummu. Akkadian *mummu* has taxed the skills of major Akkadian lexicographers. A. Heidel's important article on *mummu* summarizes earlier literature. See *JNES* 7 (1948), 88–105. More recent material may be found in van Dijk Götterlieder 2, 115; AHw., 672; *CAD M/II*, 197–98; M. Held, *AOAT* 25 (1976), 232, n. 10. Heidel correctly understood *mummu* in our passage as an epithet of Ea (*op. cit.*, 102) who is elsewhere referred to by the compound name Ea-mummu. Furthermore, since lines 5–6 compare Ištar to Anu and Enlil, it is to be expected that Ea would complete the triad. Indeed, he is mentioned by name rather than by epithet in the very next line. Other gods were also designated by the

23 The well known midrash on the fifty names of Marduk in tablets vi–vii of *enūma eliš* is probably an elaboration of god-list. See W. G. Lambert, *Or* 36 (1967), 108.

epithet *mummu*. For references see Tallqvist Götterepitheta, 129–130. For the translation "primal one" see Held, *AOAT* 25, 232, n.10.

1.8 *taklimti*. In general see AHw., 1307; *CAD T*, 80. Note further: *taklimtum ta-ki-ir-tum tāšertum naplusum u dummuqum kumma Eštar* "Instruction, oversight(?), inspection and approving scrutiny are Yours Eštar." (*ZA* 65 (1976), 190:124. Sjöberg, *ibid.*, 235) For reasons of metre we prefer the reading *riksāti* to *riksī* and read it as appositional to *taklimti*. The bands mentioned here are probably identical with the *rikis tâmāti* "band of the seas." (Ebeling Handerhebung 50:10) By comparing Ištar with Anu, Enlil and Ea, the worshipper attributes to the goddess dominion over each of the three major divisions of the Babylonian "world," *šamû* "heaven," *dadmū* "inhabitated earth" (Gk. *oikoumene*, Hebrew *tebel*) and *apsû* "subterranean waters."

1.10 *ša pâ šaknū*. Seux (*Hymnes*, 322) translates "qui sont concertés" noting "sans doute passif de'lexpression *pâ šakānu itti* "s'aboucher," "s'entrendre (avec)." Without doubt *šaknū* is passive. The absence of *itti* however, militates against Seux's translation. Note the examples of *pâ NN itti NN2 šakānu* in Oppenheim's study of Akkadian body idioms (*JAOS* 61 [1941], 260–261). The idiom *pâ šaknū* has the sense of "those endowed with a mouth." Cf. the formally similar *šūt napišti šaknā* "whatever has breath." (Lambert BWL, 126:25)

1.13 Von Soden suggests (*ZA* 42 (1934), 224) that a verb has been elided before *lupnu* "poverty." Indeed, in one of the exemplars *lupnu* is absent. The restoration of a suitable verb would provide a poetic balance between lines 13 and 14. Cf. *lupna tabalma ḫēgalla šurka* "Remove poverty and grant prosperity." (PBS 1/1 17:22 cited in *CAD L*, 252a; Cf. Ebeling, Handerhebung, 22:23 with n. 4.)

1.14 *tuštepellī šīmatamma idammiq lemnu*. Cf. the sentiment with that in another šu-íl-lá to Ištar, *enšam ana danni tele"ī turra*[*m*] *šīmat lā dumqi dummuqu bašû ittik*[*i*] "You are able to turn the weak into the strong. It rests with You to make fortunate an unfortunate lot." (Ebeling Handerhebung 128:11–12; Cf. *CAD L*, 153b.) We may likewise compare a passage in Šurpu iv:19 in which Marduk is praised for the quality of *šīmti lemuttim šupêlu* [d]*lamassi dumqi ana amēli šarāki* ... [d]*Marduk ittikāma* ... "It is in Your power O Marduk, to alter a bad lot, to bestow Good Fortune upon a man" ... A different line of interpretation has been proposed by Haldar who suggests that "we are in the sphere of 'to be propitious with regard to omens or oracles.'" A. Haldar translates 1.14, "You portion the fates unequally—it is an expression ... being powerless in relation to the divine will. The expression *idammiq lemnu* will mean 'so that the evil one is propitious' i.e. his omens are propitious." (*Or* 33 [1964], 35) This interpretation is unlikely. First, because *šupêlu* means "alter," "change," "exchange" (references in AHw., 1279–1280; *CAD Š/III*) not "portion out" or "apportion" which would be expressed by some form of *zâzu*. See *CAD Z*, 82. Note especially [d]*bēl šarrāni nūr amīlūtu muza''iz isqētu* "Lord of kings, light of humanity, who apportions the lots." See RAcc. 149:14; cf. *ibid.*, 129, n. 6. Secondly, there is no mention here of signs or omens (*bīru, ittu, têrtu, purussû, šīru, tamītu, ūrtu* and the like). Cf. VAB 4: 224:34–5, 226:18–19; Cagni Erra, 90:42; YOS 1 45 i:16 (*CAD B*, 264b); CH xliii:26.

It is difficult to find an English equivalent of Akkadian *šīmtu* (references in AHw., 1238–1239; *Š/III, 11–20*). "Fate" and "destiny" are often reasonable approximations but these English terms carry connotations of predetermination and finality that are largely foreign to *šīmtu.* Contrast W. G. Lambert, *Oudtestamentische Studien* 17 (1972), 65–72. Our passage, as well as those cited above, demonstrates that the *šīmtu* of an individual was subject to alteration by a benevolent deity. Conversely, a deity might change the *šīmtu* of an individual for the worse. King Yaḫdun-Lim of Mari for example, curses any would-be despoiler of the Šamaš temple, *Ea šar šīmtim šīmtašu lillemin* "May Ea, king of destiny make his destiny unfavorable." (*Syria* 32,[1955], 17:v:23–4; For the reading, see AHw., 1239 c) 2; Cf. *ANET*³, 557; Contrast G. Dossin, *Syria op. cit.*; *CAD L*, 117.) Oppenheim has suggested that *šīmtu* be viewed as "a disposition originating from an agency endowed with power to act and to dispose, such as the deity, the king or any individual may do." (*Ancient Mesopotamia* [Chicago, 1964], 202) The notion of "disposition" has philological support. As Seux Epithètes notes (285, n. 119), the verb *šâmu*, "fix," "determine" from which *šīmtu is* derived, is sometimes replaced by *šakānu*, "fix," "place," "establish" which carries no special connotation of predetermination or permanence. Further philological evidence may be adduced from the way *šīmtu* functions as a legal term. In an OB document from Alalakh we read, *ᴵAmmitakumma awīl Alalaḫᵏⁱ ina bulṭišūma maḫar Yarim -Lim šarrim bēlišu šīmti bītišu išīmma*... "During his lifetime Ammitakum governor of Alalakh determined the disposition of his estate in the presence of King Yarim-Lim his lord ..." (Wiseman, Alalakh 6:1–6) Though it is true that this particular legal usage appears restricted to peripheral Akkadian (AHw., 1225a), the expression *šīmti X šâmu* "dispose" seems appropriate to theological usage as well. Note further that *šīmtu* is associated with *isqu* "lot," "share," "fortune," "nature," (references in *CAD I/J*, 198) itself synonymous with *zittu* "portion," "share." (*CAD ibid.*, lexical section) Indeed, *isqu* and *šīmtu* occur as synonyms together with *uṣurtu* "design" in a prayer to Ea, Šamaš and Asalluḫi: *dāinū dīn māti mušimmū šīmāti muṣṣirū uṣurāti mussiqū isqēti ša šamê u erṣeti attunūma šīmāti šâmu uṣurāti uṣṣuru ša qātēkunūma*... "You are the only ones who render judgement for the land, who determine the destinies, lay out the plans and allot the portions of heaven and earth. The power to determine destinies and lay out plans is Yours alone ..."(*JRAS* 1929, 285:2–6) It is of interest that the Hebrew words often translated as "fate," "destiny" *ḥeleq, gorāl, mānāh* are literally "share," "lot," "portion," much like Akkadian *šīmtu* and its associated terms. (See Jer 13:25; Ps 11:6, 16:5; Qoh 3:22, 5:17, 9:9.) Similarly, the Classical Greek words for "fate," *moira* and *aisa*, meant originally "share" and "portion." See OCD, 430; M. Nillson, *A History of Greek Religion* (N.Y., 1964), 168–172; *idem*, *Greek Piety* (N.Y., 1964), 52; E. R. Dodds, *The Greeks and the Irrational* (London, 1971), 6–8. For bibliography of other comparative studies on "fate" and "destiny" see Oppenheim, *Ancient Mesopotamia* 366, n. 29; S. Paul in *The Gaster Festschrift* (N.Y., 1973), 352, n. 56.

1.15 *eš'ēma … asḫurma.* Note the similar parallelism below in ll. 29–30. See further Lambert BWL 76:72–73; Sperling in *The Gaster Festschrift* (N.Y., 1973), 401–402; M. Held, *AOAT* 25, 233.

1.16–19 The worshiper describes the goddess as surrounded completely by desirable qualities and perquisites which he wishes were his own (cf. ll. 29–32 below). These are treated by the poet in a concrete manner rather than as abstractions. The ^{d}*šēdu* and ^{d}*lamassu* are divinities. Though *mēšaru* in contrast, is written in our text without the divine determinative, it occurs with it elsewhere in the šu-íl-lá series (Ebeling Handerhebung, 50:112). See further AHw., 659–660; *CAD M/II*, 118b. For the Canaanite divinity Mysor, see *Wörterbuch der Mythologie* (Stuttgart, 1961) I, 310. The Hebrew Bible in a similar fashion, treats as persons *ṭob* "goodness," *ḥesed* "steadfast love," *ṣedeq* "righteousness," *mišpāṭ* "justice," and *'emet* "faithfulness." See Ps 23:6, 48:3, 85: 11–14, 89:15. Note especially Ps 25:21, *tom wᵉyošer yiṣṣrūni kî qiwwitīkā* "May Integrity and Uprightness protect me for I await You." Cf. C. and E. Briggs, *The Book of Psalms* (New York, 1957), 212, 233, 257; T. H. Gaster, in "The Religion of the Canaanites," in *Ancient Religions*, ed. V. Ferm (New York, 1965), 123; *idem*, *Myth, Legend and Custom in the Old Testament* (New York, 1969), 670; *idem*, *Thespis* (New York, 1961), 158.

kâšīma ša bâli. Enclitic *-ma* has the force "alone," "solely," "only." See A. Ungnad, MVAG 20 Heft II (1915), 63; T. Jacobsen, *AfO* 12 (1937/9), 364, n. 9; M. Held, *JAOS* 88, (1968), 94, n. 81. For a similar statement of uniqueness cf. the Ištar prayer which reads in part, *ayyu ina ilī imṣa malāki lā amra kima kâti māḫir teslīti* "Who among the gods is of Your caliber? There has never been seen one who accepts prayer like You." (*AfO* 19, 1960, 51:75–76) The claim that Ištar alone is worthy of prayer or is alone disposed to it favorably should be treated as an example of protocol rather than of theological rigor. In ancient Near Eastern prayer, divinities were often approached in turn as though each were the sole object of devotion and the only effective force. Cf. Morton Smith, *JBL* 71(1952), 137–139.

1.20 *ki ṭābu suppûki.* For the image cf. Hebrew *kî ṭob … kî nā'im* "How good … how pleasant" describing prayers to Yahweh; see Ps 135:3, Ps 147:1.

1.21 *napluski tašmû.* J. Laessøe (*Bi.Or.* 18 [1961], 71) argues for a "rendering to the effect that looking towards Ištar is an act which in itself ensures the acceptance of one's prayer." Grammatically not impossible, Laessøe's translation is dubious. The vast majority of attestations of *naplusu* in prayer texts refer to the favorable glance of the divinity not to the searching look of the worshiper (*še'û, saḫāru, bu''û*). We may cite several occurrences in the large Ištar piece (Ebeling Handerhebung, 130:26, 132:40, 44, 54); See conveniently, Mullo Weir Lexicon, 256–257 for additional references. Secondly, we may not ignore the line's internal poetic parallelism, for *qibītki* surely refers to the word of the goddess. Note finally that the poet has effected a chiastic transfer of properties between the faculties of seeing and hearing.

1:24 *erdi uski*. It is unclear why Laessøe (*Bi.Or.* 18, 71) preferred to read *še-pak-ki* in preference to the clearly superior *-US*. (See already Mullo Weir Lexicon, 281.) Akkadian *ūsu* (AHw., 1438) is a virtual synonym of *rid(d)u* "way," "path," "direction." Note the expression *ūsam kīnam u rīdam damqam* "proper road and goodly way." (CH Rs. xxiv:6–8; See B. Landsberger, *ZA* 41 [1933], 297, n. 2; G. R. Driver, *The Babylonian Laws* II [Oxford, 1955], 282.) Reminiscent of our passage is Nabonidus' description of himself as *murteddû ūsi Ištar* "constant follower of Ištar's way." (See *RA* 22 (1925), 58:21–22; Cf. Seux Epithètes, 242.) Note as well the advice given in the Babylonian Theodicy, *ridīma ūs ili uṣur māsīšu* "Follow the way of a god observe his rites." (See Lambert BWL 82:219 and Lambert's comment *ibid.*, 308.)

1:25 *serdâki āḫuz*. The variant *āḫuz* is preferable grammatically to *āḫuzu*. For references to *serdû* /*sirdû* "pole of a sedan chair," "pole of a chariot," see AHw., 1037b; *CAD S*, 312; MSL 3:222:5; 7:52:319. Cf. AHw., *op. cit.*; *CAD K*, 588a–b, lexical section. The native lexica associate the *kussû serdê* with *šadittu*, literally, "pulled chair" (cf. AHw., 1123b) and *arattû*, literally "Arattian chair," but having the more general sense "throne," especially one appointed for the gods. (*CAD A/II*, 238) Perhaps the closest usage to that of our own passage is Sennacherib's expressed goal, *palāhu aḫāzu serd*[*û*] "to revere, and seize the poles [of the gods] …" See H. Tadmor, *ErIsr* 5 (1958), 154:5. The same sense of servility is conveyed by *serdâ šâṭu* "to pull the poles," (VAB 4 150:A Col, III:3–4; 88:11; 262:14) or *serdâ šadādu* "haul the poles." (VAB 4:124:9) For a possible artistic representation of this image see E. Strommenger, *5000 Years of the Art of Mesopotamia* (New York, 1964), Nr. 217.

1.26 *ūbil abšānaki*. The poet provides a nice play on *lubēl* in line 25 and *ūbil* in 1.26. The precise identification of *abšānu* is difficult. The word is an early loan from Sumerian and occurs only as a literary term in Akkadian and never in lists of implements. (See *CAD A/I*, 65–66; A. Salonen, *Agricultura Mesopotamica* [Helsinki, 1968], 99.)

1.27 *ueq'i rēški*. Literally, "I have awaited Your head." The idiom frequently refers to a human being waiting in readiness upon a god (Lambert BWL 315;

AHw., 931b, 9). The idiom *rēša qu"û* is virtually synonymous with one nuance of *rēša kullu* "to be in readiness," literally, "to hold the head." (See Goetze LE, 44; A. L. Oppenheim, *JAOS* 61[1941], 255; *CAD K* 516–17; AHw., 503b, 12d.) We may also compare *panī qu"û* (Streck Asb. 124:52; Oppenheim, *op. cit.*, 258). Idioms of this sort originate in the physical realm. Thus *rēša qu"û /kullu and pānī qu"û* describe the inferior waiting upon every nod or gesture of the superior in order to anticipate his wishes and fulfill them as quickly as possible.

1.28–9 *šarūrūki*... *namrirrīki*. The luminosity of divinities is widespread in religious imagery. See Oppenheim, *JAOS* 62 (1942), 31–34; *idem*, *Ancient Mesopotamia*, 98; E. Cassin, *La Splendeur divine* (Paris, 1968); W. von Soden, *ZA* 61 (1972), 312–314. For the rabbinic concept of *ziw ha-šekinā* "divine splendor" see E. Urbach, *The Sages-Their Concepts and Beliefs* (Jerusalem, 1971), 35–36.

The above prayer may be analyzed in line with the structural scheme outlined originally by Kunstmann and generally followed by more recent scholarship.[24]

I. Address
   (a) Invocation of the deity with honorific titles (1–4)
   (b) Praise (5–21)
II. Prayer section
   (c) Lamentation
   (d) Transition formula
   (e) Petition (22–37a)
III. Thanksgiving
   (f) Offering of thanks with inclusion of benediction formula (37b–38)

Lines 1–4 of this Ištar šu-íl-lá contain the invocation of the goddess and her honorific titles. A major part of the composition consists of what von Soden has termed "ein besonderes schönes Loblied."[25] (ll. 5–21) Though most of the extant šu-íl-lá texts contain a lamentation section, the present one makes no mention, at least not directly, of the sufferings of the worshiper.[26] In the petition proper the worshiper makes mention of his past pieties and requests that the goddess reward him in return.

24 See Dalglish, *Psalm Fifty-One*, 43–47; Mayer Gebetsbeschwörungen, 34–36.

25 SAHG, 402.

26 For other members of the series without a lamentation section see Mayer Gebetsbeschwörungen, 68.

The author shows a literary flair, in particular when he draws linguistic connections between his righteous conduct and his expected reward. Thus he claims to have looked for the rays of the goddess and now wishes his face to shine to return, playing on the successive cognates *namrirrū limmirū*. Similarly, in lines 25–26 he puns on *ūbil* and *lubēl*. In line 30 he requests life (*balāṭu*) for he has sought out the dominion (*bēlētu*) of Ištar. A lesser poet would have preferred "Your glance is light, Your word is light" to the present form of line 21. Nor is it accidental that "Justice" (*mīšaru*) at Ištar's right (1.17) is replaced by "wealth" (*mešrâ*) in 1.32.[27]

Other literary devices are employed by the writer. There are of course banal rhymes of the sort common in incantations (ll.4–8, 11–13). Others have a genuine lyrical quality. Among these are: *kanût ilāti … šarūr kibrāti* (ll.1–2) and *ema bašmūma asurrû nadât libittu* (1.9).[28] In some cases the lines rhyme internally (ll.20–23). J. V. Kinnier Wilson (*JSS* 13 (1968), 97) has called attention to the avoidance of assonance in Akkadian, a phenomenon that he terms "desonance." He noted that in ll.16–17 of our text we have such an example. The author alternated the case endings chiastically in order to avoid assonance:

panukki … arkatuk
imnuk … šumēlukki

Synonymous parallelism is also employed extensively. Thus for example

dipār šamê u erṣeti	// *šarūr kibrāti*	(1.2)
bukrat Sîn	// *ilitti Ningal*	(1.3)
bašmūma asurrû	// *nadât libittu*	(1.9)

and the entire ll.11–12, 15, 16, 17, 20, 31–32, 47b–48.

Poetically the closing lines are the least interesting in that they employ standardized formulae in a conventional way.[29] For the most part though, our ancient poet managed to rise above cliché and artistically to convey the sense of genuine religious devotion.

27 CF. Seux, *Hymnes*, 323, n. 21.
28 Cf. Lambert BWL, 58:37–42.
29 See Mayer Gebetsbeschörungen, 307–361.

CHAPTER 6

An Arslan Tash Incantation: Interpretations and Implications

In 1933 two small limestone plaques came to light at Arslan Tash in northern Syria. Arslan Tash, as Ḫadattu ("New Town"),[1] had been the seat of an Assyrian governor in the eighth century BCE. The plaques themselves had probably been made in the seventh century BCE.[2] Both bore similar reliefs of demons, and contained incantations written in an Aramaic script. The longer of the two incantation plaques was published by du Mesnil in 1939.[3] Though it was studied by numerous scholars,[4] many difficulties in interpretation remained. Du Mesnil was unable to fulfill his promise to publish the second plaque until 1971.[5] Itself highly problematic, this second plaque has reawakened scholarly interest in the first.[6] The present paper is an attempt to resolve some of the scholarly controversies surrounding the main inscription of the earlier publication. Several points of interpretation depend on establishing the language of composition, and so I will begin with that question. Afterwards a new translation will be offered, philological observations will be made, and attention drawn to parallels in related ancient Semitic literature. Finally, the paper will discuss briefly some implications of the covenant terminology employed by the author of the incantation.

---

* This paper is a revised version of my presentation at the meeting of the American Oriental Society on March 16, 1981. I am delighted to dedicate it to Dr. Fritz Bamberger.

1 W. F. Albright, *BASOR* 76 (1939), 5. Cf. *qrtḥdšt* "New City," the native name of Carthage.

2 For the date see B. Haines *apud* F. M. Cross and R. Saley, *BASOR* 197 (1970), 42 n. 2.

3 Le Comte du Mesnil du Buisson, "Une tablette magique de la région du Moyen Euphrate," in *Mélanges … Dussaud* (Paris, 1939), 421–434.

4 For bibliography see *KAI* II, 43; Z. Zevit, *IEJ* 27 (1977), 110; E Lipiński in *Near Eastern Religious Texts Relating to the Old Testament* (=*NERTOT*), ed. W. Beyerlin (Philadelphia, 1978), 248.

5 A. Caquot and R. du Mesnil du Buisson, Syria 48 (1971), 391–406; see further, T. H. Gaster, BASOR 209 (1973), 18–26; F. M. Cross, *CBQ* 36 (1974), 486–490; E. Lipiński in *NERTOT*, 249–250 (with bibliography); Y. Avishur, *UF* 10 (1978), 29–36 (with bibliography).

6 A. Caquot, *JANES* 5 (1973), 45–51, employed squeezes of the original; Cross and Saley obtained new photographs for their study in *BASOR* 197, 42–49; Cf. further, F. M. Cross, *Canaanite Myth and Hebrew Epic* (Cambridge, 1973), 17; W. Röllig, *NESE* 2 (1974), 17–28; Zevit, *IEJ* 27, 110–118; Lipiński, *NERTOT*, 247–248.

 | DOI 10.1163/9789004340879_007

Lack of precision has characterized several discussions of the text. Albright's important study bore the title "An Aramaean Magical Text in Hebrew from the Seventh Century BC."[7] In the body of the article, however, Albright wrote: "the text is almost throughout pure Phoenician in Grammar."[8] Still later in the paper he designated the language as "pure Canaanite of classical Phoenician type."[9] Tur-Sinai (Torczyner) interpreted the text in light of Hebrew grammar and lexicography.[10] Cross and Saley, though considering the incantation Phoenician, suggested renderings which diverged from the Phoenician, at least as understood at present.[11] The same may be said of the article by Zevit.[12] Lipiński described the Arslan Tash texts as written in a "mixed dialect of Aramaic and Phoenician."[13] H. L. Ginsberg never devoted a special publication to these texts. Nonetheless, his designation of their language as "a special variety of Standard Phoenician"[14] is accurate. The translation offered in the present paper presupposes no Aramaisms. The only Aramaic forms are the proper names *ʿÂpātâ and Lilyân.* As Gaster noted long ago,[15] later Aramaic incantations were often addressed to Greek and Persian deities. The language of those texts did not become, thereby, a *Mischsprache.*

The Arslan Tash incantations manifest a combination of orthographic and linguistic features which occur together only in Phoenician but in no other Northwest Semitic dialect of the first pre-Christian millennium. The most obvious of these features are: 1) the relative pronoun *ʾš* (I. 16; 1.4 of the second text); 2) The pronominal suffix *yod* for the third person masculine and feminine.

7 *BASOR* 76, n. 5.

8 *Ibid.*, 7.

9 *Ibid.*, 11.

10 N. H. Tur-Sinai, *The Language and the Book* vol. I (1954), 53–65. He maintained that the text of the incantations represented a translation into Hebrew of an Aramaic original (*ibid.*, 55). Many of his observations nevertheless were correct. The photographs in his edition are a useful supplement to those of du Mesnil and Cross.

11 *BASOR* 197. Cross and Saley identify two *lameds* as vocatives (45, 46) in spite of the fact that even in Ugaritic where *lamed* vocative is certain, it is employed only before a name or epithet of at least two units. See A. Singer, *JCS* 2 (1948), 6. Similarly the divine name *ʾšr* can hardly be Asherah as Cross and Saley claim (*BASOR* 197, 45 n. 7). See Zevit, *IEJ* 27, 115.

12 See below.

13 *NERTOT*, 247.

14 *JANES* 5 (1973), 145.

15 *Or* 11 (1942), 43.

Thus, l. 16, *tm py*; l. 17, *ṣrty*; ll. 1–2 of the second text, *bʿl ʾsr mrkbty wrbʿn ʾty*[16]; 3) the form *šmm* for heaven (l. 13); 4) The form *ʾšr* as the name of the eponymous god of Assyria.

In light of the above, two other features point to Phoenician as the language of composition for they are not Aramaic and there is no warrant for explaining them as Hebraisms: 1) The noun *ʿn* "eye" (obv. ll. 2, 4 of the second text and ll. 5–6 of its reverse). 2) the negation *bl* (11. 6–8).

One departure from Phoenician practice must be noted. The scribe writes *heh* where a final vowel of -*e*- quality is expected. The numeral "eight" appears as *šmnh* in l. 16. In the second text we find *mzh* "sprinkler" in l. 1 and *šdh* "field" in 11. 4, 5.

In the commentary that follows the text and translation, reference will be made to elements of Phoenician not indicated thus far.

Text and Translation

1-	*lḥšt lʿ <p>tʾ. ʾlt*	Incantation against the flyers
2-	*ssm. bn pdr*	The conjuration of Sasom b. Pidar:
3-	*šʾ ʾlt(!).*	Pronounce the conjuration
4-	*wl. ḥnqtʾ*	And to the stranglers say:
5-	*mr. bt ʾbʾ*	The house I enter
6-	*bl tbʾn*	You shall not enter
7-	*wḥṣr . ʾdrk*	And the court I tread
8-	*bl. tdrkn. k*	You shall not tread.
9-	*rt. ln. ʾlt*	Eternal covenants were made for us.
10-	*ʿlm ʾšr. krt*	Asshur made them with us, as
11-	*ln. wkl bn ʾlm*	Did every divinity
12-	*wrb. dr kl. qdšn*	And great one, the council of all our holy beings.
13-	*bʾlt. šmm. wʾrṣʿ*	By the conjuration of Heaven and
14-	*[d] ʿlm bʾlt bʿl*	Earth forever, by the conjuration of
15-	*[zb]l ʾrṣ. bʾl[t]*	Baal, prince of the earth, by the
16-	*[ʾ]št ḥwrn. ʾš. tm. py*	Conjuration of Hauron's wife whose
17-	*wšbʿ. ṣrty. wšm*	Word is true and her seven rivals too,
18-	*nh. ʾšt. bʿl q[d]š*	And the eight wives of Holy Baal . . .!

16 "Baal has harnessed his chariot and the one of the great eye is with him." Pace Avishur, *UF*, 10, 33. *ʾty* cannot be translated as "comes." Only in Byblian Phoenician was third radical *yod* retained. See *KAI* 4:1; 7:1; Ginsberg, *JANES* 5, 142, n. 52.

Comments on the Text

1—It is not impossible that *lḥšt* is a plural "incantations." More likely, though, the vocable is a singular, standing as it does in the position of *šiptu* in the contemporary Akkadian incantations.[17] Earlier studies have noted Semitic cognates to *lḥšt*.[18] It must be emphasized that in the meaning "incantation" no feminine noun formed from the root *lḥš* is attested in a classical Semitic language.[19]

lʿ<p>tʾ—This restoration, accepted by most scholars, is certain in light of the clear reading *lʿptʾ* on the sphinx on this very plaque. Two other suggestions require comment. One is to retain the reading *lʿtʾ*, to explain *ʿtʾ* as an Aramaic form of Anat, and to translate *ʾlt* as "goddess."[20] This interpretation is unlikely. First, a divinity *ʿtʾ* is unknown in Aramaic documents outside of the compound name Atargatis attested in the Hellenistic period.[21] Secondly, if the *ʿtʾ*-element in that divine name is derived from Anat,[22] there is no evidence that assimilation of the *nun* had occurred by the seventh century BCE. Indeed, Phoenician[23] and Aramaic[24] sources indicate that this was not the case. Thirdly, so far as is known, Anat was not depicted as a demon. Finally, surviving Phoenician inscriptions show that the expression "incantation for the goddess X" would appears as *lḥšt lrbt l-X* or **lḥšt lrbt X*.[25]

---

17 Cf. Tur-Sinai, *Language*, 55. Akkadian incantations sometimes employ the construct in similar circumstances. Note, e.g., *šipat utukkī lemnūti* "incantation against the evil demons." (AS 16, 309).

18 Du Mesnil, *Mélanges ... Dussaud*, 425; KAI II, 44.

19 Cf. Tur-Sinai, *Language*, 55. An interdialectal distribution of "incantation" yields Hebrew *lḥš* (Isa 3:3; Jer 8:17; Qoh 10:11); Ugaritic *mnt* (MRS 16 [1968], 565:4[=KTU^3 1.100:4]); see Gaster, JANES 7 [1975], 41); Akkadian *šiptu* (AHw., 1247), *minûtu* (AHw., 657a; CAD M/II, 99), *tû* (En. el. iv:91; Šurpu iv:99; JCS 9 [1955], 17 n. 6); *tudukkû* (AS 16, 312; Šurpu v-vi:50–51). Most of the Aramaic sources are late. For a survey of significant Aramaic terms see Montgomery *Aramaic Incantation Texts from Nippur* (Philadelphia, 1913), 51–52.

20 Zevit, IEJ 27, 111; cf. du Mesnil, *Mélanges ... Dussaud*, 424–425. Albright translates *ʾlt* by "goddess" in BASOR 76, 7 while Cross and Saley prefer the plural "goddesses" in BASOR 197, 45.

21 For extended discussion of Atargatis, with bibliography, see R. A. Oden, Jr., *Studies in Lucian's De Syria Dea* (Missoula, 1977), 47–107.

22 See the references cited by Zevit, IEJ 27, 112–13.

23 See Röllig, NESE 2, 19.

24 Cowley, *Aramaic Papyri* 44:3. See the discussion in H. Haussig, ed., *Wörterbuch der Mythologie*, (Stuttgart, 1965), vol. I, 237.

25 E.g. KAI 78:2; 79:1; 81:1; 83; 85:1; 86:1; 87:1; 88:1. Indeed, *ʾlt* "goddess" is poorly attested in Phoenician. Surviving texts employ mostly either *rbt* or the neuter *ʾlm*.

Even more unlikely is Lipiński's suggestion that *lʿtʾ* is to be translated as "for the right moment."[26] The word *lmzh* at the beginning of the second incantation shows that the initial *lamed* in each instance means "against" as was noted by du Mesnil in 1939.[27] Furthermore, in neither component of Lipiński's alleged "mixed dialect" does *ʿt* mean "right moment." Phoenician *ʿt* means "season,"[28] "allotted life-span."[29] In Aramaic, *ʿt* is found only in petrified forms with bound *-k, kʿnt* and *kʿt*.[30]

ʾlt—This same word occurs in lines 1, 3(!), 9, 13, 14, 15. I have translated it by "conjuration" except in line 9 where "covenant" is more appropriate. Phoenician *ʾlt* shares with Hebrew *ʾlh*[31] the meanings "oath" and "covenant." Conjurations, like covenants, are specialized oaths. In each case the terms include the nuance of "penalty" or "curse" for oath violation. For semantic parallels note Akkadian *māmītu* and *nīšu*, Syriac *mumtā* and Hebrew *šᵉbuᶜāh*.[32]

2—For the reading see Caquot, *JANES* 5, 47.

3—As Caquot[33] and Tur-Sinai[34] have recognized, the phrase begins with *šʾX*, and concludes with *ʾmr* and means "pronounce X and say." A careful examination of the published photographs and copies shows that the final sign of the last word on the third line is a partially obliterated *taw*.[35] It is neither *heh* nor *waw* as maintained in earlier studies. The vocable in question is *ʾlt* exactly as in the first line. In fact, the idiom *šʾ ʾlt* is the expected Phoenician correspondent of Hebrew *nśʾ ʾlh* "pronounced an oath" / *nšʾ ʾlh* "bound by oath" attested in 1Kings 8:31 and 2Chron 6:22.[36] The entire phrase is *šʾ ʾlt wlḥnqt ʾmr*. This reading eliminates the alleged *ḥnqt ʾmr* "lamb strangler"[37] from consideration, as well

26 *NERTOT*, 248.

27 *Mélanges … Dussaud*, 425.

28 *KAI* 26 A:III:2; C:IV:5; 62:4; 69:1.

29 *KAI* 14:3, 12.

30 E.g., Ezra 4:10, 11; 6:6; 7:12; *KAI* 224:24; see further, E. Y. Kutscher, *Hebrew and Aramaic Studies* (Jerusalem, 1977), 54. In none of the Aramaic instances does the word mean "right moment" but "now," "now then."

31 The major study of Hebrew *ʾlh* is by H. C. Brichto, *The Problem of "Curse" in the Hebrew Bible* (Philadelphia, 1963), 15–17, 22–71; cf. G. R. Driver, *JSS* 10 (1965), 93–94; Cross, *Canaanite Myth*, 266–267; *Zevit*, IEJ 27, 114.

32 See the dictionaries.

33 *JANES* 5, 47.

34 *Language*, 57.

35 Note especially the table of letters provided by du Mesnil in *Mélanges … Dussaud*, 429.

36 See the variants in BHS.

37 There would be nothing strange about an incantation against stranglers of lambs. Akkadian texts refer to *ḫiniq immeri*, translated by *CAD Ḫ*, 195a as "sheep stricture." Note

as the comparison with Arabic *ḫanuq al ḥamal*.[38] At the same time the suggested comparison with Ugaritic *iltm ḫnqtm*[39] "two strangler goddesses" gains in probability. Last, but not least, the alleged *lamed* vocative of Phoenician vanishes.[40]

5–8—Others have remarked on the poetic pair *bt/ḥṣr* attested in Hebrew and Ugaritic.[41] Note further that the verbal pair *bʾ/drk* "enter/tread" occurs in synonymous parallelism in Mic 5:4, 5.

krt ln ʾlt ʿlm—The verb *krt* might be read as a passive plural, but is most naturally parsed as a third person active plural with indefinite, hence passive, sense. Zevit, in contrast to most scholars, has proposed reading the stich as *krt ln ʾlt ʿlm ʾšr*.[42] It must be objected that his proposed word order of verb, indirect object, direct object, subject would be most unusual in Phoenician.[43] A further objection is that one must then read the following line as *krt ln wkl bn ʾlm*. Zevit attempts to deal with the second objection by discovering a Phoenician pleonastic *waw* (attested only here)![44]

ʾšr—This is the expected Phoenician spelling for which compare KAI 24:8. Aramaic always spells the name with medial *waw*. See KAI 215: 11, 12, 13, 15, 16, 17, 216:9, 217:9.[45]

---

also those texts which mention sheep dying *ina ḫunnuqim* (CAD Ḫ, 238a). Nonetheless, the attention given in actual incantations to female stranglers of humans, especially children, is considerable. See Gaster, *JNES* 6 (1947), 86; Montgomery, *Incantation Texts*, 240; H. Gollancz, *The Book of Protection* (London, 1912), 58:65, 67, 62:78 (identified with Lilith); C. Isbell, *Corpus of the Aramaic Incantation Bowls* (Missoula, 1975), 19:4.

38 Du Mesnil, *Mélanges . . . Dussaud*, 426.

39 Dahood apud Zevit, *IEJ* 27, 112, 115–116.

40 Contrast Albright, *BASOR* 76, 7; Cross and Saley, *BASOR* 197, 45.

41 M. Dahood in *Ras Shamra Parallels*, ed. L. Fisher (Rome, 1972), 153–154 (with bibliography.).

42 IEJ 27, 112, 115–116.

43 Note the following examples: *ytn ln ʾdn mlkm ʾyt dʾr* "the Lord of Kingships gave us Dor" (KAI 14:18–19); *wpʿl ʾnk lšrš ʾdny nʿm* "I treated well the seed of my lord" (KAI 26:A:I:10); *wbrk* DN *ʾyt* RN *bḥym wbšlm* "DN blessed RN with life and health." (*ibid.*, C:III:16–18) In the above cases the verb begins the phrase. Another possibility is to begin with the direct object and to follow with the subject in third or fourth position (KAI 10:6–7; 12:1–3; 19:1–4; 29:1–2). A Phoenician writer may also begin with the subject (KAI 14:16–17; KAI 16). There seem to be no examples of the construction which Zevit assumes for this passage, namely verb, indirect object, direct object, subject. His translation (*IEJ* 27, 112), "Aššur has established an eternal covenant with us" would require a Phoenician: *krt ln ʾšr ʾlt ʿlm, or: ʾšr krt ln ʾlt ʿlm*, or: *ʾlt ʿlm krt ʾšr ln.*

44 *IEJ* 27, 116.

45 The alleged defective spelling of *ʾšr* at Sefîre is doubtful. See J. Fitzmyer, *The Aramaic Inscriptions of Sefîre* (Rome, 1995), 84.

The presence of the god Asshur requires comment. In Assyrian incantation texts Asshur is usually not mentioned.[46] It is extremely likely that the name of a Phoenician god stood here in an earlier form of this incantation. The most likely candidate would be *ʾl qn ʾrṣ*,[47] El, Creator of Earth. The talents of El as an exorcist were celebrated as early as the Keret epic.[48] Asshur displaced some native Phoenician divinity in the present text because Ḫadattu was an Assyrian province.[49] It will be recalled that Asshur replaced Marduk as hero in the Assyrian recension of *enūma eliš.*

The first subject of the phrase *ʾšr krt ln* is singular. It follows that the verb *krt* is singular and that the following *kl bn ʾlm* refers to each individual divinity rather than to their aggregate. Phoenician *ʾlm* "divinity," "god," "goddess" is attested as early as the Karatepe inscriptions.[50] It need hardly be pointed out that the Semitic words for "son" appear often in the construct-genitive in the sense "belonging-to-the-category-of." Note in addition that the Ugaritic *bn ilm* is a regular epithet of the god Mot and singular in number.[51]

wrb—Phoenician *rb* is a well-attested title. The feminine *rbt* is very commonly applied to goddesses. Accordingly, it is not surprising to find *rb* alongside *bn ʾlm.*[52]

dr kl qdšn—Tur-Sinai's observation[53] that the last word must be read as *qᵉdôšenu* has, unfortunately, been all but ignored. In the Eshmunazor inscription Phoenician *qdšm* stands in apposition to *ʾlnm* "gods."[54] In the Arslan

46 Röllig, *NESE* 2, 21–22.

47 For this Phoenician god see conveniently F. Bron, *Recherches sur les inscriptions phéniciennes de Karatepe* (Geneva, 1979), 186–187.

48 *CTA* 16:v:10 ff (=*KTU*³ 1.16:v:25f.).

49 On Assyrian religious policy in subject territories see M. Cogan, *Imperialism and Religion: Assyria, Judah and Israel in the Eighth and Seventh Centuries, B.C.E.* (Missoula, 1974).

50 *KAI* 26: A:I:8, II:6, III:10, C:III:11, 19. For discussion, with bibliography, see Bron, *Recherches*, 49–50.

51 *CTA* 3A: i:3–4; 5:vi:10; 6:1:42–43; iii: 3, 9, 21; iv:29, 40 [=*KTU*³ 1.3:i:3–4; 1.5:vi:10; 1.6:i:42–43; 1.6:iii:1,3,9,21; 1.6:iv:5, 6,16). It has been suggested that the same term occurs in Ammonite. But see P. Dion, *RB* 82 (1975), 31 (with bibliography).

52 Cf. Tur-Sinai, *Language*, 58.

53 *Ibid.*, 59; A. van den Branden (apud *Röllig*, *NESE* 2, 22) translated "tutti nostri santuari" which is grammatically and linguistically unexceptionable but unlikely in context.

54 In *KAI* 14:9 *hʾlnm hqdšm* is to be understood as "the gods, the holy ones." It is well known that Phoenician, unlike Hebrew, does not duplicate the definite article before both noun and adjective, nor does it repeat the definite article before both the noun and the demonstrative pronoun. The author of *KAI* 14 observed this rule as shown by the phrases *ʾrṣt dgn hʾdrt* "the great corn lands" (l. 19) *hmmlkt hʾ* "that ruler" (l. 22) and *hʾdmm hmt* "those

Tash text *qdšn* "our holy beings" understood as a suffixed form,[55] eliminates recourse to an alleged Aramaism *qaddišîn.*[56]

13–14—Caquot's[57] recovery of an *ʿayin* at the end of line 13 virtually demands the restoration of *dalet* at the beginning of line 14. Cf. *yrḥ md yrḥ ʿd ʿlm*[58] "from month to month, forever"; *ybrky wyšmʿ ql ʿd ʿlm*[59] "May they bless him and hear his voice forever!"

15—Caquot[60] was able to discern a *lamed* at the beginning of the line. The title *zbl bʿl ʾrṣ*, "the prince, the lord of earth" is known from Ugaritic.[61] The "prince of demons" Beelzebub[62] has, of course, been known much longer from the New Testament. If the restoration suggested here, *bʿl [zb]l ʾrṣ*, proves correct, then it provides a transitional form[63] between an Ugaritic epithet of Baal and a Christian epithet of Satan.

16–17—The restoration of [*ʾ*]*št* "wife" appears certain.[64] It is best to understand *ṣrty* as "her rivals," namely, as the rivals of Lady Hauron, rather than as "his wives" as has usually been suggested. Though the same individuals are involved, it is smoother on poetic grounds to oppose the Lady Hauron and her rivals to the eight wives of Baal. In Hebrew, *ṣrh* does not refer to the status of wives with regard to their husband but rather to the status of rival wives of a single husband to one another.[65]

ḥwrn-The spelling of the name of this well-known god with medial *waw* may reflect a dialectal pronunciation. Note that in the Mesha inscription the place

---

commoners." (*ibid.*). Finally, note the warning *lm ysgrnm hʾlnm hqdšm ʾl* "lest the gods, these holy ones deliver them over." (*ibid.*, 21–22).

55 Cf. the suffixed forms of *qdš* referring to a divinity in Isa 43:15, 49:7.

56 Contrast Cross and Saley, *BASOR* 197, 48.

57 *JANES* 5, 48.

58 KAI 43:12.

59 KAI 78:1.

60 *JANES* 5, 48.

61 See the references and the important remarks of M. Held in *JAOS* 88 (1968), 91.

62 Matt 10:25, 12:24, 27; Mark 3:22; Luke 11:15, 18–19.

63 See further the Punic feminine name Bʿlʾzbl (*KAI* 67:1–2). See *KAI* II, 82; Cf. N. Slouschz, *Thesaurus of Phoenician Inscriptions* (Tel-Aviv, 1942), 139.

64 The *šin* and *taw* are very clear. In contrast to du Mesnil (*Mélanges . . . Dussaud*, 422, 428), and Albright (*BASOR*, 76, 9), who first suggested *ʾšt*, Caquot (*JANES* 5, 49) restores [*lḥ*]*št*. Though graphically possible his restoration leaves *bʿl*[*t*] in mid-air.

65 For Biblical Hebrew see 1Sam 1:6. Cf. the verbal form *liṣrôr* "marry a woman as a rival to her sister" in Lev 18:18. In later Hebrew *ṣrh* as "rival wife" is particularly well-attested. See e.g. *m. Yeb.* 1:1 (*passim*), 2 (*passim*), 4, 15:4; *t. Yeb.* 1:1–10.

name *ḥwrnn* (*KAI* 181:31, 32), which is, in all likelihood related to the name of the god, is spelled with a medial *waw.*

13–18—At first blush the closing formula seems incomplete. The prepositional *bet* of *bʾlt* in lines 13, 14, 15 leads the reader to anticipate a final verb such as "be conjured," "be gone" or the like. This is especially true if one compares such formulae as Old Babylonian *utammīki māmīt Ea lū tattalakī*[66] "I have conjured you with the conjuration of Ea, be gone!" One might also cite texts closer in time to the Arslan Tash incantations such as *māmīt nīš šamê lū tamâti nīš erṣeti lū tamâti*[67] "Oath, by the life of heaven be conjured! By the life of earth be conjured!" Yet the present closing phrase is not without parallels. A closing formula in the nearly contemporary Maqlu series is: *ina qibīt iqbû* DN "By the command spoken by god-so-and-so."[68]

ʾš tm py wšbʿ ṣrty—The *yods* are third person feminine pronominal suffixes. Ginsberg has shown that in Standard Phoenician, original *-h-* was eliminated by syncopation under some phonetic conditions. In the Arslan Tash variety of Standard Phoenician the third person suffix became *-y-* under all conditions. Note the writings *mrkbty* "his chariot," *ʾty* "with him," and *mnty* "its spell."[69]

Much scholarly discussion in recent years had been devoted to the question of when the notion of Yahweh's covenant with Israel first arose. Some writers have argued that the biblical idea is early and quite possibly Mosaic. Others have held it to be a much later development.[70] The Arslan Tash incantation studied in this paper has been adduced in the controversy but its implications have not been fully realized.[71] First, it must be noted that although the inscription was found in Syria, the fact that it was written in Phoenician brings it into close connection with ancient Israel. That Phoenician mythology and cultic terminology greatly influenced the religious conceptions of ancient Israel scarcely requires demonstration. Secondly, though the present inscription dates from the seventh century BCE. there are several indications that its

---

66 *Or* 23 (1954), 338:20–21.

67 Šurpu v–vi:58; cf., e.g., CT 16:12:ii:4, 13;ii:10, BMS 53 r. 29.

68 Maqlu I:36.

69 See his discussion in *JANES* 5, 141–146; contrast Cross and Freedman, *JNES* 10 (1951), 228–230.

70 For a discussion with extensive bibliography see D. McCarthy, *Treaty and Covenant* (Rome, 1978).

71 See Zevit, *IEJ* 27; Cross and Saley, *BASOR* 197. M. Weinfeld, "berith," in G. Botterwick and H. Ringgren eds., *Theological Dictionary of the Old Testament* (Grand Rapids, 1975), 278, writes, "the idea of a covenant between a deity and a people is unknown to us from other religions and cultures." Yet *ibid.*, 259 the idiom *krt ln ʾlt* is correctly cited from our inscription.

origins are older. It will be recalled that it is common for incantations to reflect commonly accepted and popular beliefs rather than the rarefied speculations of theologians. If so, then it was not novel to speak of a covenant between divinities and human beings well before the incantation was composed. In fact, the second incantation bears a colophon indicating that its source was an older scroll.[72] The derivative character of the present text of the incantation is shown by the mention of Asshur, rather than a Phoenician deity, as the first god whose covenant protects the house and courtyard against the Flyers.[73] At the same time the notion of a covenant between gods and mortals would not have sounded odd to native Mesopotamian ears. The verb *salāmu* is well attested in Akkadian prayer literature in the sense of reconciliation between a worshiper and his gods.[74] The selfsame verb is employed regularly in the terminology of political alliance and covenant.[75] Of particular interest is a twelfth century "prophecy" uttered by Marduk, who said of a certain prince: *rubû šû mātāti kalîšina ibêl u anākūma ilū kalâma ittišu salmāku Elamta iḫeppe*, "That prince shall rule all the lands. For I alone, all you gods, have a covenant with him. He shall destroy Elam."[76]

The Israelite idea of covenant with a god was not, in itself, a departure from ancient Near Eastern religious ideas. The innovation lay in the impetus which the covenant notion gave to the gradual rise of Israelite monotheism, a process described in detail elsewhere.[77]

---

72 See Gaster, *BASOR* 209, 19; cf. Cross, *CBQ* 36, 487, 489.

73 See the discussion of ll. 5–8, above.

74 For references see Mullo Weir Lexicon, 293; AHw., 1013.

75 See AHw., 1014; further, M. Held, *BASOR* 200 (1970), 33.

76 For the text and the date see R. Borger, BiOr 28 (1971), 11:Col. III: 21'–22, 21. Whether the reform text of Uru-KA-gina actually refers to a covenant with the god Ningirsu is uncertain. See McCarthy, *Treaty*, 31, n. 6.

77 S. D. Sperling, "Monotheism and Ancient Israelite Religion," in *A Companion to the Ancient near East*, ed. D. Snell (Malden, 2005), 408–420.

CHAPTER 7

KAI 24 Re-Examined

The Phoenician inscription[1] of King Kilamuwa has been studied many times since its discovery at Zenjirli in 1902. Nonetheless, numerous problems of interpretation remain. Ironically, the most difficult passages are the similes in ll. 6–7, 10, and 13 and the cliché in 1. 8, which were no doubt employed by the royal scribe to make king's message clear and accessible. The method employed in the present paper[2] is based on the well-known facts that two dialects of Aramaic were spoken at ancient Zenjirli and that political alliance with Assyria had linguistic impact. The Phoenician employed by Kilamuwa's scribe is examined here against Zenjirli literary tradition as well as against the multilingual background. It is hoped that the new interpretations offered will add to our understanding of this most interesting ancient text.[3]

1 ʾnk. klmw. br. ḥy<ʾ>[4]
2 mlk.gbr.[5] ʿl. yʾdy. wbl. p[ʿl]
3 kn bnh.[6] wbl°. pʿl. wkn. ʾb°. ḥ°y°. wbl. pʿl. wkn. ʾḥ

---

1 This is Kilamuwa's only extant Phoenician inscription. The king's shorter inscription, erroneously included in the Phoenician section of KAI as KAI 25, is Samalian. See H. L. Ginsberg, "Ugaritico-Phoenicia," in *The Gaster Festschrift*, ed. D. Marcus (New York, 1973), 146–147; More recently, J. Gibson, *Textbook of Syrian Semitic Inscriptions* (hereafter TSSI; Oxford, 1982), III, 39 has described the shorter inscription as "an Aramaic inscription with Phoenician orthography."

2 I thank Ziony Zevit, whose paper "Phoenician *nbš/npš* and its Hebrew Semantic Equivalents," delivered to the 1984 meeting of the American Oriental Society, reawakened my interest in KAI 24. Professor Zevit kindly provided me with a pre-publication copy of that paper, which subsequently appeared in *Maarav* 5–6 (1990), 337–344.

3 For bibliography see ANET, 654–655; KAI III, 31; Gibson, TSSI III, 33.

4 The photograph in KAI I (pl. xxvii; reproduced from *Cahiers de Byrsa* 8 [1958/59], pl. II) shows that the mason left no space for the *aleph* in the name of Kilamuwa's father, an omission indicated by M. Lidzbarski, *Ephemeris für semitische Epigraphik III* (Giessen, 1909–1915), 224–225, but not by KAI or TSSI. In lines 3 and9, the name is spelled with final *aleph* (the writing with initial *heh*, rather than *ḥet* in TSSI III, 34, 9, is a misprint). In KAI 25 it occurs once again as *ḥy*.

5 The photograph shows that the mason left enough space for a single letter between the *lamed* and the *kaph*. The *kaph* of *mlk* almost touches the *gimel* of the next word, but is separated from it by a word divider.

6 The second letter of the royal name appears clearly as *nun* in the photograph. The copy in S. Birnbaum, *The Hebrew Scripts Part Two the Plates* (London, 1954–1957), pl. 014, reproduced

 | DOI 10.1163/9789004340879_008

4 š'l. wbl. pʿl. w'nk°. kl°mw. <g>br. t°m- m'š. pʿlt
5 bl. pʿl. hlpnyhm. kn. bt 'by. bmtkt. mlkm. 'd
6 rm. wkl. šlḥ. yd. lld°m. wkt. byd. mlk° m km'š. 'klt
7 zqn. w°[km] 'š. 'klt. yd. w'dr ʿly mlk. d[n]nyn. wškr.
8 'nk. ʿly. mlk 'šr. ʿlmt.[7] ytn. bš. wg° br. bswt.

---

9 'nk. klmw. br ḥy'. yšbt. ʿl. ks'. 'by. lpn. hm
10 lkm. hlpnym. ytlnn. mškbm. km. klbm. w'nk. lmy. kt. 'b. wlmy. kt. 'm.
11 wlmy. kt. 'ḥ. wmy. bl ḥz. pn. š. šty. bʿl. ʿdr. wmy bl ḥz. pn. 'lp. šty. bʿl
12 bqr. wbʿl. ksp. wbʿl. ḥrṣ. wmy. bl. ḥz. ktn. lmnʿry. wbymy. ksy. b
13 ṣ. w'nk. tmkt. mškbm. lyd. whmt. št. nbš. km. nbš. ytm. b'm. wmy. bbn
14 y 'š. yšb. tḥtn. wyzq. bspr z. mškbm. 'l ykbd. lbʿrrm. wbʿrr
15 m. 'l ykbd. lmškbm wmy. yšḥt. hspr z. yšḥt. r'š. bʿl. ṣmd. 'š. lgbr
16 wyšḥt. r'š. bʿlḥmn. 'š. lbmh. wrkb'l. bʿl. bt.

Translation

I am Kilamuwa bar Hayya. Gabbar ruled over Ya'diya but did no[t] (what I have done). Thereafter followed Bnh who did not (what I have done). And thereafter followed my father Hayya who did not (what I have done). And thereafter followed my brother Š'l who did not (what I have done). But I Kilamuwa, perfect <hero>, what I have done, the predecessors did not. My father's household was in the midst of mighty kings, and all set a hand to their extirpation. But I in the hand of those kings was like a beard-consuming fire and [li]ke a hand-consuming fire. But the King of the Danonians was too powerful for me,[8] so I hired against him the King of Assyria. He gave a maid for barley and a man for groats.

I Kilamuwa, succeeded to my father's throne. In the presence of the kings, the predecessors, the Mškbm had bedded down like dogs. But I, to whomever, was a father, and to whomever, was a mother, and to whomever, was a brother. And whoever had not seen the face of a sheep, him I made a flock-owner. And whoever had not seen the face of an ox, him I made a herd-owner and an owner of

from F. von Luschan, *Ausgrabungen in Sendschirli* 4 (1911), likewise has a clear *nun*. Either the form here or *bmh* in l. 16 is a mason's error.

7 The reading *wʿlmt* in *TSSI*, III, 34 is a misprint.

8 For the construction of the comparative with *ʿl* see M. Held, "A Faithful Lover in an Old Babylonian Dialogue," *JCS* 15 (1961), 24.

silver and gold. And whoever had not seen linen from his very youth, why in my day, they covered him with byssus. And I held on to the hand of the Mškbm and them I gave life, like the life the fatherless child gives the mother. And if any of my sons who succeeds me slights this inscription, may the Mškbm not show regard for the Bʿrrm and may the Bʿrrm not show regard for the Mškbm. And whoever smashes this inscription, may Baal Ṣmd, who is Gabbar's (personal god) smash his head, and may Baalhamman who is Bmh's (personal god) smash his head, and likewise Rakkubel, Lord of the dynasty.[9]

Commentary

I. 2 *bl pʿl*—The above translation is based on Landsberger's: "machte es nicht (anticipativ)."[10] Long ago, Torrey observed that the king "would hardly have committed the *faux pas* of boasting that he 'did more' than those who had 'done nothing.'"[11] The accuracy of that observation is bolstered by Akkadian royal inscriptions, which influenced Northwest Semitic inscriptional style.[12] In the closest verbal parallels to the Kilamuwa inscription, those in which Akkadian *epēšu*, semantically equivalent to Phoenician *pʿl*, is employed, the royal speakers do not say that their predecessors did nothing. Instead, they boast that their specific achievements outweigh those of the previous kings.[13] Thus, Shamshi-Adad I refers to a temple tower: *ša eli maḫri qadmišu nēpešu rabû naklu lū ēpuš bītam ša kiʾam mimmūšu šuklulū šarrum mannama ana Ištar ina Ninua lā īpušu* "whose workmanship was greater and more skillful than before, I built; a temple so completely adorned, no other king had ever

9 The same title recurs at Zenjirli in *KAI* 215:2.

10 B. Landsberger, *Samʾal I* (Ankara, 1948), 51; cf. A. Poebel, *Das appositionell bestimmte Pronomen der 1. Pers. Sing. in den westsemitischen Inschriften und im Alten Testament*, (Chicago, 1932), 34–35.

11 C. C. Torrey, "The Zakar and Kalamu Inscriptions," *JAOS* 35 (1915–17), 366.

12 The stylistic and linguistic connections between the Mesopotamian and West-Semitic royal inscriptions were first demonstrated by Poebel, *Pronomen* and have been elaborated by numerous scholars. For a recent statement see M. Barré, "A Note on *ršʾt* in the Karatepe Inscription," *JANES* 15 (1981), 1–3. Any lingering doubts should be dispelled by the Assyrian-Aramaic royal inscription from Tell Fakhariyeh. For bibliography of studies on Fakhariyeh see S. Kaufman, "The Pitfalls of Typology," *HUCA* 57 (1986), 8, n. 17; Add M. Fales, "Le double bilinguisme de la statue de Tell Fekhyere," *Syria* 60 (1983), 233–250.

13 The comparisons don't always employ *epēšu*. For a study of the motif of superiority to the earlier kings see R. Gelio, *apud* F. M. Fales, "Kilamuwa and the Foreign Kings: Propaganda vs. Power," *WO* 10 (1979), 7, n. 6.

built for Ishtar in Nineveh."[14] Similarly Hammurapi: *dūram ṣīram lū ēpuš ša ištu um ṣi'ātim šarru in šarrī manāma lā īpušu ana* DN *bēliya rabîš lū ēpussum* "Truly, I constructed a majestic wall; one like no king among kings whoseoever from days of old had built, I built magnificently for him, my lord Shamash."[15] Yahdun-Lim makes a like claim about a city: *ša ištu ūm ṣi'ātim šarrum šumšu ālam lā īpušu anāku lalâm aršīma ālam ēpuš* "From days of old no king had ever built a city (in that arid place) but I realized my desire and built the city."[16] Of greatest interest are the Kapara inscriptions from Tell-Halaf.[17] These furnish the closest parallel to Kilamuwa's use of the superiority motif by referring to the immediate ancestors: *ša Ad-ya AD-AD-ya DINGIR-lim lā ēpušūni anāku ētapša*[18] "That which my departed father and grandfather did not do, I did." In two of these inscriptions,[19] the words *ša AD-ya AD-AD-ya* precede a partially-broken reference to a stone construction and continue: *lā e-pa* (for *-pu*) *šu-ni anāku e-*[*tapša*]. Meissner translated "was mein Vater und mein Großvater aus [Basalt]st[ein?] nicht getan haben, habe ich ge[tan]."[20] In other words, Kapara bested his ancestors in the specific area of stone-constructions. Kilamuwa, for his part, bested his ancestors in his specific socio-political gains. The general sense of the superiority motif is conveyed most clearly in a statement by Nabopolassar: *šarru ša epšētušu eli šarrāni abbēšu šūtuqā anāku* "That king whose deeds surpass those of his royal ancestors am I."[21]

l. 2–3 *mlk RN*... *kn RN2*... *kn RN3..wkn RN4*—Phoenician *kn* has here a technical meaning "reigned," "succeeded to the throne." Cf. Byblian *km'š lmklyt 'š kn lpny*[22] "in the manner of the queens who reigned before me." For Hebrew *hāyâ* employed similarly see Jer 34:5. Cf. too, the phrase *we'aḥarâw hāyâ* to describe the "judgeship" of Shamgar in Judg 3:31.[23]

---

14 Borger Einleitung 1:11:4–12; cf. Grayson ARI I, 23.

15 See I. Gelb, "A New Clay-Nail of Hammurabi," *JNES* 7 (1948), 269:18–23; cf. F. Thureau-Dangin, "L'inscription bilingue B de Samsu-iluna," *RA* 39 (1942–1944), 8:54–61.

16 F. Thureau-Dangin, "Iahdunlim, Roi de Hana," *RA* (1936), 51:ii:12–17.

17 See B. Meissner, "Die Keilschrifttexte auf den steinernen Orthostaten und Statuen aus dem Tell Halâf," in *Festschrift Max Freiherrn von Oppenheim zum 70. Geburtstag* (=*AfO Beiband 1*), ed. E. Weidner (Berlin, 1933), 71–81.

18 *Ibid.*, 72:2–3.

19 *Ibid.*, 75–76.

20 *Ibid.*

21 VAB 4 66:18–20.

22 *KAI* 11.

23 The word *yihyû* in Ps 45:17 is correctly translated "succeed" by NJPS. In Ps 89:37 *yihyeh* should probably be translated "reign" or "rule."

l. 4 *<g>br tm*—The general tendency has been to understand *br tm-* as a matronymic to distinguish Kilamuwa from his brother S'l.[24] Torrey however, seeing here an epithet, translated "man of integrity."[25] An epithet would indeed seem to be in place at this point in order to provide a transition to Kilamuwa's claim that he accomplished what his predecessors had not. Rather though, than introduce the blatant Aramaism *br* outside of the royal patronymic,[26] we should read *<g>br*[27] *tmm*,[28] "perfect man," "flawless hero," which is attested in Hebrew,[29] and which would provide a Phoenician reflex of such Akkadian royal epithets as *qarrādu gitmālu* "flawless hero,"[30] *zikaru dannu*, "strong male,"[31] *eṭlu dannu* "valorous man,"[32] and Sennacherib's self-characterization: *eṭlum gitmālu*[33] "perfect male," "flawless hero."

l. 5 *hlpnyhm*—cf. *hlpnym* in l. 10. The phrases *šarrānu pānuttu*[*m*] at Mari[34] and *šarrānu pānû* attested at Amarna[35] apparently reflect West-Semitic usage of the type found here. The presence in the inscription of both forms, *hlpnyhm* and *hlpnym*, is clear in the photograph and has been affirmed by Hermann

---

24 So, most recently, *TSSI* III, 36. Landsberger (*Sam'al*, 51) offers the variant theory that *tm-* is a tribal name.

25 Torrey, *JAOS* 35, 365–366. The translation was based on the reading *bar tummat*; H. Bauer, "Die *klmw*-Inschrift aus Sendschirli," *ZDMG* 67 (1913), 685, offers "der Mann der Ganzheit." Among recent scholars to take this tack is T. Collins, "The Kilamuwa Inscription—A Phoenician Poem," *WO* 6 (1971), 184–185, who translates: "a man of perfection."

26 The "Samalian patronymic was regarded as an untranslatable proper name." So, Ginsberg, "Ugaritico-Phoenicia," 146.

27 In the inscription itself, the noun *gbr* "man" is opposed to *'lmt* "maid" (l. 8; cf. Prv 30:19). Cf. too, the proper name Gabbar, which is probably etymologically related. The noun *gbrth* "his strength" is attested at Zenjirli in the Samalian inscription KAI 214:32.

28 Both *tm* and *tmm* are possibilities. For references in Phoenician and Punic see R. Tomback, *A Comparative Semitic Lexicon of the Phoenician and Punic Languages* (Missoula, 1978), 340–341, 342.

29 Hebrew vacillates between *gibbôr tāmîm* in 2Sam 22:26 and *gĕbar* (Aramaism?) *tāmîm* in Ps 18:26. On these verses see G. Schmuttermayr, *Psalm 18 and 2Samuel 22:Studien zu einem Doppeltext* (Munich, 1970), 99–103; see further, A. Abou Assaf, P. Bordreuil and A. Millard, *La Statue de Tell Fekherye et son inscription bilingue assyro-araméenne* (Paris, 1982), 32–33.

30 For *qarrādu gitmālu* "flawless warrior" see Borger Esarh. 96:22; cf. Streck Asb. 176 no. 5:1; Lambert BWL, 268, rs. iii:5; see also Seux Epithètes, 97, 231.

31 *For references see Seux, Epithètes*, 378. Both *eṭlu* and *zikaru* share overlapping semantic ranges of "maleness" and "heroism."

32 See *CAD E*, 410b.

33 OIP 2 55:3.

34 ARMT I:3:10'.

35 EA 129:46.

who re-examined the original.[36] Lidzbarski's suggestion to read in both lines *hlpnym*, a gentilic formed from *lepanim* "previously," thus *hlpnym*, "the previous ones"[37] was opposed by Poebel on the ground that gentilics formed from prepositions in this manner were unattested anywhere in Semitic.[38] Ugaritic *qdmym* however, a gentilic formed from the preposition *qdm*, vitiates Poebel's objection. Note: *qrʾu rpʾim qdmym* "Summon the most ancient Rephaim," and *tḥt rpʾim qdmym* "below the most ancient Rephaim."[39]

kn bt ʾby—Beginning here, the writer employs themes and expressions that were, or became, customary in the royal inscriptions at Zenjirli, regardless of their language of composition. For the *bt ʾb*, see *KAI* 214:9 (Samalian dialect);[40] 215:2 (Samalian); 216:7, 12 (Standard Aramaic).

bmtkt mlkn ʾdrm—Lidzbarski[41] already remarked on the identity of the phrase with Bar-Hadad's *bmṣʿt mlkn rbrbn*.[42] The equivalence of *bmṣʿt* and *bmtkt* is demonstrated by the translation of Hebrew *bĕtôk haggan* (Gen 3:3) by *Tg.Onq.* as *bimṣīʿût gintâ*. In all likelihood, the form *bmtkt* acquired its preformative *mem* on the analogy of Aramaic *bmṣʿt*.[43] Note that in Ugaritic the form is *btk*.[44]

mlkm ʾdrm—For the motif of the rival mighty kings in Phoenician cf. *mmlk<t> ʾdr* "mighty ruler." (*KAI* 14:9) Cf. Hebrew *mĕlākîm ʾadirîm //gĕdolîm* (Ps 136:17–18).[45] The mighty kings recur in the Standard Aramaic of Zenjirli as *mlkn rbrbn*[46] and in the Samalian of Zenjirli as *mlky kbr*.[47]

36 S. Hermann, "Bemerkungen zur Inschrift des Königs Kilamuwa von Senğirli," *OLZ* 48 (1953), 295–297.

37 Lidzbarski, *Ephemeris* III, 227. Lidzbarski was unsure how to explain the intrusive *heh* in *hlpnyhm*.

38 Poebel, *Pronomen*, 34, n. 4.

39 *KTU*³ 1.161:8, 24. On the text see B. Levine and J.-M. Tarragon, "Dead Kings and Rephaim: The Patrons of the Ugaritic Dynasty," *JAOS* 104 (1984), 650–659. For a possible reflex in Eblaite, see P. Steinkeller, "The Eblaite Preposition *qidimay* 'Before'," *Oriens Antiquus* 23 (1984), 33–37.

40 For a discussion of the dialect see R. Garr, *Dialect Geography of Syria-Palestine, 1000–586 B.C.E.* (Philadelphia, 1985), 230–231.

41 *Ephemeris*, 227–228.

42 *KAI* 216:9; cf. *KAI* 215:10.

43 The *mem* of *bmṣʿt* of course is radical.

44 *CTA* 15:III:14 (=*KTU*³ 1.15:iii:14); cf. also the form *btkt* in *KAI* 10:5 (Byblian).

45 Cf. also Heb *mĕlākîm ʿaṣûmîm* (Ps 135:10).

46 Note that targum and Peshitta to Ps 136:17–18 translate *mĕlākîm gĕdolîm* by *malkîn rabrĕbîn* and *malkê rawrĕbê* respectively, but translate *ʾadîrîm* a.l. by *gewtānîn* and *ʿašînê*.

47 *KAI* 215:12; cf. *ibid.*, 10.

I. 6 *wkl šlḥ yd. lld°m-* Tawil has aptly compared the idiom *šlḥ yd* with Akkadian *qāta (w)abālu*.[48] In his opinion however, the Akkadian idiom carries "at least two different connotations": The physical sense "touch, harm" and "to plot/scheme (mentally)." Accordingly, Tawil who reads *wkl šlḥ yd llḥm*, translates the phrase: "My father's dynasty was in the midst of mighty kings, everybody conspired/schemed to do battle."[49] But although some occurrences of *qāta wabālu* and Hebrew *šlḥ yd*[50] might be best translated "conspire,"[51] the fact that the Kilamuwa text goes on to say *wkt byd mlkm* "but I was in the kings' hand…" shows that *kl*[52] *šlḥ yd* in KAI 24 describes a physical action.[53]

In the following word the two *lameds* are clear in the photograph, as is the final *mem*. Scholars have generally read the unclear letter as a *ḥet* and explained the vocable in one of two ways.[54] O'Connor, to cite a recent example, turns to the well-attested *lḥm* "to do battle"[55] and translates "each stretched forth

48 H. Tawil, "Two Notes on the Treaty Terminology of the Sefîre Inscriptions," CBQ 42 (1980), 35–37.

49 *Ibid.*, 35.

50 For a study of biblical Hebrew *šlḥ yd* see P. Humbert, "Étendre le main," VT 12 (1962), 383–395. See further, E. Greenstein, "Trans-Semitic Idiomatic Equivalency and the Derivation of Hebrew *ml'kh*," UF 11 (1979), 334–335.

51 See Tawil, "Two Notes," 35–37 for some suggestions. Certainly, most of the Hebrew attestations of *šlḥ yd* are physical. See e.g. Exod 22:7, 10, 24:11; Deut 25:11; Judg 5:26; 1Sam 26:9; 2Sam 15:5; 1Kgs 13:4; Job 28:9. The fact of the matter is that for the ancients, words, and expressions for physical actions could express intent. Conversely, terms for thought and volition could describe physical action. See W. Moran, "The Conclusion of the Decalogue (Ex 20.17, Dt 5.21)," CBQ 29 (1967), 543–554. Within the Semitic languages, anatomical expressions in particular lend themselves to idiomatic construction. Only careful attention to context enables us to decide among literal, semi-literal and idiomatic renderings. See M. Gruber, "The Many Faces of Hebrew *nś' pnym* 'lift up the face,'" ZAW 95 (1983), 252–260, with references to earlier literature.

52 For *kl* without a qualifying substantive elsewhere in Zenjirli, cf. *wbyt 'by* [˺]*ml mn kl* "My dynasty exerted itself more than any other." (KAI 216:7–8).

53 Indeed, in many instances Heb *šlḥ yd* bears the connotation "do harm." See Humbert, VT 12, 387–388; Greenstein, UF 11, 335. (Note that *Tg.Onq.* to Exod 24:11 translates *lô' šālaḥ yādô* by *lâ' hawâ nizqâ*.) In Ugaritic as well, *šlḥ yd* has a literal sense. See CTA 15:iv:24–25 (=KTU^3 1.15:iv:24–25). For *šlḥ yd* in the literal sense in the Aramaic of Sefire see J. Fitzmyer, *The Aramaic Inscriptions of Sefire* (Rome, 1995), 50, line 27; A. Lemaire and J.-M. Durand, *Les Inscriptions araméennes de Sfiré et L'Assyrie de Shamshi-ilu* (Paris, 1984), 115–117.

54 See DISO, 137.

55 For the dialectal distribution of "to do battle" see M. Held, "*mḫṣ/mḫš* in Ugaritic and other Semitic Languages (A Study in Comparative Lexicography)," JAOS 79 (1959), 172.

his hand to fight."[56] Others who concur in reading *llḥm*, relate the vocable to the homographous *lḥm*, meaning "eat" in Ugaritic and "dine" in Hebrew,[57] and translate approximately: "everyone stretched out his hand to consume (it)."[58] Actually, the photograph shows the outlines of a *dalet*, yielding a reading *lldm*, to be interpreted as a suffixed infinitive of *lwd*[59] "eradicate." As demonstrated by the Assyrian-Aramaic bilingual from Tell Fakhariyeh, a text roughly contemporary[60] with the Kilamuwa inscription, *lwd* is the interdialectal equivalent of Akkadian *nasāḫu*, "remove," "expel," "extirpate,"[61] a meaning that would be most appropriate in the present context.

II. 6–7 *wkt byd mlkm*[62] *km'š 'klt zqn w°[km] 'š 'klt yd*—There is no doubt that some simile, introduced by *km*, and involving "hand" and "beard" is found here.[63] There is much disagreement, however, about whether *'š* is to

56 O'Connor, *BASOR* 226, 19. For other recent translations in this vein cf. *KAI* II, 31. Cf. further, Hermann *OLZ* 48, 298–299. Hermann claims that his personal examination revealed the remnants of a *ḥet*. He however, emends the text to: *l<h>lḥm*, by moving the anomalous *heh* from *hlpnyhm* in the line above. Contrast Tawil, "Two Notes," 36, n. 31; *TSSI* III, 36.

57 The verb *lḥm* is more poetic than *'kl*. On *lḥm* in Hebrew and Ugaritic see, Y. Avishur, *Stylistic Studies of Word-Pairs in Biblical and Ancient Semitic Literatures* (= AOAT 210; Kevelaer, 1984), 379–380, with references to earlier literature.

58 See e.g. Rosenthal, *ANET*, 654; D. Marcus, "The Term 'Chin' in the Semitic Languages," *BASOR* 226, 57; *TSSI* III, 34. Cf. Collins, *WO* 6, 85: "Everyone stretched out his hand to the morsel." Poebel, *Pronomen*, 35 offers the grammatically difficult: "um mich zu verschlingen," which would require **llḥmn*.

59 For discussion of the etymology of *lwd* (alternatively: *ldd*), see Fitzmyer, *Sefîre*, 119.

60 For the ninth-century date see Kaufman, *HUCA* 57 (1986), 8–10.

61 See Fakh Aramaic 9 = Akkadian 12–13. Cf. Lemaire and Durand, *Sfiré*, 142. Note however, that the occurrences of *lwd* in Sefîre have the sense "remove text," "efface" (IIC 2,6,9, [obj. *spry'*]; IC, 18 [obj. *mn mly'*]) and thus correspond more closely to Akkadian *nukkuru* (references in *CAD N/I*, 166–167) "remove an inscription" (cf. Fakh Akkadian 16–17 = Aramaic 11–12) and *pašāṭu* (references in AHw., 844) "erase," "efface" (cf. Fakh Akkadian 26–28 = Aramaic 16–17) than to Akkadian *nasāḫu*.

62 Marcus, BASOR 226, 57 translates "now I was under the control of kings."

63 Collins (*WO* 6, 183–188) may have overstated the case in describing *KAI* 24 as a Phoenician poem (M. O'Connor, "The Rhetoric of the Kilamuwa Inscription, *BASOR* 226 [1977], 15–18), but the inscription does employ parallelism and other poetic techniques. O'Connor's rendition of *wkt byd mlkm* as an independent clause, "And I was in the hand of th(os)e kings" (*ibid.*, 19), makes the author of *KAI* 24 much less of a poet than necessary. It seems more plausible to follow the general approach of Fales, who finds in the Kilamuwa inscription an opposition between "the age before the king" and the "age of the king" (*WO* 10, 7). Two units of approximately equal length contrast the age of Kilamuwa's *bt 'b* with his own. The first is described beginning *kn bt 'by* "My father's dynasty was ..." and ending with *lldm*. The second begins with the contrasting *wkt* "But I was ...," and ends with *yd*.

be understood as the word for "fire,"[64] as the Standard Phoenician relative pronoun,[65] or even as the grammatically difficult "man."[66] Scholars have attempted to support their respective positions by appealing to parallels, but their choice of alleged parallels has been determined by the prior interpretation of the lexeme *ʾš*. Thus, Avishur for example, compares *kʾš ʾklt* "(Yahweh's presence on the mountain top was) like a raging fire," (Exod 24:17)[67] but while the text examined here contains the objects "beard" and "hand" there is no object in the biblical texts cited by Avishur. Gevirtz[68] understands *ʾš* as a pronoun, translating, "and I was… as one who eats (his) beard and as one who eats (his) hand." He compares an Akkadian text: *maḫḫūtiš illikma ina miqit ṭē[m]e unaššak rittīšu*[69] "he went insane and in his madness[70] gnawed[71] his hands." Gevirtz's parallel is superior to Avishur's because it refers to a rival king and contains the object "hand." In addition, although Gevirtz adduced no parallel to the beard-simile, a good example of beard-plucking associated with the motif of the enemy-gone-mad is attested in the Assyrian annals.[72] Problematic though for Gevirtz is the rhetorical structure of the inscription

---

64 So, already some of the earliest commentators on the inscription. See references in Bauer, *ZDMG* 67, 686. For a more recent scholar to understand *ʾš* as "fire" see *TSSI* III, 34.

65 Fales, explains *km ʾš* differently in each case: "My father's house was in the midst of mighty kings, and everybody stretched forth his hand to eat it. And I (myself) was in the hand of the kings, *as if I were eating (my) beard; but like fire, I devoured the hand (itself)*." See *WO* 10, 12 (italics in original). Fales's ingenious suggestion does not explain the meaning of the simile "as if I were eating (my) beard." In addition, were Fales correct, we would expect the second simile to read: **wkm ʾš ʾklt yd mlkm*.

66 See H.-S. Schuster, "Der Relativsatz im Phönizischen und Punischen," Studies Landsberger (=*AS* 16), 443. See *ibid.* for Schuster's attempt to account for the gender disagreement between "man" and *ʾklt*.

67 Y. Avishur, "Studies of Stylistic Features Common to the Phoenician Inscriptions and the Bible," *UF* 8 (1976), 15. He also cites Isa 30:27.

68 S. Gevirtz, "On the Etymology of the Phoenician Particle *ʾš*," *JNES* 16 (1964), 127; cf. Schuster, "Relativsatz," Studies Landsberger, 443.

69 AAA 20, pl. xcvi–xcvii; cf. *CAD N/II*, 55b; *M/II*, 104b.

70 *CAD M/II*, 104b translates *miqit ṭēmi* by "desperation." For the translation "affective loss" see J. Kinnier Wilson, "An Introduction to Babylonian Psychiatry," Studies Landsberger, 293.

71 Marcus (*BASOR* 226, 57), raises the valid objection that "bite" "gnaw" (*našāku/nuššuku*) must be distinguished from Phoenician *ʾkl*=Akk *akālu*. Note however, that phrase: *kīma kalbī itananakkalū aḫameš* is translated in *CAD K*, 70b as: "(The people of Babylonia) were gnawing at each other like dogs."

72 See Streck Asb. 124–54–56: *šanê ṭēme iṣbassunūti* PN *ibquma ziqnašu PN2 ina paṭri parzilli šibbišu isḫula karassu* "Madness seized them. PN plucked out his beard. PN2 slit his belly

in which Kilamuwa alternates between past failures and present triumphs. As such, context demands that a description of earlier difficulties be followed here by triumph so that we would expect Kilamuwa to boast here of harming the enemy kings who attempted to harm his *btʾ b*, and not himself succumb to madness. A similar objection may be raised against KAI II, 31: "Und ich war in der Hand der Könige so, *als ob* ich gegessen hätte meinen Bart und [*als*] *ob* ich meine Hand gegessen hätte." An additional objection is that although *km ʾš* surely means "just as," "in the manner of," "inasmuch as," "according to," (German: demgemäß wie) it is less certain that *km ʾš* can express a condition contrary to fact (German: als ob).[73] Thus, Byblian: ... *pʿl ʾnk lrbty* DN *kmʾš qrʾt ʾt rbty* DN *wšmʿ ql wpʿl ly nʿm* "(These items) made I for my mistress, the Lady of Byblos, inasmuch as I called on my mistress, the Lady of Byblos and she heard my voice and treated me kindly."[74] Similarly: ... *kmʾš lmlkyt ʾš kn lpny* "(With all the trappings) in the manner of the queens who reigned before me."[75] In Standard Phoenician we find: *km ʾš bn ʾyt kl ʾḥry* [ ]*m ʾš bʾrṣ*[76] "Just as they built all the other [...] in the land."

It seems best to understand Kilamuwa's characterization of himself as "a beard-consuming fire and a hand-consuming fire," because this image of injurious humiliation has parallels in Semitic literature. The image of humiliating one's adversary by burning his beard is found in the Babylonian Talmud[77] in a fanciful homiletic exposition of Isa 7:20 attributed to Rabbi Abbahu (died early fourth century). According to the story, God disguised himself as an old man and maneuvered King Sennacherib into a situation so that: *ʾtly byh nwrʾ bdyqnyh* "his beard caught on fire," after which God shaved all the remaining hair of the king's body. Abbahu's narrative is interrupted[78] by a citation from R. Papa (later fourth century) who quotes a folk-saying: *hyynw dʾmry ʾynšy grytyh*[79] *lʾrmʾh špyr lyh*[80] *ʾytly lyh nwrʾ bdyqnyh wlʾ śbʿt ḥwkʾ mynyh* "Thus do

with his iron girdle-dagger." Thus, we have gnawing of hands and plucking of beard as signs of madness but no "eating" or "consumption" of the beard as part of the motif.

73 Note that in the two later comparisons, the writer says *km klbm* (l. 10) and *km nbš ytm* (l. 13).

74 KAI 10:6–8.

75 KAI 11.

76 KAI 19:9.

77 *b. Sanh.*, 95b–96a. See also L. Ginzberg, *The Legends of the Jews* (Philadelphia, repr. 1968), vol. iv, 269; vol. vi, 364.

78 The connection between R. Abbahu's story and R. Papa's comment is redactional.

79 Variants: *grydtyh, gryrtyh.*

80 Rashi reads: *wšpr bʾpyh* "and it pleased him."

people say: If you have shaved an Aramaean[81] and it pleased him, set his beard on fire and you won't be able to laugh at him enough."[82]

Closer to Kilamuwa's own time, burning the hand of the adversary has a parallel in the call on the fire to burn and consume the harmful hand of the sorcerer in the ritual series Maqlu:[83] *kaššāpu u kaššaptu rittakunu Girra liqmi Girra līkul Girra lišti* "O sorcerer and sorceress! May the fire god burn your hand! May the fire god make a meal of your hand!"

ll. 7–8 *wškr ʾnk ʿly mlk ʾšr*—The phrasing is identical to *śākar ʿālêynû* "hired against us" in the similar context of 2Kgs 7:6.[84] Landsberger questioned the usual understanding of *škr* because it struck him as a "prahlerischer Frechheit" (boastful insolence) that a minor king would speak of "hiring" the king of Assyria.[85] Garbini raised the reverse objection that the presence of Assyrian "hired" aid would have belittled Kilamuwa in the face of the public.[86] But if the eighth century prophet Isaiah (7:20) could speak of the King of Assyria as a "hired razor,"[87] then such might have been the fashion.[88]

---

81 I.e. any gentile.

82 See L. Goldschmidt, *Der babylonische Talmud Vol 7* (Berlin, 1925), 414, but contrast n. 290 *ibid.* For a different interpretation of this proverb see J. Neusner, *A History of the Jews of Babylonia* vol. 5 (Leiden, 1970), 27. I thank Baruch Levine for discussing the talmudic passage with me.

83 III:165–166. For the translation of the merism *līkul* … *lišti* as "make a meal" see CAD A/I, 254a.

84 Cf. Deut 23:5; Neh 13:2.

85 *Sam'al*, 51. His own explanation is grammatically difficult. See *KAI* II, 32–33.

86 G. Garbini, "L'iscrizionie fenicia di Kilamuwa e il verbo škr in semitico nordoccidentale," *BeO* 111–112 (1977), 113–118. Garbini translates (*ibid.*, 118) "…(sono) opulento sopra il re di Assiria." Such a translation requries us to accept Garbini's unlikely analysis of the semantic development from *škr* II "was drunk" "was full" > "was abundant" "opulent", as well as his analysis of *ʿly* "over", rather than as "over me" or "over him" as required by the orthography. Cf. Fales, *WO* 10, 16, n. 25, 17, n. 29. We may also question the enthusiasm of the ancients to sacrifice their own lives or property on the field of battle. See e.g. *CTA* 14:II:96–103 (=*KTU*³ 1.14:ii:42–49) and parallels; Judg 5:15–16, 23, 8:6; 1Sam 8:11–12, 11:7. Accordingly, we may question Garbini's premise about the negative attitude toward "hired" armies. The Israelite standing army, for example, included non-Israelite mercenaries and foreign units. See R. de Vaux, *Ancient Israel* (New York, 1965) 218–225.

87 Cf. the American use of "hired gun." See further, H. Tadmor and M. Cogan, "Ahaz and Tiglath-Pileser in the book of Kings: Historiographic Considerations," *Biblica* 60 (1979), 503. According to Tadmor and Cogan (*ibid.*, n. 43) the verb *škr* in the Kilamuwa inscription has a "different nuance" from the negative biblical *śkr*. But see below.

88 Heb *śkr* does not necessarily have a negative connotation. If, for example, one compares Abimelech's *reqîm* "lowlifes" (Judg 9:4) who were *śkr* "hired," with Jephtah's *reqîm*

ʿlmt ytn bš wgbr bswt—This statement cannot refer literally to the troops supplied by the king of Assyria because women were normally not expected to fight alongside men in the ancient Near East.[89] Indeed, the possession of women as troops was considered a curse.[90] Among recent interpreters, there is a good deal of disagreement over the sense of this passage. Collins, for example, reads *ytn* impersonally and translates: "they gave a slave girl for a sheep and a man for a garment." On Collins's analysis, after the defeat of the Danonians, prisoners were so plentiful and their price so low, that a girl could be bought as cheaply as a sheep and a man as cheaply as a garment.[91] *KAI* likewise treats *ytn* impersonally, but understands the phrase as a parenthetical reference to the terrible economic conditions of the time. Thus, sheep and clothing were as expensive as humans.[92] Gibson understands *ytn* as a reference to the king of the Danonians, who had to settle with Kilamuwa on a loser's terms.[93] Each of these suggestions requires eisegesis. In contrast, Rosenthal's[94] interpretation that we have here a proverbial expression indicating that the King of Assyria supplied Kilamuwa with troops cheaply, neatly and logically makes the last individual mentioned, *mlk ʾšr*, the subject of *ytn*. Nonetheless, Rosenthal's suggestion too, requires modification. First, it must be emphasized that *š* "sheep" and *swt* "garment" are an odd parallelism, especially when it is recalled that in l. 11 of the inscription, *š* "sheep" is balanced by *ʾlp* "ox," just as we might expect.[95] It must also be remarked that *swt* is attested elsewhere in Phoenician as a royal

(Judg 11:3) who were *lqṭ*, "collected," it becomes obvious that their unsavory reputations had nothing to do with how they entered the service of their leaders. The basic sense of *śkr* is, to pay for the services of individuals who are otherwise not obligated to perform them. See e.g. Gen 30:16; Judg 18:4; 2Sam 10:6; 2Chr 25:6. O'Connor's "engage" (*BASOR* 226, 19) is apt.

89 See e.g. Judg 4:8–9; CTA 17:VI:39–40 (=*KTU*[3] 1.17:vi:39–40) Note how Shamshi-Addu berates Yasmah-Addu for lying around with women while the good son Ishme-Dagan is out making war. See ARMT I:69:rs. 8–11.

90 See *AfO* 8 25 v 9; cf. Wiseman Treaties 617.

91 Collins, *WO* 6, 186. He compares Joel 4:3.

92 *KAI* II, 33. So too, O'Connor, *BASOR* 226, 24. As O'Connor himself acknowledges (*ibid.*, 25), his interpretation requires a readjustment of the chronological sequence. For an undoubted attestation of the inflation motif at Zenjirli see *KAI* 215:6.

93 *TSSI*, III, 37.

94 *ANET*, 654; cf. Fales, *WO* 10, 19.

95 Cf. the Heb pair *śr/śh* (Isa 7:25; see further Avishur, *Word-Pairs*, 95). Note also the Phoenician pair *ʾlpm/ṣʾn* "cattle and flocks" in *KAI* 26:A:III:8–9, C:III:8–9; for its reflexes, see *Word-Pairs*, 580–581.

garment[96] and as a temple veil,[97] and thus unlikely to be a catchword for a cheap object. In the Panamuwa Samalian inscription grains are singled out as examples of everyday commodities that are supposed to be cheap and readily available.[98] One such specified grain is is *šʾh*, corresponding to Akkadian *šeʾu* "barley."[99] In Phoenician the same word would have been pronounced *šê* and written as a homograph of the word for "sheep." If so, then a very good parallelism would be discerned here by interpreting the grapheme *swt* as a loan from Akk *samīdu*, a type of groats.[100] It should be noted that writing of the vocable with final *t* rather than *d* are attested in Hittite-speaking areas,[101] areas geographically proximate to Zenjirli. In addition, the medial *waw* for Akkadian medial *mem* would be normal in an area of Aramaic speech.[102]

l. 9 *yšbt ʿl ksʾ ʾby*—Cf. Samalian: *yšbt ʿl mšb ʾby*[103] and Standard Aramaic at Zenjirli: *hwšbny ʿl krsʾ ʾby.*[104]

ll. 9–10 *hmlkm hlpnym*—As we know from l. 5, *hlpnym* can stand by itself. Accordingly, these two words are nouns in apposition.[105]

l. 10 *ytlnn mškbm km klbm*—Athough *waw* seems clear in the photograph,[106] Hermann's personal examination led him to prefer *ytlnn* to *ytlwn.*[107] Because there is no lack of dog-similes in ancient Near Eastern literature[108] one must resist the temptation to arrive at a prior understanding of the simile and then justify it by recourse to etymology or parallels. First, it must be noted that the exact form (*w*)*ytlnn* in the sense "make a resting-place" is attested in the hendiadys with *yškn* "dwell"[109] in Job 39:28, where it refers to an eagle. Second,

96 *KAI* 11.

97 *KAI* 76:A:4.

98 *KAI* 215:6–9.

99 References in AHw., 1222a–b.

100 See *CAD S*, 115b–116a.

101 See *CAD*, *ibid.*

102 See S. Kaufman, *The Akkadian Influences on Aramaic* (Chicago, 1972), 34. For *smydʾ* "fine flour" in the later Aramaic dialects see *ibid.*, 90.

103 *KAI* 214:8; note also Karatepe: *wyšb ʾnk ʿl ksʾ ʾby* (*KAI* 26a:I:11).

104 For parallels see Avishur, *UF* 8, 11; Gruber, "Faces," 257.

105 Cf. S. D. Sperling, "An Arslan Tash Incantation: Interpretations and Implications," *HUCA* 53 (1982), 7, n. 53.

106 So too, O'Connor, *BASOR* 226, 22.

107 *OLZ* 48, 295.

108 For Akkadian see e.g., *CAD K*, 70b; OIP 2 54:54, 57:13. See further, M. Held, "Philological Notes on the Mari Covenant Rituals," *BASOR* 200 (Dec., 1970), 38–39. For Ugaritic, see *CTA* 16:I:2–3, 15–17 (=*KTU*³ 1.16:i:1–2, 15–17). See further, B. Margulies, "A New Ugaritic Farce (RS 24.258)," *UF* 2 (1970), 135. For Hebrew, see Judg 7:5; Ps 59:7, 15; Prv 26:11.

109 In Ps 91:1, *ytlnn* is parallel to *yšb* "dwell."

the inscription contrasts the protected status of the *mškbm* in the reign of Kilamuwa, who was their father … mother … brother"[110] with their canine existence earlier. In this light, Landsberger's connection with Hebrew *lwn* "spend the night"[111] is most convincing. In pre-Kilamuwan times, the *mškbm* spent their nights the way dogs do. The specific sense of the comparison may be seen in the Akkadian curse to which Landsberger drew attention: *kīma kalbi libtaʾita ina ribīt ālišu*[112] "May he spend the nights in the square of his city like a dog."[113] Thus, *ytlnn … km klbm* means "they used to bed down, like dogs, (in the streets)." The alleged parallel between Ps 59:16 and the phrase under discussion[114] is based on a mistranslation of the Psalms passage.[115]

ll. 10–11 *lmy..wlmy..wlmy-* Gibson (*TSSI*, III, 38) rightly terms *lmy* "a peculiar usage of the interrogative." The peculiarity of *lmy* (and of *my* below) is explained by the native Aramaic background. A learned scribe whose native language was Aramaic expanded the semantic range of Phoenician *my* to conform to the general relative pronominal use of Aramaic *mn*, as documented at Sefîre[116] and Tell Fakhariyeh.[117]

ll. 11–12 *bʿl bqr wbʿl ksp wbʿl ḥrṣ*—The pairing of *ksp* and *ḥrṣ* is just what we would expect in these parallelistic lines,[118] and corresponds to Zenjirli Samalian *bʿl ksp … bʿl zhb* (*KAI* 215:11) as well as to Zenjirli Standard Aramaic

---

110 Cf. *pʿln* DN *ldnnym lʾb wlʾm* "DN made me father and mother to the Danonians." (*KAI* 26A:I:3) For a similar expression of familial treatment employing a verb of existence corresponding to Phoenician *kt*, cf. *anāku kīma abim u aḫim abaššêkum* "I, for my part have been like a father and a brother to you." For the text see J. Sasson, "Yarim-Lim's War Declaration," in *Miscellanea Babylonica mélanges offerts à Maurice Birot*, eds. J.-M. Durand and J.-R. Kupper (Paris, 1985), 237–255.

111 Cf. Poebel, *Pronomen*, 36.

112 Text cited in *CAD B*, 170b.

113 See *Samʾal*, 52; Landsberger Kult. Kalender, 108, n. 2 observes that the *hitpolel* of *lwn* corresponds to the I/2 of Akkadian *bâtu: libtaʾita.* Note further that the link between Hebrew *ytlnn* and the I/2 of Akkadian *bâtu* is assured by the Aramaic translation of *wytlnn* in Job 39:28 as *wybyt.* Cf. targum to Ps 91:1.

114 So Hermann, 296; *KAI* II, 33; *TSSI*, III, 37.

115 As ibn Ezra observed, in Ps 59:16, in the phrase *ʾim lôʾ yiśbeʿû wayyālînû*, the negation governs both of the following verbs: Vss. 15–16 are to be translated as follows: "They return at evening howling (*yehemû*) like dogs, prowling about town. They roam about in order to eat. If they are not satisfied, they will not rest."

116 See Fitzmyer, *Sefîre*, 165.

117 Fakh Aram: 10 *mn ʾḥr kn* (= Akk 15: *mannu arku*), Aram 16: *mn yld šmy* (= Akk 26–28: *mannu ša šumi … ipaššiṭu*). Note that the Akkadian employs the relative *ša* in the verbal construction.

118 See Avishur, *Word-Pairs*, 761.

bʿly ksp wbʿly zhb (*KAI* 216:10–11).[119] The lack of transition to "silver and gold" however, may be due to homeoteleuton. I suggest a restoration on the order of: *wmy bl ḥz mnm mšd štyʿ bʿl ksp wbʿl ḥrṣ* "and whoever had not seen any precious object, him I made owner of silver and owner of gold."[120]

l. 13 *wʾnk tmkt mškbm lyd*—The construction is anastrophic[121] to be understood as though it read: **wʾnk tmkt lyd*[122] *mškbm*. The Samalian reflex is *ʾḥz byd* (*KAI* 214:3–4).

whmt št nbš km nbš ytm bʾm—Each individual word in this simile is clear, but the sense of the phrase continues to elude commentators.[123] Only Torrey has understood *hmt* as the grammatical object[124] whereas most scholars take *hmt* as the grammatical subject. Nonetheless, the tendency of Near Eastern royal inscriptions to enumerate the deeds of the sovereign, rather than the reactions of the people, supports Torrey's view. If so, then Kilamuwa is the grammatical subject, and *št* is to be parsed as a first person singular perfect. We know from Hebrew that the semantic range of *šyt* "place" "put" "replace" "restore"[125] overlaps that of *ntn*[126] "give." As far as *nbš* is concerned, the scholarly tendency has been to seek an appropriate meaning from cognates as far afield as Tigre.[127] In Zenjirli itself however, *nbš* in the Samalian inscriptions is attested in the meaning of "spirit."[128] Accordingly, *št nbš* is similar to such phrases as Hebrew *mešîb*

119 See also, N. Tur-Sinai, *The Book of Job A New Commentary* (Jerusalem, 1967), 62.

120 See *KAI* 13:3–4. The vocable *mšd* is found, pointed incorrectly, in Hos 9:6. See H. L. Ginsberg, "Lexicographical Notes," VTSup 16 (1967), 78.

121 Anastrophe in Northwest Semitic is much more widespread than generally realized. Note e.g. the much discussed Moabite: *lk ʾḥz ʾt nbh ʿl yšrʾl*, which simply should be translated "Go up against Israel and seize Nebo." See *JAOS* 101 (1981), 449. For biblical examples see e.g. Exod 2:5a; 1Sam 2:11a; see further, J. Sasson, "Wordplay in the OT," *IDBSup*, 968–970.

122 Heb *tmk* may likewise take an indirect object. See e.g., Exod 17:12; Isa 33:15, 42:1; Ps 41:13, 63:9.

123 For previous translations, see e.g. Lidzbarski, *Ephemeris III*, 238; Poebel, *Pronomen*, 37; Landsberger, *Samʾal* 53; *TSSI*, III, 35; *KAI* II, 31; Collins, *WO* 6, 187; O'Connor, *BASOR* 226, 19; Rosenthal, *ANET*, 655; Bauer, *ZDMG*, 67, 691; Torrey, *JAOS* 35, 366; A. Dupont-Sommer, *Les Araméens* (Paris, 1949), 43.

124 Torrey, *JAOS* 35, 365.

125 Gen 4:25.

126 For *šyt* and *ntn* in synonymous parallelism see Job 38:36. Note how the two verbs alternate in the parallel verses Gen 41:33 and Gen 41:41. Note further the equivalent idioms, Hebrew *šyt pnym* "direct oneself" (Num 24:1) = Ugaritic *ytn pnm* (e.g. *CTA* 6:I:32=*KTU*[3] 1.6:i:32).

127 See Lidzbarski, *Ephemeris*, *III*, 235.

128 See *KAI* 214:17, 21, 22. The best translation of the Zenjirli attestations of *nbš* is "ghost" in its archaic sense, or German "Geist."

nepeš "reviver," said of humans and God;[129] *notên nĕšāmâ*,[130] "giver of life" said of God; and Akkadian *nādin napištim* used similarly of rulers and divinities.[131] As such, the phrase *whmt št nbš* means: "And them gave I life." Kilamuwa's boast is thus equivalent to Azatiwada's claim: *yḥw*[132] *ʾnk ʾyt dnnym* "I revived the Danonians."[133] With this understanding, we may proceed to the comparison: *km nbš ytm bʾm*. Zevit has emphasized,[134] that *ytm* refers to one bereft of a father, whose mother is still living. As we know from biblical sources, a childless woman counted for very little. Rachel's outburst to Jacob "Bring me children, for if not, I am a dead woman,"[135] (Gen 30:1) puts the matter succinctly: To a woman, having a child was the difference between her life and her death. The same notion is expressed positively in Ruth (4:15) when Obed's birth[136] occasions the statement by the women: *wĕhāyâ lāk lĕmešîb nepeš* "he shall revive you." Kilamuwa extravagantly claims that he gave life to the *mškbm* the way that a child whose father is dead, provides the only life that the mother has.[137]

129 Ps 19:8; Ruth 4:15; Lam 1:16 (cf. 1:11). Cf. also the *polel* form in Ps 23:3, traditionally: "He restoreth my soul."

130 Isa 42:5.

131 CH iiia:65–66 (cf. iva:1–2: *napšata qâšu*). In the Yarim-Lim war declaration of Yarim-Lim of Halab, found at Mari (Sasson, "Yarim-Lim," 238, and see 240, n. 9), we read: *ālam Bābilim ušēzibu u napištam ana mātika u kâta addinu* "I saved the city of Babylon and gave life to your people and you." For *mātu* "people/populace" see M. Held, "On Terms of Deportation in the OB Royal Inscriptions with Special Reference to Yahdunlim," *JANES* 11 (1979), 55. For Akkadian references to goddesses as *nādinat napištim* see Tallqvist Götterepitheta, 138; cf. *ibid.*, 160, s.v. *qâšu*.

132 On the form and its congeners see D. Marcus, "The Verb 'to live' in Ugaritic," *JSS* 17 (1972), 79.

133 *KAI* 26A:I:4–5. For a Nabatean parallel, see F. Bron, *Recherches sur les inscriptions phéniciennes de Karatepe* (Paris, 1979), 38. For Akkadian references to the king as dispenser of life and reviver of the dead, see *CAD B*, 60–61. The king is himself "the breath of the nostrils" of the people. See Lam 4:20; EA 147:9. See further, W. F. Albright, "The Egyptian Correspondence of the Abimilki, Prince of Tyre," *JEA* 23 (1937), 198; T. H. Gaster, *Myth, Legend, and Custom in the Old Testament* (New York, 1969), 826–827.

134 AOS meeting, 1984. Cf. the phrase *ytm bn ʾlmt* in *KAI* 14:3, 13. For Hebrew see Exod 22:23; Ps 109:9; Lam 5:3.

135 The form *mētâ* is a participle, to be translated as a noun. See S. Mandelkern, *Hekal Haqqodesh* (Photo repr. of 1896) 662d. See further, *Tg.Onq.*; cf. Rashi a.l.

136 Obed is called Naomi's son in 4:17.

137 Observe that the claim follows on *tmkt mškbm lyd*, a phrase with two well-known parallels (*CTA* 17:I:30–31 and parallels =*KTU*^{3} 1.17: i:30–31; Isa 51:18) to the benefits supplied by an offspring.

ll. 14–15—*wyzq . . . ʾl ykbd . . . ʾl ykbd*—Given the writer's enthusiasm for parallelism, we would expect *wyzq* to be balanced by *ʾl ykbd* just as *yšḥt spr* (the crime) is balanced by *yšḥt rʾš* (the punishment) in ll. 15–16. Neither the well-known senses of Late Hebrew and Aramaic *nzq* "harm" "injure" "damage," nor the West-Semitic reflexes of Akk *nazāqu* "trouble" provide this balance.[138] It will be recalled however, that Akkadian inscriptions, beginning with the OAkk. period, often include a warning near their conclusions along the lines of: *ša tuppam/narâm šuʾā(ti) ušazzakū(ni)*,[139] "Whoever fails to show due regard for this tablet/stele. . . ."[140] Whatever the actual etymology of the verb,[141] a learned scribe from an Aramaic-speaking area, writing in Phoenician, could have derived *ušazzakūni* from *nzq*, and employed it as an antonym of *kbd*.

138 For West-Semitic *nzq* = Akk *nazāqu* see Ginsberg, VTSup 16, 81.

139 For OAkk. see H. Hirsch, "Die Inschriften der Könige von Agade," *AfO* 20 (1963), 1–82; MAD III, 209. For later examples see *CAD N/I*, 19.

140 See Held, *JCS* 15 (1961), 35; cf. B. Landsberger, "Assyrische Königsliste und 'dunkles Zeitalter,' "*JCS* 8 (1954), 10. For other interpretations see Edzard and von Soden apud Goetze, *JAOS* 88 (1968), 56, n. f; *CAD N II*, 19; AHw., 752b.

141 See the previous note.

CHAPTER 8

Aramaic *nzh* and Akkadian *nesû*

From the first publication of the Aramaic incantation bowls it was clear that these artifacts of the early medieval period[1] contained much material of interest to comparatists. Over the years, scholars have drawn attention to linguistic and cultural parallels with ancient Egypt,[2] the Aegean, Jewish Palestine, the Jewish diaspora, Persia, the Hellenistic world and Mesopotamia.[3] In keeping with the philological interests of my lamented friend and colleague Stanley Gevirtz, the present paper concentrates on a comparison between the Northwest Semitic vocable preserved in the bowls, Aramaic *nzh* II[4] "depart," and its hitherto unrecognized etymological and semantic correspondent, Akkadian *nesû*.[5]

---

1 Generally these earthenware bowls are thought to date from the third or fourth to the sixth or seventh centuries of the Christian Era. See J. Naveh and S. Shaked, *Amulets and Magic Bowls, Aramaic Incantations of Late Antiquity* (Jerusalem: Magnes, 1985), 1; cf. T. Harviainen, "A Syriac Incantation Bowl in the Finnish National Museum, Helsinki," *Studia Orientalia* 51 (1981), 4–5.

2 For similarities between some ancient Egyptian letters to the dead written on pottery bowls and the medieval Aramaic incantation bowls see S. Keller, "Letters to the Dead," in *By Study and also by Faith, Essays in Honor of Hugh Nibley*, ed. J. Lundquist (Provo: Deseret, 1990), 119–120.

3 See J. Montgomery, *Aramaic Incantation Texts from Nippur* (hereafter: *AIT*; Philadelphia: University Museum, 1913), 106–116. For a brief history of research on the bowls see Naveh and Shaked, *Amulets*, 19–21 and especially the bibliography *ibid.*, 243–264; C. Müller-Kessler, *Die Zauberschalentexte in der Hilprecht-Sammlung, Jena, und weitere Nippur-Texte anderer Sammlungen* (Wiesbaden: Harrassowitz, 2005), 1–7, 155–164.

4 See *DJBA*, 739; For I נזה /נזח see *ibid.*, but cf. below.

5 The etymology proposed here drives a final, albeit redundant, nail into the coffin of the old identification of Akkadian *nesû* and Hebrew נסע "to journey." See e.g. BDB, 652; Gesenius[17], 508; *KBL*, 620, rejected in AHw., 781b and in *HALAT*, 665. The identification would never have been made if scholars had attended to the principle of interdialectal distribution. The interdialectal distribution of "to journey" is Hebrew נסע; Jewish Palestinian Aramaic (JPA) נטל, סלק. See *DJPA*, 348, 379b; JBA סלק. See Kasowski, *Thesaurus Talmudis* (Jerusalem: Ministry of Education and Culture & Jewish Theological Seminary), 27, 215; Syriac *šql mn.* See e.g. Peshitta to Judg 3:14; 2 Kgs 3:27; 19:8; Ezra 8:31; Arabic *raḥala*. See e.g. Saadia to Gen 11:2; 12:9; 13:11; 20:1; 35:21 in J. Derenbourg, ed., *Version arabe du Pentateuque de R. Saadia ben Iosef Al-Fayyoûmî* (Paris: Leroux, 1893); see further, J. Kafaḥ[Kafiḥ], תהילים עם תרגום ופירוש הגאון סעדיה בן יוסף פיומי זצ'ל (Jerusalem: American Academy for Jewish Research, 1965), 333; S. Skoss, ed., *The Hebrew-Arabic Dictionary of the Bible … of David Ben Abraham Al-Fasi II*, (New Haven: Yale, 1945), 337; Akkadian *etēqu* (*CAD E*, 348–395); *eqla/girra/ḫarrāna/urḫa*

 | DOI 10.1163/9789004340879_009

Because of the rarity of *nzh* II outside of the bowls,[6] it was only natural for Montgomery to misread a number of the vocable's attestations and to explain its etymology[7] incorrectly. Accordingly, before proceeding to the body of our discussion, we must critically summarize Montgomery's conclusions. The glossary to *AIT*[8] lists *nzḥ* (with final *ḥet*) "depart." Elsewhere[9] Montgomery observes "also Talmudic" (no references)[10] and adds = *zḥḥ*, which in his opinion is at the root of BH ולא יזח "does not come loose,"[11] (Exod 28:28; 39:21) and related as well to the Aramaic verbum movendi *zwḥ*.[12] Each element of this equation is questionable. First, although Montgomery's posited semantic link between "come loose" said of a breastpiece (BH לא יזח) and "depart" said of demons in the incantations and of other animate objects (see below) is not impossible,[13] it cannot simply be assumed. Second, a connection between BH זחח and Aramaic *zwḥ* is far from certain. In point of fact, the root of the BH dis-legomenon יזח, has been in doubt at least since the Middle Ages. Indeed, even

---

alāku CAD A/I, 313–314. The Ugaritic interdialectal correspondent is probably *ʿtq*. (See *KTU*³ 2.36:17 and RS 17.434:26ʹ as read by D. Pardee, "Ugaritic," *AfO* 30 [1983/84], 322, 325.) For an extremely lucid description of the interdialectal approach in Semitics see Ch. Cohen, "The 'Held Method' for Comparative Semitic Philology," *JANES* 19 (1989), 9–23.

6 In the course of researching this paper, I consulted with two prominent talmudists, neither of whom recalled the vocable off-hand. Kasowski (*Thesaurus* vol. 25, 1176) cites only six attestations of this root: *b. Šabb.* 48a (twice); *b. Pesaḥ* 112b (three times); and *b. Sanh.* 41b (once). Of these attestations four are nominal and two verbal. Kasowski's rubric for the verbal form is not the root, but the suffixed form נזחיה. See further, Jast, 890–891; Dalman, Handwörterbuch, 266; AC, vol. 5, 325; Levy, TMW, vol. 3, 364.

7 For another etymology see Levy, TMW vol. 3, 364. Levy translates talmudic נזח as "anschreien" ("scream" or "shout at"), for which there is good exegetical tradition (see below). As an etymology he offers Syriac *nhz*. But that vocable does not mean "anschreien," (Syriac: *qʿʾ* see e.g. Peshitta to Gen 39:14,15) but rather "disturb," "annoy," "trouble," and sometimes refers to creaking or grating sounds. See Payne Smith, II, 2295.

8 *AIT*, 295.

9 *Ibid.*, 139.

10 In all likelihood, Montgomery found talmudic נזח in Jast, 890b, translated as "to be unsteady," "shift." Thanks now to Kasowski, *Thesaurus* vol 25, 1181, it becomes possible to examine quickly all six attestations of "talmudic" נזח and to see that all are paraphrases of Exod 28:28, 31:29. There is no independent attestation of the verb in JBA. As for JPA, there is no entry for נזח in *DJPA*.

11 So NJPS and, approximately, RSV and REB.

12 *AIT*, 130.

13 Note for example Syriac *prq*.

a grammarian of the stature of Ibn Janah was uncertain.[14] Among the modern biblical lexicographers, BDB,[15] Gesenius,[16] and *KBL*[17] are in agreement with Montgomery that the root of BH יזח is *zḥḥ*. In contrast, *HALAT*[18] derives BH יזח from the root *zwḥ*, thus making a closer connection between the Hebrew and Aramaic. On semantic grounds however, that connection is extremely tenuous. Observe that within the later dialects of Aramaic, *zwḥ* seems best attested in Syriac[19] where it has the senses "to put in motion," "move," "stir," "rouse oneself into action" and the like.[20] At the same time, the verb does not seem to be the antonym of Hebrew רכס (= Syriac *dbq*), which we should expect in Exod 28:28, 39:21. Significantly, the Peshitta to Exod 28:28 renders לא יזח by *lʾ nhwʾ ʿbr* while translating Exod 39:21 לא יזח by *lʾ prq hwʾ*.[21] As for the Jewish Aramaic versions, note that *Tg. Onq.* translates יזח by יתפרק in both instances, while *Tg. Neof.* I translates the Hebrew by לא יזוע in both instances.[22] Given the above, it seems best to dissociate the verb under discussion both from BH לא יזח and Aramaic *zwḥ*.

In his review of *AIT*, J. N. Epstein,[23] well aware that the orthography of the bowl inscriptions, and presumably the pronunciation of the bowls writers and

---

14 See W. Bacher, *Sepher Haschoraschim .. von .. ibn Ǧanah* (Reprint Amsterdam: Philo, 1969): 129–130; cf. *ibid.*, 294–295.

15 BDB, 267.

16 Gesenius[17], 196.

17 *KBL*, 254.

18 *HALAT*, 255.

19 On the verb in other Aramaic dialects as well as Late Hebrew see M. Moreshet, *A Lexicon of the New Verbs in Talmudic Hebrew* (Ramat-Gan: Bar-Ilan, 1980), 147.

20 See PSmCom, 112; Cf. Payne Smith, II, 1098–1099. A meaning "stir," "rouse oneself" would be appropriate in Naveh and Shaked *Amulets*, Bowl 13:20 which reads *ʾtyzḥ qṣry* "the sick bestir themselves."

21 Peshitta Institute ed., *The Old Testament in Syriac According to the Peshitta Version* Part I. Fascicle I (Leiden: Brill, 1977), 183, 215.

22 For זוע "move," "tremble," "shake" see A. Diéz-Macho, *Neophyti I; Targum Palestinense MS de la Biblioteca Vaticana* (Madrid-Barcelona: Consejo Superior de Investigaciones Científicas, 1970), 185, 265. It must be noted however, that according to Diéz-Macho (*ibid.*, 265) there is a targumic manuscript variant to Exod 39:21 with the reading יזח. See further *DJPA*, 174.

23 J. N. Epstein, "Glosses Babylo-araméennes," *REJ* 73 (1921), 40, republished in Hebrew translation in J. N. Epstein, *Studies in Talmudic Literature and Semitic Languages*, 2 vols. ed. E. Z. Melamed (Jerusalem: Magnes, 1983), vol. 1, 339. All *AIT* readings cited below were checked against Epstein's review article, which appeared in two parts in *REJ* 73 (1921), 27–58; *REJ* 74 (1922), 40–72 (= Epstein, *Studies* vol. 1, 339–374). It is necessary in general to

their clients, did not distnguish between *heh* and *ḥet*,[24] preferred *nzh* (with *heh*). In fact, in commenting on a magical text treated earlier by Montgomery, Epstein had already corrected Montgomery's reading *wnyzḥwn* to *wnyzhwn* and had at the same time drawn attention to attestations of *nzh* in the Babylonian Talmud.[25] In order to move toward a solution, it will be useful first to collect the attestations of *nzh* in Montgomery's corpus:

(A) *AIT* 3:2
dyzh wytrḥq mynyh dywʾ byšʾ wsṭnʾ dmytqry . . .
"That departed and distanced from him be wicked devil[26] and wicked satan called . . ."

(B) *AIT* 5:1–2
wtynzh mynhwn (2) *kl lylytʾ bšytʾ wkl šydy wdywy wʾsry,*
"And may there depart from them all evil Liliths and all demons and devils and spells."

(C) *AIT* 8:2
dtyzh mynh lylytʾ byštʾ byšmyh dpzʾr ʾl lylytʾ
"That depart from her wicked Lilith in the name of DN."

(D) *AIT* 10:6
wyzdhwn wybṭlwn wypqwn wytrḥqwn mynhwn wmn bythwn wmn d[*yrty*] *hwn*
"And shall depart and cease and go out and be distant from them and from their house and dwellings . . ."

(E) *AIT* 12:10
. . . *wkl mydʿm byš dyzhwn wypqwn mn* . . .
"And let every evil thing depart and go out of . . ."[27]

(F) *AIT* 25:1
ʾswtʾ mn šmyʾ lgwryn br ṭʾty wlʾḥt bt dwdʾ ʾyttyh dyzh mnhwn k[*l*] *dy*[*wʾ wyts*]*n brḥmy dyšmyh*

---

check Epstein before citing texts from *AIT*. See J. Greenfield, "Notes on Some Aramaic and Mandaic Incantation Bowls," *JANES* 5 (1973), 149 n. 3.

24 See *AIT*, 29; cf. B. Levine apud J. Neusner, *A History of the Jews of Babylonia*, 5 vols. (Leiden: Brill, 1965–1970), vol. 5, 345 n. 1.

25 Epstein, "Zum magischen Texte," *JAOS* 33 (1912), 279, republished in Hebrew translation in Epstein, *Studies*, vol. 1, 313.

26 Aramaic *dywʾ* is a loan from Iranian *dēw*, "demon."

27 For a similar phrasing cf. *wnyzhwn wnypqwn*. See Epstein, *Studies* vol. 1, 314 (originally published in *JAOS* 33 (1912), 280.

"Healing from heaven for PN son of PN2 and PN3 daughter of PN4 his wife that every devil depart from them and that they be healed through heaven's mercies."

(G) *AIT* 31:3–4
wtyzh mnh wmn byth mbklt' wlwṭt' wḥylm' byš' 'myn
"And may there depart from him and from his house, climber[28] and curse and bad dream. Amen."
Cf. *ibid.*, 9–10
wtyzh mnh wmn byth mbklt' wlwṭt' wḥylm' byš'

(H) *AIT* 32:2–3
dtyzh mynh mbklt' wlwṭt' wḥlm' byš'
"That there depart from him climber and curse and bad dream."

(I) *AIT* 34:12
wtyzh mynh mbklt' wḥlm' byš' wlwṭt' wnydr' wḥrš'
"That there depart from him climber and bad dream and curse and oath and sorcery."

To the references available to Epstein we may add citations from bowls published later. In one bowl published by Gordon[29] we read:

(J) *dtyzhwn wt'brwn wtbṭlwn kl ḥršy wkl ptkry*
"That you depart and pass away and desist, all sorceries and idols."[30]

28 The exact sense and etymology of this term have long been obscure. For a discussion of earlier opinions and a new suggestion see M. Geller, "Four Aramaic Incantation Bowls," in *The Bible World. Essays in Honor of Cyrus H. Gordon* ed. G. Rendsburg, R. Adler, C. Gottlieb and S. Keller (New York: Ktav & Institute of Hebrew Culture and Education, New York University, 1980), 50–51. My translation "climber" is based on a derivation from Akkadian *mubbalkitu*, participle of the quadriliteral verb *nabalkutu*, "cross over a wall, a mountain, an obstacle," said among other things of demons and spirits. Note e.g. an Akkadian incantation text from Ugarit in which it is said of demons: *b·tāti ētanarrubā ūrāti ittanabalkitā* "They constantly enter the houses, they constantly climb over the roofs." (*Ugaritica* 5 17:31) For references to *nabalkutu* see *CAD N/I*, 11–20; AHw., 694–696.

29 C. Gordon, "Aramaic Incantation Bowls," *Or* 10 (1941). The quotation is from Bowl 6:15. The bowl has since been republished as text 15 in W. Rossell, *A Handbook of Aramaic Magical Texts* (Ringwood Borough, NJ: Shelton College, 1953); and as text 43 in C. Isbell, *Corpus of the Aramaic Magic Bowls* (Missoula: Scholars, 1975).

30 For *ptkr*, derived from Old Persian *patikara*, "image," and its reflexes in later Iranian dialects as well as other languages see G. Driver, *Aramaic Documents of the Fifth Century B.C.* (Oxford: Clarendon, 1965), 72–73; *DJBA*, 948.

(K) In another bowl likewise published by Gordon[31] we read:
wtyzhyn… wtypqwn mn byth wmn dyrth
"May you (f. pl.) depart and go away from her house and from her dwelling."

More recent attestations occur in bowls published by Geller:[32]

(L) Geller A:7
dtyzhyn wtpqyn mynyh wmn bytyh wdyrtyh
"That you (f.pl.) depart and go away from him and from his house and his dwelling."

(M) Geller D:2
ʾšbʿyt ʿlykwn ʾysry ʿlm[ʾ] *wtyzhwn wtpqwn mn hdyn bytyh byth d.…*
"I have adjured you, princes of the world,[33] that you depart and go away from this his house,[34] the house of…"

(N) Naveh-Shaked Bowl 1:11 (Syriac):
…wtyzh mnh mbkltʾ wḥylmʾ byšʾ
"That there depart from him climber and bad dream."[35]

What was not observed by Epstein, nor by subsequent scholars was that this Aramaic *nzh* "depart," is identical etymologically[36] and semantically with

31 The text is from Bowl 2 in Gordon "Bowls," republished in Isbell *Corpus* as text 39.

32 Geller, "Four Aramaic Incantation Bowls," in Rendsburg, *Essays Gordon*, 47–60.

33 Cf. *ibid.*, 58–59; see already, *AIT*, 86, n. 22. The translation is based on the talmudic passage (correct reference to: *b. Pesaḥ* 111b): איסרא דמזוני נקיד שמיה איסרא דעניותא נבל שמיה. "The prince of food provisions is named NQYD (Mr. Clean). The prince of poverty is named NBL (Mr. Filth)." (With NQYD cf. Syriac *nqd*, "clean, pure." With NBL cf. JPA נבל in *y. Kil.* 9:3 [32a]: רבי יוחנן יהב מפה על מנוי ואינו אסור משום כלאים דלא ינבלון מאנוי, "Rabbi Johanan would place a cloth over his garments so that they might not be soiled. This does not fall under the prohibition [Lev 19:19] against wearing a garment made of two kinds of fabric.") Note further the writing with *ʿayin* in the expression עיסרא דאוריתא עיסרא דנורא "prince of icy wind, prince of fire." (אוריתא=Akkadian *ēriyātu*. See *CAD E*, 239b); Hyvernat apud Naveh and Shaked *Amulets*, 83.

34 Geller, "Four Magic Bowls," 58 smoothes the syntax by translating "from his house-the house of." The text may be a conflation of two formulas: 1) *wtpqwn mn hdyn byth d…*; 2) *wtpqwn mn bytyh d.…*

35 The glossary in Naveh and Shaked *Amulets*, 265, incorrectly lists this reference under *ʾzl*, "to go."

36 For the correspondence of Akkadian [s] and Aramaic [z] cf. e.g. Akkadian *salāḫu* "sprinkle water" and Syriac *zlḥ* with the identical meaning.

Akkadian *nesû*. According to the definitions and references in CAD[37] the verb *nesŭ* in the I-form has the intransitive senses "step back," "withdraw," "depart," "recede"; as well as the transitive sense "remove." In the II form *nussû*, the verb means "remove," "deport," "take far away." It is likewise attested in the III and IV.

More significant than dictionary definitions, however, are examples of actual usage. In Akkadian, *nesû* is a regular synonym of *rêqu* "to be distant," "become distant,"[38] a fact demonstrated by the native synonym lists,[39] and by poetic parallelism. Note for example: *ilšu ittišu ittesi ištaršu ina zumrišu irtēq* "His personal god departed from him. His personal goddess distanced herself."[40] Particularly instructive is the well-attested parallelism of *rêqu* and *nĕsû* in the incantation literature. Note for example: *linessi pušqu … lirēq murṣu* : "May DN remove trouble, may DN2 keep sickness far away."[41] Similarly, Maqlû V: 166–168 reads : *isâ isâ rēqa rēqa bēša bēša ḫilqa duppira atlaka isâ u rēqa* "Depart, depart, be distant, be distant, move away, move away, flee, be absent, get away, depart and be distant!" The incantation continues: *ina zumriya isâ ina zumriya rēqa ina zumriya bēša ina zumriya ḫilqa ina zumriya duppira ina zumriya atlaka*[42] "From my body depart, from my body be distant, from my body move away, from my body flee, from my body go far away, from my body be gone!" Similarly, another text has the pair in hendiadys: *miḫru lā ṭābu lissû lirīqū* "May mishap and trouble depart and be distant."[43]

Given that Akkadian *rêqu*[44] is universally acknowledged to be etymologically and semantically equivalent to Aramaic *rḥq*, it should now come as no surprise that the correspondence of Akk *nesû* and *rêqu* is neatly mirrored above in our Aramaic text A, in the phrase *dyzh wytrḥq*. Of even greater interest is text D, which strings together the synonyms[45] *rḥq, npq, bṭl, nzh*. Note additionally, that in text E we have the all-purpose apotropaic phrase[46] *wkl myd'm byš dyzhwn wypqwn*, where *nzh* "depart" and *npq* "go out" occur in hendiadys.

---

37 CAD N/II, 185–189.

38 See conveniently, AHw., 781–782; *ibid.*, 971–972.

39 See, *ibid.*; CAD N/II, 186.

40 CAD I/J, 271b.

41 See Šurpu IV: 96–97; Note as well the adjectival parallelism: *ša ālsu rūqu ḫarrānšu nis*[*â*]*t*, "him whose city is distant, whose road is far away." See *ibid.*, IV:33–34.

42 Maqlu V: 170–175.

43 Šurpu VIII: 80.

44 See e.g. AHw., 971 and the various Bible dictionaries.

45 For the style, cf. Maqlu V:166–168 cited in the previous paragraph.

46 With the Aramaic formula *kl myd'm byš* cf. the functional equivalent Akkadian *mimma lemnu*. For references see conveniently, CAD L, 121b–122a.

This mirrors the parallelism between *nesû* "depart" and *aṣû* "go out" attested in an Akkadian incantation: *ina zumrišu lissû ina zumrišu*[47] *liṣû* "May they depart from his body, may they go out of his body."[48]

With the equivalency of Aramaic נזה and Akkadian *nesû* demonstrated, we may more precisely determine the meaning of the Aramaic vocable in its attestations in the Babylonian Talmud.

b. Pesaḥ 112b:

אמר רב ניזהא דתורא הן הן ניזהא דאריה זה זה ניזהא דגמלא דא דא ניזהא דארבא
הילני הייא הילא והילוק הוליא

Commenting on this passage, Rashi translated ניזהא by לחש "incantation." But because this does not fit the other talmudic attestations (as we shall see presently)[49] Rashi's grandson Samuel b. Meier (Rashbam) wrote: "It appears to me that this is not an incantation but a rebuke (גערה) uttered in these words to chase the animal away from him (להבריחו מעליו) or in order to make it (the animal) perform labor." But Rashbam's equation of גערה = ניזהא does not seem quite appropriate for the boat (ארבא). In contrast, "departure" would fit all of the instances. We should translate as follows "(For) the departure of an ox: 'hen hen'; (for) the departure of a lion 'za za'; (for) the departure of a camel 'da da'; (for) the departure of a boat etc." In other words, although Rashi's translation of ניזהא as "incantation" is imprecise, his explanation that we have to do with an incantatory formula stands.

b. Šhabb. 48a:

רבה ורבי זירא איקלעו לבי ריש גלותא חזיוה לההוא עבדא דאנח כוזא דמיא אפומא
דקומקומא נזהיה רבה א"ל ר' זירא מאי שנא ממיחם על גבי מיחם א"ל התם אוקומי
קא מוקים הכא אולודי קא מוליד הדר חזייה דפרס דסתודר אפומיה דכובא ואנח
נטלא עילויה נזהיה רבה א"ל ר' זירא אמאי אמר ליה השתא חזית לסוף חזייה דקא
מעצר ליה א"ל מאי שנא מפרונקא א"ל התם לא קפיד עילויה הכא קפיד עילויה

---

47 The Aramaic reflex is mn gwph. See Naveh and Shaked Amulets, A 9:2.

48 CT 16 14 iii 47.

49 In fact, Rashi's commentary to *b. Sanh.* 41b is much closer to Rashbam in *b. Pesaḥ.* 112b. "נזיהות refers to someone speaking harshly and forcefully (בקושי ובחזקה) as in the expression ניזהא דאריה".

Rabbah (var. Rava)[50] and R. Zera happened to be in the house of the exilarch (on a Sabbath). They saw a certain slave putting a water jug on the mouth of a kettle.[51] Rabbah drove him away. R. Zera said to him (Rabbah): how does this differ from (the permissible activity of putting) one boiler atop a second boiler? He answered him: there (in the case of the boiler) he is only retaining (the heat). Here (in the case of the jug) he is surely creating it. Another time he saw him spread a דסתודר[52] on the mouth of a cask and lay a ladle on top of it. Rabbah drove him away. R. Zera said to him: why? He said: you shall see presently. He (R. Zera) saw him wringing it out. He (R. Zera) said: how does this differ from covering the cask with a rag[53] (which Rava elsewhere permitted)? He answered him: there (in the case of the rag) he doesn't care about it (and won't bother to wring it out). In this case he cares.[54]

b. Sanh. 41b:

אי הכי אמריתו בה טובא אמריתו בה אמרי ליה מטיבותוה דמר אמרינן בה טובא מניזיהותיה דמר לא אמרינן בה ולא חדא.

If thus you said (about witness law), you said much about it. They say to him: Because of the master's kindness we say much about it (witness law). Had he put us at a distance, we would not have said a single thing.

Accordingly, the identification of Aramaic *nzh* of the bowls with Akkadian *nesû* provides us with the etymology of the Akkadian term, while the bowl

50 For the historico-political significance of the variant in this passage see M. Beer apud Neusner, *History* vol. 4, 94; It is difficult to determine which fourth century scholar is meant. Printed editions of the Talmud conventionally have רבא for R. Abba b. Joseph b. Hama (*EncJud* 13, 1579) and רבה for Rabbah b. Nahmani (*EncJud* 13, 1442). But both רבה and רבא are contractions of the PN Abba and the honorific R. (I thank Professor David Weiss-Halivni for calling this to my attention.).

51 Aramaic *qwmqwm* is a loan from Latin *cucumis*. See *DJPA*, 482.

52 The word is middle Persian *dastudar* "shawl." See S. Shaked, "Iranian Loanwords in Middle Aramaic," in E. Yarshater, ed., *Encyclopedia Iranica* (Boston: Routledge and Kegan Paul, 1986), vol. 2, fasc. 3, 261. (I thank Dr. O. Skjaervo of the Center for Iranian Studies at Columbia University for this reference.) There is a variant reading with the much more common סודר "scarf," a loan from Latin *sudarium*. See *DJPA*, 370. For other variants see AC vol. 4, 179, n. 1.

53 For other citations of פרונקא see Kasowski *Thesaurus*, vol. 32:461. For the variant spellings see AC vol. 6, 433.

54 Cf. the translation of Freedman apud Neusner *History*, vol. 4, 106–108.

references together with the information supplied by the Akkadian, enable a more precise definition of the Aramaic word in its talmudic contexts.

As to the question of *heh* versus *ḥet*, in terms of the clear attestations in the Talmud and in the Syriac bowl (Text N, above), Epstein was correct to prefer *heh*. At the same time, the fact that Akkadian *nesû* contains an [e] vowel, points sooner to an etymological *ḥet* in Northwest Semitic.[55] We may compare e.g. Akkadian *petû* = Hebrew פתח "to open"; Akkadian *leqû* = Hebrew לקח "to take"; as opposed to Akkadian *qalû* = Hebrew קלה "to burn," "to roast"; and Akkadian *manû* = Hebrew מנה "to count." In all likelihood, we have here to do with an etymological *ḥet* that was weakened to *heh*, a phenomenon attested elsewhere in Babylonian Aramaic. Examples such as להמא/נהמא for לחמא "bread" and הדדי[56] for חדדי "mutually" come readily to mind.

55 Epstein himself (*Studies* vol. 1, 339) notes two examples of *nzḥ* with *ḥet* from the medieval work *Sword of Moses*.

56 See J. Epstein, *A Grammar of Babylonian Aramaic* (Jerusalem: Magnes, 1960), 18; Dalm, Gr 58–59; E. Kutscher, *Studies in Galilean Aramaic* (Ramat-Gan: Bar-Ilan, 1976), 69–70.

CHAPTER 9

Ḥbr and Friends

The problem of distinguishing among the various senses of BH חבר and defining the vocable's inner semantic ranges, has taxed the resources of biblical lexicographers from the medieval period onward.[1] A significant paper[2] elucidating some passages in which the consonantal sequence ח-ב-ר is attested was published more than thirty-five years ago by J. J. Finkelstein, late colleague of our *Jubilar* at Yale. Ten years ago a colleague of Professor Hallo's from student days at Chicago, my own lamented teacher Moshe Held, accepted some of Finkelstein's suggestions but took issue with others.[3] My entry into the discussion is offered in modest tribute to William Hallo, whom I consider one of my teachers although I never had the privilege of formal study with him.

Among the phrases studied by Finkelstein were חבר חבר Deut 18:11; חובר חברים in Ps 58:6 (// מלחשים); ברב כשפיך בעצמת חבריך in Isa 47:9; בחבריך וברב כשפיך in Isa 47:12; בית חבר in Prv 21:9 and 25:4 and אחבירה עליכם במלים in Job 16:4. Finkelstein argued that each of these passages employed a verb *ḥbr* II, with an initial consonant that was not etymological [ḥ] (*ḥet*) normally corresponding to a vowel in Akkadian,[4] but with etymological Semitic [ḫ].[5] Specifically, Finkelstein attempted to explain the forms of חבר in each of these passages on the basis of Akkadian *ḫabāru*, "to be noisy, to make noise."[6] In some of these cases Finkelstein's explanation did not greatly alter the

---

1 See *e.g.* M Wagner in VTSup16 (1967), 360–361; *HALAT*, 276–277; H. Cazelles, "chabar, chaber," *TDOT* IV, 193–197.

2 J. J. Finkelstein, "Hebrew חבר and Semitic ḪBR," *JBL* 75 (1956), 328–331.

3 M. Held, "Studies in Biblical Lexicography in the Light of Akkadian," *ErIsr* 16 (1982), 76–85 (in Hebrew; English abstract *ibid.*, 254*).

4 Accordingly, it is odd that *HALAT*, 276, s.v. II חבר, cites Finkelstein's article for the meaning "Schlangenbeschwörer," but derives the חובר חברי(ם) in Deut 18:11 and Ps 58:6 from a stem meaning "sich binden," "zusammengefügt sein." As correctly noted in *HALAT* itself (277 *s.v.* חבר), Akk. *ibru/ebru* "friend," "colleague" (see *CAD I/J*, 5–7) and Ug. *ḥbr* "companion" (see *UT* Glossary, 834= *DLU*, 172) demonstrate that the Hebrew stem חבר which includes words for "binding," "attachment," "friend" and the like, derives from a stem with etymological *ḥet*.

5 Mari *ḫibru(m)* is a loan word from West-Semitic *ḫbr*. See A. Malamat, *JAOS* 82 (1962), 145–147; Contrast AHw., 344a.

6 Finkelstein *JBL* 75, 329. Cf. *CAD Ḫ*, 7, s.v. *ḫabāru* A; AHw., 302b s.v. *ḫabāru* I translates *ḫabāru* "lärmen," i.e. make a noise or uproar. The entry appeared a decade after Finkelstein's article. As observed by Held (*ErIsr* 16, 84, n. 79), Loretz arrived at a nearly identical conclusion,

 | DOI 10.1163/9789004340879_010

traditional understanding of the verse. Thus, "the חובר חבר of Deut 18:11 may still be translated 'charmer' but the connotation is…'one who mutters sounds, mutterer.'"[7] As for Isa 47:9, 12, Finkelstein modified the standard interpretation[8] of the verse (ב) חבריך//(כשפיך) by seeing a reference to the charmers themselves rather than their charms.[9] In contrast, Finkelstein's translation of Job 16:4 was a new departure.[10] On his interpretation that the Heb. אחבירה reflects Akkadian *ḫabāru*, the phrase אחבירה עליכם במלים means "I could harangue you[11] with words, I could shake my head[12] at you."[13] Finally, the enigmatic בית חבר in Prv 21:9 and its virtual duplicate in Prv 25:24 could be understood as "noisy household."[14]

Whereas Held allowed that Finkelstein's solution to the long-standing crux in the Proverbs passages might have been on the mark, he devoted the bulk of his remarks to refuting Finkelstein's understanding of חובר חבר in Deuteronomy and בחבריך in Isa 47:9, 12. On the negative side, Held astutely observed that neither the verb *ḫabāru* "to make noise" nor its cognate noun *ḫubūru*, "noise, uproar" (German: Lärmen[15]) was ever attested in the vast

---

apparently independently of Finkelstein. See O. Loretz, "Miscellanea Biblica ḪBR in JB 16:4," *CBQ* 23 (1961), 293–294.

7 Finkelstein, *JBL* 75, 331.

8 See e.g. translations of KJV, JPS, NJPS, NEB, REB.

9 Finkelstein, *JBL* 75, 331.

10 Cf. KJV: "heap up words"; JPS: "join words together"; NJPS: "barrage you with words."

11 NEB and REB "how could I harangue you" reflect their acceptance of Finkelstein's proposal.

12 Accordingly, Finkelstein agrees with those scholars who see "shake my head" in the verse as a gesture of contempt. See e.g. E. Dhorme, *A Commentary on the Book of Job* translated by H. Knight (New York: Nelson, 1984), 229–230; Cf. M. Gruber, *Aspects of Nonverbal Communication in the Ancient Near East* (Rome: Biblical Institute Press, 1980), 408. For a statement of the contrary view that shaking the head in this passage is meant sympathetically, see e.g. A. Hakam, *Sefer Iyyob* (Jerusalem: Mossad Harav Kook, 1981), 124.

13 *Ibid.*

14 *Ibid.* This interpretation was accepted by A. Malamat, *JAOS* 82 (1962), 145, n. 10. Additional supporting arguments were offered by two other Israeli scholars. See O. Margalit, *Beth Mikrâ* 21 (1976), 6–7; Ch. Cohen, *ibid.*, 598–599.

15 AHw., 352b, s.v. *ḫubūru(m)* II. For more recent discussions of *ḫubūru* see W. Moran, "Some Considerations of Form and Interpretation in Atra-Hasis," in *Language, Literature, and History: Philological and Historical Studies presented to Erica Reiner*, ed. R. Rochberg-Halton (New Haven: American Oriental Society, 1987), 245–255, especially 251–254; P. Michalowski, "Presence at the Creation," in *Lingering Over Words. Studies in Ancient*

Akkadian literature of incantation. To Held's objection we may add that "noise" or "uproar" would be most inappropriate[16] in a native[17] context of charm and incantation in which attention to specific words and their manner of recitation would be crucial.[18] Indeed, as Finkelstein was surely aware, the verb most commonly employed to describe the oral aspect of a charm or spell is *manû* "recite," the very same word that means "count."[19] Its cognate noun *minûtu*[20] "recitation" also serves in the meanings "amount, number, string of beads of fixed number." Akkadian spells are frequently followed by a specific instruction as to how often[21] and with what ritual accompaniment[22] they are to be recited. Charms, spells and incantations in Mesopotamia and elsewhere

---

Near Eastern Literature in Honor of William L. Moran, eds. T. Abusch, J. Huehnergard and P. Steinkeller (Atlanta: Scholars, 1990), 381–396, especially, 385–388.

16 Note the occurrences of forms of לחש "whisper" in incantational settings.. For BH in addition to Ps 58:6 see Jer 8:17; Qoh 10:11. Cf. S. Loewenstamm, *Comparative Studies in Biblical and Ancient Oriental Literatures* (Kevelaer: Butzon & Bercker, 1980), 222; for Late Hebrew see *Mishnah Sanhedrin* 10:11. For Phoenician see *KAI* 27:1. For Jewish Palestinian Aramaic see *DJPA*, 281; J. Naveh and S. Shaked, *Amulets and Magic Bowls* (Leiden: Brill, 1985), Amulet I: 16; see also Akkadian *luḫḫušu* (*CAD L*, 40b, s.v. *laḫāšu*). Note also Ug. *mlḫš* // *ydy ḥmt* "(snake) charmer // expeller of venom." (*KTU*³ 1.100 I:5–6 etc.).

17 Thus, Finkelstein would have had to demonstrate that the author of Deut 18:11 was employing a reflex of Akk *ḫabāru* in an outsider's polemical or satirical sense, much like *Tg.Onq.* to this passage who translated חבר חבר by רטין רטן. For the targum text see A. Sperber, *The Bible in Aramaic* I (Leiden: Brill, 1959), 322. For a thorough study of the use of the term רטן, see J. Greenfield, "רטין מגושא" in *Joshua Finkel Festschrift*, eds. S. Hoenig and L. Stitskin (New York: Yeshiva University, 1974), 63–69; Cf. E. S. Rosenthal, "For the Talmudic Dictionary- Talmudica-Iranica (in Hebrew)," in *Irano-Judaica*, ed. S. Shaked (Jerusalem: Ben-Zvi Institute, 1982), 72.

18 As opposed to the אוב וידעני of Deut 18:11 who are known to "chirp and mutter." (Isa 8:19) Significantly, the verb "mutter" in this passage is not חבר but הגה. On the entire passage see H. L. Ginsberg, *ErIsr* 5 (1958), 61*–65*; on הגה see *idem*, VTSup 16 (1967), 80.

19 See *CAD M*/1, 221–227.

20 See *CAD M*/2, 98; Ugaritic *mnt* "incantation" seems to be identical. See T. Gaster, *JANES* 7 (1975), 41.

21 See references in Mullo Weir, *Lexicon*, 202; *CAD M*/1, 223, meaning 3; *CAD M*/2, 99.

22 See S. D. Sperling, *WO* 12 (1981), 8, n. 6 (with earlier literature); *idem*, in *Jewish Spirituality from the Bible through the Middle Ages*, ed. A. Green (New York: Crossroad, 1986), 19. For text references to specific ritual acts see *CAD E*, 244b, s.v. *epištu; CAD K*, 353a, s.v. *kikkiṭṭû*.

usually refer "to the authorized use of rhythmically organized words of power"[23] and not to uproarious noises.[24]

On the positive side, Held, after dismissing earlier etymologies from classical rabbinic times[25] down through Finkelstein, realized the significance of the fact that in Akkadian itself *ubburu* "to bind magically" is attested in parallelism

23 So T. Ludwig, "Incantation," *The Encyclopedia of Religion* (New York: MacMillan, 1987) 7, 147. See *ibid.*, 147–152 for a convenient cross-cultural summary.

24 Some Mesopotamian rituals called for silence and the absence of ominous utterances. As Erica Reiner has observed, one reason for the existence of nocturnal rituals is that "human hubbub (Reiner's felicitous translation of *ḫubūr nišē*) is effectively avoided." See *idem, Studies Landsberger*, 250.

25 Held (*ibid.*, 78) cites BT Sanhedrin 65a as the source of a rabbinic etymology. He seems to have misunderstood the text, which provides no etymology at all. The phrase חובר חב' אחד חבר גדול אח' חבר קטן אפ' נחשים ועקרב'. (text from H. Strack, *Der babylonische Talmud nach der einzigen vollständigen Handschrift München Codex Hebraicus* 95 [Leiden: A. W. Sijthof, 1912], II, 346b) is a legal midrash, which infers from the repetition of the root חבר in cognate accusative structure, that the Deuteronomic prohibition "applies equally to one who charms large objects, and to one who charms small ones, even snakes and scorpions." See D. Epstein, *The Babylonian Talmud Seder Nezikin III* (London: Soncino: 1935), 444; Cf. L. Goldschmidt, *Der Babylonische Talmud* VII (Berlin: S. Calvary, 1903), 276; See further J. Levy, *Wörterbuch über die Talmudim und Midraschim* (Berlin, 1924) I, 8; L. Finkelstein, ed., *Siphre ad Deuteronomium* (Berlin: Jüdischer Kulturbund, 1939), 219:9–10; and the translations of Reuven Hammer, *Sifre A Tannaitic Commentary on the Book of Deuteronomy* (New Haven: Yale, 1986), 200; J. Neusner, *Sifre to Deuteronomy an Analytical Translation* II (Atlanta: Scholars, 1987), 49. It is Rashi to BT Sanhedrin 65a who provides the etymology by defining the חובר חבר as שמחבר את השדים "one who brings the demons together," and then by explaining אחד חובר גדול as מאסף חיות ובהמות גדולות "who gathers together large wild and domestic animals," and אחד חבר קטן as מחבר שקצים ורמשים "one who gathers together vermin and insects." In his Bible commentary Rashi offers essentially the same etymology: שמצרף נחשים ועקרבים או שאר חיות למקום אחד "One who collects in one place, snakes, scorpions or other wild animals." (text cited from H. Chavel, *Perush Rashi al Hattorah* [Jerusalem: Mossad Harav Kook, 1985], 558). The rabbis identified the biblical חובר חבר with חבר/חברא, which in late Hebrew and various Aramaic dialects translates Pahlavi *moγ-mard*, "magus." For the correspondences see Rosenthal, "Iranica-Talmudica," n. 23; see further, *DJPA*, 184, 186. I thank Professor James Russell of Columbia University for suggesting (oral communication, Jan. 17, 1992) that speakers may have made a semantic connection between the Semitic and Iranian terms. The Pahlavi corresponds to Old Persian *magu* (attested in LB Akk. as *magušu*. See *CAD M/I*, 48–49). Of uncertain etymology, the term may have originally meant "member of the tribe" and then come to mean "member of the priestly tribe." See M. Boyce, *A History of Zoroastrianism* (Leiden: Brill, 1982), 19. The suggestion of M. Schwartz (*Acta Iranica 25* [1985], 496) that *magu* meant "people who share a gift" would likewise facilitate a connection with Hebrew and Aramaic חבר/חברא (regardless of their etymology).

with *kuššupu* "to bewitch, to cast an evil spell." The Akkadian parallelism is perfectly mirrored in the Hebrew parallelism of חבר//כשף in Isa 47:9, 12.[26] In other words, Finkelstein's interpretation of the Isaiah verses was essentially correct, but his etymology was wrong. Similarly, the work of the חובר חבר of Deuteronomy 18:11 could now be understood with greater precision as referring to one who binds by enchantments.

Additionally, although Held did not discuss Ps 58:6, we may apply his conclusions to that verse as well. The entire verse reads: אשר לא ישמע לקול מלחשים חובר חברים מחכם Finkelstein translated: "He hears not the voice of the whisperer(s) who mutters crafty sounds." It is readily apparent that the translation is flawed by a grammatical misconstruction, because מחכם is singular and חברים is plural. Secondly, Finkelstein's translation "mutters,"[27] allegedly based on Akk. *ḫubūru*, contradicts his own renditions of the Akk. verb and its nominal cognates. Thus, he translates *ḫubūru* as "noise, uproar" noting that *ḫubūrum* is synonymous with *rigmum* "clamor." He observes additionally that it is this "din of mankind … which disturbs the gods' sleep and impels them to send down the Deluge." In like manner, Finkelstein translates *ḫabrātum nišū* as "clamorous mankind" and *ḫubūrša* "as the land's uproar."[28] But English "mutter," which means "to speak in low tones,"[29] is a virtual antonym of Akkadian *ḫabāru* as (correctly) translated by Finkelstein. In all likelihood, Finkelstein took refuge in "mutter"[30] because "clamorers" would not fit semantically[31] in parallelism with the "whisperers" of the first stich. Finally, he ignored the poetic structure of the verse by which the phrase אשר לא ישמע governs both stichs. The entire verse must be analyzed semantically as: אשר לא ישמע לקול מלחשים [אשר לא ישמע לקול] חובר חברים מחכם

The translation therefore should be: "Who hears not the voice of the conjurers; of the skilled spellbinder."[32]

26 The same observation was made independently by Y. Avishur *UF* 13 [1981], 22–23, who argued that the very same parallelism occurs in Ugaritic. Interestingly, the comparison is not found in *idem, Stylistic Studies of Word-Pairs in Biblical and Ancient Semitic Languages* (Kevelaer: Butzon & Bercker, 1984).

27 Followed by NJPS.

28 *JBL* 75, 330–331.

29 See *The Compact Edition of the Oxford English Dictionary* (Oxford: Oxford University, 1971), 1885.

30 The various nuances of English "mutter" are covered by Akkadian *dabābu, laḫāšu.*

31 See e.g. A. Hakam, *Sefer Tehillim* (Jerusalem: Mossad Harav Kook, 1979), 337.

32 Scholars have attempted to find other early Northwest Semitic attestations of חבר in the sense of "enchanter," "spellbinder." F. Vattionis's (*Or.* 36 [1967]) reading: חברי תנת and his translation "*incantatori di Tinit*" in a Phoenician inscription from Spain are accepted by M. Dahood (*Psalms* III 51–100 [Garden City: Anchor Doubleday, 1986], 60), but rejected

Because his primary concern was with the Isaiah passages, Held did not discuss Job 16:4, but ruled out any connection with אחבירה עליכם במלים with *ḫabāru*. Held wrote: "Whoever is compelled to translate 'make a noise with words' is virtually admitting that his interpretation is extremely farfetched."[33] But contra Held, the interpretation is not farfetched at all[34] and receives support from Jewish Aramaic and Late Hebrew.

According to the Palestinian Talmud (hereafter, PT),[35] R. Yohanan (third century) devised a method by which some restrictions of tithing laws might be eased. The story continues:

נחת עולא לתמן ואמרה בשם ר' יוחנן וחברון עלוי

In another story[36] this one involving the testimony of a dying husband in a potential levirate case, R. Samuel said "he is believed … R. Yohanan said 'he is not believed.' " Once again the story continues:

נחת עולא לתמן ואמרה בשם ר' יוחנן וחברון עלוי

Sokoloff[37] includes these examples in his dictionary, s.v. חבר vb., which he defines as: "to combine against, gather together, be associate of." He translates both of the above passages as "PN went there (=to Babylonia), and they combined against him."[38]

---

by F. Cross (*HTR* 64 [1971], 189–195); see further, R. Tomback, *A Comparative Semitic Lexicon of the Phoenician and Punic Languages* (Missoula: Scholars, 1978), 97. Both Avishur (*UF* 13, 22–23; contrast *idem, Word Pairs*, 523) and Mark Smith (*RB* 91 [1984], 377–376) have argued that Ug. *ḫbr // dʿt* attested in Ras ibn Hani 78/20:9–10 and *KTU*[3] 1.6 VI:49–50 means "spell-caster"// "knower," i.e. one who knows ghosts or spirits. Their interpretation would provide a parallel to the association of Heb. חובר חבר and ידעוני in Deut 18:11. See further, T. Lewis, *Cults of the Dead in Ancient Israel and Ugarit* (Atlanta: Scholars, 1989), 37, n. 102.

33 Held, *ErIsr* 16, 84, n. 79. Held quotes Loretz's formulation (*CBQ* 23, 294) rather than Finkelstein's more elegant, "I could harangue you with words." In fairness to Loretz, it must be noted that the published article was translated from the author's German manuscript.

34 The interpretation is accepted in *HALAT*, "Nachträge und Berichtigungen," LIII.

35 PT Demai 1:4 (22b). For ease of reference, we follow the chapter divisions and pagination of the standard reprints, which are based on the Venice-Krotoschin edition. Actual text citations are from *The Palestinian Talmud Leiden Ms. Cod. Scal.* 3 (Jerusalem: Kedem, 1970). All other PT references in this paper are cited from the same manuscript.

36 PT Qiddushin 3:10 (64b).

37 *DJPA*, 186.

38 Contrast J. Neusner, *The Talmud of the Land of Israel* Vol. 26 (Chicago: University of Chicago, 1984), 196. Neusner translates "they joined with him," which, in the context of the pericope, seems inappropriate.

Sokoloff attributes his interpretation to Saul Lieberman on his comment to a much discussed[39] passage from the Tosefta,[40] which reads:

פעם אחת חל ארבעה עשר בשבת שאלו את הלל הזקן פסח מהו שידחה את השבת אמ' להם וכי פסח אחד יש לנו בשנה שדוחה את השבת הרבה משלש מאות פסחים יש לנו בשנה ודוחין את השבת חברו עליו כל העזרה

Once the fourteenth (of Nisan) fell on the Sabbath. They asked Hillel the Elder: "Does the requirement of Passover sacrifice override the Sabbath (prohibition on slaughter)?" He replied to them: "Do we have just one Passover sacrifice a year? We have over three hundred Passover(-type) sacrifices throughout the year which override the Sabbath (prohibition on slaughter)." The entire temple court חברו against him.

But Lieberman had not actually translated חברו by "combined against." In his comment to the above passage Lieberman wrote: "That is to say, they attached themselves to him,[41] because they disagreed with him."[42] In support of his interpretation of חברו in the above story, Lieberman cited another Tosefta passage, also involving Hillel:

מעשה בהלל הזקן שסמך על העולה וחברו עליו תלמידי שמיי אמ' להם בואו וראו שהיא נקבה וצריך אני לעשותה זבחי שלמים הפליגן בדברים והלכו להם

There is the case of Hillel the Elder, who laid hand on the holocaust (-animal) in the temple-court and the disciples of the Shammai school (who prohibited the ritual) וחברו against him. He said to them: "Come and see[43]

39 For an analysis from a formal and literary critical perspective see J. Neusner, *The Rabbinic Traditions about the Pharisees Before 70, Part I: The Masters* (Leiden: Brill, 1971), 230–235. For other relevant bibliography see H. Strack and G. Stemberger, *Introduction to the Talmud and Midrash* (Edinburgh: T&T Clark, 1991), 71–72.

40 Tosefta Pisha 4:13. Text (punctuation added) cited from Saul Lieberman, *The Tosefta Order of Mo'ed* (New York: Jewish Theological Seminary, 1962), 165: 80–83.

41 Contrast Neusner, *Pharisees*, 231: "The whole courtyard collected against him."

42 Lieberman, *Tosefta Ki-fshutah A Comprehensive Commentary on the Tosefta Part IV Order Mo'ed*, 566. In the original Hebrew, Lieberman's comment reads: כלומר, נטפלו לו, מפני שלא הסכימו לו. Lieberman himself always told those of us who were fortunate to be his students that whenever a rabbinic commentator began with "that is to say," it was the reader's obligation to be especially cautious.

43 On this technical term see B. Z. (Wilhelm) Bacher ערכי מדרש (Tel-Aviv: Achdut, 1923), 6. For its Aramaic reflex see *ibid.*, 191; *DJPA*, 205b.

that this is a female, and I need to offer it as the sacrifice of sacred greeting."[44] Thus, he evaded them with talk, and they went on their way.[45]

There can be little doubt that Lieberman, whose contribution to talmudic philology was monumental,[46] translated "that is to say, attached themselves to him" and avoided "collected against" (Neusner) and "combined against" (Sokoloff) for good reason: absent the disputed passages, the Hebrew and Aramaic[47] verb *ḥbr* I[48] is not attested directly[49] in the hostile sense: "to gang up on someone,"[50] but only in the positive sense.[51]

---

44 For this translation of שלמים see B. Levine, *In the Presence of the Lord* (Leiden: Brill, 1974), 3–52; *idem, The JPS Torah Commentary Leviticus* (Philadelphia: Jewish Publication Society, 1989), 15.

45 Tosefta Hagigah 2:10. Text from Lieberman, *Tosefta … Mo'ed* 385:80–82; closely parallel text in PT Hagigah 2:8 (78a); PT Bezah 2:4 (61c); BT Bezah 20a.

46 See E. Y. Kutscher, ed., *Archive of the New Dictionary of Rabbinical Literature* vol. I (Ramat-Gan: Bar-Ilan, 1972), 12–13.

47 Thus, e.g. the Dead Sea targum to Job 34: 8 translates וארח לחברה עם פעלי און by ומתחבר לעבדי שקר. See K. Beyer, *Die aramäischen Texten vom Toten Meer* (Tübingen: Vandenhoeck & Ruprecht, 1984), 292, cf. *ibid.*, 571. In *Tg. Onq.* forms of חבר translate יחדו, (Deut 22:11; composite weave); צמד, (Num 25:3; sexual union); and לוה (Gen 29:3; love/sexual union). For Syriac references see Payne Smith, 1183. The same positive sense seems to hold for Mandaic. See E. Drower and R. Macuch, *A Mandaic Dictionary* (Oxford: Clarendon, 1963), 130.

48 This is true of its synonyms as well as far as the simple stem is concerned. Thus, to convey the sense of "gang up on," the verb קהל (not attested in BH in the qal), is likewise employed in the nip'al with the preposition על. See Exod 32:1; Num 16:3, 17:7, 20:2; Jer 26:9. Likewise, the verb יעד is employed in the nip'al with the preposition על. See Num 14:35, 16:11, 27:3.

49 Thus in Gen 14:3 כל אלה חברו, the association is for hostile purposes but the indirect object of the verb in the verse is the Siddim valley. Similarly, in Job 16:9 צרי ילטוש עיניו לי is translated by the Peshitta: בעלדבבי חברו עיניהון עלי (reflecting a reading of plural subjects), but the direct object of the verb is "eyes."

50 An interdialectal distribution of "gang up on" includes Heb. נקהל along with Aramaic כנש. See e.g. *Tg.Onq.* and *Tg.Neof.* to Exod 32:1; Num 16:3, 20:2, (For *Tg.Onq.* see A. Sperber, *The Bible in Aramaic I* [Leiden: Brill, 1959]; for *Tg.Neof.* see A. Diéz-Macho, *Neophyti I* [Madrid-Barcelona: Consejo Superior de Investigaciones Cientificas, 1968–1978]). Cf. further M. Klein, *Genizah Fragments of Palestinian Targum to the Pentateuch* (Cincinnati: HUC, 1986), I, 325; D. Rieder, Targum Jonathan ben Uziel to the Pentateuch (Jerusalem: 1974–1985) I, 131; II, 216, 222. Cf. further Heb. נועד על in Num 14:35, 16:11 and Num 27:3 with its correspondents in the targums and the Peshitta. In Akkadian "gang up" is *paḫāru* with the dative. See e.g. *Syria* 32: 14: 18; see further AHw., 810b.

51 Much like its Arabic semantic counterpart *ṣaḥiba*. For the correspondence see A. Neubauer, ed., *The Book of Hebrew Roots by … ibn Janâh* (reprint Amsterdam: Philo,

Thus, to cite a Late Hebrew[52] example, a midrashic comment puns on Ps 58:6 and applies the verse to Jeroboam.[53]

אמר ר' חונה חובר חברים מחוכם כל מי שהיה חוברו היה חוברו

R. Huna said: "A cunning enchanter of friends."—He enchanted those who befriended him.[54]

It should be obvious to the reader, however, that the translation "clamored" would be more contextually appropriate in the problematic passages as "attached themselves." Note, for example, another passage alluded to by Lieberman, from the Babylonian Talmud:[55]

תניא א"ר כשהלכתי ללמוד תורה אצל ר' אליעזר בן שמוע חברו עלי תלמידיו כתרנגולים של בית בוקיא ולא הניחוני ללמוד אלא דבר אחד במשנתינו רבי אליעזר אומר אנדרוגינוס חייבין עליו סקילה כזכר

1968), 207; Saadia to Ps 45:8, 94:20, 119:63 (cited from Y. Kafah [Kafih] ed., *Tehillim 'im Targûm u-Feruš ha Gā'ôn Rabbenû Sa'adyah ben Yôsef Fayyumî* [Jerusalem: American Academy for Jewish Research, 1965]).

52 Specifically, our example is from the academic dialect of Hebrew classified as *Mittlehebräisch2* (mhe2) by E. Kutscher. See *idem*, ed., *Archive of the New Dictionary of Rabbinical Literature* I (Ramat Gan: Bar-Ilan, 1972), 3–28 (in Hebrew; English summary *ibid.*, iii–xxvii).

53 PT Abodah Zarah 1:1 (39b).

54 Cf. M. Kosovsky, *Concordance to the Talmud Yerushalmi* (Palestinian Talmud), vol. 3 (Jerusalem: Israel Academy of Science and Humanities and Jewish Theological Seminary), 482: שהיה מתחבר [אליו] היה מצרפו[לעבודה זרה]. "Whoever associated [with him], he would attach [to idolatry]."; Cf. further, J. Neusner, *The Talmud of the Land of Israel Volume 33 Abodah Zarah* (Chicago: University of Chicago, 1982), 11: "Whoever was associated with him [Jeroboam] he [Jeroboam] would cast a spell over him [in the sin of the bull-calves]." Our translation as well as those of Kosovsky and Neusner can claim support from the variant attested in the Yalqut Shimoni 428c: א"ר הושעיא, חובר חברים מחוכם : כל מי שהיה לחברו היה חוברו (punning on Ps 58:6) said: A " 'A clever enchanter of associates.' He would enchant anyone who became his associate." Contrast the translation of G. Wewers, *Avoda Zara Götzendienst* (Tübingen: J. Mohr, 1980), 4: *"jeder, der sein (Jeroboams) Genosse war, dessen Genosse war er."* Despite their differences, all three translations understand חבר in a positive sense "to associate with," "to befriend." Cf. further the paraphrase in M. Schwab, *Le Talmud de Jérusalem* (reprint Paris, 1960), vol. 6, 173.

55 BT Yebamot 842. For the text, see A. Liss, ed., *The Babylonian Talmud with Variant Readings Tractate Yebamoth III* (Jerusalem: Institute for the complete Israeli Talmud, 1989), 230–231.

> It was taught: Rabbi (Judah I) said, "When I went to study torah with R. Elazar b. Shammua, his students clamored around me like the roosters of Beth Buqia and permitted me to learn only one thing in our Mishnah (namely), 'Rabbi Eliezer (sic) says (sexual relations with) a hermaphrodite are as liable to (execution by) stoning as (homosexual) relations with a male.'"

The parallel in the Palestinian Talmud[56] reads:

א"ר ביקשתי ולא מצאתי דברי בן שמוע באנדרוגינוס וחברה[57] עליו חבורה

> Rabbi (Judah the Prince) said, I tried unsuccessfully to discover ben Shammua's statements about the hermaphrodite, and an uproar[58] broke out against him.

The talmudic passages are instructive as regards Job 16:4. Whereas in the absence of Akk. *ḫabāru* it was possible to argue that חבר על in the rabbinic sources might mean "assemble against," no such option is available in Job 16:4, where the subject is 1st person singular.[59] It seems preferable therefore to accept Finkelstein's interpretation of the Job passage and to apply his insight to the elucidation of the disputed rabbinic selections.

56 PT Yebamot 8:5 (9d).

57 This is the clear reading of Leiden Ms. Cod. Scal 3. Lieberman (*Tosefta ... Commentary*, 566) cites the text as וחברו עליו חבורה without indicating the source of his reading. The printed editions agree with the Leiden MS. Cf. also M. Kasovsky, *Concordance to Talmud Yerushalmi* (Jerusalem: Jewish Theological Seminary and Israel Academy of Sciences and Humanities, 1985), III:482. The passage is included by Kasovsky under the rubric: התקהל והיוועד כנגד מי "To gather oneself (=German: sich versammeln) and meet together against (=German: sich versammeln gegen) someone."

58 Late Hebrew חבורה is a reflex of Akkadian *ḫubūru*. Cf. also OB *ḫabarratum*, on which see Held, *JANES* 11 (1979), 55, n. 19.

59 As for the alternation between the hifʿil and qal patterns, Moreshet has suggested that when no semantic distinction was involved the hifʿil pattern was employed for purposes of poetic diction. See M. Moreshet,"Hifʿil Undifferentiated in Meaning from Qal in Rabbinic Hebrew in Comparison to Biblical Hebrew," (in Hebrew) in M. Bar-Asher, ed., קובץ מחקרים בלשון חזל חלק ב (Jerusalem, 1979), 263–295, especially 265–266.

CHAPTER 10

Aramaic Spousal Misunderstandings

In Babylonian Talmud Nedarim 66b there is a humorous tale about a native of Babylonia who settled in Israel and married a local woman. Trouble began when he asked her to prepare meals for him and she misunderstood all four of his instructions. The present paper explains the misunderstandings as the result of real or perceived dialectal differences between Jewish Babylonian Aramaic and Jewish Palestinian Aramaic.

Personal experience teaches that some of the greatest confusion in communication occurs when two parties wrongly assume that they are speaking the same language. Different dialects of the same language abound in opportunities for confusion. That this was true for Aramaic in late antiquity and during the Middle Ages is proved by the existence of translations from one Aramaic dialect to another, e.g., the Peshitta to Daniel and the targumic toseftot originating in Palestine and translated into the Onqelos dialect.[1] The difficulties of mutual understanding between and among dialects are greatest in oral communication, where there are abundant variations in diction and pronunciation that are masked by the written language. We should not be surprised that the problem of mutual intelligibility of the Aramaic dialects spoken by Jews in late antiquity is raised in the Talmuds. Just as the writer of Judges 12 poked fun

---

* Note the following abbreviations: CTB=C. Kasowski, *Thesaurus Talmudis* (Jerusalem: Jewish Theological Seminary, 1954–1978); CTY=M. Kosovsky, *Concordance to the Talmud Yerushalmi* (Jerusalem: Jewish Theological Seminary, 1982–2004). (N.B. the members of the קוסובסקי family who provided several concordances to classical rabbinic literature were not consistent in transliterating the family name.); *HALAT* =*Hebräisches und aramäisches Lexikon zum alten Testament* (Leiden: E.J. Brill, 1967–1990); JBA = Jewish Babylonian Aramaic; JPA = Jewish Palestinian Aramaic.

1 "Most of the Tosefta texts ... have undergone a *conscious* (emphasis in original) dialectal transformation to the language of Onqelos." So, M. Klein, *Genizah Manuscripts of Palestinian Targum to the Pentateuch*, vol. 1 (Cincinnati: Hebrew Union College, 1986), xxvii; cf. M. Klein, "Targumic Toseftot from the Cairo Geniza," in *Salvación en la Palabra: Targum, Derash, Berith: En Memoria del Professor Alejandro Diez Macho*, ed. D. Muñoz León (Madrid: Inst. Francisco Suarez, 1985), 409–418. On theories about the Peshitta Pentateuch's origin in other dialects, see P. Dirksen, "The Old Testament Peshitta," in *Mikra*, ed. M. Mulder (Philadelphia: Fortress Press, 1988), 264–285.

 | DOI 10.1163/9789004340879_011

at the Ephraimite pronunciation of "shibboleth,"[2] so Babylonian Jews poked fun at Palestinian pronunciation and vice versa. But while the failure of the Ephraimites to speak Gileadite proved fatal, in the story presented here the dialectal confusion produced only two disappointing meals and, perhaps, a minor head injury.

The presence of the sage Baba b. Buta sets the story in BT Nedarim[3] 66b[4] in the first century.[5]

ההוא בר בבל דסליק לארעא דישׂראל, נסיב איתתא, אמר לה בשילי לי תרי טלפי, בשׁילה ליה תרי טלופחי. רתח עלה. למחר אמר לה בשׁילי לי גריוא בשׁילה ליה גריוא אמר לה זילי אייתי לי תרי בוציני, אזלת אייתיאת ליה תרי שׂרגי. אמר לה זילי תברי יתהון על רישׁא דבבא. הוה יתיב בבא בן בוטא אבבא וקא דאין דינא, אזלת ותברת יתהון על רישׁיה, אמר לה מה הדין דעבדת? אמרה ליה, כך ציוני בעלי אמר, את עשׂית רצון בעליך, המקום יוציא ממעיך שני בנים כבבא בן בוטא.

In the standard English version, H. Freedman translates as follows:

> A certain Babylonian went up to the Land of Israel and took a wife [there]. "Boil me two [cows'] feet," he ordered and she boiled him two lentils, which infuriated him with her. The next day he said, "Boil me a *griwa*," so she boiled him a *griwa*. "Go and bring me two *beẓuni*," (*sic*) so she went and brought him two candles. "Go and break them on the head of the *baba*." Now Baba b. Buṭa was sitting on the threshold (*baba*)

2 The entire story appears to be an anti-Ephraim slur. See D. Marcus, "Ridiculing the Ephraimites: The Shibboleth Incident (Judg 12:6)," *MAARAV* 8 (1992), 95–105.

3 BT Nedarim shares with Nazir, Keretot, Tamid, Meʿilah, and the "alternative formulations" that occur frequently in Temurah, a subdialect of JBA with its own characteristics. On this subdialect, see M. Schlesinger, *Satzlehre der aramäischen Sprache des babylonischen Talmuds* (Leipzig: Asia Major, 1928), 1–2; E. Y. Kutscher, *Studies in Galilean Aramaic* (Ramat-Gan: Bar-Ilan University, 1976), 58; J. N. Epstein, *A Grammar of Babylonian Aramaic* (Jerusalem: Magnes, 1960), 14; J. N. Epstein, *Prolegomena ad Litteras Amoraiticus* (Hebrew; Jerusalem: Magnes, 1962), 72–74, 131–144; H. Strack and G. Stemberger, *Introduction to the Talmud and Midrash* (Edinburgh: T&T Clark, 1991), 214–215.

4 For a full critical apparatus, see M. Hirshler ed., *Babylonian Talmud with Variant Readings: Tractate Nedarim II* (Jerusalem: Inst. for the Complete Israeli Talmud, 1991), 172–173.

5 The tale is of no historical value for the first century. The only reason that Baba b. Buta was brought into the story was that his name was necessary for the play on words. See J. Neusner, *The Rabbinic Traditions about the Pharisees before 70*, part I: *The Masters* (Leiden: E. J. Brill, 1971), 390.

> engaged in judging a lawsuit. So she went and broke them on his head. Said he to her, "What is the meaning of this that thou has done?" She replied, "Thus my husband did order me." "Thou has performed thy husband's will," he rejoined; "may the Almighty bring forth from thee two sons like Baba b. Buṭa."[6]

We may compare the more recent translation by Jacob Neusner:

> A. Once a Babylonian came up to the Land of Israel and married a woman there. "Boil me two cow's feet," and she boiled him two lentils. [Freedman: The Babylonian pronunciation of the word for cow's feet sounded to her like lentils.]
> B. He got mad at her.
> C. The next day he said to her, "Boil for me a large measure [of lentils," and she boiled for him something [which bore the same name as the word he used for "large measure."]
> D. "Bring me two melons," and she brought him two candles [which bore the same name].
> E. "Go and break them on the head of the threshold [*baba*]."[7]
> F. Baba b. Buta was in session at the threshold, judging a case. She went and broke them on his head. He said to her, "What's going on?"[8]
> G. She said to him, "That's what my husband told me to do."
> H. He said to her, "You have done what your husband wanted. May the Omnipresent bring forth from you two sons like Baba b. Buta."[9]

---

6 *Babylonian Talmud Seder Nashim*, vol. 3 (London: Soncino Press, 1936), 214–216.

7 It is unclear why Freedman and Neusner translated "threshold," rather than "gate," especially since the town gate had long been a court venue. See *KTU*[3] 1.17:iv: 6–8; Deut 21:19, 22:15; Ruth 4:1 etc. As regards "threshold," although not attested in BT, the term *ʾysqwptʾ* (various spellings) "threshold," a loan from Akkadian *askuppu/atu*, appears in magic bowls written in Babylonian Aramaic. See C. Müller-Kessler, *Die Zauberschalentexte in der Hilprecht-Sammlung, Jena und weitere Nippur-Texte anderer Sammlungen* (Wiesbaden: Harrassowitz, 2005), 170.

8 In addition to being inaccurate, Neusner's "what's going on?" detracts from the repartee of the story: "What is this you have done?—Thus my husband commanded me—You did your husband's will …"

9 J. Neusner, *The Talmud of Babylonia, An American Translation*, vol. XVb: *Tractate Nedarim Chapters 5–11* (Atlanta: Scholars Press, 1992), 69. The bracketed quotation from Freedman is reproduced from Neusner.

There are four spousal misunderstandings in the tale. It is best to begin with the least difficult, which require only minimal clarification, and to proceed to those that require more, or have eluded satisfactory explanation.

The confusion between the "lamps" and the "squashes" or "pumpkins" is the clearest to modern readers. In JBA בוצינא meant "lamp" as well as "pumpkin/squash" or the like. In JPA the vocable is attested only in the meaning "lamp" or "light."[10] Accordingly, the wife would only have known the meaning "lamp."[11] By taking this incident as a guide, we may proceed to view the other three misunderstandings as resulting from confusion over dialect.

In the burlesque climax to the story, the wife sees Baba at the בבא and breaks the lamps over the head of Baba b. Buta. Rather than taking the episode as an indication that the woman was none too bright, it is more likely that, like the lamp/squash confusion, here again is a joke whose punchline depends on a dialectal misunderstanding.[12] As suggested by von Soden[13] and bolstered by Kaufman,[14] Aramaic בבא is probably a loan from Akkadian *bābu*, "opening, doorway, door, gate." Attested at Elephantine,[15] the term persists in Eastern Aramaic and, as an allograph, represents Pahlavi *dar*, "door, palace, chapter, subject."[16] In contrast, בב is unattested in the Western Aramaic

10 See *DJPA*, 88.

11 In all likelihood, the two meanings in JBA have their origin in Akkadian *buṣinnu*, which refers to *verbascum thapsus*, a plant whose leaves were used to make candles and lamp wicks, as well as the wicks themselves. In Akkadian proper, *bīt buṣinni* means "lamp." See *CAD*, *B*, 348; S. Kaufman, *The Akkadian Influences on Aramaic* (Chicago: Univerity of Chicago, 1974), 45. The comment that the Palestinian wife supplied her husband with two lamps, שׂרגי, synonymous with בוציני, is also of interest. JBA שׂרגא is a loanword from Pahlavi *čirāγ*, "lamp," and is unattested in JPA. See AAC, 403. As might be expected, the vocable is found in Mandaic and Syriac. When Palestinian sources require a synonym for בוצינא, they employ the Greek loanword φανός. Especially illuminating (if the pun be pardoned) is the JPA line from a poem: פנסיה דכיסליו דמי לבוצינין, "The lights of Kislev (on Hanukkah) resemble lamps." (The citation is from *DJPA*, 438.) JPA פנסיה דכיסליו corresponds to JBA שרגא דחנוכתא (BT Shabbat 45a).

12 This seems to have been recognized by Shamma Friedman, *EncJud*, 4:339.

13 AHw., 95, s.v. *bābu*. The first to characterize *bāba* as an Akkadian loanword was apparently Zimmern Fremdw., 30.

14 Kaufman, *Influences*, 40–41.

15 See B. Porten and A. Yardeni, *Textbook of Aramaic Documents from Ancient Egypt*, vol. 2, (Winona Lake: Eisenbrauns, 1989), 90 (B 3.11: 3, 4). See further, *DISO*, 32.

16 The Pahlavi phonetic writing *dl* (=Manichean Middle Persian *dr*) alternates with the allographic writing *BBA*. See D. MacKenzie, *A Concise Pahlavi Dictionary* (London: Oxford

dialects.[17] JPA prefers instead the vocable תרע,[18] cognate to Hebrew שׁער, *tǵr* and the EA[19] gloss to Akkadian *abullu*, "city gate," *šaḫri*.[20] The joke is that the Palestinian woman would not have known the Eastern Aramaic common noun בבא and obediently, smashed the lamps on the head of the only Baba in sight.

The first misunderstanding in the story has been correctly understood in its essentials. As Neusner and Freedman, following Rashi, have observed, the misunderstanding arose because the unfortunate bride mistook טלפי (=Mishnaic Hebrew טלפים[21]) for טלופחי.[22] Rather than the substantial meal of two bovine hooves which the husband had requested, he got only two lentils to eat. That cows' feet were regularly consumed by Jews in late antiquity is well attested,[23] but the linguistic reality behind the story is a bit more difficult to establish. The vocable טלפחן, "lentils," is already attested in Elephantine Aramaic.[24] But whereas the Talmudic tale indicates that a Palestinian speaker might confuse the vocable with the word for "hooves," other evidence shows that the distinction between טלפי "feet," "hooves" and טלופחי "lentils," was preserved in Eastern

---

University, 1971), 24; B. Utas and C. Toll, *Frahang i Pahlavīk* (Weisbaden: Harrassowitz, 1988), 2 (par. II:16).

17 Kosovsky lists no references in CTY; nor does *DJPA*, or LSp. The divison of the Talmudic tractate Nezikin into three sections, each called *bābā*, is found in current editions of both Talmuds. In the original editions however, Nezikin was one tractate which was divided in three in Babylonia. See Friedman, *EncJud*, 4:339.

18 See *DJPA*, 592.

19 EA 244:16 (from Megiddo).

20 For these and other cognates see *HALAT*, 1491.

21 For references see Y. Kasovsky, *Thesaurus Mishnae* II (Jerusalem: Massadah, 1957), 771.

22 The alternation between *ṭalpē* and *ṭelôpḥē* has broad manuscript support. See Hirshler, *Nedarim*, 172–173. Some Talmud editions have *ṭelôpḥē* twice: "Cook me two lentils. She cooked him two lentils." Scholars accepting this inferior reading have had to complicate their explanations. L. Goldschmidt (*Der babylonische Talmud*, vol. 5 [Berlin: Jüdischer Verlag, 1931], 500) translates: "sagte … zu ihr, dass sie ihm ein paar Linsen koche. Da kochte sie ihm ein paar Linsen." To this he adds the note: "Aus Dummheit nahm sie seinen Auftrag wörtlich." Indeed, Goldschmidt regards the woman's stupidity as the main point of the anecdote; cf. a recent Spanish translation: "'Cuéceme un par de lentejas', y ella le coció dos lentejas." A note explains: "Tomándolo al pie de la letra." See M. Cales, *El Talmud de Babilonia Tratado Nedarim* (Buenos Aires: Acervo Cultural Editores, 1978), 265; similarly, A. Steinsaltz, *Talmud Babli Maseket Nedarim* II (Jerusalem: Israel Inst. for Talmudic Publications, 1992), 325.

23 See, e.g., Mishnah Zebahim 3:4; Tosefta Uqṣin 2:6; BT Hullin 114a.

24 For references see Porten and Yardeni, *Textbook*, xxvi.

and Western Aramaic. Thus, to cite another spousal spat in an Eastern Aramaic source,[25] Rab's wife (third century) always reversed his bean requests, giving him חימצי/חומצי[26] when he wanted טלופחי. Similarly, Syriac *ṭelāpḥā* translates Hebrew עדשים in Gen 25:34; 2 Sam 17:28; and elsewhere.[27] At the same time, טלופחה is well attested in Palestinian Jewish Aramaic, Christian Palestinian Aramaic and even in late Western dialects,[28] as is טלף. Note that in Neophyti טלף translates Hebrew פרסה.[29] It appears therefore that BT Nedarim 66b is not describing Aramaic dialectal realities as far as the words for "lentils" and "hooves" are concerned. Instead, the joke is based on Babylonian perceptions about Palestinian weakening of the gutturals. It suffices to cite the well-known anecdote in BT Erubin 53b:

> A certain Galilean once went about inquiring "Who has *amar?* Who has *amar?*" "Foolish Galilean," they said to him, "do you mean an ass for riding, or wine to drink, wool for clothing or a lamb for slaughtering?"[30]

For the inner-intelligibility of the Erubin passage and the present passage, it was sufficient that the putative Babylonian audience assumed that Palestinians were careless about the gutturals, whether or not that was actually true with regard to the words under discussion.

What has completely eluded explanation is the difficulty over the גריוא.[31] Unlike the other requests, there is no discrepancy in the wording of the text between what the husband requested and what he received. Freedman's interpretation[32] is more complicated than necessary:

---

25 BT Yebamot 63a. For the text see A. Liss ed., *Babylonian Talmud with Variant Readings Tractate Yebamoth* II (Jerusalem: Inst. for the Complete Israeli Talmud, 1986), 113–115.

26 A species of small peas, perhaps chickpeas. See Jast, 458; G. Dalman, *Aramäisch-neuhebräisches Handwörterbuch* (Frankfurt am Main: J. Kaufmann, 1922), 152. See also Syriac *ḥemṣâ*, "small pulse, vetches," in PSmCom, 147.

27 See Payne Smith, 1479. Similarly, *Tg.Neof.* has טלופחין. See vol. 1, 157. The vocable is also employed by *Tg.Onq.* to Gen 25:34. See M. Katzenellenbogen, ed., *Torat Hayyim Hammishah Humshe Torah*, II (Jerusalem: Mossad Harav Kook, 1986), 9.

28 See *DJPA*, 224.

29 Lev 11:3, 4, 5, 6, 7, 26; Deut 14:6. *Tg. Neof.* 3: 63–66; 5: 131.

30 For translation of the passage, see Kut, SGA, 69. For the problem of gutturals in Galilee, see *ibid.*, 67–96.

31 For references see CTB, 9:324.

32 Similarly, Rashi, Goldschmidt, Cales, and Steinsaltz.

> A large measure of lentils. Thinking that she had intentionally boiled only two the previous day through laziness or meanness, he asked for an extraordinary large quantity, believing that she would scale it down.

Neusner comes closest to explaining what is at issue, but we must reverse the order of his translation as follows:

> The next day he said to her
> Boil me something (which bore
> the same name as the word for
> "large measure") so she boiled him
> a large measure of lentils.

The husband, in his request for cows' feet, had already demonstrated a fondness for meat that one gnaws off the bone. Receiving only two lentils, and "seething,"[33] he made another request, using a word that in Babylonian Aramaic meant both the food he wanted and "a large measure."[34] The wife knew only the meaning "large measure"[35] and thought her husband wanted a large measure of lentils. But her husband spoke a dialect rich in loanwords of Iranian origin,[36] and just such a one confused her. In Pahlavi,[37] *grīw* means

---

33 In Job 30:27 Biblical Hebrew רתח approaches the figurative sense well attested in BT sources. See *HALAT*, 1211; Cf. AC, 7:313. Note that JPA apparently does not attest רתח in a figurative sense. See *DJPA*, 531.

34 Aramaic גריוא refers both to the grain measure and to a field measure based on the amount of seed necessary to sow it. גריוא corresponds to the Biblical seah < Akkadian *sūtu*. See *HALAT*, 696. See further Jast, 268; Dalman, *Wörterbuch*, 87; E. Melamed, *Millon Arami-Ivri leTalmud Bavli* (Jerusalem: Feldheim, 1992), 107. A text from the geonic period glosses the Aramaic field measure גריוא by Hebrew בית סאה. See J. N. Epstein, "Geonic Responsa" [Hebrew], in E. Melamed, ed., *J. N. Epstein Studies in Talmudic Literature and Semitic Languages* (Jerusalem: Magnes, 1983), 165.

35 According to CTY II, 727, the term occurs twice in PT, each time with *bet*, rather than *waw*.

36 See the programmatic article by E. Rosenthal, "For the Talmudic Dictionary-Talmudica Iranica," (Hebrew) in S. Shaked, ed., *Irano-Judaica*, (Jerusalem: Ben-Zvi Inst., 1982), 38–134.

37 For forms in other Iranian dialects see M. Kanga, *Čitak Handarz ī Pōryōtkešān* (Bombay: Kanga, 1960), 111.

"neck," "throat," "self," and "soul."[38] But Pahlavi attests a homonym *grīw* meaning "grain measure."[39] In phonetic orthography both are written *glyw'*.[40]

As for the "grain measure," the term may have entered Aramaic as early as the beginning of the fifth century BC. In a delivery contract dated February 17, 483, the quantity of "2 ג" appears following "2 ardabs."[41] J. N. Epstein's plausible explanation of the abbreviation as representing גריוא[42] has been generally accepted.[43] In both Pahlavi and Parthian inscriptions, *g* serves as an abbreviation for *grīw*.[44] It is of interest that in the inscription of Šābūr I at Ka'aba-ī Zardošt, the *grīw* of the Middle Persian corresponds to the μόδιον of the Greek.[45]

In conclusion, we offer the following translation of the pericope:

> There was a certain Babylonian who went up to the land of Israel and took a wife. He said to her: "Boil me two [cows'] feet." She boiled him two lentils. He raged at her. The next day he said: "Boil me a neck." She boiled him a bushel (of lentils). He said to her: "Bring me two squashes." She brought him two lamps. He said to her: "Go and break them on top of the gate." Baba b. Buta was sitting at the gate and was judging a case. She went and broke them (the lamps) on his head. He said to her: "What is this you have done?" She said: "Thus my husband commanded me." He said: "You have done the will of your husband. God will bring forth from your belly two sons like Baba b. Buta."

---

38 MacKenzie (*Dictionary*, 37) has three listings: 1) *grīw*, "neck, throat"; 2) *grīw* "self, soul"; 3) *grīw* "a grain measure, modius, peck." Professor James R. Russell of Harvard University sees no need to separate the first two (oral communication). Note that both vocables may be written allographically as *CWLE* = צולה <צורה; Aramaic *lamed* regularly represents Iranian *r*.

39 Unconvincing Semitic etymologies based on the variant spelling גריבא (see below) are given by Levy in TMW, 358; Jast, 238; and Kosovsky, CTY II, 727, 730. Contrast M. Back, *Die sassanidischen Staatsinschriften* (Leiden: E.J. Brill, 1978), 213.

40 The term for "measure" may be abbreviated *g'*, while the word for "neck" is often written allographically as *CWLH*. Cf. n. 38 above.

41 Porten and Yardeni, *Textbook*, 2:110 (B.4.4:7).

42 *Epstein Studies*, 1:165.

43 So Porten and Yardeni, *Textbook*, 2:111. There is some confusion here. The Hebrew translation of the document has the expected spelling גריו. But the index (xxii) gives the spelling גריב, which is the regular form in Syriac. See Payne Smith, 780; for JPA spelling with *bet*, see CTY I, 727.

44 See P. Gignoux, *Glossaire des inscriptions pehlevies et parthes* (London: Lund Humphries, 1972), 22, 51.

45 See Back, *Staatsinschriften*, 367. Levy, TMW I, 358, translates גריוא by "Modius."

CHAPTER 11

Talmud: East and West

The relations between the two Talmuds, the Babylonian and the Palestinian, have engaged scholars since the middle ages. Whereas much of pre-modern scholarship concentrated on harmonizing contradictions, usually in favor of the Babylonian recension, more recent effort has been directed to utilizing the disparate sources for purposes of historical reconstruction and for understanding the literary history[1] of the talmudic pericope, or sugya.[2] At the same time, much significant work has been done in providing reliable texts,[3] and in talmudic philology and lexicography.[4] We are now at the stage where it has become

---

* I am very grateful to Professor David Weiss Halivni for reading this paper and for offering extremely helpful suggestions. Abbreviations of references to rabbinic literature and relevant secondary sources follow DJPA and Melamed Millon.

1 For a survey of personalities and methods in modern Talmud criticism, see J. Neusner ed., *The Formation of the Babylonian Talmud* (Leiden: Brill, 1970); D. Goodblatt, "The Babylonian Talmud," in *Aufstieg und Niedergang der römischen Welt* II. 19. 2, ed. W. Haase (Berlin and New York: De Gruyter, 1979), 257–336, especially 281–318; B. Bokser, "The Palestinian Talmud," *ibid.*, 139–256; H. Strack and G. Stemberger, *Introduction to the Talmud and Midrash* (Edinburgh: T&T Clark, 1991; translation of a German original published in 1982), 5–52; "Accumulative Bibliography," in *The Literature of the Sages, Part 1*, ed. S. Safrai, (Philadelphia: Fortress, 1987), 415–432; More recent work on the literary history of the Talmud may be found in J. Hauptman, *Development of the Talmudic Sugya: Relationship between Tannaitic and Amoraic Sources* (Lanham: University Press of America, 1987); R. Kalmin, *The Redaction of the Babylonian Talmud: Amoraic or Saboraic?* (Cincinnati: Hebrew Union College Press, 1989); See further the programmatic article, M. Chernick, "Contemporary Talmudic Studies: The Continuing Agenda," in *The Literature of Early Rabbinic Judaism: Issues in Talmudic Redaction and Interpretation*, ed. A. Avery-Peck (Lanham: University Press of America, 1989), 73–80; M. Chernick ed., *Essential Papers on the Talmud* (New York: New York University, 1994).

2 The term may mean "course" or "lesson." See A. Goldberg, "The Babylonian Talmud," in Safrai, *Sages*, 337–339 (with references to earlier literature).

3 See the bibliography in Strack and Stemberger, *Introduction*, 225–233; Cf. Goodblatt, "Talmud," 268–273.

4 There is an excellent bibliography on lexical and philological work on PT by B. Bokser in *Aufstieg*, 201–208; For BT see Goodblatt, *ibid.*, 273–281. Among the more recent significant publications are DJPA (See the review by M. Tal in *Tarbiz* 60 [1991], 227–287; Cf. S. Kaufman, JAOS 114 [1994], 239–248); D. Sperber, *Essays on Greek and Latin in the Mishna, Talmud, and Midrashic Literature* (Jerusalem: Makor, 1982); *idem, A Dictionary of Greek and Latin Legal Terms in Rabbinic Literature* (Ramat-Gan: Bar-Ilan University, 1984); *idem, Nautica Talmudica* (Ramat-Gan: Bar Ilan University, 1986); *idem, Material Culture in Eretz Israel During the*

 | DOI 10.1163/9789004340879_012

possible to combine philological efforts with source-critical studies[5] to clarify the process of the transmission of traditions between the scholars of Palestine and Babylonia. Writing in 1990, Jacob Neusner stated: "A study of the relationship between the Talmud of the Land of Israel and the Talmud of Babylonia, particularly how the latter receives and reworks what it receives from the former will pay attention to the two kinds of Aramaic[6] that were available to the writers."[7]

Talmudic Period (Jerusalem: Ben Zvi, 1993); M. Moreshet, *A Lexicon of the New Verbs in Tannaitic Hebrew* (Ramat-Gan: Bar-Ilan, 1980); S. Morag, *Babylonian Aramaic: The Yemenite Tradition* (in Hebrew with English summary; (Jerusalem: Ben Zvi Institute, 1988); M. Kaddari and S. Sharvit eds., *Studies in the Hebrew Language and the Talmudic Literature Dedicated to the Memory of Dr. Menahem Moreshet* (Ramat-Gan: Bar-Ilan University, 1989); Important programmatic articles are, E. S. Rosenthal, "For the Talmudic Dictionary-Talmudica Iranica," in *Irano Judaica* I, ed. S. Shaked (Jerusalem: Ben Zvi Institute, 1982), 38–134; M. Bar Asher, "The Different Traditions of Mishnaic Hebrew," in *"Working with No Data"; Semitic and Egyptian Studies Presented to Thomas O. Lambdin*, ed. D. Golomb (Winona Lake: Eisenbrauns, 1987), 1–38; *idem*, "L'hébreu mishnique; esquisse d'une description," *CRAIBL* 1990, 199–237; *idem*,"Introduction to Mishnaic Hebrew," in *Rabbi Mordecai Breuer Festschrift Collected Papers in Jewish Studies*, ed. M. Bar-Asher (Jerusalem: Academon, 1992), 657–688. Access to the philological studies of Saul Lieberman has been greatly facilitated by the appearance of the well-indexed *Saul Lieberman Studies in Palestinian Talmudic Literature*, ed. D. Rosenthal (Jerusalem Magnes, 1991); of related interest to talmudic philology and lexicography is the appearance of C. Müller-Kessler, *Grammatik des Christlich-Palästinisch-Aramäischen Teil 1* (Hildesheim: Georg Olms, 1991).

5 Important work in this direction is being done by Y. Ellman. See *idem, Authority and Tradition: Toseftan Baraitot in Talmudic Babylonia* (Hoboken: Ktav, 1994).

6 In addition to the basic division into Palestinian and Babylonian Aramaic, the BT tractates Nedarim, Nazir, Keretot, Tamid, Meʿilah and the "alternative formulations" that occur frequently in Temurah, share a sub-dialect with its own characteristics. See M. Schlesinger, *Satzlehre der aramäischen Sprache des babylonischen Talmuds* (Leipzig: Asia Major, 1928), 1–2; Kut, SGA, 58; Z. Rabinovitz, *Shaʿare Torat Eretz Yisraʾel* (Jerusalem, 1939/40); J. N. Epstein, *A Grammar of Babylonian Aramaic* (in Hebrew; Jerusalem: Magnes, 1960), 14; *idem, Prolegomena ad Litteras Amoraiticus* (in Hebrew; Jerusalem, Magnes, 1962), 72–74, 131–144; Strack and Stemberger, *Introduction*, 214–215; S. Rybak, "The Aramaic Dialect of Nedarim." (unpublished Ph.D. thesis New York: Yeshiva University, 1980) There is evidence for regional dialects as well as school dialects. See Epstein, *Amoraiticus*, 141; *idem, Grammar*, 14. According to BT Ketubot 54a, R. Nahman was able to discern from a certain woman's speech that she was native of Mahoza on the Tigris rather than Nehardea on the Euphrates.

7 J. Neusner, *Language as Taxonomy The Rules for Using Hebrew and Aramaic in the Babylonian Talmud* (Atlanta: Scholars, 1990), xi, n. 4; Cf. *ibid.*, 24, n. 20.

In this statement, Neusner was echoing a slightly earlier call by David Weiss Halivni who had written the following: "As yet there has been no examination of the accuracy with which statements made in Babylonia in Jewish Babylonian Aramaic[8] were translated into Jewish Palestinian Aramaic[9] in the Palestinian Talmud.[10] Conversely, we lack studies of the accuracy with which statements[11] made in Palestine in Palestinian Aramaic[12] were translated into Babylonian Aramaic in the Babylonian Talmud."[13] The present paper, in response to the calls of Neusner and Halivni, provides some examples of how such a study might proceed. It is offered humbly, in modest tribute to Professor Isaac Barzilay who introduced me to the historical study of Hebrew literature. Professor Barzilay's own works have become in Judaics what Akkadian speakers call *alpē ša parzilli*, and Hebrew speakers צאן ברזל.

The need for translation from one related dialect to another becomes obvious when we consider the role of orality in ancient learning,[14] and in Jewish

8 Hereafter, JBA.

9 Hereafter, JPA.

10 In a different category are anecdotes that employ dialectal features for "atmosphere." In PT Sanhedrin 18c for example, an anecdote about the odd behavior of R. Kahana, a Babylonian visitor to Palestine has him say קאתינא "I come," in good JBA. In BT Baba Batra 117a (=BT Berakot 5b) we have an enigmatic four-word statement by R.Yohanan preserved in JPA: דין גרמא דעשיראה ביר "This very bone is from my tenth son." But most of R. Yohanan's statements in BT are in JBA. The background of the above statement is supplied, probably by conjecture, in a gaonic responsum. See S. Abramson, *Talmud Babli Maseket Baba Batra* (Jerusalem: Razal, 1958), 136.

11 Note that Halivni refers to "statements," while Neusner had referred to "writers." Cf. Shamma Friedman, "On Method in the Study of the Talmudic Pericope," in *Texts and Studies Analecta Judaica vol. I*, ed. H. Dimitrovsky (in Hebrew; New York: Jewish Theological Seminary, 1977), 310–312; *idem*, "On the Origin of Textual Variants in the Babylonian Talmud," *Sidra* 7 (1991), 67–102. The problem of the reduction of the talmuds to writing may be very significant for our inquiry. For a survey and bibliography see Strack and Stemberger, *Introduction* 35–49; See further Chernick in *idem*, ed., *Papers*, 11.

12 A "basic study of the language of the Palestinian Amoraim quoted in the Babylonian Talmud" was called for by E. Kutscher in Kut, SGA, 58. (Actually, Kutscher's call came in the Hebrew original published in 1952.).

13 D. Weiss Halivni, *Meqôrôt u-Mesôrôt, Shabbat* (Jerusalem: Jewish Theological Seminary, 1982), 22 (my translation of Halivni's Hebrew statement); Cf. *idem, Midrash, Mishnah and Gemara* (Cambridge: Harvard, 1986), 95–96.

14 "In antiquity all texts were intended to be perceived by ear." So, H. S. Nyberg, *A Manual of Pahlavi* Part II (Wiesbaden: Harrassowitz, 1974), 175b; For a recent study on orality in early Christian literature (with bibliography) see I. Henderson, "Didache and Orality

learning in particular. There is evidence from Jewish sources that in late antiquity, even among those who knew how to read, most did not know how to write.[15] This factor, combined with the high cost of books,[16] limited the number of writings in circulation. Adding to these circumstances was the great value placed on oral transmission of traditions within rabbinic circles, and the related reluctance to commit rabbinic tradition to written[17] publication.[18] Whatever the origin of this reluctance, it is certain that by the third century AD[19] the Amoraim of Palestine and Babylonia asserted that their traditions were "oral torah,"[20] or literally, "torah in the mouth,"[21] as opposed to "torah in writing."[22]

---

in Synoptic Comparison," *JBL* 111 (1992), 283–306. For orality in more ancient sources, see M. Vogelzang and H. Vanstiphout, eds., *Mesopotamian Epic Literature Oral or Aural?* (Lewiston: Edwin Mellen, 1992), 300.

15 See M. Bar-Ilan, "Scribes and Books in the Late Second Commonwealth and Rabbinic Period," in *Mikra*, ed. M. Mulder (Philadelphia: Fortress, 1988), 21–38. Second through third century scholars (BT Gittin 19a–b) argued over the permissibility of techniques (outlining the letters, tearing the paper into outlines) by which witnesses who could read but not write might affix their names to a document. Cf. PT Gittin 9:8.

16 Bar-Ilan (*Mikra*, 36) estimates the cost of a book of the Torah at 80–128 gold dinarii.

17 It has been argued that the Babylonian Talmud, even after being arranged and "edited" as to topics and content, was transmitted orally in free-flowing lecture format not bound to a fixed written tradition for a considerable period of time. Eliezer S. Rosenthal believes that the language was not fixed before the ninth century. See *idem, apud* S. Morag, "Regarding the Oral Transmission of the Babylonian Talmud," in *Meḥqerei Talmud II*, eds. M. Bar-Asher and D. Rosenthal (Jerusalem: Magnes, 1993), 334. That would make the fixing of the BT text contemporary with the writing of the Pahlavi literature. See the next note.

18 It is of interest that there was a similar reluctance to commit the Avesta, the collection of the sacred texts of Zoroastrianism, to writing. Some of these texts were transmitted orally for over a millennium but were not codified and written down before the Sasanian period, contemporary with the Amoraim. See conveniently, G. Noli, "Avesta," *Encyclopedia of Religion* 2: 16–17. The bulk of Zoroastrian literature written in "book Pahlavi," was not committed to writing before the ninth century.

19 There are no explicit prohibitions against writing down rabbinic tradition before the Amoraic period. See Safrai, *Sages*, 45.

20 For some of the different senses of the term see M. Gruber, *JSJ* 15 (1984), 112–122.

21 The actual form in the Palestinian Talmud is דברים בפה. See PT Megillah 74d. See further, G. Blidstein, *Tarbiz* 42 (1972–1973), 496–498. Cf. J. Neusner, *Torah: From Scroll to Symbol in Formative Judaism* (Philadelphia: Fortress, 1985), 75–77; D. Kraemer, *AJSReview* 14 (1989), 3, n. 3.

22 The original idioms are תורה בפה and תורה בכתב. See G. Blidstein, *Tarbiz* 42, 496–498. Cf. Safrai, *Sages*, 44.

By insisting on oral transmission,[23] the rabbis could claim that their traditions were either supplementary or complementary to Scripture[24] but not intended

23 For an attempt at discovering laws of transmission in oral rabbinic literature see W. S. Towner, *Journal of Jewish Studies* 24 (1973), 101–118.

24 These are very different notions. The supplementary notion is formulated in the doctrine that Israel received two torahs, one written, one oral. A well-known tradition (BT Shabbat 31a) represents the first century master Hillel requiring a potential proselyte to accept the doctrine of two torahs. But the story has no parallel in Palestinian sources and represents both Hillel and the proselyte speaking Babylonian Aramaic, and for over a century many scholars have doubted the accuracy of the attribution to Hillel. More recently, Blidstein (*Tarbiz* 42, 496–498) has shown that the phraseology שבעל פה attributed to Shammai in the same anecdote, was first coined by the Babylonian Amoraim. (Note that in a very similar story about a potential convert [Qohelet Rabbah 7:8], the protagonists are the third century scholars Rav and Samuel, rather than Hillel and Shammai.) The same notion of two torahs, one written and one oral is attributed to one R. Yuda in *PRK*, 207, a Palestinian Midrash no earlier than the fifth century. (On these sources see B. Z. [Wilhelm] Bacher, *Aggadot ha-Tannaim* [Berlin, 1922], 7, n. 3; E. Urbach, *The Sages Their Concepts and Beliefs* [Jerusalem: Magnes, 1971], 258, n. 18.) Other traditions, of uncertain dates, attribute a similar notion to the first century scholar Yohanan b. Zakkai. (See D. Hoffmann, ed., *Midrasch Tannaïm zum Deuteronomium* [Berlin: Itzkowski, 1908], 215; J. Neusner, *The Rabbinic Traditions about the Pharisees Before 70 Part I* [Leiden: Brill, 1971], 343.) But when this notion of two torahs is presented anonymously in I. H. Weiss, ed., *Sifra: Commentar zu Leviticus* (Vienna: Schlossberg, 1862), 112c, it is challenged by a statement attributed to R. Akiba (died *ca.* 135), that the Pentateuch (Heb: תורה) had been revealed to Moses, along with "laws, details and explanations," הלכות ודיקדוקין ופירושין. See Safrai, *Sages*, 35–60; *idem*, in "Halakha from Moses to Sinai-History or Theology?" in *Meḥqerei Talmud*, eds., Y. Sussmann and D. Rosenthal (Jerusalem: Magnes, 1990), 30–31. Neusner deduces from the above Sifra source that the Sifra is later than its generally assigned third-century date and "not only post-mishnaic, but in indicative traits, talmudic." See J. Neusner, *The Canonical History of Ideas, The Place of the So-called Tannaite Midrashim: Mekhilta Attributed to R. Ishmael, Sifra, Sifré to Numbers and Sifré to Deuteronomy* (Atlanta: Scholars, 1990), 53. Less extreme, and more likely, is the hypothesis of D. Boyarin (review of Neusner in *JAOS* 112 [1992], 455–465) who argues that the Sifra citation can just as easily be construed as proof that "sometime during the tannaitic period this notion arose, was contested and gradually won hegemony." (*ibid.*, 459) Further support for Boyarin's position that the notion of two torahs arose in the tannaitic period but was contested, is that the phrase "two torahs" is employed as a pejorative term by the second century scholar R. Yose b. Halafta to describe the poor transmission of legal traditions among the students of Hillel and Shammai. See Saul Lieberman, ed., *The Tosefta Order Mo'ed* (New York: Jewish Theological Seminary, 1962), 384:58–59; *idem*, *Tosefta-Ki-fshuṭah Part V* (New York: Jewish Theological Seminary, 1962), 1298; See further, M. Gruber, *JSJ* 15 (1984), 114; A. Rosenthal, "Oral Torah and Torah from Sinai-Theory and Practice," in *Meḥqerei Talmud II*, eds.

to displace it.[25] Second, oral transmission heightened the prestige of the rabbis by limiting the access of outsiders[26] to "Torah," which, among other things, was thought to confer what we term "supernatural powers."[27] Whether or not we are correct about the factors that encouraged oral transmission, one point is certain. Written communication tends to override dialectal differences within spoken languages by encouraging the evolution of standard literary forms, and to minimize obstacles to understanding raised by variant pronunciations. Eastern and Western Aramaic were more mutually intelligible in writing than in person.[28] Accordingly, it might often have been necessary to translate rabbinic statements made in Palestine into JBA and vice-versa.

Indeed, the question of mutual intelligibility of the Aramaic dialects is raised in the Talmuds. In one well-known story, Babylonian Jews poke fun at Palestinian pronunciation.[29] Another anecdote is a slapstick account of what happened when a Babylonian Jew went to Palestine and married a woman who misunderstood his dialect.[30]

Our first example is essentially a translation from one dialect of Aramaic to another with no elaboration. The Mishnah Taanit 1:2 describes a ritual of public fasting which begins with the instruction:

M. Bar-Asher and D. Rosenthal (Eliezer S. Rosenthal Memorial Volume; Jerusalem: Magnes, 1993), 448–487, especially n. 5.

25 This was precisely the charge against the Pharisees attributed to Jesus in Matt 15:3–8.

26 See the cogent remarks of J. Neusner, *JJS* 22 (1971), 16–18.

27 See Neusner's comparisons between rabbi and magus in *idem, A History of the Jews in Babylonia II* (Leiden: Brill, 1966), 147–150; Cf. *ibid.*, III (Leiden: Brill, 1968), 102–130.

28 For this reason additions (targumic Toseftot) were made to Aramaic targums in which the original Palestinian dialect was systematically recast into the Onkelos targum type Aramaic. See M. Klein, *Genizah Manuscripts of Palestinian Targum to the Pentateuch* Volume I (Cincinnati: Hebrew Union College, 1986), xxvi; P. Alexander, "Jewish Aramaic Translations of Hebrew Scriptures," *Mikra*, 250. Jewish law prohibited the public reading of targums during the synagogue service. The dragoman was required to recite the Aramaic orally as an accompaniment to the synagogue reader, who read the biblical selections in Hebrew from a scroll. On other consequences of orality in the targums see A. Shinan, *JQR* 81 (1991), 353–364.

29 According to BT Erubin 53b, a "foolish Galilean" could not distinguish in his pronunciation among the words for "ass," "wine," "wool," and "lamb," pronouncing them all *amar*. On the story see Kut, SGA, 69.

30 See BT Nedarim 66b. For a full treatment of that anecdote see S. D. Sperling, *JAOS* (1995), 205–209. See "Aramaic Spousal Misunderstandings" in this volume.

> The ark is taken into the town square and
> ashes are placed on the ark.

The reaction of R. Zeira to this ritual is recorded in BT Taanit 16a:[31]

א'ר זירא כי חזינן דיהבי אפר מוקלה[32] על גבי ספר תורה מזדעזע כוליה גופאי

> Rabbi Zeira said: "When I used to see them putting ashes on the torah scroll,[33] my whole body would quiver."

The parallel in PT Taanit 65a reads:

א"ר זעורה כל זמן[34]:דהווינא חמי לון עבדין כן הוה גופי רעד

> Rabbi Zeora[35] said "Every time I saw[36] them doing this my body would shake."

---

31 Text from Yad Harav Herzog, MS 1.

32 The *waw* in מוקלה is clear in the manuscript.

33 The underlined words are in Hebrew because they are a partial quotation from the Mishnah which reads: מוציאין את התיבה לרחובה של עיר ונותנין עליה אפר מקלה. The word מקלה may not have been in the original Mishnah. See Lieberman, *Tosefta Ki-fshuṭah Part V Order Mo'ed*, 1071. On some of the issues of Hebrew and Aramaic mixture in BT see Neusner, *Taxonomy*; J. Breuer, "On Language Change by the Sages in the Babylonian Talmud," in *Meḥqerei Talmud II*, 96–99 (with previous literature).

34 The phrase is as easily taken to be Aramaic as Hebrew. Ultimately of Semitic origin from Akkadian *simanu*, "season," "proper time," "time," (*CAD S*, 268) and semantically equivalent to BH עת or מועד, the vocable was borrowed into Persian whence it entered as זמן into Aramaic and Late Biblical Hebrew. The term זמן continues in use in contemporary Hebrew as do its counterparts in Farsi and Turkish. Because the term also corresponds semantically to Aramaic עדן, Pahlavi *zamān* "time" can be written with the Aramaic allograph *ODNA*= עדנא.

35 The PT form of the name is usually given as זעורא with the final *aleph*, rather than *heh* as in the printed edition here, or as זעירא with *yod* in place of *waw*. See Ch. Albeck, *Mabo la-Talmudim* (Jerusalem: Dvir, 1987), 233. A native-born Babylonian who immigrated to Palestine after studying in Babylon (*ibid.*, 233–235), Zeira was fluent in the Aramaic of both countries.

36 The form הווינא is the first singular past tense of הוה in JPA. See J. Lund, *MAARAV* 4 (1987), 191–199.

The verb חמי "to see" is found only in Western Aramaic.[37] Instances of חזי in PT are extremely rare and probably corrupt.[38] The verb רעד is not attested in the JBA of the Babylonian Talmud. The differences between the two accounts are simple adjustments made between dialects, which do not materially affect the process of transmission.

A parallel with more variation is attributed to Rav in a comment on Mishna Sanhedrin 8:6. As was true of Zeira, Rav was a Babylonian native. Rav came and went between Palestine and Babylonia, "studying in Palestine, returning to Babylonia, and going back to Palestine, before he finally took up residence in his homeland."[39]

The Mishnah reads:

הבא במחתרת ידון[40] על שם סופו

> (Exodus 21:1 permits a householder to kill a thief who enters through a breach, [implying that] "the one who enters through the breach is judged on the basis of the (potential) outcome of his action."[41]

In its exposition of the Mishnah, PT cites a statement by Rav: (PT San 8:8, p. 26c. [Leiden MS])

> רב אמ' כל דייתי עלי אנא קטל ליה חוץ מחנניה בן שילא דאנא ידע דלא אתי אלא מיסב מגוסתיה מיניי

> Rav said: "Whoever comes upon me, I kill him, with the exception[42] of Hananiah (*sic*) b. Shila for I know that he comes only to take his dinner from me."

37 For cognates and JPA references see *DJPA*, 205.

38 See *DJPA*, 194a. The verb is attested however in JPA outside of Galilee. See Tal, *Tarbiz* 60, 286.

39 J. Neusner, *A History of the Jews in Babylonia vol.* II, (Leiden: Brill, 1966), 126; See further, I. Gafni, *The Jews of Babylonia in the Talmudic Era a Social and Cultural History* (Jerusalem: Shazar Center, 1990), 255–256.

40 So, Kaufmann MS.

41 "He may be killed because he would have killed the householder who was attempting to protect his property." (Rashi).

42 The underlined phrase is in Hebrew.

The BT parallel (Sanhedrin 72b [Munich MS]) reads:

א' רב כל דאתי עלי במחתרת' קטילנא ליה לבר מרב חנינ' [43]בר שיל'
מאי טעמ' אילימ' משו' דצדי' הו' הא קא אתי במחתרת' אלא משו' דקים לי
בגוי' דמרחם עלי כאב על הבן[44]

Said Rav: "Everyone who comes against me through the breach, I kill, with the exception of R. Hanina b. Shila (What is the reason? If we were to say:[45] Because he is a righteous individual—it would be objected: he comes through the breach! Rather it is) because it is my presumption with regard to him that he will acknowledge me the way a father does a son."[46]

It is apparent that BT and PT report the same saying attributed to Rav. The PT report is in good JPA with such characteristics as *yod* for third person imperfect. BT employs the characteristic JBA *qatilna* tense and the expression קים ל...בגו not attested in JPA. In both talmuds, Rav's statement is attached to the same Mishnah.[47] Zechariah Frankel, with no discussion, considered the BT to be the plain sense and PT far-fetched.[48] In contrast, A. Hyman, while agreeing that the story must have originated in Babylonia because Hanina was a Babylonian who never left Babylonia for Palestine, combined the two explanations.[49] Neither they, nor more recent scholars took the respective Aramaic dialects into account in examining the parallel pericopes.

Despite the fact that, so far as we know, Hanina b. Shila never studied in Palestine,[50] historical and philological data prove the PT version to be primary.

---

43 Apparently the same individual is also called חיננא בר שילת in BT Baba Meṣiʿa 15a. See B. Kosowsky, *Thesaurus Nominum vol.* II (Jerusalem: JTSA, 1977), 522.

44 For variant readings of the line see R. Rabbinovicz, *Variae Lectiones in Mischnam et in Talmud Babylonicum vol.* ix (Nuremburg: Bulka, 1926), 103a.

45 Literally, "if to say."

46 The underlined phrases are Hebrew snippets from the Bible. The first is from Ezek 18:9; the second is based on Ps 103:13. For its forensic sense in the original biblical context see Sperling, *JANES* 19 (1989), 156.

47 It need not have been directed to the Mishnah originally. The Mishnah itself explains the logic behind Exod 22:1 but does not itself offer a new law.

48 Z. Frankel, *Einleitung in den jeruschalemischen Talmud* (Hebrew: Breslau, 1870), 33b.

49 A. Hyman, *Sefer Toldot Tannaim wa-Amoraim* (Reprint Jerusalem: Kiryah Ne'emanah, 1964) II, 475.

50 No halachic rulings by him have been preserved. For what we know about the man and his family and social position see below.

First, according to the contemporary master Samuel, Rav, R. Hanina b. Shila (who may have been a relative of Rav[51]) and Samuel himself shared a fondness for postprandial delicacies.[52] Hanina particularly liked pigeons after a good meal.[53] Being attached to the exilarchate, he apparently had the means to indulge his tastes.[54] Samuel's anecdote serves to illustrate the food restraints that must be exercised after the Passover meal. Rav's statement in PT belongs in the same category of food anecdotes with legal implications. Unfortunately, recent translations of PT have made it difficult to understand the anecdote, both its legal implications and the touch of humor it contains.

First, Jacob Neusner:

> Whoever comes against me I kill, except for Hananiah b. Shila, because I know that he only comes to take my property from me.[55]

Neusner's translation requires the reading מגוסתי which is found neither in Leiden MS nor the printed editions. Second, Neusner's translation ignores the fact that this is not the JPA word for "property."[56]

51 See Hyman, *Toldot*, 475; Rav had an uncle named Shila. See BT Sanhedrin 5a. For some of the textual and consequently, historical, problems in Rav's family tree see E. S. Rosenthal, "Rav ben Ahi R. Hiyya gam ben-Ahoto?" in *Henoch Yalon Jubilee Volume* eds., Saul Lieberman, S. Abramson, E. Y. Kutscher and S. Esh (Jerusalem: Kiryat Sepher, 1963), 281–337.

52 Whether Samuel's preference was for truffles or lamb is disputed. See *DJPA*, 418; Melamed *Millon*, 56.

53 See BT Pesahim 119b and Rashbam ad loc. Cf. PT Pesahim 37d. See M. Beer, *The Babylonian Amoraim Aspects of Economic Life* (Hebrew: Ramat-Gan: Bar-Ilan University, 1982), 143; Rosenthal characterizes Hanina as הגורמנד המפונק והענוג "the finicky and spoiled gourmand." See *idem*, "Rav," 309, n. 58.

54 Hanina was one of the "rabbis of the exilarch's household," (BT Shabbat 58; Cf. Beer, *Amoraim*, 143; *idem*, *The Babylonian Exliarchate in the Arsacid and Sassanian Periods* [Tel-Aviv: Dvir, 1970], 83). Although the nature of the body רבנן דבי ריש גלותא is unclear, (Beer *ibid.*, 82–85) Hanina's standing in the group and his familial ties to the Exilarchate seem well-established. See BT Shabbat *ibid.*, and Beer, *ibid.*, 83, n. 103 with references; Contrast J. Neusner, *A History of the Jews in Babylonia III* (Leiden: Brill, 1966), 108, n. 2. This would vitiate D. Fränkel's (קרבן העדה) explanation that Rav felt that Hanina might be excused because he only broke in because he had no food.

55 J. Neusner, *The Talmud of the Land of Israel vol. 31 Sanhedrin Makkot* (Chicago: University of Chicago, 1984), 278.

56 The common words are: ממון, נכסין, קניין. The same criticism may be leveled against the eighteenth century commentator M. Margolies (פני משה) ad loc. who offers: "My meal and my possessions."

The translation by Wewers is likewise faulty:

> Jeden, der zu mir (als Einbrecher) kommt, töte ich ausser Hananya-ben Shela, weil ich weiss, dass er nur kommt, um meinen (silbernen) Tisch wegzunehmen.[57]

In contrast to Neusner, Wewers acknowledges that he is emending the text from מגוסתיה to מגוסתי, as had been suggested (with no reason applied) by Jastrow.[58] But Jastrow himself translates his emended text as "to steal my (silver) plate," and cites no references for מגיסתא in the meaning "table."[59] Second, there is no basis for Jastrow's understanding, accepted by Wewers, that the vessel known in Hebrew and Aramaic as מגס, מגיס, מגיסא, מגיסתא,[60] if that is what is involved here, was made of silver. The LH and Aramaic terms for that vessel are borrowed[61] from μἄγίς, translated as "any kneaded mass, cake;[62] lump of fat; cake offered to Hecate and Trophonius;" "kneading trough, dresser," also "round plate or pan for placing on the τρίπους,"[63] the "three-legged cauldron."[64] A מגיסא is specified as being of silver by *Tg. Onq.* only when it is necessary to translate Heb קערה when the biblical text specifies that the vessel in question was made of silver. Like its Hebrew counterpart, the מגיסא might be made of various other materials.[65]

---

57 G. Wewers, *Sanhedrin Gerichtshof* (Tübingen: Mohr, 1981), 226–227.

58 Jast, 728a, s.v. מגיסתא, מגוס.

59 It appears that Wewers misunderstood an earlier entry on the same page in Jast, 728a, s.v. מגיסתא, מגוס. In that entry Jastrow cites targum to Ezek 13:19 where Heb ובפתותי לחם is rendered ובמגוסין דלחים. Jastrow translates the phrase ad loc. "plates with morsels from the tables." Given his rendition of the other passages s.v. מגיסא, מגוסא, it is clear that in this passage as well Jastrow takes מגוס to mean "plate," (Teller) not "table." (Tisch) (The targum is probably the source of the anonymous short comment to the printed PT Sanhedrin 26c: פירש' ליקח פיתותי לחם. See below.).

60 On the forms of the vocable see Brand, *Ceramics*, 270; See further *Tosefta-Ki-fshuṭah Part V*, 163; Melamed *Millon*, 214. For the forms and functions of the vessel itself see Brand, *Ceramics*, 271–272.

61 See Levy, TMW II, 19; Krauss, Lehnw 321; Correct the reference in *DJPA*, 290a from "Löw," to "Krauss."

62 LSJ, 1071; LXX employs μἄγίς to translate the biblical hapaxlegomenon צליל/ צלול in Judg 7:13. According to E. Hatch and H. Redpath, *A Concordance to the Septuagint vol.* 2 (Oxford: Clarendon, 1897), 891 μἄγίς is a hapaxlegomenon in LXX.

63 LSJ, 1071.

64 LSJ, 1822.

65 In Exod 25:29 the קערה is made of gold, but מגיס is employed in translation by *Tg. Onq.* just the same. For the materials out of which a קערה might be made see Brand, *Ceramics*, 507–516.

In point of fact, however, the PT pericope has nothing to do with the vessel whose name is borrowed from Greek but with מגוסה, "meal," a good Semitic word from the root[66] נגס attested in the senses "eat," "bite into food," in Mishnaic Hebrew,[67] CPA,[68] JPA, and Syriac.[69] In our pericope מגוסתיה means "his meal," just as מגוסתך means "your meal"[70] in another pericope in the same tractate (PT San 72c [Leiden MS]):[71]

המכמין עידיו אחורי גדר לא עשה כלום כהדא חד בר נש אשגח למיגוס גו אריסטון
אמ' ליה הב לי מה דת[72] חייב לי. אמ' ליה אין. בתר דקמון אמ' ליה לי נא[73] חייב
לך כלום. אמ' ליה אית לי סהדין. אמ' ליה לא אמרית אלא בגין דלא מיערבב<ה>[74]
מגוסתך

(R. Abbahu in the name of R. Yohanan said:) "One who conceals his witnesses behind a fence has done nothing (legally effective)." As in this (following case). A man took care[75] to dine at a banquet.[76] He said to him (a debtor of his he knew would be present), "Give me what you owe me." He replied "yes." After they had risen he said, "I don't owe you anything." He replied, "I have witnesses." (He had designated witnesses to listen to the admission of debt during the meal.) He replied, "I only said (that) so that your meal (מגוסתך) would not be ruined." He (the creditor) came before R. Ammi who said, "This is the application of what R. Yohanan said, 'One who conceals his witnesses behind a fence has done nothing (legally effective).' "

66 The *qetulah* nominal form from a primae *nun* verb is not unique. Note that, as shown by Ugaritic *nqpt* "circuit of the year," the root of תקופה "season" is נקף. See *HALAT*, 1641.

67 See Moreshet, *Lexicon*, 222. The word is a hapaxlegomenon in Mishnaic Hebrew. See Mishnah Tevul Yom 3:6: lkwah ˜m sgnv rwhf.

68 Müller-Kessler, *Grammatik*, 296 translates, "speisen."

69 See Payne Smith II, 2284.

70 See also *DJPA*, 289 *s.v.* מגוס.

71 A synonymous noun נגיסה from the same root is found in an Aramaic context in PT Berakot 10c אינין אינין עיקר נגיסתי. "He said to them: these very things (dates with bread) are the heart of my meal." The word appears to be a hapaxlegomenon. There is no listing in *DJPA*, which apparently considers the word to be Hebrew.

72 In the MS a superlinear *aleph* has been added to correct דת to דאת.

73 Contraction of לית אנא "I don't," sometimes written as a single word. See *DJPA*, 283.

74 For the restoration of the *heh* required for gender agreement see *DJPA*, 418.

75 For אשגח see *DJPA*, 537. His action was as deliberate as the character in R. Yohanan's paradigm who hides his witnesses.

76 "Meal," "banquet," translates אריסטון which is borrowed from Greek. See *DJPA*, 75.

We are now in a position to examine Rav's statement in the context in which it is set in PT San 26c. Immediately preceding Rav's statement the compiler offers the following:

> תני ר' שמעון בן יוחי אפי' חוץ למחתרת אין לו דמים. לפי שממון שלאדם חביב עליו כנפשו
>
> R. Simon b. Yohai taught: "Even outside of the breach, he has no blood-guilt, because a person's property is as dear to him as his life."

The Tanna's statement is followed by an Amora's statement in the same vein: The theft of property might outrage a householder every bit as much as would the homicide of one of his relatives. And as the blood avenger is not culpable, neither is the householder:

> רב הונ' אמ' נטל את הכיס והפך פניו לצאת והלך לו אין ההורג נהרג מה טע' 'כי יחם לבבו[77]
>
> R. Huna said: "If he had taken the purse and turned to exit and flee and the householder stopped him and killed him, the slayer is not himself slain. On what Scriptural basis?- 'Because he is enraged.'" (Deut 19:6)

This is followed by Rav's statement, which in turn precedes the following:

> אמ' ר' יצחק מכיון דאברי ליביה עלוי למיעבד ליה דא מילתא אין זה חנניה בן שילא
>
> Said R. Isaac: "Since his (the thief's) will emboldened him to do this thing (make a breach) this is no Hananiah b. Shila."[78]

In the PT pericope, Rav's statement is placed after the discussion of the penalty for the thief caught in the breach, and within a discussion about the permissibility of slaying any thief in the heat of the moment in defense of one's own property.[79] Rav is understood to say that he would kill any thief, burrowing or

---

77 Deut 19:6.

78 Note that in Rav's statement as reported in PT, there is no reference to a "breach."

79 Rav's statement is cited after R. Huna's explanation of a barraita in which the opinion is attributed to R. Simeon b. Yohai (second century) that one who kills a thief חוץ למחתרת is not culpable. Huna was a student of Rav. He is dated to the second half of the third century.

not. But his statement is partly humorous: an exception to his practice would be Hananiah/Hanina/(Hinnena) b. Shila,[80] who, Rav knows, would be entering his home uninvited only to get his meal from him. Hananiah's intentions are therefore gustatory rather than homicidal.[81]

Strictly speaking, Rav's statement in its present position is a digression, because R. Isaac's comment continues the series of statements which expand the rights of householders to slay intruders. According to R. Isaac, an expansive reading of the biblical breach laws is justified because once a thief has proved himself bold enough to break in, he may be bold enough to kill the householder. Since reasonable doubt about such a thief's intentions exists, a householder may kill him without liability.[82] For a householder to be culpable, it must be ascertained that he was as certain of the motives of the thief as was Rav of the motives of Hananiah b. Shila. Without Rav's statement, R. Isaac's dictum would be unintelligible to the audience of the pericope, although the reference was obviously clear to the original audience of R. Isaac.

The use of Hebrew[83] חוץ מ is due to the fact that JPA expresses "except for" without prepositional *lamed*[84] simply as בר מן. In JPA the phrase לבר מן with the prepositional *lamed* means only "outside of" spatially. Similarly, within the Aramaic dialects קים... ל in JBA is an idiom "it is clear to," corresponding to JPA ידע.

In contrast to PT, the BT pericope is derivative. Unlike the PT which attributes the entire statement to Rav, BT contains the interpolative formula אילימא... אלא. This is a common BT rhetorical device in which אילימא introduces an interpretation that will be rejected and אלא marks the one that will be accepted. Thus, אילימא "if *we* say," has the sense: "If we (interpreters)[85] say that because Hanina is righteous, Rav exempts him from the application of the Torah's law ..." Second, the reason accepted by BT and introduced by אלא is simply the continuation of the Talmud's attempt to resolve a contradiction

80 All three forms have manuscript support elsewhere. See Beer, *Exilarchate*, 83, n. 102. On the various forms of Shila see Rosenthal, "Rav," 309.

81 Cf. n. 49.

82 Cf. Neusner, *Sanhedrin*, 278.

83 Already Late Biblical Hebrew. See Qoh 2:25. But see Tur-Sinai, *The Language and the Book* I (Jerusalem: Bialik, 1954), 380; *ibid.*, II, 403. Biblical sources prefer לבד מ (e.g. Exod 12:37; Num 29:39; and זולתי (Hosea 13:4; Isa 45:5; Ps 18:32; Note that זולתי in Ps 18:32 corresponds to מבלעדי in the parallel text of 2Sam 22:32. See also A. Bendavid, *Biblical Hebrew and Mishnaic Hebrew* (Tel-Aviv: Dvir, 1967), 400; Note further that the targum to the Samuel passage reads בר מן the source of the later חוץ מ. For the targum text see M. Cohen ed., *Mikraot Gedolot Haketer Samuel I and II* (Jerusalem: Keter, 1993), 262.

84 See CTY II: 549.

85 So, expressly, Hyman, *Toldot*, 475.

between two immediately preceding anonymous[86] tannaitic statements. One barraita permits a householder to kill a burrowing thief only if he is virtually certain that the thief is likely to kill him. The other asserts the right of the householder to kill the thief unless he is virtually certain that the thief is unlikely to kill him. To put it differently, in the first case the legal presumption is that the burrower is not homicidal; in the second the presumption is that the burrower is homicidal. The Talmud resolves the contradiction with the following statement:

כאן באב על הבן כאן בבן על האב

> In one case we speak of the father vis a vis the son, the other of the son vis a vis the father.

That is, a father even when caught in the act of burglarizing his son's house will not kill his son. In all other cases, including the son caught in the act of burglarizing his father's house,[87] the presumption is that the burrower is homicidal. The wording of Rav's statement in the BT pericope has been shaped by the need to show that the Talmud's immediately preceding resolution of the tannaitic contradiction was in line with a principle already enunciated by Rav.

Let us now compare the corresponding versions of Rav's statement, omitting the BT's מאי טעמא... משום.

PT Sanhedrin 26c:

רב אמ' כל דייתי עלי אנא קטל ליה חוץ מחנניה בן שילא דאנא ידע דלא אתי אלא מיסב מגוסתיה מיניי

The BT parallel (Sanhedrin 72b) reads:

א' רב כל דאתי עלי במחתרת' קטילנא ליה לבר מרב חנינ' דקים לי בגוי' דמרחם עלי כאב על הבן

As we have seen, the PT does not include the word 'מחתרת in its citation of Rav. Its presence in Rav's statement in BT is symmetrical with the use of the vocable in the אילימא section. Accordingly, it seems safe to say that Rav's original statement did not contain the term. If so, then the two Talmuds did not differ on the content of the first part of Rav's statement: "Whoever comes upon me I slay with the exception of H.b.S." As for the second part, apparently, BT had

86 Referred to as סתמא on 72a.

87 See Rashi ad loc.

no genuine tradition about the reason given by Rav[88] and was free to formulate one in conformity with the need to harmonize the barraitot. The fact that מגוסה "meal" is unattested in JBA may account for Rav's reason not surviving in the Babylonian tradition.

Our next selection involves R. Abbahu of Caesaria,[89] who died early in the fourth century. As far as we know he was never in Babylonia, but is regularly quoted in BT. Abbahu's comment is directed to a ruling in Mishnah Shabbat (Kaufmann, 6:8) which reads:

אניקטמין[90] טהורים[91] אין יוצאין בהן

> X are not susceptible to impurity, but one must not go out with them on the Sabbath.

In BT Shabbat 66b, three interpretations of X are attributed to three scholars. Two of the scholars are Babylonians and the third is R. Abbahu:

מאי לוקטמין[92] אמ' [ר' א]בהו[93] חמרא דאכפא רבא בריה דרב פפא[94] אמר קישורין[95] רבה[96] בר רב הונא אמ' משמיה דעולא[97] פדאמי[98]

---

88 Long ago, Frankel, (*Einleitung*, 41b) observed that traditions of Babylonian scholars were sometimes better preserved in PT than in BT. In the case at hand Rav probably made his original statement in Palestine.

89 Abbahu is dated ca. 229–303 by Saul Lieberman, *Annuaire de l'Institut de Philologie et d'Histoire Orientales et Slaves* VII (1939–1944), 400.

90 There are numerous variants in Mishnah citations and parallels. הגדמין, הנקטמין, אנקטמין, נוקטמין, לוקטמין are among the more interesting. See Lieberman, *Tosefta-Ki-fshuṭah Part III, Order Mo'ed*, 70, n. 7.

91 On the controversy between Mishnah and Tosefta regarding the purity of the object in question see *Tosefta-Ki-fshuṭah Part V*, 71.

92 So, Venice first printed edition and Munich MS. For the *l/n* variant between Talmud and Mishnah forms see Lieberman, *Tosefta-Ki-fshuṭah Part III Mo'ed*, 70–71.

93 Bracketed letters missing in Munich MS. In the Venice first printed edition אמר רבי אבהו is fully written out.

94 The printed editions have רבא בר פפא. We follow Munich MS.

95 So, Munich MS for קישרי of Venice printed edition.

96 So, Munich MS. Venice printed edition has רבא. Munich lacks the honorific before Huna. In PT this same scholar is called Abba b. R. Huna. See Albeck, *Talmudim*, 306.

97 The ultimate attribution to Ulla is supplied by Munich MS.

98 This is the form cited by various commentators and by Nathan b. Yehiel in AC, VI, 296. Munich MS has פרמי. For a listing of variants see Rabbinovicz, *Variae Lectiones*, VII, 141, and see below.

> What are לוקטמין? R. Abbahu said: "a shoulder-ass";[99] Rava b. R. Papa said: "stilts";[100] Rabbah b. R. Huna said: "face-coverings."

In the parallel statement in PT Shabbat 8c we read:

מהו אנקטמין טהורין א"ר אבהו הונוס קטמין חמרא דיידה

> To what does "X are pure" refer? R. Abbahu said: "The ass of the amputees—the hand-ass."

As Lieberman has demonstrated, the PT reading shows that R. Abbahu understood Mishnah's אנקטמין as a hybrid of Greek ὄνος "ass" and Aramaic קטמין "amputees."[101] The difference in the transmission of R. Abbahu's statement in PT and BT is obvious. The context of the Mishnah shows that the enumerated items do not belong to the categories of ordinary clothing or body parts, about which there is no question that it is permissible to move them from one domain to another on the Sabbath. At the same time, the items in question did not fit the clearly prohibited category of "burden." On the basis of the Mishnah's context and their own physical and linguistic realia, the Babylonian scholars offered translations of the enigmatic term. The translation suggested by Rava b. R. Papa "stilts," has an Akkadian etymology.[102] In similar fashion, the translation "mask,"[103] is best supported by Persian etymology.[104] Neither of these

99 Some kind of mechanical contrivance. See Jast, 480a; *DJPA*, 207 b. That the reference is to an aid to amputees was already seen by R. Hananel ad loc. According to LSJ, 1233 b, from "ass" as a beast of burden the meaning of Greek ὄνος passed to "windlass," "millstone," "beaker," and "spindle" or "distaff." It is of interest that Akkadian *imēru*, "ass," cognate to Aramaic חמור is attested as a mechanical device. See *CAD I/J*, 114; AHw., 376.

100 So Rashi, OF "eschases (=échasses)." Cf. Tosafot ad loc. If this interpretation is correct, then the Aramaic vocable can hardly be separated from Akk *gušūru*, "log," "beam," "plant." (See *CAD G*, 144–146; AHw., 300.) JBA attests both גשורא and כשורא. See S. Kaufman, *The Akkadian Loanwords in Aramaic* (Chicago: University of Chicago, 1974), 53; *DJPA*, 270; *DJBA*, 305, 605.

101 The word קטם is a variant of גדם, "cut," "amputate," attested in Mishnaic Hebrew, various Aramaic dialects, Akkadian and Arabic. See Lieberman, *Tosefta-Ki-fshuṭah Part III Mo'ed*, 70; Moreshet, *Lexicon*, 118; AHw., 273.

102 See n. 100.

103 So Rashi OF "talmaje." More recently, Melamed Millon, 342. Others reading פרמי with *resh*, derive the term פרם "to tear," understanding the word as "bib." See R. Hananel *ad loc.*

104 Several scholars (see e.g. AC) derive פדאמי from Pahlavi *padām* (Avestan: *paitidana*) a veil over the mouth, worn by a celebrating priest. A remarkable marble panel from the sixth century AD Northern Qi dynasty in China, portrays a Zoroastrian religious ceremony

scholars provides an etymology of the Mishnaic term, nor does R. Abbahu in the BT version. The situation in PT is different. Inasmuch as Abbahu himself spoke Greek,[105] and most of the Palestinian rabbis likewise had a reasonable command of the language,[106] Abbahu's etymology of the Mishnaic term as a hybrid of Greek and Aramaic was preserved along with his interpretation. The difference between where the "ass" was considered to be attached, the "shoulder" or the "arm," was not significant.[107] It appears however that אכפא which is found in BT's version of R. Abbahu's statement[108] was not employed in JPA.

Our brief sampling has called attention to the ways in which parallel material in the different dialects is treated in the two talmuds. In the first example we have what is essentially a translation from one dialect of Aramaic to another, with no elaboration or change. In our second example BT has apparently filled in what it lacked in the transmission of Rav's statement. The third example represents alterations that conform to the linguistic and physical realia of the Babylonians. Further study will doubtless disclose examples of alteration on the PT side, and to more detailed and precise classifications.

In conclusion, we take the opportunity to outline some suggestions for further study and to indicate some of the difficulties that will have to be overcome. In examining statements attributed to Palestinian scholars in BT and those attributed to Babylonian scholars in PT, the most significant data will come from those statements which have parallels in the two Talmuds.[109] In

---

in which a priest holds two knives in a fire brazier, while wearing a small white veil to prevent his breath from defiling the sacred flame. For the representation see figure 1d. of the catalog of the exhibition "Chinese Archaic Bronzes, Sculpture and Works of Art, June 2–June 27, 1992." (J. J. Lally and Co., New York, New York) See further the comments on the scene in her introduction to the catalog (n.p.) by A. Juliano. I thank my friend Professor James R. Russell of Harvard for bringing the exhibition to my attention. The use of the veil has persisted in Zoroastrian tradition in modern times. See F. Kotwal and J. Boyd, *A Guide to the Zoroastrian Religion A Nineteenth Century Catechism with Modern Commentary* (Chico: Scholars, 1982), 90.

105 He recommended teaching Greek to one's daughter on the grounds that it made her more attractive. See PT Peah 1:1; PT Sotah 9:15.

106 See Saul Lieberman, *Studies*, 228.

107 Note for example that English "hose" refers to footgear, while the German cognate "Hosen" refers to shorts or breeches. It is a matter of what speakers consider to be the primary body referent.

108 There is no listing in *DJPA* or in CTY.

109 In some instances it will be necessary to treat the related transmissional problem of parallel statements in Aramaic and Hebrew. On the general question see Bendavid, *Biblical Hebrew and Mishnaic Hebrew*, 134–135; E. Margaliot, "Hebrew and Aramaic in the Talmud and Midrash," (Hebrew), *Leshonenu* 27 (1963–1964), 20–33; Shamma Friedman *apud*

some instances, additional recourse will be had to the evidence of the midrashim.[110] Unfortunately, our situation is not ideal for a number of reasons: a) While we have some reliable manuscripts at our disposal, we still lack critical editions for most of BT and PT; b) Many statements attributed to Palestinian rabbis in BT have no extant parallel in PT and vice-versa; c) There are numerous disagreements in attribution,[111] some due to original oral uncertainties, others to subsequent textual uncertainties[112] or to corruption,[113] still others due to sources. A statement attributed to one scholar in one tractate may be attributed to another even within the same tractate of Talmud, let alone in the other Talmud.[114] d) Talmudic attributions are often deductions of what a scholar would or should have said rather than direct quotations;[115] a fact often admitted by the Talmud pericopes themselves);[116] e) One half or

Dimitrovsky ed., *Texts and Studies*, 301–302; For a detailed and sustained inductive study of the problem in one tractate see Neusner, *Taxonomy*.

110 Of particular interest in this regard is Genesis Rabbah, which has a close connection to PT, but also makes extensive use of BT. See J. N. Epstein, *Amoraiticus*, 287–290; Ch. Albeck, *Einleitung und Register zum Bereschit Rabba* (Hebrew; Jerusalem, 1965), 66–86, 110–126 (printed as an appendix to J. Theodor and Ch. Albeck, *Bereschit Rabba, vol.* 3 [Jerusalem, 1965]); E. Goldman, "Parallel Texts in the Palestinian Talmud to Genesis Rabbah Chapters I–V)." (unpublished M.A. thesis Cincinnati: Hebrew Union College, 1969); Strack and Stemberger, *Introduction*, 300–305.

111 The Talmud cites instances in which a scholar denies the authorship of a statement attributed to him. See Shamma Friedman *apud* Dimitrovsky ed., *Texts and Studies*, 313.

112 "At times, the name of the tradent will be different in every manuscript." So, Friedman, *ibid.*

113 As noted by Shamma Friedman (*Sinai*, 1992), it is usually impossible to distinguish between the contemporary Babylonian scholars Rabba and Rava, both forms contracted from R. Abba; See further E. Wajsberg, "The Orthography of the Names Rabba and Rava: Rav Hai's and Rivalling Rules," in, *Language Studies V–VI* ed., M. Bar-Asher (Jerusalem: Magnes, 1992), 181–213. Similarly, the names Ashi and Asi were easily confused as were those of the Palestinian scholars Yonatan and Yohanan, Abba and Abbahu. Professor Halivni observes (oral communication) that it was easy graphically to confuse רבינא and רבי ינאי. In addition some names, e.g. Judah, were quite common. See Streck and Stemberger, *Introduction*, 64.

114 See Strack and Stemberger, *ibid.*

115 See Albeck, *Talmudim*, 483. This is especially true with regard to certain fixed expressions and hermeneutical cliches which were readily transferred among pericopes and contexts. See Albeck, *ibid.*, 482; N. Aminoah, "On Developments of Statements of Amoraim in the Babylonian Talmud," *Te'uda* III (Tel-Aviv: Tel-Aviv University, 1983), 39–56.

116 See Albeck, *Talmudim*, 452; In many cases the impression of dialogue between scholars was created by scribes who would add "he said to him," when it seemed appropriate. See R. Kalmin, *HUCA* 61 (1990), 134–135 with references to previous literature. Halivni (*PAAJR*

more of BT is anonymous;[117] f) During the Amoraic period (200–500 AD) there was a good deal of Babylonian immigration to Palestine, and a good deal of return migration. Scholars traveled between the two rabbinic centers with some regularity. Others went abroad for the purpose of study without intending to relocate permanently.[118] In consequence, there must have been a good deal of bi-dialectalism among the sages.[119] g) European scribes obliterated many Palestinian Aramaic dialectal features.[120]

It is hoped that further systematic study in this vein will facilitate our understanding of the history of talmudic literature.

46–47 [1980], 67–83) calls attention to the fact that some tradents were singled out for praise because they specified when their attributions were doubtful; a clear indication that other scholars were less precise.

117 The figure is from Halivni, *Midrash* (Cambridge: Harvard, 1986), 81.

118 See M. Beer, *EncJud* 12, s.v. "Neḥutei."

119 Certainly some dialectal features such as pronunciations of specific phonemes and words could have survived through several generations of immigrants. See Saul Lieberman, "Ḥeshbon Otiyot," in *Hebrew Language Studies Presented to Professor Zeev Ben-Hayyim*, eds. M. Bar-Asher, A. Dotan, D. Teneh and G. Ben-Ami Sarfati (Jerusalem, 1983), 332; reprinted in *Lieberman Studies*, 525.

120 Regular comparison of printed editions of the Palestinian Talmud with good manuscripts demonstrates the tendency of scribes familiar with the Babylonian Talmud to insinuate its idioms and grammatical forms into PT texts. See Kut, SGA 2; A Tal, *PNWCJS* (Jerusalem: Magnes, 1988), 14.

Bible

CHAPTER 12

Joshua 24 Re-examined

The present paper is a detailed analysis of the language and themes of Joshua 24:1–28. On the basis of this analysis, it is concluded that the chapter is the work of a single author, not identical with the Deuteronomist as argued by Perlitt, nor, as maintained recently by van Seters, with the Yahwist. The author of Joshua 24:1–28 utilized sources of the Pentateuch and other parts of the Bible but differed from them on significant points of history and theology. The chapter preserves pre-monarchic Shechemite traditions, but was written in the eighth century BCE. before the fall of Samaria.

The scholarly literature on Joshua 24 is voluminous. The chapter has been studied from the viewpoints of classical source criticism, form criticism, and tradition-history, but little consensus has emerged with regard to its authorship, the date of its composition, the antiquity of its traditions, its *Sitz im Leben* or its historical value.[1] The present paper was written primarily in response to the analysis of Joshua 24 by Lothar Perlitt in his *Bundestheologie*[2] and the paper by John van Seters in the Ahlström Festschrift.[3]

---

1 For bibliography to 1970 see J. Soggin, *Joshua* (Philadelphia: Westminster, 1972), 222–223; Y. Kaufmann, *Sepher Yehoshua* (Jerusalem: Kiryat Sepher, 1970, 248–256. Other relevant studies include F. Cross, *Canaanite Myth and Hebrew Epic* (Cambridge: Harvard, 1973), 84, n. 15; A. van Selms, "Temporary Henotheism," in *Symbolae Biblicae et Mesopotamicae Francisco Mario Theodoro de Liagre Böhl Dedicatae*, eds., M. Beek A. Kampman, C. Nijland and J. Ryckmans (Leiden: Brill, 1973), 341–348; D. McCarthy, *Treaty and Covenant* (Rome: Biblical Institute, 1978), 221–242, 279–284; R. Boling and G. Wright, *Joshua* (AB; Garden City, NY: Doubleday, 1982), 527–545.

2 L. Perlitt, *Bundestheologie im Alten Testament* (Neukirchen-Vluyn: Neukirchener, 1969), 239–284.

3 J. van Seters, "Joshua 24 and the Problem of Tradition in the Old Testament," in *In the Shelter of Elyon Essays on Ancient Palestinian Life and Literature in Honor of G. W. Ahlström*, eds. W. B. Barrick and J. R. Spencer ([JSOTSup 31] Sheffield: JSOT, 1984), 139–158.

 | DOI 10.1163/9789004340879_013

On the basis of his literary analysis, Perlitt attributes Joshua 24 to the Deuteronomist and traces its historical background to the Assyrian crisis of the seventh century. In contrast, it will be argued here that a) Joshua 24:1–28[4] is a unified literary work by a single author who is not to be identified with the Deuteronomist or any other Pentateuchal source;[5] b) that author was able to utilize the sources of the Pentateuch and other parts of the Bible and at the same time to deviate from them for literary or ideological purposes; c) the author of Joshua 24 differed with the Pentateuchal sources as well as with traditions preserved elsewhere in the Bible on significant points of history and ideology; d) Joshua 24 preserves pre-monarchic Shechemite traditions[6] but was written sometime in the eighth century before the fall of Samaria.

The setting of Joshua 24 is Shechem,[7] a city not connected with the conquest traditions of the books of Joshua and Judges. Joshua has summoned all of Israel to stand before God (האלהים). In their presence he relates the story of Israel's ancestors who "lived beyond the river... and served other gods."[8] Joshua speaks of Jacob's descent into Egypt, the dispatch of Moses and Aaron, the striking of Egypt, the drowning of the Egyptian army in the darkness, the sojourn in the wilderness, the conquest of Transjordan, the battle with Balak

4 For the treatment of 1–28 as the extant literary unit, see M. Noth, *Das Buch Josua* (HAT; Tübingen: Mohr, 1953), 135–140; Kaufmann, *Yehoshua*, 248–255; H. W. Hertzberg, *Die Bücher Josua, Richter, Ruth* (ATD; Göttingen: Vandenhoeck & Ruprecht, 1959), 131–138; McCarthy, *Treaty*, 221–234.

5 Cf. Kaufmann, *Yehoshua*, 248.

6 On Shechemite traditions in general, see E. Nielsen, *Shechem, A Traditio-Historical Investigation* (Copenhagen: Gad, 1969); on the city itself, see E. Campbell, "Shechem (City)," *IDBSup*, 821–822; cf. *idem*, "Judges 9 and Biblical Archaeology," in *The Word of the Lord Shall Go Forth: Essays in Honor of David Noel Freedman in Celebration of his Sixtieth Birthday*, eds. C. Meyers and M. O'Connor (Winona Lake: Eisenbrauns, 1983), 263–271.

7 LXX reads "Shiloh" in vs. 1 and vs. 25. The Greek reading is secondary. "Shiloh" may be an attempt at harmonization with 18:1 or the result of a later anti-Samaritan bias. Boling and Wright, *Joshua*, 533; See further Nielsen, *Schechem*, 295–357.

8 The phrase "other gods" of vs. 2 recurs in vs. 17. In vss. 20 and 22 these divinities are replaced by "foreign gods." For the alternation of אחר "other" and נכר "foreign," cf. Exod 34:14 and Ps 81:10.

aided by Balaam the curser,[9] the crossing of the Jordan, the battle at Jericho, the dispatch of the צרעה,[10] and God's gift of the land.

After completing the narration, Joshua turns to the people, admonishing them to remove the "foreign gods" and serve Yahweh exclusively. He notes that they have the option of serving other gods if they do not wish to serve Yahweh. He and his household, however, will serve Yahweh. The people then affirm that they too will serve Yahweh. Joshua then warns them that Yahweh's service is "impossible" because as a jealous god Yahweh will not forgive them if they "sin in their rebelliousness" and serve the "foreign gods." The people protest that they are prepared to serve Yahweh and to bear their own witness to their choice. Once the people have agreed to abandon all the "foreign gods," Joshua makes a covenant in their behalf. There in Shechem he provides them with a fixed rule. All these matters he sets down in writing in a document of God's teaching (ספר תורת אלהים). Finally, Joshua erects a large stone under the oak in Yahweh's sanctuary that he designates as witness to Yahweh's words to the people.

The structural unity of Josh 24:1–28 is most obvious in the rhetorical progression of Joshua's argument. Speaking in Yahweh's name in the manner of a prophet,[11]Joshua begins with a recital of the *magnalia dei* performed in the people's behalf. Inasmuch as Yahweh has always aided his people, fought for them, and given them unearned victories and unworked for prosperity, they

---

9 The reference to Balaam and Balak is not significant for dating. The Deir 'Allā texts show that Balaam was a character of folklore, who like Gilgamesh and Ahiqar was popular in more than one culture. For studies of the Deir 'Allā Balaam material with bibliography, see J. Hackett, *The Balaam Text from Deir 'Allā* (Chico: Scholars, 1984); A. Lemaire, "Les inscriptions de Deir 'Allā et la littérature araméenne antique," *CRAIBL* (1985), 270–285; S. Ahituv, *Echoes from the Past* (Jerusalem: Carta, 2008), 433–465. The reference in Mic 6:5 to Balaam and Balak as ancient figures who would be known to Micah's listeners is probably older than the Deir 'Allā text. According to Lemaire ("Deir 'Allā," 272–273), the Deir 'Allā text dates from ca. 750 BCE but is based on an original a century or two older.

10 Aside from Joshua 24, צרעה is attested only in Exod 23:28 and in Deut 7:20 which is derived from it. On the relation between these passages, cf. G. Schmitt, *Du sollst keinen Frieden schliessen mit den Bewohnern des Landes*, (Stuttgart: Kohlhammer, 1970), 17–20; The traditional translation of צרעה as "hornet" is supported by an Egyptian pun in an early text. See J. Wilson in *ANET* 477, n. 36; For an attempt to explain the significance of the צרעה, see O. Borowski, "The Identity of the Biblical *ṣir'â*," in *Essays Freedman*, 315–319.

11 Kaufmann, *Yehoshua*, 251, terms the entire chapter "a prophetic story."; cf. McCarthy, *Treaty*, 239 and van Seters, "Joshua 24," 147.

must serve Yahweh alone and remove all other objects of worship. In 24:15 Joshua gives the people a "choice" of worshipping the gods "beyond the river" (left behind by their ancestors) or the local gods (whose people were delivered into Israelite hands). Here, Joshua of necessity speaks for himself and not Yahweh asserting that he and his household will serve Yahweh. The people respond appropriately, virtually summarizing the long account of Yahweh's saving acts. Joshua eggs on the people by telling them that they cannot possibly serve Yahweh, thus making his exclusive worship a goal to be attained. He is then able to reiterate the demand of verse 14 to remove all the other gods and to bring about the people's compliance. The actions of covenant and its accompaniments follow.

The logical structure of Joshua's rhetoric is heightened by the repetition of key words and phrases. Not surprisingly, the name Yahweh occurs eighteen times.[12] Forms of אלהים occur sixteen times.[13] The verb עבד "worshipped" also occurs sixteen times.[14] Other significantly repeated words are forms of אב "ancestor" (eight times),[15] עבר "crossed/ across" (seven times),[16] מצרים "Egypt/ Egyptians" (seven times)[17] ישב "dwelt" (six times),[18] נתן "gave, granted" (six times),[19] and שלח "sent" (four times).[20] In addition, Giblin's important study has demonstrated how the placement of significant words and the repetition of grammatical forms serve to tighten the structure of the chapter.[21]

When Perlitt wrote in 1969, he noted the great variety of earlier opinion regarding the source identification of Joshua 24,[22] but made the generally accurate observation that recent scholars, even those who maintained the antiquity of its traditions, acknowledged its Deuteronomic/Deuteronomistic

12 Vss. 2, 7, 14 (twice), I5 (twice), 16, 17, 18 (twice), 19, 20, 21, 22, 23, 24, 26, 27.

13 Vss. 1, 2 (twice), 14, 15, 16, 17, 18, 19, 20, 23 (twice), 24, 26, 27.

14 Vss. 2, 14 (3 times), I5 (4 times), 16, 18, 19, 20, 21, 22, 24, 31.

15 Vss. 2 (3 times), 3, 6 (twice), 14, 15.

16 Vss. 2, 3, 8, 11, 14, 15, 17.

17 Vss. 4, 5, 6, 72, 14, 17.

18 Vss. 2, 7, 8, 13, 15, 18.

19 Vss. 3, 42, 8, 11, 13.

20 Vss. 5, 9, 12, 28.

21 C. Giblin, "Structural Patterns in Joshua 24:1–25," *CBQ* 26 (1964), 50–69; cf. Boling and Wright, *Joshua*, 533.

22 Perlitt, *Bundestheologie*, 238; cf. Nielsen, *Shechem*, 90–92.

language.[23] Proceeding from this literary "consensus,"[24] Perlitt attempted to show that the historical circumstances underlying the chapter fit the seventh century only.[25] More recently, John van Seters has correctly noted that Perlitt's historical argument is flawed.[26] For his part, van Seters[27] identifies the author of Joshua 24 with the Yahwist of the Pentateuch, whom he dates to the exilic Period.[28] Our study begins therefore with a detailed analysis of the language of the chapter.[29]

24:1: As Nielsen[30] and Hertzberg[31] have noted, the leadership elements enumerated here are characteristic of Deuteronomy. The phrase ויתיצבו לפני האלהים "they stood themselves before God" is unique. Its closest parallel is התיצבו לפני יהוה "stand yourselves before Yahweh" in 1Sam 10:19.

24:2: בעבר הנהר "beyond the river" recurs in vss. 14–15. From the Syro-Palestinian perspective, the expression means "east of the Euphrates." See 2Sam 10:16; 1Kgs 14:15.[32] The claim that Israel's ancestors were settled "beyond the river" contradicts Deut 26:5 in which the unnamed ancestor of Israel was a "wandering[33] Aramean" whose ultimate origin was unknown. Perlitt makes much of this geographic datum: "Von jenseits des Stromes droht Israel Lebensgefahr! Jenseits des Stromes aber leben die Assyrer, deren Götter hier und heute mitten in Israel zur Anbetung aufgestellt sind. Dafür kommt nur e i n e Zeit in Betracht: die des 7 Jh.s, und das ist die Zeit, in und aus deren religiösen Nöten die dt Predigt erwuchs."[34] There are a number of problems

23 Perlitt, *ibid.*, 239; Kaufmann, *Yehoshua*, 248, whose work was apparently not consulted by Perlitt, calls the writer of Joshua 24 "an independent author, writing in an archaic style containing linguistic ingredients from various 'sources.'"

24 McCarthy refers to "the rather uncritical assumption that the text is Dtistic." See *Treaty*, 283, cf. *ibid.*, 221–234.

25 See below.

26 van Seters, "Joshua 24," 145–146; cf. my comments to vs. 2 below.

27 van Seters, *ibid.*, 149.

28 van Seters, *ibid.*, 153.

29 The method followed here is similar to McCarthy's (*Treaty*, 221–234), whose treatment of the language is much less detailed.

30 Nielsen, *Shechem*, 79, 87.

31 Hertzberg, *Josua*, 133.

32 Cf. L. Toombs, "Beyond the River," *IDB* 1, 405–406.

33 "Fugitive" may be a better translation. Borger (BAL vol. I, 138), compares the ארמי אבד of Deut 36:5 with Sennacherib's characterization of Mušēzib-Marduk as *aramê ḫalqu munnabtu* "fugitive Aramaean runaway," (OIP 2 42 v 22); cf. G. Mendenhall, *The Tenth Generation* (Baltimore: Johns Hopkins, 1973), 137.

34 "From beyond the river Israel is fatally threatened. Beyond the river though, live the Assyrians whose gods have been set up here and now in Israel's midst for the purpose of

with this analysis. First, the danger from Assyria was not limited to the seventh century. Assyria's first incursion into Israelite territory was in the ninth century and continued for the next two.[35] Second, were Perlitt correct, some reference to the fall of Samaria, however veiled, would be expected. Third, Joshua 24 does not refer to any "mortal danger" (Lebensgefahr) from "beyond the river." Mortal danger, described in vague terms, comes from Yahweh if one chooses to worship gods from that region, or any other, along with him (vs. 20). Fourth, there is no evidence that Assyria demanded the adoration of its gods in its conquered or tributary territories.[36]

בעבר הנהר ישבו אבותיכם מעולם "your ancestors had always dwelt beyond the river." The term מעולם connotes antiquity and permanence.[37] The closest parallel[38] to this verse is in the ninth century Mesha inscription (*KAI* 181:10): ואש גד ישב בארץ עטרת מעלם "The Gadites had lived in the land of Ataroth from of old."

תרח אבי אברהם ואבי נחור "Teraḥ, father ofAbraham and father of Naḥor." Neither the name Teraḥ, nor the name Naḥor is mentioned in Deuteronomy.

ויעבדו אלהים אחרים "they served other gods."[39] No other biblical tradition says explicitly that the immigration of Israel's ancestors was responsible for their rejection of the foreign gods and their adoption of Yahweh worship. According to J, Yahweh had been worshipped everywhere from earliest

---

worship [by the Israelites]. Therefore, only o n e time period can come under consideration: that of the seventh century, and that is the time period in which the Deuteronomic preaching arose out of the religious emergency." Perlitt, *Bundestheologie*, 251.

35 See P. Machinist, "Assyria and its Image in the First Isaiah," *JAOS* 103 (1983), 720–721.

36 See M. Cogan, *Imperialism and Religion* (Missoula: Scholars Press, 1974); cf. van Seters, "Joshua 24," 146.

37 West-Semitic *ʿlm* is semantically equivalent to Akkadian *dârû* "everlasting." (*CAD D*, 115) Phoenician *šmš ʿlm*, Ugaritic *špš ʿlm* and Amarna *šamaš darītum* "sun from of old/everlasting" attested at Amarna and Boghazköy (*CAD D*, 114b) prove the antiquity of West- Semitic *mʿlm*. See also S. Gevirtz, "West-Semitic Curses and the Problem of the Origin of Hebrew Law," *VT* 11 (1961), 143 and n. 5; *idem*, "On Canaanite Rhetoric: The Evidence of the Amarna Letters from Tyre," *Or* 42 (1973), 177; H. Tawil, "Some Literary Elements in the Opening Sections of the Hadad, Zakir, and the Nerab II Inscriptions in the Light of East and West Semitic Royal Inscriptions," *Or.* 43 (1974), 42, n. 10; F. Bron, *Recherches sur les inscriptions phéniciennes de Karatepe* (Geneva: Droz, 1979), 187–188.

38 1Sam 27:8 may be parallel. Note however that NJPS a.l. translates מעולם as "from the region of Olam."

39 The notice about the service of other gods led later Jewish tradition to depict Terah as the proprietor of an idol shop and Abraham as an idol smasher. Cf. L. Ginzberg, *The Legends of the Jews* (Philadelphia: Jewish Publication Society, 1937) vol. 1, 213–217; cf. Nielsen, *Shechem*, 87.

times.[40] In consequence, Abraham's departure from Haran did not represent a departure from previous religious practice. According to P, the god known to Abraham as El Shaddai was not distinct from Yahweh whose name was revealed first to Moses.[41]

בכל ארץ כנען "in all of Canaan-land." כל ארץ כנען occurs only in P but is not distinctive. Cf. Amarna *māt kinaḫḫi gabbaša* (EA 162:41).

וארב את זרעו "I made his offspring numerous." Cf. Gen 16:10; Exod 32:13; Jer 33:22.

Vs. 4 ואתן לעשו את הר שעיר לרשת אותו "I gave Mt. Seir to Esau as his inheritance." For the thought, cf. Deut 2:5. The closest linguistic parallels, however, are Lev 20:24 and Num 33:53.

Vs. 5: ואשלח את משה ואת אהרן "I sent Moses and Aaron."

Cf. the early tradition in Mic 6:4 and the late one in Ps 105:26. In Deuteronomy nothing is said of Aaron's mission. He is recalled only in connection with Yahweh's anger against him (9:20) and his death (10:6, 32:50).

ואגף את מצרים "I struck Egypt." The verb נגף appears in Deuteronomy only in the *nif'al*.[42] Deuteronomy does not employ נגף for the smiting of the Egyptians, preferring instead "the mighty hand" (6:21), accompanied by "the outstretched arm." (11:3, 26:8) The phrasing here is closest to Exod 7:27, 12:23.

כאשר עשיתי בקרבו "as I did in its midst." As Nielsen has noted, this looks like an abbreviation.[43] Cf. Exod 3:20, 10:1; Num 14:11.

ואחר הוצאתי אתכם "then afterwards I brought you out." The construction ואחר + verb immediately following does not occur in Deuteronomy. Cf. Deut 21:13 with Lev 14:8.

Vs. 7: ויצעקו אל יהוה "they[44] cried out to Yahweh." Cf. Exod 14:10.

---

40 See Gen 4:1, 26.

41 See Gen 17:1; Exod 6:2–3. For a survey and discussion of the different modern theories about religion in the patriarchal narratives, see G. Wenham, "The Religion of the Patriarchs," in *Essays of the Patriarchal Narratives*, eds. A. Millard and D. Wiseman (Winona Lake: Eisenbrauns, 1983), 161–195; to the bibliography add J. van Seters. "The Religion of the Patriarchs in Genesis," *Biblica* 61 (1980), 220–223.

42 Deut 1:42, 28:7, 25.

43 *Shechem*, 88. He does however, not rule out its originality.

44 In vss. 6–7 there is an alternation between third person (ancestors) and second person (present generation). Van Seters ("Joshua 24," 147) claims that "this is not a feature of early prophecy so that one must conclude that it is a special feature of the Dtr tradition." Naturally, this requires him (*ibid.*, 157) to assign a late date to Amos 2:4: על מאסם את תורת יהוה וחקיו לא שמרו ויתעום כזביהם אשר הלכו אבותם אחריהם.

The late dating of Amos 2:4 is in agreement with a number of other scholars who assign the verse to the Dtr redaction of Amos. See e.g. J. L. Mays, *Amos, A Commentary*

וישם מאפל "he put darkness." Nowhere else in the Bible does this form of the word for "darkness" appear. In its version of this event Exod 14:19–20 refers to עמוד הענן "the cloud-pillar" and הענן והחשך, "the dark cloud." Deut 11:4 makes no mention of darkness.

ויבא עליו את הים ויכסהו "he brought the sea over him, covering him." There is no exact parallel, but cf. Exod 15:10; Ps 78:53. Deut 11:4 has the interesting reading: הציף את מי ים סוף על פניהם "He caused the waters of the Red Sea to overflow them."

ותראינה עיניכם את אשר עשיתי במצרים "Your own eyes beheld what I did to Egypt." The closest parallels are Exod 19:4; Deut 29:1.

ימים רבים "many days." The figure may be indeterminate. Cf. Deut 1:46, 2:1, and see Driver, *Deuteronomy*, 31–34. It is possible however, that the writer is referring to the ancient forty-year wilderness tradition (Amos 2:10). In the Mesha stele the ימן רבן "many days" (*KAI* 181:5) during which Omri humbled Moab are equivalent to the ארבען שת "forty years" during which he occupied Medeba (*KAI* 181:8).

Vs. 8: ואביאה אתכם אל ארץ האמרי היושב בעבר הירדן "I brought you to the land of the Amorite who dwells on the far side of the Jordan." Amos 2:9, 10 refer to the conquest of ארץ האמרי "land of the Amorite" as a well-known tradition. According to Nielsen, "the word אמרי does not appear in any *ancient* [emphasis his—SDS] tradition"[45] about the Transjordanians. Nielsen believes that אמרי was applied secondarily "to the Transjordanian population as a consequence of the policy of the house of Joseph, from the period of Judges until the kingdom of Jeroboam II, and more probably in the latter."[46] (But see Num 32:39; Judg 10:8.) Van Seters holds a more extreme view: "It is very difficult to date any Old Testament source which uses the term 'Amorite' ... for inhabitants of Palestine before the eighth century BC."[47] Biblical sources, argues van Seters, were influenced by the term *amurrû* "Westerner" in cuneiform sources which began in the early eighth century to employ *amurrû* for the kingdoms of Syria ... Palestine, including Phoenicia, Israel, Moab, Ammon, Edom and the

(Philadelphia: Westminster, 1969), 40–42. It must be noted however, that the similar כי מאסו את תורת יהוה צבאות occurs in Isa 5:25 and that כזב and תעה are unattested in Deuteronomy. But even if we grant the lateness of Amos 2:4 this so called "special feature" of alternation between third person (ancestors) and second person (present generation) is found in Amos 2:6–15 and very prominent in Hosea 12–13.

45 Nielsen, *Shechem*, 94, n. 3.

46 *Ibid.*

47 J. van Seters, "The Terms 'Amorite' and 'Hittite' in the Old Testament," *VT* 22, (1972), 81.

Philistine cities."[48] It must be replied first that the fluidity of Akkadian *amurrû* is much earlier than the eighth century;[49] that the use of biblical אמרי, however fluid, does not designate the same groups as Akkadian *amurrû*;[50] that it is unlikely that Hebrew writers learned from outsiders how to apply their own local designation.

<שני מלכי האמרי> "<The two Amorite kings>[51] did battle with you." The reference to the two Amorite kings must be moved here from vs. 12 where it is difficult syntactically and contextually. The two kings are not named, in contrast to Josh 2:10, 9:10, 12:2, 4, 5, 13:10, 12, 21, 27.

ותירשו את ארצם "you took possession of their land." Cf. וירש עמרי את כ[ל אר]ץ מהדבא "Omri had taken possession of all Medeba Land." (*KAI* 181:7–8)

ואשמידם מפניכם "I destroyed them before you." The phrase is very similar to the description of the destruction of the Amorites in Amos 2:9.

Vss. 9–10: Mic 6:5 cites an exchange between Balak, King of Moab, and Balaam, son of Beor, as a familiar tradition but mentions no battle between Israel and Moab. The narrative of Judg 11:25 explicitly says that Balak did not engage Israel in battle. Accordingly, both differ with Josh 24:9–10. There is some linguistic resemblance between Josh 24:9–10 and Deut 23:5 which refers to Balaam as being called on to "curse" קלל Israel and to Yahweh's (lack of) "desire" אבה to comply. Nonetheless the phrase ויברך ברוך is unique to Joshua 24. At the same time the derivative character of Deut 23:5 is apparent because the Deuteronomist cites the episode as a legal precedent to justify the exclusion of Ammonites and Moabites from the Israelite community.

---

48 *Ibid.*, 66.

49 See AHw., 46a; *CAD A/II*, 93–95; There is a similar fluidity in early Egyptian sources. Rameses II, in a text ca. 1296 speaks of "the shore in the land of Amurru" with reference to the Phoenician coast. See *ANET*, 256, n. 9; contrast van Seters, "Amorite," 65.

50 Note, for example, that Phoenicia and Edom are never called "Amorite" in the Bible and that biblical "Amorite" never means "Westerner." On the problems involved in the relation between the Hebrew and Akkadian terms, see N. Tur-Sinai, *The Language and the Book: Beliefs and Doctrines* [Hebrew] (Jerusalem: Bialik Institute, 1955), 134–139; H. Huffmon, "Amorites," IDBSup, 20–21; J. Luke, " 'Your Father was an Amorite' (Ezek 16:3, 45): An Essay on the Amorite Problem in OT Traditions," in The Quest for the Kingdom of God: Studies in Honor of George E. Mendenhall, eds. H. Huffmon and Alberto Green (Winona Lake: Eisenbrauns, 1983), 221–237; A. Altman, "The Original Meaning of the Name Amurru 'Ha'emori,' " in Studies in Hebrew and Semitic Languages Dedicated to the Memory of Professor Eduard Yechezkel Kutscher, eds. G. Sarfati and P. Artzi (Ramat-Gan: Bar-Ilan, 1980), 76–102.

51 LXX to vs. 12 refers to "twelve Amorite kings."

וישלח ויקרא ל "he sent a call for..." Not distinctive. Cf. e.g. Gen 27:42; Judg 4:6, 16:18.

Vs. 11: וילחמו בכם בעלי יריחו "the inhabitants of Jericho did battle with you." The battle with the Jerichonians contradicts the narrative of chapter 6, which, as Soggin has noted, has "a completely ritual context [in which] there is hardly room for any kind of military action."[52]

בעלי יריחו "the inhabitants of Jericho." The plural of בעל for inhabitants of a place is confined to the books of Judges and Samuel. See e.g., Judges 9 (passim); 1Sam 23:11, 12; 2Sam 21:12. There is a similar use in late Phoenician texts. See *KAI* 60:6; 101:1; 137:1. Deuteronomy employs (13:16) ישבי העיר and אנשי עירו (Deut 21:21, 22:21).

The list of the seven nations is apparently a gloss designed to mitigate the contradiction between the beginning of vs. 11 and the tradition of chapter 6. It may be noted however, that the sequence "Amorite, Perizzite and Canaanite" is unique.[53]

Vs. 12: ואשלח לפניכם את הצרעה ותגרש אותם מפניכם "I sent the hornet ahead of you and it drove them out before you." Structurally this verse resembles Exod 23:28: ושלחתי את הצרעה לפניך וגרשה את ... מלפניך. The צרעה is also mentioned in Deut 7:20. The idiom גרש מפני "drove out before" recurs in vs. 18. McCarthy correctly describes גרש as "un-Dtistic."[54] See e.g., Exod 34:11; Judg 2:3. Once again there is a ninth century Moabite parallel: ויגרשה כמש מפני "Chemosh drove him out before me." (*KAI* 181:19)

לא בחרבך ולא בקשתך "Not by your sword nor by your bow." The hendiadys "sword and bow" means "warfare." Cf. Gen 48:22; 2 Kgs 6:22.

Vs. 13: ארץ אשר לא יגעת בה "a land for which you did not toil." The phrase is unique. But see e.g., Isa 62:8; Ps 6:7.

וערים אשר לא בניתם ותשבו בהם כרמים וזיתים אשר לא נטעתם אתם אכלים "(I have given you) cities which you inhabit although you did not build them. You enjoy olive groves and vineyards which you did not plant." This verse has a close parallel in Deut 6:10–11:

> והיה כי יביאך יהוה אלהיך אל הארץ אשר נשבע לאבתיך לאברהם ליצחק וליעקב לתת לך ערים גדלת וטבות אשר לא בנית. ובתים מלאים כל טוב אשר לא מלאת וברת חצובים אשר לא חצבת כרמים וזיתים אשר לא נטעת ואכלת ושבעת.

52 J. Soggin, "The Conquest of Jericho through Battle," *ErIsr* 16 (1982), *215.

53 The order differs in the versions. See Nielsen, *Shechem*, 89.

54 McCarthy, *Treaty*, 232. In Deuteronomy גרש "expel" appears only in 33:27, in a poetic chapter whose relation to the rest of the book is questionable. Deuteronomy prefers forms of ירש. See, e.g., Deut 11:23, 12:2, 29, 18:14, 19:1.

> When Yahweh your god brings you into the land which he swore to your ancestors Abraham, Isaac and Jacob to give you; great prosperous cities which you did not build, and houses filled with every delight which you did not fill, and hewn cisterns[55] you did not hew, and you enjoy to satiety olive groves and vineyards which you did not plant.

The Joshua passage is obviously primary. In Josh 24:13 the "land" and "cities" are the objects of ואתן. In Deut 6:10–11, the "cities" and "houses" stand without a governing verb (לתת complements נשבע). In addition, Deuteronomy explicitly assigns the promises to the Patriarchs. The primacy of Joshua 24 is also reflected in its realistic picture of a victorious force occupying the territory of the defeated. This picture is elaborated by the Deuteronomist, who describes the cities as great and prosperous, populated with houses which are filled with delights and which contain private cisterns. The Israelites do not merely eat, but eat to satiety. The Deuteronomist apparently employed Joshua's words as part of Moses's prophetic warning.

Vs. 14: ועתה יראו את יהוה "Now then, fear Yahweh." Cf. 1Sam 12:24; Ps 34:10.

ועבדו אתו בתמים ובאמת "and serve him with wholehearted devotion." The phrase occurs nowhere else. The pair is attested in reverse order in Judg 9:16, 19, likewise set in Shechem. In Deuteronomic language the concept of wholehearted devotion is expressed by בכל לבבך[ם] ובכל נפשך[ם]. See Deut 6:5; 11:13.

והסירו את אלהים אשר עבדו אבותיכם בעבר הנהר ובמצרים "and remove the gods your ancestors served beyond the river and in Egypt."[56] Cf. vs. 23 below.

---

55 For these private cisterns, cf. Isa 36:16. Cf. also Moabite: ואמר לכל העם עשו לכם אש בר בביתה "So I said to the entire people: Each of you make a cistern for yourselves in your own home." (*KAI* 181:24–25).

56 *Pace* Nielsen (*Shechem*, 102) and van Seters ("Joshua 24," 149), there are no explicit statements in Joshua 24 that Israel served Egyptian gods in Egypt. Vs. 14 refers to Israel's persistence in the service of its ancestral gods in Egypt. In vs. 15 Joshua tells the people to choose between the ancestral gods from beyond the river and the local Amorite gods if they do not approve of Yahweh's service. The writer of the chapter believes that Joshua's contemporaries might continue in the service of their ancestral gods and that they might be drawn to the service of the local gods, but that they presumably would not be tempted to serve the gods of those who put them in the "slave house." (vs. 17) It was the Deuteronomist who first suggested that Israel might be tempted to worship the gods of Egypt (Deut 29; 15–17). He was followed by Ezek 20:5–8, which explicitly attributes the worship of Egyptian gods to Israel in Egypt.

For similar removals of offending gods, see Gen 35:3; Judg 10:16; 1Sam 7:3–4. A. van Selms refers to this action as "temporary henotheism" and cites parallel phenomena in other Near Eastern cultures.[57]

Vs. 15: בחרו לכם היום את מי תעבדון "choose now whom you will serve." In Deuteronomy it is Yahweh who chooses, not the people. See Deut 4:37, 7:6, 7, 10:15, 14:2. For the people choosing gods, see Judg 5:8, 10:14; Isa 1:29.

היום "now, right away, presently." The expression is common in Deuteronomy. See e.g., Deut 1:10, 39, 4:4, 8, 5:1. It is also well- attested elsewhere. See e.g., Gen 19:37, 21:26, 22:14, 24:12, 30:32; Exod 13:4; Lev 9:4; Judg 21:6.

אלהי האמרי אשר אתם ישבים בארצם "the gods of the Amorite in whose land you dwell."[58] Cf. Judg 6:10.

ואנכי וביתי נעבד את יהוה "but I and my household shall serve Yahweh." The phrase is unique.

Vs. 16 חלילה לנו מעזב את יהוה "far be it from us to forsake Yahweh." חלילה does not occur in Deuteronomy.

Vs. 17: כי יהוה אלהינו הוא המעלה אתנו ואת אבתינו מארץ מצרים "for Yahweh our god is the one who brought us and our ancestors up out of the land of Egypt." The verb העלה "brought up" is found in exodus traditions of all periods. For early examples, see Amos 2:10, 3:1, 9:7; Hos 12:14; Mic 6:4. For other attestations see Gen 50:24; Exod 32:4, 7, 8, 33:1; Lev 11:45; Num 14:13, 20:5; Deut 20:1; Judg 6:13; 1Sam 12:6; 1Kgs 12:28; 2Kgs 17:36; Jer 16:14; Neh 9:18.

בית עבדים "slave-house." The term occurs in the Bible in texts of all periods as an epithet of Egypt. See e.g., Exod 13:3, 14, 20:2; Deut 5:6, 7:8, 13:6; Judg 6:8; Jer 34:13; Mic 6:4. The image conveyed by the term is that Egypt is one big slave barracks. Even native Egyptians are slaves. See Gen 47:19–25.

וישמרנו בכל הדרך אשר הלכנו בה "who protected us throughout our entire journey." Cf. Gen 28:20. See further Exod 18:20; Deut 1:31.

---

57 A. van Selms, "Temporary Henotheism," in *Symbolae Böhl*, 341–348; As far as the author of Joshua 24 was concerned, the removal of the foreign gods was meant to be permanent. Most Israelites apparently accepted the notion that it was sinful to worship other gods in the presence of Yahweh (Exod 20:3). At the same time however, the priesthood taught that all sins could be expunged (Lev 16:30). In consequence, it was popularly believed that a (temporarily) reformed thief, murderer, adulterer, liar under oath, or Baal worshipper could participate in the cult with a clear conscience. See Jer 7:9–10.

58 "Amorite" clearly refers to the earlier Cisjordanian population as it does in vs. 18. See Kaufmann, *Yehoshua*, 253, 254; The "gods of the Amorite" are the Baals and Astartes. See O. Eissfeldt, "El and Yahweh," *JSS* 1(1956), 31.

Vs. 19: לא תוכלו לעבד את יהוה "you will be unable to serve Yahweh." The statement is unique.[59]

אלהים קדשים הוא "He is a holy god." The plural קדשים with אלהים in reference to Yahweh is unique. It is more at home in polytheistic language. Cf. Dan 4:5, 6, 15.

אל קנוא הוא "He is a jealous god." The closest parallel is Nah 1:2. Cf. Exod 20:5, 34:14; Deut 5:9, 6:15.

לא ישא לפשעכם ולחטאותיכם "He will not forgive your sins of rebelliousness." For the language, cf. Gen 50:17; Exod 23:21, 34:7. The singular פשעכם in hendiadys with חטאותיכם is to be understood adjectivally. It must be emphasized that although פשע is already attested in Ugaritic[60] and very frequently found in Biblical Hebrew, it does not occur in Deuteronomy.[61]

Vs. 20: ושב והרע לכם "He will turn and do you harm." The phrase is unique. For the construction, see Deut 23:14, 30:3; 1Kgs 8:47; Isa 6:10, 12; Jer 18:4; Mic 7:9; Mal 3:18; Ps 78:34.[62]

וכלה אתכם "he shall destroy you." The verb כלה "destroy, annihilate" is found in all periods of Hebrew and is attested earlier as *kly*, in the same sense in Ugaritic.[63] The threat is general and lacking in specific historical allusions.

אחרי אשר היטיב לכם "after having dealt kindly with you."

אחרי אשר Cf. Deut 24:4; Josh 7:8, 9:16, 23:1; Judg 11:36, 19:23; 2Sam 19:31. For the thought of the passage, cf. Deut 28:63.

Vs. 21: לא כי את יהוה נעבד "Not so! We shall serve Yahweh!" For examples of the emphatic denial formula לא כי see Gen 19:2; Josh 5:14; 1Sam 12:12; 1Kgs 3:22.

Vs. 22: עדים אתם בכם...ויאמרו עדים "You are your own witnesses... They replied 'We are.'"[64] Cf. 1Sam 12:5; See also Ruth 4:11.

Vs. 23: ועתה הסירו את אלהי הנכר אשר בקרבכם "Now remove those foreign gods that are among you." Cf. vs. 4 above; Gen 35:2–4; Judg 10:16; 1Sam 7:3.[65]

---

59 The notion is completely incompatible with the thinking of the Deuteronomist. See McCarthy, *Treaty*, 229, 240.

60 *CTA* 17:vi:43 (= *KTU*³ 1.17:vi: 43) // *g'an*; The virtually identical parallelism is attested in Ben-Sira. See Y. Avishur, *Stylistic Studies of Word-Pairs in Biblical and Ancient Semitic Languages* (Neukirchen: Neukirchener, 1984), 409–410.

61 This observation also argues against Perlitt's assignment of Hos 8:1b to the "dtr redigierten Hoseabuch." (*Bundestheologie*, 147).

62 There are similar constructions in Akkadian and post-biblical Hebrew. See S. D. Sperling, "Late Hebrew *ḥzr* and Akkadian *saḫāru*," in this volume.

63 See J. Patton, *apud* Avishur, *Word-Pairs*, 46.

64 So, Hertzberg, *Josua*, 132, and see below at vs. 27.

65 On the relation between the demand for removing the foreign gods in Joshua 24 and Gen 35:2–4, see A. Alt "Die Wallfahrt von Sichem nach Bethel," in *idem*, Alt, *Kleine Schriften*

והטו את לבבכם אל יהוה אלהי ישראל "and direct your heart to Yahweh, god of Israel."[66] Despite the many attestations of לבב in Deuteronomy the idiom הטה לבב אל does not appear there. Deut 32:46 has שימו לבבכם אל for "turning toward." "Turning/directing the heart (away)" is expressed by סור (Deut 17:20. The parallel in 1Kgs 11:2–4 has הטה), and פנה (Deut 29:17).

Vs. 24: את יהוה אלהינו נעבד ובקולו נשמע "We shall serve Yahweh our god and obey him." The closest parallel is 1Sam 12:14.

For the reverse sequence of שמע קול and עבד, see Deut 13:5.

Vs. 25: ויכרת יהושע ברית לעם ביום ההוא "On that day Joshua made a covenant for the people." Although כרת ברית ל- has several meanings,[67] the sense here is "in behalf of."[68] Cf. Hos 2:20. Joshua acts as mediator in behalf of the people. He himself requires no covenant because he is already committed to Yahweh's service.

וישם לו חק ומשפט בשכם "He established a fixed rule for them at Shechem." See 1Sam 30:25; cf. Exod 15:25; Ps 81:5; Ezra 7:10.[69] The hendiadys חק ומשפט is not attested in Deuteronomy.

---

zur Geschichte des Volkes Israel (Munich: Beck, 1953), vol. 1, 79–89. Outside of Joshua 24, the demand for removal of the foreign gods is followed by an explicit statement of compliance. In Joshua 24 in contrast, that notice is absent because it is the only case in which the demand is not connected to a military threat. It appears that the writers of these other pericopes wanted to demonstrate that obedience to the call for the physical removal of competing deities in wartime would result in Yahweh's full military cooperation.

66 Cf. Gen 33:20; see Noth, *Josua*, 139. The repetition of "Yahweh, god of Israel" from vs. 2 serves to frame the words of Joshua and the people and to provide a transition to the next series of actions.

67 Perlitt, *Bundestheologie*, 261–262.

68 L. Koehler, "Problems in the Study of the Language of the Old Testament," *JSS* 1 (1956), 4; cf. Soggin, *Joshua*, 225. The לעם is balanced by לו in the next phrase. Both mean "for," "in behalf of."

69 As Perlitt notes (*Bundestheologie*, 268, n. 3), in the first three passages חק ומשפט refers to a specific custom; 1Sam 30:25 to spoils division; Exod 15:25 to water purification; and Ps 81:5 to sounding the ram's horn. In Ezra 7:10 however, חק ומשפט seems to have a more general sense of "statutes and decrees" somehow associated with the written תורת יהוה referred to in the same verse. Perlitt argues from the proximity of ספר תורת אלהים in Jos 24:26 to חק ומשפט in vs. 25 that חוק ומשפט in vs. 25 carries a meaning similar to חק ומשפט in Ezra 7:10, thus reflecting late usage. It is, however, much more natural to understand חק ומשפט in Josh 24:25 as a reference to the specific action of covenant making in the same verse. See NJPS and Boling and Wright (*Joshua*, 529) ad loc. In addition, the MT of Ezra 7:10 is uncertain. Both LXX and Peshitta indicate a plural חקים ומשפטים, which unlike חק ומשפט, is well-attested in Deuteronomy (e.g., Deut 4:5, 8, 13, 5:1, 6:1, 7:11, 11:32, 12:1) and a sure sign of Deuteronomy's influence elsewhere. See e.g., 2Kgs 17:37; Mal 3:22.

Vs. 26: ויכתב יהושע את הדברים האלה בספר תורת אלהים "Joshua wrote these words words down in a document[70] of God's teaching."[71] The expression ספר תורת אלהים occurs only here. The similar ספר תורת האלהים is found in Neh 8:18.[72] It is difficult to determine whether ספר תורת אלהים refers to an already existing document to which Joshua added or whether his record constituted that[73] ספר תורת אלהים. The Peshitta to this passage reflects the reading: ספר תורת משה. Inasmuch as the historical summary earlier in the chapter makes no mention of Moses as lawgiver, it is likely that the Peshitta's reading was influenced by the better attested ספר תורת משה of Josh 8:31, 32, 23:6. No mention is made of the disposition of the document such as we might have expected from a comparison with 1Sam 10:25 and similar passages.

ויקח אבן גדולה ויקימה תחת האלה במקדש יהוה "he took a large stone[74] and stood it up at the foot of that oak[75] which is in Yahweh's sanctuary." Joshua's action violates Deuteronomy's prohibition against dedicating standing stones

---

70 *spr* is the common West Semitic word for "document." For comparisons, see Y. Muffs, *Studies in the Aramaic Legal Papyri from Elephantine* (Leiden: Brill, 1969), 207. In Biblical Hebrew ספר can refer to a written document of any length. See Gen 5:1; Num 5:23; Deut 24:1; Josh 1:8; 2Kgs 5:5, 22:8; Isa 29:11; Jer 32:11.

71 On the differences among MT, Peshitta, and LXX with regard to ספר תורת אלהים, see Nielsen, *Shechem*, 108.

72 Cf. Neh 8:8, 9:3; Neither the expression תורת אלהים, nor the concept of written divine תורה are significant for dating. For early examples see Isa 1:10; Hos 4:6, 8:12. Perlitt (*Bundestheologie*, 270) takes ספר תורת אלהים as proof of the lateness of Josh 24:26 because it employs terminology similar to Neh 8:8, 9:3. Perlitt understands that usage to reflect the conceptions of Deuteronomy and those works composed under its influence. He is surely correct with regard to Nehemiah but in that book much more than the phrase תורת ספר אלהים is involved. The Nehemiah references are to some form of the Pentateuch, i.e. the same document referred to in Neh 8:1 as ספר תורת משה "the book of the Law of Moses"; in Neh 8:2, 9 as התורה "the Law," and in Neh 8:3 as ספר התורה "the Book of the Law." Unlike the author of Joshua 24, the writer of Nehemiah 8–9 describes the public reading of divine תורה. His heroes however, do not write in that תורה or write a תורת אלהים of their own.

73 In either case, Joshua's action would be opposed to the ideology of Deuteronomy (4:2; 13:1) which views its teachings as complete and unalterable. Early Jewish sources attempted to resolve the contradiction. See Kaufmann, *Yehoshua*, 254, n.7; note the targum's translation: "He secreted them in the Torah-book."

74 The excavations at Shechem uncovered a great standing stone and its socket in the forecourt of the temple precinct there dated 1450–1100 BCE. See the discussion by E. Campbell, "Judges 9 and Biblical Archaeology," in *Essays Freedman*, 263–271.

75 Cf. Gen 12:6, 35:4; Judg 9:6.

(Deut 16:22). In addition, the Deuteronomist prohibits trees in the Yahweh sanctuaries.[76]

Vs. 27: הנה האבן הזאת תהיה בנו לעדה כי היא שמעה את כל אמרי יהוה והיתה בכם לעדה פן תכחשו באלהיכם "This stone then shall be a witness in our midst for it has heard all of Yahweh's words. Indeed it will witness against you should you deny your god." This is a play on עד ב- "witness to" (see e.g., 1Sam 12:5) and עד ב- "witness against." (e.g., Num 5:13) For the stone as witness, see Gen 31:52. The phrase אמרי יהוה is unique. It must also be noted that the verb כחש does not occur in Deuteronomy in the sense "deny."[77]

Vs. 28: וישלח יהושע את העם איש לנחלתו "Joshua then dismissed the people, all of them, to their allotted portions." Cf. the dismissal of the people in 1Sam 10:25. For the expression איש לנחלתו, see Judg 2:6, 21:24; Jer 12:15. The writer of Judg 2:6ff. borrowed this verse in order to begin his tale of the people's infidelity after Joshua's death.

This detailed study of words, expressions and grammatical constructions in Josh 24:1–28 leads to the conclusion that Perlitt's attempt to link Joshua 24 to Deuteronomy on linguistic grounds has virtually no basis. The language of the chapter is not Deuteronomic or Deuteronomistic. Aside from the tribal leadership terminology of vs. 1, in those passages in which genuine resemblances to Deuteronomy were observed, it was shown that the Deuteronomist was the borrower. Other elements were seen to have parallels in Deuteronomy as well as in other parts of the Bible and therefore are not distinctive. Indeed, several parallels to the ninth century Moabite inscription of King Mesha were noted. At the same time, we have found no words, phrases, grammatical constructions, or historical allusions which indicate a date later than the eighth century BCE.[78]

In his recent article, John van Seters makes some observations on the form of Joshua 24, arguing that it is based on the Deuteronomistic parenesis. He begins by citing similarities to 1Sam 10:17ff. which also contains the formula "Thus says Yahweh, the God of Israel," and noting that it is followed by a (very brief) recital

76 Deut 16:21. The medieval Jewish commentators were troubled by Joshua's violation of this law and attempted to mitigate the difficulty. The targum, for example, translated אלה by Aramaic אלתא "doorpost." In contrast, Rashi and Qimhi explained that Shechem had acquired temporary sanctity by serving as host to the Ark. As such, it could accurately be called a מקדש without housing an altar.

77 The verb כחש in Deut 33:29 is probably related to post-biblical כחש "was weak/meager." For references, see Jast, 629a.

78 According to Campbell, "Shechem," 821, Shechem was continuously occupied from ca. 1000 BCE. until it suffered a major destruction in 724. Joshua 24 is set in a flourishing Shechem oblivious to any impending doom.

of the sacred history, which in turn is followed by Samuel's rebuke (vs. 19) that the people have rejected Yahweh. But as van Seters himself remarks, the order of elements in 1Samuel 10 is not the same as in Joshua 24.[79] We may add that Joshua 24 in contrast to 1Samuel 10, contains no rebuke nor does it call for an array of Israel according to its tribal elements. In sum, 1Samuel 10 and Joshua 24 share the motifs of divine speech and recital of sacred history. But these are also combined in prophetic speeches uninfluenced by the Deuteronomistic parenesis such as Hos 12:1–13:10; Amos 6:1–5, and Mic 6:1–8. To prove that 1Sam 10:7f. is "thoroughly" Deuteronomistic van Seters compares that passage to Judg 6:8–10 which "contains the prophetic speech: Thus says Yahweh the God of Israel," followed by a summation of the salvation history and a divine admonition against worshipping "the gods of the Amorites in whose land you dwell." But as van Seters himself observes, this pericope differs from both Joshua 24 and 1Samuel 10 in lacking an assembly.[80]

Van Seters then turns for further proof to 1Sam 12:7ff. where a "convocation is presupposed." Samuel calls on the people to take their stand before Yahweh and then recounts to them God's acts of deliverance towards them and their forefathers. At the end of this is a warning against disobedience and disloyalty."[81] Van Seters is certainly correct to compare Joshua 24 with the Samuel pericope but that section is generally considered to belong to the early stratum of the Book of Samuel.[82]

According to van Seters, all of the above texts and Joshua 24 are dependent on the Deuteronomistic paranesis: "It is not just a question of some vague prophetic influence ... This reference back to the fathers, whether in terms of what God has done for them or how they sinned against Yahweh by serving other gods and the consequences for the present generation addressed in the second person by prophet or speaker, is found most frequently in Dtr preaching."[83] Indeed, van Seters is correct with regard to frequency, but frequency does not mean invention. The technique is already found in Hosea[84] and Amos.[85]

Believing that he has demonstrated that the form of Josh 24:1–27, is derived from the Deuteronomic parenesis, van Seters turns to the contents of its historical summary. He draws the questionable inference that the historical

79 Van Seters, "Joshua 24," 146.

80 *Ibid.*, 147.

81 *Ibid.*

82 See N. Gottwald, "Samuel, Book of," *EncJud* vol. 14, 792.

83 Van Seters, "Joshua 24," 147.

84 See Hosea 9:10–17, 10:9–13:10.

85 Amos 2:6–15. Cf. n. 44 above.

summary in Joshua 24 "must be later than all the Dtr examples"[86] because it is so elaborate, and observes that vss. 2–13 depart radically in matters of detail from the Deuteronomistic tradition and agree substantially with the Yahwistic source of the Pentateuch. In consequence, van Seters concludes, "the author of Jos 24:1–27 is none other than the Yahwist of the Pentateuch," whose work, according to van Seters, was composed during the exilic period as an addition to the Deuteronomic history.[87]

The exilic dating leads van Seters to understand Joshua 24 as reflective of exilic concerns. The people assembled at Shechem are no longer a nation but simply individual households who are bidden to follow Joshua's example. The references to the foreign gods must also be understood in this vein. "The theological crisis of the exile meant that the Jews in these regions of the diaspora were sorely tempted to worship the gods of these regions."[88]

We cannot enter here into the literary-critical problems involved in dating the Yahwist[89] and must be content with the following observations. First, that Jews, and earlier, Israelites, were tempted to serve other gods is no indication of date. Unless Yehezkel Kaufmann was correct in his radical view that biblical descriptions of Israel's worship of other gods than Yahweh are merely prophetic exaggerations,[90] there was always a "theological crisis" in Israelite Canaan. Second, there is an important ideological difference between the J source of the Pentateuch and Joshua 24. According to J, Yahweh worship was instituted during the first human generation.[91] Joshua 24 in contrast, and specifically that section which van Seters views as the contribution of the Yahwist to the Deuteronomic history,[92] connects Yahweh worship with Abraham's immigration to Canaan. This tradition, by the way, would seem to be a bad lesson for the exile. Why cite a precedent which justifies the worship of the

86 Van Seters, "Joshua 24," 148.

87 *Ibid.*, 149.

88 *Ibid*, 153. Note however, that the gods of the Amorites are local, the ancestral gods are traditional, and the gods of the Egyptians are not mentioned. In sum, the gods of the diaspora regions are not the concern of Joshua 24.

89 For a discussion with bibliography see W. Schmidt, "A Theologian of the Solomonic Era? A Plea for the Yahwist," in *Studies in the Period of David and Solomon and Other Essays*, ed. T. Ishida (Winona Lake: Eisenbrauns, 1982), 55–73.

90 Y. Kaufmann, *The Religion of Israel* (Chicago: University of Chicago, 1960); For my own critique see S. D. Sperling, "Israel's Religion in the Ancient Near East," in *Jewish Spirituality from the Bible to the Middle Ages*, ed. Arthur Green (New York: Crossroad, 1986), 16–21; *idem*, "Monotheism and Ancient Israelite Religion," in this volume.

91 See n. 40 above.

92 Van Seters, "Joshua 24," 148.

gods of the nations in the lands of the nations?[93] Third, Joshua 24 makes no reference to any earlier covenant or law associated with Moses at Sinai, Horeb, or the plains of Moab. In the exilic period, why stress a covenant made in the land? A far better lesson for the exiles would have been the Horeb or Sinai covenant traditions in which Israel bound itself exclusively to Yahweh outside of Canaan. Fourth, the covenant to serve Yahweh alone is a monolatrous, not monotheistic, notion.[94] The consistent monotheism which began to assert itself in the exilic period preferred different religious imagery.[95]

Joshua 24 clearly does not fit the conditions of the exile. At the other extreme, the chapter cannot be contemporary with the events it describes because it accepts the fall of Jericho to the Israelites as a real event and views Joshua as a full-fledged leader of all Israel. These traditions would have taken some time to develop. In addition, it seems as though the author of Joshua 24 had access to the JE literature in some form.[96]

By combining our analysis with the results of earlier scholarship and with what is known about Shechem from biblical and extra-biblical sources, we may draw certain conclusions about the date of the chapter: Shechem was an important city with ancient religious traditions dating back well into the second millennium. The Israelites reinterpreted those traditions in the light of their own historical, mythical and cultic traditions. It is well-known that the worship of a god El/Baal Berith is attested at Shechem. Joshua 24 is based on an early northern Israelite reinterpretation of that tradition in which Yahweh, the god of the exodus, became the covenant-god at Shechem.[97] The language of Joshua 24, however, points to the ninth through eighth centuries and this agrees with the historical perspective of the chapter. The people live in peace and comfort. We have noted that destruction is threatened only in general terms and that there is no reference to exile. The historical setting fits nicely with the conventional dating of JE as earlier than D. In consequence, we would date the composition of Joshua 24 to a period early in the long and prosperous reign of Jeroboam II (ca. 786–746).

---

93 Note that Jeremiah's adversaries in Jer 44:17 justify their worship of the Queen of Heaven by citing ancestral precedent.

94 See Sperling, "Irael's Religion," 16.

95 See S. D. Sperling, "Rethinking Covenant in Late Biblical Books," in this volume.

96 See the Pentateuchal citations in the detailed comments above. There are no specific indications that the author of Joshua 24 had access to P.

97 See McCarthy, *Treaty*, 222.

CHAPTER 13

Deuteronomy 6:4-יהוה אחד: A New Proposal

The "oneness of God" is a fundamental tenet of Judaism. Deut 6:4-שמע ישראל יהוה אלהינו יהוה אחד, normally translated "Hear O Israel the Lord our God, the Lord is One," has been traditionally understood to be a monotheistic credo that affirms the existence of the sole god YHWH. Not without some trepidation, the present brief study examines Deut 6:4 in quest of the meaning assigned by the ancient author of the verse, at the expense of the significance the verse has held for succeeding generations.

Deut 6:4 is followed by the command to love YHWH (ואהבת את יהוה אלהיך) wholeheartedly. Because early intepreters understood the verse as an expression of Jewish monotheism, the Mishnah (Berakot 1:1–2) prescribed its recitation twice daily.[1] In the New Testament, Jesus tells an inquiring scribe, "the first of all the commandments is 'Hear O Israel, the Lord our God, the Lord is One.'" The scribe commends Jesus saying, "You are right in saying that God is one and beside him there is no other."[2] But as Nielsen[3] has noted, a monotheistic formulation in Deuteronomic language would more likely have read: יהוה הוא האלהים אין עוד[4], "YHWH is *the* God. There is no other"; or perhaps אין אלהים עמדו[5], "there is no god beside him."

Indeed, careful attention to the wording and context of Deut 6:4 requires the reader to confront two crucial questions. First, what can the phrase יהוה אחד mean in classical Hebrew? Second, what connection is there between what Israel is supposed to "hear" and the command to love YHWH wholeheartedly? Driver[6] proposed two possible answers to the first question: יהוה אחד may mean that YHWH "is in essence indivisible, cannot ... assume different phases or attributes, as presiding over different localities." Second יהוה אחד might refer to the uniqueness of YHWH as "the only deity to whom the true

1 Deut 6:4 is the opening verse of the Shema liturgy which is recited twice daily. The Shema comprises Deut 6:4–9, Deut 11:13–21; Num 15:37–41.

2 Mark 12:29, 32.

3 E. Nielsen, "Weil Jahwe unser Gott ein Jahwe ist," in *Beiträge zur Alttestamentlichen Theologie: Festschrift für Walther Zimmerli zum 70. Geburtstag*, eds. H. Donner, R. Hanhart and R. Smend (Göttingen: Vandenhoeck & Ruprecht, 1977), 291.

4 See Deut 4:35, 39.

5 See Deut 32:39.

6 S. R. Driver, *A Critical and Exegetical Commentary on Deuteronomy* (Edinburgh: T&T Clark, 1895), 90.

 | DOI 10.1163/9789004340879_014

attributes of the Godhead really belong." Both suggestions take אחד as predicative of YHWH who is thus described as being אחד.

Driver's first proposal is philologically unsound because אחד does not mean "indivisible," in Biblical Hebrew. That notion is expressed by שלם (e.g. Deut 27:6; Josh 8:31; 1Kings 8:61); or by the negation of verbs on the order of בדל "differentiate" (e.g. Lev 1:17; Ezra 9:2); פרד, "part" (2Sam 1:23); חצה "split" (Ezek 37:22); or חלק "divide." (Josh 18:2) In other words, the designation of YHWH as אחד does not, as Driver would have, it rule out the existence of "YHWH ... as presiding over different localities." A writer wishing to deny the existence of local YHWHs, say at Samaria or Teman, who, in fact, are now known to have been worshipped in preexilic Israel[7] would have written something along the lines of Zech 14:9, a verse cited by Rashi and Nachmanides as a parallel to Deut 6:4 and almost as significant in Jewish liturgy. That verse reads: והיה יהוה למלך על כל הארץ ביום ההוא יהיה יהוה אחד ושמו אחד. "YHWH shall become king of the entire land (of Israel).[8] On that day there will be one YHWH with a single name." But despite the occurrence of יהוה אחד in both verses, the fact that אחד is not repeated in Deut 6:4 makes Zech 14:9 irrelevant to its interpretation. The actual parallels to Zech 14:9 are Gen 11:1 and Num 15:16. The first reads ויהי כל הארץ שפה אחת ודברים אחדים "It was the case that the whole earth had the same language with the same words." The second reads: תורה אחת ומשפט אחד יהיה לכם ולגר הגר אתכם "You and the alien who resides among you shall have the same ritual and the same rule." As for Driver's suggestion that אחד in Deut 6:4 indicates the unique[9] divinity of YHWH, grammar would require a copula, in this case the third person pronoun הוא.[10]

The difficulties with the predicative explanation impelled many scholars from Abraham ibn Ezra to the NJPS translators to understand Deut 6:4 as a monolatrous command along the lines of "YHWH is our God, YHWH alone."[11]

---

7 See J. Emerton, *ZAW* 94 (1982), 1–20.

8 That is what כל הארץ means in the very next verse, Zech 14:10. See A. Ehrlich, *Randglossen zur hebräischen Bibel* vol. 5 (Leipzig: J. C. Hinrich,1912), 353.

9 2Sam 7:23 reads in part: ומי כעמך כישראל גוי אחד בארץ. NJPS translates "And who is like Your people Israel, a unique nation on earth?" Note however that LXX *ethnos allo* indicates a Hebrew גוי אחר* "another nation." Even if we retain MT we must follow the lead of Ehrlich and understand the text anastrophically as, ומי בארץ גוי אחד כעמך כישראל "And is there one nation on earth like your people, like Israel?" In other words, אחד does not refer to Israel as unique. Israel is unique because there is not one nation גוי אחד like them. See A. Ehrlich. *Mikrâ ki-Pheschutô* vol. 2 (Ktav reprint: NY, 1965), 203.

10 Cf. Cant 6:8–9.

11 The NJPS was criticized in Orthodox circles for translating "The Lord alone." See S. Hoenig, *Tradition* 5/2 (Spring, 1963), 200.

In other words, Israel is commanded by Deut 6:4 to worship YHWH to the exclusion of all other gods. But as often noted[12] ancient Hebrew does not employ אחד attributively. Instead, biblical authors expressed the sense alleged here for אחד by suffixed forms of לבד, "alone."[13]

The solution to the difficulty lies in the second question we asked at the outset; namely, what is the connection between Deut 6:4 and Deut 6:5? Moran has remarked that "love in Deuteronomy is a love that can be commanded."[14] That observation led him to read Deuteronomy's calls to love YHWH in the light of ancient Near Eastern treaties in which minor kings are commanded to "love" their overlords wholeheartedly. Just so is Israel commanded to love YHWH in Deut 6:5.[15] It appears to me that hidden in the the text of Deut 6:4 is the introduction to the love-command. Underlying the perplexing אחד is the imperative of the verb "love" to be restored as אֱהָב. The same imperative to love YHWH is expressed by the second person plural of אהב in Ps 31:24-אֶהֱבוּ אֶת־יְהוָה כָּל־חֲסִידָיו, "Love YHWH all his faithful." That an imperative of אהב can follow its object we know from Zech 8:19:

> כֹּה־אָמַר יְהוָה צְבָאוֹת צוֹם הָרְבִיעִי וְצוֹם הַחֲמִישִׁי וְצוֹם הַשְּׁבִיעִי וְצוֹם הָעֲשִׂירִי יִהְיֶה
> לְבֵית־יְהוּדָה לְשָׂשׂוֹן וּלְשִׂמְחָה וּלְמֹעֲדִים טוֹבִים וְהָאֱמֶת וְהַשָּׁלוֹם אֱהָבוּ׃[16]

> Thus said YHWH of Hosts. The fast of the fourth month, the fast of the fifth month, the fast of the seventh month, and the fast of the tenth month shall become for the House of Judah occasions for joy and gladness and happy festivals. Now, love true integrity.

The textual corruption in Deut 6:4 is easily explained by the graphic similarities between *heh* and *ḥet* and *bet* and *dalet* respectively in the ancient Hebrew script.

The emendation suggested here provides the connection between Deut 6:4 and 6:5. I translate: "Hear O Israel. YHWH our God—love YHWH. You shall love YHWH your God with all your being and with all your might." On this understanding Deut 6:4 is not a declaration of divine unity or an expression of Israelite monolatry. Instead it is a command to every Israelite to love YHWH.

---

12 See e.g. F. Perles, *OLZ* 11 (1908), 537.

13 See Deut 8:3; 1Sam 7:4.

14 W. Moran, *CBQ* 25 (1963), 78.

15 Cf. Deut 11:13, 22, 13:4, 19:9, 30:6, 16, 20.

16 The author of Esther 9:30–31 made midrashic use of this verse. See H. L. Ginsberg in, *The Five Megilloth and Jonah. A New Translation* (Second Revised Edition; Jewish Publication Society of America, 1974), 88.

CHAPTER 14

Biblical *rḥm* I and *rḥm* II

In memory of Professor Moshe Held: *ina ṣilli ilāni rabûti linūḫ eṭemmaka*

A distinction between a verb *rḥm* I, "be compassionate, show mercy," and *rḥm* II, "love," in Biblical Hebrew (BH) was virtually forced on lexicographers by *ʾerḥāmĕkā yhwh ḥizqî* (Ps 18:2). Although Psalm 18 is a parallel recension of 2Samuel 22,[1] *ʾerḥāmĕkā*[2] *yhwh ḥizqî* has no parallel in the Samuel version.[3] In addition, *ʾerḥāmĕkā* is the sole biblical attestation of *rḥm* in the *qal*.[4] More important, Ps 18:2 is unique in making Yahweh the object of the verb *rḥm*. The theological enormity of Yahweh as object of human compassion impelled translators and commentators to other solutions.[5] The Septuagint's *agapeso se* and the Vulgate's *diligam te* employ the respective Greek and Latin verbs normally used to translate Hebrew *ʾhb*.[6] Among the Jewish scholars who wrote

1 For a comprehensive treatment of these two chapters, with extensive bibliography, see G. Schmuttermayr, *Psalm 18 und 2 Samuel 22 Studien zu einem Doppeltext* (Munich, 1971).

2 The form *ḥizqî*, presumably derived from the noun *ḥēzeq*, is likewise unattested except for the PNs *ḥizqî* (1 Chr 8:17) and *ḥizqîyāhû*, "Hezekiah." (passim) Note, however, that King Hezekiah's name appears in Akkadian transcription as *ḫa-za-qi-a-ú, ḫa-za-qi-ya-ú* and *ḫa-za-qi-ya-a-ú.* See OIP 2 31, n. 4; M. Noth, *Die israelitischen Personennamen im Rahmen der gemein-semitischen Namengebung* (Stuttgart, 1928), 11, n. 1.

3 This holds for MT, Vulg., Saadia, targum and most LXX texts but not for Lucianic LXX and Peshitta. See Schmuttermayr, *Psalm 18*, 34–35; *idem*, "RḤM—Eine Lexikalische Studie," *Bib* 51 (1970), 523, n. 2. It has generally not been noted that Peshitta's *ʾerḥāmāk māryā ḥayl wĕtûklan* at both 2 Sam 22:2 and Ps 18:2, reflects a Hebrew: *erḥāmĕkā YHWH ḥizqî ûmaḥsi* (cf. Peshitta to Ps 73:28, 91:2, 9). Schmuttermayr (*ibid.*) is of the opinion that the text of Peshitta to 2 Sam 22:2 has been harmonized with that of Ps 18:2, but this does not seem to be the case. Note that Peshitta to Psalm 18 lacks the prose rubric found in MT and LXX at both 2 Samuel 22 and Psalm 18, while Peshitta to 2 Samuel 22 has it. Note further that *ʾeḥseh* in vs. 3 is translated by a form of Syriac *tkl* in Psalm 18 but by a form of *sbr* in 2Samuel 22.

4 The singularity of *rḥm* in the *qal* was first remarked by Ibn Ezra.

5 Ibn Ezra attempted to interpret *erḥāmĕkā* as "I seek your mercy." See also A. Darom, ed., *R. David Kimhi* (RADAK) *ha-Pēruš ha Šalem ʿal Tehillim* (Jerusalem, 1974), 41.

6 See e.g. LXX and Vulg. to Gen 22:2, 25:28; Deut 6:5; Hos 3:1; Amos 5:15; Mal 1:1–2.

 | DOI 10.1163/9789004340879_015

in Arabic, both the Rabbinite Saadia[7] and the Qaraite David Alfasi[8] translated *ʾerḥāmĕkā* by forms of *ḥabba*, "loved," used elsewhere to render BH *ʾhb*.[9] For his part, ibn Janah[10] specifically differentiated Ps 18:2 from the other attestations of *rḥm* in the Bible: "(This is) targumic[11] language (i.e., Aramaic) such as translates *wayyeʾĕhab Yaʿăqōb* (Gen 29:18) by *ūrĕḥēm Yaʿăqōb*." H. Chajes, one of the earliest modern critical Jewish Bible scholars, followed this line of exegesis and made an additional observation: "In Assyrian as well, *rʾm* is equivalent to Hebrew *ʾhb*." In illustration, Chajes cited the Akkadian form *tarâmanni*, "you (shall) love me."[12]

The presence of *rḥm*, "love," in Ps 18:2 may be taken as assured.[13] Several questions, however, arise from this recognition. First, it is well known that Aramaic *rḥm* means both "be compassionate" and "love." Is *ʾerḥāmĕkā*, "I love you," of Ps 18:2 to be regarded as a biblical "Aramaism"[14] or is *rḥm* "love" more developed in BH than is commonly acknowledged? Second, are the senses

7 Y. Kafah/Kafih, ed., *Tĕhillîm ʿim Targûm u- Fērûš ha-Gāʾôn Rabbēnû Saʿadyāh ben Yôsēf Fayyumî* (Jerusalem, 1965), 77.

8 S. Skoss, ed., *Kitåb Jåmiʿ Al-Alfāẓ of David ben Abraham Al-Fasī* ed., S. Skoss (New Haven, 1945), 2:604.

9 E.g., Saadia to Gen 22:2, 25:8, 27:14, 37:3, 4, 44:20, Deut 6:15; cited from J. Derenbourg, ed., *Version arabe du Pentateuque* (Paris, 1893).

10 A. Neubauer, ed., *The Book of Hebrew Roots by … ibn Janah* (Oxford, 1875), 676 = W. Bacher, ed., *Sepher Haschoraschim … von ibn Ganah* (Berlin, 1896), 477.

11 Cf. Rashi, who cites *Tg. Onq.* to Lev 19:18; the targum to Ps 18:2, unlike the Peshitta, translates *rḥm* by *ḥbb*, employed by *Tg. Onq.* for the cognate Hebrew *ḥōbēb* in Deut 33:3 and *sĕgūllâ* elsewhere (Exod 19:5; Deut 7:6, 14:2, 26:18). Doubtless, the Aramaic translator chose *ḥbb*, "love," to translate Hebrew *rḥm* in Ps 18:2 because of his theological sensitivity to the possible confusion of Aramaic *rḥm*, "love," and Aramaic *rḥm*, "have compassion."

12 H. P. Chajes, *Sefer Tehillim* (Zhitomer, 1902), 33. His suggestion, however, that *rḥm* has the primary sense of "delicate, pleasant" is unlikely. The claim is based solely on Arabic *raḫuma* (with *ḫa*) "was soft or pleasant of voice."

13 F. Hitzig first proposed emending *ʾerḥāmĕkā* to *ʾarômimĕkā* and has been followed by numerous scholars. See bibliography in Schmuttermayer, *Bib* 51 (1970), 500, n. 4; cf. *idem*, *Psalm 18*, 32–34. The emendation finds no support in the versions. It is also unlikely that the more common *ʾarômimĕkā* would have been "corrected" to *ʾerḥāmĕkā*; cf. "RḤM," 503.

14 Note the equivocal statement of C. and E. Briggs, *A Critical and Exegetical Commentary on the Book of Psalms*, ICC (Edinburgh, 1906), 51: "Possibly an early and rare use in Hebrew, but probably a later one, an Aramaism." See further the bibliography in Schmuttermayr, "RḤM," 501, n. 3. On the problem of Aramaisms in Biblical Hebrew in general see bibliography *ibid.*; add A. Hurvitz, "The Chronological Significance of Aramaisms in Biblical Hebrew," *IEJ* 19 (1968), 234–240.

"love" and "be compassionate" sufficiently discrete in Hebrew and the classical Semitic languages to warrant insistence on a distinction between them? Huffmon,[15] for one, denies any fundamental difference, speaking instead of a "common Semitic *rḥm* 'love,' 'have mercy.'" Schmuttermayr, somewhat similarly, views "lieben" as the basic sense of *rḥm*. For him, the decision to understand *rḥm* as "love" or "compassion" in a particular verse depends on its direction;[16] "von unten nach oben," attested biblically only in Ps 18:2 indicates a meaning "love" whereas in all other instances *rḥm* is directed "von oben nach unten," and denotes "be compassionate."[17] In contrast, Wallenstein[18] asserts that there are many biblical passages in which the sense "love" rather than "compassion" is called for (although he does not document the assertion).

It is best to begin with the situation in English. The *OED*[19] defines "compassion" as "the feeling or emotion when a person is moved by the suffering or distress of another, and by the desire to relieve it." The same dictionary[20] defines "love" as "that disposition or state of feeling with regard to a person which (arising from recognition of attractive qualities, from instincts of natural relationship, or from sympathy) manifests itself in solicitude for the welfare of the object, and usually also in delight in his presence and desire for his approval; warm affection, attachment." In other words although love may arise out of compassion (= sympathy), the two English terms are by no means synonymous. It will be argued here that BH *rḥm* is to be divided in two etymologically and semantically distinct vocables[21] fairly corresponding to English

15 *Apud* Schuttermayer, "RḤM," 523, n. 1.

16 Cf. H. J. Stoebe, "*rḥm* pi. 'sich erbarmen,'" *THAT*, 2:761, who attributes to *rḥm* the primary sense "love," in the main directed from the high to the lowly thus, "love" > "sympathize." In Aramaic, claims Stoebe, *rḥm* expanded its more general sense of "love" without regard to direction; contrast R. Dentan, "The Literary Affinities of Exodus xxxiv 6f," *VT* 13 (1963), 40: "The finite verb [*rḥm*] is used in Hebrew … in the intensive stem with the meaning 'to show mercy' but it carries strong overtones of the meaning "to love' which the simple stem normally has in Aramaic and Syriac."

17 Schmuttermayer, "RḤM," 499, 523.

18 M. Wallenstein, "Some Aspects of the Vocabulary and Morphology of the Hymns of the Judean Scrolls," *VT* 7 (1957), 213, n. 2. In several instances, the NEB and NJPS translations reflect a similar understanding; see below.

19 *The Compact Edition of the Oxford English Dictionary* (Oxford, 1971), 489.

20 *Ibid.*, 1669.

21 There is a similar problem in the Hebrew root *šlm*. Some of its attestations have the sense "peace, alliance, reconciliation"; others mean "well-being" and "wholeness." For Hebrew *šlm* in general, see M. Eisenbeis, *Die Wurzel šlm im Alten Testament* (Berlin, 1969). Although

"love" and "be compassionate." In some verses the change from "love" to "be compassionate" does not greatly alter the meaning. Here, however, I treat passages in which the distinction is crucial. Some of these verses were selected for the further reason that our lamented teacher Professor Moshe Held had contributed to their interpretation in other respects.

Among the classical Semitic languages the distinction between "love" and "compassion" is most obvious in Akkadian. "Love" is expressed most often by *râmu*[22] with thematic vowels (a, a). The vocable and its derivatives are employed both verbally and nominally to connote "love" and "desire" (emotional and sexual), "prefer(ence)," "recognition," and "favor." The semantic range of *râmu* and its derivatives coincides at various points with *ḫašāḫu*,[23] "like, desire"; *dādū*,[24]

it is possible to draw semantic connections among these concepts in English, the situation in Akkadian strongly militates against classifying all forms of Hebrew *šlm* under a single heading. Akkadian expresses "peace, alliance, reconciliation" by forms of *salāmu* (with *s* and thematic vowels i/i) and "well-being" and "wholeness" by *šalāmu* (with *šin* and two sets of thematic vowels; i/i and a/a). Akkadian documents of West-Semitic provenience began to confuse the two in the mid-second millennium. See P. Haupt apud Mullo Weir, *Lexicon*, 293; B. Landsberger, "Zu neuveröffentlichten Geschichtsquellen der Zeit von Asarhaddon bis Nabonid," ZA 37 (1927), 86, n. 2; M. Held, "Philological Notes on the Mari Covenant Rituals," *BASOR* 200 (1970), 33, n. 9; H. Tadmor, "Bĕrît û-Šĕbû'at Ne'emānîm ba-Mizrāḥ ha-Qadmōn: Gišātô šel Hisṭoryôn," *Shnaton* 5–6 (1981–1982), 155, n. 16; W. von Soden regards *salāmu*, "freundlich, friedlich sein, werden" as a "Sekundärwurzel" (AHw., 1013) to *šalāmu* "(sem.) unversehrt, heil, gesund sein, werden." (*ibid.*, 1143).

22 For references see AHw., 951–952.

23 Cf. such phrases as: *ša epšēt qātišu u nadān zībīšu ilāni rabûti ša šamê erṣeti irāmūma*... "Whose deeds and offerings the great gods of heaven and earth loved." (AKA 262, I;24–25); and *ša nīš qātišu nadān zībīšu iḫšuḫū* [*ilū*] *rabûti*, "Whose prayers and offerings the great [gods] desired." (CAD Z, 105b) Like *râmu*, *ḫašāḫu* is opposed to *zêru*, "hate, loathe." See M. Held, "A Faithful Lover in an Old Babylonian Dialogue," *JCS* 15 (1961), 17. Note further that *hašāḫu* and *râmu* are attested in synonymous parallelism: *bēlūti iḫšuḫū irāmū epeš šarrūtiya* "They desired my lordship, loved my rule." (Streck Asb.260: ii:12).

24 Note the alternation of *kuzbi u râmi* and *kuzbi u dādī*, "(goddess of) sexual joy and lovemaking." (CAD D, 20a) Both *dādū* and *râmu* share the logogram KI.AĜ; see AHw., 149a, 951a. The synonymity of *dādū* and *râmu* corresponds to the parallelism of Hebrew *dōdim*//*'ohābîm* (Prov 7:18) and Aramaic *raḥamātā*//*rig'atātā* (targum ad loc.; cf. Peshitta). For the similar Ugaritic *ahbt*//*dd* see M. Held, "Additional Pairs of Words in Synonymous Parallelism in Biblical Hebrew and in Ugaritic," *Leš* 18 (1953), 146; Y. Avishur, *Stylistic Studies in Word-Pairs in Biblical and Ancient Semitic Literatures*, AOAT 210 (Kevelaer, 1984), 354–355.

"love-making"; *kuzbu*,[25] "charm, sexual vigor"; *ṣâḫu*,[26] "dally amorously, caress"; and *ḫadû*,[27] "like, be well-disposed, rejoice over." Akkadian *râmu* is most often opposed to *zêru*,[28] "dislike, hate, reject, repudiate." In an interdialectal distribution[29] within ancient Semitic, *râmu* corresponds to Hebrew *rḥm* II, Hebrew and Ugaritic *ʾhb*, and Aramaic *rḥm* II, "love."

---

25 See, e.g., the conclusion to a potency incantation: *i[na qibīt DN₁] bēlet ruʾame DN₂ bēlet kuzbi* (ḪI.LI), "Acc[ording to the command of Ištar], goddess of feminine charms (and) Nana, goddess of sexual attractiveness." (Biggs Šaziga, 31:22 and see Biggs, ad loc.); cf. further: *Ištar mēliṣim ruʾamam labšat zaʾnat inbī miqiʾam u kuzbam*, "Ištar of pleasure is clothed in sensuousness, adorned and made up with voluptuousness and sex appeal." (*RA* 22 [1925], 170:7–8; cf. Held, "Faithful Lover," 14).

26 Akkadian *ṣâḫu*, primarily "smile, laugh," shares various sexual nuances with its Semitic cognates. See Held, *ibid*., 20. Note the parallelism: *rāmka lū ṣurru ṣiḫātuka lū ḫurāṣu*, "Your love is true obsidian, your caress the very gold." (KAR 158, VII:43–44); cf. *CAD* Ṣ, 258a; AHw., 1114.

27 Thus the legal phrase *ašar ḫadê inaddin*, "He may give as he pleases" = *ša irammu inaddin*, "He may give as he likes"; i.e., there is no restriction on his giving. See Y. Muffs, *Studies in the Aramaic Legal Papyri from Elephantine* (Leiden, 1969), 139; cf. Muffs, "Joy and Love as Metaphorical Expressions of Spontaneity in Cuneiform, Ancient Hebrew and Related Literatures" in *Christianity, Judaism and other Greco-Roman Cults: Studies for Morton Smith at Sixty*, ed. J. Neusner (Leiden, 1975), vol. 3:1–36; Muffs, "Love and Joy as Metaphors of Volition in Hebrew and Related Literatures: Part II:The Joy of Giving," *JANES* 11 (1979), 91–111; see further J. Rabinowitz, "A Legal Formula in the Susa Tablets, in an Egyptian Document of the Twelfth Dynasty, in the Aramaic Papyri, and in the Book of Daniel," *Bib* 36 (1955), 76–77. Like *râmu, ḫadû* is an antonym of *zêru*. Note the following: *ka[ru ay iḫ]dīka nēbiru lizīrka* "May the harbor not welcome you, may the ford reject you." (Gilg. XI:235) Note also the sequence *râmu*… *ḫadû* in an OB letter: *mannum ša kima yâti irammūka u ana zi[krika] iḫaddu* "Who is there who loves you the way I do and delights at your mention?" (AbB 11, 9:3–5) The sequence recalls the pairing of Hebrew *ḥpṣ* "delight, desire" and *ʾhb* (e.g., 1Sam 18:22; 1Kgs 10:9; Ps 34:13).

28 E.g., *ina bītim PN₁ bītam ša irammu lissuqma lilqi bītam ša izirru PN₂ lilqi*, "Let PN₁ choose from the house the room he prefers; the room he rejects let PN₂ take." (Wiseman *Alalakh* 7:19–23) Similarly, we read in a well-known poetic text: *aššatka ša tarammu lā tanaššiq aššatka ša tazerru lā tamaḫḫaṣ māraka ša tarammu lā tanaššiq māraka ša tazerru lā tamaḫḫas* "Do not kiss the wife you love. Do not beat the wife you dislike. Do not kiss the son you love. Do not beat the son you dislike." (Gilg. XII:24–27).

29 Cf. *aššatka ša tarammu* (above n. 28) with *ʾiššâ ʾašer ʾāhabtā* (Qoh 9:9 = Targum *ʾittĕtā dî rĕḥimtā*) and *māraka ša tarammu* with *binĕka*… *ʾašer ʾāhabtā* (Gen 22:2 = *Tg. Onq. bĕrāk dî rĕḥîmtā*); cf. DN *ʾôhēb ṣĕdâqâh û u mišpāṭ* "Lover of justice and equity" (Ps 35:5 = Targum *raḥēm ṣidqātā wĕdînā*) and *DN rāʾim kittum u mīšaru* (Tallqvist Götterepitheta, 167; Late Hebrew *ʾôhēb ʿammô*, "Lover of his people" (prayerbook) and Akkadian *rāʾim nišēšu* (Tallqvist Götterepitheta, 167, Aramaic *rḥm ʿmh* (AH 1/1, 48: 3:7, 7:3). Ugaritic and

A common Akkadian verb for “be compassionate, show compassion” is *rêmu*[30] (e, i). It is a synonym of *napšuru*[31] (verb), “relent, show mercy”; *aḫulap qabû*,[32] “speak ‘compassion,’” and *epēqu*,[33] “be merciful.” As nouns, *rēmu* and its derivatives mean “mercy” and “compassion.” Semantically, *rēmu* is associated with *unnīnu*,[34] “grace”; *napšuru*[35] (noun), “mercy”; *nasḫuru*,[36] “pardon”; and *tay*(*y*)*āru*, “mercy.”[37] The epithet *rēmēnû*,[38] “merciful one” is a synonym of

---

Hebrew *ʾhb* are clearly equivalent. They share a synonym (above, n. 24) and an antonym *ś/šnʾ* (CTA 4, iii:17–18=KTU[3] 1.4: iii:17–18). In classical Phoenician *ʾhb* is not yet attested, although *ḥmd*, “desire,” is found in KAI 26, A III:14–17. For references to Neo-Punic *ḥbb*, “love,” see KAI III, 8.

30 References in AHw., 970; Mullo Weir Lexicon, 283.

31 E.g., *ana āliku GN napšer ana TN bītiku rišê rēma* “Show forbearance to Babylon your city, have mercy on Esaggila your temple.” (RAcc. 134:246–47); see further Ebeling Handerhebung 72:1–2.

32 E.g., [*š*]*absu kišādi ul utiraššum*[*m*]a [*u*]*l ipšaḫu ezzetu kabatti* [*a*]*ggu libbi ul inūḫma rēmu ul aršišūma ul aqbīšu aḫulap* “I did not turn my angry face (lit., neck) back to him; neither did my raging mood quiet down for him, nor my angry heart become pacified for him. I had no mercy on him. I spoke no word of compassion.” (Borger Esarh. 104, i:34–35); cf. *rēma ar<šī>šunūtīma utninnīšunu alqi atmūššunu ša tēninti ašmīma aqbīšunu aḫulap*, “Because I had mercy on them I accepted their supplications and harkened to their cries for grace. I said ‘Compassion’ to them.” (TCL 3, 59).

33 The verb *epēqu* is restricted to the lists and the onomasticon; see CAD E, 184b.

34 E.g., *rēma unnīna balta lamassa qabâ šemâ šukna yâši*, “Mercy, grace, dignity, a good spirit, and the power to speak with authority grant me.” (Ebeling Handerhebung 108:21–22 = Mayer Gebetsbeschwörungen, 477:23–24); AHw., 1421b, translates *unnīnu* in such usages as “Gebetserhörung.”

35 For the equation of *napšuru* and *rēmu* see CAD N/1, 319a, s.v. *napšuru*, lex. section.

36 For references see CAD N/2, 25. CAD ad loc. translates *nasḫuru* as “benevolent attention.”

37 References in AHw., 1304a; cf. the sequence *gammalāta … tayyarāta … muppalsāta rēmēnâta*, “(Because) you are forbearing … relenting … gracious … merciful.” (Mayer Gebetsbeschwörungen, 480:15–18); Akkadian *rēmēnû* and *tayyāru* are reflected in the Palmyrene divine epithet *rḥmnʾ wtyrʾ* (AH 1/1, 43, 14:1; see S. A. Kaufman, *The Akkadian Influences on Aramaic* (Chicago, 1974), 106.

38 The epithet *rēmēnû* is mainly applied to gods. See AHw., 970a; Tallqvist Götterepitheta, 169. Aramaic *rḥmnʾ* is its loan-translation. See Kaufman, *Influences*, 106; cf. *idem*, “Reflections on the Assyrian-Aramaic Bilingual from Tell Fakhariyeh,” *Maarav* 3 (1982), 165. The Aramaic epithet *ʾlh rḥmn* “compassionate god,” is attested at an early date in the Hadd-Yithʿi bilingual, corresponding to *ilu rēmēnû* (written LID-*ú*) in the corresponding Akkadian line. See D. Gropp and T. Lewis, “Notes on Some Problems in the Aramaic Text of the Hadd-Yithʿi Bilingual,” BASOR 259 (1985), 45:5; cf. Kaufman, “Bilingual”; see further, Grayson ARI, II, 119, n. 485; P. Dion, “Ššbṣr and Ssnwry,” ZAW 95 (1983), 111–112.

gāmilu,[39] "forbearing one." Antonyms of *rêmu* and its congeners are *lā padû*,[40] "without pity"; and *lā gāmilu*,[41] "merciless." The vocable *rēmu* is also cognate with the noun *rēmu*,[42] "womb," corresponding to Hebrew *reḥem* and Arabic

---

39 E.g., *rēmēnâta gāmilāta*, "You are merciful. You are forbearing." (CAD G, 33a).

40 See AHw., 808b.

41 See CAD G, 33a.

42 See AHw., 970a. The vocable is now attested at Ebla; see M. Krebernik, "Zu Syllabar und Orthographie der lexikalischen Texte aus Ebla," ZA 73 (1983), 14. In all likelihood, the phrase *ʿl rḥm* attested at Deir ʿAllâ means "new born child"; see J. Hackett, *The Balaam Text from Deir ʿAllâ* (Chico, 1984), 26:13; *ibid.*, p. 70. The connection between *rēmu*, "mercy," and *rēmu*, "womb," is more transparent in Akkadian than is the connection between *reḥem* and *raḥămîm* in Hebrew. First, the pointing of *raḥămîm* (assuming the accuracy of Masoretic tradition) distances the singular from from the plural. Second, in Akkadian *rēmu* (noun) is employed in the singular for both the physical organ and the associated emotion of compassion. Thus, the concept "show mercy, have compassion" may be expressed in Akkadian by *rēmu* accompanied by the verb *rašû* or *šakānu*; less frequently by *ṣabātu* (AHw., 970b). In Hebrew, the singular noun *reḥem* is never employed in an emotional sense. Accordingly, the translation of Akkadian *rēma šakānu* into Hebrew yields the well-attested *nātan raḥămîm* (e.g., Gen 43:14; Deut 13:18) or the unique *śām raḥămîm* (Isa 47:6). The equivalence holds regardless of whether *śām raḥămîm* is originally Hebrew or a calque from Akkadian; on the problem see Y. Avishur, "*lōʾ śamtā lāhēm raḥămîm* (Isaiah 47:6)—Biblical Style or Translated Idiom," *Shnaton* 5–6 (1978–1979), 91–99. Both the difference in vocalization and the avoidance of *reḥem* in the singular in figurative use, argue against the claims of P. Trible, *God and the Rhetoric of Sexuality* (Philadelphia, 1978), 31–59, who maintains that ancient Hebrew speakers were fully conscious of the etymological relation between *reḥem*, "womb," the verb *rīḥam*, and the noun *raḥămîm* and viewed them as an extension of primary uteral imagery; see further the strictures of M. Gruber, "The Motherhood of God in Second Isaiah," RB 90 (1983), 352, n. 4. Trible's related claim that the semantic development from *reḥem* to *rīḥam* and *raḥămîm* grew out of the notion of the womb as a place of protection and care, has no basis in the Hebrew Bible, which never speaks of the womb in imagery of protection and care. Metaphorically, to exist in the womb is to be in a state inferior to life, parallel to the shadowy existence of the dead in the grave. The difference is temporal: existence in the womb is pre-life (Isa 49:1, 5; Jer 1:5), while existence in the grave is post-life. (For Akkadian parallels to the existence in the womb as pre-life, see S. Paul, "Deutero-Isaiah and Cuneiform Royal Inscriptions," JAOS 88 [1968], 184–185.) The common Hebrew words for "womb," *reḥem* and *beṭen*, are poetic synonyms of *qeber* (see Jer 20:17–18; Job 10:18–19; cf. Job 1:21; Qoh 5:14). Contra Trible, the sense "compassion" for *raḥămîm* does not derive from uteral imagery but from the primary sense of *raḥămîm* (cf. its synonym *mēʿayîm*), which is "bowels, innards, or guts," without necessary reference to a specific organ. Note the wordplay in Prov 12:10: *wĕraḥamē rĕšāʿîm ʾakzārî* "The very innards/mercies of the wicked are cruel."

raḥim. In an interdialectal distribution within ancient Semitic, *rêmu* would correspond to Hebrew *rḥm* I, Ugaritic *rḥm*, and Aramaic *rḥm* I.

Long ago, Barth demonstrated that the inner-Akkadian semantic difference between *râmu* and *rêmu* as well as their different thematic vowels were reflected in Arabic *ra'ima*, "treated with love" (=Akk. *râmu*), and *raḥima*, "was compassionate." (=Akk. *rêmu*)[43]

Early Aramaic[44] orthography does not enable us to determine whether there was a difference in vocalization between *rḥm* I and *rḥm* II, but the semantic difference is clear. Thus, after describing the successful audience of Nadin before Esarhaddon the author of Ahiqar 11 says *'ḥr rḥmh RN mlk GN* "Then King Esarhaddon of Assyria loved (accepted) him." Similarly, Ah. 51 reads: *RN mlk' rḥmny 'lzy hḥytk wl' qṭltk*[45] "King Sennacherib showed me favor because

---

It is well known that the Semitic languages usually describe emotions in terms of bodily states, actions, and physical sensations; see in general M. Gruber, *Aspects of Nonverbal Communication in the Ancient Near East* (Rome, 1980); *idem*, "The Many Faces of Hebrew *nś' pnym* Lift up the Face," *ZAW* 95 (1983), 252–260; and see further, M. Petruck, "Body Part Terminology in Hebrew: A Study in Lexical Semantics" (Ph.D. dissertation; Berkeley, 1986), ch. 6. Hebrew *raḥămîm* derives its emotional connections from ellipsis as may be seen in fuller expressions such as *nikmĕrû raḥamāw/raḥamêhā* (Gen 43:30; 1Kgs 3:26) or *hamon me'êkā wĕraḥămēka*, "the rumbling of your very guts." (Isa 63:15); see I. Eitan, "An Unkown Meaning of Raḥamim," *JBL* 53 (1934), 269–271; N. H. Tur-Sinai, *The Language and the Book* (Jerusalem, 1954), 1:355 [Hebrew].

43 See J. Barth, "Babl.-assyr. *ra-a-mu* 'lieben,'" *ZA* 22 (1909), 1–5; Mullo Weir Lexicon, 278, 283–284; T. Jacobsen, "Sumerian Mythology: A Review Article," *JNES* 5 (1946), 132; Y. Muffs, *Studies*, 132, n. 2; *idem*, "Joy and Love," 5, n. 13; AHw., 951, s.v. *râmu, ra'āmu*, "lieben"; *ibid*., 970, s.v. *rêmu*, "sich erbarmen." AHw., 952, also lists a third verb *râmu* III /*ri'amu*, "(be)schenken." On its derivation, its relation to the other two verbs and possible reflexes in Aramaic, see Muffs, *Studies*, 132, n.2; W. von Soden, "Mirjām-Maria '(Gottes)-Geschenk,'" *UF* 2 (1970), 269–272, has argued that *râmu* III provides the etymology of the names Miriam and Jeremiah and of the Hebrew cultic term *tĕrûmâ*; contrast B. A. Levine, "Assyriology and Hebrew Philology: A Methodological Re-Examination," in H. Nissen and J. Renger, eds. *Mesopotamien und seine Nachbarn* (Berlin, 1987), 521–530.

44 For references to *rḥm* in early Aramaic, see *DISO*, 276–278; K. Beyer, *Die aramäischen Texte vom Toten Meer* (Göttingen, 1984), 693–694. Note that *rḥm*, "love," shares with Akkadian *râmu* the nuance of "desire sexually, lust after"; see 1QapGenar 20:8.

45 With the parallelism *hḥyh* // /*l' qṭl*, cf. *hḥyh* //*l' hrg* in Judg 8:19. For the phenomenon x// negation of y, see M. Held, "The Action-Result (Factitive-Passive) Sequence of Identical Verbs in Biblical Hebrew and Ugaritic," *JBL* 84 (19650, 282, n. 71; Ch. Cohen, "The Phenomenon of Negative Parallelism and Its Implications for the Study of Biblical Poetry," *Beer Sheva* 3 (1988), 69–107 [Hebrew]; contrast A. Berlin, *The Dynamics of Biblical Parallelism* (Bloomington, 1985), 40. A similar form of parallelism is found in Egyptian;

I had kept you alive and not killed you." The proverb in Ah. 92 reads: *trtyn mln špyrh*[46] *wzy tlt' rḥymh lšmš*[47] "two things are proper[48] and a third pleasing to Shamash."[49] Ah. 53, however, describes the tender mercies of the Assyrian king by saying: *RN mlk' rḥmn hw* "King Sennacherib is merciful." Later Aramaic speakers continued to be conscious of the difference as witness the pun preserved in the Talmud:[50] *kl dsny ly lḥdy ly wktyb . . . wdrḥym ly lyb'y 'ly rḥmy* "Let whoever hates me rejoice for it is written . . .(Prov 24:17–18 is cited to prove that the gloating of your enemies causes God to improve your lot) and let whoever loves me pray for mercy in my behalf."

Let us turn now to some biblical passages. Hos 1:6 reads: *qĕrā' šĕmâh lō' rūḥāmâ kî lō' 'ôsîp 'ôd 'araḥēm 'et bēt yiśrā'ēl*. RSV translates: "Call her name Not-pitied, for I will no more have pity on the house of Israel." As Ginsberg[51] has shown however, this is one of serveral passages in Hosea where *rḥm* in some nuance of "love" must be recognized.[52] First, Hos 2:6 reads: *wĕ'et bānêhā lō' 'araḥēm kî bĕnê zĕnûnîm hēmā* "I will disown/repudiate her children because

see N. Shupak, "Stylistic and Terminological Traits Common to Biblical and Egyptian Literature," *WO* 14 (1985), 230.

46 The association of *špr* with *mlt'* continued in later Aramaic; see the Gamaliel letters in D. Pardee, S. D. Sperling, P. Dion, and J. D. Whitehead, *Handbook of Ancient Hebrew Letters* (Chico, 1982), 192.

47 The Akkadian parallel to the expression of *rḥymh lšmš* is *ṭāb eli šamaš*, "pleasing to Shamash"; see Lambert BWL, 314:60. The inner Aramaic equivalence of *špr* and *ṭb* seems attested as early as the eighth century in Sefire III:29.

48 For the translation "just, proper," note that Syriac *špyr* translates Hebrew *yšr*; e.g., Peshitta to Judg 14:3, 19:25.

49 The saying is composed in synonymous parallelism and employs the well-known x/x+1 number scheme. See J. Lindenberger, *The Aramaic Proverbs of Ahiqar* (Baltimore, 1983), 65. On poetic elements in Ahiqar, see the summary of J. Greenfield, "Early Aramaic Poetry," *JANES* 11 (1979), 46; see further J. Kselman's review of Lindenberger in *JBL* 105 (1986), 115.

50 *b. Ned.* 40a; cf. the Akkadian pun: *bēlu rēmēnû ša bulluṭu irammu*, "merciful lord who loves to heal."(Mayer Gebetsbeschwörungen, 461; cf. *ibid.*, 12).

51 H. L. Ginsberg, "Hosea, Book of," *EncJud* 8:1010–11; cf. the translations of JB and NEB *ad loc.*

52 G. Rendsburg, "Hebrew *RḤM*= Rain," *VT* 33 (1983), 359–369, who wrongly translates *rḥm* in these passages by "pity," nonetheless offers an interesting suggestion that merits further study. On the basis of *rḥm*, "rain," attested in some South Arabian dialects, Rendsburg argues that the author of Hos 1:6, 7, 2:6, 25 was punning intentionally.

they are the issue of whoredom."[53] Second, the older brother of Lo-Ruhama is Lo-Ammi, "Not-my-people/kin," a name transparently indicating repudiation. Third, Hos 2:25, which constitutes the happy ending to 1:6, promises: *wĕriḥamtî ʾet lōʾ rūḥāmâ weʾāmartî lĕlōʾ ʿammî ʿammî ʾattâ*, "I will acknowledge (Ms.) Unacknowledged and declare to (Mr.) Not-my-people 'You are My-people.'" In none of these passages is "compassion" at issue. It is rather "love," with a formal connotation of paternal recognition or acceptance, necessary because the identity of the father is otherwise unknown. The sense of *rḥm* is exactly that of *rḥmh* in Ah. 11, which describes the king's official acceptance of Nadin as Ahiqar's successor. There is a similar use of *râmu* in the annals of Ashurbanipal (Streck Asb., 258: 30): *ittanaplas abu bānûʾa qarrādūtu ša išimmūinni ilāni rabûti ina qibīt ilāni rabûti puḫur aḫḫēya* [....] *MEŠ mādiš irāmanni aššu epēš šarrūtiya imḫur Aššur šar ilāni bēl gimri* "My natural father beheld with joy the heroism with which the great gods had endowed me. At the command of the great gods he favored me in the midst of my brothers.... He prayed to Aššur, king of the gods, lord of all, for my rule as king." Note that *mādiš irāmanni* in the Ashurbanipal passage corresponds to *rēša ullû*[54] in Esarhaddon: *abu bānûʾa ina puḫur aḫḫēya rēšiya kīniš ullīma* "My natural father formally raised my rank in the presence of all my brothers." (Borger Esarh. 40, 1:10)

A generally unrecognized use of *rḥm* II is found in Hos 14:4: *ʾašer bĕkâ yĕruḥam yātôm*. Here, NJPS, which earlier followed Ginsberg, errs in its rendition: "In You alone orphans find pity." The NEB is closest to the mark with its "In Thee the fatherless[55] find a father's love." The more precise sense is: "In You only, the fatherless find paternal recognition." With this notion we may compare the divine epithet *ʾabî yĕtômîm* (Ps 68:5).

Surely Jer 31:20 is one of the most poignant passages in the Hebrew Bible. MT reads: *habēn yaqqîr lî PN ʾim yeled šaʿašûʿîm kî middê dabbĕrî bô zākōr ʾezkĕrennû ʿôd ʿal kēn hāmû mēʿay lô raḥēm ʾaraḥamennu nĕʾūm YHWH*. Various commentators have correctly understood parts of the verse. Nonetheless, its full meaning can only be grasped by recognizing the following: a) As Held demonstrated, the passage contains a triple rhetorical question;[56] b) *dabbēr*

53 Cf. the paraphrase by R. Johanan b. Nappaha (3rd century) cited in *b. Pesaḥ* 87b: "If you, whose wife is a whore and whose children are the issue of whoredom so that you don't know if they are yours or someone else's ..."

54 For *rēša ullû* and its associated idioms see A. L. Oppenheim, "Idiomatic Accadian," *JAOS* 61 (1941), 252–256.

55 For "fatherless" rather than "orphan," see Exod 22:23; Ps 109:8; Lam 5:3. "Fatherless" is the sense of *ytm* in Phoenician and Ugaritic as well; see Avishur, *Word-Pairs*, 373–374.

56 M. Held, "Rhetorical Questions in Ugaritic and Biblical Hebrew," *Eretz-Israel* 9 (1969), 79.

bĕ means "defame,[57] repudiate, disown"; c) *ʿal kēn* here and elsewhere[58] has an asseverative rather than a causal sense; and d) *raḥēm* means "acknowledge as an offspring."[59] The entire verse should be translated: "Is Ephraim my darling son, or is he my cherished child? Why then, whenever I disowned him, have my thoughts dwelt on him still? Surely my innermost being yearns for him. I will take him back for certain—Yahweh's word."

The author of Psalm 103 shares with Hosea[60] and Deutero-Isaiah the belief that human constancy (*ḥesed*)[61] is insufficient to permit faithfulness to God.[62] Vss. 11–13 are a literary unit expressing the superiority of Yahweh's *ḥesed*;[63] the removal of Israel's iniquity; Yahweh's reclamation of Israel. Vs. 13 expresses this notion by a simile comparing Yahweh to a human father. Here, too, *rḥm* II, "love," is employed technically, just as in Jer 31:19. MT reads: *kĕraḥēm ʾāb ʿal bānîm riḥam YHWH ʿal yĕrēʾā* "Just as a father reclaims his children, so Yahweh has reclaimed his worshippers." Yahweh, in other words, legally (re)affirms his own.[64]

---

57 Cf. Num 12:1, 8b; Ps 78:19. Cf. Held, "Questions," 79; S. Paul, "Literary and Ideological Echoes of Jeremiah in Deutero-Isaiah," in *Proceedings of the Fifth World Congress of Jewish Studies* (Jerusalem, 1969), 118.

58 See Jer 29:28 and 38:4, in which "therefore" is supplied by *kî*. For Isa 9:16, see below. For other examples of asseverative *ʿal-kēn*, see R. Frankena "Einige Bemerkungen zum Gebrauch des Adverbs ʿal-kēn," in *Studia … Vriezen*, eds. W. van Unnik and A. van der Woude (Wageningen, 1966), 98.

59 The NEB translator ad loc. doubtless sensing the inappropriateness of "compassion" in context, offers "filled with tenderness," probably on the basis of Arabic *raḥuma*; cf. above, n. 13.

60 See Ginsberg, "Hosea," 1011; cf. NJPS to Hos 2:21–22 and the note ad loc.

61 On *ḥesed* see the detailed study by K. Sakenfeld, *The Meaning of Hesed in the Hebrew Bible: A New Inquiry* (Missoula, 1978).

62 In Hos 6:4, the impermanence of Ephraim's *ḥesed* is compared to a morning cloud. Isa 40:6, in similar fashion, compares human *ḥesed* to the impermanence of flowers (cf. vs. 7). For a recent discussion of the passage, with bibliography, see Sakenfeld, *Hesed*, 189–191. Sakenfeld follows several earlier scholars in emending this verse unnecessarily.

63 Vs. 11 reads: *kî kigĕbōah šāmayîm ʿal hāʾāreṣ gābar ḥasdô ʿal yĕrēʾāw*, "for his constancy surpasses that of His worshippers as heaven towers over earth"; *gābar ḥasdô ʿal yĕrēʾaw* is elliptical for **gābar ḥasdô ʿal ḥesed yĕrēʾāw*; for *gābar ʿal*, "overpowered, surpassed, was greater than," see Gen 7:18, 19, 24, 49:26; 2 Sam 11:23; Ps 117:2. Cf. Chajes, *Tehillim*, 219. Human constancy is limited by sinfulness (vs. 10) and short life (vss. 14–16); see Rashi ad loc.

64 Chajes, *Tehillim*, 219, compares Ps 103:13 to Mal 3:17; *wēḥāmaltî ʿălêhem kaʾăšer yaḥmōl ʾîš ʿal bĕnô hā-ʿōbēd ʾōtô*, "I will spare them the way a man spares the son who serves him." The similes, however, are different. As Qimhi explains, the son who serves his father

The same senses of reclamation and formal acknowledgement are demonstrable from poetic verses in which *rḥm* II is associated with *šāb šĕbût*,[65] "restore the fortunes." Deut 30:3, for example, reads: *wĕšāb YHWH lōhêkā ʿet šĕbûtĕkā wĕriḥamekā wĕšāb wĕqibbeṣĕkā mikkōl hāʿammîm ʾašer hepîṣĕkā YHWH ʾelōhêkā šāmâ.* Inasmuch as *šāb šĕbût* means "restore the fortunes" and *qibbēṣ* means "gather in," the associated verb *wĕriḥamekā* must mean "take you back, restore your standing," or the like. The passage should be rendered: "Yahweh will restore your fortunes and take you back. He will once more gather you from among all the peoples where Yahweh your god has scattered you." Similarly, Ezek 39:25 reads: *ʿattâ ʾāšîb ʾet šĕbît (Qere: šĕbût) Yaʿaqōb wĕriḥamtî kôl bēt Yiśrāʾēl wĕqinnēʾtî lĕšēm qodšî* "Now I shall restore Jacob's fortunes and take back the entire household of Israel, zealously acting in behalf of my holy name." The same association occurs in Jer 30:18, a verse composed entirely in synonymous parallelism: *hinnĕnî šāb šĕbût ʾohālê Yaʿăqōb ûmiškĕnōtāw ʾăraḥēm*[66] *wĕnibnĕtâ ʿîr ʿal tillâh wĕʾarmôn ʿal mišpāṭô yēšēb*, "Behold I will restore Jacob's tents and treat his dwellings lovingly so that the city shall be rebuilt on its own mound with each fortress in its proper place."

There is a similar association in Isa 14:1, where *rḥm* II occurs in synonymous parallelism with two verbal phrases denoting restoration: *kî yĕraḥem YHWH ʾet Yaʿaqōb ûbāḥar*[67] *ʿôd bĕ-Yiśrāʾēl wĕhinnîḥām ʿalʾ admātām*, "When Yahweh takes Jacob back and reclaims Israel and resettles them on their land."

It should be obvious that Hebrew *rḥm* II is employed in these passages exactly the way *ʾhb* is employed elsewhere. We may compare Mal 1:2b–3a: *halôʾ ʾāḥ* PN_1 *l*PN_2 *nĕʾūm YHWH wāʾōhab ʾet* PN_2 *weʾet* PN, *śānēʾti.* It is instructive to examine the targum to this unit: *halāʾ āḥ* PN_1 *l*PN_2 *ûrĕḥimat yat* PN_2 *wĕyat*

merits sparing because he is both a son and a servant. In the Malachi passage *ḥāmal* refers to the sparing of the God-fearers (vs. 16) who are righteous (vs. 18) from the coming conflagration (vs. 19). On that dreadful day, Yahweh Ṣeba'ot will secrete those who fear him (vs. 17a; for *sĕgūllâ* see HALAT, 701; for the anastrophic construction see ibn Ezra and Qimhi ad loc.), treating them the way a man treats a son who is at the same time his servant.

65 The oldest attested example of this idiom occurs as *hšbw ʾlhn šybt* (Sefire III:24), "the gods restored the fortunes." The spelling of *šybt* agrees with the unique *šybt* of Ps 126:1. For a discussion of the idiom, with bibliography, see M. Greenberg, *Ezekiel, 1–20* (Garden City, 1983), 290.

66 Cf. *drḥym lhyklʾ* "whoever cares for the palace." (KAI 242:4–5).

67 At the same time, note that *bḥr* is a poetic synonym of *ʾhb.* See Ps 47:5, 78:68. Thus, we find the parallelism of *bḥr//ʾwh*, "choose"// "desire." (Ps 132:13). Note further the parallelism of *ḥmd//bḥr* "lust after," //"choose." (Isa 1:29; cf. Ezek 23:6, 12, 23) The verb *bḥr* is an antonym of *śnʾ* (Prov 1:29), as is *ʾhb.*

PN₁ rĕḥîqêt. The Aramaic translator was aware that the verbs *ʾhb* and *śnʾ* had a legal[68] sense in this passage because he translated *śnʾ* by *rḥq*. In Aramaic and Late Hebrew, *rḥq*[69] serves as a technical term for "dispossession, renunciation, repudiation." If *śnʾ*, the antonym of *ʾhb*, is equivalent to *rḥq*, "disposses," then *ʾhb/rḥm* means "give title."[70] The passage translates as: "Was not Esau brother to Jacob—word of Yahweh? Yet I accepted Jacob and repudiated Esau."

Isaiah 9:16, although not difficult to translate, has long been considered problematic because of the parallelism *śmḥ/rḥm.*[71] MT reads: *ʿal kēn ʿal baḥûrāw lōʾ yiśmaḥ ʾădōnāy wĕʾet yĕtōmāw wĕʾet ʾalmĕnōtāw lōʾ yĕraḥēm kî kullô ḥānēp ûmērāʿ wĕkol pê dōbēr nĕbālâ.* NJPS, for example, clearly sensitive to this difficulty, followes a suggestion made by Perles[72] and translates *lōʾ yiśmaḥ* as "will not spare" on the basis of Arabic *samuḥa.* The Arabic vocable however means "was liberal, bountiful, generous."[73] "Spare" in Arabic is *safaqa*, the verb employed regularly by Saadia to translate Hebrew *ḥml.*[74] JB adopts the Dead Sea Scroll Reading *yḥml*,[75] itself in all likelihood an emendation.[76] I suggest another

---

68 Otherwise Aramaic *rḥm* and *śnʾ/sny* would have been employed to express the opposition of Hebrew *ʾhb-śnʾ*. See, e.g., targum to Judg 14:16; 2Sam 13:15, 19:6; Amos 5:15; Ps 119:113. Note further two typical talmudic usages: *mʾn drḥym lyh ... mʾn dsny lyh*, "one who loves him, one who hates him" (*b. Ketub.* 105b); similar is: *bhʾy ʾtrʾ rḥmw ly ... bhʾy ʾtrʾ snw ly*, "In this place they love me ... In this place they hate me." (*b. Qidd.* 50a).

69 Cf. Rabinowitz, "A Legal Formula" (see n. 27), 75; for Aramaic *rḥq* see references in Muffs, *Studies*, 231; for Late Hebrew see, e.g., *m. ʿEd.*, 8:2, 3, 7.

70 This has been rightly termed "the forensic sense" of *ʾhb*; see H. M. Orlinsky, "The Biblical Concept of the Land of Israel," *Eretz-Israel* 18 (1985), 53*, n. 5.

71 The parallelism *bāḥûr//yātôm ʾalmānâ* is also unusual. Most often, *bāḥûr* is paralleled by, or found in hendiadys with, *bĕtûlâ.* See Deut 32:25; Isa 23:4, 62:5; Jer 31:12, 51:22; Ezek 9:6; Amos 8:13; Zech 9:17; Ps 148:12; Lam 1:18 (cf. 1:15), 2:21. In Jer 15:8 *ʾalmĕnōtāw* and *bāḥûr* appear to be associated poetically, but the text is problematic; see the commentaries.

72 F. Perles, "Critical Notices. Gesenius' Hebrew Dictionary," *JQR* 11 (1899), 689.

73 See Lane, 1/4, 1422–23, who offers: "was liberal, bountiful generous, going an easy pace (of a camel)."

74 See, e.g., Saadia to Gen 19:16; Exod 2:6; Deut.13:9; Job 20:13. Saadia also employs *safaqa* for *ḥûs*; see e.g., to Gen 45:20; Deut 7:16; Ps 72:13.

75 For a good photograph of the variant, see J. C. Trevor, *Scrolls from Qumran Cave I* (Jerusalem, 1972), pl. 9.

76 See Wildberger, *Jesaya*, BK 10/1 (Neukirchen-Vluyn, 1972), 206; an earlier *yḥml* was "corrected" to *yḥmwl* in this text. See H. M. Orlinsky, "The Textual Criticism of the Old Testament," in *The Bible and the Ancient Near East*, ed. G. E. Wright (Garden City, 1965), 156. On the general unreliability of the textual variants from this source, see Orlinsky *apud* "P. Miller, A Selective Bibliography of the Writings of Harry M. Orlinsky," *Eretz-Israel* 16 (1982), items, 63, 76, 79, 91, 92.

solution. We have seen that *rḥm* II, "to love," has the sense of legal acceptance and recognition. In all likelihood therefore, the word *yiśmaḥ* is to be connected with Akkadian *samāḫu*,[77] a synonym of *zâzu*,[78] "to share as an heir." Thus, a Nuzi text reads in part: *ana eqlētiya bītātiya u mimma šunšuya lā isemmeḫū*,[79] "they shall not share in my fields, houses or anything else of mine." The intensive form *summuḫu*, means "to include as an heir." In one case an individual swears: *šumma* ... *ana eqlētišunu u bītātišunu lā ussemmiḫūnimma*[80] "(I swear that) they included me as an heir to their fields and houses." The negation of *summuḫu* means "to disinherit." Thus, in another case from Nuzi we read concerning the sons by a second wife: *ina eqlētišu bītātišu ina mimma šunšu ša PN lā summuḫū*[81] "they shall be disinherited with regard to his fields, his houses or anything else." Closer to Israel, a text from Ugarit reads: *ina gabbi mimmu* [*ša PN*] *lā summuḫū lā iqarrubū*,[82] "They have no share or right in any of PN's property." In this light, Isa 9:16 should be translated: "Surely my Lord will disinherit His youths[83] and not be responsible for His widows and orphans; for all are evil and wicked and every mouth speaks impiety."

Finally, we turn to Amos 1:11, well known as a difficult verse. Held demonstrated that the problematic *wayyiṭrōp* ... *šĕmārâ* sequence in the final stich concealed a Hebrew pair corresponding to Akkadian *šamāru/nadāru*, "rage/be furious."[84] Our concern here is with the previous stich *ʿal rodĕpô baḥereb ʾāḥîw wĕšiḥēt raḥamāw*. Scholars have long realized the difficulty of *raḥamāw*, "his mercy" or "compassion" in context. A century ago Krochmal[85] proposed the translation "Verwandten" on the basis of Aramaic *rahmā*, "friend." More recently Fishbane offered a similar suggestion. In addition to citing Aramaic parallels, Fishbane noted that Akkadian *râmu* was widely employed in treaty contexts. He concluded therefore that *šiḥēt raḥamāw* was to be translated as "destroyed his allies." The heinous crime of Edom was to be understood

77 See references in *CAD S*, 107–109; AHw., 1016–1017.

78 Cf. the hendiadys *lā summuḫū lā izuzzū* (*CAD S*, 109a).

79 See E. A. Speiser, "A Significant New Will from Nuzi," *JCS* 17 (1963), 65:29–31; cf. *CAD S*, 108a.

80 See *RA* 23 (1926), 148, no. 29:10: 5–10; cf. *CAD S*, 108b.

81 See *RA* 23, 145, no. 12:20–24; cf. *CAD S*, 109a.

82 *Ugaritica V*, 3:3–5.

83 Perhaps read: *ʾet baḥûrāw lōʾ yĕśammaḥ ʾădōnāy.*

84 Held, "Questions," (see n. 56); 73, n. 19; *idem*, "Studies in Biblical Homonyms in the Light of Akkadian," *JANES* 3 (1970–1971), 46–55.

85 *Apud Gesenius* 17, 755.

as betrayal of treaty-relations.[86] Paul[87] and Coote[88] objected on the grounds that etymological *ḥet*, *ʿayin*, and *ğayn* are reflected in Akkadian in a vowel of *e*-quality so that a Hebrew *rḥm* could correspond only to *rêmu*, but not to *raʾāmu/râmu*. Fishbane then retreated somewhat, contending that he had intended to suggest only a functional but not an etymological parallel.[89] Actually, Fishbane should not have given ground on the etymological objections although Paul and Coote were correct with regard to the normal phonetic correspondence,[90] there are exceptions.

Thus, Akkadian *daʾāpu*, "push, push away," can hardly be separated from Hebrew *dḥp*.[91] In addition, the Akkadian word for "kill, slay," *naʾāru/nâru/nêru*, is attested with middle *aleph* or *a*-vowel as well as with middle *e*.[92] Yet, as shown by Late Hebrew, Aramaic, and Arabic, the vocable's etymology is *nḥr*, with medial *ḥet*.[93] Accordingly, Hebrew *raḥamāw* in Amos 1:11 corresponds etymologically[94] and semantically to *rā ʾmūšu*, "his friends,[95] those who love him." From Aramaic sources Fishbane correctly noted the Elephantine phrase

86 M. Fishbane, "The Treaty Background of Amos 1:11 and Related Matters," *JBL* 89 (1970), 313–318; cf. M. Barré, "The Meaning of *lʾ ʾšybnw* in Amos 1:3–2:6," *JBL* 105 (1986), 617–620.

87 S. Paul, "Amos 1:3–2:3: A Concatenous Literary Pattern," *JBL* 90 (1971), 397–403. Paul's own suggestion is to explain *raḥamāw* on the basis of Ugaritic *rḥm*, "girl," a synonym of *btlt*; see A. Caquot. M. Scnycer and A. Herdner, *Textes ougaritiques* (Paris, 1974), 1:258; see further M. Gruber, "Ha-tiškaḥ ʾiššâ ʿûllâh?" *Tarbiz* 51 (1982), 491, n. 2. It is attested in Moabite as *rḥmt* (*KAI* 181:18). At the present state of our knowledge, however, the pairing of "brother"//'girl" in poetic parallelism seems unlikely. For more likely complements of *ʾāḥ* see Avishur, *Word-Pairs*, 753. The most convincing occurrence of Hebrew *rḥm*, "girl," is Isa 49:15; see Gruber, "Ha-tiškaḥ,", 491–492. For *rḥm rḥmtym* in Judg 5:30, see N. H. Tur Sinai, *The Language and the Book* (Jerusalem, 1959), 2:227–229 [Hebrew].

88 R. Coote, "Amos 1:11 RḤMYW," *JBL* 90 (1971), 206–208.

89 M. Fishbane, "Additional Remarks on RḤMYW (Amos 1:11)," *JBL* 91 (1972), 391–393.

90 See von Soden GAG, §9a.

91 See AHw., 146; *HALAT*, 210.

92 See *CAD, N/2*, 182a.

93 See AHw., 780b.

94 The irregular etymological correspondence of Aramaic *rḥm*, "love," and Arabic *raʾima* is not unique. Syriac *raḥēp*, "to have compassion," can hardly be separated from Arabic *raʾafa* with the same meaning. It is instructive to compare the respective translations of the Peshitta and Saadia to Ps 86:16, 145:8.

95 This interpretation causes Amos 1:11 to fit neatly into traditional patterns. Cf. the parallelism *ʾḥ//rʿ*, "brother//friend," attested in Hebrew, Ugaritic, and Akkadian; see Avishur, *Word-Pairs*, 557–558. Note that *Tg. Onq.* and Peshitta to Gen 38:12, 20, translate Hebrew *rʿ* by *rḥmʾ*.

bʿly ṭbtk wrḥmyk, "your allies and friends."[96] Additional parallels should also be mentioned. From Sefire we have *wkl mlky᾽ zy sḥrty ᾽w kl zy rḥm h᾽ ly* "and any kings in my vicinity[97] or whoever is an ally of mine." Similarly, the *baʿalê bĕrît* of Gen 14:13 are referred to as *rḥmy* in 1QapGenar 21:21. As to the pairing of *᾽ḥ* and *rḥm*, it is well-attested in Aramaic. We read for example in a Syriac incantation: *᾽ḥ᾽ l᾽ḥ᾽ nhw᾽ wrḥm᾽ ldyr᾽ byt᾽*[98] "He is brother to brethren and friend to the house-dwellers." Similarly, the pair *᾽ḥ/rʿ* (Jer 9:3) is rendered *᾽ḥ᾽/rḥm᾽* by targum and Peshitta.[99] The reverse sequence is attested in the phrase *kl rḥmwhy wkl ᾽ḥwhy*, "all his brethren and all his friends." (11QtgJob 42:11). Accordingly, we translate Amos 1:11: "For with the sword he ran down his brother[100] and annihilated his friends.[101] His anger seethed forever, his wrath raged for eternity."[102]

---

96 Fishbane, "Treaty Background," 416.

97 See S. D. Sperling, "Late Hebrew *ḥzr* and Akkadian *saḫāru*," *JANES* 5 (1973), 398, n. 6; contrast *TSSI*, 2:47.

98 J. Naveh and S. Shaked, *Amulets and Magic Bowls* (Leiden, 1985), 125:8.

99 Cf. Peshitta to Ps 122:8.

100 Accompanying *ḥrb*, *rdp* must have a perfective connotation; cf. Jer 29:18. There are several instances where *rdp* alone should be translated by "run down"; see, e.g., 1Sam 25:29; Ps 143:3. For the construction *rdp b* plus verb of destruction, cf. Lam 3:66.

101 The idiom *šḥt rḥmym* should be restored in Ps 78:38; see T. H. Gaster, *Myth, Legend and Custom in the Old Testament* (New York, 1969), 718; NEB ad loc. With Gaster read: *wĕhu᾽ yĕkapper ʿāwôn wĕlō᾽ yašḥit raḥāmāw*, but translate: "But He—He shrives wrongdoing and destroys not those who love him."

102 For the translation of Amos 1:11b, see Held, "Studies in Biblical Homonyms," 51.

CHAPTER 15

Rethinking Covenant in Late Biblical Books

Scholars have long debated the antiquity of the biblical conception that Israel was related to Yahweh by a conditional covenant[1] according to which fidelity to the god would be rewarded and infidelity severely punished.[2] In a recent monograph, *God and His People*, Ernest Nicholson provides an excellent summary of a century of research into biblical covenant.[3] Although Nicholson's book gives the impression of finality, most readers are likely to agree with Mays that "the issues posed by Wellhausen have been posed anew for discussion, but the issues are not settled; they have been simply reopened."[4]

The present paper reopens the issue of covenant in the exilic and post-exilic periods. One brief preliminary remark is in order: The respective advocates of early and late dates for conditional national covenant have agreed in construing ברית with Yahweh as a monotheistic metaphor. Mendenhall once wrote: "The population of the twelve tribes were predominantly native Palestinians who had *converted*[5] *to monotheism* [emphasis added] under the covenant with

1 For a recent survey of the varieties of divine-human covenant in the Bible see F. Bruce, *apud* H. Orlinsky, "The Biblical Concept of the Land of Israel: Cornerstone of the Covenant between God and Israel," *ErIsr* 18 (1985), 53* n. 4. On the retention of "covenant" as a translation of Hebrew ברית, see J. Barr, "Some Semantic Notes on the Covenant," in *Beiträge zur Alttestamentlichen Theologie*, eds. H. Donner, R. Hanhart and R. Smend (Göttingen, 1977), 36; D. McCarthy, "Covenant Relationships," in *idem, Institution and Narrative. Collected Essays* (Rome, 1985), 54, n. 1.

2 In itself the presentation of binary alternatives is no indication of early or late date. The epilogues to the Holiness Code (Lev 26:3–45) and to Deuteronomy (Deut 28:1–48) are nicely paralleled in the epilogue to Hammurapi's laws in their use of binary alternatives. See B. Levine, "The Epilogue to the Holiness Code: A Priestly Statement on the Destiny of Israel," in *Judaic Perspectives on Ancient Israel*, eds. J. Neusner, B. Levine and E. Frerichs, (Philadelphia, 1987), 22.

3 E. Nicholson, *God and His People. Covenant and Theology in the Old Testament* (Oxford, 1986); and more briefly, *idem*, "Covenant in a Century of Study since Wellhausen," *OTS* 24 (1986), 54–69. See further the review of *God and His People* by J. L. Mays, *JBL* 107 (1988), 119–120. For an earlier survey see K. Baltzer, *The Covenant Formulary in Old Testament, Jewish and Early Christian Writings* (Philadelphia, 1971), 1–8.

4 Mays, *JBL* 107 (1988), 120.

5 The very possibility of religious conversion in pre-exilic Israel has been denied by J. Milgrom, "Religious Conversion and the Revolt Model for the Formation of Israel," *JBL* 101 (1982), 169–176; Cf. the rejoinder by N. Gottwald, "Religious Conversion and the Societal Origins of

 | DOI 10.1163/9789004340879_016

Yahweh."[6] Weinfeld, like Mendenhall an advocate of an early date, has termed covenant a "perfect metaphor" for loyalty in a monotheistic religion, claiming that the notion was unique to Israel.[7] In fact, there is no necessary connection between divine-human covenant and monotheism. It may be argued that if biblical covenant owes anything at all to political models, then we would expect the opposite to be the case. The multiplicity of political entities was what required the making of covenants. Covenant in religious imagery reflects a like multiplicity of divine entities. Indeed, texts in Phoenician and Akkadian show that the language of divine-human covenant and alliance was employed in religious imagery in polytheistic cultures outside of Israel.[8] The biblical writers surely knew that one might covenant with other gods than Yahweh, hence the prohibition: "You shall not make a covenant with them (the inhabitants of the land) or with their gods." (Exod 23:22)[9]

The objection to linking covenant and monotheism is even stronger when applied to Wellhausen and more recent scholars who argued that the conditional covenant between Yahweh and Israel was the late[10] legalistic expression

---

Ancient Israel," in *Perspectives on the Hebrew Bible: Essays in Honor of Walter J. Harrelson*, ed. J. Crenshaw (Macon, 1988), 49–65. (I am very grateful to Professor Gottwald for providing me with a pre-publication copy of his essay.)

6 G. Mendenhall, "'Change and Decay in All Around I See': Conquest, Covenant and *The Tenth Generation*," *BA* 39 (1976), 156. Cf. *idem*, "Biblical History in Transition," in *The Bible and the Ancient Near East*, ed. G. E. Wright (Garden City, 1965), 40.

7 M. Weinfeld,"Berith," *TDOT* II, 278. Contrast S. D. Sperling, "An Arslan Tash Incantation: Interpretations and Implications," *HUCA* 53 (1982): 9, n. 70.

8 For references, see S. D. Sperling, "Israel's Religion in the Ancient Near East," in *Jewish Spirituality from the Bible to the Middle Ages*, ed. Arthur Green (New York, 1986), 24–25. In addition, note the prediction: *ilū EN.MEŠ SILIM-mi-šú* "the gods will be his allies," cited in *CAD S*, 103b.

9 It must be emphasized that the conditional "Mosaic" covenants in the Pentateuch and the covenant of Joshua 24 insist that Israelites must worship Yahweh exclusively (monolatry) but do not insist that Yahweh is the only god in existence (monotheism). As most graphically put by A. Ehrlich, *Mikrâ Ki-Pheshutô* vol. I (Reprint; New York, 1969), 172: "From this verse (Exod 20:5) we derive that the earliest worshippers of Yahweh did not claim that the other gods were insubstantial, for if that were the case, how would we construe Yahweh's jealousy of other gods? After all, no man gets jealous towards his wife on account of a eunuch." For monolatry in Israel and elsewhere in the ancient Near East see A. van Selms, "Temporary Henotheism," in *Symbolae Biblicae et Mesopotamicae Francisco Mario Theodoro de Liagre Böhl Dedicatae*, eds. M. Beek and A. Kampman (Leiden, 1973), 341–348.

10 See especially, A. Jepsen, "Berith-Ein Beitrag zur Theologie der Exilszeit," in *Verbannung und Heimkehr: Beiträge zur Geschichte und Theologie Israels im 6. und 5. Jahrhundert v. Chr. Wilhelm Rudolph zum 70. Geburtstage*, ed. A. Kuschke (Tübingen, 1961), 161–169; L. Perlitt,

of the originally prophetic teaching of ethical monotheism. Were the argument well-founded, we should expect some late biblical writings that are clearly monotheistic and at the same time enthusiastic about law to emphasize the conditional covenant between Yahweh and Israel. The present paper examines ברית in biblical texts of unquestionably late date[11] to demonstrate instead that at least as regards conditional covenant, we must agree with Noth "that in the late Old Testament literature the word 'covenant' (used in the figurative sense of the relationship between God and the people) was emptied of all its meaning."[12] It is therefore understandable that the author of Ps 119 who surely loved the law and the commandments found no use for ברית in 176 verses.[13] Of even more importance is the way in which ברית is treated in the books of Ezra and Nehemiah, which are generally considered the epitome of the monotheistic exclusiveness of Palestinian Judaism in the fifth through fourth pre-Christian centuries.[14] In Ezra-Nehemiah we find an insistence on the binding character of the law, on its punctilious observance and on the separation of Jews from Gentiles. The term ברית is attested five times in all in Ezra-Nehemiah.

In Ezra 10:3 some Jews approach Ezra to confess their[15] sinfulness in taking gentile wives. In a penitent mood they resolve on a covenant (נכרת ברית לאלהינו) to divorce these women and to oust any children born of the sinful unions. Ezra (10:5) then places all the leading priests and Levites and all Israel under oath (וישבע) to do what they have resolved. An announcement is made that in three days' time an assembly of all the exilic returnees will be convened for the purpose of dealing with the intermarriages. Excommunication (יבדל) from the community and confiscation (יחרם) of property are threatened for all who fail to attend. In his study of the pericope McCarthy[16] correctly noted that "the addition of *hišbiʿa* (vs. 5) to *kārat berît* (vs. 3) is unnecessary," without realizing the full significance of his observation. Simply stated, the pleonasm

Bundestheologie im Alten Testament (Neukirchen-Vluyn, 1969); E. Kutsch, *Verheissung und Gesetz* (Berlin-New York, 1973).

11 For a recent study with different results, cf. D. McCarthy, "Covenant and Law in Chronicles-Nehemiah," *CBQ* 44 (1982), 25–44, reprinted in *idem, Institution and Narrative*, 92–111.

12 M. Noth, *The Laws in the Pentateuch and Other Studies* (Philadelphia, 1967), 93.

13 Cf. Barr, "Some Semantic Notes," 34.

14 It is now clear that the insistence on purity, separation from foreigners and re-establishment of traditional religious observances during the Persian period were values not unique to the Jews. See J. Blenkinsopp, "The Mission of Udjahorresnet and those of Ezra and Nehemiah," *JBL* 106 (1987), 409–421.

15 The speaker is Shechaniah b. Jehiel, a member of an Elamite Jewish family. His father is specifically named as one who had brought home a gentile wife in Ezra 10:26.

16 McCarthy, "Covenant and Law," 33.

indicates that *kārat berît* in this pericope has lost its earlier precise technical sense. It is the oath which gives binding force to the community's action. We may note further the absence both of ceremonial cursing and rituals involving animals such as are found in indubitably pre-exilic covenants within[17] and without the Bible. Instead, a commission is established to examine the marriages case by case (Ezra 10:14–17).

That conditional ברית has lost its technical significance may be readily seen by examining Nehemiah's prayer in Neh 1:5–11. In vs. 5, ברית appears in a borrowing from Deut 7:9 in a string of divine epithets: יהוה אלהי השמים האל הגדול והנורא שמר הברית וחסד לאהביו ולשמרי מצותיו "Yahweh God of heaven, the God great and fearful, keeper of the[18] covenantal loyalty to those who love him and keep his commandments." Nehemiah then confesses the sins of Israel as well as those of himself and his family in vss. 7–9:

> We have acted wrongfully (חבלנו) and not observed the commandments (מצות) statutes, (חקים) and rules (משפטים) with which you charged (צוית) Moses your servant. Remember the word (הדבר) you gave[19] (צוית) your servant Moses: "Just you be unfaithful (אתם תמעלו), I will scatter you among the peoples. But just you return to me (ושבתם אלי) and carefully observe my commandments (ושמרתם מצותי ועשיתם אתם), then even if your dispersed are at the end of heaven (בקצה השמים) I will gather them from there and bring them to the temple[20] wherein I have chosen to establish my name."

Ginsberg has observed of Nehemiah "that the only Torah he reflects when he prays or wishes to speak quasi-biblically is Deuteronomy."[21] It is, therefore, noteworthy that although Nehemiah's confession employs deuteronomic

---

17 See e.g. Jer 34:8–22.

18 LXX (2 Esdras 11:5) Φυλάσσων τήν διαθήκην καί τό ἔλεος reflects the definite article just as in Deut 7:9.

19 For the various senses "give," "commission," "designate," "assign," of Heb צוה (not merely "command"), see J. Hoftijzer, *Die Verheissungen an die drei Erzväter* (Leiden, 1956), 75, n. 24. Hoftijzer's observations undermine Weinfeld's defense of Kutsch, *TDOT*, 255, that the association of ברית and צוה requires the abandonment of the translation "covenant" in favor of "obligation."

20 That is surely what "the place" (המקום) must mean here. Cf. Deut 12:5,11, 14, 26, 16:2,6, 7,11,15.

21 H. L. Ginsberg, *The Israelian Heritage of Judaism* (New York, 1982), 18.

language,[22] there is no mention of the sin of covenant violation foreseen in Deuteronomy.[23] It is even more remarkable that in vs. 8, where ברית would have been the natural choice, the writer employed דבר instead.

The use of ברית is even more striking in Nehemiah 9.[24] Although ברית occurs twice in the chapter (9: 8, 32), the term is avoided just where in deuteronomic writing it would have been an excellent choice. Chapter nine depicts the penitent Jewish community listening to a public reading of the law, and a confessional review of Israel's history, in which, as usual, Yahweh's mighty deeds are contrasted with Israel's stubbornness. Yahweh is described as sole creator of all the heavens, of the heavenly host, of the earth and the seas. He gives life to all and the heavenly host all worship him. This same Yahweh:

> chose Abram ... found him faithful and made that covenant with him (וכרות עמו הברית לתת את ארץ הכנעני ... לזרעו) to give the land[25] of the Canaanites ... to his seed. You fulfilled your words (דבריך) because you are righteous (6–8).

The history continues with the wondrous exodus and the deliverance at the sea and then proceeds to the gift of the law:

> You descended on Mount Sinai, speaking with them from heaven. You gave them right rules (ותתן להם משפטים ישרים), reliable teachings (תורות אמת) and worthwhile statutes and commandments (חקים ומצות טובים). And your holy Sabbath you proclaimed to them. Commandments, statutes and the law (תורה) you ordained for them (צוית) through your servant Moses (13–14).

The writer then recounts the wilderness wandering and the conquest of the land. He summarizes Israel's continued stubbornness and its consequent divine punishment continuing into the present, mitigated only by Yahweh's

22 Cf. vs. 9 with Deut 12:11, 16:2, 30:3–4; see further, M. Fishbane, *Biblical Interpretation in Ancient Israel* (Oxford, 1985), 471, n. 34.

23 E.g. Deut 17:2, 31:16, 20; Cf. also 1Kgs 19:10.

24 On the chapter in general with references to earlier literature see S. Mowinckel, *Studien zu dem Buche Ezra-Nehemiah*, vol. 1 (Oslo, 1964), 50–61. Mowinckel attributes the chapter to a late redactor.

25 On the intimate connection between covenant and land, see Orlinsky, "Biblical Concept," 43*–55*.

mercy. In this long and detailed account the writer employs ברית once more (vs. 32), in a manner similar to what we encountered in Neh 1:5:

> Now, our God, the great mighty and fearful God, keeper of the covenantal loyalty (שומר הברית והחסד)[26] let not appear to you insignificant the hardship that has befallen us, our kings, our princes, our priests, our ancestors, and all your people, from the days of the kings of Assyria until this very day.

The source of שומר הברית והחסד in Nehemiah 9 is, once more, Deut 7:9.[27] According to Deut 7:8–9, Yahweh brought the exodus generation out of Egypt on two accounts. First, because he loved them (מאהבת יהוה אתכם) and second, because he observed the oath (ומשמרו את השבעה) that he had long before made to their ancestors. The exodus proved that Yahweh was the "divine faithful keeper of the covenantal loyalty (האל הנאמן שמר הברית והחסד לאהביו ולשמרי מצותו לאלף דור) for a thousand generations of those who love him and keep his commandments." The reference, those "who love him and keep his commandments," is to the ancestors, who according to a tradition found elsewhere in the Pentateuch, already kept the law.[28] That tradition is fully consonant with the deuteronomic notion that human love for God is a love that can be commanded, and therefore that keeping the commandments proves one's love of God.[29] Had the ancestors not demonstrated that they loved Yahweh and kept his commandments, their descendants would not have been redeemed. The moral is stated in Deut 7:11: "You (the descendants) shall keep the commandment and the statutes and the customary laws which I command you this day to perform." That שמר הברית והחסד in Deut 7:9 is conditional, is conclusively demonstrated by Deut 7:12, which reads: "If you obey these rules and keep

26 We translate the term as a hendiadys in which חסד serves adjectivally. See M. Weinfeld, הברית והחסד—המונחים וגלגולי התפתחותם בישראל ובעולם העתיק, *Leš* 36 (1971–72), 85. The Greek (2 Esdras 19:32) translation: φυλάσσων τήν διαθήκην σου κάι τό ελεός σου, reflects *Heb: שומר בריתך וחסדך.

27 The term occurs again in 1Kgs 8:23 = 1Chr 6:14 and Dan 9:4. In 1Kgs 8:23 = 1Chr 6:14, the beneficiaries of Yahweh's "covenantal loyalty" are David's descendants. Cf. J. Gray, *I & II Kings A Commentary* (Philadelphia, 1976), 220. Gray translates "loyal love." For previous studies of הברית והחסד, see Weinfeld, *Leš* 36, 85–105; Kutsch, *Verheissung*, 122–123.

28 See especially Gen 26:5; cf. Hoftijzer, *Verheissungun*, 49. The anachronistic notion is no stranger than Noah's distinction between clean and unclean animals (Gen 7:2,8, 8:20).

29 E.g. Deut 10:12–13, 11:1, 22, 13:4–5, 19:9, 30:16; cf. 1-John 5:2–3. See W. Moran, "The Ancient Near Eastern Background of the Love of God in Deuteronomy," *CBQ* 25 (1963), 78. See further, M. Noth, *Exodus* (Philadelphia, 1962), 163.

them faithfully (ושמרתם ועשיתם אתם), Yahweh your God will keep with you that covenantal loyalty (ושמר ... לך את הברית ואת החסד) which he swore to your ancestors." In other words, the covenantal loyalty sworn to the ancestors was conditional. For that covenantal loyalty to remain in force, the descendants must emulate their ancestors.[30] It is of interest that other late texts dependent on Deut 7:9 preserve the restriction of divine covenantal loyalty to "those who love him and keep his commandments."[31] In contrast, Neh 9:32 quotes only שומר הברית והחסד but not the restriction.[32] Significant as well is the writer's placement of שמר הברית והחסד at the point where it frames the chapter's summary of Israelite history, which had begun with the ברית made with Abraham in Neh 9:8. It will be observed that by associating the Abrahamic ברית with the change of Abram's name to Abraham, Neh 9:8 recalls the covenant of Gen 17:8 (P), according to which the land was promised in perpetuity (לאחזת עולם) and unconditionally. The formula, שומר הברית והחסד at the end of the summary of Israel's history, thus serves to reinforce Neh 9:8 by recalling the unconditional ברית rather than its conditional versions. Because Nehemiah 9 speaks only of an unconditional ancestral covenant,[33] we do not find violation of the covenant among the details of Israel's sins. Thus according to vs. 16, the Israelites have been "malicious," (הזידו)[34] "stiff-necked," (ויקשו את ערפם) and "disobedient" (ולא שמעו אל מצותיך) but they are not accused of transgressing a covenant. This despite the fact that the writer of the chapter surely had access to earlier passages in which the notion occurs, especially in Deuteronomy.[35]

30 Indeed, as Deut 7:9–10 makes clear, Yahweh's "enemies," meaning those who do not show their love by keeping his commandments, will be immediately requited with destruction, despite Yahweh's earlier oath to their ancestors.

31 In 1Kgs 8:23 (=2Chr 6:14) Yahweh's covenantal loyalty is limited to "your servants who served you whole-heartedly." Dan 9:4, in the manner of Neh 1:5, simply borrows "those who love him and keep his commandments" from Deut 7:9.

32 The writer of Jonah 4:2 (cf. Joel 2:13) employed the same technique in omitting "he does not remit all punishment" from his quotation of the formula of Exod 23:7. Cf. Y. Kaufmann, *The Religion of Israel* (Chicago, 1960), 285.

33 Cf. Deut 4:31: "He will not forget the covenant which he made under oath with your ancestors." The verse is universally regarded as part of the latest additions to Deuteronomy; cf. further the line in Jehosaphat's prayer (2 Chr 20:7): "Surely, you our God dispossessed the inhabitants of this land in behalf of your people Israel and gave it forever (לעולם) to the descendants of Abraham your friend."

34 Cf. vs. 29. The writer pointedly employs the same verb that he had applied to the Egyptians in vs. 10.

35 See above, n. 23.

The final occurrence of ברית in Ezra-Nehemiah is in Neh 13:28–29. Certain priests and Levites who have taken gentile wives are accused of being "contaminators of the priesthood and the covenant of the priests and Levites." (גאלי הכהנה וברית הכהנה והלוים)[36] This appears to be a special covenant between Yahweh and the clergy, related to the ברית of the Levite priests in Jer 33:21; the ברית הלוי of Mal 2:8 (cf. 2:4,5) and the ברית כהנת עולם given Phineas and his descendants (Num 25:12).[37]

Perhaps most instructive for the whole matter of ברית in Ezra-Nehemiah is the account (Neh 10:30) of the written assent by the Jews to "join with their noble brothers, and take an oath with sanctions (באים באלה ובשבועה) to follow the law of God, given through Moses the servant of God and to observe carefully all the commandments of Yahweh our lord, his rules and laws." The written assent itself is described (10:1) by the phrase: כרתים אמנה, best translated as "we make a pledge."[38]Although the vocable אמנה[39] occurs in the Bible again only in Neh 11:23,[40] its meaning is clear from the many attestations in mishnaic and talmudic Hebrew. In the Mishnah (Sotah 9:12), אנשי אמנה are "trustworthy individuals."[41] In the Babylonian Talmud, אמנה is attested as a legal term for "loan deed of trust."[42] In the Palestinian Talmud[43] שטר אמנה

36 On the passage see Ginsberg, *Israelian Heritage*, 8.

37 Cf. Noth, *Laws*, 94; Kutsch, *Verheissung*, 118–121. It is uncertain whether Deut 33:9 refers to the specific Levite covenant or to the zealous adherence of the Levites to the Israelite covenant.

38 There is no basis for McCarthy's statement that, "ʾamānâ is an excellent surrogate for the usual berît." ("Covenant and Law," 34, n. 22).

39 According to J. C. L. Gibson, *Textbook of Syrian Semitic Inscriptions*, vol. II (Oxford, 1975), 66, *wʾmn krt by* is to be read in lines 11–12 of the Hadad inscription. Gibson *ibid.*, 67, translates: "and a sure covenant struck with me."

40 Possibly the word vocalized *ʾemunâ* in 2Kgs 12:16, 22:7 is identical to *ʾamanâ.* Note the defective writing *ʾmnh* in 2Kgs 12:16. Cf. M. Weinfeld, "The Covenant of Grant in the Old Testament and in the Ancient Near East," *JAOS* 90 (1970), 191, n. 58.

41 For similar usage in the midrash Mekilta see N. Cohen, "Analysis of the Exegetic Tradition in the 'Mekhilta de-Rabbi Ishmael': The Meaning of 'Amanah in the Second and the Third Centuries," *AJS Review* 9 (1984), 1–25.

42 See e.g. *b.B.Bat.*48b. According to R. Nahman, witnesses who signed a loan-deed were not believed if they testified: אמנה היו דברינו that is, if they testified that they had signed the document without actually witnessing the loan, in the belief that the loan would later be made.

43 Ketubot 26b.

is associated with שטר פיסטיס (Greek: πίστις), "assurance," "pledge of good faith."[44] Indeed, the LXX[45] to Neh 10:1 translates אמנה by πίστις.

The author of Nehemiah 10 avoided ברית in its formal classical sense and thus ignored the conditional national covenant so graphically described in Deuteronomy,[46] in favor of the allegedly older[47] unconditional covenant by which Yahweh had given the land to Abraham in perpetuity. The formal sense of ברית is likewise avoided in descriptions of divine law in Ezra-Nehemiah. In contrast to the pre-exilic Israelites, the exilic and post-exilic Jews did not view law as primarily a matter of adherence to the covenant, but as an entity in its own right. Accordingly, when chapter 9 speaks of the law, ברית is conspicuously absent. Thus Yahweh "gave (ותתן) right rulings and teachings" (vs. 13), "proclaimed (הודעת) the Sabbath," and ordained/prescribed (צוית) commandments, statutes and laws." (vs. 14)

The same ideology is summarized in the injunction at the end of Malachi (3:22): "Be mindful of the Torah of Moses my servant, to whom I assigned (צויתי) at Horeb[48] statutes and rules for all Israel."[49] By the post-exilic period the "law stood upon its own feet as an independent entity."[50] Its statutes were binding because the sole God of monotheistic Judaism had given them to his people at Horeb through the agency of Moses. It must be emphasized that the independence of law represents not the triumph of "legalism" over covenant[51] but the triumph of monotheism over polytheism and monolatry.[52] To enter a

44 The less-than-formal sense of אמנה survives in contemporary Israeli usage where the term refers to a financial agreement entered into by a couple who do not wish to marry officially according to Orthodox Jewish law.

45 2Esdras 19:20; Cf. Peshitta: ימין (ח)נן בשררא "We swear in truth."

46 E.g. Deut 8:18, 9:9, 11, 15, 17:2, 29:8, 11, 13, 31:16, 20.

47 For a summary of scholarly opinion on the age of the patriarchal covenant and promise traditions see C. Westermann, "Promises to the Patriarchs," *IDBSup*, 690–693, with bibliography; See further, H. Schmid, *Der sogennante Jahwist* (Zürich, 1976), 119–153; R. Rendtorff, *Das Überlieferungsgeschichtliche Problem des Pentateuch* (BZAW 147; Berlin–New York, 1976), 37–65.

48 Rather than the Sinai of Neh 9:13. On the significance of the difference see Ginsberg, *Israelian Heritage*, 18.

49 The verse is generally considered a redactional addition. See the literature cited in W. Schottroff, *'Gedenken' im alten Orient und im Alten Testament* (Neukirchen-Vluyn, 1964), 157.

50 So, Noth, *Laws*, 95.

51 Cf. J. Levenson, "The Hebrew Bible, the Old Testament and Historical Criticism," in *The Future of Biblical Studies*, eds. R. Friedman and G. Williamson (Atlanta 1987), 18–59.

52 Monolatry is inherently polytheistic in that it does not deny the divinity of gods to whom it denies worship. See Sperling, "Israel's Religion," 27; See further, M. Tsevat, *The Meaning of the Book of Job and Other Biblical Studies* (New York, 1980), 131–147.

covenant to serve only Yahweh made little sense in the post-exilic period, when for monotheistic Judaism there were no competing gods to serve. Indeed, Sara Japhet's summation of the central theological teaching of Chronicles applies to the entire post-exilic notion of "covenant," and points to a proper understanding of the Chronicler's references to the ברית between Israel and Yahweh:[53]

> In the history of the people, the author stresses several points, above all the tie between the people and their God. This tie exists not in consequence of any deed but in and of itself, as a reality existing from the beginning without need for reasons or explanations. The tie is mutual: The people serve their God and God watches over and provides for his people.[54]

Accordingly, the confessions of Israel's past sins in Chronicles agree with their counterparts in Ezra-Nehemiah[55] in omitting covenant violation. At the same time, the Chronicler differs on this point with the deuteronomistic history. Thus, where 2Kgs 17:15 includes the rejection of "his covenant" (בריתו) among the sins which resulted in the fall of the Northern Kingdom, 1Chr 5:25 refers to "trespass" (וימעלו) and "whoring after" (ויזנו) the local gods, but not to covenant violation. In contrast, when the Chronicler refers to covenant in the hymn of praise in 1Chr 16:8–36, he employs the term exactly as in Ezra-Nehemiah:

> Be mindful of his covenant (בריתו)
> The word he ordained (צוה) for a thousand generations[56]
> Which he accorded (כרת את) Abraham
> —His oath to Isaac—
> Which he confirmed (ויעמידה) to Jacob by decree (חק)
> To Israel[57] by eternal covenant (ברית עולם)
> Saying, "To you I shall give the land of Canaan
> As your allotted heritage." (vss. 15–17)

---

53 Our discussion does not deal with the Chronicler's references to covenants among humans (e.g. 1Chr 11:3; 2Chr 16:3, 23:1, 3), the role of ark of the covenant (e.g. 1Chr 16:37) and the covenant between Yahweh and the Davidids (2Chr 13:5; 21:7).

54 S. Japhet, "Chronicles, Book of," *EncJud* 5, 530.

55 The relation of the authorship of Chronicles to that of Ezra-Nehemiah does not materially affect our discussion.

56 I.e., "forever."

57 I.e., the patriarch of that name.

As in the Ezra-Nehemiah passages, the covenant in 1 Chronicles 16 is the unconditional land-grant to the remote ancestors.

The Chronicler's attitude to divine ברית becomes especially clear when one examines the way in which Chronicles rewords or refashions earlier sources. Thus, for example, in Solomon's dedicatory prayer (2Chr 6:11) the reference to "the ark containing the covenant of Yahweh (ברית יהוה) which he made with Israel" omits the phrase "when he took them out Egypt" found in the Chronicler's source (1Kgs 8:21). Even more striking is Yahweh's response to Solomon's prayer in 2Chr 7:21b–22:

> Everyone passing by it shall be appalled and say, "Why did Yahweh do thus to this land and to this house?" And they shall reply, "It is because they forsook Yahweh, (עזבו את יהוה) God of their ancestors, who took them out of Egypt, adopting other gods, worshipping and serving them. Therefore, he brought all this calamity on them."

The above passage is based on Deut 29:23–25. In Deuteronomy however, the answer to the question, "why did Yahweh do thus to this land?" is, "because they *forsook* (עזבו) *the covenant* of Yahweh (ברית יהוה), the God of their ancestors, which he made with them when he took them out of Egypt, going and serving other gods and worshipping them."[58]

2Chr 15:12, set in the reign of Asa, speaks of the people entering a covenant (ויבאו בברית) to: לדרוש את יהוה אלהי אבותיהם. In 15:13 execution is threatened for anyone who fails to comply. In 15:15 the people's whole-hearted action is rewarded by Yahweh who responds immediately (וימצא) and brings them

58 Cf. further Jer 22:8–9 where the gentiles ask why the great city was destroyed. As in Deuteronomy, the answer is: "They forsook the covenant (עזבו את ברית יהוה) of Yahweh their God." The covenant backgrounds of Deut 29:23–25 and Jer 22:8–9 are assured by the close parallel in the annals of Ashurbanipal where the Arabs ponder the reason for their land's destruction. To their own question they reply: *aššu adê rabûti ša Aššur lā niṣṣuru niḫṭû ana ṭābti Aššur-ban-aplu šarri narām libbi Enlil* "Because we did not adhere to the great covenant of (the god) Asshur; we violated the kind agreement of Ashurbanipal, the beloved of Enlil." The text is from M. Streck, *Assurbanipal und die letzten assyrischen Könige bis zum Untergange Niniveh's*, vol. II (Leipzig, 1916), 78; On the relevance of Assyrian treaties to Deuteronomy, see R. Frankena, "The Vassal Treaties of Esarhaddon and the Dating of Deuteronomy," OTS 14 (1965), 153–154. Note that the parallel terms *adû* and *ṭābtu* correspond very closely with the Heb ברית and חסד. See Weinfeld, *Leš* 36, 92.

respite (וינח). The entire story[59] becomes clear once the meaning of דרש[60] within the Asa narrative is explained. In this pericope, דרש attests the sense of "turn to for help," depend on."[61] Thus, דרש in 14:6 is synonymous with נשען על "lean on" and בא בשם "come in the name of" in 14:10. Similarly, within the same narrative the Chronicler provides two anecdotal illustrations of Asa's flawed faith in Yahweh. First (15:7), we learn that Asa preferred dependence on (נשען על) the king of Aram to dependence on (נשען על) Yahweh. In the second anecdote (16:12) we learn that when Asa developed a leg malady he "turned not to Yahweh" (לא דרש) but to the physicians. In like manner the verb דרש in 15:2 is opposed to עזב "forsake," and replaced by בקש "seek" in 15:4. Similarly, בקש in 15:15 replaces דרש in 15:12–13. Recent scholarship to the contrary notwithstanding, the ברית in this chapter is not a formal "covenant renewal"[62] but a sworn agreement to a specific course of action; namely, to rely on Yahweh in time of crisis.[63] Only in 2Chr 34:31 is there a reference to a real ברית between Israel and Yahweh that Israel follow Yahweh. But this verse, set in Josiah's reign, is merely copied from 2Kgs 23:3. Significantly, the phrase ויעמד כל העם בברית "All the people entered the covenant" (2Kgs 23:3) is missing from the Chronicler's account.

In the manner of Ezra-Nehemiah and Chronicles, other post-exilic writings consistently avoid suggesting that Israel violated ברית, and avoid collocating ברית and law. Psalm 106, clearly an exilic composition,[64] provides a detailed account of Israel's sinfulness and Yahweh's contrasting loyalty (חסדו) and mighty deeds (גבורות). The writer dwells at some length (vss. 14–33) on the negative wilderness traditions related in detail in the Pentateuch, especially in Numbers. The sordid narrative continues (vss. 34–39) with Israel's failure to eliminate the sinful inhabitants of the promised land and the consequent adoption by Israel of their ways, including the sacrifice of children (vs. 37) to demons (שדים) and the worship of idols. Naturally, Yahweh punished the

59 The pericope has been aptly characterized as "aggadic exegesis," of passages from the Pentateuch and old prophecies. See Fishbane, *Biblical Interpretation*, 388–392.

60 On דרש in Chronicles see E. Ruprecht, *TWAT* 1, 466; Cf. S. Wagner, *TDOT* 3, 301.

61 Possibly, the semantic range of the verb was expanded in post-exilic Hebrew under the influence of such Akkadian verbs as *saḫāru* and *še'û*, both of which mean "seek," "search," "look for," but which are attested in the additional senses "turn to," "depend on." On these verbs and their links to דרש and its Hebrew synonyms see M. Held, *AOAT* 25 (1976), 233, notes 23–24.

62 Contra, e.g., McCarthy, "Covenant and Law," 29 (=*Institution*, 96); Cf. Kutsch, *Verheissung*, 163.

63 Cf. Peshitta: וימיו מומתא דנצלון קדם מריא "They swore oaths that they would pray to the Lord."

64 See vss. 27,47.

Israelites by giving them over to conquerors and oppressors (vss. 41–44). But after they relented and prayed, Yahweh too relented, remembering his ברית (vs. 45), and caused their captors to be merciful towards them. As in Nehemiah, for all its sins, Israel of Psalm 106 has failed to break a ברית.[65]

The "liturgical gem"[66] that is the prayer of Dan 9:4–19, shows the same attitude to ברית as the previous selections. Yahweh is (vs. 4): שמר הברית והחסד. From 9:6 we learn that the errant Israelites "did not heed the prophets." Consequently, the Lord (Adonai) has "justice" (צדקה) on his side while (vss. 7–8) Israel has "shamefacedness" (בשת הפנים) on its side. Israel (vs. 10) did not obey Yahweh nor follow "his teachings (תורתיו), which he set before us (נתן לפנינו) through his servants the prophets."

The studied avoidance of Israel's covenant violation is especially striking in vs. 11: "All Israel has transgressed your law (עברו את תורתך) and gone astray, disobeying you; so the curse of the oath (hendiadys: האלה והשבעה)[67] which is written in the Torah of Moses, has poured down (ותתך) upon us." But if Israel has "transgressed law," in Deut 29, a chapter surely known to the writer of Daniel 9, it is hardly a coincidence that Israel of Daniel's day is bearing the consequences of "the curse of the oath,"[68] rather than the "curses of the covenant" (אלות הברית) of Deut 29:20.

The post-exilic prophets follow a similar pattern. Haggai does not employ the term ברית,[69] although there is a broken reference (Hag 2:5) to: הדבר אשר כרתי אתכם בצאתכם ממצרים "The matter which I covenanted with you when you left Egypt."[70]

The book of Zechariah likewise avoids reference to a conditional national ברית even when it might have been expected. The prophet instead attributes

---

65 Contrast N. Richardson, "Psalm 106: Yahweh's Succoring Love Saves from the Death of a Broken Covenant," in *Love and Death in the Ancient Near East. Essays in Honor of Marvin H. Pope*, eds. J. Marks and R. Good (Guilford, 1987), 191–203. As the title indicates, Richardson reads the Psalm as a tale of Israel's breach of covenant. See especially, *ibid.*, 201–203.

66 So, J. Montgomery, *A Critical and Exegetical Commentary on the Book of Daniel* (ICC; Edinburgh 1927), 361. For a detailed study of the chapter see A. Lacocque, "The Liturgical Prayer in Daniel 9," *HUCA* 47 (1976), 119–142.

67 Cf. H. Brichto, *The Problem of 'Curse' in the Hebrew Bible* (SBLMS 13; Philadelphia 1963).

68 Cf. Num 5:21; Neh 10:30.

69 The phrase זאת הברית "this is the covenant" is arbitrarily restored to Hag 2:5 by K. Elliger, *Das Buch der zwölf kleinen Propheten*, vol. II (ATD; Göttingen, 1959), 91.

70 The phrase has no counterpart in LXX, which reflects no break between צבאות of Heb vs. 4 and ורוחי of Heb vs. 5b. For recent studies of the verse see D. Petersen, *Haggai and Zechariah 1–8* (Philadelphia, 1984), 61; C. Meyers and E. Meyers, *Haggai, Zechariah 1–8* (AB; Garden City 1987) 51–52.

Israel's misfortunes to failure to heed the earlier prophets. Thus he reminds his listeners (1:6), "my prophecies and decrees (דברי וחקי) with which I commissioned (צויתי) my servants the prophets surely overtook (השׂיגו) your ancestors, so that they were brought to conclude: 'Yahweh Ṣeba'ot has dealt with us according to our customary manner (כדרכינו וכמעללינו), just as he purposed.'" Because Zechariah's proof is from earlier prophecy, vss. 4 and 6 employ language verbally close to Jeremiah's calls to his contemporaries to improve their "customary manner."[71] But although the verb (השׂיגו) recalls the language of Deuteronomy 28, where the curses accompanying the covenant[72] overtake the violators,[73] in Zechariah דברי וחקי are responsible. The same theme recurs in 7:12: "They made their hearts adamant against hearing the instruction and the prophecies (את התורה ואת הדברים)[74] which Yahweh Ṣeba'ot had sent them by his spirit through the earlier prophets; so a great wrath issued from Yahweh Ṣeba'ot."

In the latter part[75] of the book of Zechariah (9:11) there is an obscure reference to "blood of your covenant" (דם בריתך) which might refer to the covenant in Exod 24:8, but given the setting of the hellenistic period (vs. 13)[76] when circumcision might call for martyrdom, could as easily refer to the blood of circumcision.[77] Finally, the extremely difficult Zech 11:10 reads: "Taking my staff Favor (נעם) I cleft it in two, so as to annul the covenant I had made (בריתי אשר כרתי) with all the peoples." The specific content of the ברית in Zech 11:10 must be discerned both from what precedes and from what follows. In vs. 6 the prophet says:

> For I will show mercy no more (לא אחמול) to the inhabitants of the land—Yahweh's word—but I will place every human being (האדם) in the hand of every other and in the royal hand. They shall break the land to bits (וכתתו) and I will not rescue it from their hands.

---

71 See especially Jer 35:15; see further Jer 7:3, 5, 18:11, 26:13.

72 See Deut 28:15, 45.

73 See Meyers and Meyers, *Haggai, Zechariah 1–8*, 96.

74 The exact phrase occurs nowhere else.

75 "The latter part of the book of Zechariah presents vast and, in part, insoluble problems in respect of authorship, date and interpretation." See W. Neil, "Zechariah, Book of," *IDB* 4, 945.

76 Ibn Ezra and Rashi a.l. already referred this prophecy to the Hasmonean period.

77 See 1Macc 1:15, 48, 60–63, 2:46.The medieval Jewish scholars were unsure which covenantal blood was involved. Rashi preferred a connection with Exod 24:8, Qimhi, the blood of circumcision. Ibn Ezra suggests both possibilities. For modern opinions see Kutsch, *Verheissung*, 83–85.

According to vs. 6, without Yahweh's mercy all humans would attack each other. The same thought recurs in the metaphor of the sheep in vs. 9:

> So I declared; "I am not going to tend you; let the one that is to die, die and the one that is to get lost, get lost; and let the rest devour each other's flesh."

The instrument of Yahweh's mercy, which under normal circumstances keeps the people from devouring each other and the land intact, is the covenant mediated by Yahweh among all the peoples. Yahweh's power enables him to maintain all of creation harmoniously or to let chaos reign.[78] Further elucidation of Zech 11:10 is provided by the parallel action of the prophet described in vs. 14: "Then I cleft in two my second staff, Union, so as to annul the brotherhood (אחוה) between Judah and Israel." There is no mention of ברית between Judah and Israel because their relation is familial, whereas the language of ברית serves fictitiously to create a familial relation.[79] Accordingly, the mention of ברית in v. 10 is homologous to the mention of אחוה in vs. 14, recalling such Akkadian combinations such as *aḫḫūtu/ṭabūtu* "brotherhood/friendship" and *aḫḫūtu/salāmu/sulummû/ra'amūtu* "brotherhood/alliance/peace/love."[80] Just as the cleaving of the second staff annuls the fraternal relation (vs. 14), the cleaving of the first annuls the artificial relation established by covenant. The covenant whose threatened annulment (להפיר) in vs. 10 materializes in vs. 11 (ותפר) is not related to the specific national covenant between Yahweh and Israel. The ברית of this chapter is akin instead to the ברית in such passages as Hos 2:20, Ezek 34:25 and Job 5:23[81] where it is an instrument of security.

There is likewise no reference to a conditional covenant with the nation of Israel in the exilic and post-exilic sections of Isaiah.[82] The famous ברית

78 Cf. F. Anderson and D. N. Freedman, *Hosea* (AB; Garden City, 1980), 280–282.

79 See Amos 1:9. NJPS translates "covenant of brotherhood" and calls attention to the use of "my brother" in 1Kgs 9:13 in light of the covenant of 1Kgs 5:26. For extra-biblical parallels to the use of familial vocabulary in ancient Near Eastern diplomacy and politics, see Weinfeld, "Covenant of Grant," 194; H. Tadmor, "Treaty and Oath in the Ancient Near East: A Historian's Approach," in *Humanizing America's Iconic Book*, eds. G. Tucker and D. Knight (Chico, 1982), 131, 141.

80 For examples and references see Tadmor, "Treaty," 131.

81 Cf. ברית שלום in Ezek 34:25 with the parallelism בריתך//השלמה לך in Job 5:23. See Kutsch, *Verheissung*, 132 with the literature cited *ibid.*, n. 177. Note, however how Kutsch forces the sense of "Verpflichtung" (obligation) into Zech 11:10 and these other passages.

82 The question of the existence of a Trito-Isaiah alongside of Deutero-Isaiah does not affect the present inquiry. For bibliography on the question see N. Snaith, *Isaiah 40–66. A Study of the Teaching of the Second Isaiah and Its Consequences* (VTSup 14; Leiden, 1977), 219–221.

passage in Isa 40–55 is also the most difficult.[83] Isa 42:6[84] reads: "I Yahweh have triumphantly (בצדק)[85] summoned you and guided you (ואחזק בידך).[86] When I created you[87] I made you a luminary to a people, (ברית עם) a light to the nations." As noted by Rashi, the prophet is the one to whom these words are addressed. The prophet is to be a ברית to a people (singular) as well as a light to the nations (plural).[88] Obviously, the more common English rendering[89] "covenant(ed) people" would have to be expressed by עם ברית*.[90] Parallelism and context demand a term synonymous or compatible with אור. Ehrlich's suggestion[91] that some vocable from the root *brr*, "shine," "be bright," is attested here is extremely plausible.

The other examples of ברית in the exilic sections of Isaiah refer to the unconditional covenant between Yahweh and Israel:

> For this to me is like the waters (var.: days[92]) of Noah
> As I swore that the waters of Noah would never again flood the earth
> So I swear that I will not be angry with you nor rebuke you
> For the mountains may move
> And the hills be shaken

83 See the commentaries cited in Kutsch, *Verheissung*, 133–134. For the passage in the context of Deutero-Isaiah's theology see H. Orlinsky, "'A Covenant [of] People, A Light of the Nations'—a Problem in Biblical Theology," in *Essays in Biblical Culture and Bible Translation*, ed. H. Orlinsky (New York 1974), 166–186; *idem, Studies on the Second Part of the Book of Isaiah. The So-Called 'Servant of the Lord' and 'Suffering Servant' in Deutero-Isaiah* (VTSup 14; Leiden 1977 [revision of 1967 version]), 97–117.

84 MT of Isa 49:6 has only the second phrase: לאור גוים. One LXX recension reads both phrases in Isa 49:6 as well.

85 See Ehrlich, *Mikrâ* vol. III, 91; Cf. Orlinsky, "Servant," 107: "I the Lord have summoned you in triumph." Cf. Isa 45:13 where any other translation than "triumphantly" is forced. Note further that Ps 17:15 should be translated: "I shall triumphantly see your face."

86 For extra-biblical parallels to this phrase see S. Paul, "Deutero-Isaiah and Cuneiform Royal Inscriptions," *JAOS* 88 (1968), 182, n. 19.

87 The root is יצר, "create," "form." See S. Paul, "Literary and Ideological Echoes of Jeremiah in Deutero-Isaiah," in *Proceedings of the Fifth World Congress of Jewish Studies*, ed. P. Peli (Jerusalem, 1969), 109, n. 29.

88 For the parallelism: עם/גוים cf. Num 23:9; Rashi's observation that גוים is frequently applied to Israel has been underscored by Orlinsky, "Servant," 112.

89 For a sampling of translations see Orlinsky, "Covenant," 180.

90 Cf. the expressions אות ברית "covenant sign" (Gen 9:13); נקם ברית "covenant vengeance" (Lev 26:25); and נגיד ברית "covenant prince." (Dan 11:22); Peshitta to Isa 42:6 translates: קימא לעמא "covenant to a people."

91 Ehrlich, *Mikrâ* vol. III, 92; Cf. NEB: "To be a light to all peoples, a beacon for the nations."

92 See Peshitta a.l.

But my loyalty (חסדי) shall not move from you.
Nor my covenant of friendship (ברית שלומי) be shaken
Says Yahweh, who takes you back in love (Isa 54:9–10).

The sense of this passage is that in contrast to Yahweh's anger, which was temporary (Isa 54:6–8), his covenant will now be permanent.[93] As surely as the flood was a singular event that will never again disrupt creation, so too will Yahweh never again rebuke his people in anger. Both the order of creation (Gen 9:11–16) and Yahweh's relation to Israel are guaranteed by unconditional ברית.

The author of Isa 55:3 explicitly derives the new unconditional permanent covenant between Yahweh and Israel from the Davidic royal ideology:

Incline your year and come to me
Listen and you shall be revived
And I will make with you an everlasting covenant (ברית עולם)
The inviolable commitments[94] (חסדי דוד) to David.[95]

The Davidids had viewed Yahweh's covenant with them as unconditional.[96] The "very ancient"[97] text 2 Sam 23:5 refers to Yahweh's ברית עולם[98] with David.

93 Cf. C. Westermann, *Isaiah 40–66. A Commentary* (Philadelphia, 1969), 276.

94 One might even translate: "covenants." Cf. N. Glueck, *Hesed in the Bible* (translation by A. Gottschalk of the 1927 German edition; Cincinnati, 1967), 77–78.

95 The syntax of the passage is captured by K. Sakenfeld, *The Meaning of Hesed in the Hebrew Bible: A New Inquiry* (Missoula 1978) 201–202:
"I will establish for you an everlasting covenant.
The trustworthy *heseds* which were for David."

96 McCarthy's statement that "the promise turns out not to be quite so unconditional as usually claimed" is unsubstantiated. See D. McCarthy, "Compact and Kingship: Stimuli for Hebrew Covenant Thinking," in *Studies in the Period of David and Solomon and Other Essays*, ed. T. Ishida (Winona Lake, 1982), 87; Cf. the ideology expressed in Ps 89:4–5. Although the final form of that Psalm is late, the promise belongs to its older stratum. See N. Sarna, "Psalm 89, A Study in Inner Biblical Exegesis," in *Biblical and Other Studies*, ed. A. Altmann (Cambridge, MA, 1963), 29–46. On Ps 132:12, which presents a contrary ideology, that the permanence of the dynasty is conditional, see M. Tsevat, "The Steadfast House," in *idem, Meaning of Job*, 109; Cf. Weinfeld, "Covenant of Grant," 196.

97 So, G. von Rad, "The Royal Ritual in Judah," in *idem, The Problem of the Hexateuch and Other Essays* (London, 1966), 227. For bibliography on the dating of the passage see Sarna, "Psalm 89," 39–40.

98 According to Perlitt, *Bundestheologie*, 50, ברית עולם is an indication of lateness because the expression "ist nicht vor der Mitte des 6. Jhdts. dann aber breit und typisch belegt." Presumably, saying that the phrase only becomes widespread after the middle of the sixth

Weinfeld has shown that it was the deuteronomic redactor of Kings who first put the promise to David under condition (1Kgs 2:4, 8:25, 9:4).[99] The fall of the kingdom of Judah and the subsequent exile facilitated the extension of the permanent unconditional covenant to the entire people. "With his chosen people God intends to make a lasting (or permanent) covenant, the content of which is defined in the words that follow, the steadfast, sure tokens of grace vouchsafed to David."[100] It is this unconditional covenant with the entire people, not the older conditional ברית, that is found in the exilic portions of Isaiah.

The other interesting use of ברית in exilic Isaiah is found in 56:1–7:

1. Thus said Yahweh: Keep (שמרו) justice
And do (ועשו) righteousness.[101]
For soon my salvation shall come,
And my victory be revealed.
2. Happy the person who does (יעשה) this
And the mortal who holds to it (יחזיק בה)
Who keeps (שמר) the Sabbath
Rather than profane it
And keeps (שמר) his hand from doing (מעשׂות) any evil.
3. For let not the foreigner who has cleaved to Yahweh say:
Yahweh will always keep me separate from his people
And let not the eunuch say: I am a withered tree.
4. For thus said Yahweh: As regards the eunuchs
Who keep (ישמרו) my Sabbaths
And who have chosen that in which I delight
And who keep my covenant (ומחזיקים בבריתי)

---

century permits Perlitt to dismiss the significance of Isa 24:5, which is surely an authentic Isaianic verse.

99 Weinfeld, "Covenant of Grant," 195. The divine grant of a throne conditionally or unconditionally is, in itself, not a sufficient criterion for fixing the date of a text. A Mari letter provides an early example of a god's conditional gift of the throne. See G. Dossin and A. Lods, "Une Tablette inédite de Mari, intéressante pour l'histoire ancienne du prophétisme sémitique," in *Studies in Old Testament Prophecy Presented to Professor T. H. Robinson*, ed. H. Rowley (Edinburgh, 1950), 103, lines 9–23; Cf. W. von Soden, *Bibel und alter Orient* (Berlin, 1985), 29.

100 Westermann, *Isaiah 40–66*, 283–284, with references to earlier literature.

101 For a thorough study of "justice and righteousness" see M. Weinfeld, *Justice and Righteousness in the Nations: Equality and Freedom in Ancient Israel in Light of Social Justice in the Ancient Near East* (Hebrew; Jerusalem 1985).

5. I will give them, in my house, within my walls
A named monument—[102]
A thing better than sons and daughters.
I shall give them an everlasting name,
Which shall not perish.
6. As for the foreigners who cleave to Yahweh
To wait on him
To love the name of Yahweh
To be his slaves (עבדים)
All those who observe the Sabbath
Rather than profane it
And who keep to my covenant (ומחזיקים בבריתי)
7. I will bring them to my sacred mountain
And let them celebrate[103] in my house of prayer
Their holocausts and sacrifices
Shall be acceptable (לרצון)[104] on my altar.

As already seen by Qimhi in his commentary to Isa 56:4, בריתי means "my covenant of circumcision." The background of Isaiah 56 is the controversy during the Persian period between the parties aptly designated by Smith as the "assimilationists" and the "segregationists."[105] The segregationists refused both to obligate outsiders by the law of the post-exilic Jewish community and to grant them its benefits of membership. In contrast, the assimilationists were in favor of intermarriage and the incorporation of outsiders. Isa 56:1–7 is a compromise between the competing positions. Gentiles who cleaved to Yahweh could be incorporated into the cult-community. The author of these lines, unlike the author of Ezra-Nehemiah, does not consider genealogy to be an insuperable barrier to membership in Yahweh's people (עמו). Genealogical insufficiency may be overcome by righteous conduct (vss. 1–2), and adherence to two specific ritual requirements: observance of the Sabbath, an

102 Cf. 2Sam 18:18 where the יד memorial is erected in the absence of progeny. See Westermann, *Isaiah 40–66*, 314.

103 I.e. festivals and rituals. For the technical sense of שמח see Deut 12:18, 16:11,14, 14:26, 26:11, 27:7; Ps 118:24; Ezra 6:22; Neh 12:43.

104 For the technical sense of רצון and its associated verb רצה see e.g. Lev 1:4, 7:18, 22:20, 21,27; Jer 6:20; Amos 5:22; Mal 1:10,13; Ps 19:15, 51:18, 119:108.

105 Morton Smith, "Jewish Religious Life in the Persian Period," in *The Cambridge History of Judaism*, vol. 1, eds. W. Davies and L. Finkelstein (Cambridge 1984), 219–278, especially 244–251; cf. *idem*, *Palestinian Parties and Politics that Shaped the Old Testament* (New York, 1971), 180–182.

ancient institution whose importance had increased during the exile,[106] and circumcision.[107] It will be observed that here, as elsewhere, exilic Isaiah reflects traditions preserved in the book of Genesis.[108] Specifically, the verbal parallels between Genesis 17 and Isaiah 56 show that Isa 56:1–7 is a midrashic legal application of Genesis 17[109] to the situation of the Persian period. According to Genesis 17:10–14, 23–27, Yahweh made his covenant (בריתי) with Abra(ha)m, requiring the patriarch to maintain (שמר) the practice (vs. 13) of circumcising all his male descendants in perpetuity (ברית עולם). The requirement of circumcision as enunciated in Genesis 17 applies even to the slave[110] members of the household acquired from "every foreigner" (vs. 12: מכל בן נכר; vs. 27: מאת בן נכר). According to Gen 17:14, failure to circumcise results in excision of the individual from the people because he has broken the covenant (ונכרתה הנפש ההוא מעמיה את בריתי הפר). From the threat of excision, Isaiah 56 draws the legal inference that circumcision of the slave brings him into the people. He thus derives a mechanism of conversion: The foreigners (vs. 3: בן הנכר; vs. 6: בני הנכר) who are circumcised are considered keepers of the covenant (מחזיקים בבריתי). They serve Yahweh as slaves (עבדים) and are not to be considered separate from Yahweh's people (עמו). The success of the compromise may be seen

106 See the summary in R. de Vaux, *Ancient Israel*, 1 (New York, 1965), 475–483.

107 Contrast Snaith, *Isaiah 40–66*, 226.

108 We have discussed the reference to Noah (Isa 54:9) above. Note further that Gen 17:14–15 makes reference to Sarah, who outside of Genesis is not mentioned anywhere in the OT other than Isa 51:2. In addition, it has been demonstrated that exilic Isaiah was both aware of and opposed to the cosmology of Genesis 1. See M. Weinfeld, "The Creator God in Genesis 1 and in the Prophecy of Second Isaiah," (Hebrew) *Tarbiz* 37 (1965), 105–132.

109 For previous studies see E. Kutsch, "'Ich will euer Gott sein'" in *Proceedings of the Sixth World Congress of Jewish Studies*, ed. A. Shinan (Jerusalem, 1977), 245–254, with references to earlier literature.

110 Gen 17 does not employ the term עבד. Instead, vss. 12, 13, 23, 27 employ the technical slave categories יליד בית "houseborn," and מקנת כסף, "acquired with silver." Cf. Lev 22:11. Note however, that the pair עבד/יליד בית is attested in poetic parallelism in Jer 2:14. (See M. Held, "Rhetorical Questions in Ugaritic and Biblical Hebrew," *ErIsr* 9 [1969], 76. See *ibid.*, for יליד בית = Akk *wilid bītim*. The precise sense of *wilid bītim* is uncertain. See F. Kraus, *Königliche Verfügungen in altbabylonischer Zeit* [Leiden, 1984] 280–284.) Another slave designation employed by the author of Gen 17 (vss. 23, 27) is the summary term: אנשי בית. Cf. Aramaic נשי בית "household slaves" and Akk *nišī bīti*. See H. L. Ginsberg, *ANET*, 633, n. 4; S. Kaufman, *The Akkadian Influences on Aramaic* (AS 19; Chicago, 1974), 78. The term *nišī bīti* "serfs, retainers belonging to an estate, a household, a palace or a person" is attested in all periods of Akkadian. See references in *CAD N/II*, 287–288.

in a number of late pentateuchal passages in which the circumcised alien (גר) is permitted to participate in Israelite rituals after undergoing circumcision.[111]

In sum, late biblical texts show that in the exilic and post-exilic periods, unconditional covenant, by which Yahweh and Israel remained in permanent relation, had triumphed over the notion of conditional covenant that might be broken.

111 See especially Exod 12:43–50; cf. Smith, *Parties*, 180–182. Smith *ibid.* (cf. *idem*, "Religious Life," 271), has correctly recognized Isaiah 56 as a religious compromise. That Isaiah 56 requires circumcision as well as Sabbath observance buttresses Smith's argument.

CHAPTER 16

Pants, Persians, and the Priestly Source

The first significant critical[1] attempts to overturn the consensus established by Wellhausen that the Priestly source (P) is later than the Deuteronomic source (D) were made by Y. Kaufmann. As observed by Menahem Haran,[2] in order to show that P was preexilic, Kaufmann analyzed biblical cultic institutions in a manner that did not differ methodologically from Wellhausen.[3] More recent

---

* Author's note: To Baruch I extend the blessing of Darius: *Utā taya kunavāhi, avataiy Aurmazdā ucāram kunautuv.* In other words, *mimma mala teppušu Uramazda ina qātēka lusteššer.*

My friend and colleague Baruch Levine has long been in the forefront of the modern critical study of Torah-literature. The Priestly source (P) in particular has occupied much of his scholarly attention. This paper, which approaches the problem of the dating of P from the perspective of realia, is offered in tribute to our honoree. An earlier version of this paper was presented to the international meeting of the Society of Biblical Literature in Leuven, Belgium, in August 1994.

1 Unlike Kaufmann, the Orthodox Jewish scholar David Z. Hoffmann was doctrinally committed to the Mosaic authorship of the Pentateuch. Nonetheless, Hoffmann's work engaged the Wellhausen thesis seriously and made contributions that remain significant from a critical standpoint. See B. Levine apud S. D. Sperling, *Students of the Covenant: A History of Jewish Biblical Scholarship in North America* (Atlanta: Scholars Press, 1992), 20.

2 M. Haran, "The Character of the Priestly Source," in *Proceedings of the Eighth World Congress of Jewish Studies*, Panel Sessions, A: *Bible Studies and Hebrew Language* (hereafter *P8WCJS*; Jerusalem: Magnes, 1983), 131–138, esp. 131–132.

3 Kaufmann's thesis is elaborately articulated in his Hebrew four-volume *History of Israelite Religion* (2d ed.; Jerusalem: Bialik, 1967). The first edition was abridged and translated by M. Greenberg as Y. Kaufmann, *The Religion of Israel* (Chicago: University of Chicago Press, 1960). The Kaufmann school continues to influence Israeli scholars in particular. See, e.g., M. Weinfeld, "Social and Cultic Institutions in the Priestly Source Against Their Ancient Near Eastern Background," *P8WCJS*, 95–129; *idem*, "Julius Wellhausen's Understanding of the Law of Ancient Israel and Its Fallacies," *Shnaton* 4 (1989), 62–93 [Heb.]; *idem, Deuteronomy I–II* (AB 5; New York: Doubleday, 1991), 25–37; M. Haran, *Temples and Temple-Service in Ancient Israel* (Oxford: Oxford University, 1978; repr. Winona Lake, Ind.: Eisenbrauns, 1985); *idem*, "Judaism and the Bible in the Thinking of Yehezkel Kaufmann," *Mada'e Ha-Yahadut* 31 (1991), 69–80 [Heb.]; I. Knohl, *The Sanctuary of Silence: The Priestly Torah of the Holiness School* (Minneapolis: Fortress, 1995). Among Americans, Kaufmann's procedures and essential conclusions have found their continuators in such scholars as Richard Friedman, *The Exile and Biblical Narrative: The Formation of the Deuteronomistic and Priestly Works* (Chico, Calif.: Scholars Press, 1982); J. Milgrom, "Priestly ('P') Source," *ABD* 3:453–462. See there the references to his previous work.) It is noteworthy that in his later publications, the great American

 | DOI 10.1163/9789004340879_017

advocates of a preexilic P, notably Avi Hurvitz, Ziony Zevit, Gary Rendsburg, Robert Polzin,[4] and others have based their conclusions on reconstructions of the history of the Hebrew language. Naturally, the adherents of an exilic or postexilic date for P have countered with linguistic arguments of their own. Among these, the studies of Baruch Levine have been especially compelling.[5]

Art historical evidence has played a less significant role in determining the date of P, although material of great potential value is found in the studies of cultic appurtenances, such as the work of Carol Meyers on the menorah.[6] One such detail that has apparently been overlooked in the debate over the dating of P comes from the history of clothing.[7]

---

biblicist H. L. Ginsberg, who had supported Kaufmann's theories about preexilic P for decades, concluded from his studies of the pentateuchal cultic calendars that Wellhausen's dating of P was more likely. See H. L. Ginsberg, *The Israelian Heritage of Judaism* (New York: Jewish Theological Seminary, 1982); cf. the review by B. A. Levine in AJS *Review* 12 (1987), 143–157.

4 See e.g., A. Hurvitz, *A Linguistic Study of the Relationship between the Priestly Source and the Book of Ezekiel* (Paris; Gabalda, 1982); *idem*, "The Language of the Priestly Source and Its Historical Setting: The Case for an Early Date," *P8WCJS*, 83–94; *idem*, "Dating the Priestly Source in Light of the Historical Study of Biblical Hebrew a Century after Wellhausen," ZAW 100 (1988), 88–100; Z. Zevit, "Converging Lines of Evidence Bearing on the Date of P," ZAW 94 (1982), 481–511; G. Rendsburg, "Late Biblical Hebrew and the Date of 'P,'" JANES 12 (1980), 65–80; R. Polzin, *Late Biblical Hebrew: Toward an Historical Typology of Biblical Hebrew Prose* (Missoula, Mont.: Scholars Press, 1976). Polzin takes an intermediate position in which P's language is transitional between Early Biblical Hebrew and Late Biblical Hebrew.

5 See, e.g., B. A. Levine, "Research in the Priestly Source: The Linguistic Factor," *ErIsr* 16 (Orlinsky volume; 1982), 124–131 [Heb.]; *idem*, "Late Language in the Priestly Source: Some Literary and Historical Observations," *P8WCJS*, 69–82; *idem, Leviticus* (JPS Torah Commentary; Philadelphia: Jewish Publication Society, 1989); *idem, Numbers 1–20* (AB 4; New York: Doubleday, 1993), 101–109; *idem*, "On the Semantics of Land Tenure in Biblical Literature: The Term *'aḥuzzāh*," in *The Tablet and the Scroll: Near Eastern Studies in Honor of William W. Hallo*, eds. Mark Cohen, D. Snell and D. B. Weisberg; Bethesda, Md.: CDL, 1993), 134–139.

6 See C. Meyers, *The Tabernacle Menorah* (Missoula, Mont.: Scholars Press, 1976); *idem*, "Lampstand," ABD 4:141–43.

7 In his article "Dress and Ornaments" (IDB 1:869–871), J. M. Myers collected much of the data cited in the present article without indicating their significance for dating. He observed (870) that "breeches or drawers are mentioned only in connection with priestly vestments." He notes further that Josephus "calls these breeches ἀναξυρίδες (*Ant.* 3§152), a term used by Herodotus." (See below.) Worth quoting in full is R. Smend, "Beinkleider," in *Biblisch-historisches Handwörterbuch*, eds. B. Reicke and L. Rost; Göttingen: Vandenhoeck & Ruprecht, 1962), 1:214: "aus Leinwand, Bestandteil der nach exil (?) isr. Priesterkleidung (Exod 28: 42 u.ö.). Sonst wurden B. nicht getragen." The most recent author to overlook the full chronological significance of his observations about clothing is Nahum Sarna, *Exodus*

The Hebrew of Exod 20:23 reads as follows:

ולא תעלה במעלות[8] על מזבחי אשר לא תגלה ערותך עליו

This relatively early[9] passage concludes a larger pericope, which describes what constitutes a proper altar:

> Make for me an altar of earth[10] and sacrifice on it your burnt offerings and your sacrifices of well-being, your sheep and your oxen; in every place where I cause my name to be mentioned I will come to you and bless you. But if you make for me an altar of stones, do not fashion them hewn, for by wielding your blade upon it you have profaned it. Do not ascend my altar by steps, that your nakedness may not be exposed upon it.

The prohibition against ascent by steps to an altar is linked grammatically (ולא...אשר לא) and thematically with the exposure of nakedness. That is, one may not ascend to an altar by steps because that ascent might lead to an exposure of nakedness (Heb. ערוה).[11] In other words, it is prohibited to build a stepped altar such as those attested at some ancient Palestinian sites.[12] A simpler solution, or at least an option to the prohibition of steps, might have been a requirement for officiants to wear trousers.[13] Indeed, that is the solution offered by God to Moses in Exod 28:42–43. Exod 28:42 reads:

(JPS Torah Commentary; Philadelphia: Jewish Publication Society, 1991), 117. Sarna notes the verses in which priests are instructed to wear "linen breeches to cover their nakedness." He then remarks that "breeches are otherwise unknown in the Bible and Near East in preexilic times. The dress of the ordinary person included a shirtlike garb but not breeches." By "otherwise unknown," Sarna means: archaeologically unknown and attested only in the exilic Ezekiel and the Priestly source, which most scholars do not consider preexilic.

8 The vocable is attested in the early text Amos 9:6.

9 See Levine, *AJS Review* 12, 144–145.

10 For opinions on what is meant by an "altar of earth," see R. Haak, "Altar," *ABD* 1:163.

11 This seems to be directed against inadvertent exposure rather than ritual nudity. Contrast Sarna, *Exodus*, 117.

12 On altars in the biblical period, see Haak, *ABD* 1:162–167. On stepped altars in Canaan, see *ibid.*, 163. "Steps" are mentioned in the description of the altar in Ezek 43:17.

13 See H. Horovitz and I. Rabin eds., *Mekilta D'Rabbi Ismael* (Jerusalem: Bamberger and Wahrman, 1960), 245; cf. Rashi, ad. loc.: שעל ידי המעלות אתה צריך להרחיב פסיעותיך ואף על פי שאינו גילוי ערוה ממש שהרי כתיב עשה לך מכנסי בד.

ועשׂה להם מכנסי בד[14] לכסות בשׂר ערוה ממתנים ועד ירכים יהיו[15]

You shall also make for them linen[16] trousers to cover their nakedness; they shall extend from the hips to the thighs.

The text continues:

> They shall be worn by Aaron and his sons when they enter the tent of meeting or when they approach the altar to officiate in the sanctuary, so that they do not incur punishment and die. It shall be a law for all time for him and for his offspring to come.

There is no question that Exod 28:42 addresses the problem of Exod 20:23 and probably that text itself. The phrase מכנסי בד לכסות בשר ערוה in 28:42 seems to respond to לא תגלה ערותך in 20:23. It will be recalled that כסה ערוה and גלה ערוה are antonymous phrases.[17] Second, the conclusion of the pericope,

14 The term בד refers to the cloth made from flax = פשתן plant. The words שֵׁשׁ/בוץ refer to the linen thread. See A. Hakam, *The Book of Exodus*(Jerusalem:Mossad Harav Kook, 1991), 2:213 [Heb.]. On שש and בוץ see F. Knobloch, "Linen and the Linguistic Dating of P," in *Mishneh Todah.Studies in Deuteronomy and Its Cultural Environment in Honor of Jeffrey H. Tigay*, eds. N. S. Fox, D. Glatt-Gilad and M. J. Williams (Winona Lake, Ind.; Eisenbrauns, 2009), 459–474.

15 The LXX reads: καὶ ποιήσεις αὐτοῖς περισκελῆ λινᾶ καλύψαι ἀσχημοσύνην χρωτὸς αὐτῶν· ἀπὸ ὀσφύος ἕως μηρῶν (thigh) ἔσται. For Heb. מכנסים the Greek employs περισκελῆ, literally "round the leg," hence "drawers." See LSJ, 1386. Gk. σκέλος refers to the leg from the hip downward. See LSJ, 1606; Philo follows the LXX in his account of priestly garb in *Life of Moses* 2.143. See S. D. Robertson, *The Account of the Israelite Tabernacle and the First Priesthood in the "Jewish Antiquities" of Flavius Josephus* (Ph.D. dissertation; Annenberg Research Institute: Philadelphia, 1991), 206; The Peshiṭta to Exod 28:42 reads: ועבד להון פרזומא דבוצא למכסיו בסרא דערטליותהון מן חציהון ועדמא לעטמתהון נהוון. Syriac פרזומא is a loan from Gk. περίζωμα, a girdle around the loins worn by athletes, smiths, and priests. See LSJ, 1374. It is this term that Philo employs in his account of priestly clothing in *Special Laws* 1.83. See Robertson, *Tabernacle*, 206; both *Tg. Onq.* and *Tg.Neof.* translate by מכנסין, cognate to the Hebrew vocable; Saadia employs Arabic סראויל (=*sarāwīl*) for the Pentateuch's מכנסים. See J. Derenbourg, ed., *Version arabe du Pentateuque de R. Saadia Ben Iosef Al-Fayyoûmî* (Paris: Leroux, 1893), 123, 140, 149. The Arabic is borrowed from Persian. See below.

16 On flax (linen = *linum usitatissimum*), see I. and W. Jacob, "Flora," *ABD* 2:815.

17 Cf. Gen 9:23 with Lev 18:7, and Ezek 16:8 with 16:37.

"It shall be a law for all time (חקת עולם) for him and his offspring to come," has the appearance of an innovation meant to be permanent.[18]

We may ask when the innovation of trousers was likely to have been made and why the use of trousers was not suggested by the legislator of Exodus 20.[19] Let us first observe that the Hebrew word for "trousers" or "breeches" is attested biblically three more times in the Pentateuch. First, in Exod 39:28 we have the phrase ואת מכנסי הבד שש משזר "and the linen trousers of fine twisted linen." The next attestation is in Lev 6:3, which reads in part ומכנסי בד ילבש על בשׂרו "and linen trousers he shall wear on his flesh."[20] Finally, Lev 16:4 has ומכנסי בד יהיו על בשׂרו "and linen trousers shall be on his flesh."[21]

All of the above passages[22] describe priestly clothing and occur in what are universally agreed to be selections from the Priestly source. The sole other biblical occurrence of the term likewise describes priestly clothing and, not surprisingly, is in Ezek 44:18:

פארי פשתים יהיו על ראשם ומכנסי פשתים יהיו על מתניהם לא יחגרו ביזע

> They shall have linen turbans on their heads and linen breeches on their loins; they shall not gird themselves with anything that causes sweat.

Of the five occurrences of the term for "trousers" the attestation in Ezekiel has never been taken to be preexilic. Of course, advocates of a preexilic date for

---

18 Cf. the similar phraseology in Exod 12:17 (a new festival) and Lev 3:17. The innovative significance of the phrase is particularly clear in Lev 17:7 and Num 18:21–24, where the audience is instructed "no longer" (עוד) to practice what they had been doing. All of the above passages are from P. See further Levine, *Leviticus*, 17.

19 J. Milgrom understands Exod 20:23 as referring to "private altars attended by breechless laity," which were forbidden to have steps (*idem, Leviticus 1–16* (AB 3; New York: Doubleday, 1991), 385. If he is correct, then Exod 20:23 would not necessarily be older than Exod 39:28; Lev 6:3, 16:4; and Ezek 44:18.

20 "Flesh" בשׂר is elliptical for בשׂר ערוה "genitals" in Exod 28:42. See D. Hoffmann, *Sefer Vayyikra* (Jerusalem: Mosad Harav Kook, 1953), 1:159.

21 In these passages the LXX has περισκελές.

22 For מכנסים in later Hebrew, see the description of Aaron in Sir 45:8, in A. Hartom, *HaSefarim HaHiṣonim: Ben Sira* (Tel Aviv: Yavneh, 1963), 169; P. Skehan and A. Di Lella, *The Wisdom of Ben Sira* (AB 39; New York: Doubleday, 1987), 507. The Greek has περισκελῆ; J. Charlesworth, *A Graphic Concordance to the Dead Sea Scrolls* (Louisville: John Knox, 1991) has no listing for מכנסים; the term מכנסים is attested four times in the Mishnah: *m. Yoma* 7:5; *m. Sukk.* 5:3; *m. Tamid* 5:3; *m. Kelim* 27:6. In the Tosefta the vocable is found in *t. Ned.* 4:3; *t. Menaḥ* 1:8; Horowitz-Rabin, *Mekilta*, 244–245 (Yitro 2:11) attests the vocable solely in a quotation from Exod 20:23.

P may reply that Ezek 44:18 is simply a case of the dependence of Ezekiel on the Priestly Code. What is decisive then is the whole question of when trousers or breeches came to be worn in the Near East and who introduced them. According to the late Edith Porada, one of the leading ancient Near Eastern art historians, the answer is clear.[23]

> In Near Eastern art in general, differentiation among peoples was mostly made on the basis of dress. Here the trousers, which appeared for the first time in the Persian reliefs,[24] were an important feature documenting the inclusion of new peoples in the population of the Persian Empire in the north-west, the north and the north-east. The Medes wore tight trousers, shoes, a long coat with false sleeves, called κάνδυς, which was laid over the shoulders like a cloak, and a bulbous hat with a short tail-like appendage. Many other peoples in the reliefs wore trousers, some tight, like the Armenians and Cappadocians, some loose, like the Arians, Bactrians, Arachosians, and Drangianians. The Scythian peoples, as well as the Sogdians, Chorasmians and Skudrians, all wore trousers, they had a distinctive kind of headdress with earflaps fastened under the chin, they also wore a long-sleeved belted jacket.

The peoples mentioned in the list are all non-Semites within the sphere of Iranian culture. In a note to her text,[25] Porada approvingly cites Calmeyer's suggestion that trousers appeared somewhat earlier,[26] but in Fars, still in Iran. We may compare Porada's statement with one by Mary Boyce:

---

23 See. E. Porada, "Classic Achaemenian Architecture and Sculpture," in *Cambridge History of Iran* [hereafter *CHI*], ed. I. Gershevitch (Cambridge: Cambridge University, 1985), 2:793–827. The quotation is from 822.

24 Cf. P. Calmeyer, "Hose," *RLA* 4:472: "Fast bis zum Ende der altorientalischen Kultur ist die Hose ganz unbekannt geblieben; sie taucht erst in deren letzter Periode, der achaemenidischen, plötzlich und in vielerlei Varianten auf, und zwar *ausschließlich* (emphasis mine) bei Völkern der nordwestlichen, nördlichen, and nordöstlichen Randgebiete, die zum Teil erst jetzt in die Sphäre dieser Kultur geraten waren."

25 Porada, "Achaemenian Architecture," 822, n. 4.

26 I. Seibert (*Women in the Ancient Near East* [Leipzig: Edition Leipzig, 1974], 45) cites Diodorus Siculus, the historian who lived in the first century BCE as evidence that the invention of trousers was a military strategem of Queen Semiramis (Akkadian: Sammuramat), wife of Shamshi Adad V of Assyria (824–819 BCE). Diodorus (*Library of History* 2.6) reports that Semiramis "devised for herself a garment that made it impossible to determine if the wearer was a man or a woman." This same garment "allowed her to do whatever she wished ... and was altogether so convenient to her that later the

> There are representations from the Achaemenian period of men who appear to be magi, in that they are engaged in solemnizing ritual acts; and these men are shown wearing what used to be called "Median" garb,[27] that is, the trousers and close-fitting tunic of a horseman, sometimes with a sleeved mantle (called, in Greek rendering, the "kandys"). It has now been established … that this type of dress, with only minor variations, was in fact worn generally by Iranians of east and west in the sixth century (and presumably earlier) and that the Persians themselves kept it as their military garb, wearing the Elamite robe probably only at home and in court.[28]

In the same work, Boyce refers to

> the general Iranian garb, which was a horseman's wear and consisted essentially of trousers[29] and a short, close-fitting tunic.[30]

Medes … wore the dress of Semiramis, as did afterwards the Persians." But Diodorus's statement is unsubstantiated by literary or art-historical evidence. There are no extant depictions of trousered Assyrian women or men from the 9th century or later. The fact that Diodorus himself specifically associates trousers with Iranians is in agreement with the art-historical evidence that we do have. Diodorus's primary aim was to account for the peculiarities of Iranian dress. See E. Murphy, *The Antiquities of Asia: A Translation with Notes of Book II of the Library of History of Diodorus Siculus* (New Brunswick: Transaction, 1989), 9.

27 A document from the Nippur Murashû archive refers to TÚG *Ma-du-ʾ-i-tu* "Median garb." See R. Zadok, "Iranians and Individuals Bearing Iranian Names in Achaemenian Babylonia," *IOS* 7 (1977), 113; *idem*, "Iranian and Babylonian Notes," *AfO* 28 (1981–1982), 138. (I thank Eva von Dassow for bringing these references to my attention.).

28 M. M. Boyce, *A History of Zoroastrianism* [hereafter *HZ*] (Leiden: Brill, 1982), vol. 2, 20.

29 "The Persians thought it indecorous to leave any part of the body uncovered, and they viewed the Greeks as seminaked savages; whereas the Greeks equated trousers, which the Persians wore beneath all their other clothes, with the barbarism of the Scythian nomads." (Murphy, *Diodorus*, 9, n. 26).

30 *Ibid.*, 10. For a detailed study of the depictions of the different ethnic groups on the Persepolis reliefs, see G. Walser, *Die Völkerschaften auf den Reliefs von Persepolis* (Berlin: Deutsches Archäologischen Institut, Abteilung Tehran Bd. 2, 1966). (Persepolis was founded by Darius I [522–486 BCE] and continued by Xerxes [486–465 BCE].) For an accessible treatment of the reliefs, accompanied by very clear photographs, see R. Ghirshman, *The Arts of Ancient Iran from Its Origins to the Time of Alexander the Great* (New York: Golden, 1964), 147–223; see also *ANEP*, pls. 28 and 29 and the comments on page 253.

That the trousers of the Priestly code have a Persian connection is highlighted by the following passage from Josephus:[31]

> Moreover vestments (στολαί) were made for the priests, both for the general body, whom they called χααναίς (כהניא) and in particular for the high priest whom they entitle χάναράβαχην (כהנא רבא), signifying "high priest." Now the vestments of the high priest are as follows. When the priest is proceeding to perform his sacred ministrations, after undergoing the purification which the law provides, first of all what he puts on is called the μαχανάσην.[32] The word denotes a binder (συνακτῆρα) in other words drawers (διάζωμα) covering the loins αιδοῖα (private parts), stitched of fine spun linen (βύσσου) into which the legs are inserted (ἐμβαινόντον) as breeches (ἀναξυρίδας). This garment is cut short above the waist and terminates at the thighs, around which it is drawn tight.

As observed by J. R. Meyers, the Greek word translated "breeches,"[33] (ἀναξυρίδας)[34] is the same term used by Herodotus in his description of the troops of Xerxes:

> Firstly, the Persians; for their equipment they wore on their head loose caps called tiaras (τιάρας), and on their bodies sleeved tunics (κιθῶνας) of diverse colours, with scales of iron like in appearance to the scales of fish,[35] and breeches on their legs (περὶ δέ τὰ σκέλεα ἀναξυρίδας).[36]

---

31 *Ant.* 3. §§150–152. The quotation is cited from LCL 4 (Cambridge: Harvard University Press, 1938), 386–387. For a detailed study of the passage, see Robertson, "Tabernacle," 202–214.

32 For the different spellings in the MSS and a grammatical analysis, see *ibid.*, 204.

33 In contemporary American English the word *breeches* survives as a regionalism.

34 According to Robertson, "Tabernacle," 206, this is "the most common word that would have been most instructive to his readers."

35 Cf. the description of Goliath's armor in 1Sam 17:5. See A. Rofé, "The Battle of David and Goliath," in *Judaic Perspectives on Ancient Israel*, ed. J. Neusner, B. Levine and E. Frerichs (Philadelphia: Fortress, 1987), 132; K. Galling, "Goliath und seine Rüstung," in *Volume du Congrès International pour l'étude de L'Ancien Testament: Genève*, 1965 (VTSup 15; Leiden: Brill, 1966) 150–169.

36 Herodotus *Hist.* 7.61. Cited from LCL (Cambridge: Harvard University Press, 1928), 375–377.

In all likelihood, it was the importance of horsemanship in the Iranian cultural sphere that prompted the invention of trousers.[37] Be that as it may, the Iranian advance westward brought trousers to the attention of other peoples. The fact that, among others, magi wore trousers may have influenced the P legislator to consider them appropriate priestly garb. Short trousers such as dictated by P were more efficient in performing priestly duties[38] than were longer robes and more modest than kilts, which had the potential to expose one's nakedness.

The implications of trousers for dating the final form[39] of the Priestly source are obvious. No biblical writer would have seen Iranian garb before the 6th century BCE. The occurrence of an Iranian article of clothing[40] in Hebrew texts

37 For an illustration of a 5th-century BCE. Persian horseman wearing trousers, see O. Dalton, *The Treasures of the Oxus with Other Examples of Early Oriental Metal Work* (3d ed.; London: British Museum, 1964) following pl. 40 (catalog number 124098). Cf. also 15, pls. 18, 30. (I thank Professor James R. Russell of Harvard University for bringing this book to my attention.)

38 If Mishnaic tradition is reliable, priests often had to run. See *m. Yoma* 2:1–2; *m. Tamid* 5:6.

39 Given the conservatism of religious rites, it is hard to disagree with the scholarly consensus that P contains ancient material. As a parallel, compare the rituals published by F. Thureau-Dangin, *Rituels accadiens* (Paris: Leroux, 1921; cf. *ANET*, 331–345). The colophons date the texts to the Seleucid period, and the Akkadian is certainly postclassical. Nonetheless, archaic elements, including the use of Sumerian, are remnants of earlier times.

40 In the book of Daniel (3:21, 27), reference is made to an article of clothing termed סרבל in Aramaic. The term is also attested in *1QDan*[b] (3:27) as well as in Babylonian Talmudic sources. See K. Beyer, *Die aramäischen Texte vom Toten Meer* (Göttingen: Vandenhoeck & Ruprecht, 1984), 648; B. Kasowsky, *Thesaurus Talmudis* (Jerusalem: Jewish Theological Seminary, 1971), vol. 27:343–344; see also *HALAT*, 1753. The סרבל in Daniel refers to an article of clothing that might burn quickly and visibly. Context and etymology have justifiably led scholars to the Persian word for "trousers" that appears in Middle Persian as *šalwār* (written *šlw'l*; see D. MacKenzie, *A Concise Pahlavi Dictionary* [Cambridge:Cambridge University, 1971],79; the Middle Persian reflects an Old Persian **salavāra*; see J. Montgomery, *A Critical and Exegetical Commentary on the Book of Daniel* [ICC; Edinburgh: T.&T. Clark, 1927] 213; F. Rosenthal, *Aramaic Grammar* [Wiesbaden: Harrassowitz, 1963], §189), which survives in Modern Perisan *šalvar*, the common word for "trousers." Further support for סרבל in Daniel in the meaning "trousers" comes from Syriac שרבלא "wide trousers," which translates Aram. סרבל in Peshiṭta to Dan 3:21, 27. For other references see Payne Smith, vol. 2:4325. In addition, in several talmudic passages סרבל is found in contexts where baggy trousers would be appropriate. See, e.g., *b. B. Qam.* 99a; *b. B. Meṣ.* 81b; cf. E. Z. Melamed, ed., *Talmud Babli Maseket Baba Qamma* (Jerusalem: Razal, 1952), 165; *idem*, ed., *Talmud Babli Maseket Baba Mezia* (Jerusalem: Razal, 1960), 150; *idem, Dictionnaire Aramaéen-Hébreu* (Jerusalem: Feldheim, 1992), 325. In the passages in Daniel 3 סרבל probably refers to the wide trousers known as early as the 2d century BCE from bronze Parthian sculptures. For illustrations see R. Ghirshman, *Persian Art 249*

leads to the inescapable conclusion that the Hebrew texts in question must be no earlier than 6th century BCE. If the Northerners who were exiled to the cities of Media in the 8th century BCE. (2 Kgs 17:6, 18:11) saw breeches or trousers there, their records of such sightings have not reached us.

The etymology of מכנסים[41] is by no means clear. Josephus who, as we seen above, provides the earliest extant explanation, appears to waver.[42] His translation συνακτῆρα[43] points to BH and Mishnaic כנס "assemble, gather." But his use of the verb ἐμβαινόντων,[44] which includes the senses "step into, insert," might support a connection with Mishnaic נכנס "enter."[45] A satisfactory solution, which would require disentangling the various sense of כנס in

---

B.C.–A.D. 651 (New York: Golden,1962), 89. Chronologically later, the talmudic passages presumably refer to the baggy trousers of the Sasanian period (See, e.g., *ibid.*, pls. 165, 196, 206, 212, 218.) These סרבלין would differ from the מכנסים of P and Ezekiel, which are short and might be construed as "undergarments." Cf. Josephus above.

The complete philological and sartorial picture of סרבל is far from clear. Among the problems: (1) Not all of the talmudic attestations refer to "trousers." See Kasowski, *Thesaurus Talmudis* vol. 27: 343–344; cf. J. Levy, *Wörterbuch über die Talmudim und Midraschim* (Berlin: Harz, 1924), vol 3:585. (2) In some cases at least, talmudic סרבל appears to be synonymous with טלית, the general term for "garment." (See e.g., *b. B. Meṣ.* 112a [ed. Melamed, 219].) (3) Is the Aramaic/Late Hebrew verb סרבל "was thick, fattened, swelled up, covered with fat" relevant to the discussion? See Levy, *Wörterbuch*, 584–585; M. Moreshet, *A Lexicon of the New Verbs in Tannaitic Hebrew* (Ramat-Gan: Bar-Ilan University, 1980), 255 [Heb.]; further, M. Sokoloff, *A Dictionary of Jewish Palestinian Aramaic of the Byzantine Period* (Ramat-Gan: Bar Ilan University, 1990), 388; *idem, A Dictionary of Jewish Babylonian Aramaic* (Ramat-Gan: Bar Ilan University, 2002), 829. (4)What is the conection between סרבל and the Mishnaic hapax legomenon (*m. Kelim* 26:3) שרוול ("sleeve" in Modern Hebrew), whose precise meaning is uncertain? See E. Kutscher, *Words and Their History* (Jerusalem: Kiryath Sefer, 1961), 109–114. (5) What is the relevance of the Arabic data? Saadia's use of *sarāwīl* (plural of *sirwāl*) has been noted above, n. 15. Complete discussion of סרבל must also take into account Arabic *sirbāl* "shirt, coat of mail, garment" and its associated verb *sarbala* "to clothe with a *sirbāl*," which seems more specific in meaning than *labisa* "wear, dress." See Payne Smith vol. 2:4325; Lane book 1/part 4, 1343.

41 Dillmann's suggestion cited in BDB, 488a, to derive מכנסים from a root כנס, distinct from כנס "gather, collect" and allegedly an alloform of the (Mishnaic Hebrew) verb גנז, which is derived from the Persian noun **ganz* (→ Middle Persian *ganǰ* "treasure, treasury"; see *HALAT*, 191; Moreshet, *Lexicon*, 125), must be rejected as fanciful.

42 Contrast Thackeray in LCL, ad. loc., 387.

43 See LSJ, 1694.

44 *Ibid.*, 538. The LXX employs ἐμβηϑι to translate Heb. בואי in Nah 3:14.

45 See, for example, S. Mandelkern, *Hekal Haqqodesh* (Leipzig, 1896), 588. Note that the *Hiphil* and *Niphal* forms of the verb(s), which are extremely common in Post-biblical Hebrew, are unattested in Biblical Hebrew.

Hebrew[46] and Aramaic and כנש/כנס in the different dialects of Aramaic, is beyond the scope of this paper.[47]

Despite the general consensus to date P and thus the bulk of the Pentateuch in the Achaemenid period, biblicists have expended relatively little effort in exploring Iranian influences on Torah-literature.[48] Given that the consensus date would now appear to be supported by realia, it behooves us to call attention to other elements in the P source that invite further study against an Iranian backdrop,[49] although a full investigation is likewise beyond the scope of this paper.

First, P and Zoroastrian sources call for the avoidance of defilement and an emphasis on purity that extends to all members of the community and is not confined to periods of public ritual. For example, defilement caused by menstruating women[50] is very much of concern to P[51] and very significant in

---

46 For a good selection of references, see E. Ben Yehuda, *A Complete Dictionary of Ancient and Modern Hebrew* (Berlin: Langenschedit, 1915), vol. 5: 2442–2450.

47 Thus *HALAT*, 461 relates BH and Mishnaic כנס; in contrast, C. Kasovsky (*Thesaurus Mishnae* [Jerusalem: Massada, 1958] vol. 3:974) separates Mishnaic כנס itself into three verbal roots.

48 Cf. the statement by Barr: "It is … striking that, on the whole, biblical … studies have remained very much aloof from the study of Iranian language and literature … Comparatively few Old Testament scholars seriously study Iranian materials." So, J. Barr, "The Question of Religious Influence: The Case of Zoroastrianism, Judaism and Christianity," *JAAR* 53 (1985), 201–202). The Iranologists have proved more eager comparatists. See, e.g., Boyce's chapter, "The Priestly Code and Zoroastrian Influences," in *HZ* vol. 2, 191–195.

49 We follow Boyce (*ibid.*, 40–48), who argues that both branches of the Achaemenian royal house had accepted Zoroastrianism by the early 6th century BCE.

50 Referred to in Pahlavi sources as *zan ī daštān*, the menstruating woman is under strict prohibitions. The penalty for intercourse with her (*daštān-marz*) is as high as the penalty for killing a human being. See F. Vahman, *Ardā Wirāz Nāmag* (London: Curzon, 1986), 252.

51 E.g., Lev 12:5, 15:19–24, 18:19; cf. Ezek 18:6, 22:10. This is not to say that the impurity of menstruation originated with P. Commentators regularly cite 2Sam 11:4 as evidence of the notion in earlier Israel. Note, however, that P's term for menstruation, נדה, is apparently derived by Rashi and Saadia from Aramaic נדי "to sprinkle," a vocable whose native Hebrew reflex is נזה (with *zayin*). See their comments to Num 19:10. That a menstruating woman is a "sprinkling woman," is semantically much sounder than derivations from נדד "to wander," given that according to Gen 31:35, it was credible that a menstruant couldn't move. A similarly unsound derivation (e.g. *HALAT*, 635) is from Akkadian *nadû* "throw, cast" etc. *CAD N/I*, 68–100, has no references to a menstruant (Akkadian: *ḫarištu*) in its 30-page article, s.v. *nadû*, verb. If the derivation offered by Rashi and Saadia is correct, then BH נדה was borrowed into Hebrew from Aramaic after the inner-Aramaic shift of

Zoroastrianism.[52] As for corpse-defilement, Levine has observed that Ezek 43:7–9 contains, "for the first time outside of Torah-literature, the doctrine that corpses and bones of the dead and their flesh are potent contaminators."[53] Such a doctrine would be incompatible with earlier Near Eastern cults of the dead known to have been practiced, among other places, in Israel[54] but is chronologically compatible with the prominence of corpse-defilement in Zoroastrianism.[55] Boyce observes that, if Nehemiah served as cup-bearer to Artaxerxes as claimed (Neh 2:1), he would have had to keep Zoroastrian purity laws, so as not to bring pollution on his royal master.[56]

Second, immediately following on the instruction to wear linen trousers in Lev 6:3 we find in vss. 5 and 6 the command that "a fire shall always be burning on the altar; it shall not go out."[57] Because Hebrew תמיד may merely mean "regular" rather than "continuous," the writer found it necessary to stipulate that the fire must burn continuously and never be extinguished.[58] It is difficult to avoid seeing here the influence of Zoroastrianism, because "the cult of fire is at the very heart of Zoroastrian devotional life."[59] Zoroaster associated fire with Asha "Righteousness" and enjoined his followers always to pray in its presence. It was long assumed that the temple cult of fire belonged to

---

[ḏ]→[d], that is, not before the 6th–5th century BCE, thus furnishing another indication of P's date. For the date of the phonemic shift, see S. Kaufman, *ABD* 4:176–177.

52 See Boyce, *HZ vol.* 1, 307–308.

53 Levine, *Numbers 1–20*, 105.

54 See T. Lewis, *Cults of the Dead in Ancient Israel and Ugarit* (Atlanta: Scholars Press, 1989); *idem*, "Ancestor Worship," *ABD* 1:240–242; *idem*, "Dead, Abode of the," *ABD* 2:101–105; C. Kennedy, "Dead, Cult of the," *ABD* 2:105–108.

55 See Boyce, *HZ* vol. 1, 300–306.

56 Boyce, *HZ* vol. 2, 189; Barr ("Religious Influence," 228) is less certain. In a general caveat against overdone comparatism, Barr observes (*ibid.*, 218) that the Jews, in contrast to the Greeks, lacked "any indication of curiosity about the distinctive character of Persian religion." But the lack of an articulated curiosity is no bar to religious influence. The book of Daniel shows no overt interest in Persian religion, but some of its central teachings are otherwise unintelligible. (See e.g., L. Hartman and A. Di Lella, *The Book of Daniel* [AB 23; New York: Doubleday, 1978] 31–33.) To cite a contemporary example, many Jews who have evinced an interest in the "spirituality" that has become popular in Judaism in the past 20 years would be surprised (and perhaps upset) to learn that the notion of "spirituality" has reached them indirectly through St. Paul and Alcoholics Anonymous. This is not to demean either the saint or the organization.

57 Or as later in Pahlavi, *ātaxš <ī> hamēšag-sōz* "the ever-burning fire." See Vahman, *Ardā-Wirāz* 6:1, 86–87, 238.

58 See Levine, *Leviticus JPS*, 96.

59 M. Boyce, "On the Zoroastrian Temple Cult of Fire," *JAOS* 95 (1975), 454–465.

primitive Zoroastrianism. Even if this assumption were correct, it would have been unlikely to come to the attention of Hebrews before the rise of the Persian Empire. More recently however, the researches of S. Wikander, of M. Boyce, and of K. Schippmann have led them to the conclusion that the temple cult of fire was a late outgrowth of the older veneration of the hearth fire. Specifically, the temple fire may have originated as the fire that had burned in the royal palace transferred to a public place. On Boyce's analysis, the temple cult of fire arose in the 4th century BCE. in reaction to the image cult.[60] If so, then we would seek a date in the 4th century for Leviticus 6. It must be noted, hwoever, that there is evidence for a special category for fire-stoking priests-Elamite *haturkmakša* = Old Persian **ātrvaš*,[61] from the Persepolis fortfication tablets (509–494 BCE)[62]—which would be relevant to our discussion.[63]

One brief final remark is in order. Over the years, the supposed parallels between Genesis 1 and Mesopotamian creation accounts have proved unconvincing.[64] Boyce and other Iranologists have noted similariites between Genesis 1 and the admittedly late Bundahishn.[65] Boyce did not however, comment on a particularly significant feature of the creation account in Genesis 1, to which James Barr has called attention:

> Why is there emphasis, so evident in Genesis 1, on the fact that the creation was *good* (emphasis in original)—an element for which, so far as I know, no close Mesopotamian parallel has been found, and which is so strongly emphasized nowhere else in the Old Testament?[66]

60 For the research of Wikander, Boyce, and Schippmann mentioned above, see *ibid.*, 454–465; *idem*, *HZ* vol. 2, 221–222; G. Gnoli, "Āteshgāh," *Encyclopedia of Religion* (New York: Macmillan, 1986), 1:477–478.

61 See Schwartz, *CHI* 2:688; for detailed discussion see H. Koch, "Götter und ihre Verehrung im achämenidischen Persien," *ZA* 77 (1987), 239–278, esp. 254 n. 88.

62 For the date, see Boyce, *HZ* vol. 2, 133.

63 Boyce does not accept the suggested Old Persian equivalence of the *haturmakša* nor does she agree that the official in question was a priest (*HZ* vol. 2, 135–136).

64 See M. Weinfeld, "The Creator God in Genesis I and in the Prophecy of Deutero-Isaiah," *Tarbiz* 37 (1968), 112 [Heb.].

65 The Bundahishn is a commentary on a lost Avestan text and preserves extremely ancient material. See J. R. Russell, "Yamauchi, *Persia and the Bible*," *JQR* 82 (1992), 258.

66 Barr, "Religious Influence," 208.

To some extent, Barr was anticipated by Moshe Weinfeld, who observed that the notion of Genesis 1 that creation is "good" was opposed by Deutero-Isaiah (Isa 45:7).[67] Of Gen 1:2, Weinfeld writes:

> The darkness and the primordial water symbolize … negativity and evil. It is these that the good god has come to remove and repel. This viewpoint conforms to the priestly notion of the existence of a demonic sphere that constitutes an opposition to the divine sphere, which embodies the good.[68]

If we keep in mind the historical circumstances of P's composition, the answer to Barr's question is adumbrated in Weinfeld's observation. The "good creation" of Ahura Mazda is fundamental to the Zoroastrian dualistic world view in which Angra Mainyu (Ahreman) is characterized as "having an evil creation."[69] In Genesis 1, the Priestly writer provides a Hebrew adaptation of the Iranian notion that creation is all good. As shown by Weinfeld, Deutero-Isaiah (Isa 45:7) opposed this notion by attributing the creation of both good and evil to the Hebrew creator-god.[70]

---

67 Weinfeld, "Creator God," 123.

68 *Ibid.*, 121–122 [my translation from Weinfeld's Hebrew]. Weinfeld was apparently aware that his reading of Genesis 1 undermined his own advocacy of a preexilic P. (See n. 1 above and 70 below.) He asserts (*ibid.*, n. 89) that "It should not be concluded from this [interpretation] that the [creator] god [in Genesis 1] is doing battle with a primeval demonic-Ahremanic (Heb.: דימוני–אהורמני) force."

69 See Schwartz, in *CHI*, 2:681.

70 Weinfeld, "Creator God," 123. In no way does this support Weinfeld's claims (105–132; cf. more recently *idem, Deuteronomy 1–11*, 25–37) that P is preexilic. On the contrary, Genesis 1 and Deutero-Isaiah were both strongly influenced by Iranian culture (for Deutero-Isaiah, see Morton Smith, "II Isaiah and the Persians," *JAOS* 83 [1963] 415–420) but differed over which elements in that culture to accept.

CHAPTER 17

Miriam, Aaron and Moses: Sibling Rivalry

According to Numbers 26: 57–59, Miriam and Aaron are the siblings of Moses. In the pericope studied here (Num 11:35–12:16) Moses is challenged by Miriam and Aaron both with regard to his marital choice and to his superior prophetic status. The present article attempts to explicate some of the philological and thematic difficulties in the text. In the light of the archaeological data currently available, which demonstrate that none of the narrative of the Torah is historical, the study suggests that Num 11:35–12:16 is addressed to a Jewish audience of the Achaemenid Persian period; a period in which a written Torah, an innovation, was in competition with oral prophecy, an older traditional form of divine revelation. By composing a tale in which Yhwh *himself affirmed the superiority of his communications to Moses over his communications to other prophets, the author of the pericope was, in fact, claiming that Scripture, which contained the divine word in its clearest form, was far more reliable than prophecy orally delivered.*

The Pentateuch portrays Moses (and God) as regularly beset by opposition. This is especially true with regard to the Book of Numbers chapters 11–21, 25.[1] In the pericope studied in this paper Moses is challenged by Miriam and Aaron, who, according to the earliest level of the tradition (Micah 6:4) are his co-leaders in the exodus from Egypt, and his siblings according to Num 26:57–59. The present study attempts to explicate some of the philological and thematic difficulties present in the text, and to clarify some of the theological and ideological concerns of its author, and of the ancient audience. Before proceeding further I wish to clarify the general approach to the narratives of the Torah that will be taken in this study.[2]

It is no exaggeration to say that the Arab-Israeli Six-Day War (1967), and later the peace treaty between Israel and Jordan, had a revolutionary effect on the direction of biblical studies. For the previous thirty to forty years much of

1 See G. Coats, *Rebellion in the Wilderness* (Nashville: Abingdon, 1968). Coats (261–264) deals with the pericope studied here in an appendix because he considers it not to be part of the murmuring tradition.

2 An earlier version of this article was presented on June 12, 2000 as a Hebrew lecture to a symposium sponsored by the Department of Bible at the Hebrew University in Jerusalem. It is my pleasant duty to thank Dr. Israel Knohl and Professor Alexander Rofé for their invitation to the symposium, and the attendees for their extremely helpful comments.

 | DOI 10.1163/9789004340879_018

biblical scholarship had been heavily influenced by the "biblical archaeology"[3] school associated in the main with such American scholars as William Foxwell Albright,[4] and his disciples G. Ernest Wright,[5] John Bright,[6] David Noel Freedman[7] and Frank Cross.[8] To a lesser extent we should include Ephraim A. Speiser whose studies on the patriarchal period, and especially his commentary on Genesis,[9] continue to influence contemporary scholarship.[10] These scholars, to whose names we may add that of Benjamin Mazar[11] (Maisler)[12]

3 For a more detailed treatment of the rise and subsequent decline of the "Biblical Archaeology" school see S. David Sperling, *The Original Torah: The Political Intent of the Bible's Writers* (NewYork: New York University, 1998), 17–25 and the literature cited there.

4 For Albright's vast bibliography see D. N. Freedman in *The Bible and the Ancient Near East Essays in Honor of William Foxwell Albright*, ed. G. E. Wright (Garden City, N.Y.: Anchor, 1965), 488–524; *ErIsr* 9 (1969) 1–5; D. N. Freedman, R. MacDonald and D. Matson, *The Published Works of William Foxwell Albright: A Comprehensive Bibliography* (Cambridge, Mass.: AASOR, 1975); See further, P. Machinist, "William Foxwell Albright: The Man and His Work," in *The Study of the Ancient Near East in the Twenty-First Century. The William Foxwell Albright Centennial Conference*, eds. J. Cooper and G. M. Schwartz (Winona Lake: Eisenbrauns, 1996), 385–403; B. Long, *Planting and Reaping Albright: Politics, Ideology and Interpreting the Bible* (University Park: Pennsylvania State University, 1997).

5 See especially G. Ernest Wright, *Biblical Archaeology* (Philadelphia: Westminster, 1957).

6 J. Bright, *A History of Israel* (1st ed.; Philadelphia: Westminster, 1958). Between the late 1950s and the late 1970s Bright's *History* in its various editions was probably the most influential work of the school. The book was required reading in virtually any non-fundamentalist seminary or university course on the history of the biblical period.

7 Freedman, not himself an archaeologist, has regularly employed the models and discoveries of archaeology in his own work. See especially D. N. Freedman,"Pottery, Poetry, and Prophecy," *JBL* 96 (1977), 5–26. The essay is reprinted in D. N. Freedman, *Pottery, Poetry and Prophecy* (Winona Lake: Eisenbrauns, 1980), 1–22; On Freedman's method in general see the reviews of D. N. Freedman, *Divine Commitment and Human Obligation. Selected Writings of David Noel Freedman* (2 vols; [Eerdmans: Grand Rapids, 1997]) by R. E. Friedman in *JQR* 88 (1998), 259–261; S.David Sperling in *HS* 39 (1998), 7–13.

8 See e.g., F. M. Cross, *Canaanite Myth and Hebrew Epic: Essays in the History of the Religion of Israel* (Cambridge: Harvard University, 1973). For Cross's bibliography see *ErIsr* 26 (1999), xiii–xxiv.

9 E. A. Speiser, *Genesis*, (AB; Garden City, N.Y.: Doubleday, 1964).

10 See e.g., G. Rendsburg, *The Redaction of Genesis* (Winona Lake: Eisenbrauns, 1986); N. Sarna, *Genesis* (Philadelphia: Jewish Publication Society, 1989); *idem, Exodus* (Philadelphia: Jewish Publication Society, 1991).

11 See S. Ahituv, ed., *Benjamin Mazar, Biblical Israel: State and People* (Jerusalem: Magnes, 1982).

12 Mazar may be accounted a disciple of Albright.

and his students in Israel, employed the results of archaeology to substantiate the general historicity of the biblical accounts of Israel's origins.[13] Outside of the biblical archaeology movement, but congenial with regard to its conclusions, the Israeli scholar Yehezkel Kaufmann attempted to refute some of the central hypotheses of classical biblical criticism, especially of the German variety. Kaufmann did much to encourage the view, especially in Israeli and Jewish[14] circles, that the biblical portrayals of the origins of Israel had a strong grounding in historical fact.

But as G. E. Wright acknowledged in 1957, the potential of archaeology to verify the biblical record carried with it the "risk"[15] that archaeology could equally falsify that record. In fact, both potentials have been realized. Much material in the Prophets and Hagiographa has been substantiated and supplemented by extra-biblical sources unearthed by archaeologists.[16] With regard

---

13 It would be amiss not to include the Egyptologist K. A. Kitchen and the Semiticist A. R. Millard among those scholars of the ancient near eastern world who explicitly employ some of their researches to substantiate the general historicity of the biblical accounts. See e.g., K. Kitchen, *Ancient Orient and Old Testament* (Chicago: InterVarsity, 1966); *idem, The Bible in its World: The Bible and Archaeology Today* (Downer's Grove, Il: InterVarsity, 1978); *idem, Pharaoh Triumphant: The Life and Times of Ramesses II King of Egypt* (Warminster: Aris and Phillips, 1982); *idem*, "The Patriarchal Age: Myth or History," *BAR* 21/2 (1995) 48–57, 88, 90, 92, 94–5; A. R. Millard, "Methods of Studying the Patriarchal Narratives as Ancient Texts," in *Essays on the Patriarchal Narratives*, eds. A. R. Millard and D. J. Wiseman (Winona Lake: Eisenbrauns, 1983), 35–51; A. R. Millard, "Abraham (Person)," *ABD* 1:35–41.

14 Most of Kaufmann's output, notably his magnum opus תולדות האמונה הישראלית (8 vols.; Jerusalem: Bialik, 1937–57) was written in *Ivrit*, which in those days was not generally accessible to gentile scholars. An English translation and abridgment by Moshe Greenberg entitled *The Religion of Israel* (Chicago: University of Chicago) appeared in 1960. Kaufmann also produced a Hebrew commentary on Joshua (ספר יהושע [Jerusalem: Qiryat Sepher, 1959]) and on Judges (ספר שופטים [Jerusalem: Qiryat Sepher, 1962]) which were likewise inaccessible. The biblicists at Jewish Theological Seminary of America in New York, notably H. L. Ginsberg, who were greatly influenced by Kaufmann as well as by the Albright school, steeped several generations of rabbis and scholars in the Kaufmann-Albright tradition.

15 By "risk" (*Biblical Archaeology*, 27) Wright was referring to the potential harm to Christian faith.

16 Among these are the historical evidence for various kings, such as Mesha of Moab, Hazael of Aram, Necho and Taharqo (for the Kushite original, reflected in Hebrew as תרהקה, see L. Török, *The Kingdom of Kush* [Leiden: E. J. Brill, 1997], 131, n.3) of Egypt, Omri, Ahab, Ahaz, Jehu, Hezekiah, and Jehoiakin; and the confirmation that Sennacherib did not take Jerusalem. We might also note such accurate reflections of non-Hebrew or non-Aramaic titles in the biblical forms סריס, תרתן, אחשדרפנים, גזבר, רבשקה, רב מג, רב.

to the Hexateuch however, the opposite has proved true. At the present time it seems clear that the fundamental traditions of enslavement in Egypt, exodus therefrom,[17] the desert wandering and the armed conquest of Canaan are not "historical" in the accepted sense of the term. As such, we can no longer approach these traditions the way John Bright, for example, approached the biblical accounts of enslavement and Exodus: "It is not the sort of tradition any people would invent."[18] Rather, now that we know that the traditions were invented, we need to ask why they were and with what goals in mind. In a recent book I argued that although the narratives of the Pentateuch are all set temporally in the period before the rise of the Israelite states, they are allegorical in that they refer to events and institutions of the Israelite states and then of the Jewish communities in the years between ca. 1200–300 BCE. Second, the book maintained that these same narratives are not primarily antiquarian, but rather ideological, in that they advocate positions intended to influence the contemporaries of the authors[19] in matters which to them were of contemporary concern.[20] The definition of "allegory" employed in the book and the present study is that of Morris Abrams:

> Allegory is a narrative in which the agents and the action, and sometimes the setting as well, are contrived not only to make sense in themselves, but also to signify a second correlated order of things, concepts or events.[21]

17 The exodus seems originally to have been a northern tradition which subsequently made its way to Judah. See R. Carroll, "Psalm LXXVII:Vestiges of a Tribal Polemic," *VT* 21 (1971), 133–150; Y. Hoffman, "A North Israelite Typological Myth and a Judaean Historical Tradition: The Exodus in Hosea and Amos," *VT* 39 (1989), 169–182; *idem, The Doctrine of the Exodus in the Bible* (Tel-Aviv: Tel-Aviv University, 1983).

18 Bright, *History* (1972), 119.

19 For a thoroughly convincing example within prophetic narrative see A. Rofé, ספורי הנביאים (Jerusalem: Magnes, 1982), 111. Rofé's study of 2Kings 5 demonstrates that the gentile character Naaman's strategy of taking bags of Israelite earth to Syria reflects a practice whereby exiled Israelites adapted ritually to life outside the cultically pure land of Israel.

20 Sperling, *The Original Torah*; See the reviews by B. Porten, *HS* 40 (1999), 292–296; G. Rendsburg, *AJSR* 24 (1999), 359–362; J. Levenson, *Review of Biblical Literature* [www.bookreviews.org], (2000). Although Wellhausen, followed by recent scholars, attempted to approach many pentateuchal narratives in this fashion, neither he nor they employed the concept of allegory. *Original Torah* argues that the allegorical approach is to be applied as a general hermeneutical principle to all the narratives of the Pentateuch.

21 M. Abrams, *A Glossary of Literary Terms* (New York: Holt, Rinehart and Winston, 1971), 4.

In what follows, the story of Miriam, Aaron and Moses will be read as a historical allegory. First, however, it will be necessary to examine some of the details of the narrative.

Numbers 11:35–12:16.

לה מקברות התאוה נסעו העם חצרות ויהיו בחצרות[22]
א ותדבר מרים ואהרן במשה על אדות האשה הכשית אשר לקח כי אשה כשית לקח:
ב ויאמרו הרק אך במשה דבר יהוה הלא גם בנו דבר וישמע יהוה: ג והאיש משה
ענו [עניו] מאד מכל האדם אשר על פני האדמה: ד ויאמר יהוה פתאם אל משה ואל
אהרן ואל מרים צאו שלשתכם אל אהל מועד ויצאו שלשתם: ה וירד יהוה בעמוד
ענן ויעמד פתח האהל ויקרא אהרן ומרים ויצאו שניהם: ו ויאמר שמעו נא דברי אם
יהיה נביאכם יהוה במראה אליו אתודע בחלום אדבר בו: ז לא כן עבדי משה בכל
ביתי נאמן הוא: ח פה אל פה אדבר בו ומראה ולא בחידת[23] ותמנת יהוה יביט ומדוע
לא יראתם לדבר בעבדי במשה: ט ויחר אף יהוה בם וילך: י והענן סר מעל האהל
והנה מרים מצרעת כשלג ויפן אהרן אל מרים והנה[24] מצרעת: יא ויאמר אהרן אל
משה בי אדני אל נא תשת עלינו חטאת אשר נואלנו ואשר חטאנו: יב אל נא תהי
כמת אשר בצאתו מרחם אמו ויאכל חצי בשרו: יג ויצעק משה אל יהוה לאמר אל נא
רפא נא לה: יד ויאמר יהוה אל משה ואביה ירק ירק בפניה הלא תכלם שבעת ימים
תסגר שבעת ימים מחוץ למחנה ואחר תאסף: טו ותסגר מרים מחוץ למחנה שבעת
ימים והעם לא נסע עד האסף מרים: טז ואחר נסעו העם מחצרות ויחנו במדבר פארן:

From Qiberoth ha-Taawah the people journeyed to Hazeroth. While they were in Hazeroth, Miriam, and Aaron as well, spoke against Moses with regard to the Kushite woman he married, for he had married a Kushite woman.

22 Hazeroth frames the narrative. See 12:16.

23 The word בחידת, "in riddles," is a significant clue to the dating of the pericope. Most scholars consider the vocable חידה a loan from Aramaic, derived from the verb אחד (from Proto-Semitic < *ʾḫḏ*) "seize," "take," which also has the senses "to close," "lock." If this etymology is correct, then the Hebrew חידה could not have been borrowed from the Aramaic before the shift of *dhal* to *dalet* within Aramaic. That shift occurred in Imperial Aramaic, i.e., not before the late sixth century BCE (See S. Kaufman, "Languages [Aramaic]," in *ABD* 4:177.) In a posthumously published paper, my lamented teacher Professor Moshe Held, מנוחתו כבוד, argued for a derivation of חידה from Akkadian *ḫittu*, a noun perhaps meaning "riddle," but attested only in lexical texts. See M. Held, "Marginal Notes to the Biblical Lexicon," in *Biblical and related Studies Presented to Samuel Iwry*, eds. A. Kort and S. Morschauser (Winona Lake: Eisenbrauns, 1986), 133–154.

24 On הנה see S. Kogut, "On the Meaning and Syntax of הִנֵּה in Biblical Hebrew," in S. Japhet, ed., *Studies in Bible*, ScrHier 31 (Jerusalem: Magnes, 1986), 133–154.

They said, "Has Yhwh *spoken solely and exclusively*[25] *to*[26] *Moses? Has he not also spoken to us?" And* Yhwh *heard. Now the man Moses was very humble; more than any human*[27] *who is on the face of the earth. But* Yhwh *immediately*[28] *said*[29] *to Moses and to Aaron and to Miriam, "go out the three of you to the Tent of Meeting!"*[30] *So the three of them went out. Then* Yhwh *came down in a pillar of cloud and stood at the entrance of the Tent of Meeting. He called out: "Aaron and Miriam," so the two of them went out. Then He said: "Please!*[31] *Hear my words: If you have a prophet of* Yhwh,[32]

---

25 This is the only biblical attestation of הרק אך. The collocation of the two synonyms makes for emphasis. See A. Weiser, ed., *Ibn Ezra the Torah Commentaries* (Jerusalem: Mossad Harav Kook, 1976), 3:148.

26 In 2Sam 23:2 the phrase דבר ב said of the spirit of Yhwh, might best be translated as "spoke through." Rashbam translates בנו in our passage as על ידינו "through us." In Num 12:7, 8a, the same phrase is best rendered "spoke to." Note though that njps translates by "spoke through" in Num 12:2 and 8a. The choice between "spoke to" and "spoke through" may reflect more a problem of English translation than a difference in the sense of the Hebrew.

27 I.e., male or female.

28 The contrast is between the humility of Moses who does not respond to the criticisms, and the immediacy of Yhwh's response. Cf. lxx: παραθρῆμα "on the spot, forthwith." See *lsj*, 1331. "Forthwith" for פתאם is preferable to "suddenly" in Mal 3:1 as well. See A. B. Ehrlich, *Mikrâ ki-Pheshuto. The Bible According to its Plain Sense* (repr.; New York: Ktav, 1969), 259.

29 Inasmuch as Yhwh hadn't yet descended perhaps we should compare the voice from heaven in Dan 4:28.

30 On the different biblical traditions regarding the Tent of Meeting see A. Cooper and B. Goldstein, "At the Entrance to the Tent: More Cultic Resonances in Biblical Narrative," *jbl* 116 (1997) 201–215; I. Knohl, "Two Aspects of the Tent of Meeting," in *Tehillah le-Moshe: Biblical and Judaic Studies in Honor of Moshe Greenberg*, eds. M. Cogan, B. Eichler and J. Tigay, (Winona Lake: Eisenbrauns, 1997), 73–79.

31 For this translation of נא see S. Kaufman, "An Emphatic Plea for Please," *maarav* 7 (1991), 195–198.

32 The Hebrew is difficult. Our translation follows P. Schlessinger, ed., *S. D. Luzzatto Commentary on the Five Books of Moses* (Jerusalem: Devir, 1965), 458 who compares ידיהם "they have hands," in Ps 115:7; see further, S. Loewenstamm, "On the Predicative Use of the Suffix Joined to a Subject-Noun in Hebrew and Ugaritic," in *idem, Comparative Studies in Biblical and Ancient Oriental Literatures* (Kevelaer: Butzon & Bercker, 1980), 455–458. Another possibility is to treat אם יהיה נביאכם יהוה as an ellipsis for אם יהיה נביאכם <נביא> יהוה. Cf. ibn Ezra *ad loc*. Ehrlich arrives at the very same result by comparing the structure of נביאכם יהוה with (ולבש הכהן) מדו בד "(the priest) shall wear his tunic, the linen tunic," in Lev 6:3. See Ehrlich, *Mikrâ* 1:260; lxx ἐάν γένηται προφήτης υμῶν κυρίῳ would reflect: אם יהיה בכם נביא ליהוה. For נביא ליהוה cf. 1Kgs 22:7.

in a vision I make myself known to him, in a dream I speak to him. Not so my servant Moses, in all my household[33] *it is he*[34] *who is trusted?*[35] *Mouth to mouth I speak to him and not in riddles; and he beholds the image and likeness*[36] *of* YHWH. *Why then did you not fear to speak against my servant, against Moses?" The anger of* YHWH *burned against them and He left. When the cloud turned away from the Tent, there was Miriam, diseased in skin*[37] *white as the snow. When Aaron turned to Miriam there she was, diseased in skin. Then Aaron said to Moses, "Pray my lord, do not lay upon us the punishment for habitual sin, for we sinned in foolishness. Let her not be like one born dead, whose flesh is half-consumed when it comes forth from its mother's womb!" So Moses cried out to* YHWH, *"God, please heal her."*[38]

---

33 Several of the Aramaic versions understand "household" figuratively. *Tg.Onq.* has בכל עמי "among all my people"; *Tg.Neof.* has בכל עולמי דברית "in the entire world I created"; and *Tg.Ps.-J.* has בכל בית ישראל בכל עמי "among the whole house of Israel, among all my people." Similarly, Saadia has פי ג'מיע אמתי "among all my people." See J. Derenbourg, *Version arabe du Pentateuque de R. Saadia ben Iosef al-Fayyoûmî* (Paris: Ernest Leroux, !893), 210.

34 NEB and REB: "He alone is faithful." Luzzatto (*Commentary*, 458) explains the *beth* of בכל ביתי as בית היתרון "*beth* of superiority," as in היפה בנשים "most beautiful of women." (Cant 1:8); Cf. B. Levine *Numbers 1–20* (AB 4a; New York: Doubleday, 1993), 315: "He is most trusted," and Vulgate "fidelissimus est"; The Aramaic versions (מהימן הוא) and LXX (πιστός ἐστι) are literal with no additional nuance.

35 The identical triad עבד, נאמן, בית occurs in 1Sam 22:14 in describing the royal household, which is the context here; the image of the divine household is modeled after the palace and its personnel. See Levine, *Numbers 1–20*, 342; Contrast M. White,"The Elohistic Depiction of Aaron," *VTSup* 41 (1990), 158. Moses is called עבד יהוה in Deut 34:5; for the prophets as God's עבדים see e.g., 2 Kgs 9:7, 17:13; Jer 7:25, 26:5, 35:15, 44:4; Ezek 38:17; such praise of the reliability of Moses as God's עבד is no small thing. After all, God does not even trust his angelic עבדים. See Job 4:28 (Luzzatto, *Commentary*, 458).

36 So, approximately Ehrlich, *Mikrâ*, 261. Ehrlich understands the verse anastrophically, as though it read פה אל פה אדבר בו ולא בחידת ומראה ותמנת יהוה יביט. Note that the vocables תמנת and מראה occur in parallelism in Job 4:16.

37 Biblical Hebrew צרעת refers to a variety of skin diseases as well as to discolorations in inanimate objects. Neither the biblical term nor its Akkadian counterpart *saḫaršubbû/saḫaršuppû* (AHw., 1005; *CAD S*, 36) describes true leprosy, or Hansen's Disease, which was apparently unknown before the days of Alexander the Great. See D. Wright and R. Jones, "Leprosy," *ABD* 4:277–282; R. Biggs, *CANE* 3:1916.

38 Moses requests immediate aid. See Weiser, *ibn Ezra*, 3:149; Z. Gottlieb, ed., *Commentary on the Torah by R. Obadiah Sforno* (Jerusalem: Mossad Harav Kook, 1980), 276. Cf. the use of צעק in Exod 8:8, 17:4, 22:22, 26; Neh 9:27. The request for immediate healing is denied.

But YHWH said to Moses,"Had her father deliberately[39] *spit in her face,*[40] *she would surely bear her shame for seven days. Let her be afflicted in skin*[41] *for seven days after which she will be cured!"*[42] *So Miriam remained afflicted in skin outside the camp for seven days, and the people did not travel until Miriam was cured. Then afterwards the people traveled from Hazeroth and camped in the wilderness of Paran.*

The first question that confronts the reader is the unity of the chapter. The question arises immediately out of the first two verses. In vs. 1 Miriam and Aaron speak against Moses for marrying a Kushite woman. In vs. 2 however, where their words are quoted, the complaint is that YHWH has not spoken to Moses exclusively, but to them as well. As we learn from YHWH's rebuke in vss. 6–8, Miriam and Aaron view themselves as prophets on a par with Moses. The apparent discontinuity between the criticism of Moses in vs. 1 and the criticism in vs. 2 has led scholars from antiquity to the present time either to seek some

39 The use of the infinitive absolute followed by the finite verb is to exclude an inadvertent projection of saliva as in sneezing.

40 For spitting in the face as shaming, cf. Deut 25:9; Isa 50:6 (note the pairing מכלמות ורק); Job 30:10. For spitting in Ugarit as an act of shaming see *KTU*[3] 1.4:iii:10–22; For Akkadian see Maqlu vii:100–102. There the sorceress is told: *amahhaṣ lītki ašallapa lišānki umalla ru'ata ēnāki* "I smite your cheek, I pull out your tongue, I fill your eyes with spittle." In certain instances however, saliva could be curative. For example, in Šurpu vii:61 spittle is employed in a ritual to heal a person seized by an oath. In Roman Palestine, Jesus (Mark 8:22–26) cured a man's blindness by putting saliva on his eyes. In that same milieu, an anecdote about R. Meier (2d century CE) indicates that a woman might cure an eye ailment by spitting in the eye of the victim (*y. Soṭah* 1:4, [16d]). In sum, whether spittle was positive or negative depended on the intent of the spitter. In Egyptian myth Atum spits out Shu and Tefnut. According to Muslim tradition Muhammad spat into the mouth of his grandson Hasan at birth. See the examples cited by A. Ronnberg, "Spittle and Spitting." *EncRel* (1987), 14:37–38; see further, G. Parrinder, "Touching," *ibid.*, 582.

41 Our translation is based on the fact that in the Aramaic of *Tg.Onq.*, סגירו translates Hebrew צרעת, while סגירא translates צרוע and מצרעת. See H. J. Kasovsky, *Ozar Leshon Targum Onkelos. Concordance* (rev. ed., 2 vols.; Jerusalem: Magnes, 1986), 2:333 and the next note.

42 For this understanding of אסף as "heal from צרעת," see W. Bacher, *Sefer Haschoraschim Würzelwörterbuch der hebräischen Sprache von Abulwalid Merwan ibn Ganah* (repr.; Amsterdam: Philo, 1969), 41–42. Ibn Janah (sic) compares the use of the verb אסף in 2Kgs 5:3, 6 ,7, 11; note further that *Tg.Neof.* renders the root אסף in Numbers 12 by forms of Aramaic אסי, "heal." The same is true of recension A of the Samaritan Targum. See A. Tal, *The Samaritan Targum of the Pentateuch: A Critical Edition* (3 vols.; Tel-Aviv: Tel-Aviv University, 1981), 2:195; See further Y. Zakovitch, *Every High Official* (Hebrew: גבה מעל גבה) (Tel-Aviv: Am Oved, 1986), 142–145. Zakovitch points out several other significant parallels between 2Kings 5 and Numbers 12. See below.

thematic connection between the two elements, or to separate them. Jewish sources from late antiquity through medieval times applied midrashic technique to connect vss. 1–2 by identifying the Kushite woman with Zipporah,[43] the wife of Moses according to Exodus 2:21, 18:2, 5–6. In these midrashic traditions[44] the verb לקח is taken as a pluperfect, that is, Moses had previously married Zipporah, a beautiful women, referred to by the dysphemism "Kushite" as a precaution against the evil eye.[45] Subsequently however, he had divorced her,[46] or on another account, had stopped having sexual relations with her.[47] In either case, Miriam and Aaron had attributed Moses's dismissal of Zipporah to his haughty belief[48] that prophetic office precluded sexual intimacy. The

43 See Louis Ginzberg, *The Legends of the Jews* (7 vols.; Philadelphia: The Jewish Publication Society, 1959–1969), 3:255–256; 6:90, n.488. Some modern scholars equate Kushites and Midianites on the basis of the parallelism Kushan//Midian in Hab 3:7. See e.g., M. Noth, *Numbers* (London: SCM, 1968), 94; F. Cross, *Canaanite Myth*, 204. Although this suggestion was already anticipated by ibn Ezra in his comment to Num 12 :1 (Weiser *Ibn Ezra*, 3:147), it is rightly rejected by J. van Seters, *The Life of Moses The Yahwist as Historian in Exodus-Numbers* (Louisville: Westminster/John Knox, 1994), 238.

44 There are other traditions, including the *Tg.Ps.-J.* to Numbers 12, according to which Moses had actually married a Kushite woman in his youth, prior to the exodus. See A. Shinan, "Moses and the Ethiopian Woman Sources of a Story in the Chronicles of Moses," in *Studies in Hebrew Narrative Throughout the Ages*, eds. J. Heinemann and S. Werses (Jerusalem: Magnes, 1978), 66–67; For the targum text see E. G. Clarke, ed., *Targum Pseudo-Jonathan to the Pentateuch and Concordance* (Hoboken: Ktav, 1984), 171.

45 So, Rashi to vs. 2.

46 The divorce tradition is based on Exod 18:2–6. Although the standard Jewish medieval commentaries to Exod 18:2 (including Rashi; but see the next note) do not understand שלוחיה "her being sent away" as a reference to divorce, that is the interpretation of R. Joshua cited in H. S. Horovitz and I. Rabin, *Mechilta D'Rabbi Ismael* (Jerusalem: Wahrmann, 1970), 190 who compares the use of the *piel* of שלח in Deut 24:1.

47 See H. S. Horovitz, *Siphre D'Be Rab* (Jerusalem: Wahrmann, 1966), 98–99; Rashi in his comment to vs. 1 first relays the tradition of marital celibacy. At the end of the comment however, he expands כי אשה כשית לקח by adding the phrase ועתה גרשה "and now he has divorced her." Rashi thus conflates the traditions of Zipporah's divorce by Moses and Moses's assumption of celibacy within marriage.

48 See *'Abot R. Nat* 9 (ed. Schechter, 40): מרים אמרה עלי היה הדבור ולא פירשתי מבעלי אהרן אמר עלי היה הדבור ולא פירשתי מאשתי ואף אבותינו הראשונים היה הדבור עליהם ולא פירשו מנשותיהם והוא מפני שדעתו גסה עליו פירש מאשתו—Miriam said, "Prophecy came upon me but I did not abstain from my husband." Aaron said,"Prophecy came upon me but I did not abstain from my wife. And even our earliest ancestors—prophecy came upon them and they did not abstain from their wives, but he (Moses) because he is haughty, has abstained himself from his wife." According to *b. Šabb.*, 87a, and *b. Yebam.*, 62a, it was Moses's own idea to adopt marital celibacy after receiving the Torah, but an idea of which God subsequently approved (והסכים הקב"ה עמו). See also Rashi *ad loc.* On

complaint by Miriam and Aaron was that inasmuch as they too were prophets, and had not abandoned their spouses through either divorce or marital celibacy,[49] there was no need for Moses to abandon Zipporah his Kushite wife.

In contrast, the church father Origen saw thematic disunity in vss. 1–2, so much so that he identified Numbers 12 as an example of a scriptural pericope that demanded an allegorical rather than a literal interpretation. On Origen's analysis, had chapter 12 been intended to be taken literally, then vs. 2 would have continued the criticism voiced in vs. 1, by suggesting that Moses take an Israelite wife, preferably a Levite. The shift to an attack on the uniqueness of Moses's prophetic office demonstrates to Origen that an allegorical reading is required. In Origen's Christian allegorical reading Moses represents the spiritual law and the Kushite woman the gentile church. Miriam represents the superseded Jewish nation, while Aaron stands for the priesthood according to the flesh.[50]

Among modern scholars there is a similar diversity between those who seek to find a thematic unity in the chapter and those who wish to break the pericope into individual components or literary sources.[51] J. Licht[52] for example, sees here a (hypothetical) external tale in which Miriam alone spoke against Moses criticizing his marital choice, and a (hypothetical) internal tale in which both Aaron and Miriam denied the existence of a qualitative difference between the prophecies of Moses and their own. Others[53] connect vss. 1 and 2 in a literary fashion, viewing the criticism of the Kushite wife as a pretext employed by Miriam and Aaron in order to challenge the prophetic priority of

---

the rabbinic attitudes to marital celibacy as reflected in the rabbinic readings of Numbers 12 see D. Boyarin, *Carnal Israel* (Berkeley: University of California, 1993), 159–165.

49 These sources doubtless reflect the rabbinic reactions to diverse attitudes toward marriage, sexual conduct within marriage, and the purposes of marriage that Jews encountered in their dealings with Christians, Zoroastrians, and pagan philosophers. See the discussion and literature cited in I. Gafni, *The Jews of Babylonia in the Talmudic Era: A Social and Cultural History* (Hebrew; Jerusalem: Zalman Shazar Center, 1990), 266–273; see further, E. Pagels, *Adam, Eve, and the Serpent* (New York: Random House, 1988), esp. 18–20, 78–97.

50 See S. Kamin, *Jews and Christians Interpret the Bible* (Jerusalem: Magnes, 1991), 79–80 (Hebrew section). It appears that the medieval Jewish Bible scholar Rabbi Joseph Bekhor Shor was aware of Origen's commentary to Numbers 12 in some form. See Kamin, *ibid.*, 73.

51 For some references see van Seters, *Life*, 234–239. Van Seters himself views the entire pericope as the work of the Yahwist.

52 J. Licht, *A Commentary on the Book of Numbers* xi–xxi (Hebrew; Jerusalem: Magnes, 1991), 36.

53 E.g., J. Milgrom, *The JPS Torah Commentary: Numbers* (Philadelphia: Jewish Publication Society, 1990), 94.

Moses, which was their real concern. One important structural consideration however points to the unity of the pericope and that is the play on דבר ב the negative "spoke against" and the positive "spoke to." The phrase is negative in vs. 1; positive (twice) in vs. 2; positive in vs. 6. Finally, in vs. 8 the phrase appears twice, positive in the first occurrence and negative in the second.[54] In addition, although the content of the divine rejoinder in vss. 5–8 addresses the standing of Moses as a prophet, the language of the rejoinder ומדוע לא יראתם לדבר בעבדי במשה "why did you not fear to speak against my servant, against Moses?" returns the audience to vs. 1, that is to the question of the Kushite woman. In other words, on YHWH's authority one is to question neither the special prophetic standing of Moses nor his choice of a Kushite wife.

In light of the structural unity one may easily answer the objections leveled against the unity of the pericope: (1) The disagreement in gender and number between the subjects Miriam and Aaron in vs. 1 has been addressed by numerous scholars. As already observed in the Gesenius grammar,[55] similar phenomena appear in Genesis 31:14;[56] in Exod 15:1;[57] Judges 5:1.[58] In each case the gender and the number indicate the primary active party. (2) The fact that Miriam alone is punished with skin disease[59] while Aaron is not[60] has likewise been addressed in the past: one function of the pericope is to provide the etiology of the short prayer אל נא רפא נא לה,[61] which can apply grammatically only to a female but not to a male. Second, because Aaron himself is not diseased[62] he can mediate for Miriam.

---

54 I thank Professor Bezalel Porten for his observation that the negative use of דבר ב in vs. 8 makes for a chiasmus with vs. l.

55 Par. 146g.

56 ותען רחל ולאה ותאמרנה.

57 אז ישיר משה ובני ישראל.

58 ותשר דבורה וברק בן אבינעם.

59 A tradition that YHWH did something to Miriam on the journey from Egypt is found in Deut 24:9. No further details about what YHWH did are given. Inasmuch as the verse follows immediately upon the command to follow priestly instruction in cases of the צרעת skin disease, the author of Numbers 12 may have concluded, as have most commentators (see e.g., J. Tigay, *The JPS Torah Commentary: Deuteronomy* [Philadelphia: Jewish Publication Society, 1996] 225), that what YHWH did to Miriam was connected to the previous verse. The connection served his own purposes in composing Numbers 12. Contrast van Seters, *Life*, 239, who regards Deut 24:9 as a gloss.

60 According to *b. Šabb.*, 97a, R. Akiba expressed the opinion that Aaron too was afflicted with skin disease.

61 There is no need to emend אַל to אֵל as do Levine and others.

62 But he fears that he may be. Note the plural in vs. 11: "Pray, my lord do not lay upon us the punishment." Note further that Aaron acknowledges Moses as "lord," an admission of his

With regard to צרעת as punishment for transgression, the observations of Yair Zakovitch in his monographic study of 2Kings 5[63] need to be taken into account and expanded. Zakovitch demonstrated that in all the biblical narratives in which a person is punished with צרעת the punishment is due to his or her failure to submit to the proper[64] authority.[65] Similarly, in the treaty between Ashurnirari v and Mati'ilu, the Akkadian semantic equivalent of צרעת, *saḫaršubbû*, is threatened as punishment for not serving Ashurnirari in full loyalty.[66] In 2Kings 5 Gehazi is punished with צרעת for undermining the authority and standing of Elisha. In Numbers 12 Miriam is punished with צרעת for challenging the standing and authority of Moses. Another feature shared by Numbers 12 and 2Kings 5 is the equation between the צרעת sufferer and the dead.[67] Perhaps the most significant connection is between צרעת and prophecy. In 2Kgs 5:8, when Elisha hears that Naaman has been sent to Israel for the healing of his צרעת, Elisha says,"Let him please come to me so that he will know that there is a prophet in Israel." In Num 12:11–12 when Aaron appeals to Moses to heal Miriam he is acknowledging the high prophetic standing of Moses which he and Miriam had challenged.

With regard to the content of the criticisms leveled against Moses, we must ask two questions: first, what is problematic about marriage to a Kushite[68] woman? Second, is there a non-midrashic connection between Israelite-Kushite marriage and the prophetic standing of Moses? Ehrlich[69] suggested both a literary and thematic connection between the two:

---

own inferior status. Furthermore, in the words "do not lay upon us," he acknowledges the ability of Moses to inflict the punishment.

63 *High Official*, cited above, n.42.

64 I.e., the authority of which the author or narrator approves.

65 See e.g., 2Kgs 5:20–27; 2 Chr 26:16–21.

66 In SAA 2, p. 11 Reverse iv: 1–5, Mati'ilu is threatened with *saḫaršubbû* should he fail to serve Ashurnirari v "with his full heart." (Akk: *ina gammurti libbišu*) See further, Tigay, *Deuteronomy*, 543, Excursus 27; see also 494–498 and the notes and references *ibid.*, 543.

67 See Num 12:11 and cf. 2Kgs 5:7; note further that following King Uzziah's צרעת outbreak (2Kgs 15:5; 2Chr 26:21) he dwells in בית החפשית (*qere*), the equivalent of Ugaritic *bt ḫpṯt*, the realm of the dead. See *HALAT*, 328b.

68 Ancient Kush in Northeast Africa lies partly within modern Egypt and partly within modern Sudan. The translation "Ethiopia" in many English Bibles is based on the Greek terminology, which from Herodotus onward designated the lands south of Egypt. In Num 12:1 LXX translates (אשר לקח) הכשית by τῆς γυναικός τῆς Αἰθιοπίσσης. Ancient Kush, however, does not correspond to modern Ethiopia. See *OCD* s.v. "Ethiopia," 558; s.v. "Race," *ibid.*, 1293. For brief accounts of Kush, see W. Adams, "The Kingdom and Civilization of Kush in Northeast Africa," *CANE* 2:775–789; R. Smith,"Ethiopia," *ABD* 1:665–667; D. B. Redford, "Kush," *ABD* 4:109–111; For a comprehensive study see now Török, *Kush* (above n.16).

69 Ehrlich, *Mikrâ* 1:259.

> You know that it is regular scriptural practice to hold both extremes of a matter; the first something of little importance, the second a significant matter, with the intent to include everything in between.

In another words, we have here a merism; the matter of little importance is the marriage to the Kushite, while the significant matter is the exalted status of Moses relative to Miriam and Aaron. But Ehrlich continues:

> To me it seems that there is a connection between the two matters which Scripture details in the conversation between Aaron and Miriam. For we know about Muhammad that with regard to marrying women he permitted to himself what he prohibited to the entire people.

Doubtless, Ehrlich was referring to Sura 4:3 in which men were permitted to marry either two, three or four women. According to Muslim tradition, however, the prophet himself had fourteen wives or concubines.[70] Ehrlich then goes on to make a very interesting observation:

> Perhaps all ancient prophets among the Semites had been given such permission[71] in antiquity. If so, and marriage to the Kushite woman was a matter which Moses permitted to himself but did not permit to every Israelite, that is why Miriam (and Aaron) said "Did the Lord speak only etc.?"

In this last suggestion, however, Ehrlich had been anticipated by centuries by Rabbi Joseph Bekor Shor:[72]

> According to the plain sense: What they said was: "Couldn't Moses find a woman among the daughters of Israel to take for himself as a wife, that he went to take himself one of the daughters of the uncircumcised Kushites? Is it because the Holy (be He blessed) speaks to him that he exalts himself, not wishing to marry a woman from the daughters of Israel that he sought a wife from far off? After all He spoke with us as well, and we married within Israel rather than exalting ourselves in this"?

70 See W. M. Watt, "Muhammad," *EncRel(E)* 10:137–146, esp. 143.

71 Ehrlich cites Hosea's marriage to Gomer in Hosea 1.

72 Y. Nebo ed., *Perushe Rabbi Iosef Bekhor Shor al ha-Torah* (Jerusalem: Mossad Harav Kook, 1994), 258.

But if the truth be told, there is no biblical prohibition against marriage to a Kushite man or woman. Bekor Shor assumes that Moses sought a wife of geographically remote origins. But as is clear from the mention of Kushites in 2Samuel 18 and in Jeremiah 36 and 38,[73] Kushites can be documented as denizens of Israel over a period of centuries. It is even possible that such names as Kush b. Yemini and Zephaniah b. Kushi (the prophet)[74] demonstrate that Kushites had to some extent been absorbed within Israel.[75] Secondly, there is no indication that those Kushites who dwelt within Israel were uncircumcised. Indeed, according to the great triumphal stela[76] of the Kushite king Piye,[77] he himself appears to have been circumcised in his African homeland.[78] But even if Kushites in Israel were circumcised, their skin color[79] might have caused their total absorption into Israel to be less than complete even after several generations. Accordingly, the objection to Moses's marriage to a Kushite may be racially based, but is not a simple matter of racial discrimination. Instead, the question of race may provide a link between vss. 1 and 2 of Numbers 12. Buber[80] has argued that Moses, Aaron and Miriam constitute a family of seers. As such, the intrusion of a conspicuous foreign element might undermine the prophetic standing of the family.

---

73 Note the genealogy tracing Yehudi back three generations to an ancestor named Kushi (Jer 36:14).

74 Berlin rejects Zephaniah's Kushite connection. See A. Berlin, *Zephaniah: A New Introduction and Commentary*, (AB 25a; New York: Doubleday, 1994), 66–67.

75 See R. Smith,"Ethiopia," *ABD* 2:665–667; we might also call attention to the biblical figure Phineas son of Elazar and grandson of Aaron (see J. Spencer, "Phinehas," *ABD* 5:346–347). The name is Egyptian Panehesy, which means "the southerner," which from the perspective of Egypt implied black African. Whether the name carried that implication when borrowed into Hebrew cannot be ascertained. Coincidentally, the viceroy of Kush who rebelled against Ramesses XI was named Panehesy. On this individual see the index in Török, *Kush*, 567.

76 For a translation see M. Lichtheim, *Ancient Egyptian Literature. A Book of Readings III. The Late Period* (University of California: Berkeley, 1980), 66–84. The relevant passage is on 80; See further, P. Galpaz-Feller, "The Stela of King Piye: A Consideration of 'Clean" and 'Unclean' in Ancient Egypt and the Bible," *RB* 102 (1995), 506–521. In the older scholarly literature the name is given as Pi-ankhi or the like.

77 Török (*Kush*, 83,153) gives Piye's regnal years as ca. 746–716. Török (*ibid.*, 55) dates the stela to ca.727. Piye's descendents ruled Egypt as the twenty-fifth dynasty.

78 On the question of different kinds of circumcision see R. Steiner, "Incomplete Circumcision in Egypt and Edom: Jeremiah (9:24–25) in the Light of Josephus and Jonckheere," *JBL* 118 (1999), 497–526.

79 See Jer 13:23; Amos 9:7 seems to give "Kushite" a negative connotation.

80 M. Buber, *Moses The Revelation and the Covenant* (New York: Harper & Row, 1958), 167–168.

YHWH's appearance in vss. 6–8 defines the qualitative difference between the Mosaic prophecy and that of all other prophets, female and male. Just what is that qualitative difference? It has been customary to compare Num 12:6–8 with the closing lines of Deuteronomy (34:10–12):[81]

> י ולא קם נביא עוד בישראל כמשה אשר ידעו יהוה פנים אל פנים: יא לכל האתות
> והמופתים אשר שלחו יהוה לעשות בארץ מצרים לפרעה ולכל עבדיו ולכל ארצו: יב
> ולכל היד החזקה ולכל המורא הגדול אשר עשה משה לעיני כל ישראל:

> *There never again arose in Israel a prophet like·Moses—whom YHWH knew face to face—for the signs and the wonders that YHWH sent him to perform in the land of Egypt, against Pharaoh and all his servants and all his country, and for all the greatly terrifying deeds which Moses did*[82] *with a strong hand in the sight of all Israel.*

Despite the fact that both passages emphasize the uniqueness of Moses, it is a different uniqueness in each case. The conclusion to Deuteronomy emphasizes that in contrast to the prophets who followed him, it was only Moses who had been given divine authority to perform signs and wonders in the presence of Pharaoh. In addition, it was given to Moses alone to demonstrate his power in the sight of all Israel. But despite the fact that the author of Deut 34:10–12 emphasizes the uniqueness of Moses, he does not cast doubt on the reliability of those later prophets or their prophecies. Indeed, in Deuteronomy itself (Deut 18:15–18) YHWH promises Moses that He will raise up prophets[83] like Moses:

> טו נביא מקרבך מאחיך כמני יקים לך יהוה אלהיך אליו תשמעון: טז ככל אשר שאלת
> מעם יהוה אלהיך בחרב ביום הקהל לאמר לא אסף לשמע את קול יהוה אלהי ואת
> האש הגדלה הזאת לא אראה עוד ולא אמות: יז ויאמר יהוה אלי היטיבו אשר דברו:

---

81 See J. Tigay, "The Significance of the End of Deuteronomy (Deuteronomy 34:10–12)," in *Texts, Temples, and Traditions: A Tribute to Menahem Haran*, ed. M. Fox (Winona Lake: Eisenbrauns, 1996), 137–143.

82 This language of signs and wonders, terrifying deeds and strong hand is elsewhere applied to YHWH's role in the exodus. See Deut 4:35 and the comments in Tigay, *Deuteronomy*, 66, 340.

83 Cf. J. Hayes, "Prophecy and Prophets, Hebrew Bible," *DBI* 2, 310; note the similarity of language. Deut 34:10 has ולא קם נביא...כמשה while Deut 18:15 נביא...כמני יקים and Deut 18:18 has נביא אקים...כמוך.

יח נביא אקים להם מקרב אחיהם כמוך ונתתי דברי בפיו ודבר אליהם את כל אשר
אצונו:יט והיה האיש אשר לא ישמע אל דברי אשר ידבר בשמי אנכי אדרש מעמו:

A prophet like me will YHWH *your god raise up from among your brethren in your behalf. To him you shall listen; in keeping with all you requested of* YHWH *your god at Horeb on the day of assembly, to wit: "Let me not continue to hear the voice of* YHWH *my god, and this great fire let me see no longer, lest I die." So* YHWH *said to me: "Well have they spoken. A prophet will I raise up in their behalf from among your brethren, like you. I will put my words in his mouth and he will speak to them everything I command him to. As for the person who does not listen to my words which he (the prophet) will speak in my name I myself will call him to account."*

The point of the above pericope is that prophets are absolutely necessary because given the risk of death by exposure to the voice of YHWH there must be some alternative means of access to the divine word. YHWH, therefore, will raise up prophets like Moses and place His words in their mouths. These prophetic successors will, like Moses, transmit those divine words to the people. In contrast, the author of Numbers 12 impugns the very nature of prophecy. True, according to Num 12:6 YHWH is made to say something which most biblical writers accept; namely that YHWH reveals himself to his prophets (and even laics)[84] in visions and dreams.[85] But in vs. 8 YHWH tells Aaron and Miriam that He speaks to Moses mouth to mouth and not in riddles. The clear implication is that to all other prophets YHWH does speak in riddles. Rhetorically, this is a brilliant strategy. The author does not deny the claims of Miriam and Aaron that YHWH spoke to them as well as to Moses. YHWH has indeed spoken to female[86] and male prophets but, unfortunately, one cannot count on their reliability because YHWH's revelation to them was through dreams and riddles. By their very nature dreams and riddles require solution and interpretation,

84 See Gen 20:3, 31:24, 41:25.

85 On revelatory dreams see the references in Tigay, *Deuteronomy*, 367, n. 13; Jeremiah does not accept the validity of dreams. A genuine prophet, as opposed to a dreamer, could stand in the divine council (סוד) and have access to reliable prophecy. See Jer 23:22, 25–28; See further Zech 10:2; Rofé has observed that Deut 18:14–20 does not list revelatory dreams as sources of the prophetic word. See A. Rofé, *Introduction to Deuteronomy Part I and further Chapters* (Hebrew; Akademon: Jerusalem, 1988), 61–62; W. McKane, *A Critical and Exegetical Commentary on Jeremiah*, ICC (2 vols.; Edinburgh: T&T Clark, 1986), 1:588–593.

86 It is of interest that in the seventh century Assyrian prophecies collected in SAA 9, nine of the thirteen different prophets are female and four male.

which can be faulty. In contrast to all prophecies by all prophets, the prophecies of Moses require no interpretation. They are completely clear because YHWH speaks to Moses mouth to mouth with Moses beholding YHWH's very image.[87] Linguistically, it has been observed that the phrase פה אל פה אדבר בו...ותמנת יהוה יביט can hardly be separated from the wording of Jer 32:4:[88] ודבר פיו עם פיו ועיניו את עיניו תראינה "His (the king of Babylon) mouth shall speak with his (Zedekiah's) mouth and his eyes shall see his eyes."

There is another well-known pentateuchal tradition about the special character of YHWH's conversations with Moses in Exod 33:9–11:

ט והיה כבא משה האהלה ירד עמוד הענן ועמד פתח האהל ודבר עם משה: י וראה כל העם את עמוד הענן עמד פתח האהל וקם כל העם והשתחוו איש פתח אהלו: יא ודבר יהוה אל משה פנים אל פנים כאשר ידבר איש אל רעהו ושב אל המחנה ומשרתו יהושע בן נון נער לא ימיש מתוך האהל:

It happened that as soon as Moses entered the tent, the pillar of cloud would descend and stand at the entrance to the tent, and (YHWH) would speak to Moses. When all the people would see the pillar of cloud, all the people would rise and each of them would bow down at the entrance of his tent. Then YHWH would speak to Moses face to face, as a man speaks to his friend. Then he would return to the camp, but his assistant, the young Joshua son of Nun, would not leave the interior of the tent.

Levine[89] insists that Exod 33:11 is not to be taken literally. As proof he cites Exod 33:20 where YHWH tells Moses: לא תוכל לראות את פני כי לא יראני האדם וחי "You will not be able to see my face; for no human can see me and live."

The fact though is that Exod 33:20 is not a plain-sense interpretation of Exod 33:11, but a subversion of that passage. By placing the story of divine denial of Moses's request to see the face of God after the story of the tent where YHWH spoke to Moses face to face, the redactor of the chapter attempted to avoid the starkness of the "face to face" language. But in asserting the possibility that humans could see God face to face the writer of Exod 33:11 is not unique. Elsewhere in the Bible there are traditions that claim that humans might

87 For a similar understanding of Num 12:8 see Tigay, *Deuteronomy*, 340.

88 See Licht, *Numbers*, 2:44; The verbs ראה and הביט occur regularly in hendiadys and synonymous parallelism. See e.g., Num 23:21; 2 Kgs 3:14; Isa 42:18, 63:15; Ps 91:8, 142:5.

89 Levine, *Numbers*, 341.

behold God,[90] but in none of these cases does that special privilege undermine the reliability of prophets and prophecy the way in which Numbers 12 does.[91]

Before attempting to account for the uniqueness of Numbers 12 it is necessary to underscore one irony of the chapter. In vss. 6–9 YHWH asserts that He appears to all His prophets, including Miriam and Aaron, in dreams and visions, and that He speaks to them in riddles. In this case however, YHWH speaks to Miriam and Aaron directly and with utmost clarity. Apparently, the need of the author to impart his ideological message overrode the demands of literary consistency. To reiterate what was said at the outset of this article, no pentateuchal narrative is to be connected historically to its alleged chronological setting. Instead, it is to be connected to its time of composition and to the concerns of its author and his contemporaries. In practice this means that stories about such fictitious characters as Abraham, Sarah, Esau, Miriam, Aaron and Moses are to be read as allegories about people, events and institutions between ca. 1200 and 300 BCE.

Numbers 12 has an ideological and didactic message for its audience. The author makes clear to his audience that only the prophecies of Moses are reliable. But as the audience is aware, Moses has long been dead. Where then are his prophecies to be found? As the audience knows, the prophecies of Moses are to be found in the written Torah, from which the audience is hearing the story. If so, then our pericope must date from a period when there was some form of written Torah available, and a time when this written Torah was competing with some other form of prophecy.

The Achaemenid period (539–331 BCE) best fits these conditions. As described in Ezra-Nehemiah,[92] under the Achaemenids the Jews were given limited autonomy to govern themselves by their own laws.[93] Some of the Jewish leaders took the opportunity to collect, edit and expand their traditional

90 According to Exod 24:9–11 the privilege was given to Moses, Aaron, Nadab, Abihu and seventy elders. According to Ps 17:15 David sees God's image.

91 For the possibility that God might deliberately mislead the prophet see J. J. M. Roberts, "Does God Lie? Divine Deceit as a Theological Problem in Israelite Prophetic Literature," VTSup 40 (1988) 211–220. In Isa 6:8–13 the prophet's mission is temporarily to keep the people from comprehending the divine word. See further, R. Veenker, "Do Divinities Deceive?" in *Windows to the Ancient World of the Hebrew Bible: Essays in Honor of Samuel Greengus*, eds. B. Arnold, N. Erickson and J. Walton (Winona Lake: Eisenbrauns, 2014), 201–213.

92 See Ezra 7:11–26 esp. vss. 25–26.

93 For a thorough discussion of the literature assessing the reasons for the Achaemenid treatment of the Jews see L. Fried, *The Priest and the Great King. Temple-Palace Relations in the Persian Empire* (Winona Lake: Eisenbrauns, 2004).

literature,[94] including what would become the Torah. What was to be the relation between the old form of prophecy delivered by inspired individuals, and prophecies preserved in written form?[95] The answer given by the author of Numbers 12 was that although the older form of prophecy was indeed the word of YHWH, it was flawed because of its lack of clarity. In contrast, the prophecies of Moses were the result of direct and clear communication. One no longer needed to rely on individual prophets[96] because the Torah of Moses was the highest form of prophecy.[97] Only in the Torah were the revelations of God to be found in their purest form.

94 The process actually began with the Josianic reform. See M. Weinfeld, *Deuteronomy* 1–11, (AB 5; New York: Doubleday, 1991), 18. But Josiah was dead by 609 and the monarchy of Judah perished soon thereafter.

95 Cf. Budd's statement: "Mosaic revelation has a unique and supreme authority and thus is paved the way for the 'Mosaic law' of the post-exilic period. Miriam and Aaron appear together to represent the claims of prophetic inspiration ... Even prophetic revelation is subordinate to Mosaic religion." See R. J. Budd, *Numbers*, WBC 5 (Waco: Word Books, 1984), 38. Budd dates Numbers 12 to the seventh century, but views the chapter as paving the way for post-exilic thinking. Budd's contrast between "prophecy" and "law/Mosaic religion," is a bit more theological than necessary. Numbers 12 contrasts not law and prophecy but Mosaic prophecy and that of all others.

96 There may be some allegorical connection between Numbers 12 and Neh 6:14: וגם לנועדיה הנביאה וליתר הנביאים אשר היו מיראים אותי, "(And requite) Noadiah the woman prophet and the other prophets who were intimidating me." It is tempting to argue that "Miriam" of Numbers 12 is an allegorical reflex of Noadiah about whom there is no other extant biblical or extrabiblical material. But the reading is far from certain. See D. Marcus, "Is the Book of Nehemiah a Translation from Aramaic?" in *Boundaries of the Ancient Near Eastern World: A Tribute to Cyrus Gordon*, eds. M. Lubetski, C. Gottlieb and S. Keller (JSOTSup 273; Sheffield, U.K.: Sheffield Academic, 1998), 107–108.

97 Hayes ("Prophecy," 310) reached a similar conclusion about Numbers 12 from a canonical perspective: "With all other prophets in a subordinate position to Moses, the prophetic canon is placed in a secondary position to the Torah." Hayes notes in this connection that the end of Malachi (3:22), the last book in the prophetic section of the OT, concludes with the admonition to recall the Torah of Moses. Similarly, Rofé had already shown that, in the canonical shape of the Hebrew Bible, care has been taken to refer to Torah study in Josh 1:8; and Ps 1:2. The message is that Torah takes precedence over the Prophets and Hagiographa. See A. Rofé, "The Devotion to Torah-Study at the End of the Biblical Period: Joshua 1:8, Psalms 1:2; Isaiah 59:21," in *The Bible in the Light of its Interpreters Sarah Kamin Memorial Volume*, ed. S. Japhet (Jerusalem: Magnes, 1994), 622–628.

CHAPTER 18

The Law and the Prophet

The most significant question related to the theology of Scripture is the standing of Scripture itself within Judaism and Christianity. The present essay attempts to show how the concept of Scripture originated within the Bible. It is well known that both the canon of the Old Testament and the canon of the New Testament[1] represent the final stages of selection and collection.[2] Within the present OT and NT we see how some late authors commented explicitly on earlier literary productions that were already Scripture for them. For example, the exilic or postexilic author of Josh 8:30–31 takes pains to show that Joshua built an altar on Mount Ebal in conformity with the regulations of "the book of the law of Moses":

1 The designations "Old Testament" (OT) and "New Testament" (NT) carry theological implications. According to one NT writer the divine word to Jeremiah (31:31) that God would in the future make a "new testament" or "new covenant" (Hebrew: ברית חדשה) with Israel, was a prophecy that Christianity would supersede Judaism: "By speaking of a new testament he has pronounced the first one obsolete; and anything that is becoming obsolete and growing old will surely disappear." (Heb 8:13) By the end of the second century, OT and NT had become literary terms to distinguish the earlier, originally Jewish, collection from the later, specifically Christian, writings. (See Clement of Alexandria, *Stromateis* 1.28.2; 3.71.3. I thank my colleague Prof. Adam Kamesar for these references.) In recent years some Jewish and Christian scholars have attempted to replace OT and NT with other terminology. Some prefer the acronym "Tanak(h)," formed from the initial Hebrew letters of the threefold Jewish division *Torah* = Genesis-Deuteronomy, *Nevi'im* = Joshua-Malachi, and *Ketuvim* = Psalms-2 Chronicles but this designation seems a bit recherché. "Older Testament" and "Newer Testament" are occasionally heard, but they are too cute. In addition, "Newer Testament" (along with "New Testament," which used to pass muster with virtually all Jews) is unacceptable to many Jews because they reject the sacred character of these writings. Another proffered solution has been to refer to the OT as "Jewish Scriptures," denying the historical fact that they are Christian as well. Similarly, to call the NT "Christian Scriptures" as some Jewish writers have recently begun doing is confusing to many Christians and other Gentiles who designate the OT and NT collectively as "Christian Scriptures." In light of the above I have chosen to retain "Old Testament" and "New Testament" as convenient literary terms long sanctioned by usage.

2 See J. Sanders, "Canon, Hebrew Bible," *ABD* 1:837–852; and H. Gamble, "Canon, New Testament," *ABD* 1:852–861.

 | DOI 10.1163/9789004340879_019

> At that time Joshua built an altar to Yahweh the God of Israel on Mount Ebal. The altar was blocks of unhewn stone on which no iron tool had been used, as Moses the servant of God had commanded the people of Israel, as it is written in the book of the law of Moses, "an altar of unhewn stones, upon which no man has lifted an iron tool"; and they offered on it burnt offerings to Yahweh, and sacrificed peace offerings.

In this instance the author of Josh 8:30–31 shows how Joshua followed the law of Moses, by making specific reference to that which was written in the "book of the law of Moses," in Deut 27:1–8.[3]

Another late author, the writer of Neh 13:1–3 takes a further step:

> On that day they read from the book of Moses in the hearing of the people; and in it was found written that no Ammonite or Moabite should ever enter the assembly of God; for they did not meet the children of Israel with bread and water, but hired Balaam against them to curse them—yet our God turned the curse into a blessing. When the people heard the law, they separated from Israel all those of mixed descent.

The reference to what was read in the book of Moses is to Deut 23:4–6, verses that prohibit marriage with two specific groups for very specific reasons. Yet the reaction to the law is to separate *all* people of mixed descent from Israel.[4]

Nehemiah 8, likewise set in the fifth century BCE,[5] takes us into the realm of legal exegesis or legal midrash:[6]

> On the second day the heads of fathers' houses of all the people, with the priests and the Levites, came together to Ezra the scribe to study the words of the Torah. And they found written in the Torah that Yahweh had assigned to Moses that the people of Israel should dwell in booths during the feast of the seventh month, and they should publish and proclaim in

3 See S. Ahituv, *Joshua: Introduction and Commentary* (Jerusalem: Magnes, 1995), 141–143.

4 On the specific exegetical strategies involved here, see M. Fishbane, *Biblical Interpretation in Ancient Israel* (Oxford: Clarendon, 1985), 114–128.

5 Possibly the setting is the fourth century if Ezra's activity is dated in the reign of Artaxerxes II. On the chronological problems, see H. G. M. Williamson, *Ezra, Nehemiah* (WBC 16; Waco, Tex.: Word Books, 1985), xxxix–xliv.

6 With the following cf. Fishbane, *Interpretation*, 109–113; Cf. further, H. G. M. Williamson, "History," in *It Is Written- Scripture Citing Scripture: Essays in Honour of Barnabas Lindars SSF*, eds. D. A. Carson and H. G. M. Williamson (Cambridge: Cambridge University, 1988), 29–30.

> all their towns and in Jerusalem:[7] "Go out[8] to the hills and bring branches of olive and wild olive, myrtle and palm and other leafy trees to make booths," as it is written. So the people went out and brought them and made booths for themselves, each on his roof and in their courts and in the courts of the house of God, and in the square at the Water Gate and the square at the Gate of Ephraim. And all the assembly of those who had returned from the captivity made booths and dwelt in booths; for from the days of Jeshua the son of Nun to that day the people of Israel had not done so. And there was very great rejoicing. And day by day, from the first day to the last day, he read from the book of the Torah of God. They kept the feast seven days; and on the eighth day there was a solemn assembly, according to the ordinance. (Neh 8:13–18)

The source text that they found "written in the Torah" is apparently Lev 23:39–43:

> On the fifteenth day of the seventh month, when you have gathered in the produce of the land, you shall keep the feast of Yahweh seven days; on the first day shall be a solemn assembly, and on the eighth day shall be a solemn assembly. You shall take for yourselves on the first day the fruit of goodly trees, branches of palm trees, and boughs of leafy trees, and willows of the brook; and you shall rejoice before Yahweh your God seven days. You shall keep it as a feast to Yahweh seven days in the year; it is a statute for ever throughout your generations; you shall keep it in the seventh month. You shall dwell in booths for seven days; all that are native in Israel shall dwell in booths, that your generations may know that I made the people of Israel dwell in booths when I brought them out of the land of Egypt: I am Yahweh your God.

The author of Nehemiah 8 felt the need to make a connection between the command to dwell in booths in Lev 23:42 and the command to collect the fruit, the branches, the boughs and the willows in Lev 23:40. He made the connection by instructing his audience to use the collected objects as material with which to construct the booths. But the activity in which Ezra and his contemporaries were engaged is more important than the particular solution at which they arrived. According to Neh 8:13 the Jews assembled "to study the words

7 The LXX reads: "and that they should sound with trumpets in all their cities and in Jerusalem."

8 LXX reads: "Esdras said 'go out ...'" This appears to be a better reading because it is difficult to derive the command to go out to the mountains from Lev 23:40. For a different solution, see Williamson, "History," 30.

of the Torah." The Hebrew verb להשכיל, which we translated idiomatically as "study," literally means "look at," "gain insight into," and "seek."[9] It is especially significant that in at least one biblical passage[10] the verb is a synonym of דרש, which likewise means "seek," "look at." In the OT, דרש often takes a divinity or object of worship as its direct object with the technical or mantic sense "to inquire of a divinity."[11] In the book of Ezra however, the same verb is used with the direct object "Torah";[12] the use of the synonym להשכיל points to the same activity, the direction of mantic activity to a document rather than to a divinity.[13] "For Ezra had set his heart to study [Hebrew: דרש] the Torah of Yahweh and to observe it, and to teach his statutes and ordinances in Israel." (Ezra 7:10)

The above examples illustrate the legal application of earlier tenets by later writers. At least equally significant is the application of earlier prophecy to the situation of the later readers. A good example is provided by the author of chapter 9 of the Book of Daniel:

> In the first year of Darius the son of Ahasuerus by birth a Mede, who became king over the realm of the Chaldeans—in the first year of his reign, I, Daniel, was studying in the books the number of years which, according to the word of Yahweh to Jeremiah the prophet, must pass before the end of the desolations of Jerusalem, that is, seventy years. (Dan 9:1–2)

In this instance the writer of these verses has been studying "the books" (Hebrew: ספרים) that contain the words of the prophet Jeremiah. "Daniel"

9 See the study by M. Weinfeld, ,"דיק, עין, שכל: A Semantic Analysis," in *Tehillah le-Moshe: Biblical and Judaic Studies in Honor of Moshe Greenberg*, eds. M. Cogan, B. Eichler, and J. Tigay (Winona Lake: Eisenbrauns, 1997), 101–106 (in Hebrew section).

10 Ps 14:2= Ps 53:3.

11 E.g., Gen 25:22; Exod 18:15; Deut 18:11; 1Sam 9:9; 2Kgs 1:3, 16.

12 This is the beginning of a process that is carried further in the Dead Sea Scrolls in which דורש התורה, "explicator of Torah," appears and that reaches its culmination in rabbinic מדרש, a word from the same root. Cf. I. Gruenwald, "Midrash and the 'Midrashic Condition'; Preliminary Considerations," in *The Midrashic Imagination*, ed. M. Fishbane (Albany: State University of New York, 1993), 9. In rabbinic midrash the biblical text is viewed as an "independent entity... which can be interrogated to answer religious questions." See M. Idel, "Midrashic versus Other Forms of Jewish Hermeneutic: Some Comparative Reflections," in *Midrashic Imagination*, 49.

13 Note that in another postexilic source "the great Torah hymn," Ps 119, the object of דרש is sometimes a synonym of תורה. Thus, in Ps 119:45, 94 the object is פקודים, "commands," while in Ps 119:155 the object is חקים, "laws."

expects that once the prophetic word has been uttered, it must ultimately find fulfillment. In the words of Deutero-Isaiah (40:8), "the word of our God will endure forever." This notion "was deeply rooted in the primary mantic character of prophecy in Israel"[14] already in pre-exilic times, for, after all, the criterion for determining that an individual was a true prophet was that the words spoken by that prophet materialized.[15] In the pre-exilic period however, most prophecy was directed to the near future rather than to some time far off and distant. In addition, and no less significant, most prophecy reached its audience orally rather than in writing.[16] For reasons both technical and ideological, matters changed considerably beginning in the exilic period. First, only the written prophecies of the pre-exilic period survived, presumably those which had been "authenticated" by history. Second, the exilic and later prophets, notably Deutero-Isaiah, turned to the fulfillment of earlier prophecy as proof that Yahweh alone was divine: "The fact that only the Word of Yahweh of Israel has come true proves that he is the only true God."[17] Paradoxically, the availability of prophetic statements in written form centuries after their original utterance enhanced the value of "Scripture" at the expense of live prophecy. In the exilic period the notion developed that "every true prophecy is to be fulfilled in due time."[18] Inasmuch as true prophecy was to be found in Scripture, once there was a Scripture it was difficult for a living prophet to compete with

14 See A. Rofé, "How is the Word Fulfilled? Isaiah 55:6–11 within the Theological Debate of Its Time," in *Canon, Theology and Old Testament Interpretations: Essays in Honor of Brevard S. Childs*, eds. G. Tucker, D. Petersen and R. Wilson (Philadelphia: Fortress, 1988), 246; I. L. Seeligmann, "The Understanding of Prophecy in Deuteronomistic and Chronistic History," in *I. L. Seeligmann Studies in Biblical Literature*, eds. A. Hurvitz, E. Tov and S. Japhet (Jerusalem: Magnes, 1992), 205–228.

15 See Deut 18:21–22; cf. Rofé, "How Is the Word Fulfilled?" 250–251.

16 These two phenomena are closely related. Oral prophecies would normally not survive as long as written ones. At the divine command Jeremiah committed his prophecies to writing, but these written words were meant for oral delivery to Jeremiah's contemporaries rather than for an audience of later readers. (See Jer 36:1–8 and contrast W. Holladay, *Jeremiah 2: A Commentary on the Book of the Prophet Jeremiah, Chapters 26–52* [Hermeneia; Philadelphia: Fortress, 1989], 245–255.) Note that God tells Jeremiah to put sale documents in a pottery vessel "so that they might be preserved for many days." (Jer 32:14) He does not command Jeremiah to do the same for his collected prophecies.

17 Rofé, "How Is the Word Fulfilled?" 251; see also Zech 1:4–6; 7:8–14.

18 Rofé, "How is the Word Fulfilled?" 251. For the different terminologies expressing the concept, see n. 17. An anonymous teaching cited in *b. Meg.* 14a distinguishes between scriptural prophecy and nonscriptural prophecy: "Many prophets arose for them—the Israelites—twice as many as those (Israelites) who left Egypt. Prophecy which was necessary for future generations was written down but prophecy which was unnecessary [for

it. But where did the notion of Scripture as true prophecy originate? I suggest that the source of that notion is Num 12:1–8:[19]

> Miriam and Aaron spoke against Moses because of the Kushite woman whom he had married, for he had married a Kushite woman; and they said, "Has Yahweh indeed spoken only to Moses? Has he not spoken to us also?" And Yahweh heard it. Now the man Moses was very meek, more than all men who were on the face of the earth. But Yahweh immediately said to Moses and to Aaron and Miriam, "Come out, you three, to the tent of meeting." And the three of them came out. Then Yahweh came down in a pillar of cloud, and stood at the door of the tent and called, "Aaron and Miriam"; and they both came forward. And he said "Hear my words: If there is a prophet of Yahweh among you, I make myself known to him in a vision, I speak with him in a dream. Not so with my servant Moses; in all my household he alone is reliable.[20] With him I speak mouth to mouth, clearly, and not in riddles; and he be holds the image of Yahweh. Why then were you not afraid to speak against my servant, against Moses?"

Num 12:6–8 is often compared to Deut 34:10–12, which likewise stresses the uniqueness of Moses, but the two pericopes have a rather different message, a point that becomes clear by juxtaposing them. Deut 34:10–12 reads:

> And there never again rose in Israel a prophet like Moses, whom Yahweh knew face to face, none like him for all the signs and the wonders which Yahweh sent him to do in the land of Egypt, to Pharaoh and to all his servants and to all his land, and for all the mighty power and all the great and terrible deeds which Moses wrought in the sight of all Israel.

What is emphasized in Deuteronomy 34 is the power of the prophet Moses to perform signs, wonders, and mighty deeds.[21] That these signs and wonders

---

future generations] was not written down." On this understanding all scriptural prophecy remains relevant and ultimately applicable.

19 With the following cf. S. D. Sperling, "Miriam, Aaron and Moses: Sibling Rivalry," *HUCA* 70/71 (1999–2000), 39–55; reprinted with minor revisions in this volume.

20 So approximately, NEB and REB.

21 It has been argued that the end of Deuteronomy may have the political intent of contrasting Moses's (=Deuteronomic) opposition to syncretism with those prophetic teachings that legitimated certain forms of syncretism in the cult of Yahweh. See J. Tigay, "The Significance of the End of Deuteronomy (Deuteronomy 34:10–12)," in *Texts, Temples, and*

were done in the sight of the entire people and had the effect of freeing the people from the power of Pharaoh distinguished Moses from all subsequent prophets. Yet according to Deuteronomy 34 the fact that Moses was more intimate with Yahweh than were other prophets did not result in prophecies that were qualitatively better or more reliable—the validity of prophecies uttered by prophets other than Moses was not called into question.

In contrast, Numbers 12 undermines the validity of all non-Mosaic prophecy. The writer begins by seconding what is commonly acknowledged by prophets, namely that they receive dreams[22] and visions from Yahweh. But in the continuation the writer observes that only Moses is a reliable prophet because Yahweh speaks to him "mouth to mouth." The additional information that to him alone Yahweh speaks "clearly, not in riddles" means only one thing: that to all other prophets Yahweh speaks unclearly and in riddles. The rhetorical strategy employed by the writer is brilliant.[23] There is no opposition to the claim of Miriam and Aaron that Yahweh has not spoken to Moses alone (vs. 2). The writer concedes that Yahweh has indeed spoken to other male and female prophets. Unfortunately, none of them is reliable because Yahweh spoke to them in riddles, thereby leaving room for faulty interpretation. In contrast, the prophecy of Moses leaves nothing to the imagination. But if that is the point of the narrative, what are its implications?

It has become increasingly clear since the 1970's that nothing in the narrative of the Pentateuch is historical.[24] Although the events related in the Pentateuch are set in a period before the rise of the Israelite states, it can now be said with confidence that this temporal[25] setting is fictitious. I have suggested elsewhere

Traditions: A Tribute to Menahem Haran, eds. M. Fox, V. Hurowitz, A. Hurvitz, M. Klein, B. Schwartz and N. Shupak (Winona Lake: Eisenbrauns), 137–143.

22 Jeremiah does not accept the validity of dreams, but he does appear to believe that a genuine prophet could stand in the divine council and have access to reliable prophecy. See Jer 23:22, 25–28. On dreams, cf. Zech 10:2.

23 A similar strategy is employed by the writer of Deut 18:16–19, who provides an etiology of prophecy in Israel. He admits that all Israelites heard the divine voice at Horeb. But the Israelites themselves requested never again to hear the voice of Yahweh directly lest they perish. That Yahweh ever since that time speaks to Israel only through prophetic intermediaries is therefore not to be seen as prophetic self-aggrandizement but as Yahweh's acquiescence to Israel's request.

24 See conveniently, N. Lemche, "Israel, History of, Premonarchic Period," *ABD* 3:526–545.

25 Often this holds for the spatial setting as well. It is now clear that Israel arose through some kind of political realignment within Canaan. Archaeology has falsified the biblical claims that Israel was enslaved in Egypt, trekked through the Sinai desert, and conquered the promised land. See W. Dever, "Israel, History of, Archaeology and the Israelite

that all of the pentateuchal narrative should be categorized as "allegorical."[26] That is, stories about such fictitious characters as Abraham, Isaac, Jacob, Esau, Moses, Miriam, and Aaron refer allegorically to characters in the historical period between ca.1100–400 BCE. To take a well known example, the "discovery" by "Jacob" in Genesis 28 that Bethel is a holy place, a perfect site for a sanctuary, is a transparent legitimation of the designation of Bethel as a holy site by Jeroboam I.[27] As such, a story about the competing prophetic talents of Moses, Miriam, and Aaron should be read not simply as a statement about prophetic worthies of a fictitious past but as an ideological statement made by a writer attempting to influence an audience in a matter of contemporary importance. Viewed from that perspective the story in Numbers 12, which bears the message that all prophecy other than that of Moses is unreliable,[28] must emanate from a time in which the prophecy of Moses could be measured against all other prophetic competition. The historical period that fills that requirement is the Persian period (539–331 BCE).[29] According to the book of Ezra-Nehemiah, it

---

'Conquest,'" *ABD* 3:545–558. This means that stories set in Egypt and in the desert before the "conquest" are allegorical both temporally and spatially. See the following note.

26 For an attempt to apply allegoresis systematically as a hermeneutical tool in interpreting the narratives of the Pentateuch, see S. D. Sperling, *The Original Torah: The Political Intent of the Bible's Writers* (New York: New York University, 1998).

27 See Sperling, *Original Torah*, 95–97.

28 The biblical authors did not unanimously praise prophecy or the holders of the prophetic office. See D. Marcus, *From Balaam to Jonah: Anti-Prophetic Satire in the Hebrew Bible* (Atlanta: Scholars, 1995). It will be recalled that in 1Kgs 22:22–23 the possibility is raised that Yahweh himself might permit a deceitful spirit to mislead prophets and thus deceive their audiences. For the 1Kings 22 passage and others, see J. J. M. Roberts "Does God Lie? Divine Deceit As a Theological Problem in Israelite Prophetic Literature," in *Congress Volume: Jerusalem 1986* (=VTSup 40), ed. J. A. Emerton (Leiden: Brill, 1988), 211–220; cf. A. Rofé, *Introduction to the Prophetic Literature* (Jerusalem: Academon, 1992), 55; See further, R. Veenker, "Do Divinities Deceive?" in *Windows to the Ancient World of the Hebrew Bible: Essays in Honor of Samuel Greengus*, eds. B. Arnold, N. Erickson and J. Walton (Winona Lake: Eisenbrauns, 2014), 201–213. The story in 1Kings 22 may be late. (Rofé, *Introduction*, 61); Barstad argues that the book of Deuteronomy holds a negative view of prophecy. See H. Barstad, "The Understanding of the Prophets in Deuteronomy," *SJT* 8 (1994), 236–251; contrast K. Jeppesen, "Is Deuteronomy Hostile Toward Prophets?" *SJT* 8 (1994), 252–256.

29 Cf. P. J. Budd, *Numbers* (WBC 5; Waco, Texas: Word Books, 1984), 138: "Mosaic revelation has a unique and supreme authority and, thus it paved the way for 'Mosaic law' of the postexilic period. Miriam and Aaron appear together to represent the claims of prophetic inspiration ... Even prophetic revelation is subordinate to Mosaic religion." Budd dates

was on the authority of the Achaemenids that the Jews were given the opportunity to live by their own laws.[30] Taking advantage of this opportunity the Jews assembled their earlier literature, including prophecies that had been verified by the events of history. What was to be the relation between the prophecies of the past, which were now available in written form, and the prophetic word of living prophets? The author of Numbers 12 answered the question by writing a story in which the legitimacy of living prophecy was not directly questioned.[31] Instead, living prophecy was described as flawed because it was like a riddle that needed to be solved. In contrast, the prophecies of Moses were to be found in the Torah, which, it is claimed, was straightforward and did not need to be solved.[32]

According to Numbers 12 there is no conflict between law and prophecy.[33] Rather, the Torah of Moses, which contains the law, is the highest form of prophecy. Only in the Torah is the divine word available in clear and reliable form. Gradually this notion was extended to other writings, some of these produced within the very circles of prophecy denigrated by the author of Numbers 12. By the late first century CE, Josephus could describe the Jewish sources on which he relied for the details of his people's doings in remote antiquity as

---

Numbers 12 to the seventh century but views the chapter as paving the way for postexilic thinking.

30 See Ezra 7:25–26. The Jews were not treated uniquely in this respect. For a parallel treatment of Egyptians under Achaemenid rule, see E. Meyer and F. Altheim, cited by M. Fishbane, *Biblical Interpretation*, 37 n. 53; J. Blenkinsopp, "The Mission of Udjahorresnet and Those of Ezra and Nehemiah," *JBL* 106 (1987), 409–421; see further K. Hoglund, *Achaemenid Imperial Administration in Syria-Palestine and the Missions of Ezra and Nehemiah* (Atlanta: Scholars, 1992).

31 Numbers 12 may have some bearing on Neh 6:14, a verse in which Nehemiah mentions a certain "Noadiah the woman prophet [Heb.: נביאה] and the rest of the prophets who were used to intimidating me." Possibly, "Miriam" of Num 12 is an allegorical representative of this Noadiah of whom nothing is otherwise known. Note however, that the Peshitta and other ancient versions reflect here the masculine form נביא. See D. Marcus, "Is Nehemiah a Translation from Aramaic?" in *Boundaries of the Ancient Near Eastern World: A Tribute to Cyrus H. Gordon*, eds. M. Lubetski, C. Gottlieb and S. Keller (JSOTSup 273; Sheffield: Sheffield Academic, 1998), 107–108.

32 In contrast, classical rabbinic Judaism sometimes expressed the opposite opinion: Rabbi Yannai (third century CE) said, "The words of the Torah were not given as clear-cut decisions." (*Midr. Ps.* 12:4) The text is cited from D. W. Halivni, "From Midrash to Mishnah: Theological Repercussions and Further Clarifications of 'chate'u yisrael,'" *Midrashic Imagination*, 30.

33 Contra Budd, *Numbers*, 138.

the writings of prophets who learned what to write from "God himself by inspiration."[34] Subsequently, Jewish rabbinic tradition asserted that the canonical writings of the second and third divisions of the OT,[35] the Prophets (*Nevi'im*) and the Writings (*Ketuvim*), had been produced under the influence of the holy spirit (Hebrew: רוח הקדש).[36] Thus Rabbi Simeon b. Menasia (second–third century CE), who considered Song of Songs canonical, said:

> The Song of Songs defiles the hands [=is canonical] because it was uttered by means of the holy spirit. Qoheleth does not defile the hands [=is not canonical] because it is of Solomon's [own] wisdom.[37]

But in Jewish thinking this same holy spirit had ceased to operate directly through persons in the Persian period: "With the death of the last prophets, Haggai, Zechariah, and Malachi, the holy spirit departed from Israel."[38]

Similarly, citing Dan 11:3, "a great king shall arise," the *Seder Olam Rabbah*[39] comments:

> He is Alexander of Macedonia who reigned for twelve years. Until then the prophets used to prophesy by means of the holy spirit. [Hebrew:

34 In *Against Apion* 1.7 Josephus uses the term ἐπίπνοια, "breathing upon," "inspiration." (See LSJ, 652.).

35 On the development of the threefold division, see A. Hurvitz, "On the Borderline between Biblical Criticism and Hebrew Linguistics: The Emergence of the Term ספר משה," in *Tehillah le-Moshe*, 42 n. 18 (in Hebrew section).

36 On רוח הקדש, see A. Unterman, *EncJud* 14:364–366. As Unterman observes, the phrase occurs in the Bible (e.g., Isa 63:10), but its technical meaning is post-biblical. In Biblical Hebrew, the רוח "breath," of Yahweh (Num 11:29; 2Sam 23:2) or Elohim (Num 24:2, 1Sam 10:10) may confer the gift of prophecy. In rabbinic sources, הקדש "the Holy," served as a euphemism for the older Hebrew names for God. Consequently, the biblical term רוח הקדש could be reinterpreted as "spirit of God = Prophecy."

37 For the connection between canonical books and ritual impurity, see Shamma Friedman, "Holy Scriptures Defile the Hands," in *Minḥa le-Naḥum: Biblical and Other Studies Presented to Nahum M. Sarna in Honour of his 70th Birthday*, eds. M. Brettler and M. Fishbane (JSOTSup 154; Sheffield: Sheffield Academic, 1993), 117–132; The connection between canonicity and defilement of the hands is rejected by S. Leiman, *The Canonization of the Hebrew Scriptures* (Hamden: Archon, 1976), 102–128.

38 *b. Sanh.* 11a. Rabbi Joshua b. Korhah (second century CE) identified Malachi with Ezra. See *b. Meg.* 15a.

39 For the text, see M. Weinstock, ed., *Seder Olam Rabbah Ha-shalem* (Jerusalem: Torat Hesed, 1961), 3:466–467.

> רוח הקדש][40] From this time forth:[41] "Incline your ear and listen to the words of the sages." (Prov 22:17)[42]

Rabbinic tradition saw the period of Ezra as the beginning of rabbinic Judaism because the rabbis accepted the notion that the Torah was Mosaic. For them the cessation of prophecy was coeval with the beginning of rabbinism, not with the compilation of the Pentateuch. Ironically, nineteenth-century biblical criticism, largely a Protestant enterprise, agreed that the law and its Pharisaic-rabbinic application had put an end to prophecy.[43] Functionally of course this was true, but, in theory, prophecy survived in a new medium, that of Scripture.

Jewish scriptural thinking found its successor in Christianity. For example, 2Tim 3:16–17 reads:

---

40 In later sources some distinction is made between רוח הקדש and prophecy. See Halivni in Fishbane, *Midrashic Imagination*, 40 n. 13.

41 Cf. *t.Yad.* 2:13. Cf. further Josephus, *Against Apion* 1.8: "For we have not an innumerable multitude of books among us, disagreeing from and contradicting one another, as the Greeks have, but only twenty-two books, which contain the records of all the past times; which are justly believed to be divine; and of them five belong to Moses, which contain his laws and the traditions of the origin of mankind till his death. This interval of time was little short of three thousand years; but as to the time from the death of Moses till the reign of Artaxerxes king of Persia, who reigned after Xerxes, the prophets, who were after Moses, wrote down what was done in their times in thirteen books. The remaining four books contain hymns to God, and precepts for the conduct of human life. It is true, our history hath been written since Artaxerxes very particularly, but hath not been esteemed of the like authority with the former by our forefathers, because there hath not been an exact succession of prophets since that time; and how firmly we have given credit to these books of our own nation is evident by what we do; for during so many ages as have already passed, no one has been so bold as either to add any thing to them, to take any thing from them, or to make any change in them; but it is become natural to all Jews immediately, and from their very birth, to esteem these books to contain divine doctrines, and to persist in them, and, if occasion be, willingly to die for them."

42 In rabbinic chronology there is not much difference between the talmudic source and *Seder Olam Rabbah* because the latter source allotted only thirty-four years between the rebuilding of the temple (516/515 BCE) and the reign of Alexander. See *EncJud* 14:1092.

43 For references, see U. F. W. Bauer, "Anti-Jewish Interpretations of Psalm 1 in Luther and in Modern German Protestantism," *Journal of Hebrew Scriptures* (Electronic) 2 (1998), 1–27, esp. 12. The irony is that for the classical rabbis the end of prophecy was a positive development, divinely sanctioned.

> All Scripture is inspired by God [Greek: θεόπνευστος; lit.,"God-breathed"] and beneficial for teaching, for reproving, for setting things straight, for disciplining in righteousness that the man of God may be fully competent, completely equipped for every good work.

But the daughter religion differed with its mother in two significant ways. First, and not without controversy,[44] classical Christianity accepted the Old Testament as Scripture, while rabbinic Judaism rejected the New Testament.[45] Second, when it came to the manner of interpretation, much of the NT interprets the OT very narrowly in what is often referred to as "fulfillment exegesis." For the NT writers, OT Scripture was a coded prophecy predicting what would happen in the end of days, in which they perceived themselves to be living.[46] Accordingly, these writers viewed all of OT Scripture as a prediction of what would happen to them and their contemporaries. Here is a well-known example from the second chapter of Matthew:

> Now when they had departed, behold, an angel of the Lord appeared to Joseph in a dream and said, "Rise, take the child and his mother, and flee to Egypt, and remain there till I tell you; for Herod is about to search for the child, to destroy him." And he rose and took the child and his mother by night, and departed to Egypt, and remained there until the death of Herod. This was to fulfill[47] what the Lord had spoken by the prophet "Out of Egypt have I called my son." (Hosea 11:1)

44 The best-known opponents of the OT as Christian Scripture were the Marcionites and the Gnostics.

45 The NT writings do not "defile the hands" according to *t. Yad.* 2:13. There was some rabbinic controversy about whether the fact that NT books (presumably owned by Jewish Christians) contained the name of God obligated Jews to attempt to rescue them from a blaze. See *t. Šabb.* 13:5.

46 The roots of fulfillment exegesis are in the OT itself as may be seen in the example of Daniel 9 cited above. Two other good examples are 1Kgs 2:27 and 2Chr 36:22. The tendency is especially pronounced in the pesher literature of the Qumran community. See D. Dimant, "Pesharim, Qumran," *ABD* 5:244–251.

47 The Greek verb employed here, πληρόω, "make full," (LSJ, 1419–1420) is the same used by the Septuagint to translate Hebrew כלה, "bring to an end," "complete," and מלא, "fill up," when these verbs connote "fulfill a prophecy." See 1Kgs 2:27; 2Chr 36:21; 2Chr 36:22; See further G. Delling, "πληρόω," *TDNT* 6:286–298; C. Moule, "Fulfill," *IDB* 2:327–338; G. Tucker, "Exegesis," *IDBSup* 296–303; G. Stanton, "Matthew," in *It Is Written*, 205–219.

In contrast, the rabbis, who probably were a subgroup within the larger Pharisaic community,[48] read expansively. They applied to Scripture the same kinds of methods that Hellenistic[49] and Mesopotamian[50] scholars had brought to their texts. By inference from minor to major, inference by analogy, extension of a regulation found in one biblical passage to another passage, derivation of laws from apparently superfluous words, and the use of word play,[51] the rabbis made it possible to derive new laws from the ancient texts as well as to find support in the biblical text for traditions that had arisen independently of Scripture. By opening up the Torah in this manner, rabbinic Judaism laid the foundations for the forms of Judaism that were to survive until the end of the eighteenth century.

With the close of the NT, Christian exegesis became more complex. Hirshman observes that we can identify many more genres of written exegesis in Christian sources of late antiquity than in Jewish writings of the same period.[52] Nonetheless, because Christian polemics were often based on the desire to demonstrate that the Jews had failed to interpret their own Scripture correctly,[53] Christian reading of Scripture continued (and continues) to bind the OT and NT much more closely than Jewish reading bound the OT to rabbinic tradition.[54] Martin Luther, who spearheaded Christianity's return to Scripture, was committed to the exegetical principle that in interpreting OT texts, "the *sensus literalis* is at the same time the *sensus propheticus*, that is, refers to Jesus Christ."[55]

48 For recent bibliography on rabbinic origins, see H. Strack and G. Stemberger, *Introduction to Talmud and Midrash* (Edinburgh: T&T Clark, 1991), 1–2.

49 See Saul Lieberman, *Hellenism in Jewish Palestine* (New York: Jewish Theological Seminary of America, 1950), 47–82.

50 See Stephen Lieberman, "A Mesopotamian Background for the So-Called Aggadic 'Measures' of Biblical Hermeneutics?" *HUCA* 58 (1987), 157–225.

51 See the chapter on rabbinic hermeneutics in Strack and Stemberger, *Talmud and Midrash*, 17–34; for detailed studies, see D. W. Halivni, *Peshat and Derash: Plain and Applied Meaning in Rabbinic Exegesis* (New York: Oxford University, 1991); *idem*, "Reflections on Classical Jewish Hermeneutics," *PAAJR* 62 (1996), 21–127.

52 See M. Hirshman, *A Rivalry of Genius: Jewish and Christian Biblical Interpretation in Late Antiquity* (trans. B. Stein; Albany: State University of New York, 1996), 21.

53 See R. Hvalvik, *The Struggle for Scripture and Covenant: The Purpose of the Epistle of Barnabas and Jewish-Christian Competition in the Second Century* (Tübingen: Mohr Siebeck, 1996) and the review by R. F. Hull Jr., *JECS* 6 (1998), 325–327.

54 See J. Levenson, "Why Jews are Not Interested in Biblical Theology," in *Judaic Perspectives on Ancient Israel*, eds. J. Neusner, B. A. Levine, and E. Frerichs (Philadelphia: Fortress, 1987), 281–307, esp. 286.

55 Bauer, "Psalm 1," 5.

The adversarial history of Judaism and Christianity over the centuries has falsified the claim of Numbers 12. If the prophecy of Moses was clear and "not in riddles," succeeding generations have found matters a good deal more complicated. A live prophet may be interrogated by an audience and required to clarify a prophetic utterance. In contrast, once prophecy survived only in written texts, it became open to ever-constant reinterpretation. The result is that even sections of Scripture that were reasonably clear to their original target audiences have become overlaid with meanings inconceivable to their authors. Contemporary Christians and Jews must reckon with the theologically significant fact that their religious beliefs and practices are hardly based on plain-sense interpretations of Scripture. Our various forms of Judaism and Christianity would have made little sense to Moses, Miriam, Mary or Jesus. It appears to me that Jewish and Christian biblicists should be prepared to affirm publicly that our common goal is to recover the range of meanings that the different components of Scripture had for their original audiences, even when the scriptural texts have been assigned far different meanings by the church and synagogue. Surely there is no longer any need for Christian readers to find the Holy Ghost of the Trinity in the רוח אלהים "sprit/wind of God" of Gen 1:2 any more than for Jews to force monotheism into the verse, "let us make humans in our image." (Gen 1:26) But we should be sharing a second common goal: the dissemination of what Scripture has meant within the faith communities even when those meanings have resulted from radical recontextualization. It is probably fair to say that most Jews and Christians are largely unaware of each other's interpretative traditions. As such, it may be the task of the next generation of Bible scholars to adopt the medieval model of multiple senses of Scripture in the following way. We should encourage the continuing uses of "mainstream" biblical scholarship to recover what the NT and OT might have meant to their earliest audiences. Alongside this enterprise we should encourage the compilation of a series modeled on the Christian *glossa ordinaria* and the Jewish מקראות גדולות ("Large Scriptures") in which biblical texts are surrounded by commentaries from within the respective traditions.[56] That way Christian readers of Exod 17:11 for example, would learn that when Moses raised his hands against Amalek, they were raised in prayer. Jewish readers would learn on the same page that with his raised hands Moses made the sign of the cross. The interreligious activity of combining what have been for the most part separate academic disciplines would prove most salutary.

56 I thank Arthur Samuelson for suggesting in another context the notion of an interfaith project incorporating the insights of the great precritical Christian and Jewish commentators.

CHAPTER 19

Monotheism and Ancient Israelite Religion

The peoples of the Ancient Near East remain a source of fascination to moderns. No one can fail to be impressed by the pyramids, the ziggurats, and the artistic monuments of ancient Egypt and western Asia. But the interest in these great ancient civilizations is antiquarian. In contrast, ancient Israel, which was never the home of a great ruling power or of monumental architecture, is the ultimate birthplace of the monotheistic religions Judaism, Christianity and Islam. For good and ill the stories of Abraham and not those of Gilgamesh remain sources of inspiration and guidance for moderns. As such, the recovery of ancient Israelite religion is relevant within the academy and without, and therein lies a problem.

Scholars with personal religious attachments to the Bible must always exert themselves to avoid the kinds of apologetics that they would never offer in other fields. They must resist the temptation to explain away elements in Israelite religion, child sacrifice for example, if they find them abhorrent. Contrariwise, scholars with the opposite bent must resist emphasizing the Bible's nefarious support of ideologies and institutions of which they disapprove, if such disapproval impairs understanding of what the texts meant in their time of composition and early reception.

A second problem is the paucity of primary data, a situation in stark contrast to Mesopotamia, Egypt, Ugarit, Anatolia (Turkey), and Greece, which, in addition to their literary productions, have left us temples and temple offering lists telling us which gods were worshiped and what attention they received. Assyrian sources for example, provide detailed information on the practice of divination.[1] These same "extra-biblical" cultures have provided a wealth of pictorial representations of their divinities enabling us to visualize their gods the way they did. Different size temples to different gods in the same geographic area are another indication of relative importance, and these too are lacking in ancient Israel. Ancient Israel has thus far provided no undisputed pictorial representations of the Hebrew god Yahweh. Our only offering list from the biblical period comes from the fifth century Jewish temple at Elephantine in Egypt, a structure destroyed by hostile Egyptians in antiquity. The list indicates that offerings were made to YHW/YHH (forms of Yahweh) along with the

1 For examples see I. Starr, *Queries to the Sungod. Divination and Politics in Sargonid Assyria* (=SAA IV; Helsinki: Helsinki University, 1990).

 DOI 10.1163/9789004340879_020

goddesses (?) Anat-Yahu and Anat-Bethel.[2] Although we have ancient Hebrew letters, inscriptions, and artifacts, most of our information about Israelite religion comes from the Hebrew Bible, a selective anthology containing material written over a period of some eight hundred years and completed late in the first pre-Christian millennium. As such, the Bible's religion is not necessarily ancient Israelite religion but a later understanding of it. In contrast to the situation of other ancient Near Eastern texts, we have no originals of the Bible, only copies far removed chronologically from their original authors or scribes.

The greatest problem in studying Israelite religion is the figure of the Hebrew god, the hero of the Bible, absent only from the books of Esther and Song of Songs. Within the Bible the Hebrew god is depicted as creator, lawgiver, provider, and director of all the events of what would later be called "nature" and "history," Biblical Hebrew having no word for either concept. At some point this Hebrew divinity came to be viewed by followers as the sole god in existence. His proper name is Yahweh, usually translated "Lord," or "Eternal," the god of "Israel," a small politically insignificant people in western Asia first attested in the late second millennium BCE. Yahweh has thus far not been found in any pre-Israelite pantheons.[3] Yahweh was known by various names and epithets, among them Adonay,[4] El,[5] Eloah,[6] Elohim,[7] Shadday[8] and Elyon,[9] some of which were originally the names of other gods absorbed into the figure of Yahweh. In the course of time Yahweh became simply the only "God" of Christianity, Islam, and Judaism.[10] The figure of El is the best documented of those divinities folded into the god of Israel. In a complicated process, El, once head of a North Syrian pantheon, became so thoroughly identified with Yahweh that his separate existence was virtually unacknowledged by the Hebrew writers.

The name Yahweh is a scholarly reconstruction of the consonant cluster YHWH attested more than 6,600 times in the Hebrew Bible, and in the Moabite

---

2 See K. van der Toorn, *Numen* 39 (1992), 80–81.

3 For theories about the origins of Yahweh and the meaning of his name see K. van der Toorn,"Yahweh," *DDD*, 910–919 (with bibliography).

4 See van der Toorn,"Yahweh,"; K. Spronk, "Lord," *DDD*, 531–533.

5 W. Herrmann, "El," *DDD*, 274–280.

6 See D. Pardee, "Eloah," *DDD*, 285–288.

7 See van der Toorn, "God (I)," *DDD*, 352–365.

8 See E. Knauf, "Shadday," *DDD*, 749–753.

9 See E. Elnes and P. Miller, "Elyon," *DDD*, 293–299.

10 See van der Toorn, "God (I)," "Yahweh,"; Spronk, "Lord,"; F. M. Cross, *Canaanite Myth and Hebrew Epic. Essays in the History of the Religion of Israel* (Cambridge: Harvard, 1973), 44; P. Miller, *The Religion of Ancient Israel* (Louisville: Westminster, 2000), 2–3.

Stone of the ninth century BCE. The Hebrew writing system employed to compose what were to become the books of the Hebrew Bible is primarily consonantal; the vowel points were added during the first millennium of our era. Because Jews had come to avoid the use of the ancient divine name, the pronunciation of YHWH has not been preserved. Instead, the vowel points direct readers of the Hebrew text to pronounce YHWH as though it were another less sacred name, "Adonay," meaning "Lord."

The authors of the Bible consistently portrayed Yahweh as a unique divinity, but differed about the extent of that uniqueness. At one pole we have full-blown Yahwistic monotheism, that is, the claim that there is only one god in existence, and that his name is Yahweh. The prophet known as "Isaiah of the Exile" or Deutero-Isaiah, declared Yahweh to be the sole god in existence (Isaiah 43:10–11, 45:5–7,14,18, 21–22, 46:9).[11] For this prophet the claim that Yahweh alone is an actual god entails the cultic corollary of Yahweh's demand for exclusive worship. Other gods must cease to exist.[12] Accordingly, Yahweh demands the worship of all humanity, not just that of Israelites or Jews (Isaiah 44:6, 66:23). At the opposite pole, we find Yahweh jealous of other gods (Exodus 20:5, 34:15; Deuteronomy 5: 9; Joshua 24:19), defeating other gods (Exodus 12:12; Numbers 33:4), acting as king of gods (Psalm 95:3) or god of gods (Psalm 136: 2), and accepting the homage of other gods (Psalm 29:1–2, 96: 4). These passages all take for granted the existence, if inferiority, of other divinities. Deuteronomy chapter 4, despite its rhetorical monotheizing flourishes (4:35, 39), avers that Yahweh himself had allotted the depersonalized sun, moon, and stars to the gentiles as legitimate objects of worship (4:19). The gentiles could not worship Yahweh himself. For the author of Deuteronomy 4 the exclusive worship of Yahweh was both an Israelite obligation and an Israelite privilege.

Because the Bible is the work of many authors and not a systematic treatise, readers will find numerous disagreements about matters that are of fundamental importance to students of ancient Israelite religion. According to Genesis 4:26 the name of Yahweh was known to the earliest humans. In contrast, Exodus 6:3 claims that Yahweh first revealed his proper name to Moses, but not to the earlier patriarchs Abraham, Isaac, and Jacob, who knew him only as El Shadday. Individual contributors to the biblical anthology differed

11 See H. Wildberger, "Der Monotheismus Deuterojesajas," in *Beiträge zur alttestamentlichen Theologie. Festschrift für Walther Zimmerli zum 70. Geburtstag*, eds. H. Donner, R. Hanhart and R. Smend (Göttingen:Vandenhoeck & Ruprecht, 1977), 506–530.

12 H. Versnel, "Three Greek Experiments in Oneness," in *One God or Many? Concepts of Divinity in the Ancient World*, ed. B. N. Porter (Chebeague, Maine: Casco Bay Assyriological Institute, 2000), 79–163.

on the question of whether other gods existed, or whether gentiles were to worship Yahweh. All agreed though, that Yahweh was the sole legitimate object of Israelite worship. Israelites who worshiped other gods than Yahweh, or in addition to Yahweh, were both sinful and stupid (Jeremiah 5:19–23, 7:8–11). Despite biblical rhetoric accusing Israelites of abandoning Yahweh for other gods, it appears that it was more often the case that polytheistic Israelites viewed Yahweh as the head of an Israelite pantheon and supplemented his worship with that of other gods.

It is precisely that supplementary worship that is condemned in 1Kings 18:21 and Jeremiah 7:9–10. Nowhere in the Hebrew Bible do we find any of the "good guys" supporting Israelite worship of Yahweh's rivals. Whenever the biblical writers describe Israelite worship of other gods, male and female, which they do with considerable frequency (Exodus 32:7–8; Numbers 25:1–5; Judges 2:10–13; 1Kings 11:33; 2Kings 17:16; Jeremiah 3:6–10, 44:2–10; Ezekiel 8:5–17, 20:7–8, 27–31; Psalm 106:34–39), they characterize such worship as "backsliding," or as deviation from the worship of Yahweh alone as demanded by the "ten words"[13] (Exodus 34:28; Deuteronomy 4:13, 10:4) or decalogue, as spoken by Yahweh to Moses (Exodus 20:3–5; Deuteronomy 5:7–9 [compare Hosea 13:4]). Often, Israelite deviation is attributed to the potential and actual influence of the local and neighboring gentiles, and to Israelite sexual contact and intermarriage with them (Exodus 23:32–33, 34:11–16; Numbers 25:1–9, 31:14–18; Deuteronomy 12:2–3, 29–31). The view of the Old Testament that the worship of Yahweh alone was normative in Israel from the earliest days of the nation was canonized in the New Testament (Acts 7:35–43) and held sway until challenged during the rise of modern biblical criticism in the nineteenth century.

The best known of the early modern Bible critics, the German scholar Julius Wellhausen (1844–1918), employed analytical literary criticism, called source criticism, to distinguish earlier from later writings within the Hebrew Bible. Based on his system of dating biblical texts, Wellhausen reconstructed Israelite religious development and concluded that monotheism had evolved gradually out of polytheism, passing through a stage of monolatry, the worship of a single god at the same time that other gods are believed to exist. No humanist of the time could escape the ramifications of Darwin's theory of evolution. Whether Wellhausen was also influenced by the philosophy of Hegel is another matter.[14] According to Wellhausen, in the earlier biblical period Yahweh was

---

13 Popularly known as the Ten Commandments.

14 L. Perlitt, *Vatke und Wellhausen:geschichtsphilosophische Voraussetzungen und historiographische Motive für die Darstellung der Religion und Geschichte Israels durch Wilhelm Vatke und Julius Wellhausen* (Berlin:Topelmann, 1965).

a national god, much like Chemosh in Moab and Ashur in Assyria. The fact that as a national god Yahweh claimed the allegiance of every Israelite did not entail the rejection of other gods any more than allegiance to Ashur entailed the neglect of the cults of Shamash or Ishtar.

Wellhausen's thesis was open to an obvious objection. If Yahweh had at the outset been a god no different qualitatively from the Moabite Chemosh and the Assyrian Ashur, why did monotheism never arise in Moab[15] or Assyria? In the case of Ashur, the Assyriologist Simo Parpola has argued that underneath the apparent polytheism of Assyrian religion was a unifying monotheistic notion.[16] But even Parpola does not deny that Assyrian religion was polytheistic for all but the most sophisticated thinkers.

For Wellhausen the new direction in Israel was to be sought in the teaching of the eighth century Hebrew prophets. Only after Hosea and Amos began to interpret the political upheavals of the eighth century BCE as Yahweh's means of enforcing his demands upon Israel, demands that were primarily ethical and moral rather than cultic, did monotheism began to emerge. As interpreted by Wellhausen, the prophets Hosea and Amos, and Isaiah shortly thereafter, taught that Yahweh could move all the peoples of the earth either to punish or reward his people Israel. If so, he must be much more than a national god; he must have no rivals at all. "Ethical monotheism," though taught by succeeding prophets, took two centuries to take root among most of the populace. In Wellhausen's view only during the Babylonian exile of the sixth century BCE did the masses of Jews, prodded by a guilty conscience, begin to realize that the prophets had been right (Zechariah 1:1–6). Both the northern and southern kingdoms of Israel had fallen because of their failure to serve Yahweh exclusively. It was at that point that the demand that Yahweh alone was to be worshipped was retrojected into the laws and narratives set in earlier centuries.

Wellhausen's view was largely accepted until the 1940's when it began to be attacked by the American archaeologist William Foxwell Albright (1891–1971)[17]

---

15 Truth be told, we do not have enough Moabite material to deny categorically that other gods in addition to Chemosh were worshipped in Moab, although it seems likely. The Moabite Stone of the ninth century BCE mentions an Ashtar-Chemosh along with Chemosh. Does this indicate the merger of Chemosh with the god Ashtar known as a defunct deity in the Ugaritic texts of the thirteenth century? See H.-P.Müller, "Chemosh," *DDD* 186–189.

16 S. Parpola, "Monotheism in Ancient Assyria," in Porter, *One God*, 165–209.

17 The discussion of Albright is based on R. Gnuse, *No other Gods: Emergent Monotheism in Israel* (Sheffield: Sheffield Academic, 1997), 64–66. See *ibid.*, 62–128 for an extensive summary of recent scholarship on monotheism. Important recent works are D. Edelman, *The Triumph of Elohim. From Yahwisms to Judaisms* (Grand Rapids, Michigan:

and his followers, and the Israeli Yehezkel Kaufmann (1889–1963)[18] and his mostly Jewish followers. Wellhausen had reached his conclusions solely on the internal evidence of the Bible. Albright, in contrast, insisted that the biblical texts could be understood and dated only in the light of the Near Eastern world in which ancient Israel had emerged.

In Albright's view there was archaeological evidence that many biblical texts written centuries later than the events they portrayed had faithfully preserved ancient traditions. That being the case, the biblical claims about the roots of monotheism in the age of Moses ought to be historically credible. In his 1940 classic *From the Stone Age to Christianity: Monotheism and the Historical Process*,[19] Albright broke with the evolutionary explanations of monotheistic origins in favor of a monotheistic revolution led by Moses. For him Mosaic monotheism was "functional," rather than systematic. Nonetheless, Moses was the first Hebrew to teach

> the existence of one God, the creator of everything, the source of justice, who is equally powerful in the desert, and in Palestine, who has no sexuality and no mythology, who is human in form but cannot be seen by human eye and cannot be represented in any form.[20]

Thus, monotheism was not an evolutionary development within Israel, though the groundwork had been laid for it in the high gods of other cultures and especially in the exaltation of the solar disc, called the Aten, and the ban on all competing cults by King Ahkenaten of Egypt in the fourteenth century BCE. According to Albright, "the Aten cult was … a true monotheism."[21] The

---

Eerdmans, 1996); Porter, *One God*; K. van der Toorn, ed., *The Image and the Book. Iconic Cults, Aniconism, and the Rise of Book Religion in Israel and the Ancient Near East* (Leuven: Peeters, 1998); W. Propp, *Ugarit Forschungen* 31 (1999), 537–575; Mark Smith, *The Early History of God* (Grand Rapids, MI: Eerdmanns, 2002).

18 For general critiques of Kaufmann's work see J. Levenson, *Conservative Judaism* 36 (1982), 36–43; S. D. Sperling, "Israel's Religion in the Ancient Near East," in *Jewish Spirituality from the Bible to the Middle Ages*, ed. Arthur Green (New York: Crossroads, 1986), 5–31; J. Hayes, "Kaufmann, Yehezkel," *DBI*, vol. 2, 16–17; M. Greenberg, "Kaufmann on the Bible: An Appreciation," in M. Greenberg, *Studies in the Bible and Jewish Thought* (Philadelphia: Jewish Publication Society, 1995), 175–188.

19 W. F. Albright, *From the Stone Age to Christianity: Monotheism and the Historical Process* (=*FSAC*; Baltimore: Johns Hopkins, 1940). All citations herein are from the reprint by Doubleday Anchor of the second Johns Hopkins edition of 1946.

20 *FSAC*, 272.

21 *FSAC*, 221.

Egyptologist Donald Redford observes, "The Roman world might have called Akhenaten an 'atheist' for what was left to Egypt was not a 'god' at all, but a disc in the heavens."[22]

Albright thought that the Mosaic revolution proved to be a great success with the masses of the Israelite population. Of course there were always "ignorant" or "moronic"[23] Israelites who were attracted to polytheism. There was also the corrupting influence of the monarchy, sometimes tempted to adopt or promote gentile practices (1Kings 11:4–8, 16:30–33; 2Kings 16:10–11, 21:1–7). At the opposite pole stood zealots who felt the need to make Mosaic monotheism consistent by standardizing worship and eliminating vestiges of polytheistic practice and mythic language. But these zealots were reformers rather than innovators. Essentially, Albright held that Moses was a historical figure who brought a functional, if not systematic, monotheism to Israel in the thirteenth century BCE.

As noted by Mark Smith,[24]Albright's definition of monotheism is a composite drawn from various biblical sources of varying dates. We may add that the features enumerated by Albright do not have equal weight in regard to the question of the sole existence of Yahweh: 1) In some cultures creation is a specialized function of lower rather than higher gods. 2) In Mesopotamian sources the deities Kittu (truth) and Mesharu (justice) are gods responsible for justice. The Egyptian goddess Ma'at and a whole host of other gods are sources of justice without being unique. In Zoroastrianism, Ahura Mazda is the source of justice, but the existence of opposition by the thoroughly evil and very powerful Angra Mainyu does not permit us to call Zoroastrianism "monotheism." 3) As for the ban on images, its date is unclear. From the perspective of art history Schroer argues that the anti-image tradition arose late in Israel.[25] Mettinger believes that even the early absence of images would not itself be determinative because we must distinguish between *de facto* absence of images, a phenomenon attested widely in West Semitic polytheistic cults, and programmatic avoidance of images, the explicit prohibition of images, which did not appear in biblical sources composed before the exilic period. Indeed, several scholars have argued that the second commandment, which prohibits

22 D. Redford, *Akhenaten the Heretic King* (Princeton: Princeton University, 1984), 170; See further, J. Foster, *CANE*, 1751–1761, especially 1760; Propp, *Ugarit Forschungen* 31.

23 *FSAC*, 288.

24 Mark Smith, *The Origins of Biblical Monotheism. Israel's Polytheistic Background and the Ugaritic Texts* (Oxford: Oxford University, 2001), 150.

25 S. Schroer, *In Israel gab es Bilder: Nachrichten von darstellender Kunst im Alten Testament* (Fribourg: Universitätsverlag, 1987).

images (Exodus 20:4 = Deuteronomy 5:8), is an interpolation that interrupts the natural flow between "you shall have no gods in my presence" and "you shall not bow down to them in worship."[26]

Yehezkel Kaufmann went further than Albright. Kaufmann wrote his magnum opus in eight volumes between 1938 and 1956, a period in which few gentile scholars could read Modern Hebrew.[27] A one-volume abridgment and English translation of the first seven volumes[28] by Moshe Greenberg extended Kaufmann's influence somewhat, but mostly among those Jews whose Hebrew was not fluent.[29] The German scholar Thomas Krapf has brought renewed attention to Kaufmann's work.[30]

In Kaufmann's view the Mosaic revolution had thoroughly eradicated paganism from Israel in one fell swoop. Whereas the tales of the biblical patriarchs Abraham, Isaac, and Jacob reflect a polytheistic background,[31] Moses had successfully taught Israel that no other gods existed but Yahweh. Any biblical references to other gods in Israel subsequent to the Mosaic revolution should be understood as literary conceits, or petrified language emptied of mythic significance. Albright had attributed infidelity to Yahweh to morons, and other scholars had distinguished between "official" religion faithful to Yahweh alone and "popular"[32] religion which was polytheistic and syncretistic. But Kaufmann attempted to demonstrate that the number of morons as well as the differences between the "official" and the "popular" had been greatly exaggerated. Kaufmann conceded that the royal courts sometimes imported foreign cults.

26 T. Mettinger, *No Graven Images?* (Stockholm:Almqvist & Wiksell, 1995); T. Mettinger, "Israelite Aniconism: Development and Origins," in van der Toorn, *Image*, 173–204; R. Hendel, "Aniconism and Anthropomorphism in Ancient Israel," in van der Toorn, *Image*, 205–208.

27 Y. Kaufmann, *Toledot ha-Emunah ha-Yisre'elit* (Tel-Aviv: Devir, 1938–1956).

28 Y. Kaufmann, *The Religion of Israel* (Chicago: Chicago University, 1960).

29 The remainder of *Toledot* was translated unabridged by C. Efroymson as *Yehezkel Kaufmann: The History of the Religion of Israel* (New York: Ktav, 1997).

30 T. Krapf, *Yehezkel Kaufmann: Ein Lebens-und Erkenntnisweg zur Theologie der hebräischen Bibel* (Berlin: Institut für Kirche und Judentum, 1990); T. Krapf, *Die Priesterschaft und die vorexilische Zeit:Yehezkel Kaufmanns vernachlässigte Beitrag zur Geschichte der biblischen Religion* (Göttingen: Vandenhoeck & Ruprecht, 1992).

31 Kaufmann, *Toledot*, II/1, 25–32.

32 The terms "popular" and "official" have not been employed rigorously by students of Israelite religion. See J. Berlinerblau, *The Vow and the "Popular Religious Groups" of Ancient Israel: A Philological and Sociological Inquiry* (Sheffield: Sheffield Academic, 1996), 1–45; J. Berlinerblau, "Preliminary Remarks for the Sociological Study of 'Official Israelite Religion,'" in *Ki Baruch Hu: Ancient Near Eastern, Biblical and Judaic Studies in Honor of Baruch A. Levine*, eds. R. Chazan, W. Hallo, and L. Schiffman (Winona Lake: Eisenbrauns, 1999), 153–170.

The wives of Solomon had private chapels for their own use (1Kings 11). King Ahab had permitted Queen Jezebel to bring the gods Baal and Asherah and their prophets into the northern capital Samaria (1Kings 16:31–33, 18:19). But these were aberrations and no more.

Problematic for Kaufmann's thesis were the many denunciations of Israelite idolatry and polytheism in the prophetic books as well as in the editorial comments in the biblical narratives that give the impression that wholehearted fidelity to Yahweh was in short supply among the masses. Kaufmann's ingenious response was that biblical writers were not denouncing the real worship of other gods, which was not to be found in Israel, but the occasional superstitious resort to stick and stone fetishes. Indeed, by the eighth century BCE, Israelites had become so far removed from the worship of gods other than Yahweh that they projected their own vestigial fetishism on the gentiles, assuming the gods of the nations to be fetishes, rather than divinities with real personalities whose loves and wars were celebrated in myth and cult. In sum, Israelites could never worship the gods of the gentiles because they did not know how. According to Kaufmann, the Hebrew prophets denounced these minor lapses into superstition out of puritanical zeal for monotheism. We might compare such prophetic zeal with that of an Orthodox rabbi who equates a Jewish child's visit to a department store Santa Claus or that child's participation in an Easter egg hunt with his conversion to Christianity.

The prophets also needed to vindicate divine justice, an activity that theologians call "theodicy." Israel held the land conditionally, so biblical theology taught, through a covenant with Yahweh. The primary condition of that covenant was that Israel was to serve Yahweh exclusively. Failure to do so was a breach of that covenant punishable by destruction by foreigners and expulsion of the population from the land. Since both Israelite kingdoms came to be destroyed by foreigners and both populations suffered expulsion, Kaufmann argued that the biblical writers were required to exaggerate Israelite infidelity to Yahweh, or even to invent it, in order to show that Israel had violated the covenant, and that Yahweh had justly punished them.

The "theodicy" element and the attention paid to prophetic rhetoric surely have merit, but otherwise Kaufmann's ingenious thesis is seriously flawed. First, he claims that Israel differed so fundamentally from its neighbors that Israelites told no myths about Yahweh and assumed naively that gentiles told no myths about their gods, who were therefore no more than fetishes. But Kaufmann's claim is unsustainable. Comparative study of the Bible and Near Eastern myths shows keen Israelite awareness of gentile myth as well as the use, adaptation, and transformation of mythic motifs by Hebrew writers.[33]

33 Cross, *Canaanite Myth*, 143–144.

Kaufmann's further claims about Israelite ignorance of the religions of the gentiles are likewise flawed, for as Morton Smith has shown, the qualitative differences between Israel and its neighbors are often greatly exaggerated.[34]

Indeed, newer discussions of ancient Israelite religion stimulated by inscriptions and drawings discovered at Kuntillet Ajrud in the Sinai and at Khirbet el-Qôm on the west bank of the Jordan demonstrate that Israelite worship of gods in addition to Yahweh was not completely fabricated by the authors of the Bible. These texts from the ninth to eighth centuries BCE apparently mention the goddess Asherah in close connection to Yahweh.[35] One Kuntillet Ajrud text that was found on a jar follows the epistolary genre and is probably a school exercise text.[36] More than one reading and interpretation are possible:

> a) "I bless you by/ commend you to/ Yahweh of Samaria and his Asherah."
>
> On this interpretation "Asherah" is a proper name referring to the goddess Asherah known from the Hebrew Bible, from the Ugaritic writings of Northern Syria dating from the late second millennium BCE and, apparently, from the recent excavations at Ekron (Tell Miqne), a Philistine site of the earlier first millennium BCE.[37]

Some scholars maintain that the name of the goddess has been reduced to a common noun meaning "consort," and that the phrase is to be rendered:

> b) "I bless you by/ commend you to/ Yahweh of Samaria and his consort."[38]

Levine suggests another possibility:[39]

> c) "I bless you by/ commend you to/ Yahweh of Samaria and its <u>asherah</u>."

---

34 Morton Smith, *JBL* 71 (1952), 135–147.

35 See N. Wyatt, "Asherah," *DDD*, 99–105; W. Dever, *ErIsr* 26 (1999), 9–15*; Miller, *Religion*, 29–43; B. Becking, *Only One God? Monotheism in Israel and the Veneration of the Goddess Asherah* (London: Sheffield Academic, 2001).

36 J. Renz and W. Röllig, *Handbuch der althebräischen Epigraphik* (Darmstadt: Wissenschaftliche Buchgesellschaft, 1995–2003), vol. I, 61.

37 H.-P. Müller, *ZAH* 5 (1992), 15–51; Wyatt, *DDD*, 99–105. For a photograph of a Philistine inscription that reads "To Asherat," see *BA* 53/4 (1990), 232.

38 See D. Hillers, *ZAH* 11 (1998), 32–49, especially 44–48.

39 B. Levine (oral communication).

As do the first two renderings, this translation understands the last word as a noun with a possessive feminine suffix, but takes the antecedent to be the city of Samaria. In addition, *asherah* is not taken as the goddess but as the illicit cultic object *asherah*, said to have stood in Samaria according to 2Kings 13:6, and appearing in Deuteronomy 16:21 and Judges 6:25–26, 28, 30. The connection between the goddess and the cultic object of the same name remains a matter of dispute.[40]

Some scholars have opted to explain the final letter in the last word not as the feminine possessive suffix, but as an element of the name of the goddess:

> d) "I bless you by/ commend you to/ Yahweh of Samaria and to Asheratah/ Ashirtah."[41]

This last interpretation seems the most likely for a number of reasons. First, it is unusual, though not impossible,[42] in the Semitic languages to attach a possessive suffix to a proper name. Second, the alternative form "Ashirtah" is attested in the proper name Abdi-Ashirtah of the Amarna letters of the fourteenth century BCE. Third, it is common in greeting formulae of the ancient Near East to bless an individual by one or more gods. Indeed a very similar formula is attested in documents written by members of the Jewish colony of Elephantine in Egypt in the fifth century BCE:

> I bless you by/ commend you to YHH and to Khnum.[43]

Khnum was an Egyptian god. According to Porten the name of the sender may indicate his non-Jewish origin. Even if Porten is correct, the formal structure is the same. The sender of the Kuntillet Ajrud letter cited above was named Amariah, indicating that his origins were from a family of worshippers of Yahweh; the *-iah* suffix is a form of Yahweh. This same interpretation that the goddess was known in Israelite venues as Ashirtah/Asheratah best suits the grave inscription from Khirbet el-Qôm on the west bank of the Jordan in what was the kingdom of Judah in the eighth century BCE. The main portion of that text[44] reads:

---

40 J. Emerton, *VT* 49 (1999), 315–337.

41 Z. Zevit, *BASOR* 255 (1984), 39–47; A. Angerstorfer, *BN* 17 (1982), 7–16.

42 See G. R. Driver, *JBL* 73 (1953), 125; M. Tsevat, *HUCA* 36 (1965), 54.

43 See B. Porten, *COS* vol. 3, 210–211.

44 For the text, bibliography and other interpretations see Renz and Röllig *Handbuch* vol. 1, 207–211.

> Uriyahu the rich. His inscription:
> Uriyahu paid homage[45] to Yahweh,
> and out of his straits, to Asheratah.
> Save him!

It is especially noteworthy that in all of the proper names in the inscriptions from Kuntillet Ajrud and Khirbet el-Qôm that contain a god's name, that name is written -Yhw, a short form of YHWH, an indication that all of these individuals not only worshiped Yahweh themselves but belonged to families who worshiped Yahweh over generations.[46] As a statistical sample of worship in ancient Israel the data are insignificant. As snapshots, however, they tend to support the view best articulated by Morton Smith in his *Palestinian Parties and Politics that Shaped the Old Testament*.[47] In that book, by now a classic, Smith takes seriously the biblical portrayal of Israelite vacillation between periods of "following other gods" and periods of consistent fidelity to Yahweh. Behind that vacillation, argues Smith, is a struggle between two parties: the first, the "Yahweh-alone" party, insisted that Yahweh was the only god to be worshiped by Israelites. On the other side stood what I call the "Yahweh-plus" party,[48] which acknowledged the divinity of Yahweh within a larger grouping of gods. For example, Smith observed that even Ahab and Jezebel, notorious in the Bible for their support of Baal's cult, gave their children names with Yahweh as the divine element. The different parties struggled for power over centuries. Ultimate victory came to the "Yahweh-alone" party during the Persian period, 539–331 BCE. The grand narrative of the Old Testament was shaped by the victors, who divided the kings of Israel and Judah into the "just" and the "unjust" depending on their degree of adherence to the principles of the "Yahweh-alone" party.

In contrast to Albright and Kaufmann, by examining the Yahweh-alone theology from a political standpoint, Smith avoids any appeal to Israelite uniqueness. His thesis has the additional advantage of not having to explain the demand that Yahweh be worshiped by Israelites to the exclusion of all other gods as a retrojection. The task remains however to account in the first place for the monolatrous demand made in the name of Yahweh.

---

45 This is how the verb *brk* with indirect object is used in Biblical Hebrew. See Ps 95:6.

46 M. Heide, *WO* 23 (2002), 114–117.

47 Morton Smith, *Palestinian Parties and Politics that Shaped the old Testament* (New York: Columbia University, 1971).

48 "Yahweh-plus party" is obviously an oversimplification. In the ancient world one would not be an abstract monotheist or polytheist. Whereas the "Yahweh-alone party" would have been an identifiable group, the "Yahweh-plus party" would have been more diverse.

The demand that one god is to be worshiped even though the existence of others is not necessarily denied was not unique to the Yahweh-alone party in the ancient world. Reference has already been made to the reform of King Akhenaten, which forbade the worship of all gods but the sun-disk. Albright and Redford refer to Aten's worship as monotheistic. Others have withheld that characterization because under the reform the king and the royal family continued to receive the divine honors that had been accorded the earlier pharaohs. But the phenomenon is close enough to the demands for Yahweh's exclusive worship to warrant serious comparison. Outside of Egypt, Mesopotamian mythology refers to the worship of a single god in times of emergency. Mesopotamian prayer literature regularly employs the language of monolatry. A worshiper might approach different gods in succession, declaring that each, in turn, was the only divinity worthy of human worship. At other times worshipers would declare to the god whom they were supplicating that all the other gods were aspects or limbs of the god addressed.[49]

The cause of the monolatrous demand in Israel is to be sought in the particular historical circumstances in which Israel arose. It is clear from the archaeological researches of the past decades, especially in the wake of the 1967 Arab-Israeli war, that the Bible's central traditions of enslavement in Egypt, exodus from Egypt, and armed conquest of the promised land are not historical. While no full positive consensus on the origin of Israel has emerged, there is general agreement that:

a) There is no archaeological evidence in Egyptian sources that any elements of later Israel were ever in Egypt. Likewise, the early Israelite settlements do not contain Egyptian elements in their material culture, which an Egyptian sojourn would have produced.[50] As such we cannot speak of a historical exodus from Egypt.
b) The related tradition of Israel's journey of forty years through the desert is likewise unsupported archaeologically. Extensive exploration of the Sinai has found no evidence of occupation during the appropriate period.
c) Israel did not arise out of a group that had escaped from Egyptian servitude. Instead, the nucleus of Israel was "derived from the local Late Bronze culture through relatively normal social processes."[51]

49 See S. D. Sperling, *The Original Torah: The Political Intent of the Bible's Writers* (New York: New York University, 1998), 148, notes 35–37.

50 W. Dever, *ABD* vol. 3, 546.

51 W. Dever, *ABD* vol. 3, 553.

d) Israel was not a single unified ethnic group. Instead, "Israelite ethnic identity came about through the process whereby the indigenous population began to understand and identify itself as Israelite."[52]
e) Whatever movement of population occurred to produce an Israelite culture was internal, probably from the lowlands eastward and northward into the highlands.[53]

The biblical traditions about enslavement, exodus, and conquest must be understood as ideologically motivated accounts usually composed centuries later than the events, real or imagined, that they report. Behind these traditions it is often possible to recover historical information, usually more relevant to the account's time of composition than to its setting. Nonetheless, when judiciously combined with the data provided by archaeology and other historical sources a reasonable synthesis of early Israelite history and religion is possible.[54]

One biblical text refers to 430 years of servitude in Egypt (Exodus 12:40); Genesis 15:13 has 400. Attempts to explain the figures schematically have proved unpersuasive.[55] In contrast, the figure fits remarkably well with the chronology of the rise and decline of imperial Egyptian power in Asia.[56] The Egyptian Empire was part of the international system of the Bronze Age in the second millennium BCE during which the great powers extended their dominion well beyond their borders. Among these powers, which included the Hittites, Mitanni, Assyria, and the Minoan-Mycenean civilization in the Aegean, the Egyptian New Kingdom (about 1550–1069 BCE) was the greatest. Egypt's power extended from northern Sudan in the south and into Syria and Lebanon in the north.[57] The New Kingdom began after King Ahmose of Egypt overthrew the Hyksos invaders in the mid-sixteenth century BCE and Egypt began to campaign extensively in western Asia. At the battle of Megiddo

52 T. Thompson, *The Origin Tradition of Ancient Israel*, vol. I: *The Literary Formation of Genesis and Exodus 1–23* (Sheffield: JSOT, 1987), 37.

53 E. Bloch-Smith and B. Nakhai, *NEA* 62 (1999), 62–92, 101–128.

54 In their summary of Iron Age I (*NEA* 62, 118), Bloch-Smith and Nikhai write, "given the rather late and tendentious nature of the biblical text, it is somewhat unexpected to discover that archaeological evidence presents a similar, though not identical picture of the events of the period." See Also W. Dever, *NEA* 61 (1998), 39–52.

55 See W. Propp, *Exodus 1–18* (Anchor Bible; New York: Doubleday, 1998), 415–416.

56 Cf. Sperling, "Israel's Religion," in Green, *Jewish Spirituality*; Sperling, *Original Torah*, 53–60.

57 See A. Kuhrt, *The Ancient Near East c. 3000–330 BC* (London: Routledge, 1995), vol. I, 185–224.

Thutmose III won a decisive victory after which the local Asiatic rulers became vassals of Egypt. Though rival superpowers, first Mitanni and then the Hittite Kingdom, challenged Egyptian expansion in Asia, the Syria-Palestine coastline and the interior of Palestine remained solidly in Egyptian control. Egyptian correspondence of the fourteenth century BCE shows the heavy economic burdens of taxation and compulsory labor to which the population of Syria-Palestine was subjected.[58] Local rulers subject to the Pharaoh would round up work gangs to cultivate royal lands. Naturally, this was greatly resented by the locals who could themselves be rallied to attempt to throw off their subjugation by Egypt and by the local Canaanite rulers who cooperated with Egypt.[59]

About 1200 BCE the international system collapsed in what is termed "the catastrophe." Throughout the eastern Mediterranean, "the twelfth century BCE ushered in a dark age" in which forty-seven major sites were destroyed in Greece, Crete, Anatolia, Cyprus and Syria-Palestine.[60] In Turkey the Hittite Empire collapsed. Mass movements of population, notably the Sea Peoples, among them the Philistines, transformed the face of the Middle East. Indeed, comparison between the social and political terminology of the Bible and the Bronze Age shows an almost complete discontinuity.[61]Against the turbulent international background we see populations caught in the middle of fighting among rival city-states, traders who functioned poorly in the unstable conditions, debtors and dislocated peasants, and the ever-present pastoralists who were always potentially disruptive. In Syria-Palestine we witness "the destruction of the Canaanite urban culture and the withdrawal of Egypt from Canaan."[62] By the death of Rameses III *ca.* 1153 Egypt no longer dominated Canaan, though some sites continued a bit longer under Egyptian control.[63]

Gradually, new groups emerged out of the disorder, among them a group called "Israel." Made up of locals seeking a place in the new social order, the constituents of Israel denied their connections to Canaan and gave themselves a new "national" counter-identity.[64]They began to depict themselves as an

58 See W. Moran, *The Amarna Letters* (Baltimore: Johns Hopkins, 1992).

59 Moran, *Amarna*, EA 74, EA 365; Kuhrt, *Near East I*, 324–327.

60 See R. Drews, *The End of the Bronze Age. Changes in Warfare and the Catastrophe ca. 1200 B.C.* (Princeton: Princeton University, 1993). For a map of the destroyed sites see *ibid.*, 9.

61 A. Rainey, *JAOS* 107 (1987), 542.

62 I. Finkelstein and N. Na'aman, *From Nomadism to Monarchy: Archaeological and Historical Aspects of Early Israel* (Washington, D.C.: Biblical Archaeological Society), 12.

63 Bloch-Smith and Nakhai, *NEA* 62, 83.

64 See P. Machinist, *Scripta Hierosolymitana* 33 (1991), 196–212; Sperling, *Original Torah*, 41–60.

invading group from outside the land, much like the Philistines. The Bible's ideological claim to Israel's religious, social, and moral distinctiveness is framed in terms of geography. The Canaanite heritage is denied by the Torah in its claims that all of Israel's laws and institutions were given by Yahweh through Moses to the people when they wandered in the desert. Nothing good in terms of law, morality, or religion came from the land. In line with this ideological geography, the historical traditions about the subjugation of the people who became "Israel" to Egyptians ruling the land of Canaan were transformed into traditions of subjugation in Egypt proper. The withdrawal of Egypt from Canaan became the escape from the land of Egypt itself. Given that the name of the new polity was "Israel," a name which has El as the divine element, the god El must have been the group's patron. At an early date, however, Yahweh completely absorbed the figure of El, and it was Yahweh who became Israel's god. Because of the circumstances of its formation, as a political coalition rather than as an ethnic group, Israel constructed its mythic consciousness out of figures that we would call "political."

The notion that Israel is linked to Yahweh by a "covenant" is central to the Torah. Mendenhall was the first biblical scholar to draw attention to the fact that the biblical notion of covenant was based on treaty formulae employed already in the second millennium BCE. In the treaties a great king bound subordinate kings to exclusive loyalty. Characteristically, divinities were called upon to bear witness to the treaty. Faithful adherence to the treaty was to be greatly rewarded while disloyalty would be punished with the severest forms of destruction.[65] While subsequent scholarship has shown that several elements in Mendenhall's description require correction, there can be little doubt that his main observation was correct, namely, that the demand that Israel serve Yahweh exclusively was based on the treaty form. Ironically, Mendenhall himself saw the treaty formula as a model for monotheism: one god=one overlord. In fact, the covenant is a perfect metaphor of the religious notion of monolatry. Political treaties demanded exclusive service because there was always another great king who might be served. A Hittite king bound a minor Syrian king precisely because the minor king might serve the king of Egypt. Yahweh binds Israel because Israel might serve another god. What is of particular interest is that in biblical books of the exilic and post-exilic periods, when true monotheism emerges, the conditional covenant becomes a dead letter.[66]

---

65 G. Mendenhall, *BA* 17 (1954), 52–76.

66 S. D. Sperling, *Biblica* 70 (1989), 50–72; reprinted in this volume as "Rethinking Covenant in Late Biblical Books."

The theological construct of covenant with Yahweh mirrored the mundane fact of political union. Yahweh became, in essence, "the flag" that every Israelite saluted. Because Yahweh himself had no known prior connections to Canaanite cult and myth, exclusive loyalty to him served to strengthen the solidarity of the newly formed group. Initially an advantage, the absence of Yahweh from the local mythic traditions meant that the religious necessities served by gods of weather, agriculture, fertility, and the heavenly bodies would be unmet. In a monotheistic environment, monolatry is perfectly sensible; you worship one god because it is the only one. In contrast, restricting worship to one god when others are acknowledged to exist is difficult to uphold. In fact, ignoring powers that one knew to be potent could be dangerous, and relatively few Israelites in the early first millennium BCE took the risk. But if Morton Smith is right, there was always a minority who did.

Because the monolatrous demand as expressed in the primitive[67] notion of covenant was central to the formation of the Israelite polity, the call to serve Yahweh alone could resonate in times of crisis and serve as a general rallying point to encourage group solidarity (Exodus 32:25–29; 1Samuel 7:1–14; 1Kings 18; 2Kings 9–10, 22–23). The crisis occasioned by the fall of the last Israelite state in 586 BCE proved decisive. As wryly observed by Morton Smith, once Yahweh had proved his power by scattering his people "in a diaspora from one end of the known world to the other, what was left for him but monotheism?"[68]

67 I owe the characterization of covenant as "primitive" to D. B. Redford, *Egypt, Canaan and Israel in Ancient Times* (Princeton: Princeton University, 1992), 275.

68 Morton Smith, *JBL* 71, 147.

CHAPTER 20

Dinah, ʿInnah, and Related Matters

> Now as for the carrying off of women, it is the deed, they say, of a rogue; but to make a stir about such as are carried off, argues a man a fool. Men of sense care nothing for such women, since it is plain that without their own consent they would never be forced away. The Asiatics, when the Greeks ran off with their women, never troubled themselves about the matter; but the Greeks, for the sake of a single Lacedaemonian girl, collected a vast armament, invaded Asia, and destroyed the kingdom of Priam.[1]

Much ink has been spilled on the nature of the sexual encounter between Shechem and Dinah, especially in recent years.[2] The title of Bechtel's influential

---

1 Herodotus, *Hist.* I.4 (Godley, LCL).

2 See the bibliographies in Yairah Amit, "Implicit Redaction and Latent Polemic in the Story of the Rape of Dinah," in *Texts, Temples. and Traditions: A Tribute to Menahem Haran* eds. M. Fox, V. Hurowitz, A. Hurvitz, M. Klein, B. Schwartz and N. Shupak (Winona Lake: Eisenbrauns, 1996), *11–28* (Hebrew); E. van Wolde, "Love and Hatred in a Multiracial Society," in *Reading from Right to Left: Essays on the Hebrew Bible in Honour of David J. A. Clines*, eds. J. C. Exum and H. Williamson (London: Sheffield Academic, 2003), 435–449; T. Frymer-Kensky, *Reading the Women of the Bible: A New Interpretation of Their Stories* (New York: Schocken, 2004), 179–198 and the appended notes; M. Gruber, "The Accusations against Shechem Son of Hamor: A Reconsideration," *Beth Mikra* 44 (1998–1999), 119–127; *idem*, "On a Forgotten Meaning of the root *ayin-nun-yod* in Biblical Hebrew," in *Iyyune Mikra u-Farshanut*, vol. 7: *Menahot Yedidut ve-Hoqarah le-Menahem Cohen*, eds. S. Vergon J. Ofer, J. Penkower and J. Klein (Ramat Gan: Bar Ilan University Press, 2005), 233–244 (Hebrew).

The vocalization *Dinah* is based on the received Hebrew text, the Aramic Targums, and mirrored in LXX Δείνα and Vulgate *Dina*. Noth explains the name as "Rechtsstreit" (lawsuit) possibly chosen as a literary device (*IPN*, 10). A. Ungnad connects the biblical name with the name of a slave girl named da-a-na-a (presumably Dayyānâ) attested in a 7th-century Neo-Assyrian legal transaction from Gozan with a West-Semitic background. Another party to the transaction has a name corresponding to Hebrew Hosea, and the Akkadian of the document reflects Aramaic syntax. See *Inschriften vom Tell Halaf: Keilschrifttexte und aramäische Urkunden aus einer assyrischen Provinzhauptstadt* eds., J. Friedrich, G. Meyer, A. Ungnad and E. Weidner (Osnabrück: Biblio-Verlag, 1967), III.3; for a copy of the tablet, see pl. 25. It is likely that the Bible's consonantal *d-y-n-h* was misconstrued as "Dina" after the original form "Dayyānâ" had been forgotten.

 | DOI 10.1163/9789004340879_021

article, "What if Dinah Is Not Raped? (Genesis 34),"[3] articulates the problem. In contrast to the situation in Akkadian, for example,[4] Biblical Hebrew, as Bechtel observes, has no single specific verb for "rape."[5] Accordingly, two questions must be kept separate: (1) Does ענה, the verb used to describe Shechem's action in Gen 34:2, have a single meaning in sexual contexts? (2) Does Genesis 34

3 L. Bechtel, "What if Dinah Is Not Raped? (Genesis 34)" *JSOT* 62 (1994), 19–36.

4 Akkadian *maza'u* (AHw., 637; *CAD M/I*, s.v. *mazû*, 439–440), "squeeze," in the D-form means "rape." An Assyrian law (MAL A §55) speaks of a man, *kî da'āne batulta iṣbatma umanz'iši*, "by force seized a nubile woman and raped her." (See M. Roth, *Law Collections from Mesopotamia and Asia Minor* [2nd ed.; SBLWAW 6; Atlanta: Scholars Press, 1997], 174.) Alternatively, there is the circumlocutory phrase in MAL A §12, in which a married woman is walking in the main thoroughfare and a man *emūqamma iṣṣabassi ittiakši*, "seized her by force and fornicated with her." (See Roth, *Law Collections*, 157; Akkadian *nâku* is used only of illicit sex; see *CAD N/1*, 197.) The Akkadian sequence recalls Hebrew החזיק בה ושכב עמה (Deut 22:25) and ותפשה ושכב עמה (Deut 22:28). Two classic studies on sex offenses and related matters in Mesopotamia are J. Finkelstein, "Sex Offenses in Sumerian Laws," *JAOS* 86 (1966), 355–372; and B. Landsberger, "Jungfräulichkeit: Ein Beitrag zum Thema 'Beilage und Eheschliessung,'" in *Symbolae Iuridicai et Historicae Martino David Dedicatae*, vol. 2: *Iura Orientis Antiqui*, eds. J. A. Ankum, R. Feenstra, and W. F. Leemans (Leiden: Brill, 1968), 41–105. For an important recent study, see J. Scurlock, "But Was She Raped? A Verdict Through Comparison," *Nin* 4 (2006), 61–103.

5 Bechtel, "Dinah," 20. For this reason, the rabbis of the Mishnah and Talmuds, whose jurisprudence was more developed than that of the biblical legislators, adopted the verb אנס, also used for other kinds of force and compulsion (See C. Kasovsky, *Thesaurus Mishnae* [4 vols.; Jerusalem, Massadah, 1956–60] 1:229.) Although the verb is a technical term for "rape" in the Hebrew of the Mishnah and both Talmuds, Aramaic אנס refers to rape only in the Palestinian Talmud. See *DJPA*, 66; *DJBA*, 146. In Biblical Hebrew the verb is attested in a late source (Esth 1:8) in the context of drinking: "And the drinking was, by decree, 'no restraint' [אין אנס], for thus had the king established, to fulfill the request [רצון] of each individual." The verb is also attested in *Sirach* and in *The Damascus Document* (see *DCH* 1:344). The same verb occurs in Old Aramaic as *hns* (*DNWSI* 1:290), where it has the sense of "remove by force." In both *Tg. Onq.* and *Tg. Ps.-J.* to Gen 21:25, Lev 19:13, and Deut 28:29, 31, the verb אנס translates Hebrew גזל. The same is true of *Tg. J.* to 2Sam 23:21; see further H. Tawil, "The End of the Hadad Inscription in the Light of Akkadian," *JNES* 32 (1973), 481, n. 51. A slightly different sense, which may have led to the verb's adoption as a technical term for "rape," is attested in Biblical Aramaic in Dan 4:6, וכל רז לא אנס לך "No secret overpowers you." F. Rosenthal (*A Grammar of Biblical Aramaic* [Wiesbaden: Harrassowitz, 1963], 77) translates אנס by "subdue." This sense was already seen by ibn Ezra to Dan 4:6: "'Shall not overpower you.' Similar to it is אין אנס (Esth 1:8) in the sense of "overcome," "compel." Of particular interest is the *Tg. Ps.-J.* rendition of Hebrew גזל by אנס in Judg 21:23, where the object of the verb refers to female dancers abducted for the purpose of marriage. In Mishnaic and Talmudic Hebrew, the noun אונס "compulsion" is regularly contrasted with רצון "free will." See e.g., *m. Yeb* 6:1; and *b. Sanh.* 24b, 25a.

describe a rape? What in contemporary English is called "rape" describes forcible aggressive sexual intercourse with someone who does not consent[6] and shows obvious resistance or vigorous struggle.[7] According to Bechtel, "most analysis of Genesis 34 proceeds on the assumption of rape."[8] While this was largely true of Bechtel's predecessors,[9] more recent writers have tended to argue that Dinah was not, in fact, raped. E. van Wolde reads Genesis 34 partially as a love story, with Shechem playing Romeo to Dinah's Juliet.[10] J. Fleishman understands Shechem's act as abduction for the purpose of marriage such as the act described in Judg 21:19–25 and other ancient sources,[11] and attested in several contemporary societies.[12] In the body of his recent article on Genesis 34,

---

6 Unfortunately, the narrative of Genesis 34 fails to provide an account of Dinah's reaction (see below).

7 The OED (vol. 13:186) defines the noun "rape" as "violation or ravishing of a woman. Also in mod. usage sexual assault upon a man." For "rape" as a verb the OED characterizes the definition "to carry off (a person esp. a woman) by force" (vol. 13:187) as obsolete. Before its application to sexual crimes, the English term was used for the carrying off of ojbects, a sense that survives in "rapine," a synonym of "plunder." This was in keeping with the ultimate derivation of the word from Latin *rapio*. Primarily meaning "seize, snatch, tear away," the semantic range of *rapio* includes sexual violence. See *Harper's Latin Dictionary* eds. C. Lewis and C. Short (New York: American Book, 1907), 1523. The Latin is related to Greek ἁρπάζω (manifest in the English "harpie"), which the LXX employs to translate חטף in Judg 21:21 and גזלו in Judg 21:23. The Vulgate translates חטף by *rapite* in Judg 21:21 and גזלו by *rapuerent* in 21:23.

8 Bechtel, "Dinah," 19.

9 Almost a century ago, Skinner argued that Genesis 34 was a combination of two narratives. In one narrative Dinah was seduced by Shechem, and in the other she was raped by him. (See J. Skinner, *A Critical and Exegetical Commentary on Genesis* [ICC I; Edinburgh: T.&T. Clark, 1910], 417–422.) More recently, Frymer-Kensky wrote that the story is "probably not about a forcible rape ... Shechem saw her and lay with her ... In this way he treated her as a whore, a woman whose consent is sufficient because her sexuality is not part of a family structure. Even though Dinah may have consented to the act, the fact that he had not spoken to her parents in advance constitutes an impropriety." See T. Frymer-Kensky, "Law and Philosophy: The Case of Sex in the Bible," *Semeia* 45 (1989), 95. For a list of some other dissenters, see Gruber, "Accusations," 121 n. 13. For a fuller discussion of Gruber's article, see below.

10 "Love and Hatred," 439. In contrast, D. Marcus, in criticizing a similar interpretation, writes, "Calling the rape of Dinah 'her problematic relationship with Shechem' is simply outrageous." (review of *Harper's Bible Dictionary*, *JAOS* 110 [1990] 587).

11 Joseph Fleishman, "Socio-Legal Aspects of Genesis 34," *Shnaton* 12 (2000), 141–155; *idem*, "Shechem and Dinah-In Light of Non-Biblical and Biblical Sources," *ZAW* 116 (2004), 12–32.

12 Two noteworthy items produced by a Lexis-Nexis search were an Associated Press story on Sept. 24, 2004, about the prevalence of abduction for the purpose of marriage in

A. Rofé refers to the rape of Dinah, but in a footnote citing Bechtel and Gruber, allows for the possibility of consensual sex.[13] M. Gruber[14] agrees that Shechem did not rape Dinah. Arguing that the verb לקח "take" is elsewhere employed of marriage, Gruber claims that Shechem married Dinah.[15] He claims, in addition, that the biblical verb ענה/עני can refer to consensual sexual intercourse, as was already maintained by talmudic and medieval Jewish sources.[16] In Gruber's opinion, the classical midrash *Genesis Rabbah* did not understand Shechem's deed as a rape, nor did some medieval Jewish commentators, including Rashi.[17]

Ethiopia and a *New York Times* piece on April 30, 2005, on the practice in Kyrgyzstan. A prominent factor in contemporary abductions is the inability of the male's family to come up with the bride price or the necessary customary gifts, a situation irrelevant to Genesis 34. The brides' families often subsequently accede because despite the fact that the girls are not always sexually violated, they are nonetheless considered damaged goods and therefore often unmarriageable.

13 A. Rofé, "The Defilement of Virgins in Biblical Law and the Case of Dinah (Genesis 34)," *Bib 86* (2005), 369–374, especially 370 and n. 9.

14 Gruber, "Accusations," 119–127; *idem*, "Forgotten Meaning," 233–244. A. Shapira attempts to refute Gruber in his article, "The Accusations against Shechem Son of Hamor: A Reconsideration—A Reaction to Mayer Gruber's Article," *Beth Mikra* 44 (1998–1999), 281–282. Professor Gruber is a friend of long standing and a fine scholar from whom I always learn. My disagreements with him in this essay are in keeping with the pronouncement in *b. B. Bat.* 21a: קנאת סופרים תרבה חכמה "scholarly competition increases wisdom."

15 There is no refuting that לקח may mean "marry" when a woman is the grammatical object of that verb as shown by Gruber's citations ("Accusations," 121 n. 15), including those in Gen 34:4, 9, 16, and 21. But he himself cites *Gen. Rab.* Gen 34:26, where Rabbi Judah and Rabbi Huniah explain the fact that Dinah is the grammatical object of לקח on the part of Simon and Levi, to mean that Dinah had to be forcibly removed ("Accusations," 122). It is misleading to import words or idioms from one context to another. No one has argued, for example, that Dinah wished to conquer the daughters of the land on the basis of the meaning of ראה -ב in Ps 118:7 and *KAI* 181:7.

16 Gruber provides a thorough survey of medieval and modern commentators as well as the biblical lexica in "Forgotten Meaning." See especially the studies by A. Deem, "The Goddess Anath and Some Biblical Hebrew Cruces," *JSS* 23 (1978) 26; S. Morag, *Studies on Biblical Hebrew* (Jerusalem: Magnes, 1995), 85–90 (but compare *idem*, "The Great Metaphor of Hosea:The Words of Comfort—A Linguistic Examination," *Tarbiz* 68 [1998–1999], 4–11); N. Hakam, "ʿInnah," *Tarbiz* 69 (1999–2000), 441–444; A. Frisch, "ʿVe-Antah' (Hosea 2:17): A Secondary Meaning," *Tarbiz* 69 (1999–2000), 445–447; and E. van Wolde, "Does *ʿInnâ* Denote Rape? A Semantic Analysis of a Controversial Word," *VT* 52 (2002), 528–544.

17 "It is clear Rashi understood that the story of Dinah is not a story dealing with rape." (Gruber, "Forgotten Meaning," 237.

First, a number of terminological observations must be made. When it comes to sexual matters, language abounds in indirection; thus Hebrew שכב "lie with," English "sleep with," Latin *dormio cum* "sleep with," Greek κοιμάω "lie with," French *se coucher avec* "to go to bed with," to cite just a few.[18] This is true of the term *rape* as well. As will be seen below, rape is sometimes described by words for "dishonor," "humiliation," "shame," and "ruin." In addition, it should be noted that, whereas in contemporary English usage "rape" is a legal term for the forced sexual act itself, in earlier English "rape" could also refer to the abduction that preceded sexual activity, which might itself have been consented to for one reason or other after the abduction. According to the OED, "rape" was originally applied in English to the carrying off of objects and then extended to women.[19]

Gruber maintains that early Jewish tradition did not understand Shechem's act as a rape. Instead, he claims that it was Jerome (ca. 340–420 CE) who first depicted Shechem's act as rape by rendering Hebrew ויקח "he took," by *rapuit* in the Vulgate of Gen 34:2. According to Gruber, as late as Rashi (1040–1105), Jewish commentators saw the act as consensual and only later adopted the interpretation originated by Jerome.[20]

In his comment, Rashi writes: "'וישכבה- כדרכה; ויענה- שלא כדרכה'" "'*He lay with*[21] *her*—conventionally [vaginal penetration]; *he* ענה *her*—unconventionally [anal penetration].'"[22] From the fact that Rashi and his source in *Genesis Rabbah* understand Shechem's actions to refer to two different forms of intercourse, Gruber deduces that they did not view this as an act of rape. Indeed, Gruber argues that ענה simply means "had sexual relations."[23] But, as we will

18 Various dysphemisms come readily to mind.

19 See n. 8 above.

20 Gruber "Accusations," 122.

21 There is no difference in meaning whether the verb שכב is followed by the direct object or indirect object. See H. Orlinsky, "The Hebrew Root *ŠKB*," *JBL* 63 (1944), 19–44.

22 Anal intercourse is well attested in Mesopotamian sources. See V. A. Hurowitz, "An Old Babylonian Bawdy Ballad," in *Solving Riddles and Untying Knots: Biblical, Epigraphic, and Semitic Studies in Honor of Jonas C. Greenfield*, eds. Ziony Zevit, S. Gitin, and M. Sokoloff (Winona Lake: Eisenbrauns, 1995), 553, n. 22; and Gruber, "Accusations," 123, n. 30.

23 This neutral rendition ignores the fact that, in contrast to בוא אל "enter," with a woman as the object, the Bible never uses ענה in cases of formal marriage. Abraham is asked by Sarai to "enter" Hagar (Gen 16:2), she gives Hagar to him as a wife (16:3), and he obligingly "enters" her (Gen 16:4). Lot's daughters bemoan the fact that there is no man available to "enter" them in the proper "custom of the earth," that is, in marriage (Gen 19:31). Jacob asks Laban to "enter" Rachel (Gen 29:21). He is tricked into "entering" Leah instead (vs. 23), but subsequently manages to "enter" Rachel (vs. 30). Leah asks Jacob to "enter"

see, Jewish writers long before Jerome described Shechem's action as rape. As such, a more economical reading would be that the classical rabbis, and later Rashi, took the rape for granted. In the very pericope cited by Gruber, Dinah is compared to someone walking with a ליטרא of meat without the foresight to conceal it.[24] Naturally, a bird of prey comes and snatches[25] it. Whereas this is well in keeping with the notion that rape victims are somehow complicit in their victimization,[26] the rapist is a bird of prey (var. a dog). In the rabbinic reading, Shechem raped Dinah, not once, but twice.[27]

---

her in Gen 30:16 because her conjugal rights have been neglected on account of Jacob's favoritism toward her sister (Gen 30:15). The phrase בוא אל is also used for the "entry" of the levir into his widowed sister-in-law (Gen 38:8–9). בוא אל refers to intercourse within a marriage context between human women and male divinities (Gen 6:2–4) as well as to prostitution (Gen 38:16–18) and questionable marriage (2Sam 17:25). Gruber attempts to circumvent the problem of the nonformal use of ענה by equating the sequence of לקח "take," followed by שכב "lie with," with the sequence of לקח followed by ענה ("Accusations," 122), but this is to assume precisely what needs to be proved. The verb בעל followed by the woman as direct object describes the formal consummation of the marriage. See Deut 21:13, 24:1; Isa 62:5; and Mal 2:11. Carnal "knowledge" is expressed by ידע. A man can "know" a woman (Gen 4:1, 24:16; and 1Kgs 1:4); a woman can "know" a man (Gen 19:8 and Num 31:17–18); and a man can "know" a man (Gen 19:5 and Judg 19:22). In contrast to ענה which is only negative, the negative, positive, or neutral connotation of ידע can only be determined by context.

24 The Hebrew is borrowed from Greek λίτρα (*DJPA*, 281) but refers to meat weighing a Roman pound. For the midrash See *Gen. Rab.*, 956. See further the slight variations in the Genizah text in M. Sokoloff, *The Genizah Fragments of Bereshit Rabba* (Jerusalem: Israel Academy of Humanities and Sciences, 1982), 169–170. The *Tanḥ* parallel cited there reads, "'To see the daughters of the land (Dinah) went (to be seen) with daughters of the land.' To what is this comparable? To someone walking in the street with a piece (of meat) in his hand. A dog saw it and was following after it and snatched it. Just so was Dinah going out to see when Shechem saw her and snatched her." For other midrashic discussions of this verse see *Tanḥ*, Cf. the reading להראות in A. Tal ed., *The Samaritan Pentateuch* (Tel-Aviv: Tel Aviv University, 1994), 34; and למתחמייא עם in *Tg. Neof.*

25 The choice of the verb חטף in both Midrashim is probably due to its occurrence in the story of bridal abduction in Judg 21:21.

26 That may be implied in the biblical story itself. Gruber has observed that the only other reference to "the daughters of the land" (Gen 27:46) is highly negative ("Accusations," 121–122). Accordingly, a reader might infer that associating with these females was what got Dinah raped. As Gersonides (comment to Gen 34:1–3) puts it, "Because she acted inappropriately she got this bad outcome."

27 Rashi follows the tendency of rabbinic literature to reduce the amount of redundancy, superfluity, and embellishment in Scripture. This extends to the denial of the adverbial force of one verb seconding another. Accordingly, שכב and ענה must refer to two different

As for Jerome, Gruber is correct that he held Shechem to be a rapist but imprecise both in regard to the words Jerome used to describe the action and to his chronological primacy in characterizing Shechem's action as rape. The Hebrew of Gen 34:2–3 reads:

וַיַּרְא אֹתָהּ שְׁכֶם בֶּן־חֲמוֹר הַחִוִּי נְשִׂיא הָאָרֶץ וַיִּקַּח אֹתָהּ וַיִּשְׁכַּב אֹתָהּ וַיְעַנֶּהָ׃ 3 וַתִּדְבַּק נַפְשׁוֹ בְּדִינָה בַּת־יַעֲקֹב וַיֶּאֱהַב אֶת־הַנַּעֲרָ וַיְדַבֵּר עַל־לֵב הַנַּעֲרָ׃

The Vulgate offers:

> *Quam cum vidisset Sychem filius Emor Evei, princeps terrae, illius adamavit et rapuit et dormivit cum illa vi opprimens virginem.*
>
> And when Sichem the son of Emor the Evite, the prince of that land saw her, he fell in love [*adamavit*] with her, and took her away [*rapuit*], and lay with her [*dormivit cum illa*], ravishing [*vi opprimens*] the virgin.[28]

As we can see, Jerome moves the verb וַיֶּאֱהַב from vs. 3 to vs. 2, thus providing the motive of "love" at first sight. As for *rapuit* for וַיִּקַּח, Jerome uses the same word elsewhere to render the illegal seizure of a house (Job 20:19; Heb גזל), the wresting of a spear out of an opponent's hand (1Chr 11:23; Heb. ויגזל), and the seizure of Phillip by the Holy Spirit in Acts 8:39 (Gk. ἥρπασεν).[29] He translates ויענה by *opprimo* preceded by the adverbial use of *vi* "by force," from *vis* "force." He uses the same verb, *opprimo*, for oppressing the innocent in the Vulgate of Dan 13:53 (Susanna).[30] In other words, although *rapuit* can mean "he raped,"

---

actions. See also Gruber, "Accusations," 124. Abarbanel expands upon the rabbinic midrash to emphasize Shechem's wicked behavior (*Perush ʿal ha-Torah* [Jerusalem: Benê Arbael, 1964], 350–351). Rashi, following the midrash, uses the same technique to emphasize the virtue of Rebecca in Gen 24:16: "*Virgin*—with regard to the location of virginity—*whom a man had not known*—anally. Inasmuch as the gentile girls guarded the location of their virginity but gave themselves freely from another location, [the text] testifies about this one (Rebecca) that she was completely pure."

28 Note his addition that she was a virgin, already found in Jdt 9:2 (see below). See also ibn Ezra, Kimḥi, and Gersonides to Gen 34:2.

29 Jerome uses the plural *rapuerent* to describe the "seizure" (ויחלטו) of the Israelite king's word by the messengers of the Aramaean king in 1Kgs 20:33.

30 For a survey of Jerome's translation techniques, see Benjamin Kedar, "The Latin Translation," in *Mikra*, ed. M. Mulder (Philadelphia: Fortress, 1998), esp. 313–35. For Jerome's approach to Genesis, see J. Adam Kamesar, *Jerome, Greek Scholarship, and the Hebrew Bible: A Study of the Quaestiones Hebraicae in Genesim* (Oxford: Clarendon, 1993).

it does not mean it here. Jerome conveys the fact of rape by *opprimo* "press down," "crush," "suppress," "subdue," and so on, not by *rapio*.[31]

Yet another way in which Jerome describes Dinah's rape is in the second half of vs. 7. The Hebrew reads: כי נבלה עשה בישראל לשכב את בת יעקב וכן לא יעשה

This Jerome translates:

> *quod foedam rem esset operatus in Israhel et violata filia Iacob rem inlicitam perpetrasset.*

> For he had done a foul thing in Israel and perpetrated an unlawful act in violating the daughter of Jacob.[32]

By construing וכן לא יעשה to mean "against the law," Jerome is able to render the neutral שכב in the context of the verse *violo* "treat with violence," "violate."[33]

Early non-rabbinic Jewish sources seem to agree that Dinah was raped. We begin with the Septuagint:

> καὶ εἶδεν αὐτὴν Συχεμ ὁ υἱὸς Εμμωρ ὁ Χορραῖος ὁ ἄρχων τῆς γῆς καὶ λαβὼν αὐτὴν ἐκοιμήθη μετ᾽αὐτῆς καὶ ἐταπείνωσεν αὐτήν

The term *Vulgate* first occurs centuries after the time of Jerome. For convenience, this essay uses "Jerome" and "Vulgate" interchangeably.

31 See *Harper's Latin Dictionary*, 1272. The dictionary lists this passage under "to force a woman; commit a rape upon (late Lat.)." Jerome uses this same verb to translate ענה in the story of Amnon and Tamar in 2Sam 13:12, 14.

In the well-known tale of the Sabine women (see below), Livy uses *rapio* in the sense of abduction rather than direct sexual violation. See Livy, *Ab Urbe Condita* 1.9.10, 12, and 14. In the title of Rubens's masterpiece "The Rape of the Sabine Women," "rape" is used in the obsolete English sense of abduction. Poussin entitled his famous painting "Enlèvement [*not:* viol] des sabines," that is, "Abduction of the Sabine Women." Words regularly used to describe rape in Latin (*rapio, stuprum, violo, vim infero*) also refer to other offenses involving violence and shame. See E. Harris, review of G. Doblhofer, *Vergewaltigung in der Antike* (Leipzig: Teubner, 1994) in *Classical Review* 46 (1996), 327–328. In relating the famous tale of the rape of the Vestal Rhea Silvia, who became the Mother of Romulus and Remus, Livy uses the verb *comprimo: vi compress Vestalis* "the Vestal was ravished." (*Ab Urbe Condita* 1.4.2 [Foster, LCL]).

32 In vss. 13 and 27, Jerome translates the verb טמא "pollute," "defiled," by rephrasing the passage nominally as *ob stuprum* "on account of the defilement." The term *stuprum* is used especially for rape and other sexual improprieties. In Gen 39:10 Jerome paraphrases לא שמע אליה לשכב אצלה להיות עמה "he would not listen to her to lie with her to be with her" by *ille recusabat stuprum* "he refused the adultery."

33 See *Harper's Latin Dictionary*, 1994.

> And Sychem the son of Emmor the Horite[34] the prince of the land saw her, and took her, slept with her, and humbled her. (Gen 34:2)

The translator is quite literal, rendering ויקח by λαβὼν αὐτὴν, וישכב אותה by ἐκοιμήθη μετ' αὐτῆς, and ויענה by ἐταπείνωσεν αὐτήν.[35] This same verb, *tapeinōo* "lower," "reduce," "humble," "abase," is also used by the LXX of 2Sam 13:12, 14 and Ezek 22:10[36] to render Hebrew ענה when a woman is the object. LSJ (1757) lists these occurences under "violate a woman."[37]

In contrast to the literal translation of the LXX, Josephus paraphrases the biblical account, adding some details and omitting others.[38] In Ant. 1.337, Shechem's action is described as Φθείρει δι' ἁρπαγῆς "he defiled her by violence," according to Whiston's classic translation.[39] Thackeray translates "carried her off and ravished her."[40] More recently, Feldman translated "seduced

---

34 This is the reading of most of the MSS (see John W. Wevers, *Septuaginta Genesis* [Göttingen: Vandenhoeck & Ruprecht, 1974], 322). Others reflect חוי "Hivvite" as in the extant Hebrew texts.

35 For the Hebrew correspondence of the verb *lambanein*, see HRCS, 847–852. For the Hebrew correspondences of *koimaō*, see *ibid.*, 773–774; Orlinsky observes that in all but one of the 47 cases of שכב עם/את in the Hebrew Bible, the LXX has the preposition *meta* ("*ŠKB*," 27). In the one exception (1Sam 2:22b), the LXX lacks a correspondent to the Hebrew. For the Hebrew correspondences of *tapeinoō*, see HRCS, 1334–1335.

36 On the Ezekiel passage, see M. Greenberg, *Ezekiel 21–37* (AB 22a; New York: Doubleday, 1997) 445; and see below.

37 In each of these instances, except Ezek 22:10, which it paraphrases, the Peshitta translates ענה by the Pael of ܛܢܦ "treat shamefully," "abuse," "dishonor," "outrage a woman." See PSmCom, 482. In Payne Smith 2:3426, the author translates the Syriac of Gen 34:2, Judg 20:5, 1Sam 2:22 (Heb. וישכבון); 2Sam 13:12, 14, and 22 by *stupravit*. In the entry ܛܢܦܐ (*ibid.*, 3427), he translates the attestations *Act. Mart.* 2.161, 163 as *stupratio* (the source of the somewhat obsolete English words for rape, stuprate [verb] and stupration [noun]); and *vitiatio*, "vitiation," "corruption." Weitzman argues for a Jewish origin of the Peshitta, the completion of which he dates to ca. 200 CE (M .Weitzman, *The Syriac Version of the Old Testament* [Cambridge: Cambridge University Press, 1999], 244–262). If he is correct, this would give us another Jewish source prior to Jerome that interpreted Shechem's act as rape.

38 For a detailed study of how Josephus and other Hellenistic Jewish writers treated Genesis 34, see L. Feldman, "Philo, Pseudo-Philo, Josephus, and Theodotus on the Rape of Dinah," *JQR* 94 (2004), 253–277.

39 That is, he raped her. (William Whiston, *The Works of Flavius Josephus* (4 vols.; Grand Rapids: Baker, 1984) 2:117; LSJ *s.v.* ἁρπάγ-δην 245, lists ἁρπάγή "seizure,'" "robbery," "rape," and cites Solon 4.13: ὀφλὼν ἁρπαγῆ δικῄ "found guilty of rape."

40 Josephus, *Ant.* 1:337 (Thackeray, LCL).

her through abduction," but later in the same article wrote that, according to Josephus, Shechem "seized her and ruined her."[41] Perhaps Feldman hesitated initially because φθείρω can mean both "seduce" and "ruin." Although LSJ cites no case of the verb used for ravishing a woman, it does cite the usage of the verb in the passive mood "undone."[42] More important is the related noun φθορά, which, although it can mean "seduction," has the clear sense of "rape," "ravage" of virgins in Strabo, *Geogr.* 6.1.16. We would not be far off the mark by translating the relevant passage in Josephus as "he ruined her through rape."

Another early Jewish source is the *Biblical Antiquities* of Pseudo-Philo[43] ultimately going back to a Hebrew original written in Palestine, 50–150 CE, and surviving in a Latin translation, probably made from a Greek intermediary. In 8.7, we read:

> *Et habitavit Iacob in terra Chanaan, et Dinam filiam eius rapuit Sychem filius Emore Correi*[44] *et humiliavit eam.*
>
> Jacob dwelled in the land of Canaan. Shechem the son of Hemor the Horrite took Dinah his daughter and raped her.[45]

A retroversion of the extant Latin text into Hebrew would show it to be a paraphrase of the biblical text rather than a quotation. Whatever the reading of the Hebrew original of Pseudo-Philo, it was clearly understood by the later translator as a decription of rape. The fact of rape is conveyed by the combination of *rapuit* "seized," "snatched," and *humiliavit* "humbled."[46] In any event, the Latin precedes the work of Jerome, who translated the Pentateuch after 398,[47] and

41 "Philo," 94. Compare 263 with 272. Compare further L. Feldman in *Flavius Josephus: Translation and Commentary, vol. 3: Judaean Antiquities*, ed. S. Mason (Leiden: Brill, 2004), 123 and n. 959. Feldman describes the version of Genesis 34 transmitted by Theodotus (late 3rd to 2nd century BCE) as a portrayal of Shechem's action as rape ("Philo," 272–273). But the Jewish identity of Theodotus cannot be assumed.

42 LSJ, 1928.

43 For a brief description with bibliography, see D. Harrington, *ABD* 5:344–45.

44 Pseudo-Philo reflects a Hebrew חרי, as does the Alexandrine text of Septuagint cited above.

45 Howard Jacobson, *A Commentary on Pesudeo-Philo's Liber Antiquitatum Biblicarum* (2 vols.; Leiden: Brill, 1996), 1:102. Similarly, Feldman translates *rapuit* by "seized" and *humiliavit* by "raped." ("Philo," 261).

46 The Vulgate translates ענה by *humiliavit* in Deut 22:24, 29.

47 Kedar, "Latin," 321.

"the style is the same as the translations of the Bible which preceded that of Jerome."[48]

Yet another Jewish source asserting that Dinah was raped is *Tg. Neof.* to Gen 34:2 which reads as follows:

וחמה יתה שכם חיוויה רבה דארעא ושמש עמה וצער יתה

Shechem, the son of Hamor the Hivite, the lord of the land saw her, took her, copulated with her, and ravished her.[49]

The date of this targum is debated, but according to Philip Alexander "there are no good grounds for dating anything in Neofiti later than 3rd/4th century."[50]

Finally, from several centuries before Jerome, we have the book of Judith surviving in Greek and probably based on a Hebrew original written no later than the early first century BCE.[51] In a clear reference to Genesis 34,[52] the writer has Judith preface her prayer as follows:

> Lord God of My father Simeon, in whose hand you put a sword to take vengeance on the aliens who had unbound [ἔλυσαν] a virgin's [that is, Dinah's] womb[53] [μήτραν παρθένου] in defilement [εἰς μίασμα] and stripped [ἐγυμνωσαν] the thigh [μηρὸν] in shame [εἰς αἰσχύνην][54] and profaned [ἐβεβήλωσάν] the womb [μέτράν] in disgrace [εις ὄνειδος]; for you said "it must not be done"[55] yet they[56] did it. So you gave up their rulers to

48 Guido Kisch, *Pseudo-Philo's Liber Antiquitatum Biblicarum* (Notre Dame, IN: University of Notre Dame, 1949), 134.

49 *Copulated:* DJPA, 559; *ravished:* DJPA, 468. Sokoloff (*ibid.*, 468) translates this sense of צער as "outrage a woman." The same entry cites a line from an Aramaic poem of the Byzantine period, צער בתולן כל רמש "He outraged virgins every evening." The same verb with the same meaning is used by the Peshitta of Gen 34:2 to render ענה.

50 P. Alexander, *ABD* 6:323.

51 See C. Moore, *ABD* 3:1123.

52 See E. Zenger, *Das Buch Judit* (Gütersloh: Mohn, 1981), 492.

53 Most likely, womb should be corrected to μίτραν "sash." The corruption probably arose from the occurrence of μήτραν later in the verse. See Zenger, *Judit*, 492 n. 2b.

54 For *aisxunein* to describe an act of rape, see Harris, Review of Doblhofer, 373 n. 16. The verb primarily means "disfigure." In the moral sense, it means "dishonor," especially a woman. See LSJ, 43.

55 The author takes וכן לא יעשה of Gen 34:8 in a legal sense, as does Jerome.

56 Taking his cue from the plural טמאו "they polluted," in Gen 34:27, the author of Judith blames all the residents. (Peshitta reads plurals in vss. 7 and 13 as well.) Thus, he understands Dinah to have been gang raped, an action that justified the slaughter of the entire city's inhabitants.

> be killed, and their bed, which was ashamed of the deceit they had practiced, to be stained with blood and you struck down slaves upon princes and princes upon their thrones, and you gave up their wives to plunder and their daughters to captivity and all their spoils to be divided among your beloved sons, who were very zealous for you and abhorred the pollution of their blood and called upon you for help.

In sum, Jewish[57] tradition well before Jerome regarded Dinah as forced by Shechem. We now turn to the question of whether the traditional position or the position of the revisionists is correct. As we have seen, Biblical Hebrew has no single specific term for rape,[58] and we cannot solve the problem simply by plotting the semantic range of ענה. As Gruber has shown, certainly ענה cannot mean "rape" in the case of the betrothed young woman in Deut 22:23–27:

> If it happens that in the city a young nubile woman[59] [נערה בתולה] who is betrothed to a man is encountered by a man who lies with her, you shall take the two of them out to the city gate and pelt them with stones until they die; the young woman because she did not cry out in the city,

57 Similar is the Samaritan tradition. *Sam. Tg.* to Gen 34:2 translates ויענה by לבטה. Tal translates the Samaritan לבט (meaning 2) by Hebrew אנס "rape," and characterizes it as a euphemism. See A. Tal, *A Dictionary of Samaritan Aramaic* (Leiden: Brill, 2000), 423. Even though the date remains uncertain, the earliest tradition stratum of *Sam. Tg.* has affinities with *Tg. Onq.* and the Aramaic documents from the Judean Desert. See A. Tal, "Samaritan Literature," in *The Samaritans* ed., A. Crown (Tübingen: Mohr Siebeck, 1989), 413–467, esp. 448.

58 The verb שגל is used for sexual intercourse in Deut 28:30, Isa 13:16, Jer 3:2, Zech 14:2. It refers to forced sex in wartime in Isa 13:16 and Zech 14:2. Deut 28:30 may possibly describe a voluntary act, and Jer 3:2 surely does. If we assume the accuracy of the Masoretic tradition, which always substitutes שכב in the *Qere*, then שגל is best rendered by the well-known four-letter Anglo-Saxon vulgarism. See further P. Mankowski, *Akkadian Loanwords in Biblical Hebrew* (HSS 47; Winona Lake: Eisenbrauns, 2000), 138 n. 514.

59 See *DCH* 2:289–290. To describe a virgin in the contemporary English sense, בתולה is insufficient. Biblical Hebrew always adds to בתולה an additional phrase, "no man had known her" (Gen 24:16); or "a young nubile woman who has not known a man in lying with a male." (Judg 21:12) Indeed, when sexual inexperience is at issue, the term בתולה may be omitted entirely. In Num 31:18, where female sexual experience is a matter of life and death, the text reads "all the young women who have now known lying with a man." The situation is similar in Sumerian and Akkadian, in which physical virginity can only be expressed negatively. See Landsberger, "Jungfräulichkeit," 58.

> and the man because he humbled [ענה] the wife[60] of his fellow. But if in the field the man encounters the young betrothed woman and he has grabbed hold of her and lain with her, only the man who lay with her shall die. But you shall not do a thing to the young woman. The young woman has no mortal sin, for this is just the same as when a man attacks his fellow and has murdered him, for he encountered her in the field. The young betrothed woman screamed with none to save her.

In the above passage, the woman in the city is presumed to have consented to the sexual encounter and is not a victim of rape.[61] In contrast, as Gruber wryly observes, נשים בציון ענו בתלת בערי יהודה "Women they ענו in Zion, young women in the towns of Judah" (Lam 5:11) does not refer to honeymoons but to acts of rape.[62] The same may be said of Judg 19:24 and 20:5.

In the case of Amnon's rape of Tamar (2Sam 13:1–22), it is not simply the repeated presence of ענה[63] that is decisive. We know the action to be rape because he grabs her and summons her to lie with him (vs. 11); she protests for two verses (vss. 12–13); he does not listen to her and overpowers[64] her in order to have her sexually (vs. 14). In the case of Dinah, we have no account of any proposition by Shechem or of any assent or refusal on Dinah's part. Naḥmanides bases his interpretation that Dinah was raped on the presence of the verb ענה. In his comment on Gen 34:2, Naḥmanides writes, "every forced intercourse is called עינוי," citing as proof texts Deut 21:14 and Judg 20:5.[65] He

60 *Humbled*: Vulgate, *humiliavit; Wife*: According to Deut 20:8, the betrothal and marriage are sequential, separate acts. In pre-industrial societies, ancient and modern, full marriage bonds were completed through a series of actions over time, a procedure known as "inchoate marriage." See S. Greengus, "Redefining 'Inchoate Marriage' in Old Babylonian Contexts," in *Riches Hidden in Secret Places: Ancient Near Eastern Studies in Memory of Thorkild Jacobsen*, ed. Tzvi Abusch (Winona Lake: Eisenbrauns, 2002), 123–139.

61 Deut 22:24 presents a problem for Naḥmanides's contention that every instance of ענה refers to rape (see below). His ingenious solution (*ad loc.*) is: "The context of the verse is that once we see that the man grabs her and lies with her we judge the woman as consenting because she could have been saved from him (by screaming); and the man is considered as having raped her because he did not seduce her or talk her into consenting to him."

62 Gruber, "Accusations," 242.

63 2Sam 13:12, 14, 22, 32.

64 Which means that she resisted with both words and action. See S. Bar-Efrat, *II Samuel: Introduction and Commentary* (Tel-Aviv: Am Oved, 1996), 135.

65 See ibn Ezra on Lam 5:11; for תחת אשר עניתה Vulgate has *quia humiliasti eam*. Elsewhere (Deut 21:24), Naḥmanides writes, "עינוי is only used for one who lies (with a woman) by force (באונס)." He assumes that the captive woman of Deut 21:4 did not consent.

adds that "the verse is conveying to her [Dinah's] credit that she was raped and had not consented to [even] the prince of the land."

It is the contention of the present essay first that the verb ענה means "subdue," "play the dominant role" in sexual contexts just as it does in political contexts and that the lexicographers who do not separate the sexual from the political use are correct.[66] Second, the dominance or subjugation runs the gamut from consensual sex to outright rape.[67] Third, despite the claims by Gruber and others that ענה simply means "engaged in sexual relations with," in biblical settings describing sexual relations of unquestioned propriety, the term ענה is not employed.[68]

Let us return to Deut 22:24. The man who lay with the betrothed young woman is to be stoned because he exercised sexual dominance in an area limited to another. Obadiah Sforno (1470–ca. 1550) puts it well: "He humbled [הענה] and demoted [השפילה] her from her licit status [כשרותה], and made her invalid [פסל אותה] and not suitable [ראויה] to her husband, his fellow."[69]

Next, we turn to the other passages in which ענה allegedly has the neutral sense "have intercourse with." Deut 21:10–14 reads:

> When you go out to war against your enemy and Yahweh your god has handed him over to you and you have taken captives from him and you have seen among those captives a beautiful woman and desired her and would take her to you as wife—then you shall bring her into your house where she shall shave her head and tend to her nails.[70] She shall remove her captive clothing and stay in your house and bewail her father and mother for an entire month. After that, you shall enter her sexually and she will be a wife to you. But if it happens that you fail to delight in her then you shall send her where she wishes. But you shall surely not sell

66 It is still common, albeit crude, for English speakers to speak of sexual "conquests." For Hebrew ענה "excercise dominance," "subjugate" see, for example, Gen 15:13 and Exod 1:11; For Phoenician, see *KAI* 26.19–20; For Moabite, see *KAI* 181:5–6; For examples of the correspondence between the sexual and political contexts of ענה, see BDB, 776; *HALAT*, 807 (=*HALOT*, 852 ; Gesenius, "ענה II," 603–604.

67 See Deut 22:24, 28–29; Judg 19:24; 20:5; 2Sam 13:22.

68 See Gruber, "Accusations," 233 n. 2; see also Morag, *Studies*, 90 n. 31; Shapira, "Reaction," 28; Hakam, "ʿInnah," 442.

69 Z. Gottlieb, ed., *Beʾur ʿal ha-Torah le-Rabbi ʿOvadyah Sforno* (Jerusalem: Mossad Harav Kook, 1980), 341.

70 For this sense of עשה, see ibn Ezra and Naḥmanides on 2 Sam 19:25. Her hair and nails will have grown unsightly in captivity.

> her for silver. You shall not use her as a commodity inasmuch as you have humbled her [עניתה].[71]

Rashbam understands ענה in this passage as consensual intercourse for the purpose of marriage and is followed by Weinfeld and Gruber.[72] But this defines consent much too generously. Given the circumstances of warfare, a woman might prefer what is at heart, involuntary sexual intercourse, to involuntary sexual intercourse accompanied by torture and beating.[73]

As further proof that ענה simply means "had sexual intercourse," Gruber cites the difficult passage Ezek 22:10–11:

> עֶרְוַת־אָב גִּלָּה־בָךְ טְמֵאַת הַנִּדָּה עִנּוּ־בָךְ׃ 11 וְאִישׁ ׀ אֶת־אֵשֶׁת רֵעֵהוּ עָשָׂה תּוֹעֵבָה וְאִישׁ
> אֶת־כַּלָּתוֹ טִמֵּא בְזִמָּה וְאִישׁ אֶת־אֲחֹתוֹ בַת־אָבִיו עִנָּה־בָךְ׃

These verses and the entire pericope denouncing Jerusalem in Ezek 22:7–12 were long ago linked by scholars to passages in the Torah.[74] Greenberg translates as follows:

> One has uncovered [his] father's nakedness in you; they have forced the menstrually impure woman in you; and one has committed abomination with his fellow's wife, and one has depravedly defiled his daughter-in-law, and one has forced his paternal sister in you.

---

71 *Commodity*: so Rashbam and Hazzekuni, but the precise sense of תתעמר remains uncertain. See J. Tigay, *The JPS Torah Commentary: Deuteronomy* (Philadelphia: Jewish Publication Society, 1996), 195 and 382 n. 35. *Humbled her*: LXX :(ἐταπείνωσας); Peshitta: (ܕܡܟܟܬܗ̇); Vulgate: *humiliasti eam.*

72 M. Weinfeld, *Deuteronomy and the Deuteronomic School* (Oxford: Oxford University, 1972), 286; Gruber, "Accusations," 237.

73 See Shapira, "Reaction," 281; Hakam, "ʿInnah," 443 puts it well: "It is likely that the woman was taken against her will, because, in general, a woman whose people has been defeated in warfare is unlikely to consent to sexual relations with a fighter from the winning side." Naḥmanides on Gen 34:2 refers to this case as a rape.

74 See the comments of Joseph Kara in *Mikra'ot Gedolot Haketer, vol. 6: Sefer Yehezkel*, ed. M. Cohen (Ramat Gan: Bar Ilan University, 2000), 145; M. Greenberg, *Ezekiel* 21–37, 454–456; and Gruber, "Accusations," 240–242.

In his comment on the passage, Greenberg writes that ענה "signified unwillingness of the woman to acquiesce in the illegal union."[75] As Gruber correctly observes, both Greenberg's translation of ענה in these passages as "forced" and his justification for doing so are themselves forced.[76] Yet, it misses the point to translate simply "had sexual relations." It is rather the exercise of sexual dominance in the inappropriate settings of menstruation and adultery.

One example of ענה referring to inappropriate sexual dominance that has generally eluded detection is the story of Samson and Delilah in Judg 16:4–6.[77]

> וַיְהִי אַחֲרֵי־כֵן וַיֶּאֱהַב אִשָּׁה בְּנַחַל שֹׂרֵק וּשְׁמָהּ דְּלִילָה׃ 5 וַיַּעֲלוּ אֵלֶיהָ סַרְנֵי פְלִשְׁתִּים
> וַיֹּאמְרוּ לָהּ פַּתִּי אוֹתוֹ וּרְאִי בַּמֶּה כֹּחוֹ גָדוֹל וּבַמֶּה נוּכַל לוֹ וַאֲסַרְנֻהוּ לְעַנֹּתוֹ וַאֲנַחְנוּ נִתַּן־
> לָךְ אִישׁ אֶלֶף וּמֵאָה כָּסֶף׃ 6 וַתֹּאמֶר דְּלִילָה אֶל־שִׁמְשׁוֹן הַגִּידָה־נָּא לִי בַּמֶּה כֹּחֲךָ גָדוֹל
> וּבַמֶּה תֵאָסֵר לְעַנּוֹתֶךָ׃

> After that he fell in love with a woman in Wadi Sorek, who was named Delilah. The princes of the Philistines went up to her and said, "Beguile him and discover what makes his strength so great, and by what means we can overcome him, and bind him to subdue him, and we will each give you eleven hundred in silver." So Delilah said to Samson, "Tell me what makes your strength so great, and by what means might you be bound that you might be subdued."

Samson deludes Delilah three times, until she nags him so much that he confides to her that his strength lies in his hair. Realizing that he is finally telling the truth,

> וַתְּיַשְּׁנֵהוּ עַל־בִּרְכֶּיהָ וַתִּקְרָא לָאִישׁ וַתְּגַלַּח אֶת־שֶׁבַע מַחְלְפוֹת רֹאשׁוֹ וַתָּחֶל לְעַנּוֹתוֹ וַיָּסַר כֹּחוֹ מֵעָלָיו׃

75 Greenberg, *Ezekiel 21–37*, 455. This same reasoning apparently underlies NJPS "ravage" in both verses. KJV offers "humble," in both cases; NRSV translates ענו in vs. 10 by "violate" but ענה in vs. 11 by "defile." Luther Bible translates ענו in vs. 10, by *nötingen*, "compel." In vs.11, it translates ענה by the stronger *notzüchigen*, "rape." Vulgate offers *humilaverunt* in vs. 10 and *oppressit* in vs. 11. The LXX has (ἐταπείνουν) in both verses.

76 Gruber, "Accusations," 241 n. 53.

77 For recent studies, see J. C. Exum, "Harvesting the Biblical Narrator's Scanty Plot of Ground: A Holistic Approach to Judges 16:4–22," in *Tehillah le-Moshe: Biblical and Judaic Studies in Honor of Moshe Greenberg*, eds. M. Cogan, B. Eichler, and J. Tigay (Winona Lake: Eisenbrauns, 1997), 39–46; Frymer-Kensky, *Reading the Women*, 78–85.

She put him to sleep on her knees; she called out to the man [Samson], she cut off the seven locks of his head[78] and began to exercise sexual dominance over him/force him[79] [that is, she initiated sexual arousal] but his strength [that is, his potency, virility] had departed from him. (Judg 16:19)

Here as elsewhere[80] כוח refers to sexual vigor. Cutting Samson's hair removed his "strength" so that he experienced erectile dysfunction. Jer 31:22 depicts a woman's initiation of sex with a man as "something that will be new on earth."[81] In the present order, though, it is not a thing a decent woman would do,[82] but Delilah is not a decent woman. She makes Samson the object of ענה and thus exercises dominance[83] over him. The loss of his sexual potency is an indication that the rest of his strength has left him as well. Delilah's sexual dominance is analogous to the Philistine exercise of the dominance for which they expressed their desire in vss. 5 and 6.

It should be obvious that ענה in Gen 34:2 is in keeping with the use of the word elsewhere in the Bible. In other words, according to Gen 34:7, Shechem exercised sexual dominance over a highborn woman, "lying with the daughter of Jacob, a thing not to be done." But did he rape her or did she consent? We are ready at last to answer the question. Isaac Abarbanel and, slightly later, Obadiah Sforno, some 500 years ago, already contrasted the behavior of Shechem in Genesis 34 with that of Amnon in 2Samuel 13.[84] More recent

78 For this translation of ותקרא לאיש, see J. Sasson, "Who Cut Samson's Hair?" *Prooftexts* 8 (1988), 333–339.

79 See Luther Bible ad loc., "Sie fing an, ihn zu zwingen." Luther Bible translates the previous two occurrences of ענה by "zwingen" (to force) as well.

80 Prov 5:10; In Gen 49:3, the firstborn is the product of his father's sexual vigor. See also the use of חיל in Prov 31:3.

81 See W. Holladay, *Jeremiah 2* (Hermeneia; Minneapolis: Fortress, 1989), 195.

82 See the depiction of the brazen adulteress who grabs hold of a man, kisses him, and solicits him in Proverbs 7, especially vss. 15–20. The rabbis disapproved of Leah's solicitation of Jacob in Gen 30:16. See Rashi ad loc., and at Gen 34:2. According to rabbinic sources (*b. Ketub.* 65a and parallels), a woman should limit her consumption of alcohol because by the third drink she will ask to have sex. The rabbis taught that it is a man's place to orally articulate (תובע בפה) his desire for sex and sexual satisfaction, whereas a woman should be less direct (תובעת בלב). See *b. 'Erub.* 100b.

83 To borrow the contemporary American sports parlance, "she dominated him."

84 I thank my colleague David Marcus for pointing out that Abarbanel and Sforno were preceded by the Masoretes of the Leningrad manuscript, who connected the narratives of Genesis 34 and 2Samuel 13 by inserting catchwords between them at ויענה in Gen 34:2.

scholars have profitably compared the two stories in detail, an approach that will be followed here.[85]

First, as in 2Samuel 13, both the perpetrator and the victim are highborn. Second, in both stories a brother/brothers avenge(s) the outrage against a sister. Third, in each case the father of the victim does not take direct action. Fourth, both actions are described as נבלה (*nĕbālâ*) in Israel. As Sforno observed, the contrasts are no less significant. In Genesis 34, Shechem "loves" Dinah after the sexual act, sweet-talks her, tries to arrange a marriage, having brought her into his house, offers to pay a high bride-price for her, and has himself circumcised.[86] In contrast, Amnon "loves" Tamar before raping her, and hates her thereafter. Having refused Tamar's suggestion to ask for her hand, he says nothing to her and has her physically evicted from his house.[87] Critical to the interpretation of both stories is Jonadab's attempt to reassure David that Amnon alone has perished at the hands of Absalom and his explanation of Absalom's action:

> וַיַּ֣עַן יוֹנָדָ֣ב בֶּן־שִׁמְעָ֣ה אֲחִֽי־דָוִ֘ד וַיֹּאמֶר֒ אַל־יֹאמַ֣ר אֲדֹנִ֗י אֵ֣ת כָּל־הַנְּעָרִ֤ים בְּנֵֽי־הַמֶּ֙לֶךְ֙ הֵמִ֔יתוּ
> כִּֽי־אַמְנ֥וֹן לְבַדּ֖וֹ מֵ֑ת כִּֽי־עַל־פִּ֤י אַבְשָׁלוֹם֙ הָיְתָ֣ה שׂוּמָ֔ה מִיּוֹם֙ עַנֹּת֔וֹ אֵ֖ת תָּמָ֥ר אֲחֹתֽוֹ׃ 33
> וְעַתָּ֡ה אַל־יָשֵׂם֩ אֲדֹנִ֨י הַמֶּ֤לֶךְ אֶל־לִבּוֹ֙ דָּבָ֣ר לֵאמֹ֔ר כָּל־בְּנֵ֥י הַמֶּ֖לֶךְ מֵ֑תוּ כִּֽי־אִם־אַמְנ֥וֹן
> לְבַדּ֖וֹ מֵֽת׃
>
> Jonadab, the son of Shimeah brother of David spoke up and said, "Let not my lord say that they have killed all the young men, the king's sons; Amnon alone is dead, because according to Absalom it was an obligation [שׂוּמָה] [to kill Amnon] from the day that he raped [מִיּוֹם עַנֹּתוֹ] Tamar his sister. Now let not my lord the king take it to heart saying that all the sons of the king are dead; for Amnon alone is dead." (2Sam 13:32–33)[88]

B. Eichler, Professor Tigay's colleague at the University of Pennsylvania, refers to Genesis 34 and 2 Samuel 13 as two stories that "clearly reflect the importance

85 Abarbanel, *Perush*, 351; and Gottlieb *Beʾur*, 86–87. For more recent comparisons, see D. Fewell and D. Gunn, "Tipping the Balance: Steinberg's Reader and the Rape of Dinah," *JBL* 111 (1991), 193–211, esp. 210; Amit, "Rape," 16* n. 15; Shimon Bar-Efrat, *Narrative Art in the Bible* (Sheffield: Almond, 1997), 239–282; and Frymer-Kensky, *Reading*, 160–168.

86 For the sense of דבר על לב as "sweet talk," see 2Sam 19:3; Hos 2:16. Or, as Abarbanel puts it, "words of cheer, words of vows, and promised gifts" (*Perush*, 351); Dinah's location is intimated in vs. 17 and fully articulated in vs. 26.

87 See Fewell and Gunn, "Balance," 210.

88 For שומה, see Bar-Efrat, *II Samuel*, 142; observe the similarity of Jonadab's words to David to Absalom's words to Tamar in vs. 20 above.

of the brother in biblical society of his unmarried sister and as her champion against overpowering forces."[89] In his study, Eichler cites ancient and contemporary parallels to illustrate the special relationship between brother and sister. It is in this context that we must read both these stories. Both Dinah and Tamar were raped; both Jacob and David did not act and so it fell to the full brothers to exact vengeance. There are further corroborations of the fact of Dinah's rape; the first is from the conclusion of the story in Gen 34:30–31:

> וַיֹּאמֶר יַעֲקֹב אֶל־שִׁמְעוֹן וְאֶל־לֵוִי עֲכַרְתֶּם אֹתִי לְהַבְאִישֵׁנִי בְּיֹשֵׁב הָאָרֶץ בַּכְּנַעֲנִי וּבַפְּרִזִּי
> וַאֲנִי מְתֵי מִסְפָּר וְנֶאֶסְפוּ עָלַי וְהִכּוּנִי וְנִשְׁמַדְתִּי אֲנִי וּבֵיתִי׃ 31 וַיֹּאמְרוּ הַכְזוֹנָה יַעֲשֶׂה
> אֶת־אֲחוֹתֵנוּ׃

> Jacob said to Simeon and to Levi, "You have caused me trouble in making me odious to the inhabitant [collective] of the land—to the Canaanites and Perizzites, and I am few in men. If they [the inhabitants] gather against me and strike me, I will be destroyed, I and my household." But they said, "Will he make our sister out [יַעֲשֶׂה] to be a whore?"

Most translators and commentators understand the "he" included in the verbal form יַעֲשֶׂה in vs. 31 as a reference to Shechem. In consequence, they read the answer of the brothers as a visceral but somewhat irrational, or at least impractical, response to Jacob's question. Typical is the remark of the Tosafist Joseph Bekor Shor: "It is preferable to be in danger rather than to accept this shame."[90]

But readings of this sort ignore the fact that Shechem was last mentioned in vs. 26, making him a rather remote antecedent. More to the point is Sforno, who takes the subject of the verb יַעֲשֶׂה to be the inhabitant of the land (grammatically singular with collective sense as often in Biblical Hebrew):

> Will the people of the land take her to be a whore for whom recompense for shame is not to be claimed?[91] [They know] she is not a whore, but our sister for whom recompense for shame is to be claimed, and that because

---

89 See B. Eichler, "On Reading Genesis 12:10–20," in *Tehillah le-Moshe*, 33.

90 J. Nevo, ed., *Perushe Yosef Bekor Shor ʿal ha-Torah* (Jerusalem: Mossad Harav Kook, 1994), 62.

91 Hebrew: שאין ראוי לתבוע עלבונה. *Tg. Neof.* uses the same phrase in its expansive paraphrase of vs. 35. The targumist has Simeon and Levi say that they acted in order to keep Shechem from boasting that he could get away with raping Dinah because she had no one to claim recompense for her shame: דלית לה בר נש תבע עלבנה.

> she is our sister it is worthy of us to claim that recompense. And once the inhabitant of the land considers these matters, he will not find it worthy to rise up [against us].[92]

On this reading,[93] the response of the brothers is rational. They are reassuring Jacob that the Canaanites and Perizzites know that the brothers acted to avenge the outrage to the honor of their sister. Shechem did not treat her like a whore. He treated her like a victim and then declared his love for her. But he has "performed an enormity" (נבלה *nĕbālâ*) in Israel. As Bar-Efrat has observed, in all biblical attestations of this phrase, the perpetrator pays with his life.[94] In Gruber's view, Shechem was not a rapist because contemporary studies emphasize that rape is primarily a crime of violence and that rapists don't fall in love with their victims.[95] Shechem fell in love with Dinah, ergo Shechem was not a rapist. But the writer(s) of Genesis 34 was/were unaware of these studies, as was the Roman historian Livy in his recounting of the ancient tale of the Sabine women.

Livy tells how the Romans, having a scarcity of females and barred by their neighbors from intermarriage, abducted the Sabine women using a festival as a ruse.[96] In Livy's account, Romulus attempted to calm the despondent women and promised them:

> [They] should be wedded and become co-partners in all the possessions of the Romans, in their citizenship and, dearest privilege of all to the human race, in their children; only let them moderate their anger, and give their hearts to those whom fortune had given their persons. A sense of injury had often given place to affection, and they would find their husbands the kinder for this reason, that every man would earnestly

92 Gottlieb, *Beʾur*, 87.

93 A further advantage of this reading is that it obviates the need for highly questionable explanations on the order of Frymer-Kensky's ("Law and Philosophy," 95 [see n. 9 above]). My colleague Susan Einbinder suggests the possibility that the subject of the brothers' question is Jacob, referred to in the third person: "Will he [Jacob] make our sister out to be a whore [for whom no recompense is to be claimed]?".

94 Bar-Efrat, *II Samuel*, 134. The other passages are Deut 22:21; Josh 7:15; Judg 20:6, 10; and Jer 29:23. In all but the Joshua passage, the enormity in question is sexual.

95 Gruber, "Accusations," 127.

96 This story is regularly compared with Judges 21. See, for example, E. Ullendorf, "The Bawdy Bible," *BSOAS* 42 (1975), 436. For further parallels to both, see T. H. Gaster, *Myth, Legend, and Custom in the Old Testament* (2 vols; Gloucester, MA: Smith, 1981), 2:444–446.

> endeavour not only to be a good husband, but also to console his wife for the home and parents she had lost. His arguments were seconded by the wooing of the men, who excused their act on the score of passion and love, the most moving of all pleas to a woman's heart.[97]

Although Hamor and Shechem, unlike Romulus, do not refer to the offense, the terms of their offer to Jacob and his family after the fact are quite similar.[98] It is also not much of a leap to imagine that when Shechem sweet-talked Dinah (vs. 3), he excused his act by pleading the irresistible force of his passion and love. After all, Hamor (vs. 8) tells Jacob's sons that Shechem's very being longs for the girl (חשקה נפשו). Likewise, the narrator informs us (vs. 19) that Shechem was circumcised with alacrity because he desired (חפץ) the girl.

Of course, we need not go back to Livy to discover some of the assumptions underlying Genesis 34. Popular culture as recently as my youth taught that a woman's "no" often concealed a "yes" and, consequently, that rape might be an act of love. Once the victim was "convinced" by her "suitor's" sexual prowess and his words of love, the two might live happily ever after, or at least for a while.[99] Finally, it must be observed that, had the sexual act in Genesis 34 been consensual, it is unlikely that Dinah would have been spared by her brothers. In a celebrated biblical case of consensual sex across ethnic and religious[100] lines, Phineas the zealot kills both the Midianite woman Kozbi and the Israelite man Zimri. If, as claimed by some scholars, Genesis 34 is a polemic against sex, intermarriage, and concomitant idolatry with outsiders,[101] a consenting Dinah would have shared the fate of Zimri. Even if the religious issues were not a concern, the consenting Dinah, as depicted by Bechtel and Gruber,

97 Livy, *Ab Urbe Condita*, 1.9.14–16 (Foster, LCL).

98 Whereas the proposal that Jacob's people and Hamor's people become one (Gen 34:15, 22) came to naught, in the Roman story the Sabines and Romans in fact became one people after the women were mollified and Romulus interceded between their two peoples. See Livy: *nec pacem nodo, sed civitatem unam ex duabus faciunt*"not only did they agree on peace, but they made one people out of the two." (*Ab Urbe Condita*, 1.13.4 [Foster, LCL]).

99 The early James Bond movies of the 1960s, although not graphically explicit, provide numerous examples. See P. Reis, "Cupidity and Stupidity: Woman's Agency and the 'Rape' of Tamar," *JANES* 25 (1997). 52, n. 50.

100 Contra van Wolde ("Love and Hatred," 435–449), hardly "racial." For the incident, see Num 25:7–8.

101 See, for example, Amit, "Rape."

would probably have been killed by her brothers as a matter of "honor," a practice that, unfortunately, persists to this very day.[102]

102 Abarbanel writes:

All of this [his previous argumentation] teaches that Dinah was innocent of this sin [of consensual sex with Shechem]. Were it not so, there is no doubt that her brothers would have killed her on the day that they came upon the slain when they found her; where they would have judged according to the principle of the adulterer and the adulteress (Lev 20:10). But it became clear to them [the brothers] that she had definitely been a victim of rape [אנוסה]. (*Perush*, 351).

The New York Times on Dec. 16, 2005, reported that a Druse woman in Shfaram, Israel, had been murdered by her father and uncle for being intimate with a non-Druse Muslim man. The honor killing was widely approved within the Druse community. A Lexis-Nexis search going back only six months from May, 2006, produced 125 items on honor killings in Turkey, Pakistan, and the United Kingdom, among others.

* *Author's note*: Professor Jeffrey Tigay and I were classmates at Jewish Theological Seminary's Rabbinical School. He has gone on to become one of the leading biblicists of our generation. Professor Tigay's studies are models of what can be achieved when one approaches the Bible with a thorough knowledge of its ancient Near Eastern background and with a similarly thorough knowledge of classical rabbinic literature and the great medieval Jewish commentaries. It is a delight for me to contribute this article in his honor.

I am especially grateful to Murray Lichtenstein, far more at home than I in Greek and Latin, for his thorough reading of this manuscript and his numerous suggestions. I am likewise grateful for the comments of Susan Einbinder, Jennifer Jaech, J. Adam Kamesar, Sharon Keller, David Marcus, Ilana Sasson, David Silber, and Ben Sperling. All the above are absolved of responsibility for my errors.

History of Biblical Scholarship

CHAPTER 21

Jewish Biblical Scholarship in America: The Beginnings

The history of Jewish biblical scholarship in America cannot be divorced from its European heritage. At the same time, American Jewish biblical scholarship is inseparable from the larger political and social history of North American Jewry, a Jewry distinct, perhaps uniquely so, from all of its predecessors. The present essay, which is devoted to the history of American Jewish Bible scholarship from its rudimentary beginnings until the outbreak of the First World War, outlines those features of American Judaism which either encouraged or impeded the serious study of the Bible by Jews.

American Jewish institutions and religious movements were shaped and formed more in response to pressing needs than by religious ideology.[1] Jewish Bible scholarship in America[2] was no exception. The community of 1,500 Jews who lived in America on the eve of the Revolutionary War grew tenfold in the next half century but continued to be a tiny minority in the total population.The Jewish settlement in Canada was even smaller.[3] Whereas the large

1 See A. Karp, *Haven and Home: A History of the Jews in America* (New York: Schocken, 1985), 51–83. As one succinct formulation has it: "The intellectual and religious traditions of American Jewry ... have shallow roots." See A. Hertzberg, *The Jews in America* (New York: Simon and Schuster, 1988), 13. The figure 1,500 is from Karp, *Haven.* Appendix 1–4 provides population tables from 1790–1980. Hertzberg, *Jews*, 49 gives the figure as "perhaps 2,000."

2 For a comprehensive survey of American Jewish biblical scholarship until 1972 see the necrology by H. M. Orlinsky, "Jewish Biblical Scholarship in America," in *idem, Essays in Biblical Culture and Bible Translation* (New York: Ktav, 1974), 287–332; cf. *idem*, "Old Testament Studies," in *Religion*, ed. P. Ramsey (Englewood: Prentice-Hall, 1965), 51–109. In addition to Orlinsky's surveys, see I. Abrahams, "Bible: Exegesis among Jews in the Modern Period," *Encyclopaedia Judaica* 4, 889–904; S. Blank, "Bible," in *Hebrew Union College-Jewish Institute of Religion at One Hundred Years*, ed. S. Karff (Cincinnati: Hebrew Union College, 1976), 287–316; S. D. Sperling, "Judaism and Modern Biblical Research," in *Biblical Studies: Meeting Ground of Jews and Christians*, eds. L. Boadt and L. Klenicki (New York: Stimulus, 1980), 19–44; B. Levine, "A Decade of Jewish Bible Scholarship in North America," *Jewish Book Annual* 39 (1981–1982), 9–29; S. D. Sperling and B. Levine, "Biblical Scholarship, Modern," in *Blackwell Companion to Jewish Culture From the Eighteenth Century to the Present*, ed. G. Abramson (Oxford: Basil Blackwell, 1989), 87–91.

3 In 1871, the first census after confederation showed 1,115 Jews in Canada. For population figures see B. Kayfetz, "Canada," *EncJud* 5, 104–105.

 | DOI 10.1163/9789004340879_022

European Jewish communities had seldom lacked scholars, religious functionaries, well-trained teachers and educational materials, in America all of these were in short supply.[4] Schools conducted by Jewish congregations often made use of slightly reworded Protestant catechisms[5] and taught the Hebrew Bible to their students by means of the King James translation. Isaac Leeser (1806–1868) of Philadelphia[6] decried this state of affairs and attempted numerous solutions.

Leeser's contributions must be understood both against the background of the European Jewish community whence he came, and against the special circumstances of the United States. Born in Neuenkirchen in Prussian Westphalia, Leeser had received a good but limited gymnasium education. The same may be said of his Jewish education, which was greatly influenced by Abraham Sutro (1784–1869), a somewhat enlightened Orthodox rabbi. The period of Leeser's youth coincided with a period of revolutionary change in the structure and character of the Jewish communities. Until the late eighteenth century the nation states of Europe had related to Jews not as individual citizens of the state but as involuntary members of a corporate body, the Jewish community, which was generally autonomous in internal affairs. Individual Jews as members of the community were perforce governed by the traditional Jewish legal system (*halakhah*), which embraced all aspects of social, economic,

4 Both Karp, *Haven* and Hertzberg, *Jews* offer excellent detailed narrative histories of the American Jewish community from its beginnings to the present. For a briefer sketch of American Jewish history with extensive bibliography, see M. Atkin, "United States of America," *EncJud* 15, 1585–1671; See further, A Hertzberg, "The American Jew and his Religion," in *Understanding American Judaism* vol. 1, ed. J Neusner (New York: Ktav, 1975), 5–24; On the paucity of Jewish books and educators in mid-nineteenth century America, see M. Davis, *The Emergence of Conservative Judaism* (Philadelphia: Jewish Publication Society, 1963), 47–55. Davis notes (*ibid.*, 55) that in the 1840s some sixty men served as congregational rabbis and cantors. Of the rabbis, only the Reform Max Lilienthal and the Orthodox Abraham Rice (Reiss) were known to have genuine rabbinic ordination; cf. the material assembled in the somewhat overly polemical biography of Rice by I. H. Sharfman, *The First Rabbi* (Malibu: Joseph Simon Pannngloss, 1988). See further, E. Silberschlag, "The Primacy of Hebrew in Early America," *Hebrew Studies* 16 (1985; Katsh volume), 123. N.B. "Orthodox" will be capitalized when the reference is to instutional affiliation but not when it refers to belief or practice.

5 See L. Sussman, "Isaac Leeser and the Protestantization of American Judaism," *American Jewish Archives* 38 (April, 1986), 20, n. 49.

6 For a recent bibliography of studies on Leeser, see Sussman, *American Jewish Archives* 38, 16, n.4. For much of what follows we are indebted to *idem*, "Another Look at Isaac Leeser and the First Jewish Translation of the Bible in the United States," *Modern Judaism* 5 (1985), 159–190. For a full biography of Leeser, see L. Sussman, *Isaac Leeser and the Making of American Judaism* (Detroit: Wayne State University, 1995).

political, and religious life. Within these communities rabbis functioned less as clergy than as communal officials and judges responsible for the interpretation and application of the all-encompassing Jewish law. Although synagogues fell within rabbinic jurisdiction, rabbis preached only rarely. Daily services were led by laics, that is, knowledgeable males at least thirteen years of age. Sabbath and holiday services, especially in larger communities, were usually conducted by a *ḥazzan* (cantor), a learned layman with professional or semi-professional musical training. The Emancipation of much of Western and Central European Jewry between 1770 and 1870 enabled Jews to move out of the ghetto and, in varying degrees, to become included in society at large.[7] Emancipation amounted to a social revolution, which provided Jews as individuals with greater freedom, but at the same time narrowed the jurisdiction of the collective Jewish communities and consequently, undermined the authority of those officials who had traditionally filled leadership roles. In effect, the jurisdiction of the ordained rabbi became limited to the specific realm of Jewish religious practice, which with the decline of the power of the community to enforce a uniform pattern of observance, had been transformed into a matter of individual conscience. At the same time, as emancipated Jews increasingly took advantage of opportunities for general education, their knowledge of Hebrew and of Jewish ritual declined to the extent that synagogues increasingly came to require the services of professional clergy. Modernist seminaries[8] soon arose to produce rabbis who, despite numerous differences among themselves in theology and religious observance, were in essential agreement with the increasingly cosmopolitan laity that Jewish clerics should function much like Protestant ministers.[9] These rabbis of the newer breed, who usually had some university education, preached regularly and, if Orthodox, left the adjudication of fine points of ritual law to their more traditionally-schooled colleagues.

7 See J. Katz, *Out of the Ghetto* (New York: Schocken, 1978).

8 The earliest modernist rabbinical seminary was the Instituto Convitto Rabbinico founded in 1829 in Padua. A year later the École Centrale Rabbinique opened in Metz. Other significant seminaries were the Jüdisch-Theologisches Seminar of Breslau, founded in 1854: Jews' College in London (1855); Israelitisch-Theologische Lehranstalt in Vienna (1862), Hochschüle für die Wissenschaft des Judentums in Berlin (1873); Rabbiner Seminar für das Orthodoxe Judentum in Berlin (1874); and Orzágos Rabbiképzö Intézet (=Franz-Josef Landesrabbinerschule) in Budapest in 1877. For a historical outline with bibliography see L. Rabinowitz, "Rabbinical Seminaries," *EncJud*, 13, 1463–1466.

9 The radically innovative character of the modernist seminaries may be appreciated by observing with Rabinowitz ("Rabbinical Seminaries," 1464), that such institutions never took root in Russia, Poland, or for that matter in modern Israel, where the old style talmudical academy (*yeshivah*) retained its predominance.

Early nineteenth century American Jewry likewise required professional clergy. But given its small size, low level of education and general lack of concern for the finer points of Jewish ritual law, the American Jewish community had little need for ordained rabbis, and indeed engaged none until the 1840s. Required instead were cantors to lead services, ritual slaughterers to provide kosher meat and ritual circumcisers to initiate baby boys into the Abrahamic covenant. Often one man would serve in all these capacities. He would also be expected to teach synagogue Hebrew to the children and on the model of the American Protestant minister, to preach regularly in the synagogue.[10]

Isaac Leeser was just the kind of clergyman required in the American synagogue of his time. At the age of twenty-two, he became *hazzan* (cantor) of his Congregation Mikveh Israel in Philadelphia, a position he occupied for twenty-one years. Leeser, like his contemporary occupants of the post of *ḥazzan*, lacked rabbinic ordination and had no doctoral degree.[11] Nonetheless, American historical circumstances combined with the man's personal vision and sense of purpose to make Leeser the primary architect of American Jewish institutional life. Bertram Korn has written: "Practically every form of Jewish activity which supports American Jewish life today was either established or envisaged by this one man."[12] Among Leeser's pioneering accomplishments were the establishment of the English sermon as a fixture of the American synagogue, and the editing and publication of *The Occident*, the first successful Anglo-Jewish newspaper in the United States. Leeser also founded the first American Jewish Publication Society, and the first American rabbinic school, Maimonides College, neither of which long survived Leeser's death,[13] although his personal example inspired others to succeed where he had failed. What survived him for more than a half century was the Leeser translation of the Bible, a project that took seventeen years. The English

10 See Sussman, "Protestantization," 10–11. The job of the factotum sometimes required him to teach the native European language of the synagogue's adult members to the children. See the synagogue advertisements cited by Sussman, *ibid.*, 19.

11 In Karp's (*Haven*, 67) felicitous formulation: "Leeser … had the grace never to call himself 'Rabbi.' Others readily conferred ordination and doctorates upon themselves." Nonetheless, the introduction to the authoritative *TANAKH A New Translation of the Holy Scriptures According to the Traditional Hebrew Text* (Philadelphia: Jewish Publication Society, 1985), xvii persists in referring to Leeser as "the American rabbi."

12 B. Korn, *apud* Sussman, "Another Look," 159.

13 Maimonides College enrolled four students in 1867. By the time it closed its doors four years later, it had trained three men for the rabbinate. See Davis, *Emergence*, 59–64.

translation of the Pentateuch appeared in 1845[14] followed in 1853 by an entire Hebrew-English Bible.[15] Leeser, unlike his Reform opponents, was personally committed to the observance of Jewish ritual law. Although Leeser's orthodoxy impelled him to forswear American citizenship, which he regarded as a compromise of the ancient Jewish messianic redemptive hope, he had *volens nolens* become an American influenced by American religion. In his own words, "If ever a country other than the blessed commonwealth of Israel, had especial cause for glorifying the most holy Name, it is surely the republic of the United States."[16] In the first half of the nineteenth century, religious traditions in the American republic were evaluated according to Protestant criteria, and Protestantism itself was centered in the Bible. Between 1816–1820 the American Bible Society, itself a product of that revival movement known as the "Second Great Awakening," had distributed about one hundred thousand Bibles in the United States.[17] Leeser's biblicentrism in religion, itself an unacknowledged departure from European Jewish orthodoxy, was complemented by his anglophilism and his admiration of the Episcopalian style of worship.[18] Accordingly, Leeser looked for his model of Bible translation to the English Authorized Version, whose translators he described "as honest as men writing for their sect are likely to be."[19] Nonetheless, because "persons differing from us in religious ideas make use of Scripture to assail Israel's hope and faith,"[20] it was Leeser's conviction that Jews required an English Bible[21] that would retain the dignity of the King James Version while abandoning its Christology. On the

14 I. Leeser, *The Law of God, Edited, with Former Translations Diligently Compared and Revised* (Philadelphia: C. Sherman, 5605 [=1844–1845]).

15 I. Leeser, *The Twenty-Four Books of the Holy Scriptures: Carefully Translated According to the Massoretic Text, on the Basis of the English Version, after the Best Jewish Authorities; and Supplied with Short Explanatory Notes* (Philadelphia, 5614 [=1853–1854]).

16 Thanksgiving Day sermon, December 21, 1843, quoted by Sussman "Another Look," 171. The very act of preaching a sermon on Thanksgiving Day exemplified Leeser's Americanization as well as his acceptance of a Protestant model.

17 Sussman, *Modern Judaism*, 5, 161.

18 See Sussman, "Protestantization," 4–6. It is of interest that Leeser in collaboration with Joseph Jaquett, an Episcopalian cleric, published an untranslated *Biblia Hebraica* in 1848. See Sussman, "Another Look," 166.

19 Leeser, *Twenty-Four Books*, iii. Note the words "on the Basis of the English Version," in the full title.

20 *Ibid.*, vii.

21 Their lack of Hebrew fluency also required the production of prayer books that included an English translation. Solomon Jackson had published a prayer book in Hebrew and English in 1826. Leeser provided an edition of the Spanish and Portuguese rite with translation in 1836, and a corresponding German rite version in 1848. See Karp, *Haven*, 37–38.

one hand, Leeser can hardly be faulted for his frank attempt to give his English version a Jewish coloring by translating biblical passages in accord with the Aramaic Targums, the medieval Jewish exegetes and the "modern German Israelites" among them, Mendelssohn, Wessely, Zunz and Fürst.[22] On the other hand, it must be admitted that in his avoidance of christological interpretation Leeser often went to the other extreme by rendering biblical passages according to later Jewish law or theological doctrine while at the same time insisting that he was translating literally. In this approach Leeser differed from such outstanding medieval Jewish exegetes as Rashi who had regularly acknowledged that the plain sense of Scripture might differ from rabbinic interpretation. In the same vein, Leeser often attempted to harmonize conflicting biblical passages even when sufficient textual warrant was lacking, in order to demonstrate the unity of Scripture.[23] There can be no doubt that these flaws in his work stem from Leeser's biblicentric agenda. In the manner of some of its Protestant counterparts, early nineteenth century American Judaism had to justify itself by Scripture alone.

As regards style, Leeser's translation faithfully followed the King James Version in its elegant, if archaic, language as well as in the pursuit of extreme literalness when such did not impede the translator's religious objectives. All *waws* were mechanically rendered "and;"[24] protagonists invariably "lift up their feet" before walking and "lift up their voices" before speaking. The Judaized King James produced by Leeser proved extremely popular among the Jews in America if not among their coreligionists in England.[25] There can be no doubt that the style and format of the Leeser Bible captured the "specific synthesis" of American Jewish life in the mid-nineteenth century.[26] In the United States the Leeser translation served as the English Bible of the Jews until its replacement by the translation of the Jewish Publication Society in 1917.

Whereas Leeser succeeded admirably in his goal of translating the Bible for American Jewish use, his failure at Maimonides College provides a partial explanation of why serious American Jewish Bible scholarship took a long time to develop. In the New World, Jews were freer than they had been

22 *Ibid.*, vii–viii.

23 For numerous examples of such tendentious renditions along with a detailed appreciation and critique of Leeser as translator see M. Tsevat, "A Retrospective View of Isaac Leeser's Biblical Work," in *Essays in American Jewish History*, ed. J. Marcus (Cincinnati: American Jewish Archives, 1958), 295–313.

24 See the remarks about "'And Bibles,'" in Orlinsky, *Essays*, 410–411.

25 See I. Abrahams *apud* Tsevat, "Retrospective," 296, n. 4.

26 See Sussman, "Another Look," 169.

throughout most of their history. For much of the nineteenth century their low population[27] served to shield American Jews from much of the religious discrimination suffered by Roman Catholics[28] and the racial abuses to which Chinese, blacks and American Indians were subjected.[29] Internally, there was no autonomous Jewish governing body to coerce its members into conformity of belief and practice. But if the American Jewish community was freer than its European antecedents, it was far less schooled in the law and lore of Judaism. The lack of Jewish libraries, the scarcity of Hebrew type and the relative smallness of the American Jewish community were responsible only in part for this cultural lag. More important was the social and educational position of the Jewish community.

The Jews who had come to America were predominantly peddlers and traders rather than scholars and students.[30] For the first seventy-five years of the nineteenth century, educational and rabbinic leadership came from abroad,[31] trained according to the traditional European Jewish curriculum. It must be emphasized that whereas the Reformation had made the Bible fundamental to Protestant seminary education, Scripture played a very minor role in the training of traditional rabbis. The European Jewish curriculum prescribed Bible solely for early elementary education in the *ḥeder* (one-room schoolhouse). Older boys with the desire for higher learning whose families or communities were able and willing to support them, were spared the pressures of earning a living, so that they might continue their studies in a talmudical academy (*yeshivah*) where they concentrated on the Babylonian Talmud and its commentaries.[32] Students who desired rabbinic ordination were given the

27 See Karp, *Haven*, Appendix I.

28 See Hertzberg, *Jews*, 121.

29 This is not to say that the Jews had suffered no ethnic prejudice before the mass immigrations. See M. Selzer, *Kike* (New York: Meridian, 1972), 9–39.

30 See Orlinsky, "Scholarship," 288. Hertzberg notes (*Jews*, 250) that in the 1770's when Rhode Island College, now Brown University, offered to establish a chair in Hebrew and Oriental Languages, the wealthy Jewish merchants declined to contribute.

31 See Hertzberg, "American Jew," 9.

32 On the history, structure, and curriculum of the *yeshivah* see S. Assaf, M. Breuer and A. Steinsaltz, "Yeshivot," *EncJud* 21, 315–321. No less an authority than Elijah b. Solomon of Vilna (1720–1797), "the Gaon of Vilna" had failed in his attempt to reform the curriculum so that students might learn Bible properly before turning to Talmud. See E. Ginzberg, *Keeper of the Law: Louis Ginzberg* (Philadelphia: Jewish Publication Society, 1966), 24. Ginzberg (*ibid.*) quotes the saying that "Jews learned their Bible from Talmud."

further requirement of mastering the late medieval Jewish law codes.[33] In contrast, Bible study in the talmudical academy generally consisted of little more than following the public reading of the Torah during the synagogue service. In some pietistic circles, study of the Bible by adults, especially when unmediated by the proper medieval commentaries and the talmudic traditions, was construed with good cause,[34] as a mark of heterodoxy. Needless to say, critical study of the Bible, which questioned the accuracy of the received text, challenged traditional attributions of authorship and discovered disparate sources where tradition claimed unity of composition, was anathema to the Orthodox. But even in the circles of nineteenth century *Wissenschaft des Judentums*, there was very little attention paid to critical study of Bible for a number of reasons. First, scholars associated with *Wissenschaft des Judentums* sought citizenship rights in their native or adopted countries. For them, reconstruction of the history of the Jew in the gentile world was a scholarly task with contemporary and personal relevance. In contrast, the serious study of historic ancient Israel in its own land had embarrassingly nationalistic overtones. Second, critical Christian Bible scholarship since the days of Herder had often been couched in language highly critical of Jews and Judaism.[35] Wellhausen, for example, was notorious in Jewish circles for his negative evaluation of the late Jewish "church" to which he attributed the final form of the Pentateuch, a work he considered overly legalistic and ritualistic.[36] To be sure, Wellhausen's antipathy to legalism as expressed in his biblical scholarship was largely meant

33 In nineteenth century eastern Europe it was the practice to ordain only married students. Because the *yeshivot* had facilities only for unmarried students, married men seeking ordination united in a study-community known as *kolel*, where they and their families were supported out of communal funds for the three to four years needed to master the Jewish legal code literature. See Assaf, "Yeshivot," 769–770.

34 See Katz, *Ghetto*, 129–130.

35 Johann G. Herder, writing in the eighteenth century, set the tone for the common nineteenth century view that the restoration community of the sixth century BC was degenerate in comparison with pre-exilic Israel: "When the Jews … returned from bondage … they built a temple, as if this would have revived the times of Moses and Solomon: their religion was pharisaical; their learning a minute nibbling at syllables." (The citation is from J. Rogerson, *Old Testament Criticism in the Nineteenth Century England and Germany*, [London: Fortress, 1985], 43.) Similarly, in the first decade of the nineteenth century de Wette wrote: "Das Judenthum ist das Unglück, das Christenthum der Trost dafür." See Rogerson, *ibid.*, 41, n. 57. In describing the literature of the post-exilic period Wilhelm Gesenius wrote: "Die Bücher Daniel, Esther, Jona enthalten Legenden in einem gesunkenen jüdischen Geschmacke." See Rogerson, *ibid.*, 53, n. 16.

36 See references in Sperling, "Judaism," 23.

as an assault on his own German Protestant contemporaries who practiced what Wellhausen considered an unduly legalistic Christianity.[37] Nonetheless, his comments could be, and were, regarded as anti-Semitic by many Jewish scholars.[38] Third, we must recall that critical study of the Bible remained a sensitive topic even for educated American Christians throughout the nineteenth century.[39] American Presbyterian authorities, for example, convicted Henry Preserved Smith of heresy in 1891 because he espoused biblical criticism. C. A. Briggs, who likewise accepted biblical criticism, was removed from the Presbyterian ministry in 1893 despite being acquitted of heresy.[40]

In consequence, even when American Jewry began successfully to train its own leaders, critical study of the Bible was at first discouraged.[41] Isaac Mayer Wise (1819–1900),[42] against whose reformist approach much of Isaac Leeser's activity was directed, serves as a notable example of one who encouraged the scientific study of Judaism while at the same time institutionalizing a

37 See L. Silberman, "Wellhausen and Judaism," *Semeia* 25 (1983), 79–82. On Silberman's analysis, we must include Wellhausen in the tradition of Christians whose characterizations of their opponents as "Judaizers" has little or nothing to do with Jews or Judaism. It was Wellhausen who personally encouraged Silberman's teacher Jacob Lauterbach in the study of rabbinics in which he was to excel. It must be said nonetheless, that Jewish readers of Wellhausen and his colleagues in biblical studies might readily be discouraged from pursuing a field in which scholarly literature abounded in rhetoric inimical to Judaism.

38 Jews could easily take offense with such summaries of their religion as the following: "Judaism … is a mass of antinomies. We are struck with the free flight of thought and the deep inwardness of feeling which are found in some passages in the Wisdom and in the Psalms; but, on the other hand, we meet with a pedantic ascetism which is far from lovely, and with pious wishes the greediness of which is ill-concealed; and these unedifying features are the dominant ones of the system … The Creator of heaven and earth becomes the manager of a petty scheme of salvation … The Law takes the soul out of religion and spoils morality … The labour is done for the sake of the exercise; it does no one any good, and rejoices neither God nor man." The above is taken from Wellhausen's article "Israel" appended to J. Wellhausen, *Prolegomena to the History of Ancient Israel* (Cleveland: Meridian, 1961 [originally published in 1878]), 509.

39 This was true in Europe as well. See Rogerson, *Criticism.*

40 See E. W. Saunders, *Searching the Scriptures. A History of the Society of Biblical Literature, 1880–1980* (Chico: Scholars, 1982), 17–18. For earlier nineteenth century American controversies over Bible study see J. Brown, *The Rise of Biblical Criticism in America, 1800–1870: The New England Scholars* (Middletown: Wesleyan, 1969).

41 At the ill-fated Maimonides College, Bible had been taught by Sabato Morais, a man of strong conservative bent. See Davis, *Emergence*, 61, and see below.

42 On Wise, see M. Meyer, "In the Days of Isaac Mayer Wise," in *Hebrew Union College at One Hundred*, 7–47; for further bibliography see *ibid.*, 248, n.4.

sentimental attachment to the Bible of his own early childhood. German-born and despite his own claims to the contrary, largely self-taught,[43] Wise compensated for his lack of formal training with ambition, vision and apparently boundless energy. In 1875, after an earlier failure,[44] Wise founded the first American rabbinical seminary to survive its infancy, Hebrew Union College (HUC) in Cincinnati, Ohio. Although Wise was a religious reformer who considered such matters as the dietary laws "purely national laws for Israel, local and temporary,"[45] and denied or questioned the hallowed beliefs in resurrection and a personal god, he continued at HUC the traditional practice of moving students quickly from Bible to Talmud.[46] Wise was unwavering, if behaviorally and ritually inconsistent, in his faith that the Pentateuch had been revealed to Moses by the hand of God. For Wise it was "Mosaic and Sinaitic … or nothing."[47] In 1891 Wise published *Pronaos to Holy Writ*[48] with the aim of demolishing what the author repeatedly termed "negative criticism," in order to demonstrate the antiquity of the Pentateuch and the fact of its Mosaic authorship. According to Wise, negative criticism was to be shunned because it depicted the Bible as "a compendium of pious or even impious frauds, willful deceptions [and] unscrupulous misrepresentations."[49] Although tendentious and idiosyncratic, *Pronaos* is a much better book than one might expect. On the negative side of the ledger, Wise departs from accepted convention by never quoting any other scholar by name. In addition, Wise inconsistently, but in a manner hardly unique in Jewish scholarship,[50] accepts the critical method when its conclusions do not undermine the authenticity and Mosaic origin of the Pentateuch. Thus, Wise avers that Isaiah 40–66 is exilic (*Pronaos*, 72) and

43 See Meyer, *ibid.*, 11; Cf. W. Jacob "The Influence of the Pittsburgh Platform on Reform Halakhah and Biblical Study," in *The Pittsburgh Platform in Retrospect*, ed. W. Jacob (Pittsburgh: Rodef Shalom, 1985), 28.

44 Wise had established the Zion Collegiate Institute in 1855. It fell victim to apathy and lack of financial support. See Davis, *Emergence*, 56–67.

45 *Ibid.*, 42.

46 *Ibid.*, 20.

47 *Ibid.*, 44.

48 I. M. Wise, *Pronaos to Holy Writ Establishing on Documentary Evidence the Authorship, Date, Form and Contents of Each of the Books and the Authenticity of the Pentateuch* (Cincinnati: Robert Clarke and Company, 1891). For a detailed critique see S. Sandmel, "Isaac Mayer Wise's Pronaos to Holy Writ," in *A Bicentennial Festschrift for Jacob Rader Marcus*, ed. B. Korn (New York and Waltham: American Jewish Historical Society and Ktav, 1976), 517–525.

49 *Pronaos*, iv.

50 See below.

that Psalm 118 is Maccabean (*ibid.*, 90). On the positive side, *Pronaos* depends for its argumentation on a very detailed knowledge of the Hebrew Bible, which Wise possessed in abundance. Indeed, the work rewards its readers by demonstrating that Wise was both a man of superior intellect and a very close reader of the biblical text. In sum, Wise had the potential to make lasting contributions to biblical scholarship but lacked that openness of mind which might have accompanied a better formal education. *Pronaos* reflected a view of the Bible that other HUC faculty, better educated than Wise, and more sympathetic to critical Bible scholarship, could not accept. Nonetheless, Wise's view, that biblical instruction should concentrate on "exegesis" prevailed in the first quarter-century of HUC's existence.[51] By "exegesis," Wise meant that students should study Bible primarily in the light of the Jewish medieval commentaries and the Aramaic Targums. In Wise's lifetime professors were prohibited from suggesting textual emendations of the Pentateuch in class. During one visit to a classroom Wise heard a professor expounding Wellhausenian biblical criticism and ordered him to discontinue the lecture.[52]

A similar institutional position was taken by the Jewish Theological Seminary (JTS), organized in 1886 by the centrist forces, which had begun to coalesce in American religious Judaism as early as the 1870s and especially in the 1880s. On the left wing were scholarly rabbis such as Alexander Kohut,[53] Marcus Jastrow and Benjamin Szold who were considered by many to be Reform,[54] but who could not support the radical Reform[55] stance of the Philadelphia Conference

51 S. Blank, "Bible," in *Hebrew Union College at One Hundred*, 288–289.

52 Meyer, "Isaac Mayer Wise," 44.

53 Alexander Kohut (1842–1894) contributed significantly to Semitic lexicography with his eight volume edition of the medieval talmudic dictionary of Nathan ben Jehiel (1035–ca. 1110), which appeared as *Aruch Completum* (8 volumes, reprint New York, 1955).

54 Karp (*Haven*, 59) observes that Szold's Oheb Shalom in Baltimore "may well have been the first ... Conservative (although this term began to be used only later) congregation." Nonetheless, both Oheb Shalom and Jastrow's Rodeph Shalom in Philadelphia were members of the Union of American Hebrew Congregations organized by I. M. Wise. See Meyer, "Isaac Mayer Wise," 39. Szold gave the opening address at the first HUC ordination in 1883 (*ibid.*, 38). Hertzberg, (*Jews*, 149) refers to Szold as a "Reform rabbi." Davis, (*Emergence*, 17) characterizes Szold as theologically more radical than I. M. Wise.

55 Wise had always favored unity over ideology. (See Jacob, *Pittsburgh Platform*, 26.) Indeed, the Cleveland Conference called by Wise in 1855 included Leeser as a participant. (See Meyer, "Isaac Mayer Wise," 38.) Among the Cleveland declarations of principles were the following: "The Bible as delivered to us by our fathers and as now in our possession is of immediate divine origin and the standard of our religion. The Talmud contains the traditional legal and logical exposition of the biblical laws, which must be expounded and practiced according to the comments of the Talmud." (Jacob, *Pittsburgh Platform*, 26)

of 1869[56] and especially, the Pittsburgh Platform of 1885.[57] On the right wing were clerics more committed to traditional Jewish observance, notably the Sephardim Sabato Morais and H. Pereira Mendes, who along with like-minded German and early East and Central European immigrants who had grown up in America, were too acculturated to the United States and too disdainful of the newer immigrants[58] to be accepted by them as authentically orthodox.[59] These men and others who identified themselves with "the Historical School" founded The Jewish Theological Seminary Association in New York in 1886 "for the preservation in America of the knowledge and practice of historical Judaism." The JTS itself was opened formally in 1887. Because the Seminary's natural constituency of "acculturated East European immigrants and their children had not yet come into being," JTS barely survived into the twentieth century.[60] By 1902, when the Seminary was reorganized with Solomon Schechter as president, the American Jewish demographic situation had begun to change considerably. There were now increasing numbers of Jews, mainly of East-European origin, who were alienated from old-style orthodoxy but unwilling to reject its forms completely. These Jews favored the retention of Hebrew

---

The fact that the call for the Pittsburgh Conference came from Kaufmann Kohler demonstrated that the radical wing was in control and prompted the more traditional elements to avoid the conference entirely. (See Jacob, *ibid.*, 28–29.).

56 Among other things, the Philadelphia conference repudiated Davidic Messianism and maintained that the dispersion of the Jews was not a "punishment for the sinfulness of Israel" but a "realization of their high-priestly mission, to lead the nations to the true knowledge and worship of God." See D. Polish, "The Changing and the Constant in the Reform Rabbinate," *American Jewish Archives* (November, 1983), 270.

57 See the studies in Jacob, *Pittsburgh Platform*. No direct transcript of the Pittsburgh meetings has survived. See Jacob, *ibid.*, 28.

58 When questioned by a reporter about the plan to bring Rabbi Jacob Joseph of Vilna to New York as chief rabbi of the Association of American Orthodox Congregations, Sabato Morais stated: "I never before heard of Rabbi Joseph. I am familiar with the manner in which the Hebrews in the place when he comes are educated, and I know he is not a cultured man. He does not possess the knowledge nor the literary attainments which a rabbi should possess." See A. Karp, "The Conservative Rabbi—'Dissatisfied But Not Unhappy,'" *American Jewish Archives* 35 (1983), 199–200.

59 See Karp, "Conservative Rabbi," 196. On the question of Morais's orthodoxy see *ibid.*, 195–196. See further the discussion and bibliography in J. Gurock, "Resisters and Accommodators: Varieties of Orthodox Rabbis in America, 1886–1893," *ibid.* 162–163.

60 Karp, "Conservative Rabbi," 201. Financial difficulties at both JTS and HUC had led two of New York's wealthiest Reform Jews, Jacob Schiff and Louis Marshall, to advocate a merger of the two institutions. See Meyer, "A Theological School for Reform Judaism," *Hebrew Union College at One Hundred*, 51–52.

as their language of prayer, but at the same time demanded decorous services with frequent English accompaniment. In Orthodox fashion they preferred to cover their heads during worship. In Reform fashion and in keeping with American church style, they preferred family pews to the Orthodox requirement of separate seating for men and women. United in opposition to Reform and largely unwelcome in Reform synagogues, such people differed considerably in their own forms of personal observance and belief. It was from JTS that the rabbinic leadership of this new constituency was to come. Although the members of the "Historical School" who served on the faculty of JTS during the Schechter years and later, differed from their genuinely orthodox adversaries in their advocacy of the scientific approach to the study of Judaism, they generally adhered to the personal observance of Jewish law in greater or lesser degrees and were not entirely committed to the creation of a new religious movement within Judaism.[61] Nonetheless, the self-definition of JTS as traditionalist in opposition to Reform, was insufficient to win the support of the Orthodox who maligned JTS as "Schechter's seminary."[62] In consequence, a new Conservative[63] movement gradually emerged, with JTS as its primary source of synagogue professionals.[64]

---

61 It is significant that the Reform HUC consciously arrogated to itself the authority of the classical *yeshivah* by granting its rabbinic graduates the traditional *semikah* (judicial authorization) whose central clause is the talmudic formula: *yoreh yoreh yadin yadin* "Shall he give legal rulings? He shall give legal rulings! Shall he judge? He shall judge!" In contrast, although the English version of the JTS ordination confers the degree of "Rabbi, Teacher and Preacher" on rabbinic graduates, the Hebrew version withholds the traditional *semikah* because students are not required to master the law codes. In a similar vein, the Seminary synagogue originally differed from nearly all other Conservative synagogues in requiring separate seating for men and women in pseudo-Orthodox fashion (no physical partition or separate gallery as required by classical Jewish law) and in the use of prayer books produced under Orthodox auspices.

62 The derogation was employed at least until the nineteen sixties, long after Schechter's death. A more extreme form was "Schechter's cemetery," i.e., the place to bury one's Judaism.

63 "Schechter emphatically deprecated all attempts to have the movement which he inaugurated labelled 'Conservative.'" So, Mordecai Kaplan, *Judaism as a Civilization* (New York, 1934), 163.

64 For details of early JTS history see Davis, *Emergence*; A. Karp, "A Century of Conservative Judaism in the United States," *American Jewish Yearbook* 86 (1986), 3–61; *idem*, "Conservative Rabbi"; Ginzberg, *Keeper*; *Tradition and Change: The Development of Conservative Judaism* ed. M Waxman New York: Burning Bush, 1958); A. Hertzberg, "Conservative Judaism," *EncJud* 5, 901–906; A. Kass, "Jewish Theological Seminary of America, The (JTS)," *ibid.*, 10,

The man being "Schechter's seminary," Solomon Schechter (1847–1915), grew up in a family of Habad-Lubavitch Hasidim.[65] His given name was Shneur Zalman,[66] while the Yiddish surname "Schechter" attests to his father's position as a Jewish ritual slaughterer. Schechter had studied in traditional *yeshivot* in Galicia and Rumania before attending universities in Vienna and Berlin. Claude Montefiore (1858–1938), the British Jewish philanthropist and New Testament scholar brought Schechter to England as his private tutor. Although Schechter had not earned a doctorate,[67] a position was created for him as a reader in rabbinics at Cambridge University. It was Schechter who realized the significance of the contents of the Genizah[68] in the Ezra synagogue in Cairo. Thanks to him, some 140,000 fragmentary documents, invaluable for the reconstruction of Jewish history and culture, were brought to Cambridge. The subsequent publication of many of these finds, including a Hebrew manuscript of Ecclesiasticus, not only earned Schechter his scholarly reputation but brought him to the attention of the most prominent American Jewish lay leaders.

Leading American Jews, including Louis Marshall, Jacob Schiff, Felix Warburg, the Lewisohns and the Guggenheims had been increasingly concerned about the breakdown of traditional Jewish life in immigrant families. To be sure, these leaders, members of the Reform Temple Emanuel, who themselves were not ritually observant, did not agonize over the alienation of the immigrants from such identifiably East European traits as strict Sabbath observance and adherence to the Jewish dietary laws. They were mostly concerned with the crime rate among the immigrants and the attraction of their young to socialism and anarchism, all of which reflected negatively on their more prosperous and acculturated coreligionists. Thanks to the efforts of such Philadelphia Jewish intellectuals as Cyrus Adler, his cousin Mayer Sulzberger, and Solomon Solis-Cohen, the New York "Uptown Jews" were persuaded

95–97; *Tradition Renewed*, ed. J. Werthheimer (New York: JTS Press, 1997); M. R. Cohen, *The Birth of Conservative Judaism* (New York: Columbia University, 2012).

65 For an outline of the tenets of this sect see R. Elior, "HaBaD: The Contemplative Ascent to God," in *Jewish Spirituality II*, ed. A. Green (New York: Crossroad, 1987), 157–205; In contemporary English sources produced by the sect, and in its coverage by the media the spelling "Chabad" is preferred.

66 To this day it remains customary within Habad Lubavitch to name male children after the sect's founder Shneur Zalman of Lyady (1745–1813).

67 Schechter claimed rabbinic ordination from both I. H. Weiss of Vienna and Z. Frankel of Berlin. In 1892 Cambridge awarded Schechter the M.A. *honoris causa*. See A. Karp, "Solomon Schechter Comes to America," *American Jewish Historical Quarterly* 53 (1963), 44–62.

68 For a brief description see A. Habermann, "Genizah," *EncJud* 7, 403–407.

that the ideology of the "Historical School," which valued secular learning, and Jewish ritual law in moderation, coincided with their own social goals. The Jewish philanthropists supported JTS financially because of its potential to train American rabbinic leaders who might build stability among the East European immigrants and westernize them at the same time.[69] Schechter, a charismatic personality, combined traditional East European Jewish learning and a tolerable amount of its religious commitment with some university training, and no less important, with a fine command of written English. To this day, his essays serve as models of scholarly popularization.[70] For his part, Schechter wanted very much to come to America. He felt the need for more money for the support of his family than he could ever hope to make at Cambridge.[71] He also desired a more observant Jewish atmosphere in which to raise his children.

A far stronger scholar than Isaac Mayer Wise, but like him a man of daring and vision, Schechter succeeded in placing JTS on a firm academic foundation by actively recruiting promising young European trained scholars to its faculty.[72] Ironically, the first, and ultimately the most significant, appointment made by Schechter was that of Louis Ginzberg (1873–1953), an outstanding talmudist, whose earlier appointment to HUC had been precipitately withdrawn in part because he accepted the views of higher criticism to which he had been exposed in his university studies.[73] JTS emulated its namesake the *Jüdisch-Theologisches Seminar* of Breslau, Germany in its commitment to the "positive-historical Judaism,"[74] preached by Zacharias Frankel (1801–1875)

69 See Karp, *Haven*, 99–102; For a list of the largest contributors to the endowment of the new JTS see Ginzberg, *Keeper*, 91.

70 See e.g. S. Schechter, *Studies in Judaism* (Reprint Philadelphia: Jewish Publication Society and Meridian, 1958).

71 In Cambridge Schechter was dependent on the private support of Claude Montefiore, who in contrast to Schechter, was opposed to Zionism, favored Sunday Sabbaths and preferred English language religious services. See Karp, "Schechter," 56–57. Despite Schechter's traditionalism, Schechter's daughter Amy became an active Communist.

72 See Karp, *Haven*, 210.

73 Ginzberg, *Keeper*, 60–63. Ginzberg had earned his Ph.D. studying under Nöldeke at Strassburg and Bezold at Heidelberg. See *ibid.*, 47–58. For Ginzberg's acceptance of the documentary hypothesis see L. Ginzberg, "Law, Codification of," in *Jewish Encyclopedia* 7, 635–647.

74 See "Juedisch-Theologisches Seminar, Breslau," in *EncJud* 10; 465–466. The buildings of JTS bear a striking resemblance to the Breslau Seminary. Cf. the respective photographs *ibid.*, 97 and 465. It is of interest that Ismar Schorsch, then chancellor of JTS, in an address delivered on December 10, 1986, spoke of JTS as "founded first in Breslau and then in New

and his circle, which attempted to combine a somewhat lenient orthopraxy with the *Wissenschaft* approach[75] to all of the sources of Judaism, including, in theory, the Bible.[76] Schechter nonetheless, once characterized by an angry Ginzberg as "a Rumanian who never had a proper modern education,"[77] equated biblical criticism with "higher anti-Semitism."[78] Accordingly, his search for a Bible professor led him to orientalists whose primary focus was outside of biblical studies. In 1903 the position in biblical literature and exegesis was first offered to Samuel Posnanski (1864–1921), a Polish-Jewish medievalist especially remembered for his scholarly contributions to the study of the Karaite movement. When Posnanski rejected the offer, Schechter turned to Israel Friedlaender (1876–1920),[79] a graduate of the (Orthodox) Hildesheimer Seminary in Berlin. Friedlaender held great promise in Semitics. He had studied under Theodor Nöldeke, as had Ginzberg at an earlier date, and had come to America recommended by Nöldeke as well as by the great Islamicist Ignaz Goldziher.[80] Although Friedlaender had attended lectures given by the Assyriologist Friedrich Delitzsch and studied Bible with David Zvi Hoffmann,[81] the only Orthodox Jewish scholar of his day to engage the Wellhausenian hypothesis directly and to attempt to rebut it systematically, his scholarly interests were in Arabic and Judeo-Arabic.[82] Fully aware of the lacunae in his biblical training, Friedlaender appended to his acceptance of Schechter's offer the following promise:

York." See I. Schorsch, *Thoughts from 3080 Selected Addresses and Writings* (n.d., n.p), 24; cf. *ibid.*, 17, 49.

75 The ideology of positive-historical Judaism as advocated by Frankel and emulated by the JTS of America is quintessentially expressed in Z. Frankel, "On Changes in Judaism," in *Tradition and Change*, 43–50.

76 According to its original preamble adopted on May 6, 1886, JTS was to be a "seminary where the Bible shall be impartially taught." See Karp, *Haven*, 97.

77 Ginzberg, *Keeper*, 89.

78 See S. Schechter, "Higher Criticism-Higher Anti-Semitism," in *idem, Seminary Addresses and Other Papers* (Cincinnati: Ark, 1915), 36–37. On March 26, 1903, Schechter delivered an address in which he said: "Wellhausen's *Prolegomena* and *History* are teeming with aperçus full of venom against Judaism." See Silberman, "Wellhausen," 26.

79 For biographical details see B. Shargel, *Practical Dreamer: Israel Friedlaender and the Shaping of American Judaism* (New York: Jewish Theological Seminary, 1985).

80 See Shargel, *Dreamer*, 192.

81 See Shargel, *Dreamer*, 45.

82 Friedlaender's thesis was published as *Der Sprachgebrauch des Maimonides. Ein lexikalischer and grammatischer Beitrag zur Kenntnis des Mittelarabischen* (Frankfurt and Main, 1902).

> I shall seek to familiarize myself with the problems of biblical scholarship ... I intend to make a modest contribution to their clarification and solution.

Friedlaender did not fulfill his promise. It appears that his real interest was the Jewish community rather than the academy.[83] Friedlaender was a tireless worker for Zionism, for Jewish education for children and adults and for the amelioration of the suffering of East European Jewry. Although Friedlaender devoted much time to lecturing and writing popular articles, he nonetheless managed to complete scholarly projects begun in Europe. During his brief lifetime Friedlaender made significant contributions to medieval studies[84] but wrote little in biblical scholarship. We may cite: "The Present Position and Original Form of the Prophecy of Eternal Peace in Isaiah 2:1–5 and Micah 4:1–5."[85] In popular essays, notably in a review of Charles and Emilie Briggs's *Psalms* (New York, 1906–1907), Friedlaender polemized against higher biblical criticism.[86] Nonetheless, in other popular pieces of an ideological cast, Friedlaender regularly advocated adherence to "ceremonalism," i.e., observance of ritual law, on the grounds that Ezra:

> understood that prophetic Judaism was indispensable as an ideal ... but that it was too lofty ... to serve ... in everyday existence ... He therefore proceeded to turn the solid gold bars of prophecy into small coin.[87]

The "small coin" which Ezra made available for everyday use was the law. As Shargel correctly observes:

83 For details of Friedlaender's communal activities, see Shargel, *Dreamer*. In addition, see Ginzberg, *Keeper*, 150; Karp, *Haven*, 167–169.

84 See Orlinsky, "Scholarship," 313–316. For a complete bibliography see Shargel, *Dreamer*, 202–204.

85 *Jewish Quarterly Review* N.S. 6 (1916), 405–413. Although Friedlaender refers to Christian scholars, including Wellhausen, he does not seriously engage the critical issues of the prophetic doublet. More incisive is the brief note, "Das hebräische *seper* in einer verkannten Bedeutung," *JQR* O.S. 15 (1903), 102–103. In all likelihood, Friedlaender had written the note in Europe, because he did not arrive in America until 1903. See Shargel, *Dreamer*, 6.

86 I. Friedlaender, "A New Specimen of Modern Biblical Exegesis," *American Hebrew and Jewish Messenger* 81 (July 5, 1907); Literary Supplement, 3–7.

87 Friedlaender *apud* Shargel, *Dreamer*, 57.

> Friedlaender's ... metaphor implies a Wellhausian (sic) conception ... that the prophets preceded and were in part responsible for the composition of the Pentateuch.[88]

Accordingly, it seems that Friedlaender was more opposed to the tone of classical criticism than to its content. Classical criticism maintained that the encapsulation of prophecy in the law of the Pentateuch had killed prophecy by transforming it into "legalism." Friedlaender, along with the critics and in contrast to traditional Jewish teaching, agreed that the law had chronologically followed prophecy but as a proudly observant Jew[89] applauded the process by which the law had enabled prophecy to become common property. That the form taken by Christian Bible criticism rather than its substance was at issue, may also be seen in Friedlaender's tribute to Arnold Ehrlich, a proponent of both lower and higher criticism.[90]

Neither Schechter's death in 1915 nor Friedlaender's tragic demise at the hand of bandits while on a relief mission in the Ukraine in 1920,[91] brought about a change in the orientation of biblical studies at JTS. Although Schechter was succeeded as President by Cyrus Adler (1863–1940), who had earned his doctorate under the great orientalist and biblicist Paul Haupt,[92] editor of a classic of source-criticism, the *Polychrome Bible*, higher biblical criticism at JTS continued to be viewed with some disdain. Pentateuch criticism was avoided altogether and not taught officially at JTS rabbinical school until 1966.[93]

---

88 Shargel, *Dreamer*, 61.

89 Like Schechter, Friedlaender was not punctilious about observance. It was known that he somehow managed to come to Sabbath morning services at JTS in Manhattan from far-off Staten Island.

90 See the eulogy by Friedlaender, "A Great Bible Scholar, Arnold B. Ehrlich," *Nation*, January 10, 1920, 41. On Ehrlich see below.

91 See Shargel, *Dreamer*, 32–35.

92 See Orlinsky, "Scholarship," 304–305.

93 Louis Finkelstein (1895–1991) Friedlaender's brother-in-law, who succeeded Adler as President (later: Chancellor) of JTS in 1940, remarked on several occasions that "what was good enough for Schechter" as regards the avoidance of higher criticism was good enough for Finkelstein. This is not to say that classical Pentateuch criticism went unnoted. Students in classes dealing with the history of the biblical period were often assigned secondary sources referring to the documentary hypothesis. Nonetheless, the first course in Pentateuch employing the critical method to be offered officially in the Bible Department of JTS rabbinical school was "Exodus," given in 1966–1967 by Moshe Greenberg, then visiting from the University of Pennsylvania. Previously, there had been offered only a pre-critical preparatory course entitled "The Pentateuch with Rashi's Commentary," for students insufficiently prepared to enter the rabbinic program proper. In an oral

The negative attitude to critical Jewish biblical scholarship shown by the administration of the two modernist non-Orthodox rabbinic schools[94] in America was, fortunately, not unanimous. It is of interest that the Society of Biblical Literature, then the Society of Biblical Literature and Exegesis, founded in 1880, had three Jewish members by 1886,[95] Rabbi Marcus Jastrow (1829–1903), rabbi of Temple Rodeph Shalom of Philadelphia, who had taught at Leeser's Maimonides College and was later to produce the standard English language talmudic and targumic dictionary,[96] Gustave Gottheil, rabbi of Temple Emanuel of New York[97] and his son Dr. Richard Gottheil (1862–1936), professor of Semitic languages at Columbia University.[98]

Coincidentally, in the same year, 1886, Benjamin Szold (1829–1902) published a Hebrew commentary on Job. Szold, born in Hungary, was expelled from Vienna for his political activities in the revolution of 1848. A former student of

communication (June 20, 1987) Professor Abraham Karp and Mrs. Deborah Karp recalled that Mordecai Kaplan (1881–1983), the founder of the Reconstructionist movement, had regularly taught Pentateuch criticism in his homiletics classes at JTS as background for preaching from the Bible. Kaplan, a member of the 1902 graduating class at JTS, had been introduced to higher biblical criticism by Arnold Ehrlich who belonged to the personal circle of Kaplan's father, the Orthodox Rabbi Israel Kaplan, himself brought to America at the invitation of Rabbi Jacob Joseph. See A. Hertzberg in the introduction to Kaplan, *Judaism as a Civilization*, xxii–xxiv.

94 The first modern Orthodox rabbinic school to survive and flourish in America was Rabbi Isaac Elhanan Theological Seminary (RIETS), organized in 1897. On its background see J. Gurock, "Resisters," 129–130. RIETS eventually grew into what is now Yeshiva University.

95 Saunders, *Searching*, 6–7.

96 M. Jastrow, *A Dictionary of the Targumim, the Talmud Babli and Yerushalmi, and the Midrashic Literature* (New York, 1903).

97 Gottheil served as superintendent of an ill-fated rabbinic school in New York City known variously as the Emanu-El Theological Seminary, The American Hebrew College of the City of New York, and the Hebrew Theological Seminary Association. The school operated from 1877–1885. See Davis, *Emergence*, 57–58; Meyer, "Isaac Mayer Wise," 40–41. There is much valuable background information relevant to our topic in R. Gottheil, *The Life of Gustav Gottheil: Memoir of a Priest in Israel* (Williamsport: Bayard, 1936).

98 On Gottheil the younger see the memorial notice by J. Bloch, "Richard James Horatio Gottheil 1862–1936," in *JAOS* 56 (1936), 480–489. Gottheil's original appointment at Columbia was to a chair of rabbinical literature endowed initially (1887–1892) by Temple Emanuel. Subsequently, under Gottheil the chair developed into a Division of Oriental Languages. (See Gottheil, *Memoir*, 196–216.) During his years at Columbia, Gottheil taught in most areas of Semitic, including Bible. He served as president of The Society of Biblical Literature in 1903. The bulk of his publication, however, was devoted to Syriac rather than to Bible proper. See the bibliography by I. Pratt, *JAOS ibid*, 480–489. In addition, see the essay "The Bible at Columbia University" in this volume.

Zacharias Frankel and Heinrich Graetz at the *Jüdisch-Theologisches Seminar* in Breslau, Szold became rabbi of Congregation Oheb Shalom in Baltimore in 1858.

Szold, father of the far better known social activist Henrietta Szold, did not teach at a university or seminary, but was very much involved in communal affairs. As a progressive in religious matters, he often found himself opposed by the left and right wings of American Judaism.[99] Despite his activism, Szold found time for important scholarly contributions, including biblical studies. Of particular interest and still valuable is his commentary on Job.[100] The reader willing to engage the nineteenth century scholarly Hebrew in which the commentary is written will be rewarded with important insights and observations. Szold makes full use of the medieval Jewish commentators but also specifically acknowledges his recourse to Christian scholars including Delitzsch, Ewald, and Hitzig. Szold's approach may be characterized as conservative criticism. Textual emendation, although rare, is employed, and higher criticism is cautiously offered. Note his summary statement: "The book [of Job] is a complete whole … It was not composed at one time …[Yet] there is no doubt that it was entirely complete in its sections and in its present shape before it entered the Covenant of Scripture and has not been altered since."[101]

A younger contemporary of Szold was Arnold (b. David) Bogumil Ehrlich (1864–1919),[102] who likewise held no academic institutional position in America. An "utterly egocentric personality"[103] who weighed three hundred pounds,[104] Ehrlich affected the persona of a recluse, signing his name Shabbetai ben Yom Tob ibn Boded (i.e. "Mr. Lonely-[even] on-Sabbaths-and-Festivals") to his *Mikrâ ki-Pheschutô*. Born in Polish Russia, Ehrlich studied in *heder* and then *yeshivah*. But his narrow Jewish world held too little for him. Ehrlich's wife did not share his need to experience the larger world. Accordingly, he divorced her

99 On Szold see Davis, *Emergence*, 360–362. On Szold's work see further, Orlinsky, "Scholarship," 296–297.

100 *Sefer Iyyob Mebu'ar Mehadash-Das Buch Hiob nebst einem neuen Commentar* (Baltimore, 1886).

101 *Ibid.*, 22.

102 See Orlinsky, "Scholarship," 297–299; *idem*, "Prolegomenon" to A. Ehrlich, *Mikrâ ki-Pheschutô* (*Die Schrift nach ihren Wortlaut*) (Berlin, 1903; Reprint, New York: Ktav, 1969), ix–xxxiii; Gottheil, *Memoir*, 75–81. For Ehrlich's given name "David," a photograph of him, his second wife and his American family, as well as additional biographical details, see J. Kabakoff, "New Light on Arnold Bogomil Ehrlich," *American Jewish Archives* 36, No. 2, (Nov., 1984), 202–224.

103 Orlinsky, "Prologomenon" to reprint of *Mikrâ*, ix.

104 Ginzberg, *Keeper*, 64.

and made his way to Leipzig, where under the influence of Christian missionaries and "tempted by prospects of a better position than I could ever attain as an Israelite," he converted to Christianity at the age of twenty-three.[105] In Leipzig, Ehrlich worked with Franz Delitzsch (1813–1890) in his missionary Institutum Judaicum, helping to translate the New Testament into Hebrew for the purpose of Christian mission to the Jews.[106] After arriving in America in 1876, Ehrlich sought out Rabbi Gustav Gottheil who convened a rabbinic court, which accepted Ehrlich back into the Jewish faith.[107] Although Ehrlich loved America and was an intimate friend of the influential Louis Ginzberg, he could never attain a real academic post. Jews with academic influence suspected his Christian missionary connections. At the same time, Christians probably thought him too much a Polish Jew.[108] In order to support himself and his family, Ehrlich worked at various jobs, including social work, portraiture and private Hebrew teaching. A major scholarly work of Ehrlich's was the three volume commentary *Mikrâ ki-Pheschutô* (German title: *Die Schrift nach ihrem Wortlaut*), which appeared between 1899–1901.[109] Ehrlich derived the title from the hermeneutic dictum recorded in Babylonian Talmud Shabbat 36a: "(Despite the numerous meanings that might be teased out of it,) no scriptural verse (Heb *mikrâ*) may be permitted to escape its plain sense (Heb *p^ešûtô*)." Ehrlich chose to write in Hebrew as had Szold. Unlike Szold, Ehrlich explained his choice. With an almost missionary zeal, Ehrlich expressed in the preface his hope that the book would reach "my brethren and my people who understand only Hebrew … and demonstrate that its author was a Jew in origin and education." The author first chastises the old style Jewish scholars who worry about the minutiae of Jewish law to the exclusion of all worldly matters. He then directs

105 The quotation that indicates that Ehrlich's conversion to Christianity was opportunistic is taken from the "Minute" recorded by Gustav Gottheil on behalf of the ecclesiastical court that received Ehrlich back into Judaism. In Ehrlich's own German language letter to the Jewish ecclesiastical court dated March 7, 1876, he attributes his conversion to Christianity to a mental lapse ("von einem mir selbst nicht recht bewussten Wahne bethört.") For both documents see Gottheil, *Memoir*, 76–77.

106 Ehrlich claimed that for the most part the translation was of his doing. See Gottheil, *Memoir*, 76.

107 Ehrlich subsequently served as tutor in Bible, Mishnah, Talmud and Modern Hebrew to the young Richard Gottheil. He also taught in the preparatory school of Temple Emanuel. See Gottheil, *Memoir*, 77.

108 De Sola Pool, *apud* Orlinsky, *Mikrâ* repr., x–xi.

109 Ehrlich dedicated the commentary to the spirit of Delitzsch, Ehrlich's "unforgettable fatherly friend," who had died in 1890. The dedication reads: "Den Manen seines unvergesslichen väterlichen Freundes Franz Delitzsch widmet dieses Werk der Verfasser."

his ire against the *Wissenschaft* practitioners who "waste their days studying worthless medieval rhymes and rhymesters." Ehrlich laments the absence of Jews from biblical study, an absence attributable in his thinking, to the talmudic dictum that all intellectual development since the days of the early rabbis has been from higher to lower forms.[110] Observing that the allegedly superior ancient rabbis believed in demons and incantations, "which only fools believe in nowadays,"[111] Ehrlich faults his coreligionists for abandoning Bible study to the Christians. Needless to say, Ehrlich does not spare the Christians either. In his opinion, Christian scholarship since Reuchlin's day has benefitted from linguistic advances coupled to the spirit of inquiry. Unfortunately, Christian understanding has been limited, because Christian scholars do not respect the Old Testament on its own terms, but only as a precursor of the New Testament. In addition, because Christians are largely ignorant of post-biblical Hebrew and of the conservatism and continuity of Jewish tradition, they are unable to employ the valuable rabbinic sources in their biblical research. Unlike the Jews, Christian scholars are compelled to rely for comparative philology on the languages of ancient Israel's gentile contemporaries. Ehrlich faults such comparisons because:

> just as the resemblance between fathers and sons is greater than that among brothers, so are the later stages of a language more illuminative of the earlier than is the evidence drawn from the contemporary related languages.[112]

This linguistically dubious statement justifies Orlinsky's suspicion[113] that Ehrlich thought it necessary to defend his frequent recourse to rabbinic Hebrew and Arabic[114] as compensation for his ignorance of Akkadian and the newer discoveries in Northwest Semitic. In addition, *Mikrâ* may be faulted substantively for containing numerous scattered higher critical statements about "early" and "late" sections of the Bible, but no forthright statement about the documentary hypothesis as a whole, as well as for falsely claiming originality for interpretations already offered in medieval Jewish commentaries.[115]

---

110 *Mikrâ*, xxxvi.

111 *Ibid.*

112 *Ibid.*, xxxvii.

113 "Prolegomenon" to *Mikrâ*, xviii.

114 Ehrlich had taught himself Arabic by "working throughout the day and a good part of the night with his feet in cold water as a means of remaining awake." See Gottheil, *Memoir*, 79.

115 *Ibid.*, xxiv.

Despite these shortcomings and Ehrlich's overly polemical tone, *Mikrâ* demonstrates both its author's enormous talent as a philologist and his fervent desire to attract Jews to Bible study. Non-Jewish scholars are more familiar with Ehrlich's German Bible commentary, *Randglossen zur hebräischen Bibel* (1908–1914), a work that continues to be consulted. *Randglossen* follows the form of *Mikrâ*, but often differs in particulars. Ehrlich's scholarship has been very influential. The preface to the 1917 Jewish Publication Society Bible translation, *The Holy Scriptures*, singles Ehrlich out for special mention together with the medievals Rashi, Kimhi, ibn Ezra, and the modern conservatives, Luzzatto and Malbim.[116] Later Jewish biblicists, notably the Israeli scholar N. H. Tur-Sinai (Harry Torzcyner; 1886–1975), and H. L. Ginsberg (1903–1990), have acknowledged their debt to him.[117] The translators who produced NJPS were likewise greatly indebted to Ehrlich.[118]

Unlike Szold and Ehrlich, Morris Jastrow (1861–1921),[119] a son of Rabbi Marcus Jastrow, was very much a professional academician. The elder Jastrow, although not a Bible scholar, served as first editor of the Bible translation project undertaken by the Jewish Publication Society to replace the Leeser Bible.[120] Morris Jastrow was brought by his father to Philadelphia as a child but returned to Europe to earn the doctorate at Leipzig in 1884 with a thesis on the medieval Jewish grammarian Judah Hayyuj. Jastrow began teaching at the University of Pennsylvania in 1885 and remained there until his death in 1921. Together with Richard Gottheil of Columbia, likewise the son of a prominent rabbi, Jastrow edited the Semitic Study Series. Although his primary field of interest was Assyriology and especially Mesopotamian religion, Jastrow devoted a great deal of study to the Bible, often bringing Mesopotamian material to bear on biblical interpretation, as in his *Hebrew and Babylonian Tradition* (1919). Jastrow's publications include some forty items in biblical studies, notably books on Ecclesiastes, Job, and Canticles.[121] Jastrow also served as Bible

116 *The Holy Scriptures according to the Masoretic Text a New Translation* (Philadelphia: Jewish Publication Society, 1917), vii.

117 A major work of Tur-Sinai's follows the pattern of *Mikrâ* and *Randglossen* and is entitled *Peshutô shel Mikrâ* (Jerusalem: Qiryath-Sefer, 1962–68).

118 See the numerous references to Ehrlich in the index to H. M. Orlinsky, *Notes on the New Translation of the Torah* (Philadelphia, 1969), 273.

119 See Orlinsky, "Scholarship," 300–302; C. H. Gordon, *The Pennsylvania Tradition of Semitics* (Atlanta: Scholars, 1986), 13–32.

120 The elder Jastrow was also responsible for preparing the Job translation. See *Holy Scriptures*, v.

121 For bibliography see *JAOS* 41 (1921), 337–344.

editor of the *Jewish Encyclopedia*.[122] He was President of the Society of Biblical Literature in 1916. A great admirer of Keunen and Wellhausen,[123] Jastrow was an outspoken champion of higher criticism, maintaining that "criticism has usurped the place once taken by tradition."[124] Methodologically, Jastrow was consistent, if overly rationalistic, in his higher criticism: "Instead of assuming a combination of many documents . . . it is a sounder method to assume in many cases a single document extended by glosses, explanatory comments and other kinds of additions by later editors."[125] Jastrow's application of this method may be seen in his Ecclesiastes commentary whose full title is: *A Gentle Cynic, being a translation of the Book of Koheleth, commonly known as Ecclesiastes, stripped of later additions, also its origin, growth and interpretation*.[126] Jastrow accounts for the numerous inconsistencies in Job and Ecclesiastes by arguing that both books originated as short unorthodox works, which were later enlarged by pietists.

Max Margolis (1866–1932) was the most important American Jewish Bible scholar before the First World War in his role as Editor-in-Chief of the 1917 Jewish Publication Society translation of *The Holy Scriptures*.[127] Born in Meretz in Polish Russia into an enlightened rabbinic family, Margolis was tutored as a boy by a Greek Orthodox priest. After completing gymnasium in Berlin, he came to America in 1889 and studied at Columbia University under Richard Gottheil. Margolis earned the Ph.D. in Oriental Studies with a thesis, in Latin, on the use of Rashi's commentary to Babylonian Talmud Erubin to restore its original text.[128] Margolis's first academic position was as Assistant Professor

---

122 See below.

123 See M. Jastrow Jr., "Constructive Elements in the Critical Study of the Old Testament," *JBL* 36 (1917), 4.

124 *Ibid*, 7.

125 *Ibid*., 23. It may be noted that this approach has become newly popular, particularly in the writings of John van Seters. See e.g. his *Abraham in History and Tradition* (New Haven: Yale, 1975).

126 Philadelphia: Lippincott, 1919.

127 For biographical details see L. Greenspoon, *Max Leopold Margolis A Scholar's Scholar* (Atlanta: Scholars, 1987). A brief account of Margolis's life and essays on various aspects of Margolis's scholarship may be found in *Max Leopold Margolis Scholar and Teacher*, ed. R. Gordis (Philadelphia: Alumni Association of Dropsie College, 1952). The annotated bibliography of Margolis's publications compiled by J. Reider, originally published in Gordis, *Margolis*, 61–124 has been republished with corrections in Greenspoon, *Margolis*, 135–186. For some interesting personal anecdotes about Margolis see Gordon, *Pennsylvania*, 49–52.

128 M. Margolis, "Commentarius Isaacidis Quatenus ad Textum Talmudis Investigandum Adhiberi Possit, Tractatu 'Erubhin Ostenditur," (New York, 1891). Margolis' doctorate was the first awarded by Columbia's Oriental Department. See Greenspoon, *Margolis*, 5.

of Hebrew and Biblical Exegesis at Hebrew Union College from 1893–1897. On higher criticism he seems to have agreed with I. M. Wise. (See below.) Margolis left HUC in 1897 to teach Semitics at Berkeley where he remained until 1905. He enjoyed Berkeley's academic atmosphere greatly. In addition, while teaching there, Margolis met Evelyn Aronson, a member of one of California's oldest and most prominent Jewish families, whom he would later marry. Nonetheless, he felt the absence of Jewish community[129] and was happy to return to HUC in 1905 as Professor of Biblical Exegesis. His happiness was short-lived. Kaufmann Kohler, president of HUC, who had enthusiastically[130] invited Margolis to return to HUC, was like him, an extremely strong willed individual. On the small HUC faculty constant clashes between the two men were inevitable. To be sure the differences were often clothed in ideological garb. Thus Kohler advocated the lecture method while Margolis maintained that the inductive textual method was more effective. More significant was the issue of Zionism. Kohler had codified the classic anti-Zionist stance of early American Reform Judaism in the Pittsburgh Platform.[131] During the Kohler presidency, chapel sermons advocating Zionism were strongly discouraged or forbidden outright.[132] Margolis, previously opposed to Jewish nationalism, had become converted to Zionism shortly before returning to teach at HUC. Tensions between Kohler and Margolis finally resulted in Margolis's resignation in 1907.[133] Margolis then spent a year in Europe where he completed his *Manual of the Aramaic Language of the Babylonian Talmud.*

129 In a letter to Kaufmann Kohler Margolis spoke of "my love for Judaism . . . and the unbounded confidence in yourself" as decisive in his return to HUC. (See Greenspoon, *Margolis*, 15.) According to Gordon (*Pennsylvania*, 50), a higher salary was another factor. Indeed, in 1906 Margolis's salary of $3,600 was the highest paid by HUC to any faculty member. See Meyer, "A Theological School for Reform Judaism," *in Hebrew Union College at One Hundred*, 66. Many years after his departure from California, Margolis told Gordon that returning to HUC was the greatest mistake he had ever made.

130 See Meyer, "Theological School," 63.

131 According to the report of the Proceedings, the fifth plank of the Pittsburgh Platform read in part: "We consider ourselves no longer a nation but a religious community, and therefore expect neither a return to Palestine, nor a sacrificial worship under the sons of Aaron, nor the restoration of any of the laws concerning the Jewish state." See Jacob, *Pittsburgh Platform*, 108. It must be noted that several Reform rabbis demurred and espoused Zionism in the 1880s. See Polish, *American Jewish* Archives 35, 275–276.

132 See Polish, *American Jewish Archives* 35, 280–281.

133 Margolis's Zionist colleagues on the faculty, Henry Malter and Max Schloessinger, also resigned during that academic year. See Meyer, "Theological School," 63–64. Malter, a talmudist, would once again be a colleague of Margolis at Dropsie.

In the meantime, the death of the editor-in-chief Marcus Jastrow[134] in 1903 had effectively halted the translation project begun in 1892 by the Jewish Publication Society with the goal of replacing Leeser's Bible. Progress had been slow because individual books were first delegated to scholars in England and America and then studied by an editorial committee, which returned their comments to the original translators. In 1908 the Society in cooperation with the Central Conference of American Rabbis (Reform) agreed on the more efficient procedure of translation by which an editorial board would revise a draft translation prepared by its new editor-in-chief. The new board chose Margolis, the only professional Bible scholar among them,[135] to assume the posts of secretary to the Board of Editors and editor-in-chief of the Bible translation.[136] Margolis shared Leeser's high estimation of the Authorized Version but had the further advantage of access to the Revised Version produced by the Church of England in 1885.[137] Margolis, along with his wife who served as his secretary, proceeded to immerse himself in the literature of Elizabethan and Restoration England before beginning the work proper.[138] Far better trained as a text-critic than Leeser had been, Margolis took less than a year[139] to produce a draft translation of the entire Hebrew Bible for the use of the editors. At the same time that Margolis was working on the translation he was also carrying out extensive text-critical researches in the Septuagint, Aquila, Symmachus, Theodotion, the Targums, the Peshitta, the Vulgate and Saadia.

134 Kaufmann Kohler and the Sephardic rabbi Frederick de Sola Mendes served with Jastrow on the editorial Committee. Jastrow had prepared the Job translation, Kohler the Psalms translation and de Sola Mendes the translation of Deuteronomy. It is of interest that there was no Orthodox representation on this committee. Kohler, as we have seen, was a radical reformer; Jastrow was in the left wing of the historical school; and Mendes, one of the original members of the Jewish Theological Seminary Association, was solidly in the Reform camp by the end of his career.

135 See Orlinsky, *Essays*, 354.

136 See the account in the "Preface" to *The Holy Scriptures*. Cf. Orlinsky, *Essays*, 354.

137 The RV actually served as the basic text for the JPS revision. Indeed, Orlinsky has characterized the final product of 1917 as "an extremely modest revision of the English Revised Version of 1885, a revision that probably did not exceed more than a very few percent of the whole." See H. Orlinsky, "The New Jewish Version of the Torah: Toward a New Philosophy of Bible Translation," in *idem, Essays*, 399–400; Cf. L. Greenspoon, "Biblical Translators in Antiquity and the Modern World: A Comparative Study," *HUCA* 60 (1989), 91–113. The RV, like its predecessor KJV, had too Christian a slant to serve the Anglophone Jewish communities. See *idem, Margolis*, 65–66, and Sarna *apud* Greenspoon *ibid.*, 73.

138 Gordis, *Margolis*, 9.

139 For his speed he earned a bonus. The early completion also facilitated Margolis's appointment to the Dropsie faculty. See Greenspoon, *Margolis*, 63.

The results of Margolis's research were made available to the members of the translation committee in a privately circulated 646 page manuscript of "Notes on the New Translation of the Holy Scriptures."

In 1909, while still the beneficiary of one Leeser legacy, the JPS translation project, Margolis became heir to a second, the professorship in Biblical Philology at the Dropsie College for Hebrew and Cognate Learning. Organized in 1907 in Philadelphia and chartered in 1909, the school was funded by money provided by the will of Moses Dropsie (1821–1905), a Philadelphia lawyer and one-time disciple of Isaac Leeser. Dropsie had desired the creation of a nonsectarian[140] and nontheological school devoted to the study of Hebrew, Biblical and Rabbinic Literature, the Middle East and cognate fields.[141] Leeser's personal library became the basis of the Dropsie collection. The school's first president[142] was Cyrus Adler who had been deeply involved in the reorganization of JTS and would later serve as its president.[143] It was Adler together with Solomon Schechter, who in 1910 revived the moribund British scholarly journal, *Jewish Quarterly Review*, which had been founded in London in 1889. Under the auspices of Dropsie, JQR provided an important American outlet

140 The non-sectarianism applied to the admission of students. Although in later years such non-Jewish scholars as Morton Enslin and Morton Smith served as faculty members, Dropsie's will had stipulated that the college appoint to the faculty, "only persons who are Jews in faith." See A. Neumann, "The Dropsie College for Hebrew and Cognate Learning: Basic Principles and Objectives," in *The Seventy-Fifth Anniversary Volume of the Jewish Quarterly Review*, ed. A. Neuman and S. Zeitlin (Philadelphia: Jewish Quarterly Review, 1967), 22. For his own part, Moses A. Dropsie was vehemently opposed to Reform Judaism, which he caricatured as "Deform." See Davis, *Emergence*, 338.

141 See A. Katsh and L. Nemoy in *Essays on the Occasion of the Seventieth Anniversary of the Dropsie University* (*1909–1979*, eds. A. Katsh and L. Nemoy (Philadelphia: Dropsie University, 1979), ix–xi. The school officially became Dropsie University in 1969, after it had ceased to be an important institution. After a long period of moribundity, Dropsie was enabled by the philanthropy of Walter Annenberg to become, in 1986, the Annenberg Research Institute for Judaic and Near Eastern Studies, predominantly a postdoctoral research center. See B. Lewis and D. Goldenberg, "Annenberg Research Institute for Judaic and Near Eastern Studies Statement of Purpose," *Jewish Quarterly Review* 72 (1986), 1–4. As of this writing Dropsie's incarnation is now the Herbert D. Katz Center for Advanced Judaic Studies at the University of Pennsylvania. Dropsie's demise was largely due to the widespread availability of Judaica courses of study at major American universities.

142 Israel Friedlaender had also been a candidate for the presidency of Dropsie and for a professorship there in Semitics. See H. Parzen, "New Data on the Formation of Dropsie College," *Jewish Social Studies* 28 (1966), 131–147; Cf. Shargel, *Dreamer*, 10.

143 One early plan had envisioned Dropsie, JTS and Graetz College in Philadelphia as branches of a single university. See Shargel, *Dreamer, ibid.*

for Jewish scholarly publication. The independent, non-denominational character of Dropsie College was a great boon to Margolis who taught there until his death.

Margolis' scholarly contributions were mainly in textual criticism. Some twenty years of his life were dedicated to the goal of producing a true critical edition of the Septuagint, of which only the Greek Joshua actually materialized. Margolis also contributed commentaries on Zephaniah and Malachi to the first Hebrew multi-volume collaborative critical commentary to the Bible, A. Kahana's *Tanak ʿim Perush Madaʿi*.[144] Naturally, Margolis made use of the versions and of medieval and modern Jewish and Christian scholarship. In these brief commentaries Margolis is conservative with regard to emendations and rationalistic in approach. For example, he explains biblical prophecies of total earthly destruction as poetic exaggerations or symbols. Margolis's characteristic attitude to higher critical problems is illustrated by a comment to Malachi 3:22: "Because 'Horeb' is mentioned, Wellhausen has claimed that this is proof that Malachi had only Deuteronomy before him and that the Priestly Code had not yet appeared. But this is insufficient proof. In fact one scholar who assigns a later date [than the rest of Malachi] to verses 22–24 has stated that even after the appearance of the Priestly Code, expressions based on Deuteronomy continued to be employed. If so, we may say that *Malachi had before him the entire Torah just as we have it* [emphasis added]." Margolis's conservatism in matters of higher criticism mars the sections devoted to the history of the biblical period in the classic one-volume *History of the Jewish People*[145] written mostly by Margolis, in collaboration with Alexander Marx. In these chapters, Margolis's essentially paraphrases the biblical account, alluding occasionally to "corroborative" archaeological data. Thus, we read (*ibid.*, 15) that "the exodus took place in the spring of the year 1220," undoubtedly because of the famous reference to "Israel" in the stele that dates from Pharaoh Merneptah's fifth regnal year. It is likewise instructive to read Margolis's discussion of the differences between Deuteronomy and the Book of the Covenant (Exodus 21–24), on the issue of centralization of worship (*ibid.*, 19): "Moses now realized the

144 An English title would be: *The Bible with a Critical Commentary*. Kahana's project began in 1902–1903. Although the series was not completed, a number of important commentaries were produced by such luminaries as Samuel Kraus, H. P. Chajes, Felix Perles and M. H. Segal. Margolis was the only American scholar to contribute. Published in 1930 in Tel-Aviv, Margolis's commentaries were probably written about 1910. See F. Zimmerman in Gordis, *Margolis*, 21, and J. Reider, *ibid.*, 76.

145 M. Margolis and A. Marx, *A History of the Jewish People* (Philadelphia: Jewish Publication Society, 1927).

danger to the new and spiritual religion of his foundation, when local habits and pagan superstitions of the former inhabitants might creep in. He accordingly revised his earlier legislation in a new Book of the Covenant issued on the eve of his death in the plains of Moab opposite Jericho."

Among his many distinctions, Margolis served as editor of the *Journal of Biblical Literature* from 1914–1922 and as President of the Society of Biblical Literature in 1923. He was editor of the *Journal of the American Oriental Society* from 1922–1932.

Mention must be made here of Margolis's successor at Berkeley, William Popper (1874–1963).[146] Before coming to Berkeley, Popper had served as acting head of the Oriental Department of the New York Public Library and as an associate editor of the *Jewish Encyclopedia*. A native of St. Louis, Popper had, like Margolis, earned his doctorate at Columbia under Richard Gottheil. His 1899 dissertation was entitled, "The Censorship of Hebrew Books." Subsequently, Popper studied in Europe with the Semiticists J. Euting, T. Nöldeke, and H. Derenbourg. Early in his career, Popper devoted several studies to biblical parallelism, which can still be consulted with profit.[147] The bulk of his research however, gradually, shifted to Arabic, primarily the historical writings of Yusuf ibn Taghri-Birdi.

Shortly after Margolis's departure from Berkeley provided an opening for Popper, his departure from HUC made way for Julian Morgenstern (1881–1976), whose productive career spanned two generations. Morgenstern joined the HUC faculty in 1907.[148] Born in St. Francisville, Illinois, Morgenstern was ordained at HUC in 1902. He then studied Assyriology in Germany with such luminaries as Friedrich Delitzsch, Bruno Meissner and Carl Bezold, earning a Ph.D. at Heidelberg in 1904 with a dissertation on "The Doctrine of Sin in Babylonian Religion." Assyriology however, was soon replaced by Bible as the focus of Morgenstern's scholarly interests. Indeed, Morgenstern was the first American Jewish scholar with a primary scholarly interest in Bible to practice

---

146 For biographical information see *Semitic and Oriental Studies: A Volume Presented to William Popper on the Occasion of his Seventieth Birthday October 25, 1949*, ed. W. Fischel (Berkeley and Los Angeles: University of California, 1951), v–x; *idem*, "Popper, William," *EncJud* 13, 864. For bibliography see *idem*, *JAOS* 84 (1964), 213–220.

147 See W. Popper, "Parallelism in Isaiah, Chapters 1–10." The monograph is Part II of *Semicentennial Publications of the University of California 1868–1918: Studies in Biblical Parallelism*; *idem*, "A Suggestion as to the Sequence of Some Prophecies in the First Isaiah," *HUCA* 1 (1924), 79–96; *idem*, "Notes on Parallelism," *HUCA* 2 (1925), 63–85. Incidentally, this last piece directly addresses itself to questions of theory and method in a manner rare in early twentieth century Jewish Bible scholarship.

148 Blank, "Bible," 295.

higher biblical criticism systematically. In some respects, Morgenstern may be considered a Jewish bridge to what was then a gentile discipline. A firm adherent of the documentary hypothesis in the European tradition of critical Christian Bible scholarship, Morgenstern added a K(enite) source of his own. Morgenstern denied the Mosaic authorship of the Torah. Indeed, he called on the Reform rabbinate to take a public stand against Mosaic authorship because that would help justify Reform's stand against the binding character of Jewish law.[149] Kaufmann Kohler was himself a staunch advocate of higher criticism. Accordingly, the triumph of critical biblical study at HUC was assured. Morgenstern, unlike his predecessors of the Wise years, had no reason to be reticent. He wrote voluminously on such matters as calendar studies, Pentateuchal law, prophecy and the history of the cult.[150] Because Morgenstern contributed annually to *HUCA*, one of his articles appeared in a volume that turned out to be his own Festschrift.[151] Morgenstern's work is quite free in regard to textual emendations and rearrangements of verses and chapters. Although he began as an ardent Wellhausenian, later in his career Morgenstern began to realize the insufficiency of literary criticism alone to reconstruct the biblical world. In his presidential address to the SBL in 1941, Morgenstern referred to the "increasingly outmoded documentary techniques,"[152] and called for a synthesis of classical biblical study with archaeology, folklore studies, and religious phenomenology. As President of HUC from 1922–1947, Morgenstern was responsible for its major institutional growth. In that same capacity he was able to save many Jewish scholars from the Nazis by bringing them to HUC. Although Morgenstern's actual writings have not been very influential in recent years, the programmatic synthesis he called for in 1941 is now a universally accepted goal of Bible scholarship.

Less productive than Morgenstern but nevertheless worthy of mention is Moses Buttenwieser (1862–1939), first a teacher and later a colleague of Morgenstern's at HUC. Born at Beerfelden, Hessen Darmstadt, Buttenwieser studied at Wurzburg and Leipzig, earning his Ph.D. in 1896 at Heidelberg with a dissertation on the Hebrew Elijah Apocalypse. A year later Buttenwieser became Assistant Professor of Biblical Exegesis at HUC. Although Buttenwieser accepted Wellhausenian theory, he did not have to clash with I. M. Wise because

149 *Ibid.*, 296.

150 Morgenstern contributed to every issue of *HUCA* from 1924–1970. For bibliographical information see Blank, "Bible," 296, 313, n.5; See further, I. Berger, *Analytical Subject Index to the Hebrew Union College Annual Volumes 1–37 (1924–1966)*, 127–128.

151 "Amos Studies (Part Four)," appeared in *HUCA* 32 (1961), 295–350.

152 *JBL* 61 (1942), 1.

his interests were outside of the Pentateuch. In his personal life Buttenwieser was known as a consistent champion of social justice who took the prophets as role models. His major scholarly works were: *The Prophets of Israel* (1914), *The Book of Job* (1922) and *The Psalms, Chronologically Treated with a New Translation* (1938).[153] Blank has aptly noted, if understated, that "a fair amount of subjectivity"[154] attaches to Buttenwieser's method. Indeed, Buttenwieser believed that he could precisely date specific passages in the books he treated. Although contemporary scholars would consider his historical approach arbitrary, it must be acknowledged that Buttenwieser was a superior Semitic philologist and grammarian whose translations of poetic passages may still be consulted with benefit.[155]

We have thus far surveyed the contributions of individual American Jewish Bible scholars. It remains to comment on the most important collective effort of early twentieth century Jewish scholarship, *The Jewish Encyclopedia*.[156] A private undertaking, not sponsored by a university or seminary, *JE* was originally conceived by Isidore Singer, a journalist and promoter who hoped to enrich himself by soliciting Jewish sports figures and businessmen who might be flattered by having their biographies in print and willing to pay for the privilege.[157] Ironically, *JE* turned out to be an invaluable contribution to scholarship, with many articles that may still be consulted with profit. The twelve volume work contained contributions from scholars all over the world, mostly, but not exclusively, Jewish. To a great extent, *JE* was a summation of nineteenth century *Wissenschaft des Judentums*.[158] We have seen that Morris Jastrow served as Bible editor.[159] Nonetheless, characteristically, non-Jewish scholars predominated in the area of Bible, among them Barton, Budde, Buhl, Conybeare and Torrey. Characteristic as well was the arrangement of Bible articles in the encyclopedia. These were divided in three sections: a) biblical data, i.e. text summaries; b) comments on the particular biblical topic drawn from rabbinic

153 For bibliography see B. Bamberger, *EncJud* 4, 1542. For an assessment of Buttenwieser's contribution to Psalms scholarship, see N. Sarna's introduction to the Ktav reissue of *Psalms, Chronologically Treated* (New York, 1969).

154 Blank, "Bible," 294.

155 See for example, M. Buttenwieser, "The Importance of the Tenses for Interpretation of the Psalms," *HUCA Jubilee Volume* (Cincinnati, 1925), 89–111.

156 *The Jewish Encyclopedia* (New York: Funk and Wagnalls, 1901–1906).

157 See Ginzberg, *Keeper*, 65–68.

158 *JE* was especially strong in the rabbinics department, thanks in the main to the labors of Louis Ginzberg.

159 Richard Gottheil, who also served on the editorial board, was responsible for "History from Ezra to 1492." He left "Hebrew Philology" to Crawford H. Toy.

literature; c) critical view, as held in contemporary scholarship. Readers were thus enabled to ignore the offending section, which for most, was the third.

On the eve of the First World War, various historical factors had conspired to make Philadelphia and Cincinnati the two institutional centers of American Jewish Bible scholarship. Jewish scholarship in America, to a greater extent than Christian, remained dependent on Europe. The simple fact that Jews were a minority meant that there were many more Christian than Jewish seminaries in the United States and in consequence more opportunities for Christian scholars to study and teach. University appointments in Bible were generally held by Christians. The Jewish scholars whose work we have described thus far were few in number and either European born or European trained. Only during the next generation would the situation begin to change.

CHAPTER 22

The Bible at Columbia University

Professor Mayer Gruber and I received our doctorates under Professor Moshe Held *menuhato kavod* at Columbia University. It was at Professor Gruber's home institution, Ben Gurion University, that Held spent what was to be the last month of his life. Professors Gruber, Held and I also share a connection with the Jewish Theological Seminary (JTS). Under these circumstances it seemed appropriate to publish this study on the Bible at Columbia in fond tribute to my friend Professor Gruber. An earlier form of this paper was delivered to a meeting of the Columbia University Seminar on the Hebrew Bible on October 22, 2003. That session was occasioned by Columbia's commemoration of the 250th year of the university's founding. It is my pleasure to thank Donald Glassman, archivist at Barnard College, as well as the staff of the Columbia archives for their generous assistance. Access to the minutes of the Columbia Seminar on the Hebrew Bible over a thirty-five year period was generously provided by Professor Robert Belknap, Director of Columbia University Seminars and his staff, Amanda Roberts, Department Administrator and Alison Garforth, administrative assistant. I am likewise grateful for papers and personal recollections provided by Aaron Demsky, Stephen Geller, William Hallo, Arthur Hertzberg, Murray Lichtenstein, David Marcus, Phyllis Trible and David Weisberg.

Until the late 1980s it had hardly occurred to me to ask questions about the development of academic disciplines and academic area studies. Educated first as a Conservative rabbi, then as a Semitic philologist and then willy-nilly stumbling into the history of Israelite religion, I tended to see those educational curricula as having emerged full blown from the head of Zeus, or perhaps Yahweh. Thanks to Baruch Levine and the Society of Biblical Literature, which commissioned a series of confessional perspectives on the Bible on the occasion of the society's centennial, I was asked to write a history of Jewish biblical scholarship in North America.[1] That project led to an invitation by the Columbia Seminar on the Hebrew Bible to outline the history of biblical instruction and scholarship at Columbia.

1 S. David Sperling, *Students of the Covenant. A History of Jewish Biblical Scholarship in North America* (Atlanta: Scholars, 1992).

 | DOI 10.1163/9789004340879_023

Columbia University, a fixture in the Morningside Heights neighborhood of New York City, began life in lower Manhattan as King's College in July 1754, when Samuel Johnson (1696–1772) held the first classes in a schoolhouse belonging to Trinity Church.[2] Johnson, president of King's College from 1754–1763, was the leading Anglican minister in colonial America and aspired to be its first American Bishop. He had studied Hebrew at Yale before his conversion to Anglicanism. In a letter to a fellow cleric dated Dec 1, 1759, President Johnson wrote:

> ... and those that I can prevail upon to learn Hebrew I teach that to them twice a week, especially such as are designed for [religious] orders, that they may be able to read the Hebrew Scriptures; a thing I have much at heart, as I esteem them the only true foundations of all knowledge both natural and divine, moral and political.[3]

Johnson's successor Myles Cooper (1735–1785), president from 1763–1775), was likewise an Anglican minister. He did not teach Biblical Hebrew himself but reported in 1773 that the subject was taught by proper masters and professors.[4] The first official appointment to the post of Professor of Oriental Languages was Johann Christoff Kunze,[5] Anglicized as John Christopher Kunze (1744–1807). This was in the first year of King's College's new life as the newly patriotic Columbia College in 1784. Kunze, who held a doctorate from the University of Leipzig, came to America in 1770.

---

2 For details on Columbia's history I am especially indebted to R. McCaughey, *Stand, Columbia. A History of Columbia University in the City of New York* (Columbia University, 2003). I am grateful to Professor McCaughey for providing access to an online version of the book's earlier draft, which was likewise of great value.

3 Cited from A. Jeffery, "The Department of Semitic Languages," in *A History of the Faculty of Philosophy Columbia University*, ed. J. Barzun (New York: Columbia University, 1957), 184. It should be noted that Columbia was almost alone among the pre-revolutionary colleges in not being connected to a theological faculty. See J. van Amringe, *A History of Columbia University 1754–1904* (New York: Columbia University, 1904), 17.

4 Jeffery, "Semitic," 184.

5 On Kunze see Jeffery, "Semitic," *ibid*; P. Ritterband and H. S. Wechsler, *Jewish Learning in American Universities. The First Century* (Bloomington: Indiana University, 1994), 12; B. R. Foster, "A Mithridatic Nation: Germany and the Beginning of American Semitic Scholarship," in *Assyriologica et Semitica Festschrift für Joachim Oelsner*, eds. J. Marzahn and H. Neumann (Münster: Ugarit, 2000), 53–65; *idem*, "Yale and the Study of Near Eastern Languages in America, 1770–1930," in YCIAS *Working Papers Series. The United States & the Middle East:Cultural Encounters*, eds., A. Amanat and M. T. Bernhardsson (New Haven, 2002), 1–56.

Kunze began his American professional life as a Lutheran minister in Philadelphia where he founded a German secondary school. In this *Seminarium* he offered German and Hebrew, hoping that the institution would grow into a training center for Lutheran ministers. Unfortunately, few students signed up for either Hebrew or German, and the school Kunze founded was out of business by 1787. In the meantime though, Kunze was called to a pastorate in New York City in 1784. The new Columbia College, now under the regents of New York State and forbidden from requiring a "religious test," offered him an unsalaried professorship for the three-year term 1784–1787 (not unique at the time and for a century thereafter at Columbia and elsewhere.) In 1784 there were seven paid professorships and additional, or "extra" professorships. (These included medicine and law.[6]) He received a second appointment for 1792–1799 that carried a small stipend. In Samuel Mitchill's report to the academic senate in July 1794 Kunze's duties were described as follows:

> The Professor of Oriental languages assists students of divinity of all denominations in their pursuits to acquire a competent knowledge of the original languages of such documents of revealed religion as belong to the Old Testament. He teaches the graduates and undergraduates of Columbia College, and others who apply for the purpose at such hours as do not interfere with the usual lecture hours of the college.[7]

According to Jeffery,[8] Kunze's abilities as a scholar of Hebrew and Arabic "were recognized outside of his church and even by Jewish rabbis who came to him for information."[9] He seems though to have had few students. When the State of New York discontinued an annual grant to Columbia, the trustees of Columbia had little choice but to terminate his professorship as well as those in French and Law. Kunze was an extremely learned man with a thorough knowledge of the Semitic and classical languages, and mathematics as well. His learning was put to use in a book that appears quaint today but surely was not at the time of its publication in 1808. The work was entitled, *A New Method*

6 See. van Amringe, History, 60.

7 Cited from *ibid.*, 79.

8 "Jeffery, "Semitic," 185.

9 The state of Jewish learning in America was quite low in Kunze's time. As late as the 1840s, of the sixty-or-so men who led American congregations only the Reform Max Lilienthal and the Orthodox Abraham Rice (Reiss) were known to have genuine rabbinic ordination. See M. Davis, *The Emergence of Conservative Judaism* (Philadelphia: Jewish Publication Society, 1963), 47–55.

of Calculating all the Lunar and Solar Eclipses and New and Full Moons from the Creation of the World: Grounded upon the Scripture Chronology.[10] In the work Kunze makes critical use of Herodotus, Josephus, Targum Onkelos and the Samaritan Pentateuch, among others. The book attacks the Kantians and the Deists especially the French blasphemers (p. 6) and those biblical scholars like Johann David Michaelis (1717–1791) who were influenced by them.

Thirty years were to pass before the appointment of the Reverend Samuel Hulbeart Turner (1790–1861) as Professor of Hebrew Language and Literature in Columbia College. Turner's primary affiliation was with the Protestant Episcopal General Theological Seminary. The background to his appointment at Columbia is provided by Turner in his autobiography.[11] In 1830, the University of the City of New York, now New York University, was in formation.[12] At that point, writes Turner, "Columbia College thought it expedient to revive the old professorship of Hebrew, which many years before had been held by the Rev. Dr. Kunze ... which had continued vacant since his death. Very much to my surprise, the choice fell on me."

Turner's expression of surprise seems a bit disingenuous. Turner's colleague at General and the man who had donated the land to General was Clement Clarke Moore. Moore, best known as the author (perhaps) of "A Visit from St. Nicholas," was the son of Benjamin Moore, second bishop of New York, sixth rector of Trinity Church, and third president of Columbia College (1801–1811). C. C. Moore (1779–1863; B.A. Columbia, 1798; M.A. 1801; honorary LL.D. 1829) was by 1830 a very influential member of Columbia's board of trustees. Indeed, 12 years after the Turner appointment, C. C. Moore maneuvered the election of his cousin Nathaniel Fish Moore as Columbia's eighth president (1842–1849).[13]

Turner, born in Philadelphia, had graduated from the University of Pennsylvania in 1807 and studied privately for the Episcopal ministry with Bishop William White, who ordained him deacon in 1811 and priest in 1814. His Hebrew studies were with Rev. Samuel B. Wylie who taught Greek and Latin at the University of Pennsylvania. As Turner later came to regret, Wylie

10 The work was printed in New York on June 4, 1806, and is available as Microform MP 5 n. 10865 at the Bobst Library of New York University.

11 S. H. Turner, *Autobiography of the Rev. Samuel H. Turner, D.D.* (New York: A. D. F. Randolf, 1863), 169; Some years earlier Turner had purchased some of Kunze's library (*ibid.*, 26); For a brief outline of Turner's life and work see the entry "Samuel Hulbeart Turner," at http://www.famousamericans.net/samuelhulbeartturner/, which is scanned from *Appelton's Cyclopedia of American Biography* (New York: D. Appelton and Company, 1887–1889).

12 The first professor of Hebrew at the new institution was George Bush, from the same family as the two American presidents of the same name.

13 McCaughey, *Stand Columbia*, 92.

was one of a number of Christian Hebraists whose skepticism about the value of the vowel points led them to ignore the vowels in their Hebrew instruction. Between 1812 and 1817 Turner served in a pulpit in Maryland, and then spent a year as superintendent of a theological school in Philadelphia. It was at the end of 1818 that Turner was appointed Professor of Historic Theology at the newly opened (1817) General Theological Seminary in New York. In 1820 General relocated to New Haven. When the seminary returned to New York in 1821 and was reorganized, Turner was named Professor of Hebrew Language and Interpretation of Holy Scriptures, a post he held until his death in 1861.

In 1831, as the Columbia appointee Turner gave three public lectures on the Hebrew Language. In 1833 he gave his first Hebrew course under the aegis of Columbia. Turner's course met at General with the three students who signed up. They were apparently pleased because all three came to General following their graduation from Columbia. But as he tells us:

> After a while however, when Nordheimer[14] became known as a good Hebrew teacher, I felt it less incumbent on me to devote my time to this subject. Since then I have never been required to give lessons in Hebrew, so that the professorship has become a sinecure.[15]

Nonetheless, Turner was listed in the Columbia catalogue until 1857.[16] In fact, Turner made good use of Nordheimer's presence. Nordheimer was one of several Jewish tutors employed by Turner to instruct him in Rabbinic Hebrew and in the traditional Jewish commentaries. Turner attributed the weakening of his eyesight to "reading a Rabbinical commentary in regular small print, at night,"[17] but he felt it worth the effort, because it would aid in the Christian mission to the Jews. In his book of 1847, *Biographical Notices of Some of the Most Distinguished Jewish Rabbies*[18] *and Translations of Portions of their Commentaries and other Works with Illustrative Introductions and*

---

14 The reference is to Isaac Nordheimer (1809–1842) who held an unpaid professorship in Arabic and Other Oriental Languages at New York University. Although he was a practicing Jew, if no longer traditionally observant, thanks to Edward Robinson Nordheimer was appointed in 1838 as Instructor in Sacred Literature at Union Theological Seminary. He also taught at New Haven Theological Seminary. See S. Goldman, "Isaac Nordheimer (1809–1842): An Israelite Truly in Whom There was no Guile," *American Jewish History* 80 (1990–1991), 213–229.

15 Turner, *Autobiography*, 170–171.

16 Jeffery, "Semitic," 185.

17 Turner, *Autobiography*, 131–132.

18 The spelling "rabbies" was common in the nineteenth century.

Notes,[19] Turner expresses personal sympathy with the sufferings of the Jews through the ages, and castigates those Christians and Muslims who have brought about that suffering. He argues though, that the Christian mission to the Jews has not as been as successful as it might be because Christians do not understand that the Jews read the Bible through their own exegetical tradition. He hopes that his book with its selections from Rashi,[20] Halevi, Saadia, Targum, Aben Ezra, etc. will aid in the effort. A prolific scholar, Turner published a commentary on Genesis in 1841 and numerous articles on the New Testament. He also collaborated on the English translation of the German scholar Johann Jahn's *Introduction to the Old Testament* (1827) and on G. Planck, *Introduction to Sacred Philology and Interpretation* (1834).

Modest as were the beginnings under Kunze and Turner, matters declined yet further. It was only in 1886 that the classicist Harry Thurston Peck was named tutor in Latin and the Semitic Languages. An important turning point was reached with the appointment of Richard James Horatio Gottheil (1862–1936), who was born in Manchester, England where his father served as the spiritual leader of the Manchester Reform Synagogue.[21] The father, Rabbi Gustav Gottheil, was called to the pulpit of New York's Temple Emanuel in 1873. The move brought the younger Gottheil to Columbia Grammar School and then to Columbia College from which he graduated in 1881. Undergraduate degree in hand, Gottheil was sent to Europe in the expectation that he would return with both higher university degrees and rabbinical training, and succeed his father in the rabbinate of Temple Emanuel. The first two expectations were realized. In Berlin, Gottheil studied both at the (Reform) Hochschule für die Wissenschaft des Judenthums and at the Veitel-Heine Ephraim'sche Beth-Hamidrasch. He took his secular studies at the universities in Berlin, Tübingen and Leipzig, which last awarded him the Ph.D. for a thesis on a Syriac grammatical manuscript.

But the young Gottheil, like Felix Adler, the son of Rabbi Samuel Adler, Gustav Gottheil's predecessor at Emanuel, chose not to succeed to the pulpit of his father. Unlike Felix Adler, the founder of Ethical Culture, Gottheil did

19 New York: Stanford and Swords, 1847.

20 He refers to Rashi as Yarhi, perpetuating a centuries-old Christian error in decoding the acronym רש"י as Rabbi Shelomo Yarhi, rather than the correct Rabbi Shelomo Yitzhaqi.

21 For a biographical sketch and a bibliography see J. Bloch and Ida Pratt, "Richard James Horatio Gottheil, 1862–1936," *JAOS* 56 (1936), 472–489; See further, "Gottheil, Richard," p. 341 in the index to Ritterband and Wechsler, *Jewish Learning*; There is much useful information on Gottheil and Columbia in Gottheil's biography of his father entitled *The Life of Gustav Gottheil, Memoir of a Priest in Israel* (Williamsport: Bayard, 1936).

not found a new religion. Instead, his father Gustav Gottheil, convinced prominent members of Temple Emanuel to endow a chair at Columbia for the study of Hebrew and cognate dialects. Gottheil's account of how he got his job at Columbia is more candid than Turner's:

> On February 7, 1887 my father wrote to the Rev. Frederick A. P. Barnard, D. D. President of Columbia College, in regard to the founding of a chair for the study of Hebrew and the cognate dialects, which should be on a par with the other professorial chairs in the College. My father had long had the idea in mind, and now that the future occupant of the chair was in New York and ready for work, he thought the moment had come to make the proposal.[22]

Temple Emanuel secured from Columbia the right of presentation of a candidate for the endowed chair. The Emanuel endowment was for five years after which the university continued the position out of its own funds.[23] Bible was not named as one of the subjects to be taught. In his first letter to President Barnard (Feb 1, 1887) Gustav Gottheil outlined the subjects to be taught by the chair's occupant: "The Aramaic Version of the Scriptures, the Mishnah, the Talmud. The history of Jewish Exegesis & Hebrew Grammar, post-Biblical Poetry & Philosophy & the secular history of the Jews since their final dispersion."[24] In fact, when the chair was, not unsurprisingly, given to Richard Gottheil, his title was Professor of Rabbinical Literature and Oriental Languages. Nonetheless, Columbia announcements through the 1890s and later show that Gottheil offered a biblical program. In 1893–1894 he taught elementary Biblical Hebrew

22 *Life of Gustav Gottheil*, 196.

23 President Seth Low's letter of March 8, 1899 to Gustav Gottheil and Gottheil's reply of March 20, 1899 (*ibid.*, 204–206) show the mutual benefit to both parties. Gottheil wanted the chair continued, and Low, anxious about the expenses incurred in Columbia's expansion into a university (1896) and its relocation to Morningside Heights, wanted the cooperation of Temple Emanuel in its efforts to raise funds.

24 *Ibid*, 196. Quite possibly the proposal deliberately avoided Bible for diplomatic reasons. One of the trustees mentioned in the elder Gottheil's (*ibid.*, 197) correspondence with President Barnard was Talbot W. Chambers (1819–1896), a pastor of the Dutch Reformed Church, and a member of the American committee to revise the King James Version, who edited the conservative *Moses and his Recent Critics* (1849). He may have had some doubts about the advisability of having Bible taught by a Jew committed to higher criticism, but did support the idea of teaching rabbinic literature. Then there was the Reverend Doctor Morgan Dix (1827–1908), rector of Trinity, long term trustee of Columbia and conservative with regard to just about everything.

and an advanced course in Job. In 1894–1895 he offered Deuteronomy and Hosea. In 1895–1896 he began with the elements of Biblical Hebrew and then continued with a second course in Samuel and a third in Jeremiah. In 1896 he once again taught Job. The Barnard College announcements for 1890–1891 (Barnard opened in 1889) show two years of a special undergraduate Hebrew course, the first in principles of Hebrew grammar and the second in selections from the historical books. Both of these were given by Gottheil. In Barnard's graduate department of the same year Gottheil offered text courses in Isaiah and Jeremiah as well as the forms of Hebrew poetry and Aramaic biblical selections.

Although Gottheil published little in the biblical field, he was very much committed to teaching students about archaeology and biblical criticism. As Joshua Bloch reminds us, "No easy task, indeed, and a rather delicate one at that; for those were the days when Robertson Smith in Scotland, and Charles A. Briggs and Henry P. Smith in America were tried for 'heretical opinions on matters biblical.'"[25]

Perhaps the most important contributions to biblical studies made by Gottheil were the students he trained. Among these were Max Margolis (1866–1932; Ph.D., 1891) the outstanding text-critic who taught at Berkeley, HUC and Dropsie, Julius Bewer (1877–1953; Ph.D. 1900) who taught at Oberlin Theological Seminary, and then for many years at Union Theological Seminary, the brothers Emil and Carl Kraeling, William Popper (in the main an Arabist, but who made important contributions to the study of Isaiah) and Isaac Mendelsohn (Columbia faculty 1943–1959; see below).

Gottheil was also very much a man of affairs, a leading figure in the Zionist movement and a founder of the first American Jewish college fraternity Zeta Beta Tau, which Greek letters transliterate the Hebrew initials of Isa 1:27: *ziyon be-mishpat tippadeh* "Zion shall be redeemed through righteousness." The Gottheil years also saw the signing in 1890 of a cross registration agreement with Union Theological Seminary (UTS). By 1894 courses offered by Francis Brown and C. A. Briggs, two thirds of the BDB[26] team, were listed in the Semitics offerings at Columbia.

The 1902–1903 catalogue lists additional instruction in Bible by John Dyneley Prince (1868–1945; B.A. Columbia, 1889; two years study in Berlin then Ph.D. Hopkins, 1892; under Paul Haupt). Prince came to Columbia from NYU

25 *JAOS* 56, 473.

26 F. Brown, S. R. Driver, and C. A. Briggs, *A Hebrew and English Lexicon of the Old Testament* (Oxford: Oxford University, 1907). Although greatly outdated, *BDB* remains the most widely used biblical lexicon in the anglophone world.

where he specialized in cuneiform. He remained in the area of Semitics until 1915. But if Gottheil had been a man of affairs, he could not compare to Prince, who was a member of the New Jersey State Assembly between 1906–1909 and its speaker in 1909.This was followed by three years in the New Jersey State Senate. Prince shifted his interests to Slavonic studies and became professor of Slavonic at Columbia in 1915 where he was located between 1915–1921. Prince took a break to serve as ambassador to Denmark, and later to what was to become Yugoslavia.[27]

As to publications in Semitics and Bible, Prince wrote *Mene Mene Tekel Upharsin: An Historical study of the fifth chapter of Daniel* (Baltimore, 1893); an *Assyrian Primer, an Inductive Method of Learning the Cuneiform Characters* (Columbia University, 1909). He also translated Wellhausen's notes to the critical addition of Psalms in Haupt's Polychrome Bible series (1895; Johns Hopkins University, 1895). Other studies published by Prince were on Serbo-Croatian and Amerindian.

After some controversy with anti-Semitic overtones, following Gottheil's death,[28] his chair was filled by Arthur Jeffery (exact date of birth uncertain, d. 1959). Jeffery was a native Australian who received his B.A. in 1918 and his M.A. in 1920 from University of Melbourne, after serving as a missionary in Madras, India during WWI. It was said that he learned a new Indian dialect in each year of his sojourn in India. He took a degree in theology in 1926 and was ordained in the Methodist Church. He received the Ph.D. from Edinburgh in 1929. He spent 1921–1938 (with study breaks in Europe) in Cairo at the School of Oriental Studies of the University of Cairo, which grew out of the non-academic Language Study Center of the American Mission, and which never lost its missionary component. Jeffery's useful account of the Department of Semitic Languages published in 1957 is in need of some revision:

> With the moving to Morningside Heights of the Jewish Theological Seminary in 1903 and of the Union Theological Seminary in 1910, there was no further need for this department to carry the burden of instruction in Rabbinic or in Biblical Hebrew, which were adequately cared for in the seminaries.[29]

---

27 For a sketch of Prince's Life see *Dictionary of American Biography* (1942), 666.

28 See Ritterband and Wechsler, *Jewish Learning*, 90–105; On the more general question of Jews at Columbia see McCaughey, *Stand, Columbia*, 256–276.

29 Jeffery, "Semitic," 87.

In fact, in 1922–1923 Biblical Hebrew was still offered in the department, although advanced courses offered at UTS were listed in the Columbia catalogue. As far as the JTS connection is concerned, there was early hesitation on the JTS side to get too close to a secular institution. As far as Columbia is concerned, Gottheil, who may not have wanted competition in Rabbinics[30] had opposed the move of JTS to Morningside Heights, and he often had the ear of his classmate Nicholas Murray Butler, president of Columbia. According to Harold Wechsler, Gottheil maintained that JTS would turn out "Jesuitical, narrow-minded teachers of religion."[31] Matters were not helped by Columbia's quota system and the perception that Butler (president 1902–1945) was anti-Semitic. Relations between Columbia and JTS improved after 1940, when Louis Finkelstein, himself a Gottheil Ph.D., became president of JTS.

Jeffery himself published in the main on Arabic and Islamics, which is what he taught at Columbia. He published some articles on biblical subjects in *Harper's One-Volume Bible Dictionary*. Between 1938–1959 while serving at Columbia he served as adjunct professor of Semitic languages at Union Theological Seminary where, among other things, he taught Old Testament. His course on Psalms was singled out as extremely popular.[32] The absence of attention to the Bible and indeed to the entire ancient near east at Columbia was somewhat mitigated by the Gustav Gottheil lectureship, which had been provided to Columbia in 1903 by Temple Emanuel in memory of the good rabbi. One beneficiary of this gift was Isaac Mendelsohn.[33]

Mendelsohn (1898 or 1899–1965) as described in a Hebrew obituary by Harry Orlinsky, was part of a generation that was beginning to disappear by the mid-sixties and is represented by the fewest of survivors at the time of this writing. This is the generation of Jews born in Eastern Europe who escaped the

30 Gottheil's rabbinic learning was no match for Schechter's and especially Louis Ginzberg's. But he had no cause to fear competition in Bible thanks to the baleful influence of JTS president Solomon Schechter and his successor Cyrus Adler on biblical studies. See Sperling, *Students of the Covenant*, 42–44; I. Schorsch, "Coming to Terms with Biblical Criticism," *Conservative Judaism* 59 (2005), 3–22.

31 H. Wechsler, "The JTSA in American Higher Education," in *Tradition Renewed: A History of the Jewish Theological Seminary of America*, ed. J. Wertheimer (New York: JTSA, 1997), II:769–825.

32 See R. T. Handy, *A History of Union Theological Seminary in New York* (New York: Columbia University 1987), 205; F. C. Grant, cited from http://answering-islam.org/uk/Books/Jeffery/tribute.htm .

33 For biographical information on Mendelsohn, see the Hebrew memorial tribute by H. M. Orlinsky, "Professor Isaac Mendelsohn of Blessed Memory," in *Hadoar* 44/32 (1964–1965), 595.

poverty and backwardness of Jewish Russia and Poland and studied in central European and western European universities, where they acquired western learning and proper manners. (Mendelsohn was by all accounts a gentleman and a human being generous of spirit.) Mendelsohn's peers later found themselves in what was then Palestine, or the United States and sometimes, on different occasions, in both. Mendelsohn was born in Kremenets where his father was a tanner and a synagogue beadle. At the age of fifteen Mendelsohn went to Vienna where he spent eight years studying at the Israelitisch-Theologische Lehranstalt, a non-Orthodox seminary where he was ordained. Involved in a student Zionist movement, Mendelsohn immigrated to Palestine in the early nineteen twenties where he was a pioneer worker or *halutz*. In 1925 he became the seventeenth student at the new Hebrew University. He met his future wife in the home of Golda Meyerson, later Golda Meir, prime minister of Israel. The couple immigrated to New York, where Mendelsohn's father-in-law taught at Yeshiva College. Mendelsohn then went to Columbia, and earned his doctorate under Gottheil in 1932. His thesis, published as *Legal Aspects of Slavery in Babylonia, Assyria and Palestine A Comparative Study (3000–500 BC)*, prefigures Mendelsohn's research interests over the years. A larger study appeared as *Slavery in the Ancient Near East: A Comparative Study of Slavery in Babylonia, Assyria, Syria and Palestine, from the Middle of the Third millennium to the End of the First Millennium*.[34]

Mendelsohn did not immediately secure a faculty appointment. Instead, he served as a curator at Columbia and was responsible for compiling a catalogue of Columbia's cuneiform holdings, which appeared in 1943. The departure of two of Gottheil's doctorates, the Arabist Abraham Halkin and the classicist Ralph Marcus, who had been funded by the Gustav Gottheil lectureships, for real academic posts, opened Mendelsohn's way to a faculty position. By the late 1950s he was a member of the graduate sub-committee which oversaw the joint program with UTS in Religion. Although Mendelsohn never taught Bible *per se*, his classes in Akkadian and Ugaritic were taught with the needs of Bible students in mind.[35] Mendelsohn was involved in some dissertations in Bible, but seems not to have directed any. It was only after Jeffery's death in 1959 that Mendelsohn became full professor of Semitic languages at age

34 New York: Oxford, 1949.

35 David Weisberg, who studied as an undergraduate with Mendelsohn, recalls (personal communication) that Mendelsohn constantly referred to biblical parallels for the benefit of the UTS graduate students whose primary interest were in Bible. In my conversations with them, both Weisberg and Phyllis Trible emphasized Mendelsohn's humanity and accessibility.

62, a position that included teaching Modern Hebrew. A Zionist all his life, Mendelsohn had planned to retire from Columbia a bit early and move to Israel but died before that could be accomplished. His scholarly work in Bible focused on biblical institutions in the light of ancient Near Eastern society. Noteworthy and characteristic are his articles, "Slavery in the OT," in *Interpreter's Dictionary of the Bible* (*IDB*);[36] "The Conditional Sale into Slavery of Free-Born Daughters in Nuzi and the Law of Ex, 21:7–11,"[37] and "Samuel's Denunciation of Kingship in Light of Akkadian Documents from Ugarit."[38]

After Mendelsohn's death Moshe Held (1924–1984) came to Columbia.[39] Held, born in Poland, was brought to mandatory Palestine in 1935 and entered the Hebrew University in 1943. Held's studies, interrupted by service in the British army and resumed in 1946, were delayed a second time by the Israeli War of independence. Held then completed his M.A. in Hebrew literature at Hebrew University, where he studied under some of the greats of that generation. He studied a great deal of Arabic (what he later referred to as his *hata'at neurim*, "youthful sin") with D. Baneth, S. D. Goitein and H. J. Polotsky. After the M.A. Held spent time at the university as a research fellow and instructor. He would probably have remained in the field of medieval Hebrew studies, and in Israel, were it not for his Ugaritic teacher Umberto Moshe David Cassuto (1883–1951). Cassuto, a pioneer in comparative study of Ugaritic and biblical literature, inspired Held to change his academic direction, advising him to come to the United States to study with W. F. Albright at Johns Hopkins. Held came to Baltimore on a State Department Fellowship. After a year at Hopkins, Held was advised by Albright to study Akkadian at the Oriental Institute of the University of Chicago under the great Assyriologist Benno Landsberger. Thanks to additional fellowship support, Held was able to spend four years at Chicago. In 1957 Held submitted his dissertation to Hopkins, which awarded him the Ph.D. He then joined the faculty at Dropsie replacing Cyrus Gordon who had moved to Brandeis. In 1959 Held began his visits to Morningside Heights at Jewish Theological Seminary where he was to continue as an adjunct professor of Bible for twenty-five years. The JTS connection brought Held under the close tutelage of H. L. Ginsberg to whom Held always referred as "my mentor." In 1966 Held was called to Columbia to replace Mendelsohn. As George Landes

36 *IDB* 4:383–391.

37 *JAOS* 55 (1935), 190–195.

38 *BASOR* 143 (1956), 17–22.

39 For biographical information see Stephen Leiberman, "Moshe Held (1924–1984)," *JQR* 76 (1985), 1–3; E. Greenstein and D. Marcus, "Professor Moshe Held: Our Teacher," *JANES* 19 (1989), 1–2; See also the list of publications, *ibid.*, vii–viii; Ch. Cohen, "The 'Held' Method for Comparative Semitic Philology," *ibid.*, 9–23; Sperling, *Students*, 101–103.

wrote of Held in a letter of February 24,1989, "he proceeded to revive Semitic studies at Columbia through a truly spectacular decade."

Although he did not teach courses on specific biblical books at Columbia, Held did teach courses on biblical poetry, and the Bible in the light of the ancient Near East. In classes in Ugaritic or on Northwest Semitic inscriptions constant reference was made to biblical passages. Indeed, he rarely came to an Akkadian class without a Hebrew Bible. David Marcus and Edward Greenstein have observed that as a teacher Held was like the chef who took you into the kitchen to watch him work.[40] Held concentrated on method. He might have had students spend a semester of biblical poetry on three poetic chapters of Job or Psalms, but once they were done the students could fight their way through the remaining chapters on their own.

As a teacher Held was passionate. After a semester with him you might be convinced, as was I, that the survival of the world depended on plotting accurate interdialectal distributions. His twenty-five years at JTS teaching Bible with constant reference to ancient Near Eastern literature regularly attracted JTS students to Held's graduate courses at Columbia. UTS graduate students likewise studied with him for their Semitic language credits towards doctorates in the biblical area. I doubt that there was any Advanced Akkadian class outside of Held's days at Columbia that had more than twenty students, as did Held's classes.

Held's publication record is relatively small but the small number of bibliographical entries is deceptive.[41] Held was never happier than when he could condense an article into a footnote. (He learned some of this technique from H. L. Ginsberg.) I remember several classes when he would say, "I've written on this." I would not recall an article on the subject at hand, only to go home and find notes one to three paragraphs long, which almost anyone else would have expanded into articles. Held could be highly critical of other scholars in class, but was always polite in print. He often threatened to write a review of Dahood's *Psalms*.[42] He never did, and I suspect that it was out of fear that

40 *JANES* 19, 2.

41 The bibliography by Chaim Cohen published in *JANES* 19 (1989), vii–viii lists twenty articles and one review. To these should be added M. Held, "H. L. Ginsberg: An Appreciation," *Conservative Judaism* 30 (1976), 3–9.

42 M. Dahood, *Psalms I: 1–50, Psalms II:51–100, Psalms III:101–150* (Anchor Bible; Garden City: 1966, 1967, 1968). As numerous critics observed, Dahood misread hundreds of biblical passages by "interpreting" them in the light of the Ugaritic language, a method akin to translating *Don Quixote* with a French Dictionary. Inasmuch as these volumes were published by Doubleday, Held, depending on what language he was speaking, referred to them disparagingly as "*Doppelnacht*," or "*Double-khoyshekh*," respectively, "Double-night," and "Double-darkness."

he would not be able to keep his criticisms within the bounds of academic courtesy.

Held's speech, which was filled with malapropisms and mannerisms, could easily be imitated, and it often was. I remember once when Held called my house. My wife at the time answered the phone and was sure that it was Murray Lichtenstein doing his Held imitation. One final anecdote that I recalled only recently: Held was having lunch with some of us graduate students at a greasy spoon establishment owned by one "Irving," AKA Yitzhok, whose manner and demeanor made Held look like a graduate of Eton and Oxford. One day Yitzhok made a vulgar Yiddish comment. All of us laughed except Hayim Tawil who, as a Yemenite, knew no Yiddish. Held obligingly translated the vulgarism into Akkadian.

Held was not the only "character" at Columbia involved in the study of Bible. We cannot ignore two of Held's older contemporaries. First there was Morton Smith (1915–1991)[43] one of the founders of the Seminar on the Hebrew Bible at Columbia. His student Shaye Cohen described Smith as "a great scholar, blessed with extraordinary acuity, mordant wit and an expansive range." In that same Columbia press release of July 11, 1991 following Smith's death, Cohen was quoted as follows: "The truth was always his most important goal and if it collided with sacred beliefs so much the better." In that same release Roger Bagnall said, "it was hard to find a subject on which he was not thoroughly informed and very opinionated. The sharpness and critical candor of his work became legendary." I want to focus on his contributions to biblical scholarship and give some examples of that mordant and opinionated wit.

Smith received his A.B. at Harvard in 1936, and the S.T.B. from Harvard Divinity in 1940. At Harvard, Smith studied New Testament with Henry Cadbury, Judaism with H. A. Wolfson and Greco-Roman religion with A. D. Nock. On a traveling fellowship he spent four years at Hebrew University and at the American School of Oriental Research, studying Hellenistic Judaism with Moshe Schwabe and Hans Lewy, and Jewish magic and mysticism with Gershom Scholem. Smith came back to the United States in 1944 and continued writing his Ph.D. (in Hebrew) for Hebrew University, which awarded him the doctorate in 1948. He then taught at Brown as instructor in biblical literature 1950–1951 and as assistant professor of biblical literature 1951–1955. He served at Drew as visiting professor of History of Religion in 1956–1957. Smith later earned the Th.D. at Harvard in 1985. He came to Columbia's History

43 See S. Cohen, "In Memoriam Morton Smith," in Cohen's edition of some of Smith's articles as *The Cult of Yahweh*," vol. II, (Leiden: Brill, 1996), 279–285.

department in 1957 in ancient history. Smith retired in 1985, but taught as emeritus until 1990.

Smith was an ordained Episcopal priest. I do not know the facts behind Smith's conversion from Episcopalianism to anti-clericalism, but it was deep and sincere. He looked forward to someone writing a practical handbook entitled "Religions, their Causes and Cures."[44] Interestingly, of his seven Ph.D. graduates, Jacob Neusner and Shaye Cohen are ordained rabbis. Another, Seth Schwartz, is a graduate of Yeshiva University who taught at JTS before moving to Columbia, while Albert I. Baumgarten is an Orthodox Jew recently retired from the Israeli Orthodox university Bar-Ilan. Smith's most important contribution to the study of the Hebrew Bible was the 1973 work *Palestinian Parties and Politics that Shaped the Old Testament.* The book's significance lies in the fact that Smith took seriously both the biblical demand that Israel serve the god Yahweh exclusively, and the biblical accounts that most Israelites served other gods along with Yahweh. His solution was that the demand for Yahweh's exclusive worship was due to what Smith called the "Yahweh-alone" party, an ancient minority party that arose in the early monarchy. The party had intermittent successes and failures over the centuries, only attaining full victory in the Persian period. Until that point the majority of Israelites had accepted Yahweh as the national god whose pre-eminence did not preclude the service of other essential divinities.

An important shorter paper by Smith, "The Present State of OT Studies,"[45] contains some very constructive points of method in studying biblical text and history. In the paper Smith stresses the importance of serious text criticism, and laments that little work was being done at the time in producing critical texts.[46] He likewise criticized the misuse of comparative philology, to my mind excessively, but completely understandable in that two volumes of Dahood's pan-Ugaritic commentary on Psalms had been published by the time the essay appeared.[47] Likewise constructive, if again excessive, was his complete dismissal of comparative material from the second millennium BC for understanding the Bible. But the great pleasure of the essay comes from its sarcasm. Smith coins the term "pseudorthodoxy," to describe what he perceives to be the regnant stance of biblical scholars in the late 1960s. The reason Smith stresses the pseud-element in pseudorthodoxy is significant. He writes: "Nobody so far

44 Cohen, *Yahweh*, 45. Reprint of an article of 1968.

45 *JBL* 88 (1969), 19–35 (reprinted in Cohen, *Yahweh* I, 37–54).

46 The situation has improved significantly. See J. Sanders, "The Hebrew University Bible and Biblia Hebraica Quinta," *JBL* 118 (1999), 518–526.

47 See the discussion on Held, above.

as I know believes in the existence of Yahweh as the OT describes him—a north Arabian mountain god who traveled in thunderstorms and liked the smell of burning fat."[48] Smith decried "the constant tendency to save as much of the old [religious] positions as possible. If not true, then let the stories be 'essentially' true. If not even 'essentially' true, let them at least teach some 'higher truth.'" Smith then adds (in parentheses) "Whenever a critic makes much of a higher truth you may suppose he is trying to conceal a lower falsity. And if in the end, unpleasant facts must be admitted, they must at least be expressed in reverent language."

In addition, Smith impugned the motives of the pseud-orthodox by repeating an anecdote about the Assyriologist Friedrich Delitzsch who once asked his Old Testament professor if Deuteronomy was a forgery since it had been written in the seventh century while claiming to be the work of Moses. "For God's sake 'no' said the professor. Deuteronomy may be a forgery but you mustn't say so."

Some of Smith's best comments were embedded in his critiques of the Albright school of biblical archaeology, which had attempted to provide a concrete historical setting in the second pre-Christian millennium for the biblical patriarchs. The Albright school claimed that Israelite religion emerged as a product of "very civilized, sophisticated and cosmopolitan era."[49] In contrast to Wellhausen, the Albright school asserted that Israelite religion was not primitive in its earliest forms. What follows is vintage Smith sarcasm:

> Abraham was a theologian as well as a merchant prince; his donkey caravans could barely stagger along beneath his library of cuneiform tablets. From these little Isaac learned all that Sumerian literature of which the knowledge handed down by tradition for a whole millennium, was to appear in the Israelite works of the eighth or seventh centuries. Or, to follow another version, Joseph learned monotheism from his friend Akh-en-Aton, or better, taught it to him. Or at least Moses, schooled in all the wisdom of the Egyptians, anticipated the excavation of Tell el Amarna and recovered Akh-en-Aton's suppressed teachings.[50]

At the Hebrew Bible seminar Smith would regularly appear to doze off during the meetings only to awake with sharp, if soft-spoken attacks on the presenter

48 Cohen, *Yahweh*, 39.

49 The quotation is from George Mendenhall, a student of Albright, cited by Smith *apud* Cohen, *Yahweh*, 44.

50 *Ibid.*

of the evening. When I congratulated him on the appearance of the four-volume Festschrift, *Judaism, Christianity and other Greco-Roman Cults* edited in his honor by Jacob Neusner (Leiden: E. J. Brill, 1975), he said that he could take no credit for its production save the title, for which, he said proudly, he alone was responsible.

The third member of that triumvirate of brilliant "characters" was Theodor Herzl Gaster (1906–1992). Gaster was born in England as the eighth and youngest son of the *Hakam*, or chief rabbi, of the English Sephardic community[51] Moses Gaster, himself a scholar and bibliophile. The elder Gaster had become blind by the time of his son's youth. Because this required young Theodor to read to his father in numerous languages, the son grew up remarkably erudite. Theodor Gaster earned a B.A. in Classics (London, 1928), and the M.A. in Archaeology (London, 1936). Between 1928 and 1932 he served as Assistant Rabbi in the London Reformed Synagogue.[52] After coming to the United States he earned his doctorate at Columbia in 1943 for a thesis on the Ugaritic text, "The Beautiful and Gracious Gods." Gaster had an active, if peripatetic, career. He served as chief of the Hebraic section of the Library of Congress and taught at Fairleigh Dickinson and Dropsie. He was an adjunct professor at Columbia off and on before being appointed to the faculty in the Department of Religion at Barnard in 1966, at the age of sixty. In the days of mandatory retirement that meant that Gaster was emeritus by 1972–1973. He regularly taught the Introduction to OT at Barnard, and a graduate course on ancient Near Nastern religions. Murray Lichtenstein has aptly characterized the body of Gaster's writing as "comparative material of encyclopedic proportions."[53] At an introductory joint meeting of the Columbia and Barnard Religion departments at which I was present, each faculty member described his or her specialization. When Gaster's turn came he said simply, "the field of religion." He was misidentified more than once as a member of the "myth and ritual school." Unlike the members of that school, however, Gaster employed the grammatical model of "punctual" versus "durative," to argue that ritual and myth represent parallel expressions through two concurrent media. Two of his classics are *Thespis* and *Myth, Legend and Custom in the Old Testament*. The second especially, is of immeasurable value for biblicists.

51 According to Theodor Gaster (personal communication ca. 1975), his father told him that the family name was originally Castro.

52 Despite its name, British Reformed Judaism is closer to American Conservative Judaism, than to American Reform Judaism.

53 M. Lichtenstein, "Theodor H. Gaster: An Appreciation," *JANES* 5 (1973), 9.

Members of my generation recall a certain meeting of the Ancient Near Society, founded by David Marcus while still a student. (The Society inaugurated *The Journal of the Ancient Near Eastern Society* (JANES) likewise founded by David Marcus.) The meeting featured Held and Gaster in a debate on scholarly method that, as entertainment, could have succeeded on "Saturday Night Live." Gaster, in his best British accent, berated Held for his exclusively philological focus on the individual words of a text, and his consequent inability to see the larger picture. Held, in his booming Polish-Israeli accent returned the compliment by saying that Gaster's theoretical approach ignored scholarly method and distorted what the texts actually said. Held allowed that Gaster's imprecision led to entertaining misinterpretation. In fact, Held recommended reading *Thespis* in an armchair on a quiet Saturday night while enjoying a glass of sherry.

Gaster was not a happy man. It is common for scholars to acknowledge the aid of colleagues in the prefaces to their books. Contrast Gaster in the preface to *Myth, Legend*: "I have had no help from colleagues in preparing this book, and have been constrained, over these long years, to plow a lonely furrow." Sadly, much of this loneliness was of his own making. Gaster could never ignore the opportunity for a barb or insult. One semester when Held was on sabbatical, Gaster taught Held's Ugaritic course where he regularly criticized Held for his ignorance of classics and world literature. Similarly, when he taught a class at the New York School of the (Reform seminary) Hebrew Union College, Gaster kept referring to the *New Union Prayer Book* of the Reform movement as the *New Onion Prayer Book* because as he put it, "I cry every time I turn a leaf."[54]

It would be amiss not to include some remarks about the contribution to biblical studies made by the Columbia University Seminar for the Study of the Hebrew Bible. The first meeting of the ongoing Seminar was held in May, 1968, against the background of the Columbia student protests, at what was then the Men's Faculty Club. The idea of establishing the Seminar had come from Morton Smith who first turned to James Sanders, then a professor at UTS and adjunct at Columbia. Sanders and Smith enlisted Held to join their efforts.[55] These "founding fathers" were able to bring together a group of founding members; a list of whom reads like a *Who's Who* of biblical and related scholarship. Among those, now deceased, were Elias Bickerman (Columbia), Gerson Cohen (Columbia), Gaster (Barnard), Judah Goldin (Yale), Ginsberg (JTS), Held (Columbia), Harry Orlinsky (Hebrew Union College), Marvin Pope (Yale),

54 Oral communication from David Ellenson.

55 I thank James Sanders, Founder and President of the Ancient Biblical Manuscript Center at Claremont for his personal recollections of the early history of the Seminar.

R. B. Y. Scott (Princeton), Smith (Columbia), Samuel Terrien (UTS), Robert Bornemann, Moshe Greenberg, William Hallo,[56] and Yochanan Muffs. James Sanders as of this revision (2016) is the sole survivor of the founders.

Now in its forty-eighth year of existence the Hebrew Bible Seminar has maintained a strong comparative focus, especially with regard to the ancient Near East. Such cognate disciplines and areas as Dead Sea Scrolls, Septuagint, Targum and Midrash have also been represented. The Seminar has provided a very significant forum for scholars to discuss their work and preview their publications. Indeed, new approaches and projects that came to fruition years later were first presented at the Seminar. Among these have been psycholinguistics, structuralism, Bible as literature, advanced text-criticism and sociological theory. Of no little importance was the opportunity for Seminar participants to interact with such foreign scholars as Avi Hurvitz, Bernard Jackson, Anson Rainey, Alexander Rofé, Emanuel Tov and Moshe Weinfeld. To these I add our *Jubilar* Professor Gruber.

At the present time the Seminar remains the one significant venue at Columbia for the study of the Hebrew Bible. The fact that ever since the time of Gottheil, no appointment has been made in Bible proper, has meant that attention to Bible has depended on the individual interests of scholars in such departments as Middle East, Religion, and History. Should future appointments to Columbia's faculty include latter-day Gasters, Helds, and Smiths, the situation might change.

Permit me to close by saying there is much more that could be added. I paid little attention to the UTS contribution because I think it more properly belongs to the history of Bible at UTS.[57] The combined programs between Columbia and JTS and Barnard-JTS are likewise relevant, but as a sage once said (Ecclesiastes 12:12) "of the making of many books there is no end," and this might be one such book.

56 Hallo taught twice at Columbia when Held was on leave. He also served as advisor to several Columbia graduate students.

57 The history of biblical studies at UTS remains a desideratum. A good start has been made by J. Sanders, "The Bible at Union: 1835 to the Present," *USQR* 52/2 (1998), 123–131. As Professor Sanders informed me, he was asked to focus in the main on the ideological issues involved in Bible at UTS, rather then on the work of individual scholars. It should also be noted that well before the term "out-sourcing" had been coined, in the area of Bible Columbia relied heavily, and some might say, exploitatively, on UTS.

Bibliography

Note: An asterisk indicates articles in a language other than Hebrew in the journal *Eretz Israel* (*ErIsr*).

Abarbanel, Isaac. *Perush al ha-Torah*. Jerusalem: Benê Arbael, 1964.

Abou Assaf, A., P. Bordreuil, and A.Millard. *La Statue de Tell Fekherye et son inscription bilingue assyro-araméenne*. Paris, 1982.

Abrams, M. *A Glossary of Literary Terms*. New York: Holt, Rinehart and Winston, 1971.

Abramson, S. *Talmud Babli Maseket Baba Batra*. Jerusalem: Razal, 1958.

Aḥituv, S. *Echoes from the Past: Hebrew and Cognate Inscriptions from the Biblical Period*. Jerusalem: Carta, 2008.

Aḥituv, S. *Joshua: Introduction and Commentary*. Jerusalem: Magnes, 1995.

Albeck, Ch. *Mabo la-Talmudim*. Jerusalem: Dvir, 1987.

Albright, W. F. "Abram the Hebrew: A New Archaeological Interpretation." *BASOR* 163 (1961): 44.

Albright, W. F. "An Aramean Magical Text in Hebrew from the Seventh Century B.C." *BASOR* 76 (December 1939): 5–11.

Albright, W. F. "The Egyptian Correspondence of Abimilki, Prince of Tyre." *JEA* 23 (1937): 198.

Albright, W. F. "Some Remarks on the Meaning of SHR in Genesis." *BASOR* 164 (1961): 28.

Albright, W. F. *From the Stone Age to Christianity: Monotheism and the Historical Process*. Baltimore: Johns Hopkins, 1940.

Albright, W. F. *From the Stone Age to Christianity: Monotheism and the Historical Process*. 2nd ed. Garden City, NY: Doubleday, 1957.

Alexander, P. "Targum, Targumim." In *The Anchor Bible Dictionary*. Vol. 6, edited by D. N. Freedman, 320–331. New York: Doubleday, 1992.

Alt, A. "Die Wallfahrt von Sichem nach Bethel." In *Kleine Schriften zur Geschichte des Volkes Israel*. Vol. 1, edited by A. Alt, 79–89. Munich: Beck, 1953.

Altman, A. "The Original Meaning of the Name Amurru 'Ha'emori.'" In *Studies in Hebrew and Semitic Languages Dedicated to the Memory of Professor Eduard Yechezkel Kutscher* [in Hebrew], edited by G. B. Sarfatti and P. Artzi, 76–102. Ramat Gan: Bar-Ilan, 1980.

Aminoah, N. "On Developments of Statements of Amoraim in the Babylonian Talmud." In *Te'uda*. Vol. 3, 39–56. Tel Aviv: Tel Aviv University, 1983.

Amit, Yairah. "Implicit Redaction and Latent Polemic in the Story of the Rape of Dinah" [in Hebrew]. In *Texts, Temples and Traditions: A Tribute to Menahem Haran*, edited by M. Fox, V. Hurowitz, A. Hurvitz, M. Klein, B. J. Schwartz, and N. Shupak, 11–28. Winona Lake, IN: Eisenbrauns, 1996.

Anderson, F., and D. N. Freedman. *Hosea*. Garden City, NY: Anchor Bible, 1980.
Angerstorfer, A. "Asherah als 'consort of Jahwe' oder Ashirtah?" *BN* 17 (1982): 7–16.
Asmussen, J. "A Zoroastrian 'De-Demonization' in Judeo-Persian." In *Irano-Judaica*, edited by S. Shaked, 112–121. Jerusalem: Ben-Zvi Institute, 1982.
Avishur, Y. "The Ghost-Expelling Incantation from Ugarit (Ras ibn Hani 78/20)." *UF* 13 (1981): 22–23.
Avishur, Y. "*lōʿ śamtā lāhēm raḥămîm* (Isaiah 47:6)—Biblical Style or Translated Idiom." *Shnaton* 5–6 (1978–1979): 91–99.
Avishur, Y. "The Second Inscription from Arslan Tash." *UF* 10 (1978): 29–36, 33.
Avishur, Y. "Studies of Stylistic Features Common to the Phoenician Inscriptions and the Bible." *UF* 8 (1976): 15.
Avishur, Y. *Stylistic Studies in Word-Pairs in Biblical and Ancient Semitic Literatures*. Neukirchen: Neukirchener, 1984.
Bacher, B. ערכי מדרש. Tel Aviv: Achdut, 1923.
Bacher, B. Z. (Wilhelm). *Aggadot Hatanna'im*. Berlin, 1922.
Bacher, W., ed. *Sepher Haschoraschim: Wurzelwörterbuch der hebräischen Sprache von Ab-ulwalîd Merwân Ibn Ganâh*. Berlin, 1896. Reprint, Amsterdam: Philo, 1969.
Back, M. *Die sassanidischen Staatsinschriften*. Leiden: E. J. Brill, 1978.
Balkan, K. "Contributions to the Understanding of the Idiom of the Old Assyrian Merchants of Kanish." *Or* 36 (1967): 405.
Baltzer, K. *The Covenant Formulary in Old Testament, Jewish and Early Christian Writings*. Philadelphia, 1971.
Bar, S. *A Letter That Has Not Been Read: Dreams in the Hebrew Bible*. Cincinnati, 2001.
Bar Asher, M. "The Different Traditions of Mishnaic Hebrew." In *Working with No Data… Studies T. O. Lambdin*, edited by D. Golomb, 1–38. Winona Lake, IN: Eisenbrauns, 1987.
Bar Asher, M. "L'hébreu mishnique; esquisse d'une description." *CRAIBL* (1990): 199–237.
Bar Asher, M. "Introduction to Mishnaic Hebrew." In *Rabbi Mordecai Breuer Festschrift Collected Papers in Jewish Studies*, edited by M. Bar Asher, 657–688. Jerusalem: Academon, 1992.
Bar Asher, M, ed. קובץ מחקרים בלשון חז"ל חלק ב Jerusalem, 1979.
Bar Asher, M., and D. Rosenthal, eds. *Meḥqerei Talmud*. Vol. 2. Jerusalem: Magnes, 1993.
Bar-Efrat, Shimon. *Narrative Art in the Bible*. Sheffield: Almond, 1997.
Bar-Efrat, Shimon. *II Samuel: Introduction and Commentary*. Tel Aviv: Am Oved, 1996.
Bar-Ilan, M. "Writing in Ancient Israel and Early Judaism." In *Mikra: Text, Translation, Reading and Interpretation of the Hebrew Bible in Ancient Judaism and Early Christianity*, edited by M. Mulder and H. Sysling, 22. Philadelphia: Fortress, 1988.
Barr, J. "The Question of Religious Influence: The Case of Zoroastrianism, Judaism and Christianity." *JAAR* 53 (1985): 201–202.

Barr, J. "Some Semantic Notes on the Covenant." In *Beiträge zur Alttestamentlichen Theologie*, edited by H. Donner, R. Hanhart, and R. Smend, 36. Göttingen, 1977.

Barré, M. "The Meaning of *l'šybnw* [לא אשיבנו] in Amos 1:3–2:6." *JBL* 105 (1986): 617–620.

Barré, M. "A Note on *rš't* in the Karatepe Inscription." *JANES* 15 (1981): 1–3.

Barstad, Hans. "The Understanding of the Prophets in Deuteronomy." *SJT* 8 (1994): 236–251.

Barth, J. "Babl.-assyr. *ra-a-mu* 'lieben'." *ZA* 22 (1909): 1–5.

Bauer, H. "Die *klmw*-Inschrift aus Sendschirli." *ZDMG* 67 (1913): 685.

Bauer, U. F. W. "Anti-Jewish Interpretations of Psalm 1 in Luther and in Modern German Protestantism." *Journal of Hebrew Scriptures* 2 (1998): 1–27.

Bechtel, Lyn. "What if Dinah Is Not Raped? (Genesis 34)." *JSOT* 62 (1994): 19–36.

Becking, B. *Only One God? Monotheism in Israel and the Veneration of the Goddess Asherah*. London: Sheffield Academic, 2001.

Beer, M. *The Babylonian Amoraim Aspects of Economic Life*. Ramat Gan: Bar-Ilan University, 1982.

Beer, M. *The Babylonian Exliarchate in the Arsacid and Sassanian Periods*. Tel Aviv: Dvir, 1970.

ben Jehiel, Nathan. *Aruch Completum*. 8 vols. Reprint, New York, 1955.

Bendavid, A. *Biblical Hebrew and Mishnaic Hebrew*. Tel Aviv: Dvir, 1967.

Berger, I. *Analytical Subject Index to the Hebrew Union College Annual Volumes 1–37 (1924–1966)*. New York: Ktav, 1969.

Berger, P. "*Zur Nabonid–Inschrift und ihren Duplikaten.*" *ZA* 60 (1970): 131–133.

Berlin, A. *The Dynamics of Biblical Parallelism*. Bloomington: Indiana University Press, 1985.

Berlin, A. Review of *Mesopotamian Epic Literature Oral or Aural?* by M. E. Vogelzang and H. L. J. Vanstiphout. *JAOS* 115 (1995): 300.

Berlin, A. *Zephaniah: A New Introduction and Commentary*. AB 25a. New York: Doubleday, 1994.

Berlin, A., and Brettler, M. "The Modern Study of the Bible." In *Jewish Study Bible*, edited by A. Berlin and M. Brettler, 2084–2096. New York: Oxford University Press, 2004.

Berliner, A., ed. *Raschi der Kommentar des Salomo b. Isak über den Pentateuch*. Frankfurt am Main: J.Kauffmann, 1905.

Berlinerblau, J. "Preliminary Remarks for the Sociological Study of 'Official Israelite Religion.'" In *Ki Baruch Hu: Ancient Near Eastern, Biblical and Judaic Studies in Honor of Baruch A. Levine*, edited by R. Chazan, W. W. Hallo, and L. H. Schiffman, 153–170. Winona Lake, IN: Eisenbrauns, 1999.

Berlinerblau, J. *The Vow and the "Popular Religious Groups" of Ancient Israel: A Philological and Sociological Inquiry*. Sheffield: Sheffield Academic, 1996.

Beyer, K. *Die aramäischen Texten vom Toten Meer*. Göttingen and Tübingen: Vandenhoeck & Ruprecht, 1984.

Biesenthal, J., and F. Lebrecht, eds. *Rabbi Davidis Kimchi Radicum Liber*. Berlin, 1847.

Birnbaum, S. *The Hebrew Scripts Part Two: The Plates*. London, 1954–57.

Blank, S. "Bible." In *Hebrew Union College-Jewish Institute of Religion at One Hundred Years*, edited by S. Karff, 287–316. Cincinnati: Hebrew Union College, 1976.

Blau, L. *Das altjüdische Zauberwesen*. Budapest, 1898.

Blenkinsopp, J. "The Mission of Udjahorresnet and those of Ezra and Nehemiah." *JBL* 106 (1987): 409–421.

Blidstein, G. "A Note on the Term 'Torah she-be-al Peh'" [in Hebrew]. *Tarbiz* 42 (1972–1973): 496–498.

Bloch, J., and Ida Pratt. "Richard James Horatio Gottheil, 1862–1936." *JAOS* 56 (1936): 472–489.

Bloch-Smith, E., and B. Nakhai. "A Landscape Comes to Life: The Iron Age 1." *NEA* 62 (1999), 62–92, 101–128.

Bokser, B. "The Palestinian Talmud." In *Aufstieg und Niedergang der römischen Welt*, 2.19.2, 139–256. Berlin and New York: De Gruyter, 1979.

Borger, R. "Gott Marduk und Gott-König Šulgi als Propheten: Zwei Prophetische Texte." *Bi.Or.* 28 (1971): 3–24.

Borowski, O. "The Identity of the Biblical *ṣirʿâ*." In *The Word of the Lord Shall Go Forth: Essays in Honor of David Noel Freedman in Celebration of his Sixtieth Birthday*, edited by C. Meyers and M. O'Connor, 315–319. Winona Lake, IN: Eisenbrauns, 1983.

Boyarin, D. Review of *The Canonical History of Ideas, The Place of the So-called Tannaite Midrashim: Mekhilta Attributed to R. Ishmael, Sifra, Sifré to Numbers and Sifré to Deuteronomy* by J. Neusner. *JAOS* 112 (1992): 455–465.

Boyarin, D. *Carnal Israel*. Berkeley: University of California, 1993.

Boyce, M. *A History of Zoroastrianism*. Leiden: Brill, 1982.

Boyce, M. "On the Zoroastrian Temple Cult of Fire." *JAOS* 95 (1975): 454–465.

Breuer, E. "Post-Medieval Jewish Interpretation." In *Jewish Study Bible*, edited by A. Berlin and M. Brettler, 1900–1908. New York: Oxford University Press, 2004.

Brichto, H. C. *The Problem of 'Curse' in the Hebrew Bible*. Philadelphia: Society of Biblical Literature, 1963.

Briggs, C., and E. Briggs. *The Book of Psalms*. Vol. 2. New York, 1957.

Bright, J. *A History of Israel*. 1st ed. Philadelphia: Westminster, 1958.

Brockelmann, C. "Semitische Reimwortbildungen." *ZS* 5 (1927): 6–38.

Bron, F. *Recherches sur les inscriptions phéniciennes de Karatepe*. Geneva and Paris: Droz, 1979.

Brown, J. *The Rise of Biblical Criticism in America, 1800–1870: The New England Scholars*. Middletown, CT: Wesleyan University Press, 1969.

Buber, M. *Moses: The Revelation and the Covenant*. New York: Harper & Row, 1958.

Buber, S. *Lekach-Tob*. Vilna, 1880.

Buber, S. *Midrash Tehillim.* Reprint, Jerusalem, 1977.

Budd, P.J. *Numbers.* Waco, TX: Word Books, 1984.

Buttenwieser, M. "The Importance of the Tenses for Interpretation of the Psalms." In *HUCA Jubilee Volume*, edited by D. Philipson, 89–111. Cincinnati: 1925.

Cahiers de Byrsa 8 (1958–1959).

Cales, M. *El Talmud de Babilonia Tratado Nedarim.* Buenos Aires: Acervo Cultural Editores, 1978.

Campbell, E. "Judges 9 and Biblical Archeology." In *The Word of the Lord Shall Go Forth: Essays in Honor of David Noel Freedman in Celebration of his Sixtieth Birthday*, edited by C. Meyers and M. O'Connor, 263–271. Winona Lake, IN: Eisenbrauns, 1983.

Caquot, A. "Observations sur le Première Tablette Magique d'Arslan Tash." *JANES* 5 (1973): 45–51.

Caquot, A., and R. du Mesnil du Buisson. "La seconde tablette ou 'petite amulette' d'Arslan Tash." *Syria 48* (1971): 391–406.

Caquot, A., M. Sznycer, and A. Herdner. *Textes ougaritiques.* Paris, 1974.

Carroll, R. "Psalm LXXVII: Vestiges of a Tribal Polemic." *VT* 21 (1971): 133–150.

Cassin, E. *La Splendeur divine.* Paris, 1968.

Cazelles, H. "Chabar, chaber." *TDOT* 4 (1981): 193–197.

Chajes, H. P. *Sefer Tehillim.* Zhitomer, 1902.

Charlesworth, J. *A Graphic Concordance to the Dead Sea Scrolls.* Louisville: John Knox, 1991.

Chavel, H. *Perush Rashi al Hattorah.* Jerusalem: Mossad Harav Kook, 1985.

Chernick, M. "Contemporary Talmudic Studies: The Continuing Agenda." In *The Literature of Early Rabbinic Judaism: Issues in Talmudic Redaction and Interpretation*, edited by A. Avery-Peck, 73–80. Lanham: University Press of America, 1989.

Chernick, M, ed. *Essential Papers on the Talmud.* New York: New York University Press, 1994.

Clarke, E. G., ed. *Targum Pseudo-Jonathan to the Pentateuch and Concordance.* Hoboken, NJ: Ktav, 1984.

Coats, G. *Rebellion in the Wilderness.* Nashville: Abingdon, 1968.

Cogan, M. *Imperialism and Religion: Assyria, Judah and Israel in the Eighth and Seventh Centuries, B.C.E.* Missoula, MT: Scholars, 1974.

Cohen, Ch. "Bibliography." *JANES* 19 (1989): vii–viii.

Cohen, Ch. "The 'Held Method' for Comparative Semitic Philology." *JANES* 19 (1989): 9–23.

Cohen, Ch. "The Phenomenon of Negative Parallelism and Its Ramifications for the Study of Biblical Poetry" [in Hebrew]. *Beer Sheva* 3 (1988): 69–107.

Cohen, Ch. "The Phrase *bt br* (Prov 21:9; 25:2)." *Beth Mikrâ* 21 (1976), 598–599.

Cohen, M., ed. *Mikra'ot Gedolot Haketer Samuel I and II.* Jerusalem: Keter, 1993.

Cohen, M. R. *Birth of Conservative Judaism*. New York: Columbia University, 2012.

Cohen, N. "Analysis of the Exegetic Tradition in the Mekhilta de-Rabbi Ishmael: The Meaning of *'Amanah'* in the Second and the Third Centuries." AJS *Review* 9 (1984): 1–25.

Cohen, S. "In Memoriam: Morton Smith." In S. Cohen, *The Cult of Yahweh*. Vol. 2, 279–285. Leiden: Brill, 1996.

Collins, T. "The Kilamuwa Inscription—A Phoenician Poem." *WO* 6 (1971): 184–185.

Conybeare, F. C., J. Rendel Harris, and Agnes Smith Lewis. *The Story of Aḥikar.* Cambridge, 1913.

Cooper, A., and B.Goldstein, "At the Entrance to the Tent: More Cultic Resonances in Biblical Narrative." *JBL* 116 (1997): 201–215.

Coote, R. "Amos 1:11 RḤMYW." *JBL* 90 (1971): 206–208.

Cowley, A. *Aramaic Papyri of the Fifth Century B.C.* Oxford: Magdalen College, 1923.

Cross, F. M. *Canaanite Myth and Hebrew Epic: Essays in the History of the Religion of Israel.* Cambridge, MA: Harvard University Press, 1973.

Cross, F. M. "The Old Phoenician Inscription from Spain Dedicated to Hurrian Astarte." *HTR* 64 (1971): 189–195.

Cross, F. M., and D. N. Freedman. "The Pronomial Suffixes of the Third Person Singular in Phoenician." *JNES* 10 (1951): 228–230.

Cross, F. M., and D. N. Freedman. "A Royal Song of Thanksgiving: II Samuel 22 = Psalm 18." *JBL* 72 (1953): 33n104.

Cross, F. M., and R. Saley, "Phoenician Incantations on a Plaque from the Seventh Century B.C. from Arslan Tash in Upper Syria." *BASOR* 197 (February 1970): 42–49.

Cross, F. M., and R. Saley, "Phoenician Incantations of the Seventh Century b.c. [*sic*] from Arslan Tash in Upper Syria." *CBQ* 36 (1974): 486–490.

Dahood, M. *Psalms 1: 1–50, Psalms 2:51–100, Psalms 3:101–150.* Garden City, NY: Anchor Bible, 1966–1968.

Dahood, M. "Ugaritic-Hebrew Parallel Pairs." In *Ras Shamra Parallels*, edited by L. R. Fisher, 71–382. Rome, 1972.

Dalglish, E. *Psalm Fifty-One in the Light of Ancient Near Eastern Patternism.* Leiden, 1962.

Dalman, G. *Aramäisch-neuhebräisches Handwörterbuch.* Frankfurt am Main: J. Kaufmann, 1922.

Dalman, G. *Grammatik der jüdisch-palästinischen Aramäisch.* Leipzig: Hinrichs, 1905.

Dalton, O. *The Treasures of the Oxus with Other Examples of Early Oriental Metal Work.* 3rd ed. London: British Museum, 1964.

Darom, A., ed. *R. David Kimhi* (RADAK): *ha-Pēruš ha Šalem 'al Tehillim.* Jerusalem, 1974.

Davis, M. *The Emergence of Conservative Judaism.* Philadelphia: Jewish Publication Society, 1963.

de Boer, P. A. H., ed. *The Old Testament in Syriac According to the Peshitta Version.* Pt 1. Fascicle 1. Peshitta Institute. Leiden: Brill, 1977.

Deem, A. "The Goddess Anath and Some Biblical Hebrew Cruces." *JSS* 23 (1978): 26.

Degen, R. *Altaramäische Grammatik.* Wiesbaden, 1969.

Deller, K. "Die Briefe des Adad-šumu-uṣur." *AOAT* 1 (1969): 58:18'–19'.

De Moor, J. C. *Seasonal Pattern in the Ugaritic Myth of Ba'lu.* AOAT 16. Neukirchen: Neukirchener, 1971.

Dentan, R. "The Literary Affinities of Exodus xxxiv 6f." *VT* 13 (1963): 40.

Derenbourg, J., ed. *Version arabe du Pentateuque.* Paris: Itztikowski, 1893.

de Vaux, R. *Ancient Israel.* New York, 1965.

Dever, W. "Archaeology and the Ancient Israelite Cult: How the KH. El-Qôm and Kuntillet 'Ajrud 'Asherah Inscriptions Have Changed the Picture." *ErIsr* 26 (1999): 9–15*.

Dhorme, E. *A Commentary on the Book of Job.* Translated by H. Knight. New York: Nelson, 1984.

Dhorme, E. *L'emploi métaphorique des noms de parties du corps en Hébreu et en Akkadien.* Paris, 1923.

Dietrich, M., O. Loretz, and J. Sanmartin. *The Cuneiform Alphabetic Texts from Ugarit, Ras Ibn Hani and Other Places.* 3d ed. Munster: Ugarit-Verlag, 2013. See also *KTU* in the List of Abbreviations.

Diéz-Macho, A. *Neophyti.* Vol. 1. Madrid-Barcelona: Consejo Superior de Investigaciones Cientificas, 1968–1978.

Dimitrovsky, H., ed. *Texts and Studies Analecta Judaica.* Vol 1. New York: Jewish Theological Seminary, 1977.

Dion, P. "Notes d'épigraphie ammonite." *RB* 82 (1975): 24–33.

Dion, P. "Ššbṣr and Ssnwry." *ZAW* 95 (1983): 111–112.

Dirksen, P. "The Old Testament Peshitta." In *Mikra: Text, Translation, Reading and Interpretation of the Hebrew Bible in Ancient Judaism and Early Christianity*, edited by M. Mulder and H. Sysling, 264–285. Philadelphia: Fortress, 1988.

Dodds, E. R. *The Greeks and the Irrational.* London, 1971.

Dossin, G. "L'inscription de fondation de Iahdun-Lim, roi de Mari." *Syria* 32, no. 1 (1955): 1–28.

Dossin, G., and A. Lods. "Une Tablette inédite de Mari, intéressante pour l'histoire ancienne du prophétisme sémitique." In *Studies in Old Testament Prophecy Presented to Professor T. H. Robinson*, edited by H. Rowley, 103. Edinburgh, 1950.

Drews, R. *The End of the Bronze Age. Changes in Warfare and the Catastrophe ca. 1200 B.C.* Princeton: Princeton University, 1993.

Driver, G. R. *Aramaic Documents of the Fifth Century B.C.* Oxford: Clarendon, 1965.

Driver, G. R. Review of Proverbs and Northwest Semitic Philology by M. Dahood. *JSS* 10 (1965): 112–118.

Driver, G. R., and J. Miles. *The Babylonian Laws.* Vol. 2. Oxford: Clarendon, 1955.

Driver, S. R. *The Book of Genesis*. New York, 1904.

Driver, S. R. *A Critical and Exegetical Commentary on Deuteronomy*. Edinburgh: T&T Clark, 1895.

du Mesnil du Buisson, R. "Une tablette magique de la région du Moyen Euphrate." In *Mélanges syriens offerts à Monsieur René Dussaud*, 421–434. Paris: Paul Geuthner, 1939.

Dupont-Sommer, A. *Les Araméens*. Paris, 1949.

Ebeling, E. *Die akkadische Gebetsserie "Handerhebung."* Berlin: Akademie-Verlag, 1953.

Edelman, D. *The Triumph of Elohim: From Yahwisms to Judaisms*. Grand Rapids, MI: Eerdmans, 1996.

Efroymson, C. *Yehezkel Kaufmann: The History of the Religion of Israel.* New York: Ktav, 1997.

Ehrlich, A. B. *Mikra ki-Pheschuto: The Bible According to its Literal Meaning*. Reprint, New York: Ktav, 1969.

Ehrlich, A. B. *Mikrâ Ki-Pheschutô.* Vol. 1. Reprint, New York: Ktav, 1969.

Ehrlich, A. B. *Mikrâ ki-Pheschutô.* Vol. 2. New York: Ktav, 1965.

Ehrlich, A. B. *Randglossen zur hebräischen Bibel.* Vol. 5. Leipzig: J. C. Hinrich, 1912.

Eichler, Barry. "On Reading Genesis 12:10–20." In *Tehillah le-Moshe: Biblical and Judaic Studies in Honor of Moshe Greenberg*, edited by Mordechai Cogan, B. L. Eichler, and J. H. Tigay, 33. Winona Lake, IN: Eisenbrauns, 1997.

Eisenbeis, M. *Die Wurzel šlm im Alten Testament*. Berlin, 1969.

Eissfeldt, O. "El and Yahweh." *JSS* 1 (1956): 31.

Eitan, I. "An Unkown Meaning of Raḥamim." *JBL* 53 (1934): 269–271.

Elliger, K. *Das Buch der zwölf kleinen Propheten.* Vol. 2. Göttingen: ATD, 1959.

Elman, Y. *Authority and Tradition: Toseftan Baraitot in Talmudic Babylonia*. Hoboken, NJ: Ktav, 1994.

Elior, R. "HaBaD: The Contemplative Ascent to God." In *Jewish Spirituality II*, edited by A. Green, 157–205. New York: Crossroad, 1987.

Emerton, J. "New Light on Israelite Religion: The Implications of the Inscriptions from Kuntillet Ajrud." *ZAW* 94 (1982): 1–20.

Emerton, J. "'Yahweh and His Asherah': The Goddess or Her Symbol?" *VT* 49 (1999): 315–337.

Epstein, D. *The Babylonian Talmud Seder Nezikin* Vol. 3. London: Soncino: 1935.

Epstein, J. N. "Gaonic Responsa" [in Hebrew]. In *J. N. Epstein Studies in Talmudic Literature and Semitic Languages*, edited by E. Z. Melamed, 165. Jerusalem: Magnes, 1983.

Epstein, J. N. "Glosses Babylo-araméenes." *REJ* 73 (1921): 40.

Epstein, J. N. "Glosses Babylo-araméenes." *REJ* 74 (1922): 40–72.

Epstein, J. N. *A Grammar of Babylonian Aramaic.* Jerusalem: Magnes, 1960.

Epstein, J. N. *Prolegomena ad Litteras Amoraiticus* [in Hebrew]. Jerusalem: Magnes, 1962.

Epstein, J. N. *Studies in Talmudic Literature and Semitic Languages.* Vol. 1, edited by E. Z. Melamed, 339–374. Jerusalem: Magnes, 1983.

Epstein, J. N. "Zum magischen Texte." *JAOS* 33 (1912): 279.

Eskenazi, T., and A. Weiss, eds. *The Torah: A Women's Commentary.* New York: Union for Reform Judaism, 2007.

Exum, J. Cheryl. "Harvesting the Biblical Narrator's Scanty Plot of Ground: A Holistic Approach to Judges 16:4–22." In *Tehillah le-Moshe: Biblical and Judaic Studies in Honor of Moshe Greenberg*, edited by Mordechai Cogan, B. L. Eichler, and J. H. Tigay, 39–46. Winona Lake, IN: Eisenbrauns, 1997.

Fales, F. M. "Le double bilinguisme de la statue de Tell Fekhyere." *Syria* 60 (1983): 233–250.

Falkenstein, A. *Die Haupttypen, der sumerischen Beschwörung literarisch untersucht.* Leipzig: Hinrich, 1931.

Feldman, Louis, trans. *Flavius Josephus: Translation and Commentary.* Vol. 3. *Judaean Antiquities*, edited by Steve N. Mason, 123. Leiden: Brill, 2004.

Feldman, Louis, trans, Louis. "Philo, Pseudo-Philo, Josephus, and Theodotus on the Rape of Dinah." *JQR* 94 (2004): 253–277.

Fewell, Dana, and David Gunn. "Tipping the Balance: Steinberg's Reader and the Rape of Dinah." *JBL* 111 (1991): 193–211.

Finet, A. "Un cas de clédonomancie à Mari." In *Zikir Šumim: Assyriological Studies Presented to F. R. Kraus on the Occasion of his Seventieth Birthday*, edited by G. van Driel, Th. Krispin, and K. R. Veenhof, 48–56. Leiden, 1982.

Finkelstein, I., and N. Na'aman. *From Nomadism to Monarchy: Archaeological and Historical Aspects of Early Israel.* Washington, DC: Biblical Archaeology Society, 1994.

Finkelstein, J. J. "Hebrew חבר and Semitic ḪBR." *JBL* 75 (1956): 328–331.

Finkelstein, J. J. "An Old Babylonian Herding Contract and Genesis 31:38f." *JAOS* 88 (1968): 32.

Finkelstein, J. J. "Sex Offenses in Sumerian Laws." *JAOS* 86 (1966): 355–372.

Finkelstein, J. J. "The So-Called 'Old Babylonian Kutha Legend.'" *JCS* 11 (1957): 86:iv:12.

Finkelstein, J. J., and M. Greenberg, eds. *Oriental and Biblical Studies. Collected Writings of E. A. Speiser.* Philadelphia, 1967.

Finkelstein, L., ed. *Siphre ad Deuteronomium.* Berlin: Jüdischer Kulturbund, 1939.

Fischel, W., ed. *Semitic and Oriental Studies: A Volume Presented to William Popper on the Occasion of His Seventieth Birthday October 25, 1949.* Berkeley and Los Angeles: University of California, 1951.

Fishbane, M. "Additional Remarks on RḤMYW (Amos 1:11)." *JBL* 91 (1972): 391–393.

Fishbane, M. *Biblical Interpretation in Ancient Israel*. Oxford: Clarendon, 1985.

Fishbane, M. "The Treaty Background of Amos 1:11 and Related Matters." *JBL* 89 (1970): 313–318.

Fitzmyer, J. *The Aramaic Inscriptions of Sefîre*. Rome, 1967.

Fleishman, Joseph. "Shechem and Dinah in Light of Non-Biblical and Biblical Sources." *ZAW* 116 (2004): 12–32.

Fleishman, Joseph. "Socio-Legal Aspects of Genesis 34." *Shnaton* 12 (2000): 141–155.

Fossey, C. *La Magie assyrienne*. Paris, 1932.

Foster, B. R. "A Mithridatic Nation: Germany and the Beginning of American Semitic Scholarship." In *Assyriologica et Semitica Festschrift für Joachim Oelsner*, edited by J. Marzahn and H. Neumann. Münster: Ugarit, 2000.

Foster, B. R. "Yale and the Study of Near Eastern Languages in America, 1770–1930." In *YCIAS Working Papers Series. The United States & the Middle East: Cultural Encounters*, edited by A. Amanat and M. T. Bernhardsson. New Haven, CT, 2002.

Frank, C. *Studien Zur babylonischen Religion*. Leipzig, 1911.

Frankel, Zechariah. "On Changes in Judaism." In *Tradition and Change: The Development of Conservative Judaism*, edited by M. Waxman, 43–50. New York: Burning Bush, 1958.

Frankel, Zechariah. *Einleitung in den jeruschalemischen Talmud* [in Hebrew]. Breslau, 1870.

Frankena, R. "Einige Bemerkungen zum Gebrauch des Adverbs 'al-kēn." In *Studia Biblica et Semitica Theodoro Christiano Vriezen*, edited by W. van Unnik and A. van der Woude. Wageningen, 1966.

Frankena, R. "The Vassal Treaties of Esarhaddon and the Dating of Deuteronomy." *OTS* 14 (1965): 153–154.

Frechette, C. *Mesopotamian Ritual-Prayers of "Hand-lifting" (Akkadian Šuillas)*. Münter: Ugarit-Verlag, 2012.

Freed, Lisbeth. *The Priest and the Great King*.Winona Lake, IN: Eisenbrauns, 2004.

Freedman, D. N. *Divine Commitment and Human Obligation. Selected Writings of David Noel Freedman*. 2 vols. Eerdmans: Grand Rapids, 1997.

Freedman, D. N. "Pottery, Poetry, and Prophecy." *JBL* 96 (1977): 5–26.

Freedman, D. N. *Pottery, Poetry and Prophecy*. Winona Lake, IN: Eisenbrauns, 1980.

Freedman, D. N., R. MacDonald, and D. Matson. *The Published Works of William Foxwell Albright: A Comprehensive Bibliography*. Cambridge, MA: AASOR., 1975.

Freedman, D. N., and G. E. Wright. "Bibliography of W. F. Albright." In *The Bible and the Ancient Near East: Essays in Honor of William Foxwell Albright*, edited by D. N. Freedman and G. E. Wright, 488–524. Garden City, NY: Anchor, 1965.

Freedman, D. N. "Bibliography of W. F. Albright." *ErIsr* 9 (1969): 1–5.

Friedlaender, I. "A Great Bible Scholar, Arnold B. Ehrlich." *Nation* (January 10, 1920): 41.

Friedlaender, I. "Das hebräische *seper* in ciner verkannten Bedeutung." *JQR O.S.* 15 (1903): 102–103.

Friedlaender, I. "A New Specimen of Modern Biblical Exegesis." *American Hebrew and Jewish Messenger* 81 (July 5, 1907): 3–7.

Friedlaender, I. "The Present Position and Original Form of the Prophecy of Eternal Peace in Isaiah 2:1–5 and Micah 4:1–5." *Jewish Quarterly Review N.S.* 6 (1916): 405–413.

Friedlaender, I. *Der Sprachgebrauch des Maimonides. Ein lexikalisher and grammatischer Beitrag zur Kenntnis des Mittelarabischen*. PhD diss, University of Strasbourg, 1901.

Friedman, Richard. *The Exile and Biblical Narrative: The Formation of the Deuteronomistic and Priestly Works*. Chico, CA: Scholars, 1982.

Friedman, Richard. Review of *Divine Commitment and Human Obligation: Selected Writings of David Noel Freedman* by D. N. Freedman. *JQR* 88 (1998): 259–261.

Friedman, S. "Holy Scriptures Defile the Hands." In *Minḥa le-Naḥum: Biblical and Other Studies Presented to Nahum M. Sarna in Honour of his 70th Birthday*, edited by Marc Brettler and Michael Fishbane, 117–132. JSOTSup 154. Sheffield: Sheffield Academic Press, 1993.

Friedman, S. "On Method in the Study of the Talmudic Pericope" [in Hebrew]. In *Texts and Studies Analecta Judaica*. Vol. 1, edited by H. Dimitrovsky, 310–312. New York: Jewish Theological Seminary, 1977.

Friedman, S. "On the Origin of Textual Variants in the Babylonian Talmud" [in Hebrew]. *Sidra* 7 (1991): 67–102.

Friedman, S. "Orthography of the Names Rabbah and Rava." *Sinai* 110 (1992): 140–164.

Frisch, Amos. "'Ve-Antah' (Hosea 2:17): A Secondary Meaning." *Tarbiz* 69 (1999–2000): 445–447.

Frymer-Kensky, Tikva. "Law and Philosophy: The Case of Sex in the Bible." *Semeia* 45 (1989): 95.

Frymer-Kensky, Tikva. *Reading the Women of the Bible: A New Interpretation of Their Stories*. New York: Schocken, 2004.

Gafni, I. *The Jews of Babylonia in the Talmudic Era: A Social and Cultural History*. Jerusalem: Shazar Center, 1990.

Galling, K. "Goliath und seine Rüstung." In *Volume du Congrès International pour l'étude de l'Ancien Testament: Genève*, 1965. VTSup 15, 150–169. Leiden: Brill, 1966.

Galpaz-Feller, P. "The Stela of King Piye: A Consideration of 'Clean' and 'Unclean' in Ancient Egypt and the Bible." *RB* 102 (1995): 506–521.

Garbini, G. "L'iscrizionie fenicia di Kilamuwa e il verbo škr in semitico nordoccidentale." *BeO* (1977): 112–118.

Garr, W. R. *Dialect Geography of Syria-Palestine, 1000–586 B.C.E.* Philadelphia, 1985.

Gaster, M. "Divination (Jewish)." In *Encyclopedia of Religion and Ethics*. Vol. 4, edited by J Hastings, 813. New York, 1955.

Gaster, T. H. "A Hang-up for Hang-ups: The Second Amuletic Plaque from Arslan Tash." *BASOR* 209 (1973): 18–26.

Gaster, T. H. *Myth, Legend and Custom in the Old Testament*. New York, 1969.

Gaster, T. H. *Myth, Legend, and Custom in the Old Testament*. 2 vols. Gloucester, MA: Smith, 1981.

Gaster, T. H. "Mythic Thought in the Ancient Near East." *Journal of the History of Ideas* 16 (1955): 424.

Gaster, T. H. *The New Golden Bough*. New York, 1959.

Gaster, T. H. "The Religion of the Canaanites." In *Ancient Religions*, edited by V. Ferm, 123. New York: Citadel, 1965.

Gaster, T. H. "Sharper than a Serpent's Tooth: A Canaanite Charm against Snakebite." *JANES* 7 (1975): 41.

Gaster, T. H. *Thespis*. New York, 1961.

Geers, F. W. "*Die Gebetsbeschwörung an Ischtar Nr. 1.*" *ZA* 42 (1934): 220–222.

Gelb, I. J. *Hurrians and Subarians*. Chicago: University of Chicago Press, 1944.

Gelb, I. J. "A New Clay-Nail of Hammurabi." *JNES* 7 (1948): 269.

Gelb, I. J. *Sargonic Texts in the Ashmolean Museum, Oxford*. Chicago, 1970.

Gelio, R. "Kilamuwa and the Foreign Kings: Propaganda vs. Power." *WO* 10 (1979): 7.

Geller, M. "Four Aramaic Incantation Bowls." In *The Bible World. Essays in Honor of Cyrus H. Gordon*, edited by G. Rendsburg, R. Adler, Milton Arfa, and Nathan H. Winter, 50–51. New York: Ktav & Institute of Hebrew Culture and Education, New York University, 1980.

Gevirtz, S. "On Canaanite Rhetoric: The Evidence of the Amarna Letters from Tyre." *Or* 42 (1973): 177.

Gevirtz, S. "On the Etymology of the Phoenician Particle ʾš." *JNES* 16 (1964): 127.

Gevirtz, S. "West-Semitic Curses and the Problem of the Origins of Hebrew Law." *VT* 11 (1961): 143.

Ghirshman, R. *The Art of Ancient Iran from Its Origins to the Time of Alexander the Great*. New York: Golden, 1964.

Ghirshman, R. *Persian Art 249 B.C.–A.D. 651*. New York: Golden, 1962.

Giblin, C. "Structural Patterns in Joshua 24:1–25." *CBQ* 26 (1964): 50–69.

Gibson, J. *Textbook of Syrian Semitic Inscriptions*. Vol. 2. Oxford: Oxford University Press, 1975.

Gibson, J. *Textbook of Syrian Semitic Inscriptions*. Vol. 3. Oxford: Oxford University Press, 1982.

Gignoux, P. *Glossaire des inscriptions pehlevies et parthes*. London: Lund Humphries, 1972.

Ginsberg, H. L. *The Five Megilloth and Jonah. A New Translation.* 2nd ed. Philadelphia: Jewish Publication Society of America, 1974.

Ginsberg, H. L. "Gleanings in First Isaiah." In *Mordecai Kaplan Jubilee Volume*, edited by Moshe Davis, 252–253, 257. New York: Jewish Theological Seminary of America, 1953.

Ginsberg, H. L. "Interpreting Ugaritic Texts." *JAOS* 70 (1950): 158.

Ginsberg, H. L. *The Israelian Heritage of Judaism.* New York: Jewish Theological Seminary, 1982.

Ginsberg, H. L. *Koheleth.* Jerusalem: M. Newman, 1961.

Ginsberg, H. L. "Koheleth 12:4 in the Light of Ugaritic." *Syria* 33 (1956): 99–101.

Ginsberg, H. L. "Lexicographical Notes." VTSup 16 (1967): 78.

Ginsberg, H. L. "Psalms and Inscriptions of Petition and Acknowledgement." In *Louis Ginzberg Jubilee Volume*, 161n8. New York: The American Academy for Jewish Research, 1945.

Ginsberg, H. L. "Ugaritico-Phoenicia." In *The Gaster Festschrift*, edited by D. Marcus, 146–147. New York, 1973.

Ginsberg, H. L. "An Unrecognized Allusion to Kings Pekah and Hoshea of Israel (Isa.8:23)." *ErIsr* 5 (1958): 61–65*.

Ginzberg, E. *Keeper of the Law: Louis Ginzberg.* Philadelphia: Jewish Publication Society, 1966.

Ginzberg, L. *The Legends of the Jews.* 7 vols. Philadelphia: Jewish Publication Society, 1959–1969.

Glueck, N. *Hesed in the Bible.* Translated by A. Gottschalk. Cincinnati, 1967.

Gnuse, R. *No Other Gods: Emergent Monotheism in Israel.* Sheffield: Sheffield Academic, 1997.

Goetze, A. *The Laws of Eshnunna.* The Annual of the American Schools of Oriental Research. Vol. 31. New Haven, 1986.

Goetze, A. "An Old Babylonian List of Amorites." *JAOS* 88 (1968): 56.

Goldman, E. "Parallel Texts in the Palestinian Talmud to Genesis Rabbah (Chapters 1–5)." MA thesis, Hebrew Union College, 1969.

Goldman, S. "Isaac Nordheimer (1809–1842): An Israelite Truly in Whom There Was No Guile." *American Jewish History* 80 (1990–1991): 213–229.

Goldschmidt, L. *Der babylonische Talmud.* Vol. 5. Berlin: Jüdischer, 1931.

Goldschmidt, L. *Der babylonische Talmud.* Vol. 7. Berlin: S. Calvary, 1903 and 1925.

Gollancz, H. *The Book of Protection.* London, 1912.

Goodblatt, D. "The Babylonian Talmud." In *Aufstieg und Niedergang der römischen Welt* 2.19.2, edited by W. Hasse, 257–336. Berlin and New York: De Gruyter, 1979.

Gordis, R., ed. *Max Leopold Margolis: Scholar and Teacher.* Philadelphia: Alumni Association of Dropsie College, 1952.

Gordon, C. "Abraham of Ur." In *Hebrew and Semitic Studies Presented to Godfrey Rolles Driver ... in Celebration of His Seventieth Birthday 20 August, 1962*, ed. D. Thomas and W. McHardy, 77–84. Oxford, 1963.

Gordon, C. "Aramaic Incantation Bowls." *Or* 10 (1941): 116–141, 272–284, 339–360.

Gordon, C. *The Pennsylvania Tradition of Semitics*. Atlanta: Scholars, 1986.

Gottheil, R. *The Life of Gustav Gottheil: Memoir of a Priest in Israel*. Williamsport, PA: Bayard, 1936.

Gottlieb, Ze'ev, ed. *Be'ur 'al ha-Torah le-Rabbi 'Ovadyah Sforno*. Jerusalem: Mossad Harav Kook, 1980.

Gottwald, N. K. "Religious Conversion and the Societal Origins of Ancient Israel." *Perspectives in Religious Studies* 15 (1988): 49–65.

Gray, J. *I & II Kings: A Commentary*. Philadelphia, 1976.

Grayson, A. K. *Assyrian Royal Inscriptions, Pt. 2: From Tiglath-pileser I to Ashur-nasir-apli*. Wiesbaden: Otto Harrassowitz, 1976.

Greenberg, M. *Ezekiel, 1–20*. Garden City, NY, 1983.

Greenberg, M. *Ezekiel 21–37*. New York: Doubleday, 1997.

Greenberg, M. "Kaufmann on the Bible: An Appreciation." In *Studies in the Bible and Jewish Thought*, edited by M. Greenberg. Philadelphia: Jewish Publication Society, 1995: 175–188.

Greenfield, J. C. "Early Aramaic Poetry." *JANES* 11 (1979): 46.

Greenfield, J. C. "Notes on Some Aramaic and Mandaic Incantation Bowls." *JANES* 5 (1973): 149.

Greenfield, J. C. "רטין מגושא." In *Joshua Finkel Festschrift*, edited by S. and L. Honig and L. Stitskin, 63–69. New York: Yeshiva University, 1974.

Greengus, Samuel. "Redefining 'Inchoate Marriage' in Old Babylonian Contexts." In *Riches Hidden in Secret Places: Ancient Near Eastern Studies in Memory of Thorkild Jacobsen*, edited by Tzvi Abusch, 123–139. Winona Lake, IN: Eisenbrauns, 2002.

Greenspoon, L. "Biblical Translators in Antiquity and the Modern World: A Comparative Study." *HUCA* 60 (1989): 91–113.

Greenspoon, L. "Jewish Translations of the Bible." In *Jewish Study Bible*, edited by A. Berlin and M. Brettler, 2005–2020. New York: Oxford University Press, 2004.

Greenspoon, L. *Max Leopold Margolis: A Scholar's Scholar*. Atlanta: Scholars, 1987.

Greenstein, E. "Trans-Semitic Idiomatic Equivalency and the Derivation of Hebrew *ml'kh*." *UF* 11 (1979): 334–335.

Greenstein, E., and D. Marcus. "The Akkadian Inscription of Idrimi." *JANES* 8 (1976): 90.

Greenstein, E. "Professor Moshe Held: Our Teacher." *JANES* 19 (1989): 1–2.

Gropp, D., and T. Lewis. "Notes on Some Problems in the Aramaic Text of the Hadd-Yith'i Bilingual." *BASOR* 259 (1985): 45:5.

Gruber, M. "The Accusations against Shechem Son of Hamor: A Reconsideration." *Beth Mikra* 44 (1998–1999): 119–127.

Gruber, M. "Akkadian *labān appi* in the Light of Art and Literature." *JANES* 7 (1975): 78–83.

Gruber, M. *Aspects of Nonverbal Communication in the Ancient Near East*. Rome: Biblical Institute, 1980.

Gruber, M. "On a Forgotten Meaning of the Root *ayin-nun-yod* in Biblical Hebrew" [in Hebrew]. In *Iyyune Mikra u-Farshanut*. Vol. 7, *Menahot Yedidut ve-Hoqarah le-Menahem Cohen*, edited by Samuel Vergon, Joseph Ofer, Jordan Penkower, and Jacob Klein, 233–244. Ramat Gan: Bar-Ilan University Press, 2005.

Gruber, M. "The Many Faces of Hebrew *nś' pnym* 'lift up the face,'" *ZAW* 95 (1983): 252–260.

Gruber, M. "The Mishnah as Oral Torah. A Reconsideration." *JSJ* 15 (1984): 112–122.

Gruber, M. "The Motherhood of God in Second Isaiah." *RB* 90 (1983): 352.

Gruber, M. "Ha-tiškaḥ 'iššâ `ulâh?" *Tarbiz* 51 (1982): 491.

Gruenwald, Itamar. "Midrash and the 'Midrashic Condition': Preliminary Considerations." In *The Midrashic Imagination: Jewish Exegesis, Thought, and History*, edited by Michael Fishbane, 9. Albany: State University of New York Press, 1993.

Gunkel, H. *Genesis*. Göttingen, 1910.

Gurney, O. R. "The Poor Man of Nippur." *Anatolian Studies* 6 (1956): 154:82.

Gurock, J. "Resisters and Accommodators: Varieties of Orthodox Rabbis in America, 1886–1893." *American Jewish Archives* 35 (1983): 162–163.

Hackett, J. *The Balaam Text from Deir 'Allâ*. Chico, CA: Scholars, 1984.

Hakam, A. *The Book of Exodus*. Jerusalem: Mossad Harav Kook, 1991.

Hakam, A. *Sefer Iyyob*. Jerusalem: Mossad Harav Kook, 1981.

Hakam, A. *Sefer Tehillim*. Jerusalem: Mossad Harav Kook, 1979.

Hakam, Noah. "'Innah." *Tarbiz* 69 (1999–2000): 441–444.

Halder, A. "The Akkadian Verbal System." *Or.* 33 (1964): 35.

Hallo, W. W. "The Lame and the Halt." *ErIsr* 9 (1969): 68.

Hammer, Reuven. *Sifre: A Tannaitic Commentary on the Book of Deuteronomy*. New Haven: Yale University Press, 1986.

Handy, R. T. *A History of Union Theological Seminary in New York*. New York: Columbia University, 1987.

Haran, M. "The Character of the Priestly Source." In *Proceedings of the Eighth World Congress of Jewish Studies*, Panel Sessions, A: *Bible Studies and Hebrew Language*, 131–138. Jerusalem: Magnes, 1983.

Haran, M. "Judaism and the Bible in the Thinking of Yehezkel Kaufmann" [in Hebrew]. *Mada'e Ha-Yahadut 31* (1991): 69–80.

Haran, M. *Temples and Temple-Service in Ancient Israel*. Oxford: Oxford University Press, 1978. Reprint, Winona Lake, IN.: Eisenbrauns, 1985.

Harrington, D. "Philo, Pseudo-." *ABD* 5 (1992): 344–345.

Hartman, L., and A. Di Lella. *The Book of Daniel* (AB 23). New York: Doubleday, 1978.

Hartom, A. *HaSefarim HaHiṣonim: Ben Sira*. Tel Aviv: Yavneh, 1963.

Harviainen, T. "A Syriac Incantation Bowl in the Finnish National Museum, Helsinki." *Studia Orientalia* 51 (1981): 4–5.

Hatch, E., and H. Redpath. *A Concordance to the Septuagint*. Vol 2. Oxford: Clarendon, 1897.

Hauptman, J. *Development of the Talmudic Sugya: Relationship between Tannaitic and Amoraic Sources*. Lanham: University Press of America, 1987.

Haussig, H., ed. *Wörterbuch der Mythologie*. Vol. 1. Stuttgart, 1965.

Heide, M. "Die theophoren Personennamen der Kuntillet 'Ağrūd Inschriften." *WO* 32 (2002): 114–117.

Heidel, A. "The Meaning of Mummu in Akkadian Literature." *JNES* 7 (1948): 88–105.

Heiler, F. *Prayer: A Study in the History and Psychology of Religion*. New York, 1932.

Heinisch, P. *Das Buch Genesis*. Bonn, 1930.

Held, M. "The Action-Result (Factitive-Passive) Sequence of Identical Verbs in Biblical Hebrew and Ugaritic." *JBL* 84 (1965): 276n19, 282.

Held, M. "Additional Pairs of Words in Synonymous Parallelism in Biblical Hebrew and in Ugaritic." *Leš.* 18 (1953): 146.

Held, M. "A Faithful Lover in an Old Babylonian Dialogue." *JCS* 15 (1961): 17.

Held, M. "H. L. Ginsberg: An Appreciation." *Conservative Judaism* 30 (1976): 3–9.

Held, M. "Marginal Notes to the Biblical Lexicon." In *Biblical and Related Studies Presented to Samuel Iwry*, edited by A. Kort and S. Morschauser, 133–154. Winona Lake, IN: Eisenbrauns, 1986.

Held, M. "*mḫṣ/mḫš* in Ugaritic and other Semitic Languages (A Study in Comparative Lexicography)." *JAOS* 79 (1959): 169–176.

Held, M. "Philological Notes on the Mari Covenant Rituals." *BASOR* 200 (1970): 32–40.

Held, M. "Rhetorical Questions in Ugaritic and Biblical Hebrew." *ErIsr* 9 (1969): 79.

Held, M. "The Root ZBL/SBL in Akkadian, Ugaritic and Biblical Hebrew." *JAOS* 88 (1968): 90–96.

Held, M. "Studies in Biblical Homonyms in the Light of Akkadian." *JANES* 3 (1970–1971): 46–55.

Held, M. "Studies in Biblical Lexicography in the Light of Akkadian" [in Hebrew]. *ErIsr* 16 (1982): 76–85.

Held, M. "Studies in Comparative Semitic Lexicography." *AS* 16 (1965): 397–398, 402–405.

Held, M. "On Terms for Deportation in the Old Babylonian Royal Inscriptions with Special Reference to Yahdunlim." *JANES* 11 (1979): 55.

Held, M. "Two Philological Notes on Enūma Eliš." *AOAT* 25 (1976): 232–233.

Hendel, R. "Aniconism and Anthropomorphism in Ancient Israel." In *The Image and the Book: Iconic Cults, Aniconism and the Rise of Book Religion in Israel and the Ancient Near East* by K. van der Toorn, 205–208. Leuven: Peeters, 1998.

Henderson, I. "Didache and Orality in Synoptic Comparison." *JBL* 111 (1992): 283–306.

Hermann, S. "Bemerkungen zur Inschrift des Königs Kilamuwa von Senğirli." *OLZ* 48 (1953): 295–297.

Hertzberg, A. "The American Jew and his Religion." In *Understanding American Judaism*, edited by J. Neusner, 1:5–24. New York: Ktav, 1975.

Hertzberg, A. *The Jews in America.* New York: Simon and Schuster, 1988.

Hertzberg, H. W. *Die Bücher Josua, Richter, Ruth.* Gottingen: Vandenhoeck & Ruprecht, 1959.

Hillers, D. "Palmyrene Aramaic Inscriptions and the Old Testament, especially Amos 2:8." *ZAH* 11 (1998): 32–49.

Hirsch, H. "Die Inschriften der Könige von Agade." *AfO* 20 (1963): 1–82.

Hirshler, M., ed. *Babylonian Talmud with Variant Readings: Tractate Nedarim 2.* Jerusalem: Inst. for the Complete Israeli Talmud, 1991.

Hirshman, Marc. *A Rivalry of Genius: Jewish and Christian Biblical Interpretation in Late Antiquity.* Translated by B. Stein. Albany: State University of New York Press, 1996.

Hoenig, S. "Notes on the New Translation of the Torah—A Preliminary Inquiry." *Tradition* 5/2 (Spring 1963): 200.

Hoffman, Y. *The Doctrine of the Exodus in the Bible.* Tel Aviv: Tel Aviv University, 1983.

Hoffman, Y. "A North Israelite Typological Myth and a Judaean Historical Tradition: The Exodus in Hosea and Amos." *VT* 39 (1989): 169–182.

Hoffmann, D. *Mischnajot Teil.* Vol. 6. *Ordnung Toharot.* Basel: Goldschmidt, 1968.

Hoffmann, D. *Sefer Vayyikra.* Jerusalem: Mossad Harav Kook, 1953.

Hoftijzer, J. *Die Verheissungen an die drei Erzväter.* Leiden, 1956.

Hoglund, Kenneth, G. *Achaemenid Imperial Administration in Syria-Palestine and the Missions of Ezra and Nehemiah.* Atlanta: Scholars, 1992.

Holladay, William. *Jeremiah 2* Hermeneia. Minneapolis: Fortress, 1989.

Holma, H. *Die Namen der Körperteile im Assyrisch-Babylonischen: Eine lexikalisch-etymologische Studie.* Leipzig: Pries, 1911.

Horovitz, H. S., and I. A. Rabin, eds. *Mekilta D'Rabbi Ismael.* Jerusalem: Bamberger and Wahrman, 1960.

Horovitz, H. S., and I. A. Rabin, eds. *Mekilta D'Rabbi Ismael.* Jerusalem: Bamberger and Wahrman, 1970.

Hruška, B. "Das spätbabylonische Lehrgedicht Inannas Erhöhung." *Archiv Orientalní* 37 (1969): 484:46.

Huffmon, H. "Amorites." *IDBSup*, (1976): 20–21.

Hull, Robert F., Jr. Review of *The Struggle for Scripture and Covenant: The Purpose of the Epistle of Barnabas and Jewish-Christian Competition in the Second Century* by Reidar Hvalvik. *JECS* 6 (1998): 325–327.

Humbert, P. "Étendre le main." *VT* 12 (1962): 383–395.

Hunger, H. *Babylonische und assyrische Kolophone*. Neukirchen: Neukirchener, 1968.

Hurowitz, V. A. "An Old Babylonian Bawdy Ballad." In *Solving Riddles and Untying Knots: Biblical, Epigraphic, and Semitic Studies in Honor of Jonas C. Greenfield*, edited by Ziony Zevit, S. Gitin, and M. Sokoloff, 553. Winona Lake, IN: Eisenbrauns, 1995.

Hurvitz, A. "On the Borderline between Biblical Criticism and Hebrew Linguistics: The Emergence of the Term *sefer moshe*" [in Hebrew]. In *Tehillah le-Moshe: Biblical and Judaic Studies in Honor of Moshe Greenberg*, edited by Mordecai Cogan, Barry L. Eichler, and Jeffrey H. Tigay, 42. Winona Lake, IN: Eisenbrauns, 1997.

Hurvitz, A. "The Chronological Significance of Aramaisms in Biblical Hebrew." *IEJ* 19 (1968): 234–240.

Hurvitz, A. "Dating the Priestly Source in Light of the Historical Study of Biblical Hebrew a Century after Wellhausen." *ZAW 100* Supplement 88–100 (1988): 481–511.

Hurvitz, A. "The Language of the Priestly Source and Its Historical Setting: The Case for an Early Date." In *Proceedings of the Eighth World Congress of Jewish Studies*, 83–94. Jerusalem: Magnes, 1983.

Hurvitz, A. *A Linguistic Study of the Relationship between the Priestly Source and the Book of Ezekiel.* Paris: Gabalda, 1982.

Hvalvik, Reidar. *The Struggle for Scripture and Covenant: The Purpose of the Epistle of Barnabas and Jewish-Christian Competition in the Second Century*. Tübingen: Mohr Siebeck, 1996.

Hyman, A. *Sefer Toldot Tannaim wa-Amoraim*. Reprint, Jerusalem: Kiryah Ne'emanah, 1964.

Hyman (Heiman), D., D. Lerrer, and I. Shiloni. *Yalqut Shim'ony 'al Hattora.* Jerusalem: 1973.

Idel, Moshe. "Midrashic versus Other Forms of Jewish Hermeneutics: Some Comparative Reflections." In *The Midrashic Imagination: Jewish Exegesis, Thought, and History*, edited by Michael Fishbane, 49. Albany: State University of New York Press, 1993.

Isbell, C. *Corpus of the Aramaic Incantation Bowls*. Missoula: Scholars, 1975.

Jacob, W. "The Influence of the Pittsburgh Platform on Reform Halakhah and Biblical Study." In *The Pittsburgh Platform in Retrospect*, edited by W. Jacob, 28. Pittsburgh: Rodef Shalom, 1985.

Jacobsen, T. "The Inscription of Takil-ili-su of Malgium." *AfO* 12, (1937–1939): 364.

Jacobsen, T. "Sumerian Mythology: A Review Article." *JNES* 5 (1946): 132.

Jacobson, Howard. *A Commentary on Pesudeo-Philo's Liber Antiquitatum Biblicarum.* 2 vols. Leiden: Brill, 1996.

Jastrow, Morris. "Constructive Elements in the Critical Study of the Old Testament." *JBL* 36 (1917): 4.

Jastrow, Morris. *A Gentle Cynic, being a translation of the Book of Koheleth, commonly known as Ecclesiastes, stripped of later additions, also its origin, growth and interpretation.* Philadelphia: Lippincott, 1919.

Jeffery, A. "The Department of Semitic Languages." In *A History of the Faculty of Philosophy Columbia University*, edited by J. Barzun. New York: Columbia University, 1957.

Jeppesen, Knud. "Is Deuteronomy Hostile Toward Prophets?" *SJT* 8 (1994): 252–256.

Jepsen, A. "Berith-Ein Beitrag zur Theologie der Exilszeit." In *Verbannung und Heimkehr: Beiträge zur Geschichte und Theologie Israels im 6. und 5. Jahrhundert v. Chr. Wilhelm Rudolph zum 70. Geburtstage*, edited by A. Kuschke, 161–169. Tübingen, 1961.

Kabakoff, J. "New Light on Arnold Bogomil Ehrlich." *American Jewish Archives* 36, no. 2 (November 1984): 202–224.

Kaddari, M., and S. Sharvit, eds. *Studies in the Hebrew Language and the Talmudic Literature Dedicated to the Memory of Dr. Menahem Moreshet.* Ramat Gan: Bar-Ilan University, 1989.

Kafah [Kafih], Y., ed. *Tĕhillîm 'im Targûm u- Fērûš ha-Gā'ôn Rabbēnû Sa'adyāh ben Yôsēf Fayyumî.* Jerusalem: American Academy for Jewish Research, 1965.

Kahana, A. *The Bible with Critical Commentary* [in Hebrew]. Zhitomer, 1904.

Kalmin, R. "Friends and Colleagues or Barely Acquainted? Relations between Fourth-Generation Masters in the Babylonian Talmud." *HUCA* 61 (1990): 134–135.

Kalmin, R. *The Redaction of the Babylonian Talmud: Amoraic or Saboraic?* Cincinnati: Hebrew Union College Press, 1989.

Kamesar, J. Adam. *Jerome, Greek Scholarship, and the Hebrew Bible: A Study of the Quaestiones Hebraicae in Genesim.* Oxford: Clarendon, 1993.

Kamin, S. *Jews and Christians Interpret the Bible.* Jerusalem: Magnes, 1991.

Kanga, M. *Čitak Handarz ī Pōryōtkešān.* Bombay: Kanga, 1960.

Kaplan, Mordecai. *Judaism as a Civilization.* New York: Macmillan, 1934.

Kara, Joseph. *Mikra'ot Gedolot Haketer.* Vol. 6, *Sefer Yehezkel*, edited by Menahem Cohen, 145. Ramat Gan: Bar-Ilan University Press, 2000.

Karp, A. "A Century of Conservative Judaism in the United States." *American Jewish Yearbook* 86 (1986): 3–61.

Karp, A. "The Conservative Rabbi—'Dissatisfied But Not Unhappy.'" *American Jewish Archives* 35 (1983): 199–200.

Karp, A. *Haven and Home: A History of the Jews in America.* New York: Schocken, 1985.

Karp, A. "Solomon Schechter Comes to America." *American Jewish Historical Quarterly* 53 (1963): 44–62.

Kasovsky, H. J. *Ozar Leshon Targum Onkelos Concordance.* Rev. ed. 2 vols. Jerusalem: Magnes, 1986.

Katsh, A., and L. Nemoy. *Essays on the Occasion of the Seventieth Anniversary of the Dropsie University (1909–1979)*. Philadelphia: Dropsie University, 1979, ix–xi.

Katz, J. *Out of the Ghetto*. New York: Schocken, 1978.

Katzenellenbogen, M., ed. *Torat Hayyim: Hammishah Humshe Torah*. Vol. 2. Jerusalem: Mossad Harav Kook, 1986.

Katzenstein, H. J. "The Royal Steward (Asher 'al ha-Bayith)." *IEJ* 10 (1960): 150.

Kaufman, S. *The Akkadian Influences on Aramaic*. Chicago: University of Chicago Press, 1974.

Kaufman, S. *The Akkadian Loanwords in Aramaic*. Chicago: University of Chicago, 1974.

Kaufman, S. "An Emphatic Plea for Please." *MAARAV* 7 (1991): 195–198.

Kaufman, S. "The Pitfalls of Typology." *HUCA* 57 (1986): 8.

Kaufman, S. "Reflections on the Assyrian–Aramaic Bilingual from Tell Fakhariyeh." *Maarav* 3 (1982): 165.

Kaufman, S. Review: *A Scholar's Dictionary of Jewish Palestinian Aramaic* by Michael Sokoloff. *JAOS* 114 (1994): 239–248.

Kaufmann, Y. *History of Israelite Religion*. 2nd ed. [in Hebrew]. Jerusalem: Bialik, 1967.

Kaufmann, Y. *The Religion of Israel*. Translated by Moshe Greenberg. Chicago: University of Chicago Press, 1960.

Kaufmann, Y. *Sepher Shofetim*. Jerusalem: Qiryat Sepher, 1962.

Kaufmann, Y. *Sepher Yehoshua*. Jerusalem: Kiryat Sepher, 1970.

Kaufmann, Y. *Toledot ha-Emunah ha-Yisre'elit*. Tel Aviv: Dvir, 1938–1956.

Kedar, Benjamin. "The Latin Translation." In *Mikra: Text, Translation, Reading and Interpretation of the Hebrew Bible in Ancient Judaism and Early Christianity*, edited by M. Mulder and H. Sysling, 313–335. Philadelphia: Fortress, 1998.

Keller, S. "Letters to the Dead." In *By Study and also by Faith: Essays in Honor of Hugh Nibley*, edited by J. Lundquist, 119–120. Provo, UT: Deseret, 1990.

Kilmer, A. D. "Symbolic Gestures in Akkadian Contracts from Alalakh and Ugarit." *JAOS* 94 (1974): 177–183.

King, L. W. *Babylonian Magic and Sorcery*. London: Luzac, 1896; Hildesheim and New York: Georg Olms, 1975.

Kisch, Guido. *Pseudo-Philo's Liber Antiquitatum Biblicarum*. Notre Dame, IN: University of Notre Dame Press, 1949.

Kitchen, K. *Ancient Orient and Old Testament*. Chicago: InterVarsity, 1966.

Kitchen, K. *The Bible in Its World: The Bible and Archaeology Today*. Downer's Grove, IL: InterVarsity, 1978.

Kitchen, K. "The Patriarchal Age: Myth or History." *BAR* 21/2 (1995): 94–95.

Kitchen, K. *Pharaoh Triumphant: The Life and Times of Ramesses II King of Egypt*. Warminster, UK: Aris and Phillips, 1982.

Kitchen, K. "The Term Nšq in Genesis 41:40." *ET* 69 (1957): 30.

Klein, M. *Genizah Manuscripts of Palestinian Targum to the Pentateuch.* Vol. 1. Cincinnati: Hebrew Union College, 1986.

Klein, M. "Targumic Toseftot from the Cairo Geniza." In *Salvación en la Palabra: Targum, Derash, Berith: En Memoria del Professor Alejandro Diez Macho*, edited by D. Muñoz León, 409–418. Madrid: Inst. Francisco Suarez, 1985.

Knobloch, F. "Linen and the Linguistic Dating of P." In *Mishneh Todah. Studies in Deuteronomy and Its Cultural Environment in Honor of Jeffrey H. Tigay*, edited by Nili Fox, David A. Glatt-Gilad, and Michael J. Williams, 459–474. Winona Lake, IN: Eisenbrauns, 2009.

Knohl, I. *The Sanctuary of Silence: The Priestly Torah of the Holiness School.* Minneapolis: Fortress, 1995.

Knohl, I. "Two Aspects of the Tent of Meeting." In *Tehillah le-Moshe: Biblical and Judaic Studies in Honor of Moshe Greenberg*, edited by M. Cogan, B. Eichler, and J. Tigay, 73–79. Winona Lake, IN: Eisenbrauns, 1997.

Koch, H. "Götter und ihre Verehrung im achämenidischen Persien." *ZA* 77 (1987): 239–278.

Koehler, L. "Problems in the Study of the Language of the Old Testament." *JSS* 1 (1956): 4.

Kogut, S. "On the Meaning and Syntax of *hinneh* in Biblical Hebrew." In *Studies in Bible*, ScrHier 31, edited by S. Japhet, 133–154. Jerusalem: Magnes, 1986.

Kohut, A., ed. *Aruch Completum.* Vol. 5. Reprint, New York: Shiloh, 1955.

König, E. "Die sprachliche Gestalt des Pentateuch in ihrer Beziehung zur Ägyptischen Sprache." *JBL* 48 (1929): 342.

Kosovsky, M. *Concordance to the Talmud Yerushalmi* (Palestinian Talmud). Vol 3. Jerusalem: Israel Academy of Science and Humanities and Jewish Theological Seminary, 1985.

Kotwal, F., and J. Boyd. *A Guide to the Zoroastrian Religion: A Nineteenth Century Catechism with Modern Commentary.* Chico, CA: Scholars, 1982.

Kraemer, D. "Scripture Commentary in the Babylonian Talmud: Primary or Secondary Phenomenon?" *AJS Review* 14 (1989): 3.

Kramer, S. N. "The 'Babel of Tongues': A Sumerian Version." *JAOS* 88 (1968): 109.

Krapf, T. *Die Priesterschaft und die vorexilische Zeit: Yehezkel Kaufmanns vernachlässigte Beitrag zur Geschichte der biblischen Religion.* Göttingen: Vandenhoeck & Ruprecht, 1992.

Krapf, T. *Yehezkel Kaufmann: Ein Lebens-und Erkenntnisweg zur Theologie der hebräischen Bibel.* Berlin: Institut für Kirche und Judentum, 1990.

Kraus, F. *Königliche Verfügungen in altbabylonischer Zeit.* Leiden, 1984.

Krebernik, M. "Zu Syllabar und Orthographie der lexikalischen Texte aus Ebla." *ZA* 73 (1983): 14.

Kselman, J. Review of *The Aramaic Proverbs of Ahiqar* by J. Lindenberger. *JBL* 105 (1986): 114–115.

Kuhrt, A. *The Ancient Near East c. 3000–330 BC.* Vol. 1. London: Routledge, 1995.

Kunstmann, W. G. *Die babylonische Gebetsbeschwörungen*. Leipzig, 1932.

Kunze, J. C. *A New Method of Calculating All the Lunar and Solar Eclipses and New and Full Moons from the Creation of the World: Grounded upon the Scripture Chronology.* New York, 1806 (available as Microform MP 5 n. 10865 at the Bobst Library of New York University).

Kutsch, E. "'Ich will euer Gott sein.'" In *Proceedings of the Sixth World Congress of Jewish Studies*, edited by A. Shinan, 245–254. Jerusalem, 1977.

Kutsch, E. *Verheissung und Gesetz*. Berlin-New York, 1973.

Kutscher, E. "Mittelhebräisch und Jüdisch-Aramäisch im Neuen Köhler-Baumgartner." VTSup16 (1967): 172.

Kutscher, E. *Studies in Galilean Aramaic.* Ramat Gan: Bar-Ilan University Press, 1976.

Kutscher, E. *Words and Their History*. Jerusalem: Kiryat Sefer, 1961.

Kutscher, E, ed. *Archive of the New Dictionary of Rabbinical Literature.* Vol 1. Ramat Gan: Bar-Ilan University, 1972.

Kutscher, E. Y. *Hebrew and Aramaic Studies*. Jerusalem, 1977.

Labat, R. *Manuel d'épigraphie akkadiene*. Paris, 1976.

Lacocque, A. "The Liturgical Prayer in Daniel 9." *HUCA* 47 (1976): 119–142.

Laessøe, J. Review of *Die akkadische Gebetsserie "Handerhebung"* by E. Ebeling. *BiOr.* 18 (1961): 71.

Lambert, W. G. "Destiny and Divine Intervention in Babylon and Israel." *Oudtestamentische Studien* 17 (1972): 65–72.

Lambert, W. G. "Dingir.šà.dib.ba. Incantations." *JNES* 33 (1974): 267–322.

Lambert, W. G. "The Gula Hymn of Bullutsa-rabi." *Or* 36 (1967): 108.

Lambert, W. G. "Literary Style in First Millennium Mesopotamia." *JAOS* 88 (1968): 123–132.

Lambert, W. G. "Three Literary Prayers of the Babylonians." *AfO* 19 (1960): 51:75–76.

Lambert W. G., and R. Millard. *Atrahasis: The Babylonian Story of the Flood.* Winona Lake, IN: Eisenbrauns, 1999.

Landsberger, B. "Akkadisch-Hebräisches Wortgleichungen." VTSup16 (1967): 176–204.

Landsberger, B. "Assyrische Königsliste und 'dunkles Zeitalter.'" *JCS* 8 (1954): 10.

Landsberger, B. "The Date Palm and Its By-Products According to the Cuneiform Sources." *AfO* Beiheft 17 (1967): 25, n.7.

Landsberger, B. "Das 'gute Wort.'" *MAOG* 4 (1929): 294–315.

Landsberger, B. "Jahreszeiten im Sumerisch-Akkadischen." *JNES* 8 (1949): 285n120.

Landsberger, B. "Jungfräulichkeit: Ein Beitrag zum Thema 'Beilage und Eheschliessung.'" In *Symbolae Iuridicaie et Historicae Martino David Dedicatae.* Vol. 2, *Iura Orientis Antiqui*, edited by J. A. Ankum, R. Feenstra, and W. F. Leemans, 41–105. Leiden: Brill, 1968.

Landsberger, B. "Die Liste der Menschenklassen im babylonischen Kanon." *ZA* 41 (1933): 297.

Landsberger, B. Note to "*Zu meiner Übersetzung des Gilgameš-Epos*" by A. Schott. *ZA* 42 (1934): 129n1.

Landsberger, B. "Zu neuveröffentlichten Geschichtsquellen der Zeit von Asarhaddon bis Nabonid." *ZA* 37 (1927): 86.

Landsberger, B. *Sam'al I*. Ankara, 1948.

Landsberger, B. Review of *Sumerisch-akkadische Parallelen zum Aufbau alttestamentliche Psalmen* by F. Stummer. *OLZ* (1925): 480.

Landsberger, B. "Tin and Lead: The Adventures of Two Vocables." *JNES* 24 (1965): 295–296.

Langdon, S. "Gesture in Sumerian and Babylonian Prayer: A Study in Babylonian and Assyrian Archaeology." *JRAS* (1919): 531–558.

Leeser, I. *The Law of God, Edited, with Former Translations Diligently Compared and Revised.* Philadelphia: C. Sherman, 1844–1845.

Leeser, I. *The Twenty-Four Books of the Holy Scriptures: Carefully Translated According to the Massoretic Text, on the Basis of the English Version, after the Best Jewish Authorities; and Supplied with Short Explanatory Notes*. Philadelphia, 1853–1854.

Leiman, Shneur Zalman. *The Canonization of the Hebrew Scriptures*. Hamden, CT: Archon, 1976.

Lemaire, A. "Les inscriptions de Deir 'Allā et la littérature araméenne antique." *CRAIBL* (1985): 270–285.

Lemaire, A., and J.-M. Durand. *Les Inscriptions araméennes de Sfiré et L'Assyrie de Shamshi-ilu*. Paris, 1984.

Levenson, Jon D. "The Hebrew Bible, the Old Testament and Historical Criticism." In *The Future of Biblical Studies*, edited by R. Friedman and G. Williamson, 18–59. Atlanta, 1987.

Levenson, Jon D. Review of *The Original Torah* by S. D. Sperling. *Review of Biblical Literature* (2000): http://www.bookreviews.org.

Levenson, Jon D. "Why Jews are Not Interested in Biblical Theology." In *Judaic Perspectives on Ancient Israel*, edited by Jacob Neusner, Baruch A. Levine, and Ernest S. Frerichs, 281–307. Philadelphia: Fortress, 1987.

Levine, B. A. "Assyriology and Hebrew Philology: A Methodological Re-Examination." In *Mesopotamien und seine Nachbarn*, edited by H. Nissen and J. Renger, 521–530. Berlin, 1987.

Levine, B. A. "A Decade of Jewish Bible Scholarship in North America." *Jewish Book Annual* 39 (1981–1982): 9–29.

Levine, B. A. "The Epilogue to the Holiness Code: A Priestly Statement on the Destiny of Israel." In *Judaic Perspectives on Ancient Israel*, edited by J. Neusner, B. Levine, and E. Frerichs, 22. Philadelphia, 1987.

Levine, B. A. Review of *The Israelian Heritage of Judaism* by H. L. Ginsberg. *AJS Review* 12 (1987): 143–157.

Levine, B. A. *The JPS Torah Commentary: Leviticus*. Philadelphia: Jewish Publication Society, 1989.

Levine, B. A. "Late Language in the Priestly Source: Some Literary and Historical Observations." In *Proceedings of the Eighth World Congress of Jewish Studies*, 69–82. Jerusalem: Magnes, 1983.

Levine, B. A. *Numbers 1–20* (AB 4). New York: Doubleday, 1993.

Levine, B. A. *In the Presence of the Lord*. Leiden: Brill, 1974.

Levine, B. A. "Research in the Priestly Source: The Linguistic Factor" [in Hebrew]. *ErIsr* 16 (Orlinsky vol., 1982): 124–131.

Levine, B. A. "On the Semantics of Land Tenure in Biblical Literature: The Term *'aḥuzzāh*." In *The Tablet and the Scroll: Near Eastern Studies in Honor of William W. Hallo*, edited by M. Cohen, Daniel C. Snell, and David B. Weisberg, 134–139. Bethesda, MD.: CDL, 1993.

Levine, B. A., and J.-M. Tarragon. "Dead Kings and Rephaim: The Patrons of the Ugaritic Dynasty." *JAOS* 104 (1984): 650–659.

Levy, J. *Chaldäisches Wörterbuch über die Targumin*. Leipzig, 1881.

Levy, J. *Wörterbuch über die Talmudim und Midraschim*. Vol. 3, 2nd ed. Berlin: Benjamin Harz, 1924.

Lewis, B., and D. Goldenberg. "Annenberg Research Institute for Judaic and Near Eastern Studies Statement of Purpose." *Jewish Quarterly Review* 72 (1986): 1–4.

Lewis, T. *Cults of the Dead in Ancient Israel and Ugarit*. Atlanta: Scholars, 1989.

Licht, J. *A Commentary on the Book of Numbers* xi–xxi [in Hebrew]. 3 vols. Jerusalem: Magnes, 1991.

Lichtenstein, M. "Theodor H. Gaster: An Appreciation." *JANES* 5 (1973): 9.

Lichtheim, M. *Ancient Egyptian Literature. A Book of Readings III. The Late Period*. Berkeley: University of California, 1980.

Lidzbarski, M. *Ephemeris für semitische Epigraphik*. Vol. 3. Giessen, 1909–1915.

Lieberman, Saul. *Hellenism in Jewish Palestine*. New York: Jewish Theological Seminary of America, 1950.

Lieberman, Saul. "Ḥeshbon Otiyot." In *Hebrew Language Studies Presented to Professor Zeev Ben-Hayyim*, edited by M. Bar-Asher, A. Dotan, G. B. Sarfatti, and D. Tene, 332. Jerusalem: Magnes, 1983. Reprinted in D. Rosenthal, ed., *S. Lieberman Studies in Palestinian Talmudic Literature* [in Hebrew], 525.

Lieberman, Saul. "The Martyrs of Caesarea." *Annuaire de l'Institut de Philologie et d'Histoire Orientales et Slaves* 7 (1939–1944): 395–446.

Lieberman, Saul. *Tosefta*, 1. New York: Jewish Theological Seminary, 1955.

Lieberman, Saul. *Tosefta Ki-fshutah: A Comprehensive Commentary on the Tosefta*. Part 3, *Order Mo'ed*. New York, 1962.

Lieberman, Saul. *Tosefta Ki-fshutah: A Comprehensive Commentary on the Tosefta.* Part 4, *Order Mo'ed.* New York: Jewish Theological Seminary of America, 1962.

Lieberman, Saul. *Tosefta-Kifshuṭah: A Comprehensive Commentary on the Tosefta.* Part 5, *Order Mo'ed.* New York: Jewish Theological Seminary, 1962.

Lieberman, Saul. *The Tosefta Order of Mo'ed.* New York: Jewish Theological Seminary, 1962.

Lieberman, Saul. *Tosefta Ki-fshuṭah Order Zeraim.* Pt. 1. New York: Jewish Theological Seminary of America, 1955.

Lieberman, Saul. *Tosefta Ki-fshuṭah Order Zeraim.* Pt. 2. New York, 1955.

Lieberman, Stephen. "A Mesopotamian Background for the So-Called Aggadic 'Measures' of Biblical Hermeneutics?" *HUCA* 58 (1987): 157–225.

Lieberman, Stephen. "Moshe Held (1924–1984)." *JQR* 76 (1985): 1–3.

Lindenberger, J. *The Aramaic Proverbs of Ahiqar.* Baltimore, 1983.

Lipiński, E. "North Semitic Texts from the First Millennium B.C." In *Near Eastern Religious Texts Relating to the Old Testament,* edited by W. Beyerlin, 249–250. Philadelphia: Westminster, 1978.

Liss, A., ed. *The Babylonian Talmud with Variant Readings Tractate Yebamoth.* Vol. 2. Jerusalem: Institute for the Complete Israeli Talmud, 1986.

Liss, A., ed. *The Babylonian Talmud with Variant Readings Tractate Yebamoth.* Vol. 3. Jerusalem: Institute for the Complete Israeli Talmud, 1989.

Livius, Titus (Livy). *Ab Urbe Condita,* 1.13.4. Translated by B. O. Foster. Loeb Classical Library. Cambridge, MA: Harvard University Press, 1919.

Loewenstamm, S. *Comparative Studies in Biblical and Ancient Oriental Literatures.* Kevelaer and Neukirchen-Vluyn: Butzon & Bercker and Neukirchener, 1980.

Loewenstamm, S. "On the Predicative Use of the Suffix Joined to a Subject-Noun in Hebrew and Ugaritic." In *Comparative Studies in Biblical and Ancient Oriental Literatures,* 455–458. Kevelaer: Butzon & Bercker, 1980.

Long, B. *Planting and Reaping Albright: Politics, Ideology and Interpreting the Bible.* University Park, PA: Pennsylvania State University, 1997.

Loretz, O. "Miscellanea Biblica ḪBR in JB 16:4." *CBQ* 23 (1961): 293–294.

Luke, J. "'Your Father was an Amorite' (Ezek 16:3, 45): An Essay on the Amorite Problem in OT Traditions." In *The Quest for the Kingdom of God: Studies in Honor of George E. Mendenhall,* edited by H. Huffmon and Alberto Green, 221–237. Winona Lake, IN: Eisenbrauns, 1983.

Lund, J. "The First Person Singular Past Tense of the Verb 'hwh' in Jewish Palestinian Aramaic." *MAARAV* 4 (1987): 191–199.

Luzzatto, S. D. *Commentary on the Five Books of Moses* [in Hebrew]. Edited by P. Schlesinger. Jerusalem: Dvir, 1965.

Machinist, P. "Assyria and Its Image in the First Isaiah." *JAOS* 103 (1983): 720–721.

Machinist, P. "The Question of Distinctiveness in Ancient Israel." *Scripta Hierosolymitana* 33 (1991): 196–212.

Machinist, P. "William Foxwell Albright: The Man and His Work." In *The Study of the Ancient Near East in the Twenty-First Century. The William Foxwell Albright Centennial Conference*, edited by J. Cooper and G. M. Schwartz, 385–403. Winona Lake, IN: Eisenbrauns, 1996.

Malamat, A. "Mari and the Bible: Patterns of Tribal Organization and Institutions." *JAOS* 82 (1962): 145.

Malamat, A. "The Prophetic Experience in Mari and the Bible: A Re-examination." *Shnaton* 7–8 (1983–1984): 173–174.

Mandelkern, S. *Hekal Haqqodesh*. Leipzig 1896.

Mankowski, P. *Akkadian Loanwords in Biblical Hebrew*. HSS 47. Winona Lake, IN: Eisenbrauns, 2000.

Marcus, D. *From Balaam to Jonah: Anti-Prophetic Satire in the Hebrew Bible*. Atlanta: Scholars Press, 1995.

Marcus, D. "Is the Book of Nehemiah a Translation from Aramaic?" In *Boundaries of the Ancient Near Eastern World: A Tribute to Cyrus H. Gordon*, edited by Meir Lubetski, Claire Gottlieb, and Sharon Keller, 273. JSOTSup. Sheffield: Sheffield Academic, 1998.

Marcus, D. Review of *Harper's Bible Dictionary*, edited by Charlton Lews and Charles Short. *JAOS* 110 (1990): 587.

Marcus, D. "Ridiculing the Ephraimites: The Shibboleth Incident (Judg 12:6)." *MAARAV* 8 (1992): 95–105.

Marcus, D. "The Term 'Chin' in the Semitic Languages." *BASOR* 226 (1977): 57.

Marcus, D. "The Verb 'to live' in Ugaritic." *JSS* 17 (1972): 79.

Margaliot, E. "Hebrew and Aramaic in the Talmud and Midrash" [in Hebrew]. *Leshonenu* 27 (1963–1964): 20–33.

Margalit, O. "Four Verses in Proverbs." *Beth Mikrâ* 21 (1976): 6–7.

Margolis, M. "Commentarius Isaacidis Quatenus ad Textum Talmudis Investigandum Adhiberi Possit, Tractatu 'Erubhin Ostenditur." PhD diss., Columbia University, 1891.

Margolis, M., and A. Marx. *A History of the Jewish People*. Philadelphia: Jewish Publication Society, 1927.

Margulies, B. "A New Ugaritic Farce (RS 24.258)." *UF* 2 (1970): 135.

Mayer, W. *Untersuchungen zur Formensprache der babylonischen*. Rome, 1976.

Mays, J. L. *Amos, A Commentary*. Philadelphia: Westminster, 1969.

Mays, J. L. Review of *God and His People* by Ernest Nicholson. *JBL* 107 (1988): 119–120.

Mazar, Benjamin. *Biblical Israel: State and People*. Edited by S. Ahituv. Jerusalem: Magnes, 1982.

McCarthy, D. "Compact and Kingship: Stimuli for Hebrew Covenant Thinking." In *Studies in the Period of David and Solomon and Other Essays*, edited by T. Ishida, 87. Winona Lake, IN: Eisenbrauns, 1982.

McCarthy, D. "Covenant and Law in Chronicles-Nehemiah." *CBQ* 44 (1982): 25–44.

McCarthy, D. "Covenant Relationships." In *Institution and Narrative: Collected Essays*. Rome, 1985.

McCarthy, D. *Treaty and Covenant*. Rome: Biblical Institute, 1978.

McCaughey, R. *Stand, Columbia: A History of Columbia University in the City of New York*. New York: Columbia University, 2003.

McKane, W. *A Critical and Exegetical Commentary on Jeremiah* (ICC). 2 vols. Edinburgh: T&T Clark, 1986, 1:588–593.

Meier, G. *Die assyrische Beschwörungssamlung Maqlû*. Berlin, 1937 (self published).

Meissner, B. *Babylonien und Assyrien II*. Heidelberg, 1925.

Meissner, B. "Die Keilschrifttexte auf den steinernen Orthostaten und Statuen aus dem Tell Halâf." In *Festschrift Max Freiherrn von Oppenheim zum 70. Geburtstag* (= *AfO Beiband* 1), 71–81. Berlin, 1933.

Melamed, E. Z. *Dictionnaire Aramaéen-Hébreu*. Jerusalem: Feldheim, 1992.

Melamed, E. *Millon Arami-Ivri leTalmud Bavli*. Jerusalem: Feldheim, 1992.

Melamed, E. *Talmud Babli Maseket Baba Qamma*. Jerusalem: Razal, 1952.

Melamed, E, ed. *Talmud Babli Maseket Baba Mezia*. Jerusalem: Razal, 1960.

Mendenhall, G. "Biblical History in Transition." In *The Bible and the Ancient Near East*, edited by G. E. Wright, 40. Garden City, NY: Doubleday, 1965.

Mendenhall, G. "'Change and Decay in All Around I See': Conquest, Covenant and *The Tenth Generation*." *BA* 39 (1976): 156.

Mendenhall, G. *The Tenth Generation*. Baltimore: Johns Hopkins, 1973.

Mettinger, T. "Israelite Aniconism: Development and Origins." In *The Image and the Book: Iconic Cults, Aniconism and the Rise of Book Religion in Israel and the Ancient Near East* by K. van der Toorn, 173–204. Leuven: Peeters, 1998.

Mettinger, T. *No Graven Images?* Stockholm: Almqvist & Wiksell, 1995.

Meyer, M. "In the Days of Isaac Mayer Wise." In *Hebrew Union College–Jewish Institute of Religion at One Hundred Years*, edited by S. Karff, 7–47. Cincinnati: Hebrew Union College, 1976.

Meyers, C. *The Tabernacle Menorah*. Missoula, MT: Scholars, 1976.

Meyers, C., and E. Meyers. *Haggai, Zechariah 1–8*. Garden City, NY: Anchor Bible, 1987.

Michalowski, P. "Presence at the Creation." In *Lingering over Words, Studies in Ancient Near Eastern Literature in Honor of William L. Moran*, edited by T. Abusch, J. Huehnergard, and P. Steinkeller, 381–396. Atlanta: Scholars, 1990.

Milgrom, J. *The JPS Torah Commentary: Numbers*. Philadelphia: Jewish Publication Society, 1990.

Milgrom, J. *Leviticus 1–16* (AB 3). New York: Doubleday, 1991.

Milgrom, J. "Priestly ('P') Source." *ABD* 3 (1991): 453–462.

Milgrom, J. "Religious Conversion and the Revolt Model for the Formation of Israel." *JBL* 101 (1982): 169–176.

Millard, A. R. "Methods of Studying the Patriarchal Narratives as Ancient Texts." In *Essays on the Patriarchal Narratives*, edited by A. R. Millard and D. J. Wiseman, 35–51. Winona Lake, IN: Eisenbrauns, 1983.

Miller, Patrick. *The Religion of Ancient Israel*. Louisville: Westminster, 2000.

Miller, Philip. "A Selective Bibliography of the Writings of Harry M. Orlinsky." *ErIsr 16* (1982).

Montgomery, J. *Aramaic Incantation Texts from Nippur*. Philadelphia: University Museum, 1913.

Montgomery, J. *A Critical and Exegetical Commentary on the Book of Daniel* (ICC). Edinburgh: T&T Clark, 1927.

Morag, S. *Babylonian Aramaic: The Yemenite Tradition* [in Hebrew]. Jerusalem: Ben Zvi Institute, 1988.

Morag, S. "The Great Metaphor of Hosea: The Words of Comfort-A Linguistic Examination." *Tarbiz* 68 (1998–1999): 4–11.

Morag, S. "Regarding the Oral Transmission of the Babylonian Talmud." In *Meḥqerei Talmud*. Vol. 2, edited by M. Bar-Asher and D. Rosenthal, 334. Jerusalem: Magnes, 1993.

Morag, S. *Studies on Biblical Hebrew*. Jerusalem: Magnes, 1995.

Moran, W. *The Amarna Letters*. Baltimore: Johns Hopkins, 1992.

Moran, W. "The Ancient Near Eastern Background of the Love of God in Deuteronomy." *CBQ* 25 (1963): 78.

Moran, W. "Atrahasis and the Biblical Story of the Flood." *Biblica* 52 (1971): 51–61.

Moran, W. "The Conclusion of the Decalogue (Ex 20.17, Dt 5.21)." *CBQ* 29 (1967): 543–554.

Moran, W. "New Evidence from Mari on the History of Prophecy." *Biblica* 50 (1969): 47:16–17.

Moran, W. "Some Considerations of Form and Interpretation in Atra-Hasis." In *Language, Literature, and History: Philological and Historical Studies presented to Erica Reiner*, edited by R. Rochberg-Halton, 245–255. New Haven: American Oriental Society, 1987.

Moreshet, M. *A Lexicon of the New Verbs in Tannaitic Hebrew*. Ramat Gan: Bar-Ilan Univeristy Press, 1980.

Morgenstern, J. "Amos Studies (Part Four)." *HUCA* 32 (1961): 295–350.

Mowinckel, S. *Studien zu dem Buche Ezra-Nehemiah*. Vol. 1. Oslo, 1964.

Muffs, Y. "Joy and Love as Metaphors of Willingness and Spontaneity in Cuneiform, Ancient Hebrew, and Related Literatures." In *Christianity, Judaism and other Greco-Roman Cults: Studies for Morton Smith at Sixty*, edited by J. Neusner, 3:1–36. Leiden, 1975.

Muffs, Y. "Love and Joy as Metaphors of Volition in Hebrew and Related Literatures: The Joy of Giving." *JANES* 11 (1979): 91–111.

Muffs, Y. *Studies in the Aramaic Legal Papyri from Elephantine*. Leiden: Brill, 1969.

Müller, H.-P. "Kolloquialsprache und Volksreligion in den Inschriften von Kuntillet 'Ajrud und Khirbet el-Qom." *ZAH* 5 (1992): 15–51.

Müller-Kessler, C. *Grammatik des Christlich-Palästinisch-Aramäischen Teil 1*. Hildesheim: Georg Olms, 1991.

Müller-Kessler, C. *Die Zauberschalentexte in der Hilprecht-Sammlung, Jena, und weitere Nippur-Texte anderer Sammlungen*.Wiesbaden: Harrassowitz, 2005.

Mullo-Weir, C. J. "A Prayer to Ea, Shamash, and Marduk." *JRAS* (1929): 285–286.

Murphy, E. *The Antiquities of Asia: A Translation with Notes of Book II of the LIbrary of History of Diodorus Siculus*. New Brunswick, NJ: Transaction, 1989.

Naveh, J., and S. Shaked. *Amulets and Magic Bowls: Aramaic Incantations of Late Antiquit.* Leiden: Brill; and Jerusalem: Magnes; 1985.

Nebo, Y., ed. *Perushe Rabbi Yoseph Bekhor Shor al Hatorah*. Jerusalem: Mossad Harav Kook, 1994.

Neubauer, A., ed. *The Book of Hebrew Roots by Abu al-Walid Marwan ibn Janah.* Oxford, 1875. Reprint, Amsterdam: Philo, 1968.

Neuman, A. "The Dropsie College for Hebrew and Cognate Learning: Basic Principles and Objectives." In *The Seventy-Fifth Anniversary Volume of the Jewish Quarterly Review*, edited by A. Neuman and S. Zeitlin, 22. Philadelphia: Jewish Quarterly Review, 1967.

Neusner, J. *The Canonical History of Ideas, The Place of the So-called Tannaite Midrashim: Mekhilta Attributed to R. Ishmael, Sifra, Sifré to Numbers and Sifré to Deuteronomy*. Atlanta: Scholars, 1990.

Neusner, J. "The Christian-Jewish Argument in Fourth-Century Iran." *JJS* 22 (1971): 16–18.

Neusner, J. *A History of the Jews of Babylonia.* Vol. 2. Leiden: Brill, 1966.

Neusner, J. *A History of the Jews of Babylonia.* Vol. 3. Leiden: Brill, 1968.

Neusner, J. *A History of the Jews of Babylonia.* Vol. 4. Leiden: Brill, 1969.

Neusner, J. *A History of the Jews of Babylonia.* Vol. 5. Leiden: Brill, 1970.

Neusner, J. *Language as Taxonomy: The Rules for Using Hebrew and Aramaic in the Babylonian Talmud*. Atlanta: Scholars, 1990.

Neusner, J. *The Rabbinic Traditions about the Pharisees before 70*. Pt. 1, *The Masters.* Leiden: E. J. Brill, 1971.

Neusner, J. *Sifre to Deuteronomy an Analytical Translation*. Vol. 2. Atlanta: Scholars, 1987.

Neusner, J. *The Talmud of the Land of Israel.* Vol. 26. Chicago: University of Chicago, 1984.

Neusner, J. *The Talmud of the Land of Israel.* Vol. 31. *Sanhedrin Makkot* Chicago: University of Chicago, 1984.

Neusner, J. *The Talmud of the Land of Israel*. Vol. 33. *Abodah Zarah*. Chicago: University of Chicago, 1982.

Neusner, J. *The Talmud of Babylonia: An American Translation*. Vol. 15b, *Tractate Nedarim Chapters 5–11*. Atlanta: Scholars, 1992.

Neusner, J. *Torah: From Scroll to Symbol in Formative Judaism*. Philadelphia: Fortress, 1985.

Neusner, J, ed. *The Formation of the Babylonian Talmud*. Leiden: Brill, 1970.

Nicholson, E. "Covenant in a Century of Study since Wellhausen." OTS 24 (1986): 54–69.

Nicholson, E. *God and His People: Covenant and Theology in the Old Testament*. Oxford, 1986.

Nielsen, E. *Shechem, A Traditio-Historical Investigation*. Copenhagen: Gad, 1969.

Nielsen, E. "Weil Jahwe unser Gott ein Jahwe ist." In *Beiträge zur Alttestamentlichen Theologie. Festschrift für Walther Zimmerli: Zum 70. Geburtstag*, edited by H. Donner, R. Hanhart, and R. Smend, 291. Göttingen: Vandenhoeck & Ruprecht, 1977.

Nillson, M. *Greek Piety*. New York, 1964.

Nillson, M. *A History of Greek Religion*. New York, 1964.

Noth, M. *Das Buch Josua*. Tübingen: Mohr, 1953.

Noth, M. *Exodus*. Philadelphia, 1962.

Noth, M. *Die israelitischen Personennamen im Rahmen der gemeinsemitischen Namengebung*. Stuttgart, 1928.

Noth, M. *The Laws in the Pentateuch and Other Studies*. Philadelphia, 1967.

Noth, M. *Numbers*. London: SCM, 1968.

Nyberg, S. *A Manual of Pahlavi*. Pt. 2. Wiesbaden: Harrassowitz, 1974.

O'Connor, M. P. "The Rhetoric of the Kilamuwa Inscription." *BASOR* 226 (1977): 15–29.

Oden, R. A., Jr., *Studies in Lucian's De Syria Dea*. Missoula, MT: Scholars, 1977.

Oppenheim, A. L. *Ancient Mesopotamia*. Chicago, 1964.

Oppenheim, A. "Idiomatic Accadian." *JAOS* 61 (1941): 252–256.

Oppenheim, A. *The Interpretation of Dreams in the Anient Near East*. Philadelphia: American Philosophical Society, 1956.

Oppenheim, A. *Letters from Mesopotamia*. Chicago, 1967.

Oppenheim, A. "Sumerian: inim.gar, Akkadian: *egirrû* = Greek: *kledon*." *AfO* 17 (1954–1956): 55.

Orlinsky, H. M. "The Biblical Concept of the Land of Israel: Cornerstone of the Covenant between God and Israel." *ErIsr* 18 (1985): 53.

Orlinsky, H. M. "'A Covenant [of] People, A Light of the Nations'—a Problem in Biblical Theology." In *Essays in Biblical Culture and Bible Translation*, edited by H. Orlinsky, 166–186. New York: Ktav, 1974.

Orlinsky, H. M. *Essays in Biblical Culture and Bible Translation*. New York: Ktav, 1974.

Orlinsky, H. M. "The Hebrew Root *ŠKB*." *JBL* 63 (1944): 19–44.

Orlinsky, H. M. "Jewish Biblical Scholarship in America." In *Essays in Biblical Culture and Bible Translation*, 287–332. New York: Ktav, 1974.

Orlinsky, H. M. *Notes on the New Translation of the Torah.* Philadelphia, 1969.

Orlinsky, H. M. "Old Testament Studies." In *Religion*, edited by P. Ramsey in *Princeton Studies: Humanistic Scholarship in America*, 51–109. Englewood, NJ: Prentice-Hall, 1965.

Orlinsky, H. M. "Professor Isaac Mendelsohn of Blessed Memory." *Hadoar* 44/32 (1964–1965): 595.

Orlinsky, H. M. "Prolegomenon." In A. Ehrlich, *Mikrâ ki-Pheschutô* (*Die Schrift nach ihrein Wortlaut*), ix–xxxiii. Berlin, 1903. Reprint, New York: Ktav, 1969.

Orlinsky, H. M. "The So-Called 'Servant of the Lord' and 'Suffering Servant' in Second Isaiah." In *Studies on the Second Part of the Book of Isaiah*, 97–117. VTSup 14 and Leiden: E. J. Brill, 1977 [revision of 1967 version].

Orlinsky, H. M. "The Textual Criticism of the Old Testament." In *The Bible and the Ancient Near East*, edited by G. E. Wright, 156. Garden City, NY, 1965.

Pagels, E. *Adam, Eve, and the Serpent.* New York: Random House, 1988.

Pardee, D. "The Letter of Puduhepa: The Text." *AfO* 30 (1983/1984): 322, 325.

Pardee, D., S. D. Sperling, J. D. Whitehead, and. P. E. Dion. *Handbook of Ancient Hebrew Letters.* Chico, CA, 1982.

Parpola, S. "Monotheism in Ancient Assyria." In *One God or Many? Concepts of Divinity in the Ancient World*, edited by B. N. Porter, 165–209. Chebeague Island, ME: Casco Bay Assyriological Institute, 2000.

Parrinder, G. "Touching." *EncRel* 14 (1987): 582.

Parzen, H. "New Data on the Formation of Dropsie College." *Jewish Social Studies* 28 (1966): 131–147.

Paul, S. "Amos 1:3–2:3: A Concatenous Literary Pattern." *JBL* 90 (1971): 397–403.

Paul, S. "Deutero-Isaiah and Cuneiform Royal Inscriptions." *JAOS* 88 (1968): 184–185.

Paul, S. "Heavenly Tablets and the Book of Life." *JANES* 5 (1973): 345–353.

Paul, S. "Literary and Ideological Echoes of Jeremiah in Deutero-Isaiah." In *Proceedings of the Fifth World Congress of Jewish Studies*, edited by P. Peli, 118. Jerusalem, 1969.

Peet, T. E. Review of *Die Sprache des Pentateuch in ihrer Beziehungen zur Aegyptischen* by A. S. Yahuda." *JEA* 16 (1930): 158.

Perles, F. "Critical Notices. Gesenius' Hebrew Dictionary." *JQR* 11 (1899): 689.

Perles, F. "Was Bedeutet יהוה אחד, Deut 6:4." *OLZ* 11 (1908): 537–538.

Perlitt, L. *Bundestheologie im Alten Testament.* Neukirchen-Vluyn: Neukirchener, 1969.

Perlitt, L. *Vatke und Wellhausen:geschichtsphilosophische Voraussetzungen und historiographische Motive für die Darstellung der Religion und Geschichte Israels durch Wilhelm Vatke und Julius Wellhausen.* Berlin: Topelmann, 1965.

Petersen, D. *Haggai and Zechariah 1–8.* Philadelphia, 1984.

Petruck, M. "Body Part Terminology in Hebrew: A Study in Lexical Semantics." PhD diss., University of California, 1986.

Poebel, A. *Das appositionell bestimmte Pronomen der 1. Pers. Sing. in den westsemitischen Inschriften und im Alten Testament.* Chicago, 1932.

Polish, D. "The Changing and the Constant in the Reform Rabbinate." *American Jewish Archives* 35 (November, 1983).

Polzin, R. *Late Biblical Hebrew: Toward an Historical Typology of Biblical Hebrew Prose.* Missoula, MT: Scholars, 1976.

Popper, W. "Parallelism in Isaiah, Chapters 1–10." *SemiCentennial Publications of the University of California 1868–1918: Studies in Biblical Parallelism*, Pt 2. Berkeley: University of California Press, 1918.

Porada, E. "Classic Achaemenian Architecture and Sculpture." In *Cambridge History of Iran*, edited by I. Gershevitch. Cambridge: Cambridge University Press, 1985.

Porten, B. Review of *The Original Torah* by S. D. Sperling. *HS* 40 (1999): 292–296.

Porten, B., and A. Yardeni. *Textbook of Aramaic Documents from Ancient Egypt.* Vol 2. Winona Lake, IN: Eisenbrauns, 1989.

Porter, B. N., ed. *One God or Many? Concepts of Divinity in the Ancient World.* Chebeague Island, ME: Casco Bay Assyriological Institute, 2000.

Pritchard, J. *Ancient Near Eastern Texts Relating to the Old Testament.* Princeton: Princeton University Press, 1955.

Propp, W. *Exodus 1–18.* Anchor Bible. New York: Doubleday, 1998.

Propp, W. "Monotheism and Moses: The Problem of Early Israelite Religion." *Ugarit Forschungen* 31 (1999): 537–575.

Rabbinovicz, R. *Variae Lectiones in Mischnam et in Talmud Babylonicum.*Vol. 3. Nürnberg, 1926. Reprint, New York, 1976.

Rabbinovicz, R. *Variae Lectiones in Mischnam et in Talmud Babylonicum.*Vol. 9. Nuremburg: Bulka, 1926.

Rabinovitz, Z. *Shaare Torat Eretz Yisra'el.* Jerusalem, 1939/1940.

Rabinowitz, J. "A Legal Formula in the Susa Tablets in an Egyptian Document of the Twelfth Dynasty, in the Aramaic Papyri, and in the Book of Daniel 4:14." *Bib.* 36 (1955): 76–77.

Rainey, A. Review of *The Tribes of Yahweh: A Sociology of the Religion of the Liberated Israel: 1250-1050 B.C.E.* by N. K. Gottwald. *JAOS* 107 (1987): 542.

Redford, D. *Akhenaten the Heretic King*. Princeton: Princeton University, 1984.

Redford, D. *Egypt, Canaan and Israel in Ancient Times.* Princeton: Princeton University, 1992.

Redford, D. *A Study of the Biblical Story of Joseph.* Leiden: E. J. Brill, 1970.

Reiner, E. "Dead of Night." In *Studies in Honor of Benno Landsberger on his Seventy-fifth Birthday*, edited by Hans G. Güterbock and Thorkild Jacobsen, 250. Chicago: University of Chicago Press, 1965.

Reiner, E., and H. Güterbock. "The Great Prayer to Ishtar and Its Two Versions from Boğazköy." *JCS* 21 (1967): 255–266.

Reis, Pamela. "Cupidity and Stupidity: Woman's Agency and the 'Rape' of Tamar." *JANES* 25 (1997): 52.

Rendsburg, G. "Hebrew *RḤM* = Rain." *VT* 33 (1983): 359–369.

Rendsburg, G. "Late Biblical Hebrew and the Date of 'P.'" *JANES* 12 (1980): 65–80.

Rendsburg, G. *The Redaction of Genesis*. Winona Lake, IN: Eisenbrauns, 1986.

Rendsburg, G. Review of *The Original Torah* by S. D. Sperling. *AJSR* 24 (1999): 359–362.

Rendtorff, R. *Das Überlieferungsgeschichtliche Problem des Pentateuch* (BZAW 147). Berlin and New York, 1976.

Renger, J. "Untersuchungen zum Priestertum der altbabylonischen Zeit." *ZA* 59 (1969): 203–228.

Renz, J., and W. Röllig. *Handbuch der althebräischen Epigraphik*. Vol. 1. Darmstadt: Wissenschaftliche Buchgesellschaft, 1995–2003.

Richardson, N. "Psalm 106: Yahweh's Succoring Love Saves from the Death of a Broken Covenant." In *Love and Death in the Ancient Near East. Essays in Honor of Marvin H. Pope*, edited by J. Marks and R. Good, 191–203. Guilford, 1987.

Rieder, D. *Targum Jonathan ben Uziel to the Pentateuch*. Vols. 1 and 2. Jerusalem: 1974–1985.

Riemschneider, K. *Lehrbuch des Akkadischen*. Leipzig, 1969.

Ritter, E. "Magical Expert (=ĀŠIPU) and Physician (=ASÛ): Notes on Two Complementary Professions in Babylonian Medicine." *AS* 16 (1965): 299–321.

Ritterband, P., and H. S.Wechsler. *Jewish Learning in American Universities. The First Century*. Bloomington: Indiana University, 1994.

Roberts, J. J. M. "Does God Lie? Divine Deceit as a Theological Problem in Israelite Prophetic Literature." In *Congress Volume: Jerusalem 1986* (=VTSup 40), edited by J. A. Emerton, 211–220. Leiden: Brill, 1988.

Robertson, S. Dunbar. *The Account of the Israelite Tabernacle and the First Priesthood in the "Jewish Antiquities" of Flavius Josephus*. PhD diss., Annenberg Research Institute, 1991.

Rofé, A. "The Battle of David and Goliath." In *Judaic Perspectives on Ancient Israel*, edited by J. Neusner, Ernest S. Frerichs, and Baruch A. Levine, 132. Philadelphia: Fortress, 1987.

Rofé, A. "The Defilement of Virgins in Biblical Law and the Case of Dinah (Genesis 34)." *Bib 86*. 2005, 369–374.

Rofé, A. "The Devotion to Torah-Study at the End of the Biblical Period: Joshua 1:8, Psalms 1:2; Isaiah 59:21." In *The Bible in the Light of its Interpreters, Sarah Kamin Memorial Volume*, edited by S. Japhet, 622–628. Jerusalem: Magnes, 1994.

Rofé, A. "How is the Word Fulfilled? Isaiah 55:6–11 within the Theological Debate of Its Time." In *Canon, Theology and Old Testament Interpretation: Essays in Honor of*

Brevard S. Childs, edited by Gene Tucker, David L. Petersen, and Robert R. Wilson, 246. Philadelphia: Fortress, 1988.
Rofé, A. *Introduction to Deuteronomy Part 1 and further Chapters* [in Hebrew]. Jerusalem: Akademon, 1988.
Rofé, A. *Introduction to the Prophetic Literature*. Jerusalem: Academon, 1992.
Rofé, A. ספורי הנביאים. Jerusalem: Magnes, 1982.
Rogerson, J. *Old Testament Criticism in the Nineteenth Century: England and Germany*. London: Fortress, 1985.
Röllig, W. "Die Amulette von Arslan Taş." *NESE* 2 (1974): 17–36.
Ronnberg, A. "Spittle and Spitting." *EncRel* 14 (1987): 37–38.
Rosenthal, A. "Oral Torah and Torah from Sinai—Theory and Practice" [in Hebrew]. In *Meḥqerei Talmud*. Vol. 2, edited by M. Bar-Asher and D. Rosenthal, 448–487. Jerusalem: Magnes, 1993.
Rosenthal D., ed. *S. Lieberman Studies in Palestinian Talmudic Literature* [in Hebrew]. Jerusalem: Magnes, 1991.
Rosenthal, E. "For the Talmudic Dictionary-Talmudica Iranica" [in Hebrew]. In *Irano-Judaica*, edited by S. Shaked, 38–134. Jerusalem: Ben-Zvi Institute, 1982.
Rosenthal, E. S. "Rav ben Ahi R. Hiyya gam ben-Ahoto?" In *Henoch Yalon Jubilee Volume*, edited by S. Lieberman, A. Abramson, E. Y. Kutcher, and S. Esh, 281–337. Jerusalem: Kiryat Sepher, 1963.
Rosenthal, F. *An Aramaic Handbook*. Wiesbaden, 1967.
Rosenthal, F. *Die aramaistische Forschung*. Reprint, Leiden: 1964.
Rossell, W. *A Handbook of Aramaic Magical Texts*. Ringwood Borough, NJ: Shelton College, 1953.
Roth, Martha. *Law Collections from Mesopotamia and Asia Minor*. 2nd ed. SBLWAW 6. Atlanta: Scholars, 1997.
Russell, J. R. "Yamauchi, *Persia and the Bible*." *JQR* 82 (1992): 258.
Rybak, S. "The Aramaic Dialect of Nedarim." PhD diss., Yeshiva University, 1980.
Saadiah ben Joseph. *Version arabe du Pentateuque de R. Saadia ben Iosef Al-Fayyoûmî*. Edited and translated by J. Derenbourg. Paris: Leroux, 1893.
Safrai, S. "Halakha to Moses from Sinai: History or Theology?" In *Meḥqerei Talmud*, edited by Y. Sussmann and D. Rosenthal, 30–31. Jerusalem: Magnes, 1990.
Safrai, S, ed. *The Literature of the Sages, Pt 1*. Philadelphia: Fortress, 1987.
Sakenfeld, K. D. *The Meaning of Hesed in the Hebrew Bible: A New Inquiry*. Missoula, MT: Scholars, 1978.
Salonen, A. *Agricultura Mesopotamica*. Helsinki, 1968.
Salonen, E. "Gruss." *RLA* 3 (1957): 668–670.
Sanders, J. "The Bible at Union: 1835 to the Present." *USQR* 52/2 (1998): 123–131.
Sanders, J. "The Hebrew University Bible and Biblia Hebraica Quinta." *JBL* 118 (1999): 518–526.

Sandmel, S. "Isaac Mayer Wise's Pronaos to Holy Writ." In *A Bicentennial Festschrift for Jacob Rader Marcus*, edited by B. Korn, 517–525. New York: American Jewish Historical Society and Ktav, 1976.

Sarna, N. *Exodus* (JPS Torah Commentary). Philadelphia: Jewish Publication Society, 1991.

Sarna, N. *Genesis* (JPS Torah Commentary). Philadelphia: Jewish Publication Society, 1989.

Sarna, N. "Introduction." In *Psalms, Chronologically Treated.* New York: Ktav, 1969.

Sarna, N. "Psalm XIX and the Near Eastern Sun-God Literature." *Proceedings of the Fourth World Congress of Jewish Studies* (1969): 172.

Sarna, N. "Psalm 89: A Study in Inner Biblical Exegesis." In *Biblical and Other Studies*, edited by A. Altmann, 29–46. Cambridge, MA: Harvard University Press, 1963.

Sasson, J. "Who Cut Samson's Hair?" *Prooftexts* 8 (1988): 333–339.

Sasson, J. "Wordplay in the OT." *IDBSup* (1976): 968–970.

Sasson, J. "Yarim-Lim's War Declaration." In *Miscellanea Babylonica mélanges offerts à Maurice Birot*, edited by J.-M. Durand and J.-R. Kupper, 237–255. Paris, 1985.

Saunders, E. W. *Searching the Scriptures: A History of the Society of Biblical Literature, 1880–1980*. Chico, CA: Scholars, 1982.

Sauren, H., and G. Kestemont, "Keret, roi de Ḫubur." *UF* 3 (1971): 200.

Schechter, S. *Seminary Addresses and Other Papers*. Cincinnati: Ark, 1915.

Schechter, S. *Studies in Judaism*. Reprint, Philadelphia: Jewish Publication Society and Meridian, 1958.

Schechter, S. "On the Study of the Talmud." In *Studies in Judaism*, 112–114. Philadelphia: Jewish Publication Society of America, 1908.

Schlesinger, M. *Satzlehre der aramäischen Sprache des babylonischen Talmuds*. Leipzig: Asia Major, 1928.

Schmid, H. *Der sogennante Jahwist*. Zürich, 1976.

Schmidt, W. "A Theologian of the Solomonic Era? A Plea for the Yahwist." In *Studies in the Period of David and Solomon and Other Essays*, edited by T. Ishida, 55–73. Winona Lake, IN: Eisenbrauns, 1982.

Schmitt, G. *Du sollst keinen Frieden schliessen mit den Bewohnern des Landes*. BWANT. Stuttgart: Kohlhammer, 1970.

Schmuttermayr, G. *Psalm 18 und 2 Samuel 22 Studien zu einem Doppeltext*. Munich, 1971.

Schmuttermayr, G. "RḤM—Eine Lexikalische Studie." *Bib.* 51 (1970).

Schorsch, I. "Coming to Terms with Biblical Criticism." *Conservative Judaism* 59 (2005): 3–22.

Schorsch, I. *Thoughts from 3080: Selected Addresses and Writings*. n.d, n.p.

Schott, A. "*Zu meiner Übersetzung des Gilgameš-Epos*." *ZA* 42 (1934): 125–129.

Schottroff, W. *'Gedenken' im alten Orient und im Alten Testament.* Neukirchen-Vluyn, 1964.

Schroer, S. *In Israel gab es Bilder: Nachrichten von darstellender Kunst im Alten Testament*. Fribourg: Universitätsverlag, 1987.

Schuster, H.-S. "Der Relativsatz im Phönizischen und Punischen." In *Studies in Honor of Benno Landsberger on His Seventy-fifth Birthday*, edited by H. G. Güterbock and T. Jacobsen, 443. Chicago: University of Chicago Press, 1965.

Schwab, M. *Le Talmud de Jérusalem*. Vol 6. Reprint, Paris, 1960.

Schwartz, J. "Aliya from Babylonia during the Amoraic Period (200–500 CE)." In *The Jerusalem Cathedra*. Vol 1, edited by L. Levine, 58–69. Jerusalem: Ben-Zvi Institute, 1983.

Schwartz, J. "Babylonian Commoners in Amoraic Palestine." *JAOS* 101 (1981): 317–322.

Schwartz, J. "Tension between Palestinian Scholars and Babylonian Olim in Amoraic Palestine." *JSJ* 11 (1980): 78–94.

Schwartz, M. "Scatology and Eschatology in Zoroaster." *Acta Iranica* 25 (1985): 473–496.

Scurlock, Jo Ann. "But Was She Raped? A Verdict through Comparison." *NIN* 4 (2006): 61–103.

Seeligmann, I. L. "The Understanding of Prophecy in Deuteronomistic and Chronistic History." In *I. L. Seeligmann Studies in Biblical Literature*, edited by Avi Hurvitz, Sara Japhet, and Emanuel Tov, 205–228. Jerusalem: Magnes, 1992.

Sefer Iyyob Mebu'ar Mehadash-Das Buch Hiob nebst einem neuen Commentar. Baltimore, 1886.

Segal, M. H. *A Grammar of Mishnaic Hebrew*. Oxford: Clarendon, 1970.

Seibert, I. *Woman in the Ancient Near East*. Leipzig: Edition Leipzig, 1974.

Selzer, M. *Kike*. New York: Meridian, 1972.

Seux, M.-J. *Epithetes royals akkadiennes et sumeriennes*. Paris: Letouzey et Ane, 1967.

Seux, M.-J. *Hymnes et prières aux dieux de Babylonie et d'Assyrie*. Paris, 1986.

Shaked, S. "Iranian Loanwords in Middle Aramaic." In *Encyclopedia Iranica*, edited by E. Yarshater, 261. Boston: Routledge and Kegan Paul, 1986.

Shapira, Amnon. "The Accusations against Shechem Son of Hamor: A Reconsideration—A Reaction to Mayer Gruber's Article." *Beth Mikra* 44 (1998–1999): 281–282.

Sharfman, I. H. *The First Rabbi*. Malibu: Joseph Simon Panngloss, 1988.

Shargel, B. *Practical Dreamer: Israel Friedlaender and the Shaping of American Judaism*. New York: Jewish Theological Seminary, 1985.

Shinan, A. "Echoes from Ancient Synagogues: Vocatives and 'Emendations' in the Aramaic Targums to the Pentateuch." *JQR* 81 (1991): 353–364.

Shinan, A. "Moses and the Ethiopian Woman: Sources of a Story in the Chronicles of Moses." In *Studies in Hebrew Narrative throughout the Ages*, edited by J.Heinemann and S.Werses, 66–67. Jerusalem: Magnes, 1978.

Shupak, N. "Stylistic and Terminological Traits Common to Biblical and Egyptian Literature." *WO* 14 (1985): 230.

Silberman, L. "Wellhausen and Judaism." *Semeia* 25 (1983): 79–82.

Silberschlag, E. "The Primacy of Hebrew in Early America." In *Hebrew Studies* 16, Katsh volume, 123. Philadelphia: Jewish Publication Society, 1985.

Singer, A. "The Vocative in Ugaritic." *JCS* 2 (1948): 1–10.

Sittl, C. *Die Gebärden der Griechen und Römer.* Leipzig, 1890.

Sjöberg, A. "*inin-šà gur* A Hymn to the Goddess Inanna," *ZA* 65 (1976): 190:124.

Skehan, P., and A. Di Lella. *The Wisdom of Ben Sira* (AB 39). New York: Doubleday, 1987.

Skinner, John. *A Critical and Exegetical Commentary on Genesis.* Edinburgh: T&T Clark, 1910.

Skoss, S., ed. *Kitāb Jamiʿ Al-Alfāẓ.* Vol. 1. New Haven: Yale University Press, 1936.

Skoss, S., ed. *Kitāb Jamiʿ Al-Alfāẓ.* Vol. 2. New Haven: Yale University Press, 1945.

Slouschz, N. *Thesaurus of Phoenician Inscriptions.* Tel Aviv, 1942.

Smend, R. "Beinkleider." In *Biblisch-historisches Handwörterbuch*, edited by B. Reicke and L. Rost. Göttingen: Vandenhoeck & Ruprecht, 1962.

Smith, Mark S. *The Early History of God.* Grand Rapids, MI: Eerdmanns, 2002.

Smith, Mark S. "The Magic of Kothar wa-Hasis the Ugaritic Craftsman God in KTU 1.6 VI 49–50." *RB* 91 (1984): 377–380.

Smith, Mark S. *The Origins of Biblical Monotheism: Israel's Polytheistic Background and the Ugaritic Texts.* Oxford: Oxford University, 2001.

Smith, Morton. "The Common Theology of the Ancient Near East." *JBL* 71 (1952): 137–139.

Smith, Morton. "II Isaiah and the Persians." *JAOS* 83 (1963): 415–420.

Smith, Morton. "Jewish Religious Life in the Persian Period." In *The Cambridge History of Judaism.* Vol. 1, edited by W. Davies and L. Finkelstein, 219–278. Cambridge, 1984.

Smith, Morton. *Palestinian Parties and Politics that Shaped the Old Testament.* New York: Columbia University Press, 1971.

Snaith, N. *Isaiah 40–66. A Study of the Teaching of the Second Isaiah and Its Consequences* (VTSup 14). Leiden, 1977.

Soggin, J. "The Conquest of Jericho through Battle." *ErIsr* 16 (1982): *215.

Soggin, J. *Joshua.* Philadelphia: Westminster, 1972.

Sokoloff, Michael. *The Genizah Fragments of Bereshit Rabba.* Jerusalem: Israel Academy of Humanities and Sciences, 1982.

Sollberger, E., "Samsu-ilūna's Bilingual Inscriptions C. and D." *RA* 63 (1969): 36:29–43.

Sommer, B. "Inner-biblical Interpretation." In *Jewish Study Bible*, edited by A. Berlin and M. Brettler, 1829–1835. New York: Oxford University Press, 2004.

Speiser, E. A. *The Anchor Bible: Genesis.* Garden City, NY, 1964.

Speiser, E. "A Significant New Will from Nuzi." *JCS* 17 (1963): 65–71.

Sperber, A. *The Bible in Aramaic.* 5 vols. Leiden: Brill, 1959–1973.

Sperber, D. *A Dictionary of Greek and Latin Legal Terms in Rabbinic Literature.* Ramat Gan: Bar-Ilan University, 1984.

Sperber, D. *Essays on Greek and Latin in the Mishna, Talmud, and Midrashic Literature.* Jerusalem: Makor, 1982.

Sperber, D. *Material Culture in Eretz Israel during the Talmudic Period.* Jerusalem: Ben Zvi, 1993.

Sperber, D. *Nautica Talmudica.* Ramat Gan: Bar-Ilan University, 1986.

Sperling, S. "Aramaic Spousal Misunderstandings." *JAOS* 115/2 (1995): 205–209.

Sperling, S. "An Arslan Tash Incantation: Interpretations and Implications." *HUCA* 53 (1982): 7.

Sperling, S. "A šu-íl-lá to Ištar." *WO* 12 (1981): 8.

Sperling, S. "Biblical rhm I and rhm II." *JANES* 19 (1989): 156.

Sperling, S. Review of *Divine Commitment and Human Obligation: Selected Writings of David Noel Freedman* by D. N. Freedman. *HS* 39 (1998): 7–13.

Sperling, S. "Israel's Religion in the Ancient Near East." In *Jewish Spirituality from the Bible to the Middle Ages*, edited by A. Green, 16–21. New York: Crossroad, 1986.

Sperling, S. "Judaism and Modern Biblical Research." In *Biblical Studies: Meeting Ground of Jews and Christians*, edited by L. Boadt and L. Klenicki, 19–44. New York: Stimulus, 1980.

Sperling, S. "Late Hebrew *ḥzr* and Akkadian *saḫāru.*" *JANES* 5 (1973): 397–404.

Sperling, S. "Miriam, Aaron and Moses: Sibling Rivalry." *HUCA* 70/71 (1999–2000): 39–55.

Sperling, S. *The Original Torah: The Political Intent of the Bible's Writers.* New York: New York University Press, 1998.

Sperling, S. "Rethinking Covenant in Late Biblical Texts." *Biblica* 70 (1989): 50–73.

Sperling, S. *Students of the Covenant. A History of Jewish Biblical Scholarship in North America.* Atlanta: Scholars, 1992.

Sperling, S. "Studies in Late Hebrew Lexicography in the Light of Akkadian." PhD diss, Columbia University, 1973.

Sperling, S. D. "Ancient Near Eastern Religious Text Relating to the Old Testament." *JAOS* 101 (1981): 449.

Sperling, S. D., and B. Levine. "Biblical Scholarship, Modern." In *Blackwell Companion to Jewish Culture from the Eighteenth Century to the Present*, edited by G. Abramson, 87–91. Oxford: Basil Blackwell, 1989.

Stanton, G. "Matthew." In *It Is Written: Scripture Citing Scripture: Essays in Honour of Barnabas Lindars, SSF*, edited by D. A. Carson and H. G. M. Williamson, 205–219. Cambridge: Cambridge University Press, 1988.

Starr, I. *Queries to the Sungod: Divination and Politics in Sargonid Assyria.* Helsinki: Helsinki University, 1990.

Steiner, R. "Incomplete Circumcision in Egypt and Edom: Jeremiah (9:24–25) in the Light of Josephus and Jonckheere." *JBL* 118 (1999): 497–526.

Steinkeller, P. "The Eblaite Preposition *qidimay* 'Before.'" *Oriens Antiquus* 23 (1984): 33–37.

Steinsaltz, A. *Talmud Babli Maseket Nedarim 2*. Jerusalem: Israel Institute for Talmudic Publications, 1992.

Stoebe, H. J. "*rḥm* pi. 'sich erbarmen.'" *THAT* 2 (1976): 761.

Strack, H. *Der babylonische Talmud nach der einzigen vollständigen Handschrift München Codex Hebraicus* 95 Leiden: A. W. Sijthof, 1912.

Strack, H., and G. Stemberger. *Introduction to the Talmud and Midrash*. Edinburgh: T&T Clark, 1991.

Streck, M. *Assurbanipal und die letzten assyrischen Könige bis zum Untergange Niniveh's*. Vol. 2. Leipzig 1916.

Strommenger, E. *5000 Years of the Art of Mesopotamia*. New York, 1964.

Sussman, L. "Another Look at Isaac Leeser and the First Jewish Translation of the Bible in the United States." *Modern Judaism* 5 (1985): 159–190.

Sussman, L. *Isaac Leeser and the Making of American Judaism*. Detroit: Wayne State University, 1995.

Sussman, L. "Isaac Leeser and the Protestantization of American Judaism." *American Jewish Archives* 38 (April 1986).

Szlechter, E. "Les tablettes juridiques datées du regne d'Abi-Ešuḥ conservées au Musée d'Art et d'Histoire de Genève." *JCS* 7 (1953): 91.

Tadmor, H. "Bĕrît û-Šĕbû'at Ne'emānîm ba-Mizrāḥ ha-Qadmōn: Gišātô šel Hisṭoryôn." *Shnaton* 5–6 (1981–1982): 155.

Tadmor, H. "The Sin of Sargon." *ErIsr* 5 (1958): 154:5.

Tadmor, H. "Treaty and Oath in the Ancient Near East: A Historian's Approach." In *Humanizing America's Iconic Book*, edited by G. Tucker and D. Knight, 131, 141. Chico, CA: Scholars, 1982.

Tadmor, H., and M. Cogan. "Ahaz and Tiglath-Pileser in the Book of Kings: Historiographic Considerations." *Biblica* 60 (1979): 503.

Tal, A. "The Aramaic Dialects of Palestine and the 'Yerushalmi' Targum to the Pentateuch" [in Hebrew]. *Proceedings of the Ninth World Congress of Jewish Studies*, 14. Jerusalem: Magnes, 1988.

Tal, A. "Samaritan Literature." In *The Samaritans*, edited by Alan D. Crown, 413–467. Tübingen: Mohr Siebeck, 1989.

Tal, A. *The Samaritan Targum of the Pentateuch: A Critical Edition*. 3 vols. Tel Aviv: Tel Aviv University, 1981.

Tal, A. ed. *The Samaritan Pentateuch*. Tel Aviv: Tel Aviv University Press, 1994.

Tal, M. Review of *A Dictionary of Jewish Palestinian Aramaic* by M. Sokoloff. *Tarbiz* 60 (1991): 1): 277–287.

Tawil, H. "The End of the Hadad Inscription in the Light of Akkadian." *JNES* 32 (1973): 481.

Tawil, H. "Some Literary Elements in the Opening Sections of the Hadad, Zakir, and the Nerab II Inscriptions in the Light of East and West Semitic Royal Inscriptions." *Or* 43 (1974): 42.

Tawil, H. "Two Notes on the Treaty Terminology of the Sefîre Inscriptions." *CBQ* 42 (1980): 35–37.

Theodor J., and Ch. Albeck. *Der Midrasch Bereschit Rabba.* Reprint, Jerusalem, 1965.

Thompson, T. *The Origin Tradition of Ancient Israel.* Vol. 1, *The Literary Formation of Genesis and Exodus 1–23.* Sheffield: JSOT, 1987.

Thureau-Dangin, F. "Iahdunlim, Roi de Hana." *RA* (1936): 51.

Thureau-Dangin, F. "L'inscription bilingue B de Samsu-iluna." *RA* 39 (1942–1944): 8.

Thureau-Dangin, F. *Rituels accadiens.* Paris: Leroux, 1921.

Tigay, Jeffrey. *The JPS Torah Commentary: Deuteronomy.* Philadelphia: Jewish Publication Society, 1996.

Tigay, Jeffrey. "The Significance of the End of Deuteronomy (Deuteronomy 34:10–12)." In *Texts, Temples, and Traditions: A Tribute to Menahem Haran*, edited by Michael Fox, Victor Avigdor Hurowitz, Avi Hurvitz, Michael L. Klein, Baruch J. Schwartz, and Nili Shupak, 137–143. Winona Lake, IN: Eisenbrauns, 1996.

Tomback, R. *A Comparative Semitic Lexicon of the Phoenician and Punic Languages.* Missoula, MT: Scholars, 1978.

Toombs, L. "Beyond the River." *IDB* 1 (1966): 405–406.

Török, L. *The Kingdom of Kush.* Leiden: E. J.Brill, 1997.

Torrey, C. C. "The Zakar and Kalamu Inscriptions." *JAOS* 35 (1915–1917): 366.

Towner, W. S. "Form-Criticism of Rabbinic Literature." *Journal of Jewish Studies* 24 (1973): 101–118.

Trevor, J. C. *Scrolls from Qumran Cave I.* Jerusalem, 1972.

Trible, P. *God and the Rhetoric of Sexuality.* Philadelphia, 1978.

Tsevat, M. *The Meaning of the Book of Job and Other Biblical Studies.* New York, 1980.

Tsevat, M. "A Retrospective View of Isaac Leeser's Biblical Work." In *Essays in American Jewish History*, edited by J. Marcus, 295–313. Cincinnati: American Jewish Archives, 1958.

Turner, S. H. *Autobiography of the Rev. Samuel H. Turner, D. D.* New York: A. D. F. Randolf, 1863.

Turner, S. H. *Biographical Notices of Some of the Most Distinguished Jewish Rabbies (sic) and Translations of Portions of their Commentaries and Other Works with Illustrative Introductions and Notes.* New York: Stanford and Swords, 1847.

Tur-Sinai, N. H. *The Book of Job: A New Commentary.* Jerusalem, 1967.

Tur-Sinai, N. H. *The Language and the Book: Beliefs and Doctrines* [in Hebrew]. Vol. 3. 2nd ed. Jerusalem: Bialik Institute, 1954–1955.

Tur-Sinai, N. H. *Peshutô shel Mikrâ.* Jerusalem: Kiryat Sefer, 1962–1968.

Ullendorf, Edward. "The Bawdy Bible." *BSOAS* 42 (1975): 436.

Ungnad, A. "Materialien zur altakkadischen Sprache." *MVAG.* 20 Heft II, (1915): 63.

Ungnad, A., J. Friedrich, G. R. Meyer, and E. F. Weidner. *Inschriften vom Tell Halaf: Keilschrifttexte und aramäische Urkunden aus einer assyrischen Provinzhauptstadt*. Osnabrück: Biblio-Verlag, 1967.

Urbach, E. A. "Halacha and Prophecy." *Tarbiz* 18 (1947): 1–27.

Urbach, E. A. *The Sages—Their Concepts and Beliefs*. Jerusalem: Magnes, 1971.

Utas B., and C. Toll. *Frahang i Pahlavīk*. Weisbaden: Otto Harrassowitz, 1988.

Vahman, F. *Arda Wirāz Nāmag*. London: Curzon, 1986.

van Amringe, J. *A History of Columbia University 1754–1904*. New York: Columbia University, 1904.

van der Leeuw, G. *Religion in Essence and Manifestation*. New York, 1963.

van der Toorn, K. "Anat-Yahu, Some Other Deities and the Jews of Elephantine." *Numen* 39 (1992): 80-101.

van der Toorn, K. *The Image and the Book. Iconic Cults, Aniconism and the Rise of Book Religion in Israel and the Ancient Near East*. Leuven: Peeters, 1998.

van Dijk, J. *Sumerische Götterlieder*. Vol. 2. Heidelberg, 1960.

van Selms, A. "Temporary Henotheism." In *Symbolae Biblicae et Mesopotamicae Francisco Mariò Theodoro de Liagre Böhl Dedicatae*, edited by M. Beek and A. Kampman, 341–348. Leiden: Brill, 1973.

van Seters, J. *Abraham in History and Tradition*. New Haven: Yale, 1975.

van Seters, J. "Joshua 24 and the Problem of Tradition in the Old Testament." In *In the Shelter of Elyon Essays on Ancient Palestinian Life and Literature in Honor of G. W. Ahlström*, edited by W. B. Barrick and J. R. Spencer, 139–158 [JSOTSup 31]. Sheffield: JSOT, 1984.

van Seters, J. *The Life of Moses the Yahwist as Historian in Exodus–Numbers*. Louisville: Westminster/John Knox, 1994.

van Seters, J. "The Religion of the Patriarchs in Genesis." *Biblica* 61 (1980): 220–223.

van Seters, J. "The Terms 'Amorite' and 'Hittite' in the Old Testament." *VT* 22 (1972): 81.

van Wolde, E. "Does *'Innâ* Denote Rape? A Semantic Analysis of a Controversial Word." *VT* 52 (2002): 528–544.

van Wolde, E. "Love and Hatred in a Multiracial Society." In *Reading from Right to Left: Essays on the Hebrew Bible in Honour of David J. A. Clines*, edited by J. C. Exum and H. Williamson, 435–449. London: Sheffield, 2003.

Versnel, H. "Three Greek Experiments in Oneness." In *One God or Many? Concepts of Divinity in the Ancient World*, edited by B. N. Porter, 79–163. Chebeague Island, ME: Casco Bay Assyriological Institute, 2000.

Vogelzang, M., and H. Vanstiphout, eds. *Mesopotamian Epic Literature Oral or Aural?* Lewiston, NY: Edwin Mellen, 1992.

von Rad, G. *The Problem of the Hexateuch and Other Essays*. London, 1966.

von Soden, W. "Das akkadische t-Perfekt in Haupt- und Nebensätzen und sumerische Verbalformen mit den Präfixen ba-, imma- und u." *AS* 16 (1965): 110.

von Soden, W. "Zum akkadischen Wörterbuch 31–40." *Or* 18 (1949): 399–401.

von Soden, W. "Altbabylonische Dialektdichtungen." *ZA* 44, (1938): 32:19.

von Soden, W. "Aramäische Wörter in neuassyrischen und neu- und spätbabylonischen Texten. Ein Vorbericht. 1 (aga-*muš)." *Or* 35 (1966): 12.

von Soden, W. *Bibel und alter Orient.* Berlin, 1985.

von Soden, W. "Ergänzende Bemerkungen zum 'Liebeszauber' Text MAD 5 Nr. 8." *ZA* 62 (1973): 273.

von Soden, W. "Gebet II (babylonisch und assyrisch)." *RLA* 3 (1957): 169–170.

von Soden, W. "Der hymnisch-episch Dialekt des Akkadischen (Schluss)." *ZA* 41 (1932): 170n3.

von Soden, W. Comments to "Zu meiner Übersetzung des Gilgameš-Epos" by A. Schott. *ZA* 42 (1934): 224.

von Soden, W. "Mirjām-Maria '(Gottes)-Geschenk.'" *UF* 2 (1970): 269–272.

von Soden, W. "Zu den politischen Korrezpondenzen des Archives von Mari." *Or* 21 (1952): 76.

von Soden, W. Review of *La splendeur divine* by E. Cassin. *ZA* 61 (1972): 312–314.

Vorwahl, H. *Die Gebärdensprache im Alten Testament.* Berlin, 1932.

Wagner, M. "Beiträge zur Aramaismenfrage im alttestamentlichen Hebräisch." VTSup 16 (1967): 360–361.

Wajsberg, E. "The Orthography of the Names Rabba and Rava: Rav Hai's and Rivalling Rules." In *Language Studies.* Vols. 5–6, edited by M. Bar-Asher, 181–213. Jerusalem: Magnes, 1992.

Walfish, B. "Medieval Jewish Interpretation." In *Jewish Study Bible*, edited by A. Berlin and M. Brettler, 1876–1900. New York: Oxford University Press, 2004.

Wallenstein, M. "Some Aspects of the Vocabulary and Morphology of the Hymns of the Judean Scrolls." *VT* 7 (1957): 213.

Walser, G. *Die Völkerschaften auf den Reliefs von Persepolis.* Berlin: Deutsches Archäologischen Institut, Abteilung Tehran Bd. 2, 1966.

Watt, W. M. "Muhammad." *EncRel* (1987): 10:137–146.

Waxman, M., ed. *Tradition and Change: The Development of Conservative Judaism.* New York: Burning Bush, 1958.

Wechsler, H. "The JTSA in American Higher Education." In *Tradition Renewed: A History of the Jewish Theological Seminary of America*, edited by J. Wertheimer, 2:769–825. New York: Jewish Theological Seminary, 1997.

Weinfeld, Moshe. "Berith." In *Theological Dictionary of the Old Testament* by G. Botterweck and H. Ringgren. Grand Rapids, MI: Eerdmans, 1975.

Weinfeld, Moshe. "Bond and Grace"—Covenantal Expressions in the Bible and in the Ancient World—A Common Heritage." *Leš* 36 (1971–1972): 85.

Weinfeld, Moshe. "The Covenant of Grant in the Old Testament and in the Ancient Near East." *JAOS* 90 (1970): 191.

Weinfeld, Moshe. "The Creator God in Genesis I and in the Prophecy of Deutero-Isaiah" [in Hebrew]. *Tarbiz* 37 (1968): 112.

Weinfeld, Moshe. *Deuteronomy I–II*. AB 5. New York: Doubleday, 1991.

Weinfeld, Moshe. *Deuteronomy and the Deuteronomic School*. Oxford: Oxford University Press, 1972.

Weinfeld, Moshe. "Julius Wellhausen's Understanding of the Law of Ancient Israel and Its Fallacies" [in Hebrew]. *Shnaton* 4 (1989): 62–93.

Weinfeld, Moshe. *Justice and Righteousness in the Nations: Equality and Freedom in Ancient Israel in Light of Social Justice in the Ancient Near East* [in Hebrew]. Jerusalem, 1985.

Weinfeld, Moshe. "*śkl, yn, dyq*: A Semantic Analysis" [in Hebrew]. In *Tehillah le-Moshe: Biblical and Judaic Studies in Honor of Moshe Greenberg*, edited by Mordechai Cogan, Barry L. Eichler, and Jeffrey H. Tigay, 101–106. Winona Lake, IN: Eisenbrauns, 1997.

Weinfeld, Moshe. "Social and Cultic Institutions in the Priestly Source against Their Ancient Near Eastern Background." *Proceedings of the Eighth World Congress of Jewish Studies*, 95–129. Jerusalem: World Union of Jewish Studies, 1983.

Weinstock, Moshe, ed. *Seder Olam Rabbah Ha-shalem*. Jerusalem: Torat Hesed, 1961.

Weiser, A., ed. *Ibn Ezra*. Jerusalem, 1976.

Weiss (Halivni), D. *Meqôrôt u-Mesôrôt, Shabbat.* Jerusalem: Jewish Theological Seminary, 1982.

Weiss (Halivni), D. "From Midrash to Mishnah: Theological Repercussions and Further Clarifications of 'chate'u yisrael.'" In *The Midrashic Imagination: Jewish Exegesis, Thought, and History*, edited by Michael Fishbane, 30. Albany: State University of New York Press, 1993.

Weiss (Halivni), D. *Midrash, Mishnah and Gemara.* Cambridge, MA: Harvard University Press, 1986.

Weiss (Halivni), D. *Peshat and Derash: Plain and Applied Meaning in Rabbinic Exegesis.* New York: Oxford University Press, 1991.

Weiss (Halivni), D. "Reflections on Classical Jewish Hermeneutics." *PAAJR* 46–47 (1980): 67–83.

Weiss (Halivni), D. "Reflections on Classical Jewish Hermeneutics." *PAAJR* 62 (1996): 21–127.

Weiss, I. *Sipra d'Be Rab*. New York, 1946.

Weitzman, Michael. *The Syriac Version of the Old Testament*. Cambridge: Cambridge University Press, 1999.

Wellhausen, J. *Prolegomena to the History of Ancient Israel*. Cleveland: Meridian, 1961 [1878].

Wenham, G. "The Religion of the Patriarchs." In *Essays on the Patriarchal Narratives*, edited by A. Millard and D. Wiseman, 161–195. Winona Lake, IN: Eisenbrauns, 1983.

Westermann, C. *Isaiah 40–66: A Commentary*. Philadelphia, 1969.

Westermann, C. "Promises to the Patriarchs." *IDBSup*, (1976): 690–693.

Wevers, John W. *Septuaginta Genesis.* Göttingen: Vandenhoeck & Ruprecht, 1974.

Wewers, G. *Avoda Zara Götzendienst*. Tübingen: J. Mohr, 1980.

Wewers, G. *Sanhedrin Gerichtshof.* Tūbingen: Mohr, 1981.

Whiston, William. *The Works of Flavius Josephus*, 2:117. 4 vols. Grand Rapids, MI: Baker, 1984.

White, M. "The Elohistic Depiction of Aaron." VTSup 41 (1990): 158.

Wildberger, H. *Jesaja BK 10/1*. Neukirchen–Vluyn: Neukirchener, 1972.

Wildberger, H. "Der Monotheismus Deuterojesajas." In *Beiträge zur alttestamentlichen Theologie. Festschrift für Walther Zimmerli zum 70. Geburtstag*, edited by H. Donner, R. Hanhart, and R. Smend, 506–530. Göttingen:Vandenhoeck & Ruprecht, 1977.

Williamson, H. G. M. *Ezra, Nehemiah.* Waco, TX: Word Books, 1985.

Williamson, H. G. M. "History." In *It Is Written—Scripture Citing Scripture: Essays in Honour of Barnabas Lindars*, SSF, edited by D. A. Carson and H. G. M. Williamson, 29–30. Cambridge: Cambridge University Press, 1988.

Wilson, John. "Ancient Near Eastern Texts Relating to the Old Testament." *ANET* (1955): 477.

Wilson, J. Kinnier. "'Desonance' in Accadian [sic]." *JSS* 13 (1968): 97.

Wilson, J. Kinnier. "An Introduction to Babylonian Psychiatry." In *Studies in Honor of Benno Landsberger on His Seventy-fifth Birthday*, edited by H. G. Güterbock and T. Jacobsen, 293. Chicago: University of Chicago Press, 1965.

Wise, I. M. *Pronaos to Holy Writ Establishing on Documentary Evidence the Authorship, Date, Form and Contents of Each of the Books and the Authenticity of the Pentateuch.* Cincinnati: Robert and Company, 1891.

Wiseman, D. J. *The Alalakh Tablets.* London: British Institute of Archaeology at Ankara, 1953.

Wright, G. E. *Biblical Archaeology*. Philadelphia: Westminster, 1957.

Wright, G. E., and R. Boling. *Joshua*. AB. Garden City, NY: Doubleday, 1982.

Yadin, Y. *The Scroll of the War of the Sons of Light against the Sons of Darkness*. Jerusalem, 1957.

Yahuda, A. S. *The Language of the Pentateuch in Its Relation to Egyptian.* Oxford, 1933.

Yahuda, A. S. *Die Sprache des Pentateuch in ihren Beziehungen zum Ägyptischen.* Leipzig, 1929.

Yamauchi, E. *Mandaic Incantation Texts*. New Haven: Yale University, 1967.

Zadok, R. "Iranian and Babylonian Notes." *AfO* 28 (1981–1982): 138.

Zadok, R. "Iranians and Individuals Bearing Iranian Names in Achaemenian Babylonia." *IOS* 7 (1977): 113.

Zakovitch, Y. *Every High Official* [in Hebrew]. Tel Aviv: Am Oved, 1986.

Zenger, Erich. *Das Buch Judit*. Gütersloh: Mohn, 1981.

Zevit, Z. "Converging Lines of Evidence Bearing on the Date of P." *ZAW* 94 (1982).

Zevit, Z. "The Khirbet el-Qôm Inscription Mentioning a Goddess." *BASOR* 255 (1984): 39–47.

Zevit, Z. "A Phoenician Inscription and Biblical Covenant Theology." *IEJ* 27 (1977): 110–118.

Zevit, Z. "Phoenician NBŠ/NPŠ and Its Hebrew Semantic Equivalents." In *Sopher Mahir: Northwest Semitic Studies Presented to Stanislav Segert*, edited by Edward M. Cook, 337. Winona Lake, IN: Eisenbrauns, 1990.

Zimmern, H. "Die Beschwörung 'Bann, Bann.'" *ZA* 28 (1914): 77:60.

Index

Note: Italicized page locators denote pages that include illustrative material.